Golden Common LISP

Golden Common LISP

A Hands-on Approach

David J. Steele

ADDISON-WESLEY PUBLISHING COMPANY

Singapore · Wokingham, England · Reading, Massachusetts
Menlo Park, California · New York · Don Mills, Ontario
Amsterdam · Bonn · Sydney · Tokyo · Madrid · San Juan

The programs presented in this book have been included for their instructional value. They have been tested with care but are not guaranteed for any particular purpose. The publisher does not offer any warranties or representations, nor does it accept any liabilities with respect to the programs.

Many of the designations used by manufacturers and sellers to distinguish their products are claimed as trademarks. Addison-Wesley has made every attempt to supply trademark information about manufacturers and their products mentioned in this book. A list of the trademark designations and their owners appears on page xxxii.

Cover designed and illustrated by Mike Davidson
Text designed by Lesley Stewart
Typeset by CRB Typesetting Services, Ely, Cambs
Printed in Singapore

First printed 1989

British Library Cataloguing in Publication Data

Steele, David J.
Golden Common LISP: a hands-on approach
1. Computer systems. Programming Languages: Lisp language
I. Title.
005.13′3

ISBN 0–201–41653–0

Library of Congress Cataloging in Publication Data

Steele, David J. (David Jay)
Golden common LISP : a hands-on approach / D.J. Steele.
p. cm.
Bibliography: p.
Includes index.
ISBN 0–201–41653–0
1. COMMON LISP (Computer program language) I. Title.
QA76.73.C28S74 1989
005.13′3–dc20 89–6582
CIP

respectfully dedicated to
John McCarthy
the father of LISP

Preface

This book is about programming in LISP, a high-level language which uses list processing and symbol manipulation to solve problems in artificial intelligence (AI). Because of the remarkable flexibility afforded by these programming mechanisms, LISP has been the principal language used for AI applications since its development in 1958. Not only is LISP the second oldest (after FORTRAN) computer language still in current use, but its applications are growing rapidly as a result of the burgeoning interest in AI.

To programmers used to procedural languages such as BASIC or PASCAL, LISP initially presents something of a challenge since it operates in a very different manner. As an applicative language, LISP uses a mechanism whereby functions are applied to their arguments, returning values to higher level functions. Such function calls may be nested to any depth. The overall LISP program therefore resembles a hierarchical structure not unlike that of a corporate organization, where higher-level functions call lower level functions to get the nitty-gritty work done. Such an approach lends itself well to the complexities of AI since programs can be structured in a manner which directly reflects the cognitive steps taken by a human being in solving a real-life problem.

About this book

The purpose of this book is to help you learn LISP, either as part of an undergraduate course or on a self-study basis.

Special effort has been made to support the use of this book for self-study. In the opening pages of many LISP tutorials appears the sentence: 'This book grew out of course notes....' The book which you are now holding might alternatively be prefaced: 'This book grew out of frustration resulting from trying to understand books which grew out of course notes...,' reflecting my feeling that books targeted at a narrow academic audience – in this case computer science majors – can present real problems when used by other interested people for self-study purposes. Even if you have a tertiary degree in some other discipline you may find such books daunting, since they take for granted a certain amount of prerequisite knowledge which you may lack.

This book therefore includes several introductory chapters to provide a 'gentle' introduction, as Touretzky might say, to the occult art of LISP programming. Experienced programmers or computer science undergraduates may find these chapters somewhat simplistic, and may skip over or through them. Once you are past these chapters and 'up to speed,' as it were, the balance of the book follows in a staged and graded manner, building upon the essentials introduced in the earlier chapters.

The general organization of the book is based upon somewhat more frequent, and shorter, chapters than other works on LISP. This permits a single narrow topic, for example, streams, packages, strings, etc., to be covered without the diversionary effect of trying to cram other, unrelated material into the same chapter.

Since it is generally agreed that programming is best learned in an interactive environment, it is assumed that you have a LISP interpreter on line and accessible during your perusal of this book. The book has been based on the use of the lexically scoped Version 1.1 of *Golden Common LISP*, an MS-DOS implementation which supports a large subset of Common LISP. However it may equally well be used as a tutorial in conjunction with other LISP implementations with minor modifications depending on the extent to which these versions deviate from Common LISP standards.

Generally, when examples are prefaced with the GCLISP prompt symbol *, it is expected that you will type them into the system and satisfy yourself that the results are as illustrated. At the same time it is hoped that you will carry out your own experiments, as whimsy dictates, to enhance your familiarity with the system.

At the end of most chapters is a series of ten exercises which cover the range of concepts presented in the chapter. If you are able independently to solve all of the exercises you can feel satisfied that you have mastered the essentials of the chapter. Answers to all exercises are included at the back of the book. Since some of the answers involve rather extensive coding, a separate MS-DOS diskette is available which includes not only the answers to all exercises but also a complete summary of all functions defined during the course of the book. Ordering information for this diskette is included in Appendix C.

The book contains somewhat more detailed coverage than usual of the internal features of a LISP interpreter, for example, the manner in which a symbolic data object is represented in computer memory, the manner in which the Object List is created and maintained, etc. Having worked with various LISP interpreters at the machine language level, I feel strongly that a working knowledge of what actually 'goes on' within the interpreter will vastly enhance your understanding of LISP.

Organization of the book

The first five chapters of the book introduce you to the concepts of symbols and symbol manipulation, the manner in which lists are used as a framework for such symbol manipulation, and the nature of LISP functions and how they are applied to their arguments. Chapter headings and their contents are as follows.

Chapter 1. Intelligence Involves Symbol Manipulation
A simple everyday problem is used to illustrate the manner in which we unconsciously use and manipulate symbols in the course of problem solving. The varied use of symbols is explored: as names to represent real-world objects or properties of objects, or as descriptions of procedures to be executed.

Chapter 2. The LISP Interpreter
Our 'hands-on' experiments with LISP will be carried out in an interactive manner with a LISP interpreter. In this chapter you will develop some familiarity with the interpreter, including the kinds of error situations which may arise and how to extricate yourself from these situations.

Chapter 3. Getting Acquainted with Functions
In its role as an applicative language, LISP depends on function calls to get things accomplished. This chapter discusses the syntax of function calls, shows how functions are applied to their arguments, and illustrates the manner in which functions may be nested to reflect levels of detail in a LISP applications program.

Chapter 4. Symbols as Data Objects
In the course of working with LISP, it will be helpful if you can visualize the nature of the data structures which you are working with. This chapter concentrates on symbols, illustrates the manner in which symbols are created as data objects, and illustrates the various attributes which a symbol may have.

Chapter 5. List Creation and Manipulation
The linked list is the basic framework into which symbols and other data objects are collected into groups which reflect their functional and/or other relationships. This chapter describes the structure of a linked list and illustrates the manner in which lists can be created, modified, and otherwise manipulated.

The above preliminary chapters deal with the essence of LISP: its applicative nature, the symbols and lists which it uses to solve its problems, and the manner in which these data objects are internally represented in computer memory. Once these basic concepts are understood, the details of

LISP programming which make up the rest of the tutorial can be seen in proper context and be more easily learned.

The next four chapters address the manner in which you can define procedures in LISP, the manner in which values are bound to variables in a lexically scoped implementation, the many predicates which are available for use as testing mechanisms, and the manner in which the results of these tests can be used as a basis for if/then/else type decision-making.

Chapter 6. Defining Your Own Functions
As an applicative language, the nature of LISP is to apply a function to its arguments. An overall LISP program therefore consists of a hierarchical structure of function calls. This chapter shows you how to define your own function definitions in terms of LISP primitives and other user-defined functions.

Chapter 7. Scoping of Variables
One of the important features which distinguishes one LISP system from another is the system of rules which governs the manner in which values are bound to symbols. In this chapter we carry out experiments to illustrate how such bindings are established in a lexically scoped implementation.

Chapter 8. Predicates and Boolean Operators
Predicates are used to test whether a data object meets some particular criterion or whether two objects bear some specified relationship to one another. Predicates return **NIL** if false, or some non-**NIL** value if true. These values may then be used in LISP conditional expressions to control branching decisions.

Chapter 9. Branching Operations
LISP equivalents of the if/then/else branching decisions found in procedural languages are performed by various conditional structures such as **cond**, **if**, and **when**. Negative counterparts of these structures include **ifn** and **unless**. A **case** structure is also available which maps the value of its input against a choice of outputs.

As in any high-level language, the manner in which information can be input to the system and output from the system is of basic importance. The next three chapters explore the mechanisms available in LISP for these purposes, including features whereby output can be formatted in special ways.

Chapter 10. Input Functions
The principal mechanism for input to a LISP system is **read** which reads a single LISP form from the keyboard or other source of input. Other principal variants include **read-char**, which reads a single character from an input stream; **read-line**, which inputs a single line

of input as a string; and **read-from-string**, which reads a single token from a string.

Chapter 11. Output Functions
The principal mechanism for output from a LISP system is **print**, which generates the printed representation of a LISP data object to an output peripheral such as the console or printer. Used in conjunction with streams, data can also be directed to a selected output sink such as a file.

Chapter 12. Formatting Printed Output
Various ways are available in LISP to format the manner in which text strings and data may be integrated into an output printout, including variants on the basic **print** function as well as the use of **backquote** to incorporate values along with quoted text. A special **format** function can be used to structure the manner in which data is output to the screen.

Many computer operations require that some activity be carried out *x* number of times or until some test is satisfied. LISP provides a variety of functions for carrying out such iteration. In addition, alternative means are provided whereby powerful recursive operations may be carried out to achieve similar goals in a more elegant and/or efficient manner. Specialized mapping functions are also available to apply a function successively to the elements of a list. The following three chapters explore these facilities.

Chapter 13. Iterative Programming
The basic iterative function **do** provides a flexible method of carrying out iteration, including provision for initialization and modification of variables on each pass. Other specialized variants such as **dolist** and **dotimes** permit simple iterative operations to be carried out efficiently on lists and integer sequences.

Chapter 14. Writing Recursive Functions
One of the more powerful features of LISP is its recursive nature, whereby a function can incorporate a call to itself within its own function definition. This feature permits a problem to be broken down into smaller versions of itself, and often provides a more efficient way of solving a problem than an iterative approach.

Chapter 15. Mapping Functions
Mapping functions such as **mapcar** and **maplist** provide a means of successively applying a function to the elements of a list and accumulating the results. Other variants such as **mapcan** and **mapcon** include the ability to apply a test to every element of the list, filtering out from the accumulation those elements which do not meet the test.

The next few chapters explore more advanced features of LISP. The use of macros, which provide flexibility in that they do not immediately evaluate their arguments, is discussed. The establishment of blocks and the ability to exit from such blocks in a lexical (return) or dynamic (catch and throw) manner is discussed, along with facilities for generating and handling multiple values. The nature of property and association lists as mechanisms for storage and retrieval of data is explored.

Chapter 16. Creating and Using Macros
Macros provide a kind of template for the construction of generalized procedures in LISP. Flexibility is provided as macros do not evaluate their arguments, but rather pass through a phase of expansion before the resulting expanded expression is evaluated.

Chapter 17. Blocks, Exits, and Multiple Values
The block facility permits a return from any point within the lexical scope of the block; catch and throw permit even more flexibility in the way of dynamic exits from anywhere in the program. LISP provides facilities for the generation of multiple values returned by a function, and provides a variety of special functions to deal with such values.

Chapter 18. Property and Association Lists
LISP symbols are often used to represent real-world objects. The property list permits a variety of attributes to be associated with such an object, in the form of a list of property names along with their associated values. Another more general lookup facility is provided by the association list, in which a keyword is linked with a value.

Various other data structures are available in LISP for different purposes. Streams provide the necessary interface between the interpreter and input/output devices. Characters are used for their ASCII properties as well as for a variety of macro operations. Strings find extensive use in screen displays and natural language processing. Various kinds of integers and floating point numbers are supported by Common LISP. Arrays and structures provide alternatives to the use of lists as mechanisms for data storage and retrieval. The use of these data structures is explored in the next four chapters.

Chapter 19. Working with Streams
Streams are data objects which provide an interface with peripherals and files. Input streams typically read data from the keyboard, file, or other source; output streams print data to the console, printer, or other peripheral. Various stream-related functions are particularly helpful for manipulating strings for natural language processing.

Chapter 20. What's in a Character?
In addition to supporting the standard range of ASCII characters, GCLISP supports the use of **:control** and **:meta** bits associated with the Ctrl and Alt keys. A large subset of Common LISP macro characters are supported, and macro functions can be defined for any character.

Chapter 21. Working with Strings
A wide variety of functions are provided for manipulating strings, including the conversion of other LISP data objects to strings and the conversion of a string to a stream to be used as an input source from which characters may be read. Other functions permit extraction of substrings, lexicographical comparison, and concatenation of strings.

Chapter 22. Numbers, Arrays, and Structures
Various functions are provided to carry out exponential, logarithmic, trigonometric, and bit-wise operations on integers and floating-point numbers. Other functions provide for the creation of arrays and vectors, and for retrieval of data from an array. Finally, **defstruct** and related functions permit the creation of user-defined data structures.

A variety of other Common LISP features are provided by GCLISP, including extensive **pathname** functions for interfacing with file systems. Various tools are available for error-handling, breaks, debugging, and tracing of programs. Packages provide a means of isolating users from other users, thereby eliminating inadvertent symbol name conflicts. Other implementation-specific features of GCLISP include functions for interfacing with the system at the machine language level. These areas are covered in the next four chapters.

Chapter 23. Interfacing with File Systems
Pathnames in Common LISP provide for a standardized way of creating and accessing files. Functions such as **with-open-file** provide for automatic closing of files after use, and other functions provide for the renaming and deleting of files. A wide variety of functions are available for testing and/or returning the components of a pathname.

Chapter 24. Debugging, Tracing, and Timing
Debugging facilities in LISP include the use of **break** within which the current values of variables can be tested, **backtrace** to display contents of the control stack, **step** to step through the evaluation process, and **trace** to display the argument list of a specified function as well as the values returned by that function.

Chapter 25. Packages
Multi-user systems, in which conflicts can occur due to the use of the same symbol name for different purposes by different users, has given rise to the creation of packages which provide a user with a separate

symbol lookup table for his or her own use. Basic LISP primitives and keywords are maintained in their own LISP and KEYWORD packages.

Chapter 26. Other Features of GCLISP
Various utility functions are provided by GCLISP to allocate memory and control garbage collection activities. Low-level functions are available for interfacing with the system at the machine language level, and to retrieve or store data at specific MS-DOS base/offset addresses as well as to generate CPU interrupts for purposes such as time measurement.

The last four chapters provide additional information about the GMACS editor and about LISP in general, including the manner in which an interpreter is structured, the internal working details of the **read/eval/print** cycle, and the essential differences between dynamically and lexically scoped interpreters.

Chapter 27. Using the GMACS Editor
For purposes of program development, use of the GMACS editor, in which program changes can be tested as soon as they have been made, is essential. This chapter outlines all of the principal features of the editor, including cursor movements, transfer of blocks of text, forward/backward search, and the use of split windows for editing.

Chapter 28. Inside a LISP Interpreter
In order to fine-tune your understanding of the mechanisms of LISP, it is useful to be familiar with the general manner in which an interpreter is structured, how memory is allocated for different purposes, and how the Object List is created and maintained.

Chapter 29. The read/eval/print Cycle
The basic **read/eval/print** mechanism is examined in detail, including the manner in which **read** builds up an internal data object corresponding to the LISP input; how **eval** carries out the evaluation process; and how **print** effectively reverses the **read** process to create a printed representation of the LISP data object returned by **eval**.

Chapter 30. Lexical and Dynamic Scoping Mechanisms
One of the more confusing aspects of LISP is the manner in which dynamically scoped interpreters differ from lexically scoped interpreters. We construct working mini-interpreters of both types to compare the manner in which binding environments are handled. The use of closures is illustrated.

Appendices

Appendix A includes an index of all Common LISP functions supported by GCLISP. In addition to indicating the section in which these functions are covered in the book, cross-reference information is provided for convenient lookup in Guy Steele's *Common LISP: The Language* (referred to as CLRM), as well as the *Golden Common LISP Reference Manual* (Versions 1.0 and 1.1) (referred to as GCLRM).

Appendix B includes an index of all of the user-defined functions which have been developed during the course of the book, whether in the text or as exercises.

Appendix C contains information on how to order an MS-DOS diskette which contains all of the code for functions defined within the text as well as all of the answers to the exercises. In addition, a number of applications programs are included on the diskette covering such areas as pattern-matching, Eliza programs, the use of frames for hierarchical knowledge representation, and natural language processing using augmented transition networks.

The Bibliography includes a complete listing of books on LISP which have been published to date, as well as sources of technical papers and other information on LISP.

A Subject Index is provided for general reference.

Acknowledgements

Appreciation is expressed to the following entities for permission to quote from or extensively reference the works in question: Digital Press for Guy L. Steele, Jr's *Common LISP: The Language*; The MIT Press for Richard P. Gabriel's *Performance and Evaluation of LISP Systems*; Symbolic Technology Limited for material quoted from the tutorial on *Advanced Common LISP Programming* presented at AAAI-87 by Richard Gabriel and David Touretzky; United Feature Syndicate, Inc. for the use of the Peanuts cartoon on page 32; International Business Machines Corporation for the ASCII character chart on page 273; and Goldhill Computers for their *Golden Common LISP Reference Manual*. Goldhill's kindness in reviewing the manuscript and in fielding numerous questions about the workings of GCLISP has been particularly appreciated.

I very much appreciate the thorough review of the manuscript which was carried out by Randy Haskins. His many corrections and suggestions for improvement have been gratefully incorporated into the final text. Thanks are also due to John McCallum, Lin Yih, Aldis Skuja, Mike Smith, and Dick Steele for partial review of the text. Any errors which remain are mine, *ça va sans dire*. The continuing support and encouragement of my

Addison-Wesley editor, Stephen Troth, has been much appreciated. Finally special thanks are due to Rita for the infinite number of ways in which she has supported the course of this book.

David J. Steele
Singapore
January 1989

Contents

Chapter 27 Using the GMACS Editor 394

Chapter 28 Inside a LISP Interpreter 412

Chapter 29 The **read/eval/print** Cycle 430

Trademark notice

MS-DOS™ is a trademark of the MicroSoft Corporation.
WordStar™ is a trademark of the MicroPro International Corporation.
Common LISP
Golden Common LISP™ is a trademark of Goldhill Computers, Inc.
IBM-PC™ is a trademark of the International Business Machines Corporation.

Chapter 1

Intelligence Involves Symbol Manipulation

Computers were originally developed to carry out tasks which people find difficult to do, such as summarizing census results, developing ballistic tables, and calculating pi to the 1000th decimal place. They did these jobs very well. However by the mid-1950s people were starting to ask computers to do other kinds of things, including machine translation of languages and problem-solving activities involving some degree of common sense. They ran into unexpected problems. Some things which people find easy to do were found to be surprisingly difficult for computers.

A part of the problem was related to the fact that early high-level languages, such as FORTRAN, operate in a procedural manner. Such languages generally get numbers as input, carry out operations on these numbers, and generate numbers as output. Artificial intelligence (AI), on the other hand, deals with quite different entities. A typical AI problem has limited interest in numerical calculations *per se*, but rather deals with real-world concepts such as objects, ideas, events, and relationships. Such concepts cannot easily be represented by numbers, let alone manipulated by the mechanical techniques of procedural languages.

A new kind of language was clearly required: one which included provision for symbolic representation of the elusive components of 'common sense,' and moreover provided means by which such symbols could be manipulated to produce a manifestation of computer 'intelligence.' Building upon previous applications of list processing in the IPL family of languages, John McCarthy and his associates developed such a language in 1958 to meet these needs. They called the language LISP to reflect the fact that it used LISt Processing as a mechanism for manipulating symbols.

Since *symbol manipulation* constitutes the essence of LISP, this introductory chapter will look at the nature of symbols and how they may be used to represent real-world objects, properties of objects, and procedures. We will see how LISP can be used to solve a simple AI problem; and we will explore the structure of lists to see why they provide a natural framework for symbol manipulation.

1.1 Problem-solving typically involves symbol manipulation

We have just arrived home in the evening, after a long trip from the city, to find that we have somehow left our keys at the office. Our spouse is away visiting relatives and the kids have gone to an early movie. What to do?

A typical reasoning pattern in such a situation might survey various ways in which we could get into the house without having to go all the way back to the office to get our keys. Perhaps the front door was fortuitously left unlocked. Maybe we keep a spare key under the door mat. Possibly the back door or one of the windows of the house was left unlocked. Reasoning out the problem would likely proceed as shown in Fig. 1.1

In the course of working our way through this problem while standing in front of the door, we are unconsciously doing a lot of internal *symbol manipulation*. (We are here using the word *symbol* in its specialized LISP sense, that is, a string of characters used to represent some real-world object or concept.) Some of the symbols, like **front-door** and **spare-key**, may represent familiar objects. Other symbols, like **contents-of-pockets** or **objects-under-door-mat**, may represent collections of objects which may be searched to see if a given item (such as **door-key** or **spare-key**) is among them.

Symbols may also be used to represent attributes or properties of other symbols. The **security-status** property of a particular door may specify whether that door is locked or not, depending on whether the value associated with that property (another symbol) is '**locked**' or '**unlocked**.'

Finally, symbols can represent actions to be carried out, as **unlock-door** might stand for the steps to be taken to use a key to unlock a door.

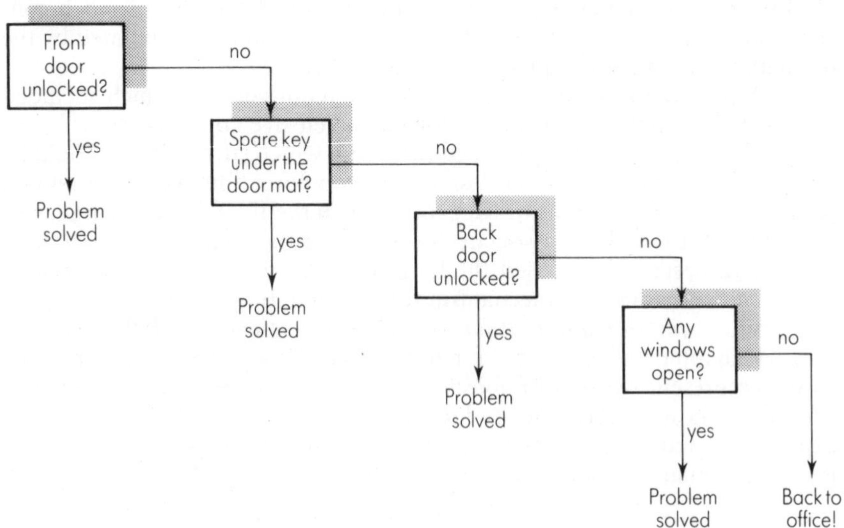

Fig. 1.1 Reasoning processes utilize symbol manipulation.

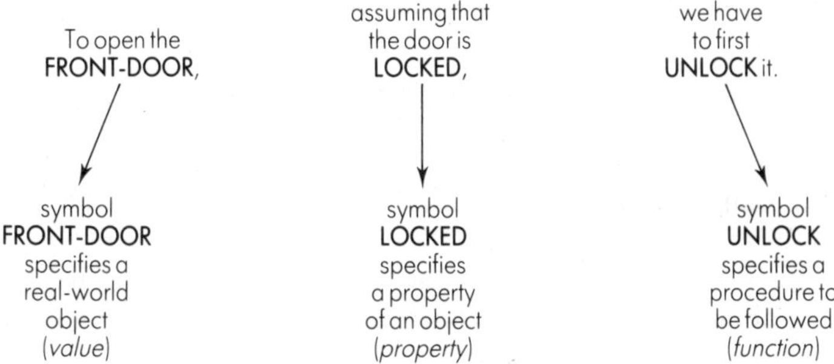

Fig. 1.2 Symbols can be used in three basic ways.

We can illustrate the three basic ways in which we use symbols as we think about how to get in the front door (see Fig. 1.2). We can think about these different ways in which a symbol can be used as being *attributes* of a symbol. We can add to these a fourth attribute: the name of the symbol itself. Provision for each of these attributes is built into the internal data object created by LISP to represent a symbol.

1.2 A LISP symbol may have a value, properties, or functional implications

The nature of the data object which constitutes a LISP symbol provides for all of these varying usages which can be summarized diagrammatically as shown in Fig. 1.3.

How do we create such symbols in LISP? Having created them, how do we give them *values*, vest them with *properties*, and define the *procedures* which are carried out when they are invoked in this context? How do we *manipulate* symbols to achieve a desired AI goal? During the remainder of this chapter we will look further at the front door problem in an attempt to provide some of the answers to these questions. In later chapters we will explore all of these concepts in greater detail.

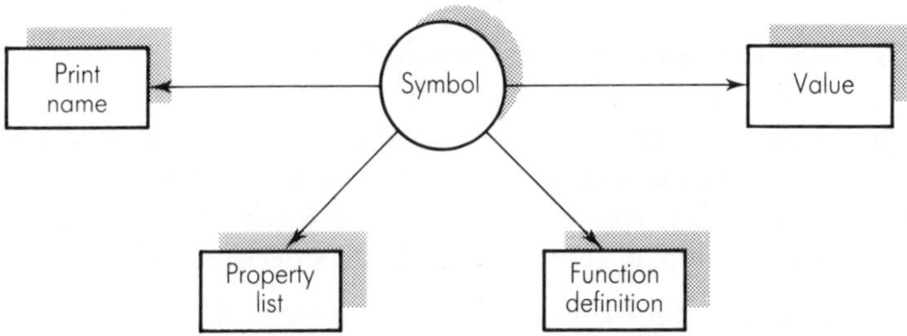

Fig. 1.3 A LISP symbol has four principal attributes.

1.3 The front door problem: robot version

Our robot neighbor R2D2 has just arrived home after a tiring day on the factory assembly line and finds himself facing his front door. He has the same basic problem that we did, but he handles the situation somewhat differently. Rather than solving the front door problem through a series of unconscious thought processes, R2D2's reasoning is very explicit and is all carried out in LISP. By examining these reasoning processes we can learn something about the manner in which LISP operates to 'manipulate' symbols and solve problems.

During the remainder of this chapter we will be illustrating a variety of expressions exactly as they would be typed into a Common LISP interpreter. *If you are a beginner to LISP, don't try to understand every last detail of what is presented.* The principal intent of this chapter is only that you become acquainted with the *flavor* of LISP, and how it deals with symbols.

Back to R2D2, we may assume that his day comprises various activities which can be represented in LISP as a series of procedures:

```
...
...
(commute-home)
(walk-from-station)
(enter-house)
(recharge-batteries)
(change-oil)
(watch-television)
...
...
```

The parentheses which demarcate each procedure name flag out that the name represents some action to be carried out. At this moment R2D2 has just finished walking from the station and is standing in front of his door. His next activity is **enter-house**. However before seeing how he goes about this we first have to create a degree of infrastructure.

1.4 Symbols can stand for real-world objects

As we have observed, symbols may be used to represent real-world objects. Referring to the previous search diagram – and assuming that we have windows in the living room, bedroom, and kitchen – we see that the following objects will play some part in R2D2's decision-making:

```
front-door   door-key    living-room-window
back-door    spare-key   bedroom-window
                         kitchen-window
```

In LISP, we can *create* these symbols by the simple expedient of including them in some valid expression which we type into our LISP interpreter. If the items are not already on the internal list of symbols maintained within the interpreter they will be added automatically. For example, we can type in a statement such as the following:

```
* (setf environment-list '(front-door back-door
   door-key spare-key living-room-window bedroom-window
   kitchen-window))
(FRONT-DOOR BACK-DOOR DOOR-KEY SPARE-KEY
  LIVING-ROOM-WINDOW BEDROOM-WINDOW
  KITCHEN-WINDOW)
```

The asterisk * represents the GCLISP **prompt** symbol, inviting us to input an expression for evaluation. The lowercase expression is our input. LISP evaluates the expression which we have typed in and returns the results of this evaluation. For consistency LISP converts all of our input into uppercase for internal use.

By using the **setf** assignment function of LISP we have taken the list of objects shown and assigned this list as the value of the symbol **environment-list**. As the interpreter reads in this expression, each of the symbols named in the list as well as the symbol **environment-list** is automatically created as a LISP data object.

We can similarly take other collections of items and assign them as values to other symbols:

```
* (setf pocket-contents '(handkerchief coins door-key comb))
(HANDKERCHIEF COINS DOOR-KEY COMB)

* (setf objects-under-door-mat '(dust dead-rat spare-key))
(DUST DEAD-RAT SPARE-KEY)
```

The quote marks ' before the lists of items tell the LISP interpreter that these lists are to be taken verbatim, that is, considered as data rather than being evaluated as nested procedures. In each instance LISP *returns a value*, which in the case of a **setf** expression corresponds to the value which has been assigned.

In all of the above cases the value to be assigned consists of a list of real-world objects. However we might equally well have assigned other kinds of values to each symbol, for example, another symbol, a number, a string, or some other more exotic LISP data object.

1.5 LISP provides facilities to manipulate symbols

Having created symbols how do we manipulate them? LISP provides various ways, a few of which we will review here.

Assuming that we have typed in the assignment statements as shown above, we can retrieve the value of any symbol by simply typing it into the interpreter:

```
* pocket-contents
(HANDKERCHIEF COINS DOOR-KEY COMB)
```

LISP evaluates the symbol, that is, looks up the value which has been assigned to it, and returns this value in the form of a printout to the console. Through a similar evaluation mechanism, whenever we use the term pocket-contents in a LISP program, the interpreter will retrieve the value (HANDKERCHIEF COINS DOOR-KEY COMB) and will *substitute* this value in place of pocket-contents.

We can check whether a given item is on the list of pocket contents:

```
* (member 'parking-ticket pocket-contents)
NIL
```

The LISP predicate member checks through the list which constitutes its second argument, comparing each element of the list against its first argument. If no match is found, member returns NIL, which is the LISP equivalent of 'false.' Otherwise it returns the remainder of the list commencing with the element:

```
* (member 'door-key pocket-contents)
(DOOR-KEY COMB)
```

We can use such a 'value returned' to trigger off a branching decision – in this case to decide what action to take depending on whether or not R2D2 has the door key in his pocket.

The above example illustrates one way in which we can manipulate symbols, that is, by assigning values to them and subsequently retrieving these values and/or testing to see whether they meet some particular criterion. In Chapter 4 we will further explore the manner in which values are assigned to symbols.

1.6 Descriptive properties can be assigned to symbols

When a symbol is used to represent a real-world object, it may be assigned any number of *properties* each of which has a *value*. In this manner a complete description can be established for the object represented by the symbol. For example, we might define various properties to describe the front-door of R2D2's house. Among these might be the property security-status, indicating whether the door is locked or unlocked. A LISP expression to establish the value of such a property might look as follows:

```
* (setf (get 'front-door 'security-status) 'locked)
LOCKED
```

To establish the rest of the environment for R2D2's entry into the house we might execute the following additional property assignments:

```
(setf (get 'back-door 'security-status) 'locked)
(setf (get 'living-room-window 'security-status) 'locked)
(setf (get 'bedroom-window 'security-status) 'locked)
(setf (get 'kitchen-window 'security-status) 'locked)
```

to reflect, in this instance, the fact that all possible entry modes into the house are locked.

LISP provides various ways to access and manipulate such properties. For example, if we want to see whether or not the door is locked we can use a property retrieval function:

```
* (get 'front-door 'security-status)
LOCKED
```

In the course of retrieving such a value, we can compare it with another symbol to test whether the two are the same:

```
* (equal (get 'front-door 'security-status) 'locked)
T
```

In this case the value of the **security-status** property of the symbol **front-door** matches the symbol **locked**, so the **equal** predicate returns **T**, or 'true.' Again, such tests can be used to activate branching decisions, such as whether or not R2D2 needs a key to get in through the (locked or unlocked) front door.

The above example illustrates a second instance of manipulating symbols by using them to represent *properties* of a real-world object. Subsequently we can retrieve these properties to provide us with information about the object, or alternatively test them to see whether they meet some particular criterion.

Other LISP functions are used to add new properties or values to the property list of a symbol, change the values of existing properties, remove a property from the list, or return the entire property list. We will further explore the creation and use of property lists in Chapter 18.

1.7 Symbol names may be used to represent procedures

Finally, symbols may be used as the names of *procedures* which describe the various steps required to carry out a given task. We will for the moment refer to such procedures as LISP *functions* and to the invoking of a procedure as a *function call*.

At any given moment any or all of the attributes mentioned previously – a value, a property list, or a function definition – may be associated with a given symbol name. How then does LISP know when a symbol is being used as a function call and when it is being used for its value or to retrieve some item from its property list? The simple answer is: when a symbol is the first element in an (unquoted) list, LISP assumes that it is being used as the name of a function. Otherwise the context in which it is used will determine whether its value or its property list is to be accessed.

We can define the procedure associated with a given symbol using the LISP function defun. A defun expression consists of three parts: the function *name*, a list of the *arguments* to which the function is to be applied, and the *body* of the function, that is, the procedure to be carried out when the function is called.

As a preliminary exercise before applying ourselves to R2D2's front door problem, let's create a function to provide us with a report on the status of all items which bear on this problem:

```
* (defun environment ()
    (format t "~%~%Front door security status:          ~a"
      (get 'front-door 'security-status))
    (format t "~%Back door security status:            ~a"
      (get 'back-door 'security-status))
    (format t "~%Living room window security status:   ~a"
      (get 'living-room-window 'security-status))
    (format t "~%Bedroom window security status:       ~a"
      (get 'bedroom-window 'security-status))
    (format t "~%Kitchen window security status:       ~a"
      (get 'kitchen-window 'security-status))
    (format t "~%Front door mat covers:                ~a"
      objects-under-door-mat)
    (format t "~%Pocket contents include:              ~a"
      pocket-contents))
ENVIRONMENT
```

Since this particular function, which we have called environment, takes no arguments, the empty list () is inserted in place of an argument list. After a function has been defined in the above manner, the interpreter stores the definition for future use and 'returns' the function name.

The body of the environment function simply consists of a number of format statements (see Section 12.5) which LISP uses to print information to the screen. As may be inferred from the above example, format provides a kind of template for the printout, printing the text contained within double quote marks, evaluating the argument which follows the text, and inserting the value in place of the *format directive* ~a. Other format directives such as ~% generate a line feed and carriage return.

Assuming that we have created the environment defined by the previous **setf** expressions, we can now call up our new function:

```
* (environment)
Front door security status:          LOCKED
Back door security status:           LOCKED
Living room window security status:  LOCKED
Bedroom window security status:      LOCKED
Kitchen window security status:      LOCKED
Front door mat covers:               (DUST DEAD-RAT SPARE-KEY)
Pocket-contents include:             (HANDKERCHIEF COINS
                                        DOOR-KEY COMB)
```

The above example illustrates the third manner in which we can manipulate symbols, that is, by using them to define procedures which may then be used to carry out operations on other LISP objects.

The ability to associate a procedure with a symbol, which is somewhat similar to defining procedures in PASCAL, is one of the most powerful features of LISP. In Chapter 6 we will explore in detail the manner in which we can define our own functions.

1.8 R2D2 manipulates symbols to solve the problem

Culminating our example, and bearing in mind that R2D2 talks to himself as he goes about his activities, we might define his **enter-house** activity as follows:

```
(defun enter-house ()
  (cond ((member 'door-key pocket-contents)
            (format t "~%Unlock door with the front door key!"))
        ((equal (get 'front-door 'security-status) 'unlocked)
            (format t "~%The door is already unlocked!"))
        ((member 'spare-key objects-under-door-mat)
            (format t "~%Use the spare key under the mat!"))
        ((equal (get 'back-door 'security-status) 'unlocked)
            (format t "~%You can get in the back door!"))
        ((setf open-window (check-windows))
            (format t "~%The ~a is unlocked!" open-window))
        (t  (format t "~%Go back and get your keys!"))))
```

The main body of the above function consists of a **cond** construct which is LISP's basic mechanism for making branching decisions. This type of construct consists of a series of if-then statements in which the first element consists of some test to be made, and the second element specifies the action to be carried out in the event the test passes, that is, returns some non-**NIL** value. If the test in any statement is unsuccessful, the next following statement is tested. Once a successful test has been found the associated action is carried out and the cond function is exited without carrying out any further tests.

The first test says in effect: *if* the door key is one of the items listed as pocket contents, *then* use it to open the front door and go in. The problem is solved and no further actions are required.

Assuming that R2D2 does not have the key in his pocket, the test fails and control passes to the next statement which includes the test:

```
(equal (get 'front-door 'security-status) 'unlocked)
```

which compares the value returned by (get 'front-door 'security-status) with the symbol unlocked. Since the status is locked this test will fail, the equal test will return NIL, and control will pass to the next clause. If all clauses fail, the final default clause (which always succeeds since its test clause is T) will be reached and R2D2 will tell himself to go back to the office and get his keys.

Assuming that the first four tests fail, the value returned by the next test clause will depend on a function call to check-windows, which we might define as follows:

```
(defun check-windows ()
  (setf window-list '(living-room-window
       bedroom-window kitchen-window))
  (loop
    (if (endp window-list)
       (return nil))
    (setf window (first window-list))
    (cond ((equal (get window 'security-status)
                 'unlocked)
           (case window
             (living-room-window
                (return "living room window"))
             (bedroom-window
                (return "bedroom window"))
             (kitchen-window
                (return "kitchen window")))))
    (setf window-list (rest window-list))))
```

check-windows collects all of the windows into a single list and then sets up a loop to examine each of them in turn to see if it is unlocked.

The terminating test (endp window-list) is set up so that if the whole list is traversed without finding an unlocked window, the function as a whole returns NIL. This in turn causes the conditional clause commencing with ((setf open-window ...) in the higher level calling function enter-house to fail. If on the other hand an unlocked window is found, the *case* statement causes an equivalent string to be returned as a non-**NIL** value to satisfy the conditional clause, after which the string will subsequently be integrated into the **format** statement in place of the format directive **~a** to generate a sentence such as:

```
The living room window is unlocked!
```

thus providing a solution to R2D2's house entry problem.

1.9 Lists are a natural mechanism for manipulating symbols

Up to now we have seen various ways in which symbols are used by LISP. We have assigned values to these symbols and later retrieved them for comparison against some criterion, or to see whether they are a member of some group. We have assigned properties to symbols along with the values associated with those properties and have later retrieved and compared these values. The results of these tests have been used in making branching decisions. We have also seen how symbols can be used to name functional procedures, and have caused these procedures to be invoked by typing them into the interpreter in the form of a list.

Before leaving this preliminary review, let us look briefly at the nature of the lists which are used as devices for manipulating symbols.

As will be noted from the previous examples, the combinations of symbols which are used to solve an AI problem form natural groups in which each symbol bears some relationship to the other symbols in the list. For instance, in the quoted list of data:

```
'(handkerchief coins door-key comb)
```

all of the symbols belong to a common category, that is, items found in a pocket. In this particular case the order of the symbols could be randomized without effecting the significance of the list.

On the other hand in a function-calling list such as:

```
(member 'door-key pocket-contents)
```

the order of the symbols must follow fixed rules. The first symbol invokes a test to be carried out to ascertain whether the second symbol is a member of the list represented by the third symbol.

Or let's take a simple English language sentence:

```
'(What time does the train leave for Westport?)
```

Such a sentence represents another natural example of a list of symbols in which all elements are related and the word order has a clear bearing on the overall 'meaning' of the list. These relationships will be exploited when we start using LISP for natural language processing.

The associative nature of all of the above kinds of symbol groupings, coupled with the unpredictable size of the groups, led to the concept of list processing as a natural mechanism for symbol manipulation.

1.10 Lists are structured as binary trees

The basic intent of a list is to provide a framework for grouping symbols in some particular order which determines their interrelationships. The printed representation of a list is not unlike a list as we use it in everyday life, that is, a listing of symbols one after another, the only obvious difference being the set of parentheses which demarcate the list.

Internally, within the computer, a list is structured as a binary tree consisting of *nodes*, which in turn each comprise two double-word cells each of which contains an *address pointer*. For example, the internal representation of the list used to invoke the **member** function call as noted above can be shown diagrammatically (see Fig. 1.4). The left-hand address cell of each node points to an element of the list, and the right-hand address cell points to the next node. This of course permits the system to traverse a list element by element by following the address pointers. The final right-hand cell points to **NIL**, which is LISP's convention for indicating when the end of a list has been reached.

The linked nature of such lists provides for a remarkable degree of flexibility in manipulating the elements which make up the lists. Additional elements can be added by creating new nodes and grafting them onto the list. Elements can be deleted from the list by adjusting address pointers to

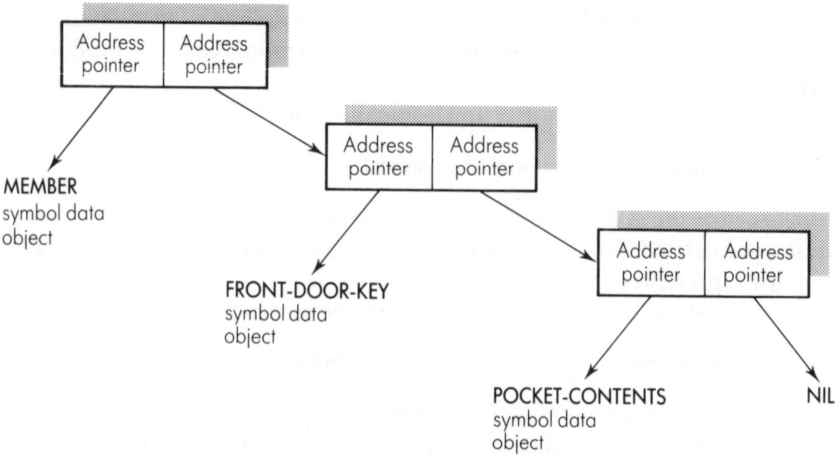

Fig. 1.4 Lists provide a useful mechanism for grouping symbols.

bypass the deleted element. As we will see, most of LISP's operations are carried out internally through the manipulation of address pointers.

We will explore this subject in more detail in Chapter 5 where we look at various ways to create and otherwise manipulate lists.

SUMMARY

Summarizing the key points of this chapter:

- *symbols* find common use in our mental processes as a means of representing real-world objects, properties of objects, collections of objects, relationships between objects, and procedures to be carried out on objects
- a computer program which purports to exhibit some degree of intelligence must have a way of *manipulating* symbols
- *assignment functions* such as **setf** can be used to *assign* a value to a symbol
- various *property list functions* permit properties and their values to be associated with a given symbol
- a *function definition* may be assigned to a symbol so that the function is activated when the symbol is included as the first element in an (unquoted) list
- since symbols may be grouped within lists in ways which reflect the relationship between them, LISP's talents at *list processing* provide a natural way to manipulate such symbols

Chapter 2
The LISP Interpreter

In the course of experimenting with LISP and/or developing LISP programs, the two principal tools which we will be using are the LISP *interpreter* and the LISP *editor*. The interpreter is the software which provides an interactive environment in which LISP expressions can be typed in for evaluation. The interpreter also provides the environment in which the editor (which is usually written in LISP) can be called up and used to create and/or edit the expressions which make up a LISP applications program.

Since this book is based on the use of Golden Common LISP, we will be using the *GCLISP interpreter* for our hands-on experiments and the *GMACS editor* for editing our programs. If you have some other implementation of LISP the basic principles outlined here will be generally applicable. However some degree of modification may be required to your procedures to reflect the extent to which the primitives built into these other versions differ from the Common LISP standard.

The GMACS editor is covered in detail in Chapter 27. The principal purpose of this chapter is to familiarize you with the use of the GCLISP interpreter.

In this chapter we will look at:

- the *interactive* manner in which a LISP interpreter works
- the way in which the **read/eval/print** cycle operates
- the fact that LISP always '*returns a value*'
- the manner in which interaction with the interpreter is carried out at the '*top level*'
- some basic nomenclature of *LISP expressions*
- how to get the *GCLISP interpreter* up and running
- various ways to handle *errors* in GCLISP
- how to get in and out of *MS-DOS* from GCLISP
- a sampling of the various kinds of expressions which we can type in to the interpreter and the values which are returned

2.1 The LISP interpreter operates in interactive mode

LISP is a highly interactive language. When we load the interpreter into our computer the first thing it does is to display a prompt symbol, in the form of an asterisk *, inviting us to type some input into the keyboard. After we have done so, the interpreter evaluates what we have typed in, 'returns a value' to the console, and displays another prompt asking for further input. This cycle continues indefinitely until we terminate the process.

While in the interpreter we can also call up the editor (which is loaded from a different diskette) and use it to edit LISP programs. Most LISP interpreters, including GCLISP, provide an ongoing interactive system where you can jump back and forth between the editor and interpreter, testing program changes as these are made.

Our interactive relationship with the GCLISP interpreter and the GMACS editor may be graphically represented as shown in Fig. 2.1. There are three basic modes in which we can operate:

(1) We can experiment interactively with the GCLISP interpreter, which is what we are going to do in this chapter. This means that we can type in a LISP expression, the interpreter will evaluate it, and the value will be returned to us in the form of a printout on the console. (Alternatively an *error message* may be generated by the system if our input is not to LISP's liking!)

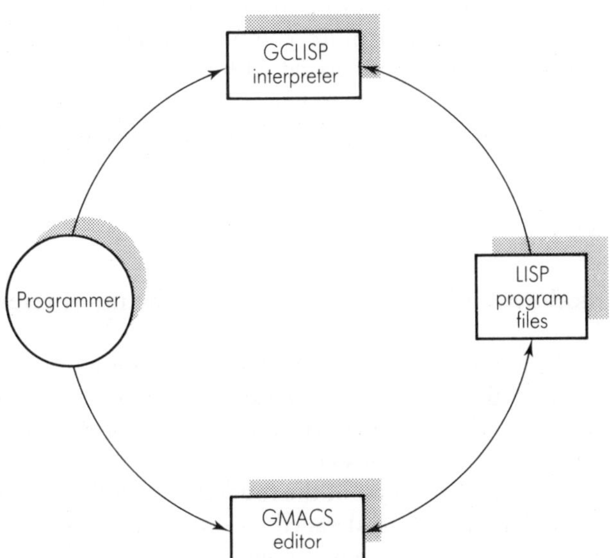

Fig. 2.1 LISP software includes the interpreter and the editor.

During such interactive sessions we can assign values to symbols, create property lists, define functions, and run short programs using such functions operating within the environment which has been created. However the list structures created by such experiments are transient and will be permanently lost when we exit from the interpreter.

(2) After loading the interpreter we can call up the GMACS editor, create a .LSP *program file*, and type our various value and property list assignments and function definitions into the editor. These can then be saved to the file.

While working with the GMACS editor we can periodically return to the interpreter, load the most recent version of the file which we have just saved, and try out our program. As errors are identified we can jump back into GMACS, make the necessary corrections, return to the interpreter, reload the modified version, and try again.

(3) Having previously created and debugged a LISP program and saved it to a .LSP file, after loading the interpreter we can directly load the file in question. This creates an operating environment in which we can then call up whatever functions are involved in running the program. Since the editor (which consists of an extremely large body of LISP code) is not resident in on-board memory we will have a lot more space in which to run our program than in option 2.

For our hands-on experiments during this chapter we will be operating as per option 1. As we get into more complex programs we will find it desirable to start becoming familiarized with the GMACS editor. Chapter 27 provides details on its use, including a 'quick and dirty' approach to master the essentials without going into detail on all its auxiliary bells and whistles. Later, and at a more leisurely pace, we can explore all of its capabilities.

2.2 The read/eval/print cycle is the heart of the interpreter

In the course of our interaction with the LISP interpreter most of the work is carried out during the so-called read/eval/print cycle, meaning that the interpreter will *read* what we have typed in, will *evaluate* it, and will *print* out the resulting value on the console.

A more detailed discussion of the read/eval/print cycle is provided in Chapter 29. Familiarity with its detailed workings contributes greatly to a general knowledge of exactly what is going on in LISP. However we will review the process briefly here as background to our initial hands-on experiments.

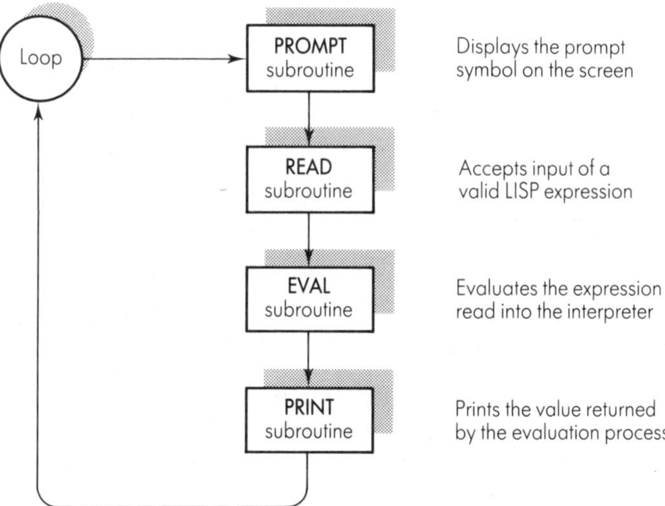

Fig. 2.2 The **read/eval/print** cycle operates in a repetitive manner.

For those familiar with assembly language programming the heart of the LISP **read/eval/print** cycle could be expressed roughly as:

```
LOOP    CALL PROMPT
        CALL READ
        CALL EVAL
        CALL PRINT
        JMP LOOP
```

that is, a repetitive operation which cycles until we jump out of the loop through an **(exit)** command or by other means. Since the **read** function may be used explicitly elsewhere in a LISP program, the **prompt** is handled as a separate subroutine, displaying the asterisk which indicates that GCLISP is waiting for input. We can express the foregoing in a diagrammatic manner (see Fig. 2.2).

After generating the prompt symbol the LISP system parses whatever is typed into the keyboard on a character-by-character basis until a complete LISP expression – be it a symbol, a number, a string, or a list – has been typed in. This input is scanned by **read**, which creates in computer memory an internal LISP data object corresponding to the expression. A pointer to this data object is then passed to **eval**.

To the extent a symbol or number is typed into the keyboard, **read** merely returns a pointer either to the location of the symbol on the Object List or to the numeric data object which has been constructed in memory. Reading in a list is a more complicated process. As each element of the list is parsed, read operates recursively to build up in memory an internal linked-list structure. When the end of the input is reached, as evidenced by a balancing right parenthesis, read returns a pointer to the first cell of the list structure which it has just created.

The eval function picks up the pointer handed over by read and evaluates the data object pointed to. If it is a number or a string, both of which evaluate to themselves, the same number or string is returned. If it is a symbol, eval returns a pointer to the value of the symbol. If the data object is a list, evaluation is much more complex and eval may generate a new list as the result of the evaluation. eval returns a pointer to the data structure representing the results of the evaluation, which pointer is then passed to the print subroutine.

The objective of the print function is to generate the printed representation of the data object returned by eval. print is therefore somewhat the reverse of read; whereas read creates an internal data object from printed input, print creates printed output from an internal data object.

As will be seen from the foregoing brief description of the LISP read/eval/print process, much of what goes on within LISP is related to passing address pointers back and forth. We will look at this in much more detail in Chapter 29.

2.3 LISP always 'returns a value'

An integral characteristic of LISP is that it always '*returns a value*' as a result of its evaluation. When operating at the 'top level,' that is, interactively typing expressions into the keyboard, this value is printed on the console immediately below the expression which has been input. For example, if we input an arithmetic expression:

```
* (+ 3 4)
7
```

the interpreter evaluates the expression (+ 3 4) and prints the results of the evaluation, 7, immediately beneath. Thereafter the prompt symbol is redisplayed, inviting another round of input.

We can make the analogy that we, as the programmer, are in a manner of speaking the 'function' which is calling the expression which we have typed in; and that the interpreter is returning the value of that expression to us in exactly the same manner as it operates at a lower level to return a value to the next-higher-level calling function. The only difference is that at the top level, since we are obviously not set up to handle internal address pointers, the value is handed over to print and winds up on the console as a printed representation of the data object.

2.4 Functions may be used for their value returned or for the side-effects they produce

A point of interest to note is that values returned may be useful in their own right and put to practical use, or may be mere LISP conventions to maintain consistency with the convention that LISP must always return a value. Let's look at a few examples to illustrate this.

When carrying out arithmetic operations, the value returned is of course the whole point of the exercise:

```
* (+ 3 4)
7
```

Whether we are using the interpreter at the top level to help us balance our checkbook, or incorporating the operation at some lower level in a LISP program, the value returned in this case is obviously useful and will be utilized by us or by the function which is calling it.

On the other hand, we often use the function **terpri** (TERminate PRInting) in print routines to output a blank line to the console:

```
* (terpri)

NIL
```

After generating the blank line, **terpri** returns a value of **NIL**. This value is of absolutely no use to anyone, aside from maintaining consistency with the above-mentioned convention that LISP always returns a value. A number of other LISP functions similarly return values which are for all practical purposes useless. Their utility lies in the changes in list structure which they produce, or in the actions they perform (like skipping a line), rather than the values they return.

Where the evaluation of a LISP expression results in some significant change in list structure within the computer's memory, we say that the evaluation has produced a '*side effect.*' For instance, a **setf** operation produces a side effect in that the value cell of a symbol has been altered to contain a new address pointer.

In line with the previous comments we will often hear of a LISP function being called 'for its value' or 'for its side effects.' The arithmetic operation shown above would be a clear instance of a function being called for its value. A **setf** function would normally be called for its side effects.

Occasionally both the side effects *and* the value returned may be useful, as in cases where a **setf** value assignment generates a non-**NIL** value which is then used to trigger a conditional clause.

2.5 Interaction with the interpreter is carried out at the 'top level'

Evaluation of LISP expressions is said to be carried out at different 'levels,' which relate to the degree to which functions are nested within other functions. When we type in an expression at the keyboard we are said to be operating at the '*top level*.' This in turn implies that the value returned to our input will be printed out on the console.

To the extent that we have included a nested expression, this expression must be evaluated before the interpreter can complete evaluation of the top-level expression:

```
* (+ 3 (* 2 2))
7
```

Upon encountering the nested expression (* 2 2), the interpreter 'drops down' one level to evaluate this expression. The resulting value, 4, is 'passed upwards' to the higher level function (+ 3 (...)) in which it is nested and is used by this function as its second argument. Since we are now back at the top level the final value returned, 7, is printed on the console.

Another way to think of levels in LISP is to visualize the stack operations which take place when a nested expression must be evaluated. All of the previous values associated with any higher level expressions must be pushed onto a stack and held in abeyance until evaluation of the lower level expression has been completed.

2.6 A quick preview of nomenclature

We will shortly boot up our system and get started on some hands-on experimentation to see how our LISP interpreter works. However before doing so let's look at the various data objects with which we will be working and define some LISP terminology associated with them.

The most basic building block of LISP is called an *atom*, which term is supposedly derived from the fact that you can't break it down into anything smaller. (This is not strictly true, since we will later learn various ways in which an atom can be decomposed into into its constituent characters.) Atoms come in two types: *numeric atoms*, which we will henceforth simply refer to as *numbers*, and *literal atoms*, which we have already met in the form of *symbols*.

Numbers come in various forms depending on the LISP implementation. GCLISP supports two types of integers and two types of floating-point numbers (see Chapter 22). The main thing to remember about numbers for the moment is the simple fact that they are constants and therefore evaluate to themselves.

We have already met *symbols* in Chapter 1; we will discuss them in greater detail in Chapter 4.

We have also already encountered *lists* in such formats as:

```
(equal (get 'front-door 'security-status) 'unlocked))
```

A list contains so-called *top-level elements*. In the above example, the top-level elements would be the symbol equal, the list (get 'front-door 'security-status), and the list 'unlocked. (Although the latter element does not superficially *look* like a list, the fact that it is preceded by a quote mark causes it to be internally expanded by the read operation into the list (quote unlocked). These top-level elements may be thought of as the basic components which make up the list.

Each of the *nested lists* has its own top-level elements. The first list contains the symbol get and, after expansion, the lists (quote front-door) and (quote security-status). The second list, after expansion, contains the symbols quote and unlocked.

Strings, which are groups of characters demarcated by double quotation marks, come in handy for displaying text on the screen. Like numbers, strings are constants and evaluate to themselves.

All of the foregoing, be they numbers, strings, symbols, or lists, may be referred to by the catch-all phrase *symbolic expression*, or *S-expression* for short, or simply *expression*.

With this basic vocabulary to get us by for the moment, let's now commence our hands-on experiments with the GCLISP interpreter.

2.7 Getting GCLISP loaded and running

For purposes of this discussion we will assume that we have installed the lexically scoped Version 1.1 of our GCLISP interpreter on a hard disk (Drive C:) and are currently in the GCLISP directory on that drive.

After entering gclisp at the keyboard, followed by a carriage return, the following screen is displayed as the interpreter is loaded:

```
GOLDEN COMMON LISP
  Version 1.1, Small Memory
  Copyright (C) 1984, 1985, 1986, 1987 by Gold Hill Computers
; Loading file INIT.FAS
; Reading file C:\GCLISP\USERINIT.LSP
Current directory is \GCLISP
Type Alt-H for help
Top-Level
*
```

The prompt asterisk * indicates that the interpreter is now waiting for us to type in something for evaluation.

We will now start to input different expressions and observe the manner in which they are evaluated and the values which are returned by the interpreter. But first let's prepare for the possibility that we will make some mistakes.

2.8 Various levels of error-handling are provided by GCLISP

As the first step in hands-on familiarization with any LISP interpreter it is a good idea to become familiarized with the kinds of errors which can be generated by the system, and how to return from these errors to normal (top level) operating mode.

As our first experiment at the keyboard, then, let's type in the integer 1000000000000 to provoke an error message from GCLISP:

```
* 1000000000000 <followed by a space>
ERROR:
Integer overflow or underflow.
1>
```

An error was generated because GCLISP only provides for **bignum** integers in the range -2^{32} to $+2^{32} - 1$. Any attempt to evaluate an integer outside of this range or to carry out an arithmetic operation which would return such an integer, will generate the above error.

The 1> below the error message refers to the 'listener level' at which the error break has occurred. In this case the number indicates that we are one level down from the top level. During such a break we can type in more LISP expressions in the normal manner and they will be evaluated. As we will discuss further in Chapter 24, this can be a useful debugging mechanism to ascertain the current values of variables and/or to carry out other operations to find out what is going wrong with the program. (In the above case, of course, the error is obvious.)

If we make yet another mistake at this listener level we will get another error message and will find ourselves in a break at a still lower listener level:

```
1> (how now brown cow)
ERROR:
Undefined function: HOW
while evaluating: (HOW NOW BROWN COW)
2>
```

We got this error because we typed in a list in which the first symbol was not a recognized function.

We can escape from a break level to the next higher level through the use of Ctrl-G, that is, by simultaneously pressing the Control key and the 'G' key. In this case, Ctrl-G will return us to the 1> error level. Another use of Ctrl-G will return us to the top level and the familiar * prompt. Alternatively, if we are several levels down we can skip over the intermediate levels and return directly to the top level with a single application of Ctrl-C. At this point you may wish to generate a series of errors such as the above and practice using Ctrl-G and Ctrl-C to return to the top level.

Another kind of error can occur when we inadvertently generate a programming loop which will continue to cycle indefinitely. The screen will hang up and there will be no response from the keyboard. Let's set up such a situation:

```
* (loop)
```

With no provision for returning from (jumping out of) the loop, the cursor will hang and the function will cycle endlessly. We can break this cycle using Ctrl-Break which returns us to the first-level listener mode with the message:

```
BREAK, (CONTINUE) or c-P to continue.
1>
```

Again, we can use Ctrl-C to get us back to the top level. (Ctrl-G doesn't work in this special case.)

Finally, there may be times when a bug within GCLISP causes the system to hang permanently, defying all efforts to break out of it. This can happen occasionally while using the GMACS editor and can be very frustrating if you have been doing a lot of editing and not gotten around to saving the changes! In such cases there is no alternative but to use the keychord Ctrl-Alt-Delete (three keys simultaneously) to warm boot the system, or simply to shut off the computer. In either case you will have to reload GCLISP and start again from scratch.

When entering expressions into the keyboard we note that as soon as a balancing parenthesis is typed the interpreter immediately carries out the evaluation and returns a value. In a similar vein, when we enter a symbol or a number evaluation will commence the instant the first space has been typed after the input. In other words, as soon as it has a valid expression in hand GCLISP gets right down to business! Initially this can be disconcerting for someone used to genteel systems which wait for a carriage return before processing the input.

2.9 Getting in and out of MS-DOS and exiting GCLISP

While we are working with the interpreter we may wish to return temporarily to MS-DOS to execute some DOS commands such as typing the contents of a file, reviewing the listings of a directory, or carrying out other command-level tasks. We can temporarily exit from GCLISP with the sys:dos command:

```
* (sys:dos)
Going to DOS, type EXIT to return to GCLISP
```

and we will be returned to the disk drive from which we have initiated the GCLISP process. While in MS-DOS we can issue DOS commands such as **type, dir**, etc. but we cannot load another command file since this would introduce memory conflicts with GCLISP. (However see Section 26.2 for ways to run an MS-DOS program from within GCLISP.) After working in MS-DOS we can return to GCLISP by typing an **exit** command without parentheses:

```
C:\GCLISP> exit
NIL
* <GCLISP prompt, ready for more input>
```

Finally, when we are through with GCLISP we can permanently return to the MS-DOS system with the exit command:

```
* (exit)
C:\GCLISP>
```

after which, should we wish to use GCLISP again, we will have to re-initiate it as a new process.

It should be noted that the above procedure can only be carried out when the bare GCLISP interpreter is loaded. When using GMACS, insufficient memory is left over to run MS-DOS commands.

With that background, let's try some hands-on experiments with the system to get familiarized with it. Our initial experimentation will take the form of typing in different kinds of LISP expressions and observing the manner in which the interpreter evaluates them.

2.10 Numbers evaluate to themselves

Numbers, being constants, evaluate to themselves. If we type in a number we will get the same number back:

```
* 13
13
```

We would not normally carry out such a redundant exercise at the top level. However the example illustrates what takes place within the LISP system when it is required to evaluate a number within a program, that is, the same number is returned as a value. Numbers will be discussed in more detail in Chapter 22.

2.11 Strings also evaluate to themselves

A string is a sequence of characters demarcated by double quote marks. Like numbers, strings evaluate to themselves:

```
* "How now brown cow!"
"How now brown cow!"
```

It will be noted that the upper- or lowercase nature of characters are preserved within a string.

Strings are useful in LISP for generating screen displays and for processing natural language. The wide variety of functions provided by Common LISP for processing strings will be reviewed in Chapter 21.

2.12 Assigning values to symbols

If we attempt to evaluate a symbol which does not yet have a value, an error message will be generated:

```
* hotdog
ERROR:
Unbound variable: HOTDOG
1>
```

Aside from the error generation, we note that although we have entered the symbol name in lower case, GCLISP has converted it to upper case. In general, LISP systems like to work with upper case for consistency and will convert all alphabetic characters to upper case unless certain specific steps are taken to maintain their identity as lower case.

After returning to the top level with Ctrl-G, let's assign a value to hotdog:

```
* (setf hotdog '(never sausage a thing!))
(NEVER SAUSAGE A THING!)
```

We can now retrieve the value:

```
* hotdog
(NEVER SAUSAGE A THING!)
```

In Chapter 4 we will review symbols in greater depth, including their nature as LISP data objects and the manner in which values may be assigned to them.

2.13 NIL and T are special symbols in LISP

Two special and often-used symbols, NIL and T, are pre-defined in LISP. Both symbols evaluate to themselves:

```
* nil
NIL
```

```
* t
T
```

NIL is frequently used to represent the Boolean truth value of 'false.' In this context it is returned by a predicate test which does not succeed, for example:

```
* (equal 5 10)
NIL
```

NIL also corresponds to the so-called 'empty list,' that is, a list from which all of the elements have been removed:

```
* ()
NIL
```

NIL is unique in LISP in that it can be considered both a symbol and a list.

T is generally used to correspond to the Boolean truth value of 'true,' and in this context is returned as the value of a successful predicate test:

```
* (equal 10 10)
T
```

2.14 Assigning properties to symbols

As we saw in our previous example with R2D2, we can assign a property to a symbol through use of the setf assignment function used in conjunction with a property retrieval function:

```
* (setf (get 'hotdogs 'meat-type) 'beef)
BEEF
```

and we can subsequently retrieve that property by using the retrieval function alone:

```
* (get 'hotdogs 'meat-type)
BEEF
```

We will be reviewing the use of property lists in more depth in Chapter 18.

2.15 Creating user-defined procedures

One of the more powerful features of LISP is the ability to create a user-defined procedure. The use of defun for this purpose is illustrated by the following example in which we define the function plus. This function takes two arguments, each of which must evaluate to a number, and adds them together:

```
* (defun plus (x y)
    (+ x y))
PLUS
```

We have typed in this definition according to normal LISP conventions. The top line contains the elements **defun** followed by the name of the function being defined and a list containing the so-called *formal parameters* to the function. After typing a carriage return plus several spaces to indent the remaining input, we have typed in the so-called *body* of the function, that is, what it is supposed to do: in this case add together its two arguments. The practice of indenting successive lines of code to indicate nesting relationships and/or improve readability is referred to as *pretty-printing* (see Section 11.7).

After evaluation the interpreter returns the name of the function. (This is another instance where an evaluation is carried out for its side effect, which in this case is the creation of a user-defined procedure. The value returned is of no particular use.)

Now that we have defined our new function we can put it to use:

```
* (plus 4 6)
10
```

In Chapter 6 we will review in more detail the manner in which new LISP functions can be defined by the user.

2.16 Quoting an argument suppresses its evaluation

The evaluation of any LISP S-expression can be suppressed by quoting it. The special form **quote** takes a single argument and returns the argument verbatim, that is, unevaluated:

```
* (quote hello)
HELLO
* (quote my dog has fleas)
MY
```

When the evaluation mechanism encounters **quote** as the first element of a list, it simply returns the second element of the list. If any additional elements are present in the list they will be ignored. Hence if we want the whole phrase in the second example to be quoted we have to enclose it in a list:

```
* (quote (my dog has fleas))
(MY DOG HAS FLEAS)
```

The quote mechanism can be simplified through use of the macro character ', which causes **read** to create a data object which is exactly the same as if the argument had been quoted:

```
* 'hello
HELLO
```

Upon parsing **'hello**, **read** creates the list **(quote hello)** in memory and returns a pointer to this object, which is then passed to **eval**.

2.17 A data list is created by quoting a list of symbols

As indicated in our earlier discussion of lists in everyday life, there are many instances in which we will want a list to contain data rather than be used for its functional implications. Since use of **quote** suppresses evaluation, such a list can be created merely by virtue of quoting it:

```
* (quote (apples pears raisins nuts flour cornflakes))
(APPLES PEARS RAISINS NUTS FLOUR CORNFLAKES)
```

As noted previously, we can get exactly the same effect as **quote** by use of the ' macro character:

```
* '(apples pears raisins nuts flour cornflakes)
(APPLES PEARS RAISINS NUTS FLOUR CORNFLAKES)
```

We will very often find ourselves using such a quoted list as the argument to a function, where the function is used to manipulate the elements of the list in some manner. For example:

```
* (reverse '(apples pears raisins nuts flour cornflakes))
(CORNFLAKES FLOUR NUTS RAISINS PEARS APPLES)
```

The function **reverse** takes a single argument, which must be a list, and returns another list in which the elements are listed in reverse order. It should be noted that in most list-manipulation operations a *copy* of the list is made, and it is the copy which is manipulated and returned. The original list is left unharmed, since other LISP data objects may be pointing to it. (LISP does provide some 'destructive' list-alteration functions (see Section 5.16) which operate directly on the original lists.)

A vast variety of other functions is available which manipulate lists in some manner. Functions such as **cons** build up lists by grafting elements onto the front of the list; **append** joins two or more lists into a single list; and **list** collects its various arguments into a single list. Other functions such as **car** and **cdr** return the first element of a list or the rest of a list (after removing the first element); and functions such as **first**, **second**, **third**, and **nth** return those respective elements of a list. We will review all of these functions in Chapter 5 which deals with list creation and manipulation.

SUMMARY

Summarizing the key points of this chapter:

- a LISP interpreter operates in an *interactive* manner, evaluating the expressions which are typed into it
- the principal work of the interpreter is carried out by the read/eval/print cycle, which reads the input, evaluates it, and prints out the value on the console
- LISP always *returns a value* after evaluating input
- LISP functions may be used for the *values* they return or for the *side effects* which they produce
- the programmer's interactions with the interpreter are generally carried out at the *top level*, but may also be carried out at a lower *listener level* during an error break
- the basic components which make up a list are referred to as the *top level elements* and may comprise numbers, symbols, or other lists
- *numbers* and *strings* evaluate to themselves
- NIL and T are special symbols in LISP
- evaluation of an expression can be suppressed by *quoting* it

EXERCISES

2.1 What are the four elements of the basic LISP interpreter cycle, and what does each do?

2.2 What is the basic purpose of the quote function in LISP?

2.3 Which data objects in LISP evaluate to themselves?

2.4 LISP functions are principally used for the sake of which two activities associated with their use?

2.5 What keychord combination is used to return to the next higher listener level after a break?

2.6 What keychord combination is used to skip over intermediate listener levels and return directly to the top level?

2.7 What keychord combination breaks out of an endless loop and returns you to the top level?

2.8 What expression is typed to exit temporarily from GCLISP to the MS-DOS operating system?

2.9 What expression is typed to return from DOS to GCLISP?

2.10 What expression is typed to exit permanently from GCLISP?

Chapter 3

Getting Acquainted with Functions

To programmers used to procedural languages such as BASIC or PASCAL the function-calling mechanisms of LISP can seem at first sight confusing. The purpose of this chapter is therefore to present a simplified introduction to LISP functions through a review of its basic arithmetic operations.

Since LISP is touted for its talents at symbolic computation, one may reasonably ask: why use numerical calculations to start off with? The reason is that arithmetic operations are the most straightforward functions of LISP and thus are easy to explain and to understand. Using them as examples we can demonstrate the essential features of LISP, including its somewhat peculiar Polish syntax, its methods of evaluation, and its recursive nature. Once the foregoing are understood it is an easy step to using more complex functions for symbol manipulation.

In this chapter we will look at:

- the use of *parentheses* to demarcate a list
- the use of *Polish notation*, in which arguments are preceded by the name of a function to be applied to them
- the structure and use of the basic LISP functions for *addition*, *subtraction*, *multiplication*, and *division*
- the kinds of *error messages* which are generated as a result of incorrect function calls
- the use of *predicates* to test for certain features of a number and to compare one number against others
- how the largest or smallest number can be extracted from a group of numbers, using max and min
- the use of 1+ and 1− to increment or decrement a number
- the manner in which functions may be *nested*

3.1 Parentheses are used to demarcate a list

The first impression that one gets when looking at a LISP program is that there seem to be an awful lot of parentheses! Inevitably, various wags have postulated that the acronym LISP is derived from 'Lots of Irritating Silly Parentheses.'

Left and right parentheses are used as a printing convention to indicate the beginning and end of a list. Since a LISP program is made up of many such lists, most of which are nested within other lists, the printed representation of such a program contains a great many parentheses. The term 'printed representation' is used here to flag out that the parentheses do not physically exist within the interpreter; rather they are an external way of representing the beginning and end of a linked network of memory cells. We will explore all of this in more detail in Chapter 5.

When you start typing in an expression and the first character is a left parenthesis you are signalling your intention to enter a list. Thereafter the interpreter keeps track of all left and right parentheses which are typed in and defers evaluation of the expression until a final balancing right parenthesis has been typed. (The GMACS editor includes a convenient feature

Fig. 3.1 Parentheses must balance in a LISP expression.

whereby, when the cursor is located just after a right parenthesis, the matching left parenthesis located earlier in the expression is displayed in flashing mode. When working with deeply nested expressions, this feature helps you to keep track of parentheses.)

3.2 Polish notation is an essential feature of LISP's syntax

We can introduce Polish notation with a shaggy dog story. We have three dogs: **fido**, **spot**, and **max**, and we are being reminded to put them out at night. If our spouse spoke LISP, he/she might put it this way:

```
(put-out fido spot max)
```

An English command like this has a lot in common with a LISP function in that the operative verb comes first in the sentence, followed by objects on which the verb is to operate. In LISP terms we can think of **put-out** as a symbol which represents a functional procedure, and **fido**, **spot**, and **max** as the objects to which the procedure is to be applied.

The foregoing illustrates a principal aspect of LISP's syntax, known as *Polish notation*, wherein the first symbol on a list is taken to be an indicator of the function to be carried out, and the remaining elements of the list – which may be atoms or other lists – are the arguments on which that function is to operate. This somewhat peculiar syntax, in which the name of a function is placed to the left of its arguments, is attributed to the Polish logician Jan Lukasiewicz and was developed before computers came onto the scene. Unfortunately for Lukasiewicz, his name was such a hassle for English-speaking people to pronounce, much less spell, that the syntax came to be known simply as Polish notation. We can express Polish notation diagrammatically, as shown in Fig. 3.2.

Polish notation comes in handy since there is never any doubt as to

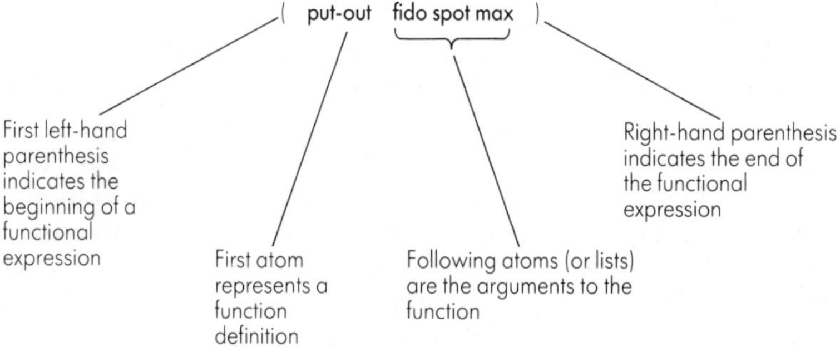

Fig. 3.2 LISP syntax utilizes Polish notation.

what function is being applied; it is always the first symbol in a list. Aside from this advantage, Polish notation is useful in that it allows any number of arguments to follow the function name. (If you wanted to add five numbers together within a list, where else would you put a single + operator?)

In summary – and subject to a few provisos as mentioned below – whenever you see a LISP expression enclosed within parentheses, the first atom can be taken to be the name of a LISP function to be called, and the elements which follow (which may be atoms or embedded lists) can be assumed to be the arguments on which that function is to operate.

3.3 Built-in LISP functions are called primitives

In preceding chapters we saw some examples of the many LISP functions which are built into the system, for example, **setf**:

```
* (setf hotdogs '(bunch of sausages))
(BUNCH OF SAUSAGES)
```

Since the symbol **setf** is built into the interpeter, along with many other functions, it is referred to as a *primitive* to differentiate it from it from the user-defined functions which we will later be creating ourselves.

The terminology associated with functions varies somewhat among LISP *cognoscenti*. Some writers take a more mathematical approach to the word 'function' on the basis that this term should be reserved for procedures which compute a value based only on their arguments, for example (+ 3 4); whereas other kinds of functions such as **setf** should more properly be referred to as 'procedures.' For the time being we will use the general term *function* to refer to any LISP primitive which is used to activate a procedure, with or without arguments. Later we will fine-tune this terminology as we differentiate between the three types of procedures used in Common LISP to carry out function-like operations, that is, normal functions, special forms, and macros.

A LISP primitive has something in common with a procedure in PASCAL or a subroutine in BASIC, in that it specifies some operation to be carried out in a pre-defined manner on its arguments. One principal difference is that, whereas procedures or subroutines can be of any degree of complexity, a LISP primitive only carries out one particular operation on its arguments. In order to achieve the complexity of a PASCAL procedure it is necessary to employ two or more of these primitives working together in combination in the form of a user-defined function.

The amount of primitives will vary with the LISP implementation. In small systems designed for CP/M, from 80 to 100 primitives will be included. In larger MS-DOS systems, the vastly increased memory permits a much wider selection of primitives. GCLISP, which is still only a subset of Common LISP, offers approximately 350 primitives.

As a first step in getting acquainted with LISP functions we will look at the four basic arithmetic functions used to add, subtract, multiply, and divide numbers. We will use simple integers for our examples, although these functions may be used to operate on floating point numbers as well.

3.4 The + function corresponds to addition

Let's look first at the + function which adds up its arguments and returns their sum. Like a number of other LISP functions + is flexible in that it can take any number of arguments. The syntax of a + function call is as follows:

```
(+ &rest <numbers>)
```

where the notation **&rest** indicates that an indefinite number of arguments can follow. Also, since no arguments are included before **&rest**, the function can be called with *no* arguments, in which case it returns 0:

```
* (+ 1 2 3 4 5 6)
21
* (+)
0
```

At this point you should experiment a bit with the + function to see what kind of errors you can generate. What happens if you include additional spaces or carriage returns in the course of typing in the input? If you use the wrong symbol in place of +? If you enter as an argument a symbol which as yet has no value? If you enter an argument other than a number?

3.5 Incorrect function calls invoke various kinds of error messages

We find that LISP is very tolerant of redundant 'whitespace' incorporated into the input, that is, carriage returns, spaces, tab stops, etc. Taking a simple example:

```
* (+ 3 4)
7
```

If we now type in the same expression, including a bunch of random carriage returns, spaces, tab stops, etc., we find that we get exactly the same result:

```
* (    +
    3     4
          )
7
```

In the course of parsing the input, the **read** function of LISP is basically looking for left parentheses, right parentheses, and atoms, the end of which are signaled by a parenthesis or a space. These considerations aside, any extra whitespace which is incorporated is completely ignored during the parsing process.

Other kinds of mischief will generally earn us an error message. If we misspell the name of the function or if the first symbol in the list does not currently have a functional definition, we will generate an 'undefined function' error:

```
* (% 3 4)
ERROR:
Undefined function: %
while evaluating: (% 3 4)
1>
```

(Remember from Chapter 2 that we can get out of the break and return to the top level with Ctrl-G.)

The + function is a 'normal' kind of LISP function in which all of the arguments are evaluated before the function is applied to them. Another kind of error can therefore occur when one of the arguments is *unbound*, that is, as yet has no value:

```
* (+ apples pears)
ERROR:
Unbound variable: APPLES
1>
```

In this case neither **apples** nor **pears** is bound to a value. Since evaluation is proceeding from left to right the interpreter will issue the error message on the first unbound argument it comes to, that is, **apples.**

When processing an arithmetic function, LISP understandably expects arguments which evaluate to numbers:

```
* (setf apples 3)
3

* (setf pears '(my favorite fruit))
(MY FAVORITE FRUIT)

* (+ apples pears)
ERROR:
+: wrong type argument: (MY FAVORITE FRUIT)
A NUMBER was expected.
1>
```

On the other hand:

```
* (setf pears 4)
4

* (+ apples pears)
7
```

Who says you can't add apples and pears? When using arithmetic functions LISP is happy so long as all of the arguments evaluate to numbers.

3.6 Quoting numbers has no effect on their value

As might be expected, since numbers evaluate to themselves, quoting them has no effect whatsoever on the end result:

```
* (+ '12 '3)
15
```

3.7 Other functions provide for subtraction, multiplication, and division

The function − provides for subtraction and takes the syntax:

```
(- <number> &rest <more-numbers>)
```

In this case, and unlike +, at least one argument is required. If we try to call − without any arguments an error message is generated:

```
* (-)
ERROR:
Wrong number of arguments for: -
while evaluating: (-)
1>
```

If a single argument is provided − returns the negative of that number. Otherwise, subsequent arguments are subtracted from the first argument:

```
* (- 13)
-13

* (- 100 20 13 4)
63
```

If we subtract one number from another number we will note that the *second* argument is subtracted from the *first* argument. In the case of the + function discussed previously the order of the arguments did not matter. However in most instances of LISP functions the order very definitely *does* matter, and this is perhaps a good place to make that point. During the creation of user-defined functions, which we will discuss in in Chapter 6, we will find that it is essential to indicate the order in which arguments are to be specified.

The function * provides for multiplication and takes the syntax:

```
(* &rest <numbers>)
```

Like the + function, * can be called without arguments, in which case it returns 1. A single argument will be returned as is. Otherwise, the arguments will be multiplied together:

```
* (*)
1

* (* 13)
13

* (* 2 3 4 5)
120
```

Like +, the order of arguments does not matter.

You may find the fact that the GCLISP prompt symbol * is the same as the name of the multiplication function mildly confusing. The two are quite different in the sense that the prompt symbol is an arbitrary character or sequence of characters displayed on the screen by the prompt subroutine. The * which you input is a LISP primitive which exists on the Object List and which has the functional implication as noted.

The function / provides for division, and takes the syntax:

```
(/ <number> &rest <more-numbers>)
```

As for −, at least one argument is required. When called with a single argument / returns the reciprocal of that argument. Otherwise, the second through the last arguments are successively divided into the first argument:

```
* (/ 4)
0.25

* (/ 10 2)
5.0

* (/ 80 8 3)
3.33333
```

It will be noted that when dividing integers GCLISP provides a floating-point number as the quotient, even when the quotient is an integer.

Furthermore, when a division operation is embedded within another arithmetic function, the overall value returned becomes a floating-point number to maintain consistency with the value returned by the division operation:

```
* (+ 2 (/ 10 5))
4.0
```

The conversion of an integer into a floating-point number in situations where the two types of numbers are being combined by an arithmetic operation is referred to as *floating-point contagion*, and will be discussed in more detail in Chapter 22.

Many other mathematical operations are provided for by GCLISP, including exponential, square root and logarithmic operations, trigonometric functions, and logical operations on numbers. These will be discussed in Chapter 22, which deals with the more complex numerical capabilities of GCLISP, including the use of floating-point numbers.

While we are discussing arithmetic functions, let's look at a few other related LISP functions which increment or decrement a number, pick out the largest or smallest number from a group, and test certain qualities of a number.

3.8 1+ and 1− increment and decrement a number

In the course of keeping count of some operation, or in counting down to zero from some initial value, it is often necessary to increment or decrement a given number by 1. The functions 1+ and 1− come in handy for this purpose. The first of these adds 1 to its single argument; the second subtracts 1. For example:

```
* (1+ 12)
13
* (1- 12)
11
```

You could of course express the above as (+ 12 1) and (− 12 1), respectively, and get the same result. However since incrementing and decrementing numbers by 1 is commonly carried out in iterative situations, 1+ and 1− have been provided as separate primitives which are computationally more efficient than the + and − functions.

3.9 max and min can be used to extract the largest and smallest number of a group

At times we may have a group of numbers and wish to extract either the largest or the smallest of these numbers. Such operations may be carried out with max and min.

max returns the argument which is greatest, that is, closest to positive infinity:

```
* (max 5 3 10 4 2 5)
10
```

min returns the argument which is least, that is, closest to negative infinity.

```
* (min 5 3 10 4 2 5)
2
```

3.10 Recognizer predicates test for features of a number

While on the subject of numbers, let's introduce a number of *recognizer predicates* which deal with numbers. A *predicate* is a function which makes some kind of test of its argument(s) and generally returns a **T** or **NIL** value, depending on whether the test succeeds. Predicates are widely used as a test for a branching operation, and we will be looking at them in much more detail in Chapter 8.

Zerop tests whether a number is zero. If it is, **zerop** returns **T**:

```
* (zerop 0)
T
```

Otherwise it returns **NIL**:

```
* (zerop 5)
NIL
```

Unlike the numerical functions which we looked at earlier, these predicates take only a single argument and will complain if more than one argument is provided:

```
* (zerop 0 0)
ERROR:
Wrong number of arguments for: ZEROP
While evaluating: (ZEROP 0 0)
1>
```

Other recognizer predicates dealing with numbers are as follows.

Predicate	*Tests whether its argument is*
plusp	a positive number
minusp	a negative number
oddp	an odd number
evenp	an even number

Zerop, **plusp**, and **minusp** work with any type of number; **oddp** and **evenp** work only with integers.

3.11 Comparator predicates compare a number against one or more other numbers

In addition to the recognizer predicates listed above, a number of *comparator predicates* are provided whereby a number can be compared against one or more other numbers.

The equal predicate = provides a test for equality of its first argument against one or more following arguments:

```
* (= 5 5 5)
T
* (= 5 6 7)
NIL
```

Other comparator predicates are as follows.

Predicate	*Tests whether all its arguments are*
/=	unequal
<	monotonically increasing
>	monotonically decreasing
<=	monotonically nondecreasing
>=	monotonically nonincreasing

Use of all these predicates without a second argument returns **T**.

The comparator predicates **eql** and **equal** (see Section 8.6) which are normally used to compare symbols may also be used on any type of number. In GCLISP **eq** may be used to compare **fixnums** (but not **bignums**).

3.12 A LISP program is similar to a corporate organization

So far we have generally been dealing with top-level function calls which demonstrate the use of one or another LISP primitive. These simple function calls return their value to the console.

A typical LISP program is of course much more complex and consists of a multitude of interrelated functional expressions, most of which are themselves nested within other functions. The whole program therefore winds up as a hierarchical structure in which 'lower' – that is, more deeply nested – functions 'report upwards' to the functions which have in turn called them.

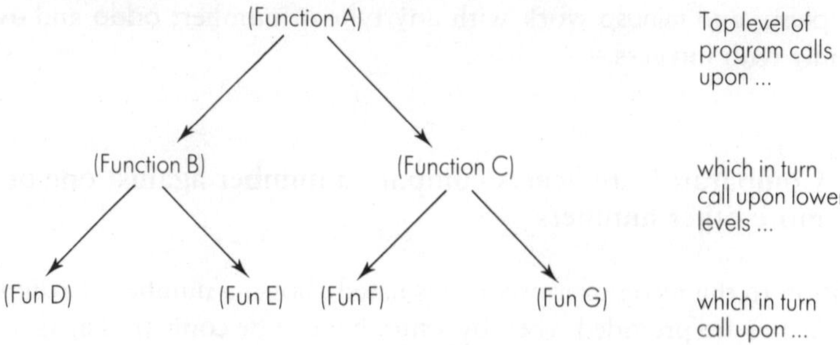

Fig. 3.3 A LISP program is hierarchically structured.

As mentioned earlier, a LISP program has much in common with a corporate organization in that various levels can call upon lower levels in order to get a specific job accomplished. These levels may call in turn upon still lower levels to handle problem solving at an even finer level of detail. The results of these collective efforts pass back upwards through the organization in the form of values returned, and eventually reach the topmost level which returns a final value to the console. Such a structure may be represented diagramatically, as shown in Fig. 3.3.

Putting all of the foregoing together in a linear manner we might expect to wind up with something like this:

```
( A ( B ( D )( E ))( C ( F )( G )))
```

wherein functions D and E are nested within B, functions F and G are nested within C, and functions B and C are in turn nested within A. And *that* is where all those Lots of Irritating Silly Parentheses come from – the need to isolate and otherwise indicate the nesting relationships of all those individual function calls!

3.13 Functions may be nested to any number of levels

What do we mean when we say that a function can call upon another subordinate function to carry out the detail work? Let's look again at some simple arithmetic functions to explore this new concept.

In an earlier experiment we observed the **read/eval/print** mechanism at work when we typed in the expression:

```
* (+ 6 5)
11
```

The LISP interpreter *read* the expression which we typed, *evaluated* the result of applying the + function to the arguments 6 and 5, and *printed* the value returned on the console screen.

We can amplify our LISP technical vocabulary at this point by defining a few additional terms.

To *enter a function* refers to the point at which the interpreter is called upon to evaluate a nested functional expression and drops down one level to commence evaluation of that expression. To *exit a function* refers to the point at which the interpreter has finished evaluating the expression and returns a value to the next higher level calling function. (For those with an interest in the machine language aspects, the act of 'returning a value' means placing a pointer to the address of a LISP data object in an appropriate register of the CPU chip, whence it may be retrieved by another LISP function.)

Let's now look at an example where one of the arguments to the above example is *replaced* by another function call:

```
* (+ 6 (- 7 2))
11
```

Although the same answer is returned, in this case a somewhat more complex evaluation process has taken place. As in the earlier example, the interpreter enters the first function, finds a valid function symbol, that is, +, and continues on to look for numerical arguments to which to apply the function. The first argument, 6, satisfies the requisites. However upon searching further for the next argument, the interpreter runs head on into another nested functional expression!

At this point the interpreter must now stop and evaluate the new functional expression. The value returned by this expression should equate to a number which will be used in turn as the next argument to the higher level function. Evaluation of (– 7 2) is straightforward and the value of 5 is returned.

It is at this point that operation at a lower level differs from operation at the top level. In this case, rather than being printed to the console, the value returned is passed upwards to the next higher level function and is used as an argument to that function. The net effect is therefore exactly the same as if we had entered (+ 6 5) in the first place.

We can conceptualize the levels involved, as shown in Fig. 3.4. All LISP programs, however complicated, are evaluated in this basic manner. Whenever a left-hand parenthesis is encountered, the program will temporarily

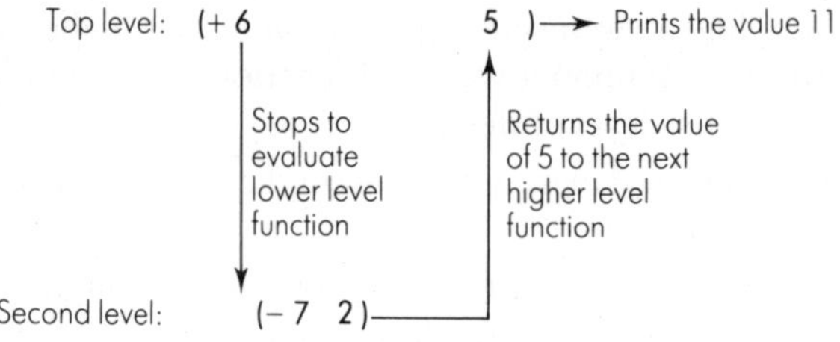

Fig. 3.4 Functions are evaluated at different 'levels'.

store the results of the current evaluation and will drop down to a lower level to explore the next list. Whenever a right-hand parenthesis is encountered, the value resulting from evaluation of that list will be passed upward one level and used as an argument by the higher level function.

Functions can be nested to any depth, subject only to the amount of memory available for the control stack, on which intermediate results are held pending while the program recurs to ever-lower levels.

SUMMARY

Summarizing the key points of this chapter:

- *parentheses* are used to demarcate a LISP list
- the first atom in a list represents the name of a *function*
- the remaining elements which make up the list are the *arguments* to which the function is to be applied
- the system of putting the function name first followed by the arguments is referred to as *Polish notation*
- basic LISP *numerical functions* include +, −, *, and /, corresponding to addition, subtraction, multiplication, and division, all of which may take an indefinite number of arguments
- LISP issues *error messages* to indicate too many or too few arguments and/or other deviations from standard syntax
- the functions 1+ and 1− may be used to increment or decrement a number
- a *recognizer predicate* tests a certain feature of its single argument
- a *comparator predicate* tests some feature of its first argument against that of its remaining argument(s)
- the functions max and min extract the largest and smallest number from a group, respectively
- LISP is like a *corporate organization* in that higher level functions call upon lower level functions to get work done at an ever-finer level of detail
- LISP *enters* and *exits* a function in the course of executing a function call
- a function always *returns a value* to the next higher level calling function or, at top level, to the console

EXERCISES

3.1 What values would the following expressions return? If any expressions are incorrect, what kind of error message would be generated?

(a) (+ 3 4 (− 2 1)(* 5 5))
(b) (/ 20 5 (plus 1 1))
(c) (/ 60 2 (* 2 3))
(d) (* (+ (− (/ 20 2) 2) 2) 10)
(e) (setf pears 3)
(f) (1+ (max 4 5 (min 8 9 3)))
(g) (evenp 4 6)
(h) (<= (+ 2 4)(− 10 3))
(i) (>= 5 4 (− 4 1))

3.2 The area of a triangle is (**base** × **height**)/2. Assuming that the symbols **base** and **height** have already been bound to their proper values, write an expression which will return the area of the triangle.

3.3 The area of a circle is (**pi** × **diameter** × **diameter**)/4. Assuming that **pi** and **diameter** have already been bound to their proper values, write an expression which will return the area of the circle.

3.4 Assuming that 2 is bound to some numerical value, write an expression which returns the value of the polynomial term $x^2 + 2x + 6$. Can you think of an alternate way to write the expression?

3.5 If the symbol **apple** has been bound to a numerical value, write two LISP expressions which can be used to bind the symbol **pear** to a number which is 1 higher than **apple**.

3.6 The symbol **grape** is bound to an unknown value. Write an expression to test whether **grape** is zero.

3.7 Taking the sequence of numbers 7, 3, 2, 6, 6, and 9, write an expression which will test whether the smallest number in the group is an odd number.

3.8 Taking the same sequence of numbers as Exercise 3.7, write an expression which will test whether the largest number in the group is an even number.

3.9 Taking the sequence of numbers 4, −3, 5, −7, −2, and 1, write an expression which will test whether the sum of all these numbers is a positive number.

3.10 Taking the same sequence of numbers as Exercise 3.9, write an expression which will test whether the cumulative difference of all these numbers is a negative number.

Chapter 4
Symbols as Data Objects

As we saw in the first chapter, LISP symbols may be used in various ways. A symbol may have a value, in which case the symbol name may be thought of as an identifier for the constant or variable which the symbol represents. Symbols may also be used to represent a real-world object, in which case property indicators and values may be put onto their property lists to describe various attributes of the object. Finally, symbols may be used to name a procedure to be carried out.

This chapter will focus on the first feature and look at ways in which values may be assigned to symbols and how these values may be later retrieved for use. At the same time we will look at the manner in which a symbol is represented as a *data object* within the interpreter.

In this chapter we will look at:

- the nature of the *Object List*, which serves as a symbol lookup table
- the manner in which a *symbol is created* as a data object and added to the Object List
- the manner in which a symbol's value is represented by a *pointer* to some LISP data object
- how a value may be assigned to a symbol using **setq**
- the use of **psetq**, which assigns values in parallel
- the use of **set**, in which both of its arguments are evaluated
- a number of functions which retrieve information about a symbol or test to see whether a data object is a symbol
- the use of **setf** to assign a value to a generalized variable
- the use of functions to test whether a symbol has a value or to wipe out any value a symbol may have

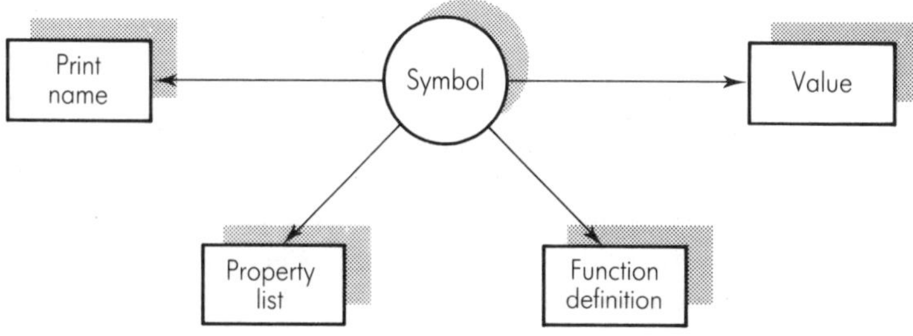

Fig. 4.1 A LISP symbol has four principal attributes.

4.1 Symbols have four principal attributes

As discussed in Chapter 1, four principal attributes can be associated with a LISP symbol (see Fig. 4.1).

(1) The *print name* is the sequence of characters which represents the name of the symbol. This name is stored as a string in memory and used by print to generate the printed representation of the symbol when required.

(2) The *property list* of the symbol is the list of property indicators and their values which may be associated with a symbol through the use of appropriate assignment functions. We will review property lists in more detail in Chapter 18.

(3) The *function definition* of the symbol is a definition of the procedure to be carried out when the symbol is used in a functional context. We will look at this aspect in Chapter 6.

(4) The *value* of the symbol is the data object which the symbol represents. This value is most commonly another symbol, a number, or a list. However symbols may also be used to represent more complex data objects such as streams, packages, closures, arrays, etc. the nature of which will be reviewed in later chapters.

A symbol is physically represented in computer memory as a short vector containing address pointers to each of the above attributes. During the evaluation process eval uses these pointers to retrieve the appropriate attribute.

4.2 The Object List functions as a symbol lookup table

When the interpreter is loaded into the computer the initialization process creates a symbol table which contains all of the symbols pre-defined by

LISP. This table is generally referred to as the Object List (Oblist). The manner in which the Oblist is physically constructed in memory is outlined in more detail in Chapter 28.

Most of the pre-defined symbols are functional primitives such as **setq**, **cons**, **quote**, etc. The remaining symbols include the special symbols **NIL** and **T**, as well as certain global parameters such as ***print-base*** and ***print-length*** (see Section 11.8) whose values affect the manner in which the interpreter carries out its operations.

Thereafter, as new symbols are defined by the user in the course of an interactive session with the interpreter, these symbols are added to the Oblist. This list may therefore be thought of as a kind of master lookup table which contains pointers to the names, property lists, function definitions, and values of all active symbols in current use.

4.3 The interpreter allocates memory during the initialization process

During the initialization process, which takes place when the interpreter is first loaded, the amount of available (on-board) memory is ascertained. In a CP/M system this might typically be 56K; in an MS-DOS system 640K. Depending on how much memory is available for use, the interpreter allocates it for specific purposes. This allocation is discussed in more detail in Chapter 28 which explores the makeup of a typical microcomputer interpreter.

The bulk of the memory is allocated to list storage, since this represents by far the largest memory requirement of a LISP system. Lesser areas are allocated for storage of strings, integers, floating-point numbers, and the control stack which is used to keep track of function calls and their values.

Within the body of the interpreter itself are two areas relevant to this discussion. One area contains the machine language subroutines associated with 'normal' LISP functions, that is, those which evaluate all of their arguments. The other area is reserved for 'special' LISP functions, such as **setq**, which require special handling during evaluation. **eval** can quickly ascertain whether it is dealing with a normal or a special function simply by testing to which area the function pointer is pointing. Memory allocation can be illustrated graphically (see Fig. 4.2).

4.4 A symbol data object contains address pointers

When a new symbol is created during the course of a LISP program, a data object corresponding to this symbol is created and added to the end of the Object List. Such a data object would typically be at least eight computer

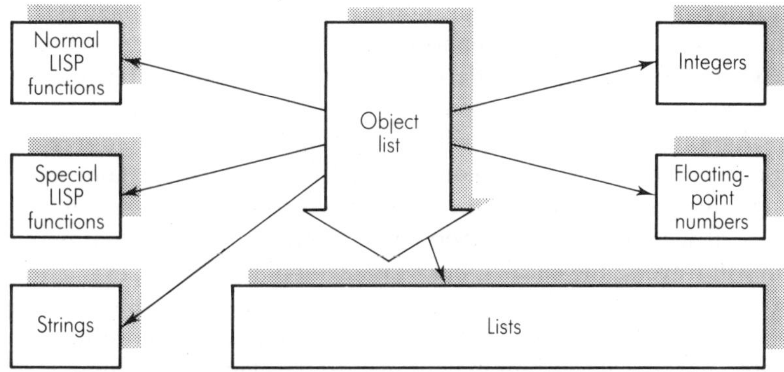

Fig. 4.2 The LISP interpreter allocates areas of memory.

words in length, as required to specify four (double-word) address locations. For instance, in a CP/M-80 implementation a symbol data object might be 8 bytes in length, corresponding to four 2-byte cells which contain address pointers to the symbol's print name, property list, function definition, and value, respectively. In an MS-DOS system, where memory is not at such a premium, symbol data objects might be somewhat longer depending on what additional information – such as pointers to documentation strings – might be tacked onto the data object.

Assuming that we have just created a new symbol with the name **hotdog**, but have as yet assigned no value, property list, or function definition to this symbol, the data object might be represented in memory as shown in Fig. 4.3, where XX XX represents a double-word address pointer.

In most microcomputer LISPs when a symbol is initially created its name is stored as a string in that portion of memory reserved for strings. The starting address of this string is stored in the print name pointer cell. Thereafter, whenever the **print** function is called upon to generate the printed representation of the symbol it will extract that address from the

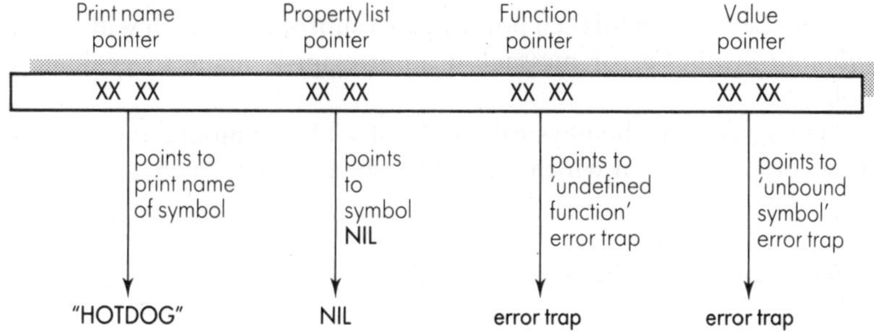

Fig. 4.3 Symbol data object contains address pointers.

print name pointer cell and print out the string which commences at that address. (In GCLISP, which supports packages, the print name is handled somewhat differently. This difference, which is not essential at this point, will be explored further in Chapter 25.)

Although other pointer cells may not hold any useful addresses, the print name pointer cell *always* contains a pointer to the print name; and it is through this print name that the data object itself is later referenced. For instance, if we now type in **hotdog** to the interpreter, the evaluation mechanism will traverse the entire Object List, symbol by symbol, extracting the print name associated with each symbol and comparing this print name with the string "**HOTDOG**". (In MS-DOS LISPs, where more memory is available, hashing algorithms may be used to speed up lookup on the Object List.) When a match is found the value address pointer is extracted by **eval** and passed over to **print**, which follows the pointer and generates a printed representation of the data object pointed to as the value returned. If no value has been bound to the symbol an error message is generated.

Depending on the circumstances in which the symbol has been created, the remaining cells may contain pointers to other data objects or (if LISP primitives) to machine language subroutines.

If the symbol has been created in the course of initializing its *property list* with a statement such as **(setf (get <property-name> <property-indicator>) <property-value>)**, the address of the property list which is created will be put into the property list pointer cell. Otherwise, this cell will be initialized to point to **NIL**.

If the symbol has been created in the course of defining a function of that name, the address of the *lambda definition* created during evaluation of the **defun** statement will be put into the function pointer cell. Otherwise, as previously noted in connection with the value, an address will be put into this cell pointing to a subroutine which will generate an *undefined function* error message if an attempt is made to use the symbol name in a functional context.

If the symbol has been created in the course of a value assignment such as **(setf <symbol-name> <value>)**, the address of the data object assigned as **<value>** will be stored in the value pointer cell. Otherwise an address will be put into this cell pointing to a subroutine which will generate an *unbound symbol* error message if an attempt is made to evaluate the symbol.

Having defined the physical nature of a LISP symbol data object, we will now look at ways in which we can assign a value to such a symbol.

4.5 setq assigns a value to a symbol

The principal traditional assignment function in LISP is **setq**, which assigns the value of its second argument to the symbol named by its first argument.

setq's basic syntax is therefore:

```
(setq <symbol-name><some-value>)
```

The combination **<symbol-name><some-value>** can be repeated indefinitely (see Section 4.6) so as to assign values to two or more symbols at the same time. However for the balance of this discussion we will assume that only one symbol is involved.

setq is an exception to normal LISP functions in that its first argument is *not* evaluated. (We can think of **setq** as an acronym for SET value to Quoted first argument). Let's type in a **setq** statement:

```
* (setq test-numb 12)
12
```

When we typed in the above expression, various operations were carried out in the course of the **read/eval/print** cycle. We will discuss these operations in detail in Chapter 29, for those with an interest in 'what goes on' within the interpreter, but will review them briefly here as a guide to what happens during the assignment of a value to a symbol.

- The **read** operation constructed an internal representation of the list **(SETQ TEST-NUMB 12)** in the area of memory allocated to lists, and returned a pointer to this data object, which pointer was then passed to **eval**.
- During parsing of the above list by **read**, the symbol **TEST-NUMB** was looked up on the Oblist, could not be found, and was therefore added to the list as a new symbol. At this time, all of its pointer cells were initialized along the lines discussed previously in connection with **"HOTDOG"** (Section 4.4).
- **eval** inspected **setq**, the first element in the expression, ascertained that it was a valid function name, and at the same time ascertained that it was a special function in which the first argument is not to be evaluated.
- The second argument **12** was evaluated, returning a value equal to itself.
- The address of the integer **12** was put into the value cell of the symbol **TEST-NUMB**, replacing the pointer to the 'unbound symbol' error trap.
- Finally, this same address was handed over to the **print** function which outputs the printed representation of **12** to the console, representing the value returned of the **setq** function.

The configuration of our newly created data object is shown in Fig. 4.4.

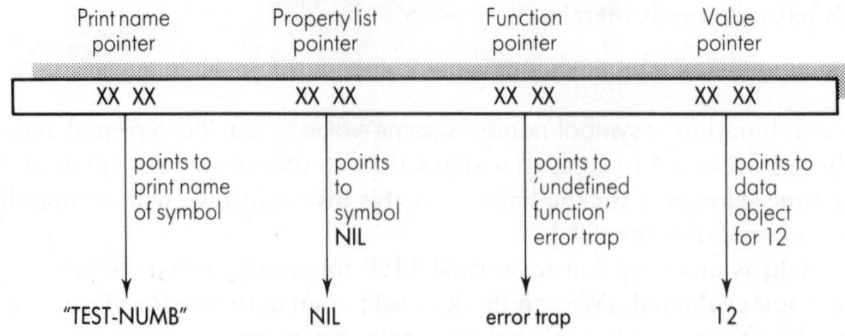

Fig. 4.4 Symbol data object for **TEST-NUMB.**

As discussed previously, the property list address would have been initialized to point to **NIL**, and the function address initialized to point to a routine which generates an undefined function error.

An error message will be generated if we try to **setq** a value to anything other than a symbol:

```
* (setq 12 'hotdog)
ERROR:
SETQ: wrong type argument: 12
A SYMBOL was expected.
1>
```

In order to illustrate the use of the Object List, and the manner in which the address pointers of a symbol reference other areas of memory, let's make a number of other **setq** assignments. These will cover a range of possibilities, that is, will assign different kinds of data objects as the value of a symbol. For consistency we will give all of these symbols mnemonic names commencing with **test–**.

Firstly, we can assign a floating-point number:

```
* (setq test-flot 123.456)
123.456
```

after which the value cell of **test-flot** will point to a new data object created in the area reserved for floating point numbers.

We can assign a list as the value of a symbol:

```
* (setq test-list '(this is a list))
(THIS IS A LIST)
```

We have quoted the list in order to suppress evaluation; otherwise the interpreter would assume that the symbol **this** represents a function name and would try to evaluate **(THIS IS A LIST)** as a function call.

We can assign a string as the value:

```
* (setq test-strg "hello!")
"hello!"
```

During the **read** operation the string is created in the area of memory reserved for strings, and a pointer to the start of the string is placed in the value cell of the symbol. For purposes of this discussion we will follow the convention used in many microcomputer LISPs in which a null byte is tacked onto the end of the string as a terminating signal. (GCLISP incorporates a special length field into the string structure which is used to determine when the end of the string is reached.)

Finally, we can assign another symbol as the value:

```
* (setq test-symb 'test-strg)
TEST-STRG
```

in which the previous symbol we created, **TEST-STRG**, has been assigned as the value of the new symbol **TEST-SYMB**. Again, we have quoted the symbol name in order that the symbol itself, and not its value, is assigned as the value of **TEST-SYMB**. Had we not quoted it, we would have had this result:

```
* (setq test-symb test-strg)
"hello!"
```

in which the *value* of **TEST-STRG**, rather than the symbol itself, would have been assigned as the value of **TEST-SYMB**.

If we could now inspect the Oblist, we would find that all of the new symbols have been added and that the addresses in their value cells are pointing to the data objects which have been assigned as their values (see Fig. 4.5). As we note from the diagram, the value pointer for **TEST-NUMB** is pointing to the data object for the integer **12**, which is located in the portion of memory reserved for integers. The value pointer for **TEST-FLOT** is pointing to the floating point number **123.456** which has just been created in the area of storage reserved for floating point numbers. The value pointer for **TEST-LIST** points to the internal representation of the (quoted) list **(THIS IS A LIST)** which has been created in the list area. The value pointer for **TEST-STRG** points to the string **"hello!"** which has been added to the strings previously created for print names. (NB: This reflects the manner of handling print names for most LISP microcomputer implementations; that is, they are incorporated into the string area along with strings created for other purposes. As we will see when we get to Chapter 25, Common LISP systems which support packages handle print name strings on a separate lookup table associated with the package name.) Finally, the value pointer for **TEST-SYMB** points to the first byte of the data object which was previously created for **TEST-STRG**.

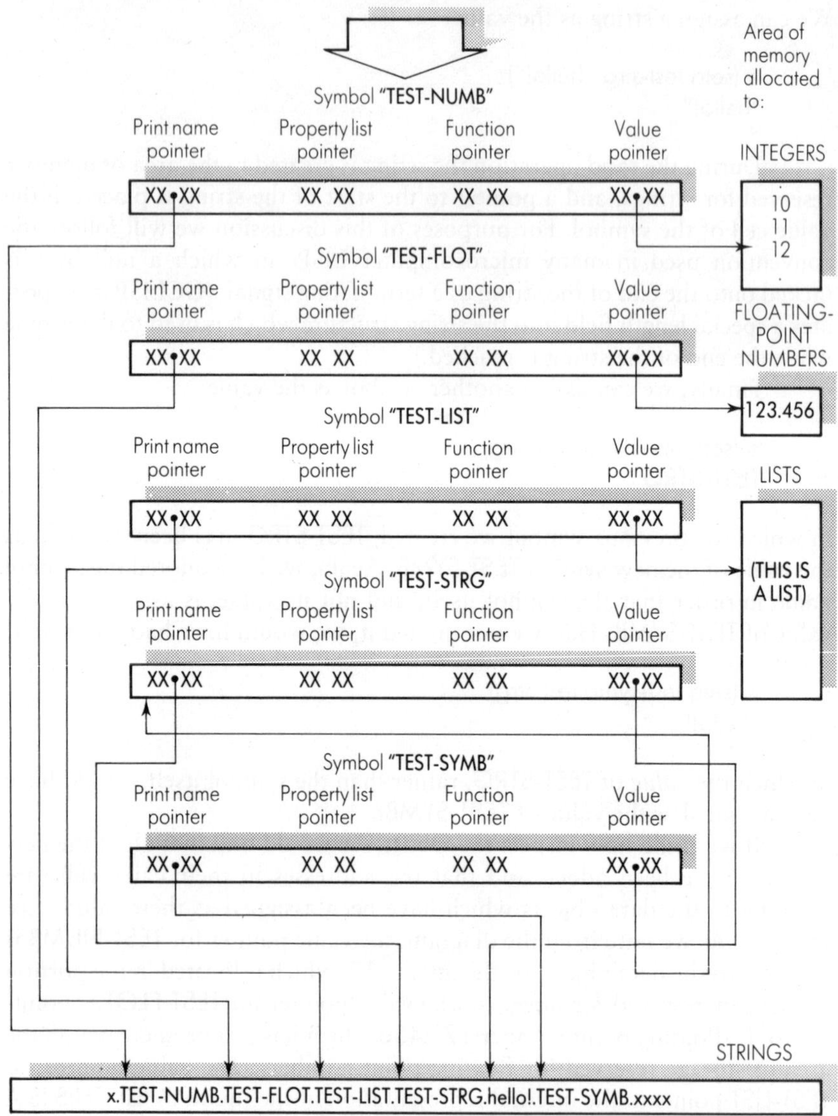

Fig. 4.5 New symbols are added to the Object List.

In addition to the symbols which we have just created by virtue of using **setq** to assign values to them, the symbols **THIS**, **IS**, **A**, and **LIST** have also been added to the Object List. (These would be sandwiched in between **TEST-LIST** and **TEST-STRG**, but have been omitted for clarity.) Although these symbols have neither values of their own, nor property lists, nor functional definitions they must nonetheless be included on the Oblist as symbols since they are referred to by the list (THIS IS A LIST) and must be available as data objects when required to print the list.

4.6 setq assigns multiple values sequentially

Although most often used to assign a value to a single symbol, setq can also be used to assign values simultaneously to two or more symbols. The assignment is carried out sequentially, that is, each successive value is assigned to its symbol before carrying out the next assignment. For example:

```
* (setq one 10 two (* 2 one) four (* 2 two))
40
```

The value of the last assignment is returned. If we now retrieve the values of two and four we will find that they are 20 and 40 respectively, reflecting the fact that values have been assigned to the preceding symbols prior to carrying out the assignments which follow.

Note that the sequential manner of assignment permits the value of one, which is set to 10, to be used in the following assignment which evaluates (* 2 one) to obtain a value of 20 which is in turn assigned to the symbol two. This contrasts with the parallel nature of psetq assignments (see Section 4.7).

4.7 psetq assigns multiple values in parallel

As illustrated above, setq assigns values to symbols in a sequential order in which each form is evaluated and assigned to its corresponding symbol before evaluating the values associated with the next assignment. The related function psetq is similar but with the difference that evaluation of the <value> arguments is carried out in *parallel.*

Hence, if we try to make a similar group of assignments using psetq:

```
* (psetq ten 10 twenty (* 2 ten) forty (* 2 twenty))
ERROR:
Unbound variable: TEN
1>
```

When trying to evaluate (* 2 ten) in parallel, an error message is generated since the symbol TEN does not yet have a value.

Once all of its second arguments have been evaluated (in parallel), psetq carries out the value assignments, working from right to left, and returns NIL. (Note that GCLISP carries out such assignments in reverse order from the Common LISP standard.)

4.8 set assigns the value of one argument to the value of another

set is similar to **setq** except that it evaluates *both* the first and second arguments, and then assigns the value of the second argument to the *value* of the first argument (which must equate to a symbol). Only one assignment at a time may be made with **set**:

```
* (setq first-number 'second-number)
SECOND-NUMBER
* (set first-number 50)
50
* first-number
SECOND-NUMBER
* second-number
50
```

In this case we have assigned the quoted name of the symbol **second-number** as the value of **first-number**. The value cell of the latter now points to another symbolic data object, **second-number**. By using **set**, we assign the value **50** to the *value* of **first-number**, that is, to **second-number**.

It can be seen from comparison of **set** and **setq** that the following expressions are equivalent:

```
(set 'symbol value) <==> (setq symbol value)
```

4.9 symbol-name and symbol-value retrieve information about a symbol

Once a symbol has been created, various functions are available which retrieve information about the symbol.

symbol-name returns a string that contains the print name of the symbol which comprises its single argument:

```
* (symbol-name 'first-number)
"FIRST-NUMBER"
```

Note that we have quoted the single argument **'first-number**, since this argument will be evaluated. (If we didn't quote it **symbol-name** would return the print name of the *value* of **first-number**; and an error message would be generated if this value was not itself a symbol.)

symbol-value returns the value of the variable named by the symbol:

```
* (symbol-value 'first-number)
SECOND-NUMBER
```

Again we have quoted the argument, for the same general reasons as noted in connection with the use of **symbol-name**.

4.10 symbolp identifies a symbol

symbolp is a predicate which returns a value of **T** if its argument evaluates to a symbol (as opposed to some other kind of data object):

```
* (symbolp 'second-number)
T
```

Since the (quoted) symbol name refers to the symbol itself, the predicate of course returns **T**. However:

```
* (symbolp second-number)
NIL
```

The function returns **NIL** since the *value* of **second-number** is currently **12**, which is a number (not a symbol).

4.11 setf assigns a value to a generalized variable

The assignment functions which we have looked at so far, **setq** and **set**, can only be used to assign a value to a symbol, that is, to place an address pointer to some data object in the value cell of the symbol. However there may be times when we would like to have the option of changing the address pointer in some other location.

setf (an acronym for SET Field) is a very flexible assignment function (actually a macro). Rather than being limited to assigning a value to a specific symbol, **setf** inserts the pointer to the value at any location specifed by **<access form>**. **setf** takes the syntax:

```
(setf <access form><update value>)
```

where **<access form>** defines the location into which a new pointer will be inserted and **<update value>** defines the new pointer. Note that **<access form>** must be of a type supported by **setf**; see the GCLRM p. 64 and the CLRM pp. 95–7 for a list of access forms which are supported by GCLISP and Common LISP, respectively.

We have briefly seen an example of **setf** as applied to property lists in Chapter 1, where we assigned a property value by using the expression:

```
(setf (get 'front-door 'security-status) 'locked)
```

In this case, **(get 'front-door 'security-status)** constituted the *access form*, which found (or created, if necessary) the symbol data object for **front-door**, found (or created) the property list for that symbol, found (or created) the particular property on that list corresponding to **security-status**, and accessed the **value** field corresponding to that property. If we had been using the expression **(get 'front-door 'security-status)** by itself, that pointer would have represented the value, which in turn would have been printed on the screen (for example, **LOCKED**) or passed upward to some higher level calling function.

If the calling function happens to be **setf**, the pointer is interpreted as pointing to a field which **setf** intends to update. Upon evaluation of the **setf** function, the pointer in that field is *replaced* by a pointer to **setf**'s second argument.

Where **setf** is used to assign a value to a symbol, it operates like **setq** in the sense that its first argument is unevaluated:

```
* (setf test-numb 12)
12
* test-numb
12
```

We can also use **setf** in place of **set**, in which case we would use **(symbol-value <symbol>)** for the first argument, eg:

```
* (setf test-numb 'next-numb)
NEXT NUMB
* (setf (symbol-value test-numb) 12)
12
```

Note that **(symbol-value test-numb)**, which evaluates its argument, returns a pointer to **next-numb**; and it is therefore the value cell of **next-numb** which is updated by the **setf** operation.

```
* next-numb
12
```

setq was introduced previously since it is the traditional assignment function of LISP and appears frequently in examples of older LISP code and in implementations which do not support Common LISP. You should therefore know how it operates. However in writing your own LISP programs you are encouraged to use **setf** for all such assignments. For the balance of this book we will use **setf** exclusively in lieu of **setq**.

4.12 boundp tests as to whether a symbol has a value

The predicate **boundp**, when applied to a symbol, tests as to whether the symbol has a value:

```
* (boundp 'test-numb)
T
```

If no value has as yet been assigned through the use of **setq**, **set**, or **setf**, **boundp** will return **NIL**. This predicate is used as a preliminary check in situations where you want to do something with the value of a symbol, provided that it has a value. If the predicate returns **NIL** you then have the option of doing something else to avoid the fatal 'unbound error' that you would otherwise get from trying to evaluate a value-less symbol.

The function **makunbound** can be applied to a symbol to wipe out any value which the symbol may have. The symbol name is returned as a value:

```
* (makunbound 'test-numb)
TEST-NUMB
* (boundp 'test-numb)
NIL
```

As the GCLRM points out, a better name for **makunbound** might have been **make-valueless**, since any local bindings the symbol may currently have remain unaffected. This points up a source of some confusion in LISP terminology as regards 'assignment' and 'binding,' which subject will be explored later in Chapter 6.

SUMMARY

Summarizing the key points of this chapter:

- a symbol is used in LISP for three basic purposes: to represent the data object which has been assigned to it as a *value*; as a means of accessing the *property list* which has been associated with it; and as the name of a *function*
- a symbol is a full-fledged *data object* in LISP, typically consisting of four pointer cells which contain the addresses of its print name, its property list, the function definition associated with it, and its value
- a value may be assigned to a symbol using the assignment function **setq**
- where **setq** is used to assign values to two or more symbols, evaluation of the values is carried out in series
- the assignment function **psetq** is similar to **setq**, but carries out its value assignments in parallel
- the assignment function **set** is similar to **setq** except that it evaluates *both* of its arguments, and can only be used to make a single value assignment
- the functions **symbol-name** and **symbol-value** may be used to retrieve a symbol's print name and its value
- the predicate **symbolp** tests a data object to see whether it is a symbol
- the assignment function **setf** provides for assigning a value to a generalized variable
- the predicate **boundp** tests as to whether a symbol has a value; the function **makunbound** wipes out any value a symbol may have

EXERCISES

4.1 What is the Object List and how is it used?

4.2 What are the four attributes associated with a symbol and how is each one used?

4.3 We have just added the symbol **new-symbol** to the object list with the assignment expression: **(setf new-symbol 'old-symbol)**. Draw a diagram of the data object which has been created, indicating the data object or machine language subroutine which each pointer cell is pointing to.

4.4 After executing the following expressions:

(a) (setq x 3)

(b) (setq x (+ 1 x) y (+ 2 x))

what value is returned by (b) and what is the value of **y**?

4.5 After executing the following expressions:

(a) (setq x 3)

(b) (psetq x (+ 1 x) y (+ 2 x))

what value is returned by (b) and what is the value of **y**?

4.6 Using **setq**, assign the following values to the given symbols:

Symbol	*Value*
symbol-one	"this is a string"
symbol-two	'symbol-three
symbol-three	'(one two three four)
symbol-four	'symbol-two

After carrying out the following assignments with **set**:

(a) (set symbol-two symbol-three)

(b) (set symbol-four 'symbol-three)

(c) (set symbol-four symbol-one)

(d) (set 'symbol-four symbol-three)

(e) (set 'symbol-two symbol-four)

(f) (set 'symbol-one symbol-two)

what are the current values of the four symbols?

4.7 After executing the assignment expressions **(setq test-symbol 'next-symbol)** and **(setq next-symbol 12)**, what values would be returned by the following expressions:

(a) (symbolp 'test-symbol)

(b) (symbolp test-symbol)

(c) (symbolp 'next-symbol)

(d) (symbolp next-symbol)

4.8 Further to Exercise 4.7, what values would be returned by the expressions:

(a) (symbol-value 'test-symbol)

(b) (symbol-value 'next-symbol)

(c) (symbol-value next-symbol)

4.9 Further to Exercise 4.7, what values would be returned by the expressions:

(a) (symbol-name 'test-symbol)

(b) (symbol-name 'next-symbol)

(c) (symbol-name next-symbol)

4.10 Use **setf** to write expressions which create the same side effects as the following:

(a) (setq test-symbol next-symbol)

(b) (setq test-symbol 'next-symbol)

(c) (set test-symbol next-symbol)

(d) (set test-symbol 'next-symbol)

What constraints apply to the values of **test-symbol** in (c) and (d)?

Chapter 5
List Creation and Manipulation

As we have discussed in earlier chapters, the list is the basic data structure of LISP. Using lists as a structural framework, symbols may be collected into meaningful groups which establish the relationship between them. Such symbol groupings may take the form of function calls, for example, **(put-out fido spot max)** or of data, for example, **'(apples grapes pears)**. In either case the general structure of the list is the same, giving rise to one of the more useful features of LISP, that is, that *data* and the *programs* which manipulate the data take the same form and hence may be interchanged.

The purpose of this chapter is to take a closer look at the nature of lists, how they are physically represented in computer memory, how they are created, and how they may be modified. This information in conjunction with what you have already learned about symbols will provide you with a solid foundation for understanding the subjects covered in the remainder of this book.

In this chapter we will look at:

- the nature of a *list* data object in computer memory
- how **cons** adds an element to the front of a list, **append** concatenates two or more lists, and **list** joins symbols or lists into a single list.
- the use of **car** and **cdr** in splitting lists apart
- the manner in which multiple **car/cdr** functions can be condensed into a single function **c---r**
- the use of other auxiliary list selector functions such as **first**, **rest**, **second**, **third**, **nth**, and **last**
- how **length** can be used to measure the number of top-level elements in a list
- the use of list surgery functions **nconc**, **rplaca**, and **rplacd**, and the manner in which they modify original list structures

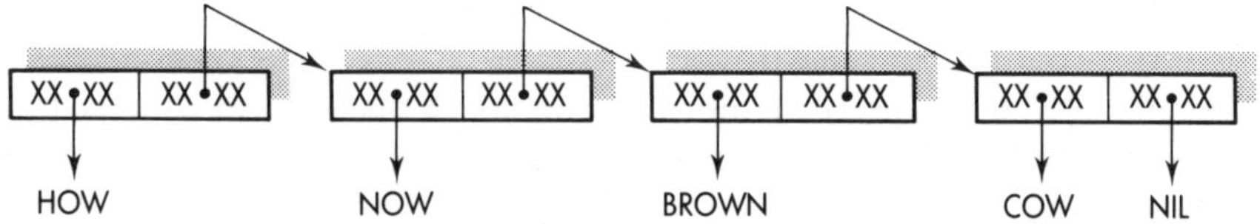

Fig. 5.1 A list is a linked chain of address cells.

5.1 A list is a linked chain of double address cells

As we mentioned in Chapter 1, a list is represented in computer memory as a linked data structure consisting of a series of one or more double address cells, or **nodes**. The left-hand address of each node points to some data object and the right-hand address points to the next node in the chain. In LISP usage, such nodes are more commonly referred to as *cons cells*, since they are created by a **cons** operation (see Section 5.3). We will use this terminology from now on.

For example, the list **(HOW NOW BROWN COW!)** would be represented in memory by four cons cells (see Fig. 5.1). The right-hand address cell of the last cons cell in the chain points to **NIL** as an indication that the end of the list has been reached.

In our top-level experiments in the preceding chapters we created a number of lists by simply typing them in as input. Keeping in mind the physical nature of a list as illustrated in Fig. 5.1, we will now look at ways in which lists can be built up, modified, and otherwise manipulated under program control.

5.2 The smallest list is the empty list

The smallest theoretical list is the *empty list*, which is equivalent in all respects to **NIL**. If you type in the empty list it will be evaluated to **NIL**:

```
* ()
NIL
```

The empty list is somewhat of a maverick among lists. Since there is no data object to point to, there is no need for a cons cell and therefore no list structure need be created. As mentioned previously, **()** or **NIL** both meet the tests for being simultaneously a **list** and a **symbol**. Considered as a *symbol*, the empty list **()** may be thought of as an alternative way to represent the symbol **NIL** in print. Considered as a *list*, **()** may be thought of as a nucleus to which other data objects may be **cons**'d (see below) to create a (nonempty) list.

5.3 cons is used to build up a list

We can build up the empty list into a list containing one element with the list CONStructor function **cons**, which takes the syntax:

```
(cons <object1> <object2>)
```

cons creates a cons cell in which the left-hand address points to **<object1>** and the right-hand address points to **<object2>**. Normally **<object2>** is a list. It is possible to create a structure called a *dotted pair* (see Section 5.7), in which the right-hand address points to a symbol instead of to a list, by **cons**'ing something to a symbol. For the moment we will limit our discussion to 'normal' **cons** operations in which the second argument is a list.

Let's now create a simple one-element list by **cons**'ing a symbol – say, **SYMBOL-01** – to the empty list:

```
* (cons 'symbol-01 nil)
(SYMBOL-01)
```

cons returns as its value the list structure which has just been created in that area of memory reserved for lists. Fig. 5.2 illustrates this structure, where the left-hand address points to the location of the symbol data object for **SYMBOL-01** on the Object List, and the right-hand address points to the symbol data object for **NIL**, which is also on the Object List.

Although we have created the list **(SYMBOL-01)** in memory, we find that we have a problem: there is no way that we can *access* it! In legitimate LISP terminology – as well as the practical vernacular – it has become *garbage*, and will be reclaimed the next time the garbage collector (Section 28.5) comes around!

Let's therefore go back and repeat the exercise, except that this time we will assign the list **(SYMBOL-01)** as the value of some symbol, say, **TEST-CONS**:

```
* (setf test-cons (cons 'symbol-01 nil))
(SYMBOL-01)

* test-cons
(SYMBOL-01)
```

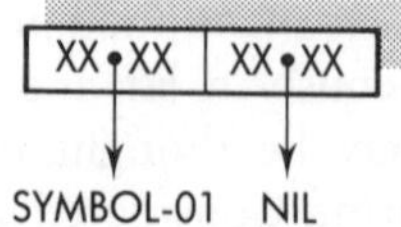

Fig. 5.2 List data object for **(SYMBOL-01)**.

We now have a way to access the structure via the symbol **TEST-CONS**, the value cell of which contains a pointer to the list **(SYMBOL-01)**. The relevant additions to the Object List and to the area reserved for lists are shown in Fig. 5.3.

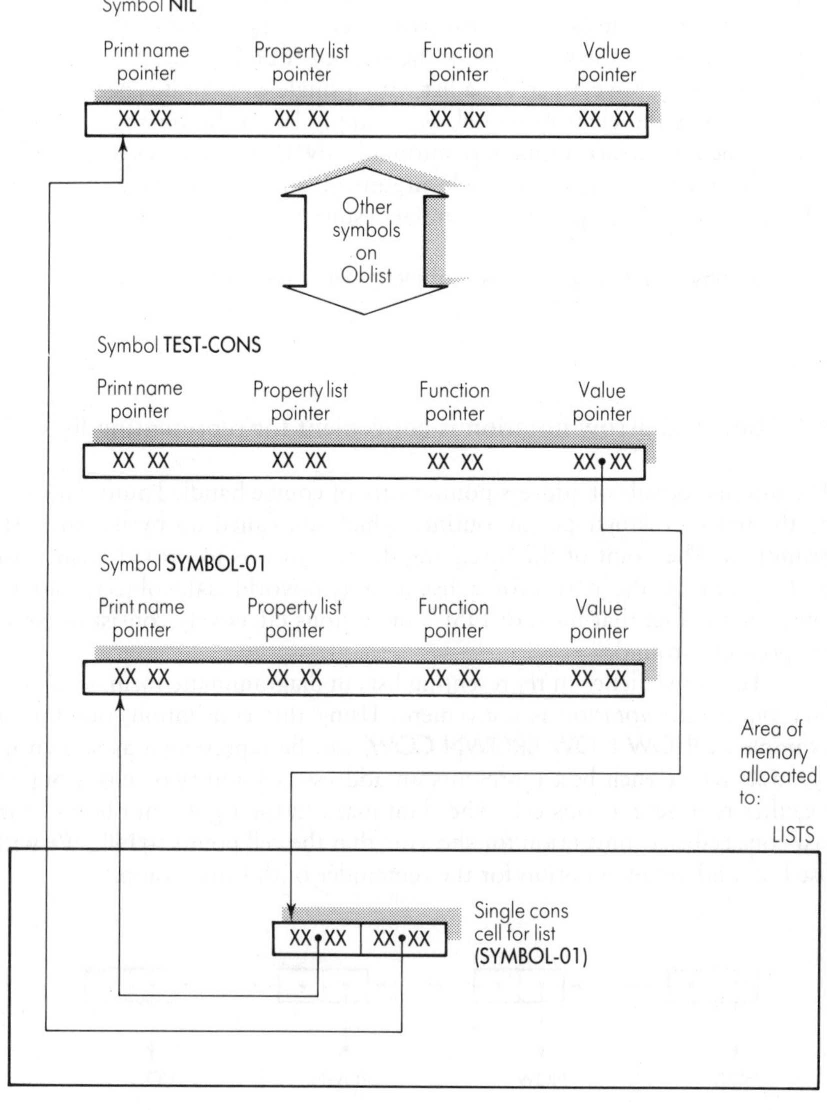

Fig. 5.3 Data structures associated with **(SYMBOL-01)**.

To complete our illustration, let's use **cons** again to add another **cons** cell to the front of the existing list. At the same time, we will use **setf** again to revise the value of **TEST-CONS** so that it now points to the (expanded) list:

```
* (setf test-cons (cons 'symbol-02 test-cons))
(SYMBOL-02 SYMBOL-01)
```

If you find the two references to **test-cons** confusing, keep in mind that the innermost list **(cons 'symbol-02 test-cons)** is evaluated first, returning as a value a pointer to the expanded list structure. This pointer then replaces the previous pointer in the value cell of the symbol **TEST-CONS**.

As noted above, to create a list with a single element it is necessary to explicitly **cons** the element to **NIL** or to apply **list** to the object. A related function **ncons** performs this step automatically, that is, creates and returns a cons cell whose **car** is its single argument and whose **cdr** is **NIL**. The following expressions produce a similar result:

```
(ncons <object>) = (cons <object> nil) = (list <object>)
```

5.4 Box-and-arrow notation is convenient for representing lists

The internal details of address pointers are of course handled automatically by the machine language subroutines which are called up by use of LISP primitives. The point of the foregoing discussion was to provide you with background on the nature of a list as a real-world data object, and to illustrate the fact that most of LISP's operations effectively consist of passing pointers around.

For convenience in representing lists in diagrammatic form, so-called *box-and-arrow notation* is convenient. Using this convention, our initial example of **(HOW NOW BROWN COW)** can be represented as shown in Fig. 5.4, where each box represents an address cell and two cells grouped together represent a cons cell. The slant mark in the right-hand box of the last cons cell is a convention for showing that the cell points to **NIL**. We will use box-and-arrow notation for the remainder of this discussion.

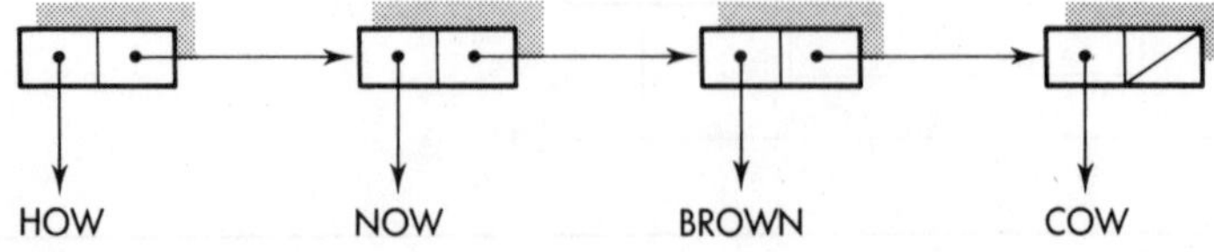

Fig. 5.4 Box-and-arrow representation of **(HOW NOW BROWN COW)**.

5.5 List structures may be shared by more than one symbol

We have seen that it is possible to assign the value of one symbol to another symbol:

```
* (setf symbol-01 '(how now!))
(HOW NOW!)

* (setf symbol-02 symbol-01)
(HOW NOW!)
```

such that the value cells of both symbols wind up pointing to the same data object – in this case the list **(HOW NOW!)**.

Data structures may also be shared by more than one symbol. If for instance we execute the following:

```
* (setf test-01 (cons 'symbol-01 nil))
(SYMBOL-01)

* (setf test-02 (cons 'symbol-02 test-01))
(SYMBOL-02 SYMBOL-01))

(setf test-03 (cons 'symbol-03 test-02))
(SYMBOL-03 SYMBOL-02 SYMBOL-01)
```

we find that the resulting list structure is shared by the three symbols (see Fig. 5.5). Each **cons** operation creates a new **cons** cell, the left address of which points to its first argument and the right address of which points to the original list structure which makes up its second argument. Should the values of **TEST-01** or **TEST-02** subsequently be changed, the list data structures to which they were previously bound will not be subject to garbage collection since they are still being used by **TEST-03**. As we shall see, some functions such as **append** also make use of shared list structures in the interest of memory conservation.

The intent of the foregoing has been to familiarize you with the physical nature of a list in computer memory. We will now go on to review some of the principal functions for creating and modifying lists, as well as for accessing the components of a list.

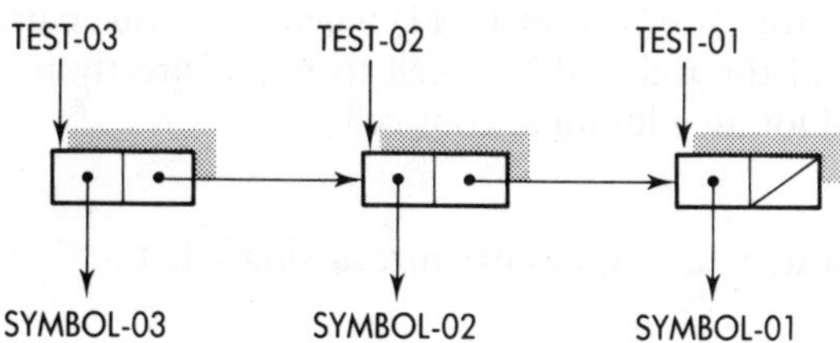

Fig. 5.5 List structures may be shared by more than one symbol.

5.6 append joins two lists together

append joins two or more lists together so that the elements of the individual lists are combined into a single list. All of the arguments to **append** except the last one must be lists; the last can be any data object. (However if it is a symbol, the list will end with a dotted pair; see Section 5.7.) Since **append** evaluates its arguments before carrying out its operation, a symbol can appear in the list of arguments provided it evaluates to a list. The syntax is:

(append &rest <lists>)

In line with the list-sharing philosophy mentioned earlier, **append** makes a copy of all of its arguments *except* the last, and then grafts these structures onto the front of the last argument in much the same manner as **cons** previously grafted additional cells onto the list pointed to by TEST-01. The manner in which such list structures are shared is explored in more detail in connection with **nconc** (see Section 5.16).

Given no arguments, **append** returns NIL.

5.7 consing an object to an atom creates a dotted pair

In the 'normal' lists we have considered so far, the right-hand address of the cons cell points either to another cons cell or to NIL, indicating that the end of the list has been reached. An object known as a dotted pair can be created by **cons**'ing an object to a symbol instead of to another list or NIL:

```
* (cons 'dave 'rita)
(DAVE . RITA)
```

The resulting pair is printed out with a dot separating the two elements to indicate that the structure is a dotted pair. In box-and-arrow terms we have:

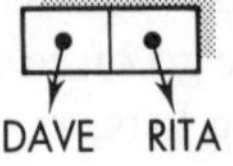

Dotted pairs find extensive use in applications such as property lists and association lists (see Section 18.11) where key/value pairs are involved; the utilization of the right address cell to point directly to the value precludes the need for an additional cons cell.

5.8 list combines its arguments into a single list

The function **list**, which takes the syntax:

(list &rest <data-objects>)

encapsulates a single argument into a list, or joins two or more expressions together to form a list in which each element, after evaluation, retains its individual character as either an atom or a list:

```
* (list 'supercallifragilistic)
(SUPERCALLIFRAGILISTIC)

* (list 'hot 'dog)
(HOT DOG)

* (list 'dave '(likes rita))
(DAVE (LIKES RITA))

* (list '(my friend) '(likes apples))
((MY FRIEND)(LIKES APPLES))
```

Given no arguments, list returns NIL.

A related function list*, which takes the syntax:

```
(list* <data-object> &rest <other-objects>)
```

is similar to list except that it builds up a list by cons'ing the next-to-last object to the last object; and thereafter, working from right to left, conses the remaining objects onto the resulting list. This may result in a so-called *dotted list* if the last argument is an atom (see the CLRM p. 267–8 for some examples).

5.9 reverse returns the elements of a list in reverse order

reverse takes a single argument – usually a list of elements which has been returned by some lower level function – and returns a copy of the list with the order of elements reversed:

```
* (reverse '(apples pears lemons grapes))
(GRAPES LEMONS PEARS APPLES)
```

reverse is often helpful in AI applications when, during the course of the program, a list of items is being built up by cons'ing the latest item onto the front of a growing list. After the entire list has been generated it can be operated on by reverse to put all of the items back into the order in which they were originally generated.

The related function nreverse is similar to reverse, but permits the implementation to modify the original argument directly rather than making a copy of it for reversal purposes.

5.10 car returns the first element of a list

The two most basic functions for taking lists apart are **car** and **cdr** (pronounced *could-er*). **car** returns as its value the first top-level element of a list, whereas **cdr** returns whatever is left after removing the first element. These non-mnemonic names are relics from the original implementation of LISP on the IBM 704 computer: **car** stood (approximately) for Contents of Address Register and **cdr** for Contents of Decrement Register (see McCarthy, 1977).

car takes a single argument which must evaluate to a list and returns the first top-level element of that list:

```
* (car '(how now brown cow))
HOW
```

We have quoted the list argument since it is not intended to be evalated as a function call. We could have achieved the same result by:

```
* (setf test-list '(how now brown cow))
(HOW NOW BROWN COW)

* (car test-list)
HOW
```

since the argument to **car** is evaluated. (For the rest of this chapter we will use quoted arguments to list manipulation functions since the operations are more obvious and comprehensible.)

If the single argument to **car** does not evaluate to a list, **car** will complain:

```
* (car 'hotdog)
ERROR:
CAR or CDR of non-LIST object: HOTDOG
1>
```

When applied to the empty list **()**, **car** returns **NIL**. (This is a convention of Common LISP. Other dialects such as SCHEME may not permit a **car** or **cdr** operation on an empty list.)

Used in conjunction with **cdr**, in however many successive applications as may be required, any element of a list can be isolated. As far as top-level elements are concerned, we will normally be using **car** only to isolate the first element of a list and **cdr** to return the balance of the list; for more exotic retrievals – say, the seventh element of a list – more specific functions are available.

5.11 cdr returns the rest of the list

cdr returns a pointer to the remainder of a list after **car** has removed the first-level element. Furthermore, whereas the value returned by **car** may be either an atom or a list, depending on the nature of the first element, the value returned by **cdr** is *always* a list. (But note the single exception that **cdr** of a dotted pair (see Section 5.7) returns an atom.) Using our previous example:

```
(cdr '(how now brown cow))
(NOW BROWN COW)
```

If applied to a list like **(cow)** which contains only a single element, **cdr** will return **NIL**, on the not unreasonable assumption that once **car** has removed the single element there is nothing left to **cdr**!

When applied to the empty list **()**, **cdr** returns **NIL**.

5.12 car/cdr combinations may be condensed into a single function

When trying to extract an element from somewhere in the middle of a long list, successive applications of **car** and **cdr** can be used. For instance, to extract the word **MOTHER** from the quoted list **(Does your mother chew betel nut?)** one could take the **car** of the result of two successive **cdr** operations:

```
(car (cdr (cdr '(Does your mother chew ... etc)))))
MOTHER
```

Since this is somewhat awkward, most implementations of LISP include auxiliary functions of the form **c---r** where the dashes are replaced by **d** or **a**, starting from the right side and working backward in the same order in which **car** and/or **cdr** operations work backward from the list being worked on. The above example of **(car (cdr (cdr '(...** could therefore be replaced by a single function **caddr**, which would effectively condense them all into a single operation, as shown in Fig. 5.6.

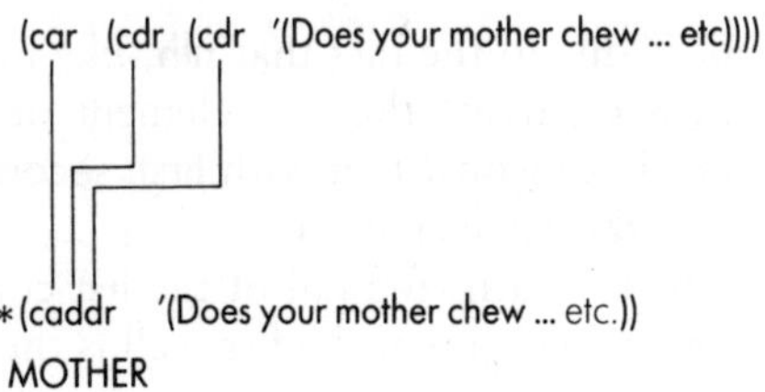

Fig. 5.6 Auxiliary functions combine **car** and **cdr** operations.

GCLISP provides all possible combinations of **car** and **cdr** up to three combined function calls, that is, **caaar, caadr, caddr**, etc. (However, the function **nth** (see Section 5.14) provides an easier way of extracting an intermediate element from a list.)

5.13 first and rest are modern equivalents of car and cdr

Given the nature of their distant (and un-nmemonic) origins, **car** and **cdr** are somewhat anachronistic names. Common LISP provides the more modern equivalents **first** and **rest**, which do exactly the same thing as **car** and **cdr**:

```
* (first '(how now brown cow))
HOW
* (rest 'how now brown cow))
(NOW BROWN COW)
```

Due to their long-standing established usage, we will generally be using **car** and **cdr** throughout the rest of this book. You can however substitute **first** and **rest** if you prefer these terms.

5.14 Other functions provide for retrieving a specific element or sublist from a list

In addition to **car** and **cdr** and their variants, other *selector functions* are available to extract any element from a list. **second** and **third** take a single list argument and respectively extract the second or third elements from that list.

```
* (third '(how now brown cow!))
BROWN
```

A more general function, **nth**, takes the syntax:

```
(nth <number> <list>)
```

where **<number>** is an integer, and extracts the **nth** element of the list:

```
* (nth 4 '(four score and seven years ago our fathers))
YEARS
```

The unexpected result is due to the fact that **nth**, like many LISP functions which deal with sequences, treats the first element of the list as the 0th element. (This is somewhat inconsistent with **first, second**, and **third**, which treat the first element as the 1th element.)

The function **nthcdr** returns the tail of the list commencing with the **nth** cons cell. Again remembering that the first cell is the 0th cell:

```
* (nthcdr 4 '(four score and seven years ago our fathers))
(YEARS AGO OUR FATHERS)
```

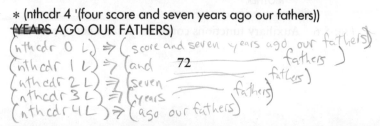

Finally, the function **last**, which takes a list as its single argument, returns the last **cons** of the list. Like the conventions for **car** and **cdr**, **last** returns **NIL** when applied to the empty list.

5.15 length measures the number of elements in a list

length takes a single argument, which must be a list (or other object of type **sequence**), and returns the number of top-level elements of the list:

```
* (length '(apples grapes lemons pears))
4
```

length may also be used to measure the number of characters in a string:

```
* (length "How now brown cow!")
18
```

The more specialized function **list-length** is specifically designed to work with lists. It returns the number of elements in the list, or returns **NIL** if the list is circular (see Section 5.17).

5.16 nconc destructively concatenates lists

The list manipulation functions which we have reviewed up to now have where necessary made *copies* of the original lists with which they worked. The original lists (which may have been pointed to by other symbols) therefore remain unchanged.

However there are a number of functions in LISP which *destructively* modify the lists on which they work. That is to say, they work directly on the *original* lists. Such a capability can be convenient if there is no further use for the original list and modifying it is quicker than copying it. Generation of garbage is minimized also. However such functions must be used with caution.

The first of the three 'list surgery' functions we will look at is **nconc**, which concatenates two or more lists together in much the same manner as **append**. **nconc** takes the syntax:

```
(nconc &rest <list1> <list2> ... <listn>)
```

The final resulting list is exactly the same as would have been obtained with **append**; however it is achieved in a quite different manner. Let's compare the two operations.

As noted previously, **append** may utilize an existing list for the tail end of a larger list structure which is being created. This conserves memory and introduces no change to the values of existing symbols. Where a list is to be appended to another list, a *copy* of the first list is made for this purpose.

For instance:

```
* (setf abc '(a b c))
(A B C)

* (setf def '(d e f))
(D E F)
```

If we now append these two lists together and **setf** the result to the new list **abcdef**:

```
* (setf abcdef (append abc def))
(A B C D E F)
```

we get the desired result. If we check the values of the original symbols **abc** and **def**, we find that they remain unchanged:

```
* abc
(A B C)

* def
(D E F)
```

append has in fact made a *copy* of the first list **(A B C)** and has altered the final pointer of this (copied) list so that it points to the first cons cell in the original list **(D E F)**.

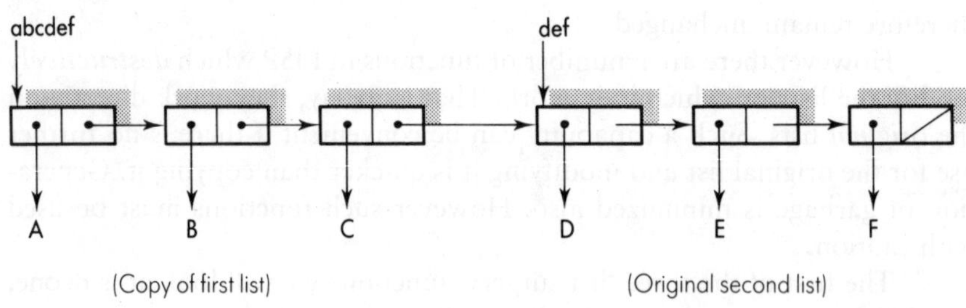

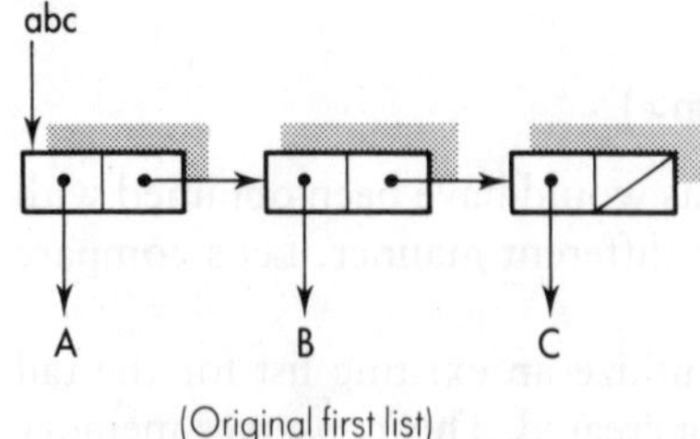

Fig. 5.7 **append** makes copies of its list arguments.

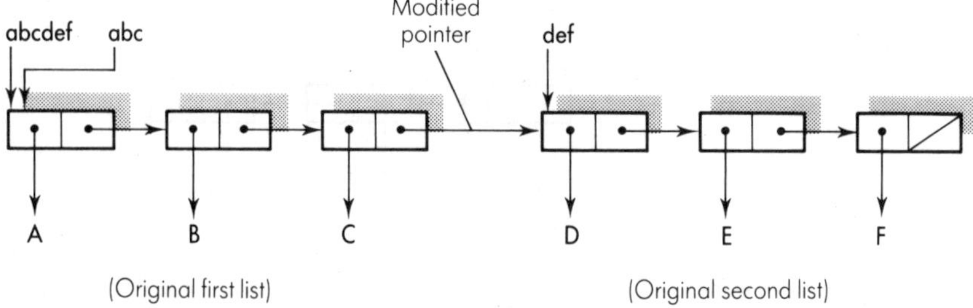

Fig. 5.8 **nconc** alters original list structure.

The above operation achieves the desired results without changing the values of the original symbols **abc** and **def**, while at the same time minimizing the amount of additional cons cells required to provide the structure corresponding to the new symbol **abcdef**. This can be expressed in box-and-arrow notation (see Fig. 5.7).

nconc, on the other hand, does *not* make a copy of the first list, but rather alters the tail-end pointer of this list so that instead of pointing to **NIL** it now points to the first cons cell of the second list:

```
* (setf abcdef (nconc abc def))
(A B C D E F)
```

The results are at first glance similar to those achieved with **append** (see Fig. 5.8). However although the value of the new symbol **abcdef** is valid and the value of symbol **def** remains unchanged, the surgery has had fatal effects on symbol **abc**:

```
* abc
(A B C D E F)
```

whose value is now the same as the new symbol **abcdef** due to having had **def** grafted onto it as a tail! Hence, to paraphrase Pope, a little list surgery can be a dangerous thing (if the consequences are not fully understood).

5.17 rplaca and rplacd destructively replace the car or cdr of their argument

rplaca, which takes the syntax:

```
(rplaca <some-list> <some-object>)
```

is similar to **nconc** in that it carries out surgery on an original list rather than making a copy. In this case the **car** pointer of its first argument is altered to point to its *second argument* rather than whatever it was pointing to before.

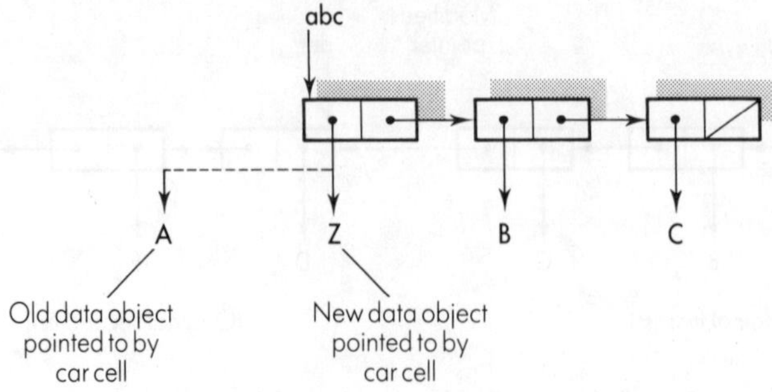

Fig. 5.9 **rplaca** distinctively replaces the **car** pointer.

Taking our previous example in which the symbol **abc** had the value of the list **(A B C)**:

```
* (rplaca abc 'z)
Z
```

The pointer in the car cell of **abc** is now replaced with a pointer to the new object **Z** (see Fig. 5.9). This change would affect any other structures in the system which point to **abc**, or to programs which reference **(car abc)**.

rplacd is similar to **rplaca**, except that the **cdr** rather than the **car** is involved. In this case the **cdr** pointer is altered to point to the second argument rather than whatever it pointed to before, with similarly permanent effects on other list structures which point to **abc** or which reference **(cdr abc)**.

GCLISP also provides the un-Common LISP function **rplacb**, which takes the syntax:

```
(rplacb <some-list> <another-list>)
```

and which replaces *both* the car and the **cdr** of its first argument with the **car** and the **cdr** of its second argument.

One of the odd phenomena which can occur through misuse of destructive modification functions is the *circular list*, which comes about when the tail of a list is modified such that it points at itself! Printout of such a list will cycle endlessly. Try this experiment:

```
* (setf abc '(a b c))
(A B C)

* (rplacd abc abc)
(A A A A A A A A A A A A A A A A A ......
```

(Remember to break the cycle with Ctrl-Break followed by Ctrl-C to get back to the top level.) See Exercise 5.10 for a box-and-arrow diagram of the **rplacd** operation.

Note that circular lists *do* have their uses in LISP, since you can utilize them as a special type of lookup table in which the next element beyond the end of the list is the first element of the list. Just don't try to print one out!

5.18 make-list creates a list and initializes its elements

The function **make-list**, which takes the syntax:

```
(make-list <size> &key :initial-element <initial-element>)
```

creates a list of length **<size>** whose elements are all initialized to **<initial-element>** (which defaults to **NIL**), for example:

```
* (make-list 5 :initial-element 'apple)
(APPLE APPLE APPLE APPLE APPLE)
```

SUMMARY

Summarizing the key points of this chapter:

- *lists* are represented in memory as chains of double address cells, or *cons cells*, in which the left-hand address points to some data object and the right-hand address points to the next node in the chain
- **cons** adds an element to the front of a list by creating a new cons cell whose **car** points to the element and whose **cdr** points to the list
- **append** concatenates two or more lists together into a single list
- **list** joins two or more s-expressions into a single list, while maintaining the identities of the individual elements
- **car** and **cdr** can be used to extract the first element of a list or the tail of a list
- multiple **car/cdr** functions can be condensed into a single function **c---r**
- other auxiliary list selector functions such as **first**, **rest**, **second**, **third**, **nth**, and **last** are available to extract elements from a list
- **length** measures the number of top-level elements in a list
- the list surgery functions **nconc**, **rplaca**, and **rplacd** modify original list structures and therefore must be used with caution

EXERCISES

5.1 We can assign the value (THIS IS A LIST) to the symbol sentence with a setf operation. Write a single expression which achieves the same result using a series of cons operations.

5.2 If TEMP is the value of the temperature, which let's say is 68 degrees, use append to write an expression which will generate the list (THE TEMPERATURE IS 68 DEGREES).

5.3 Is it possible to produce the same result as Exercise 5.2 using the function list? If so, what must be done differently?

5.4 A palindrome is an expression which reads the same way backward as forward. If palindrome is a symbol representing such a list of words, write an expression to say it backward.

5.5 Write four different ways to extract the symbol THE from the list (NOW IS THE TIME).

5.6 What are the values returned by the following expressions:

(a) (car '(how now brown cow))
(b) (car '((this is a list)))
(c) (cdr '((how now) brown cow))
(d) (car (car '(a list)))
(e) (cdr (cdr '(a list)))

5.7 What are the values returned by the following expressions:

(a) (caddr '(my dog has fleas))
(b) (caadr '(how now brown cow))
(c) (caaar '(((now is the time) for) all))

5.8 Write an expression to extract the 5th word from the list (NOW IS THE TIME FOR ALL GOOD MEN).

5.9 Write an expression to return the number of top-level elements in the list '(one (two) three (four) five).

5.10 After making the assignment (setf abc '(a b c)), draw a box-and-arrow diagram showing why the printout from the function (rplacd abc abc) will cycle endlessly.

Chapter 6

Defining Your Own Functions

One of the most interesting and powerful features of LISP is the ability of the user to create function definitions. Such definitions may range from a simple function call using a few LISP primitives to a complex hierarchy of nested function calls built up from LISP primitives and other user-defined functions.

In this chapter we will look at:

- the various kind of procedural constructs which are provided by LISP
- the manner in which a *user-defined function* can be created
- how *lambda expressions* may be used to create a nameless function for on-the-spot evaluation
- the use of let for creating bindings for auxiliary variables
- the use of the lambda-list keywords &optional and &aux
- how setf may be used together with symbol-function to initialize or update a function definition
- how eval may be used to resuscitate a quoted function call
- the use of funcall and apply to invoke functions and apply them to their arguments

6.1 LISP provides for various kinds of procedural constructs

Up to now we have been referring generally to 'functions' as the mechanism by which LISP manipulates symbols. At this point we can define a more specific vocabulary, which we will use for the remainder of the book, to differentiate the various mechanisms which are actually used in practice. These include three kinds of constructs which come pre-defined within the interpreter and two kinds which we can define ourselves (see Fig. 6.1).

Functions take a varying number of arguments all of which are evaluated prior to applying the functional procedure to them. These represent the bulk of the procedures in LISP. We have already encountered a number of functions in the form of the arithmetic functions, **set**, **car**, **cdr**, **cons**, **append**, etc. The user can define his or her own functions, which differ from built-in primitives in that the latter are written in machine language whereas user-defined procedures must be interpreted. It follows from this that LISP primitives are executed much more rapidly than user-defined functions. (Compilation of user-defined functions, which greatly speeds up execution, is not yet supported by GCLISP.)

Special forms are generally more complex constructs used for environmental and control purposes. These have no fixed syntax; their arguments may or may not be evaluated. We have already encountered two special forms: **quote** and **setq**. The user cannot define additional special forms. The (relatively small) set of special forms which are built into a Common LISP interpreter are enumerated in CLRM Table 5-1 p. 57. As will be noted from p. 39 of the GCLRM, GCLISP has chosen to implement numerous Common LISP macros as special forms.

Macro calls represent a flexible mechanism in which the interpreter computes a new form through *macro expansion* and then evaluates the expanded form. We will discuss macros in more detail in Chapter 16.

In all of the above cases a symbol is used to represent the functional procedure, and a pointer to the procedure is placed in the function pointer

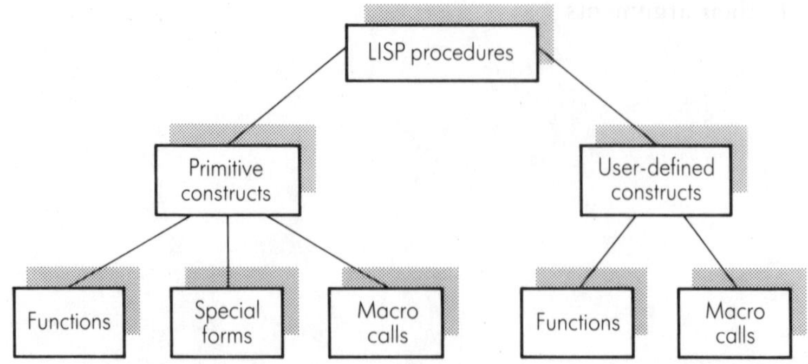

Fig. 6.1 Primitive and user-defined procedural constructs.

cell of the symbol. At the time of evaluation the nature of the procedure pointed to will be recognized by the interpreter and appropriate steps taken to apply it as a function or to evaluate it as a special form or macro call.

The balance of this chapter will deal with the manner in which the user may define his or her own functions.

6.2 defun creates a user-defined function

In the course of developing a function definition to suit some particular purpose, three specific things have to be defined:

(1) The *name* of the function: Every function must be represented by a single symbolic name. LISP primitives are represented by their corresponding symbol names such as **setf**, **cons**, etc. The name of a user-defined function can be any symbol, and is usually chosen to have some mnemonic value which indicates its purpose and makes it easy to remember. In our previous example we illustrated a function to check whether any windows of the house were left open. We called the function **check-windows**, but could as easily have called it **check** or **windows** or even **see-if-any-windows-are-open.** Since names take up space in memory they should be kept reasonably short, consistent with mnemonic considerations.

(2) The *parameters* of the function: The parameters of a function represent the variables on which the value returned by the function depends. In an earlier exercise we created an expression which calculated the area of a triangle, given the values bound to **base** and **height**, that is:

```
(/ (* base height) 2)
```

If we had a special function called **triangle-area**, which would calculate this area for us, we would likely use the symbols **base** and **height** as the two parameters of the function (see example below).

(3) The *body* of the function: The body of the function consists of one or more LISP expressions which describe the manner in which the parameters to the function interact with constants and/or other input to generate the side effects associated with the function and/or the value returned by the function.

The body of a function can be immensely long – an entire LISP program, in fact – or can be as short as a simple arithmetic operation or a formula of some kind.

A function can be defined by use of the special form **defun** followed by the function name followed by a list of the parameters to the function followed by the body of the function:

```
(defun <function-name> <parameter-list> <body-of-function>)
```

where **defun** is the primitive which causes a function definition to be created; **<function-name>** is the symbol which names the function; **<parameter-list>** is a list of the formal parameters to the function; and **<body-of-function>** is one or more expressions which describe the procedure to be carried out on the arguments to the function.

Let's create a function to illustrate the example of calculating the area of a triangle:

```
* (defun triangle-area (base height)
     (/ (* base height) 2))
TRIANGLE-AREA
```

As mentioned above, **base** and **height** are the parameters of the function. The symbols **base** and **height** are also referred to as *dummy variables*, since their names have no significance outside of the definition of the function. We can name them **jack** and **jill** or anything else, just so long as we maintain consistency with their use within the body of the function.

We see that the function has been defined in accordance with the format noted above: **defun** followed by the name followed by the parameter list followed by the body of the function. We have followed the normal convention of entering the name and parameter list on the first line followed by the body of the function on the next and/or following lines. As discussed previously, we can indent the expressions in the body of the function to make them more readable by pretty-printing (see Section 11.7).

After storing the function definition in memory, LISP returns the name of the function. Having defined the function, we can now use it to calculate the area of a triangle:

```
* (triangle-area 5 10)
25.0
```

(As noted previously in our discussion of integer operations, the answer is expressed in floating-point notation because a division operation was involved in the calculation.)

6.3 Arguments are bound to the formal parameters of a function

When we called the function **triangle-area** in the previous example we provided the two necessary *arguments* 5 and 10. Upon entering the function, these arguments became *bound* to the parameters **base** and **height**. By 'bound' we mean that during the period that the functional expression was being evaluated the dummy variable **base** temporarily took on the value of

5, and **height** the value of 10. The bindings were carried out in the same order as the parameters were specified and the arguments were input, that is, 5 was bound to **base** and 10 was bound to **height**.

After the function has been exited and the value returned, what happens to the values of **base** and **height**? Let's see:

```
* base
ERROR:
Unbound variable: BASE
1>
```

The same result will be observed with **height**. If we were to repeat the experiment, but this time assigning values – say, 30 and 40 – to **base** and **height** prior to calling **triangle-area**, we would get the same area as before, 25.0. Upon exiting the function and testing the values of **base** and **height** we would find them to be 30 and 40. In other words, if a symbol is used as a formal parameter within a function, whatever prior value it may have will be saved at the time the function is called. The symbol will then be used as a dummy variable and temporarily take on the value of its corresponding argument. Upon exiting the function its old value will be restored.

Since the nature of this temporary binding is an essential feature of LISP, we will run another experiment to illustrate it. However to provide some additional flexibility in our function definitions, let's first review a basic primitive with which we can explicitly *output* information other than values returned at the top level.

6.4 format is convenient for generating printed output

Before proceeding further, let us define **format** (Section 12.5), a function which will permit us to print out the values which exist within a nested function call. As we will use it here, **format** takes the syntax:

```
(format t "~%<some-string> ~a" <some-argument>)
```

The **format** statement causes the string enclosed within the quote marks to be printed to the console (the **t** following the function name instructs the system to print the information to the console, rather than to some other output device). So-called *format directives* may be included within the string. The directive ~% causes a line feed and carriage return to be generated, and the directive ~a causes the value returned by the argument following the string to be spliced into the string. For example:

```
* (setf some-arg "for all men")
"for all men"
* (format t "~%Now is the time ~a" some-arg)
Now is the time for all men
```

As will be noted, format prints the string in a 'natural' manner, that is, without quote marks.

Now that we have format at our disposal, we can alter our previous function so that we can see what is going on with the values of the dummy variables during the evaluation process.

6.5 Dummy variables take on temporary bindings during evaluation of a function

If we redefine the function triangle-area in the manner shown below, the new definition automatically replaces the old one:

```
* (defun triangle-area (base height)
    (format t "~%Base = ~a" base)
    (format t "~%Height = ~a" height)
    (format t "~%Area = ~a" (/ (* base height) 2)))
TRIANGLE-AREA
```

The new function definition now contains three format expressions which will be evaluated in sequential order when the function is called. The argument to the last expression is the original formula for calculating the area (/ (* base height) 2), the value of which will be printed in the same manner as the values for base and height.

We can now conduct our experiment with parameter bindings:

```
* (setf base 30 height 40)
40
* base
30
* height
40
* (triangle-area 5 10)
Base = 5
Height = 10
Area = 25.0
NIL
* base
30
* height
40
```

where the NIL after the call to triangle-area represents the value returned by the last format statement.

Hence, although base and height had values prior to calling the function triangle-area, upon entry into that function these values were stored and the two variables took on temporary bindings within the function. After the function was exited, the values of the symbols **base** and **height** were restored to what they were previously.

The physical manner in which bindings are established and previous values are saved and later restored is outlined in detail in the course of developing LISP mini-interpreters in Chapter 30.

6.6 Arguments to a function are evaluated

In the above example we provided numerical constants as the arguments to **triangle-area**. Since the arguments to any user-defined function are evaluated, we can provide symbols as arguments provided that they evaluate to numbers:

```
* (setf apples 5 pears 10)
10

* (triangle-area apples pears)
Base = 5
Height = 10
Area = 25.0
NIL
```

6.7 lambda creates a kind of anonymous function

There is a certain amount of overhead involved in defining and using functions as described above, in that a specific symbol must be used to *name* the function and a certain amount of processing time must be expended in retrieving the address from the symbol's function pointer cell.

We can create the same effect as a function call by creating a sort of anonymous function definition which will be evaluated on the spot using a **lambda** expression. The syntax is:

```
((lambda <lambda-list><body-of-function>) <arguments>)
```

We have changed <parameter-list> to <lambda-list>, which is the technical name for the list of parameters.

Use of **lambda** in this context is the only example in LISP where a list containing another embedded list as its first element can be evaluated as a valid stand-alone LISP expression. The whole embedded lambda expression in effect replaces the name of a user-defined function. We can convert our **triangle-area** function to a lambda expression:

```
(lambda (base height)(/ (* base height) 2))
```

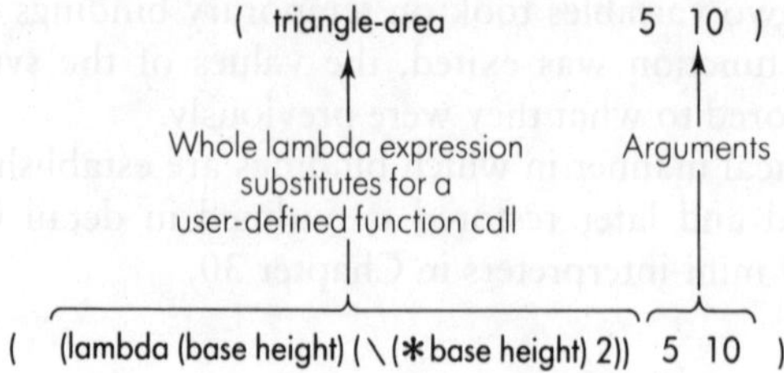

Fig. 6.2 A lambda expression substitutes for a function call.

The symbol **lambda** itself is *not* a function name, and the above expression will earn an error message if you try to evaluate it. Since a lambda expression is an on-the-spot function call, it must be embedded, as noted previously, within another list of which the second and succeeding elements comprise the arguments being provided to the function:

```
* ((lambda (base height)(\ (* base height) 2)) 5 10)
25.0
```

During the evaluation process, when **eval** encounters a nested list where it expects to find a functional symbol, it makes a further check to see if the first symbol of the nested list is **lambda**. If the symbol is anything other than **lambda**, an error message is generated, for example:

```
* ((setf test-numb 12))
ERROR:
Bad function: (SETF TEST-NUMB 12)
while evaluating: ((SETF TEST-NUMB 12))
1>
```

However if **lambda** is the next symbol, **eval** acts as if the entire lambda expression replaced a call to some anonymous function with the same **<lambda-list><body-of-function>** elements; and the arguments which follow are treated as being the arguments supplied to that function call, as shown in Fig. 6.2.

While the **lambda** function is being evaluated, the dummy variables are bound to the arguments in exactly the same manner as for a user-defined function call.

6.8 let and let* provide separate variable bindings

In the course of defining a procedure we will often have need for supplementary 'scratch-pad' variables for use in storing intermediate values while the function is being executed. Let's look at an example in which we want to count the number of elements in a list:

```
* (defun count-list-elements (some-list)
    (setf count 0)
    (loop
      (cond (some-list
              (setf count (1+ count))
              (setf some-list (cdr some-list)))
            (t (return count)))))
COUNT-LIST-ELEMENTS

* (count-list-elements '(how now brown cow!))
4
```

count-list-elements contains some constructs which we have not yet studied, but we can trace through it to get the gist of how it operates. The scratch-pad variable which we are using is **count**, which keeps track of the number of elements in the list. After initializing this variable to zero, we set up a loop which contains a *conditional* structure like the one we encountered earlier with R2D2's front door problem. If there are any elements left in the list we are working with, **some-list** evaluates to a non-**NIL** value, **count** is incremented by 1, and we chop one element off the front of the list before returning to the loop. At such time as there are no elements left in the list, control passes to the default clause, which jumps out of the loop and returns the current value of **count**.

The above function works, but could cause problems in a dynamically scoped interpreter (such as GCLISP's Version 1.0) because **count** is used as a so-called *free variable*. Supposing that **count-list-elements** was deeply nested in a program, and that some higher level calling function had also inadvertently used **count** as a formal parameter. The use of **count** as a free variable by a lower level nested function could come back and interfere with the binding of **count** at the higher level.

It is therefore desirable to avoid the use of free variables in a function definition. We can achieve this through the use of **let**, which is a special form designed to establish temporary bindings for scratch-pad variables such as **count**. The general syntax of **let** is:

```
(let ((var-1 val-1)
      (var-2 val-2)
         ...
      (var-n val-n))
  form-1
  form-2
  ...
  form-n)
```

let establishes temporary bindings of **val-1** .. **val-n** to the corresponding variables **var-1** .. **var-n** in a manner generally similar to the way in which local bindings are established between the arguments and parameters of a function. After establishing such bindings, the forms are evaluated, and let is then exited. This construct provides for *localizing* the bindings associated with scratch-pad variables in such a manner that they cannot affect the values of variables bound within higher level functions.

Further experiments to illustrate the behavior of variable bindings in the context of let constructs will be covered in the next Section 7.10.

Restructuring our earlier function definition to include let:

```
(defun count-list-elements (some-list)
  (let ((count 0))
    (loop
      (cond (some-list
              (setf count (1+ count))
              (setf some-list (cdr some-list)))
            (t (return count))))))
```

The final value of count is the value returned by the whole let construct. Since the end of this construct coincides with the end of count-list-elements, the same value is returned by this function.

Instead of embedded (var-1 val-1) lists, the symbol names of the variables can be used alone in which case they will be initialized to NIL.

let carries out its bindings in a manner analogous to psetq, in that it evaluates all of the values in parallel and then binds them to the corresponding variables from left to right. An associated form let* operates like setq, in that bindings are performed sequentially rather than in parallel. Like local bindings within a function, any previous values which let variables may have had are restored upon exit from the let construct.

6.9 Lambda-list keywords may be included

LISP includes provision for a number of *lambda-list keywords* which may be included in the lambda-list. These keywords, which are prefixed by &, provide an additional degree of flexibility in the specification and use of parameters.

The &optional keyword indicates that any parameters which follow are optional, that is, when calling the function their corresponding arguments may be included or left out. If included they will of course be bound to their corresponding parameters; if left out, the parameters will be initialized to NIL.

The &aux keyword allows an alternative way of providing bindings for auxiliary variables, similarly to the use of let* (see Section 6.8). The first lines of our count-list-elements function might alternatively have been defined as:

```
(defun count-list-elements (some-list &aux (count 0))
  (loop ...
```

Whether to use **&aux** or a **let** construct is largely a question of style and individual preference.

Extensive discussion on the use of lambda-list keywords is provided in the CLRM pp. 59–65. Note that Version 1.1 of GCLISP supports **supplied-p** parameters (in spite of the notice on p. 42 of the GCLRM) but does not yet support **&key** keywords.

6.10 **symbol-function** returns the function definition of a symbol

Having assigned a function definition to a symbol, we can retrieve this definition with **symbol-function**, which takes the syntax:

```
(symbol-function <symbol>)
```

and which returns the lambda definition pointed to by the function cell of the symbol. First let's redefine our **triangle-area** function to its original form:

```
* (defun triangle-area (base height)
    (/ (* base height) 2))
TRIANGLE-AREA
```

Using **symbol-function** to retrieve the current definition:

```
* (symbol-function 'triangle-area)
(LISP::SCANNED LAMBDA ((BASE HEIGHT)(/ (* BASE HEIGHT) 2)))
```

The **LISP::SCANNED** prefix denotes a special GCLISP construct used to generate the printed representation of a user-defined functional object. The main thing to note is that a lambda expression is being returned. Is this unexpected? It can be seen that the mechanism of creating a definition for a function consists of creating the corresponding lambda expression in memory and putting a pointer to that definition in the function pointer cell of the symbol name. When required to apply the function to its arguments, **eval** retrieves and evaluates the lambda definition in exactly the same manner as discussed previously.

We therefore have the option of using a lambda definition directly or using **defun** to associate the lambda definition with a particular symbol name. Normally we will use **defun**, since it is more convenient and far more comprehensible to use a mnemonic function name as opposed to typing in a (possibly complex) lambda expression every time the function is to be called in a program. However we may find instances involving short and infrequently used functions where an on-the-spot lambda expression makes more sense.

Used with LISP primitives, **symbol-function** returns an appropriate message:

```
* (symbol-function 'car)
#<COMPILED FUNCTION 19F6:4400>
```

6.11 setf can be used to revise a function definition

We can revise a function definition by virtue of redefining it with **defun** at the top level. However there may be instances in which we would like to be able to redefine the definition under program control. This can be done with **setf**, which uses **symbol-function** to access the lambda definition associated with the symbol and then uses its update mechanism to replace the old lambda definition with a new one.

As a highly contrived example, let's say we want to change the names of the dummy variables in **triangle-area** from **base** and **height** to **jack** and **jill**:

```
* (setf (symbol-function 'triangle-area)
    '(lambda (jack jill)(/ (* jack jill) 2)))
(LAMBDA (JACK JILL)(/ (* JACK JILL) 2))
```

The lambda expression which forms the second argument to **setf** must be quoted. We can verify that the replacement has been carried out, and that the redefined function works as before:

```
* (symbol-function 'triangle-area)
(LISP::SCANNED LAMBDA ((JACK JILL)(/ (* JACK JILL) 2)))
* (triangle-area 5 10)
25.0
```

If we experiment we will find that we can similarly use **setf** to create an initial function definition for a symbol, as well as revise an existing definition. (In fact, at the machine language level the primitive **defun** calls upon the other primitives **setf** and **symbol-function** to achieve the identical effect.)

6.12 eval resuscitates a quoted function call

As we noted earlier, one of the unusual features of LISP is that the same kinds of expressions may be considered as either 'data' or as 'program', depending on the context in which they are used.

For instance, a quoted list of any kind is by its nature data since it is not subject to evaluation. Thus:

```
* (quote (triangle-area 5 10))
(TRIANGLE-AREA 5 10)
```

The list (**TRIANGLE-AREA 5 10**) has become a simple list of data with three symbolic elements, and has – for the moment, at least – lost its functional implications. Since we are using **quote** at the top level, the pointer to the list in question is being passed to **print** and the list itself is returned to the console in the form of a printout.

However we can 'resuscitate' the ailing function by explicitly forcing evaluation with **eval**:

```
* (eval (quote (triangle-area 5 10)))
25.0
```

The purpose of the foregoing exercise is to introduce the concept that a list can be shifted back and forth between being 'data' and being 'program' depending on how it is being handled. Let's look at a more interesting example:

```
* (eval (cons 'triangle-area (cons 5 (list 10))))
25.0
```

Here we have built up the function call from scratch by **cons**'ing the two arguments into a list and then **cons**'ing the function name onto the front of the list. Up to this point, the value returned by the higher level **cons** operation is strictly data. But in one fell swoop, by a single application of **eval**, we have suddenly turned it back into 'program' again!

The above exercise is somewhat academic; in practice, one would probably use either **funcall** (see Section 6.14) or **apply** (see Section 6.15) to achieve a similar effect.

6.13 function returns a functional object

As mentioned previously, the Common LISP interpreter assumes that the functional object associated with a symbol name is being invoked when the symbol (or an equivalent lambda expression) is the first element of an unquoted list. However there are other instances in which we may wish to use a functional object:

- as a function to be applied to its arguments in the context of a **funcall** expression (see Section 6.14)
- as a function to be applied to a list of arguments in the context of an **apply** expression (see Section 6.15)
- as a function to be applied to a list of arguments by one of the available **mapping** functions (see Chapter 15)
- as a function to be used to test an argument in connection with a keyword such as **:test** (see Section 8.7)

In the above instances we must explicitly indicate to the system that a functional interpretation is required by using **function**, which takes the syntax:

```
(function <function-name>)
```

The printed representation of the value returned will reflect whether the function is user-defined or a primitive:

```
* (function triangle-area)
(LISP::SCANNED LAMBDA ((JACK JILL)(/ (* JACK JILL) 2)))
* (function car)
#<COMPILED FUNCTION 1A1F:4495>
```

Since this expression is used frequently, the sharp-sign macro #' has been provided as an abbreviation. Thus **#'equal** is equivalent to **(function equal)**.

6.14 funcall applies a function to its arguments

In normal situations, where we know what function is to be applied to what arguments, the function call can be incorporated into the program and evaluated in the usual manner. However there are times when neither the name of the function nor its arguments are known until run time.

We can build up such a function call piece by piece, as illustrated in Section 6.12 and then apply **eval** to the resulting expression. Another way is to use **funcall**, which takes the syntax:

```
(funcall <function-name> &rest <arguments>)
```

The **<function-name>** may be a symbol, which in turn represents a LISP *primitive* or a *user-defined function*, or it may be a *lambda expression*, or a more exotic functional data object such as a *stack-group* or a *closure* (which we will look at in more detail in Chapter 30.)

Again using our previous example, we can bind some general symbols to the name of the function as well as to the arguments, and use **funcall** to tie them all together:

```
* (setf func-name 'triangle-area apples 5 pears 10)
10

* (funcall func-name apples pears)
25.0
```

6.15 apply applies a function to a list of arguments

apply is somewhat similar to funcall in that it applies a function to its arguments. The difference is that the arguments must be supplied in the form of a list, whereupon the function is apply'd to the elements of the list. The syntax of apply is:

```
(apply <function-name> <arg> &rest <more-arguments>)
```

apply comes in handy when a list of elements has been accumulated during the course of the program and you want to apply some particular function to these elements.

If the (minimal) single argument is supplied, it must be in the form of a list. If more than one argument is supplied, the last argument must be a list, and the effect is as if list* were used to cons the previous arguments to the front of that list.

```
* (apply func-name 5 (list 10))
25.0
```

At the machine language level, eval calls upon apply in the course of evaluating a normal function call (as opposed to a special form or macro). This process is elaborated on in detail in Chapter 30.

6.16 Predicates may be used to identify a functional procedure

Several predicates are available which test whether a certain type of functional procedure is associated with a symbol.

fboundp is a general test which will return T if the symbol has any sort of functional implication, be it as a normal function, a special form, or a macro call:

```
* (fboundp 'triangle-area)
T
```

If the function definition associated with the symbol is of the autoloading type, a call to fboundp will cause the definition to be autoloaded. The associated un-Common LISP function %fboundp works similarly but will not cause an autoload.

special-form-p tests for a special form, and macro-function tests for a macro call. If fboundp returns T and the former two functions return NIL, the procedure must be a normal function.

Similarly to the manner in which makunbound (see Section 4.12) wiped out the value associated with a symbol, the related function fmakunbound wipes out any function definition which may be associated with a symbol.

SUMMARY

Summarizing the key points of this chapter:

- users can define their own functions with **defun**, which takes three arguments: the *name* of the function, the *parameter list*, and the *body* of the function
- the *body* of a function definition comprises one or more expressions which define the procedure to be applied to the function's arguments
- the (evaluated) arguments to a function are temporarily bound to the symbols, or *dummy variables*, which represent the formal *parameters* of the function; after the function has been exited, the previous values are restored to the symbols
- *lambda expressions*, which are used to store the function definition associated with a symbol, can be used to create an anonymous sort of function to be evaluated on the spot
- a **let** construct can be used to provide temporary bindings for auxiliary variables used by a function definition
- the *lambda-list keyword* **&optional** provides for optional arguments; the keyword **&aux** permits bindings to be established for auxiliary variables similarly to **let***
- **symbol-function** can be used to retrieve the function definition associated with a symbol
- **setf**, used in conjunction with **symbol-function**, can be used to initialize or update a function definition
- **eval** can be used to resuscitate a quoted function call
- **function** (abbreviated #') returns a functional data object
- **funcall** may be used to apply a function to its arguments, whereas **apply** is used to apply a function name to a list of arguments
- the predicates **fboundp, special-function-p,** and **macro-function** test whether a symbol represents a functional procedure

EXERCISES

6.1 Define the function **circle-area**, which takes the diameter of the circle as its single argument and returns the area. (Area = 3.14 × diameter × diameter/4.)

6.2 Define the function **trapezoid-area**, which takes the bottom, top, and height as parameters and returns the area. (Area = (bottom + top)/2 × height).

6.3 Assuming that the diameter of the circle in Exercise 6.1 is 10, write a lambda expression which will return an equivalent value.

6.4 Assuming that the bottom of the trapezoid in Exercise 6.2 is 20, the top is 16, and the height is 8, write a lambda expression which will return an equivalent value.

6.5 Define the function **square-area** with the statement **(defun square-area (base)(* base base))** and write an expression to retrieve this function definition from memory.

6.6 We wish to revise the body of the **square-area** function of Exercise 6.5 to **(expt base 2)**. Write two expressions which would effect the desired modification.

6.7 Write an expression which uses **funcall** with the **trapezoid-area** definition used in Exercise 6.4 to return an equivalent value.

6.8 After doing Exercise 6.1, write an expression which will cause the quoted expression **(quote (circle-area 10))** to return the area of the circle.

6.9 Write an expression which uses **apply** to apply the **trapezoid-area** definition given in Exercise 6.4 to the arguments indicated.

6.10 Given the symbol **test-symb**, write three expressions to test:

(a) whether the symbol has a functional procedure associated with it

(b) whether the functional procedure associated with the symbol is a special form

(c) whether the functional procedure associated with the symbol is a macro call

Chapter 7
Scoping of Variables

In the previous chapter (see Section 6.5) we reviewed the manner in which the lambda-list variables of a LISP function temporarily take on the values of the arguments passed to the function. When the function is exited, any previous values of these variables are restored.

When we are only experimenting with a single function at the top level, the above convention seems clear enough and gives rise to little confusion. However in real life a LISP program consists of a hierarchy of ever-more-deeply-nested function calls. How are the above-mentioned temporary bindings affected by value assignments and/or further bindings taking place at lower levels of the program?

The manner in which this question is resolved is potentially one of the more confusing aspects of LISP. The confusion is compounded by the fact that two separate sets of rules may be applied, depending on whether your implementation of LISP is *lexically scoped* or *dynamically scoped.*

Variable bindings in Common LISP are normally lexically scoped, and the latest Version 1.1 of GCLISP follows this practice. This discussion will therefore center on lexical scoping. Later we will compare the differences between the two kinds of scoping and, in Chapter 30, develop some mini-interpreters to illustrate these differences in a hands-on manner.

In this chapter we will look at:

- the meaning of the term '*scope*' as it applies to variable bindings
- the use and global nature of *special variables*, as well as the various ways in which special variables can be created and/or initialized at the top level
- the nature of locally bound or *lexical variables* and how their values are only visible within the lexical scope of the function in which they are bound
- how global variables created by **setf** or **setq** assignments differ in their behavior from true special variables

7.1 The scope of a variable is the area of the program in which the variable is bound to a certain value

The term 'scope' relates to the area of the LISP program in which the name of a symbol is bound to a particular value. This term is in turn related to the so-called 'establishing construct,' that is, the expression which creates the binding of the variable. Common LISP in general provides three types of 'constructs' which establish an ever-narrower 'scope' over which their variable bindings may be referenced:

- top-level declarations of *special variables* in which the scope is effectively the entire program
- lower level *special declarations* in which the scope includes all lower level functions which are directly or indirectly nested within the function in which the special declaration is made
- *lexically bound variables* in which the scope is limited to the lexical body of the function in which the variable is bound

Special variables created at the top level are in effect global variables whose values are 'visible' at all levels of the program. We can also create variables whose values are globally visible through assignment functions such as **setf** and **setq**; however the behavior of such variables differs somewhat from that of special variables, as we will see in Section 7.10.

In this chapter we will be conducting a number of experiments which will demonstrate the manner in which scope is established within a lexically scoped interpreter. In Chapter 30 we will look at the ways in which a dynamically scoped interpreter differs and will explore some programming problems which can arise when working with such an interpreter.

7.2 **defvar**, **defparameter**, and **defconstant** define special variables at the top level

Special variables find three kinds of uses in LISP. They may be used as true *variables*, that is, values which may be expected to vary during the course of the program; as *parameters*, that is, values which may be set before a program and thereafter used to control the manner in which the program operates; or as *constants*, that is, constant values such as 3.1416 which may be used for calculations throughout the program.

As a Common LISP convention, special variables begin and end with an asterisk, for example, ***print-base***, to identify them as such. GCLISP provides about 40 special variables as built-in parameters to control various aspects of interpreter operation. We can of course create our own special variables with the macros described below.

Three assignment macros are used to create and/or initialize the values of special variables at the top level. With minor variations all of these macros do essentially the same thing; the principal reason for giving them different names is to indicate the intended use of the variables to someone who is reading the program listing.

defvar, which takes the syntax:

```
(defvar<variable-name> <init-value> <doc-string>)
```

is used to create the symbol <variable-name>, (optionally) initialize its value and (optionally) specify a documentation string which provides further information about the intended use of the variable. The symbol name is returned. The use of defvar implies that the value of the variable will be subject to change during the course of the program.

The evaluation of this expression is somewhat unusual in that, if for some reason the variable *already has a value* at the time of calling defvar, this value will be left unchanged; otherwise <init-value> will be evaluated and the result assigned to the variable. Called without <init-value>, the variable will be created as an (unbound) data object with no initial value.

An (optional) document string can be included in a defvar statement to provide additional information about the intended use of the variable. For example:

```
(defvar *name* 'john-doe
  "The name of the graduate student")
```

The document string, which is otherwise completely ignored by the interpreter, is internally associated with the variable name and can be retrieved using the *documentation function* (see Section 26.5). (NB: This feature is not yet supported by GCLISP.)

defparameter takes the same syntax as defvar and does essentially the same thing, the only difference being that the <init-value>, which must be specified, will override any previous value. The use of defparameter implies that the variable will be used to control program operation in some way. For example, a program designed to read integers in base 10 and print out their equivalents in hexadecimal might be prefaced with the statement:

```
(defparameter *print-base* 16)
```

defconstant takes the same syntax as defparameter. As the name implies, the use of defconstant is intended to indicate to the reader that the value of the variable will not be changed during the program. For example:

```
(defconstant *pi* 3.1416)
```

defconstant differs from the previous two macros in that an error message will be generated if an attempt is made to update a variable previously declared to be a constant. (NB: GCLISP does not enforce this convention.)

7.3 Special variables may also be created by proclamation

Another way to create special variables at the top level is through use of **proclaim** in conjunction with a *special declaration*, for example:

```
(proclaim '(special *var-01* *var-02* ... *var-n*))
```

The **special** construct is a so-called *declaration specifier*, which we will explore in more detail in Section 7.7 below. When used by itself, within a special form, it specifies that all of the named variables are to be considered as special within the body of the special form. When used in conjunction with a top level proclamation statement the named variables become special on a global basis.

As will be noted, **proclaim** does not provide for initialization of values nor does it provide for documentation strings; it merely creates the variables and tags them as being special in nature.

The CLRM advises against the use of **proclaim** for this purpose: 'As a matter of style, use of special proclamations should be avoided. The **defvar** and **defparameter** macros are the conventional means for proclaiming special variables in a program.'

7.4 Special variables are 'visible' at all levels of a program

As our first experiment, let's use **defvar** to create the special variable ***hotdog***, and design a function to demonstrate that the value of such a variable is visible at all levels of a program:

```
* (defvar *hotdog* '(never sausage a thing!))
*HOTDOG*
```

Unlike **setf**, **defvar** returns the symbol itself rather than the value assigned. The value can now be retrieved through evaluation of the symbol:

```
* *hotdog*
(NEVER SAUSAGE A THING!)
```

and will remain in effect until such time as we update it with another assignment function.

Using **format** to print out the current binding of a variable within a function, we can set up the following experiment:

```
* (defun scope-01 ()
    (format t "~%Now in scope-01")
    (format t "~%Value of *hotdog* is ~a" *hotdog*)
    (scope-02))
SCOPE-01
```

```
* (defun scope-02 ()
    (format t "~%~%Now in scope-02")
    (format t "~%Value of *hotdog* is ~a" *hotdog*))
SCOPE-02
```

Having defined the above functions, we can call **scope-01** to check whether the value of ***hotdog*** can be accessed from within lower level nested functions:

```
* (scope-01)
Now in scope-01
Value of *hotdog* is (NEVER SAUSAGE A THING!)

Now is scope-02
Value of *hotdog* is (NEVER SAUSAGE A THING!)
NIL
```

The results indicate that the value of ***hotdog*** is indeed globally 'visible'; otherwise we would have gotten an *unbound variable* error message when the **format** statement within either function tried to evaluate ***hotdog***. Hence, when we create and assign a value to a special variable at the top level, we are in effect creating a global variable whose value is visible at all nested levels of the program.

(NB: Henceforth we will ignore the final **NIL** returned by the last format statement.)

7.5 The values of locally bound variables 'shadow' the global values associated with these variables

As we noted during our earlier experiment with parameter bindings (see Section 6.5), dummy variables take on temporary bindings during the evaluation of a function. These new bindings 'shadow' any previous values which the variables might have had, whether as special variables or locally bound variables. After the function is exited, the previous values are restored:

```
* (defvar *cow* 'moo)
*COW*

* (defun scope-03 ()
    (format t "~%Now in scope-03")
    (format t "~%Value of *cow* is ~a" *cow*)
    (scope-04 'elsie)
    (format t "~%~%Back in scope-03")
    (format t "~%Value of *cow* is ~a" *cow*))
SCOPE-03
```

```
* (defun scope-04 (*cow*)
    (format t "~%~%Now in scope-04")
    (format t "~%Value of *cow* is ~a" *cow*))
SCOPE-04
```

Executing our experiment with **scope-03**:

```
* (scope-03)
Now in scope-03
Value of *cow* is MOO

Now in scope-04
Value of *cow* is ELSIE

Back in scope-03
Value of *cow* is MOO
```

Hence the local binding of ***cow*** in **scope-04** takes precedence, or shadows, any previous binding until such time as **scope-04** is exited.

The demonstration is an academic one, since hopefully you would *not* use the name of a special variable as a formal parameter to a user-defined function!

7.6 Locally bound values are accessible only within the lexical scope of a function

We have seen that the local binding of a variable shadows any value it might have had previously. But if a variable is locally bound, can some yet-lower-level function access it? We can devise the following experiment to see:

```
* (makunbound 'baz)
BAZ

* (defun scope-05 (baz)
    (format t "~%Now in scope-05")
    (format t "~%Value of baz is ~a" baz)
    (scope-06))
SCOPE-05

* (defun scope-06 ()
    (format t "~%~%Now in scope-06")
    (format t "~%Value of baz is ~a" baz))
SCOPE-06
```

If we now call **scope-05** with some argument, say **50**:

```
* (scope-05 50)
Now in scope-05
Value of baz is 50
```

```
Now in scope-06
ERROR:
Unbound variable: BAZ
1>
```

We see that the binding of the variable **baz**, which is bound within **scope-05**, is not visible within **scope-06**. An error message was therefore generated when the format statement within **scope-06** tried to evaluate **baz**. This is a characteristic of a *lexically scoped* LISP: the value of a bound variable (assuming that it has not been declared special) is only visible within the so-called *lexical scope* of the function in which it is bound.

7.7 A local variable can be declared 'special' and thus made accessible to lower levels

There are times when it may be useful for a lower level function to be able to access and/or change the value of a variable bound in a higher level function. This situation can be handled through use of a *special declaration*, which causes the variable in question to temporarily act if it were a special variable. The declaration takes the syntax:

```
(declare (special <var-01> <var-02> ... <var-n>))
```

For example:

```
* (makunbound 'bar)
BAR

* (defun scope-07 (bar)
    (declare (special bar))
    (format t "~%Now in scope-07")
    (format t "~%Value of bar is ~a" bar)
    (scope-08)
    (format t "~%~%Back in scope-07")
    (format t "~%Value of bar is ~a" bar))
SCOPE-07

* (defun scope-08 ()
    (format t "~%~%Now in scope-08")
    (format t "~%Value of bar is ~a" bar)
    (format t "~%Assigning value of 90 to bar")
    (setf bar 90)
    (scope-09)
    (format t "~%~%Back in scope-08")
    (format t "~%Value of bar is ~a" bar))
SCOPE-08
```

```
* (defun scope-09 ()
    (format t "~%~%Now in scope-09")
    (format t "~%Value of bar is ~a" bar)
    (format t "~%Assigning value of 150 to bar")
    (setf bar 150))
SCOPE-09
```

Calling scope-07 with an arbitrary argument, say 100:

```
* (scope-07 100)
Now in scope-07
Value of bar is 100
Now in scope-08
Value of bar is 100
Assigning value of 90 to bar
Now in scope-09
Value of bar is 90
Assigning value of 150 to bar
Back in scope-08
Value of bar is 150
Back in scope-07
Value of bar is 150
```

Hence by declaring the locally bound variable bar in scope-07 to be special, the binding has been made visible within the lower level functions scope-08 and scope-09. Furthermore if we update the value within either of these nested functions we find that the updated value persists upon return to the higher level functions.

Variables declared to be special within a nested function, as in the above example, appear to fall half-way between being globally special variables and lexical variables. They are like globally special variables in that they can be accessed and/or updated by any lower level functions which may be called within the body of the function in which they are declared special. However they are like lexical variables in that their previous values are restored upon exit from that function. In the above case, since bar had no value prior to calling scope-08 its value-less status is restored upon exit from that function:

```
* bar
ERROR:
Unbound variable: BAR
1>
```

In a *lexically scoped interpreter*, such as GCLISP Version 1.1, the explicit use of a *special declaration* is necessary if a locally bound variable is to be accessed and/or updated by some lower level function. (In a *dynamically scoped* interpreter, *all* such bound variables are freely visible and accessible at lower levels, giving rise to potential problems. We will explore the nature of these so-called *functional argument* problems in Chapter 30.)

A special declaration, if used, should be placed at the beginning of a lambda expression or the body of a special form. Such a declaration may be preceded only by other **declare** statements or by documention strings. The GCLISP special forms which support declarations include **defun, do, do*, do-all-symbols, do-external-symbols, do-symbols, dolist, dotimes, labels, let, let*, multiple-value-bind, prog,** and **prog***. (Common LISP supports a few additional special forms which are not supported by GCLISP: see p. 154 of the CLRM.)

7.8 Local bindings established by let and multiple-value-bind are lexically scoped

We have reviewed the manner in which the special form **let** could be used to create and/or initialize variables required for temporary use (see Section 6.8). Let's look at the manner in which higher level variable bindings are affected by a **let** construct:

```
* (defvar *foo* 50)
*FOO*
* (defun scope-10 (bar baz)
    (format t "~%Now in scope-10")
    (format t "~%Values of *foo*/bar/baz are ~a/~a/~a"
       *foo* bar baz)
    (let ((bar 80))
          (format t "~%~%Now within let construct")
          (format t "~%Values of *foo*/bar/baz are ~a/~a/~a"
             *foo* bar baz)))
SCOPE-10
```

If we now call **scope-10** with two arbitrary arguments:

```
* (scope-10 60 70)
Now in scope-10
Values of *foo*/bar/baz are 50/60/70
Now within let construct
Values of *foo*/bar/baz are 50/80/70
```

We see that the special variable **foo** is visible, as expected, and that the **let** binding of **bar** has shadowed the previously established binding. The binding of **baz** is also visible since we are still within the lexical scope of **scope-10**. Hence, and assuming that no shadowing takes place, the bindings established by **let** effectively augment the bindings established by the function in whose body the **let** construct appears. In fact, and as noted in Section 6.9, the bindings established by the **let** can alternatively be established by use of the **&aux** keyword within the lambda list of the function in which it appears.

Let us now look at whether bindings established by a **let** construct are in turn visible within other functions called within the body of the construct:

```
* (makunbound 'foo)
FOO
* (defun scope-11 ()
    (let ((foo 10))
      (format t "~%Now within let construct in scope-11")
      (format t "~%Value of foo is ~a" foo)
      (scope-12)))
SCOPE-11
* (defun scope-12 ()
    (format t "~%~%Now in scope-12")
    (format t "~%Value of foo is ~a" foo))
SCOPE-12
```

Calling **scope-11**:

```
* (scope-11)
Now within let construct in scope-11
Value of foo is 10
Now in scope-12
ERROR:
Unbound variable: FOO
1>
```

Hence the scope of variable bindings established by a **let** construct is similar to that of bindings established during a user-defined function call, that is, limited to the lexical scope of the construct. (Note that we have again preceded the experiment with a **makunbound** statement to assure that no global binding of **foo** existed; otherwise such a value would have been visible within **scope-12**.)

The related special form **multiple-value-bind** (see Section 17.10) combines the facilities provided by a **let** construct with multiple assignment features. Scoping is similar as for the above **let** example:

```
* (makunbound 'x)
X
* (defun scope-13 ()
    (multiple-value-bind (x y) (values 5 10)
      (format t "~%Now within multiple-value-bind ~
                     construct in scope-13")
      (format t "~%Value of x is is ~a" x)
      (scope-14)))
```

```
SCOPE-13
* (defun scope-14 ()
    (format t "~%~%Now in scope-14")
    (format t "~%Value of x is ~a" x))
SCOPE-14
```

If we now call scope-13:

```
* (scope-13)
Now within multiple-value-bind construct in scope-13
Value of x is 5
Now in scope-14
ERROR:
Unbound variable: X
1>
```

Hence multiple-value-bind behaves like let as regards the lexical scoping of the bindings which it establishes.

7.9 labels and flet encapsulate local function definitions

Whereas let establishes temporary bindings for the auxiliary variables which are required by that part of the program, the special form labels can be used to encapsulate local function definitions. For example:

```
* (makunbound 'x)
X
* (defun scope-15 (x)
    (labels ((add-em-up (y z)
               (format t "~%Now in add-em-up")
               (if (fboundp 'add-em-up)
                   (format t "~%Add-em-up meets ~
                           fboundp test")
                   (format t "~%Add-em-up does not meet ~
                           fboundp test"))
               (format t "~%Value of x is ~a" x)
               (+ y z)))
             (add-em-up 10 5)))
SCOPE-15
```

Calling scope-15 with the arbitrary argument 20:

```
* (scope-15 20)
Now in add-em-up
Add-em-up does not meet fboundp test
Value of x is 20
15
```

```
* (fboundp 'add-em-up)
NIL
```

The function **add-em-up**, which is encapsulated within the **labels** construct, has a short life span: the body of the construct. As a matter of interest it should be noted that such a localized function does not meet the **fboundp** predicate test even during its active life span. Similarly to **let** and **multiple-value-bind**, the bindings established by **scope-15** are visible within the **labels** construct.

The associated special form **flet** (not supported by GCLISP) is similar to **labels**; there are subtle differences which are elaborated upon in more detail in the CLRM p. 113.

7.10 Variables created with setf statements at the top level behave differently from special variables

The bindings of variables created with **setf** assignment statements at top level (which for purposes of this discussion we will refer to as 'global' variables) are visible at all levels of a program. In this sense they behave similarly to special variables. However we can see a difference in behavior between the two types of variables when we use them as parameters of a function or as variables within a **let** construct and then try to reference them at a lower level, for example:

```
* (defvar special 10)
SPECIAL

* (setf global 20)
20

* (defun scope-16 ()
    (let ((special 2)(global 4))
     (format t "~%Now in scope-16")
     (format t "~%Value of special is ~a" special)
     (format t "~%Value of global is ~a" global)
     (scope-17)))
SCOPE-16

* (defun scope-17 ()
    (format t "~%~%Now in scope-17")
    (format t "~%Value of special is ~a" special)
    (format t "~%Value of global is ~a" global))
SCOPE-17
```

If we then call scope-16:

```
* (scope-16)
Now in scope-16
Value of special is 2
Value of global is 4
Now in scope-17
Value of special is 2
Value of global is 20
```

we see that, whereas the value of the special variable remains the same as the let binding in the higher level function, the value of the global variable has reverted to its top level value. We may therefore conclude that, although it is possible to use setf or setq assignments at top level to create global variables, it is not good practice to do so since such variables will exhibit behavior inconsistent with that of special variables.

7.11 Global variables can be created at lower nested levels

As a final experiment with global variables, let's create one at a lower nested level of the program using setf:

```
* (makunbound '*blah*)
*blah*
* (defun scope-18 ()
    (format t "~%Now in scope-18")
    (if (boundp '*blah*)
        (format t "~%Value of *blah* is ~a" *blah*)
        (format t "~%Variable *blah* is not bound"))
    (format t "~%Assigning value of 66 to *blah*")
    (setf *blah* 66))
SCOPE-18
```

Executing our experiment with scope-18:

```
* (scope-18)
Now in scope-18
Variable *blah* is not bound
Assigning value of 66 to *blah*
66
* *blah*
66
```

Again we have preceded our call to scope-18 with a makunbound statement to ensure that any previous top-level experiments with *blah* are not left over to distort the results of the current experiment.

Upon return to the top level we see that ***blah*** now exists as a global variable and, as such, will now be visible to all nested portions of the program. Creation of a global variable within a nested function is an example of something that 'works' in LISP but should be avoided. Someone reading somebody else's program listing should be able to determine what global (special) variables exist in the program merely by scanning the opening **defvar/defparameter/defconstant** statements. They should not have to worry about maverick global variables which may subsequently be created 'on the run' by **setf** statements buried somewhere within the program.

7.12 GCLISP's special-p predicate tests for special variables

GCLISP provides an un-Common LISP predicate, **special-p**, which can be used to test whether or not a variable is special. As pointed out earlier, in GCLISP variables may for all practical purposes be global – for example, variables created by use of **setq** or **setf** – without necessarily being special:

```
* (defvar *var-01* 'first-var)
*VAR-01*
* (special-p '*var-01*)
T
* (setf *var-02* 'second-var)
SECOND-VAR
* (special-p '*var-02*)
NIL
```

SUMMARY

Summarizing the key points of this chapter:

- the term '*scope*' relates to the area of a program in which a variable is bound to a particular value
- *special variables* may be defined at the top level of Common LISP by **defvar**, **defparameter**, or **defconstant** statements, the respective use of which provides an indication of the intended use of the symbol
- special variables are *global* in nature, that is, may be accessed and/or updated at any nested level of the program
- special variables may also be created at the top level by means of a *proclamation statement*
- *lexical variables* are created when arguments to a function are bound to the formal parameters of the function
- the bindings of lexical variables '*shadow*' any previous bindings the variables may have had, whether global or local
- the bindings of lexical variables are only visible within the lexical scope of the functions for which they are formal parameters, unless specific arrangements are made to declare them special
- constructs such as **let**, **labels**, and **multiple-value-bind** establish local bindings which are lexically scoped
- global variables created by **setf** or **setq** assignments should be avoided since their behavior is inconsistent with that of special variables

EXERCISES

7.1 Describe the difference between a special variable and a lexical variable.

7.2 Name the three functions which should be used to create and/or initialize special variables at the top level, and indicate the intended use of each.

7.3 Describe another way in which special variables can be created at top level. What if any are its shortcomings?

7.4 Write a statement to test whether variable ***cow*** is special. Would this statement return **NIL** or **T** if applied to variables created by **setf** or **setq** assignments?

7.5 After executing the two consecutive statements:

```
(defvar x 10)
(defvar x 20)
```

what will be the value of **x**? Why?

7.6 After executing the two consecutive statements:

```
(defparameter y 10)
(defparameter y 20)
```

what will be the value of **y**? Why?

7.7 How should a Common LISP interpreter be expected to react to the two consecutive statements:

```
(defconstant z 10)
(defconstant z 20)
```

7.8 If function **B** is nested within function **A**, is a lexical variable of function **A** visible within function **B**? If not, what statement would you incorporate at the beginning of function **A** to make it visible?

7.9 What is the meaning of the term 'shadows' as applied to variable bindings? Does a lexical binding shadow a previous global binding? Devise an experiment similar to that shown in Section 7.5 to demonstrate whether a lexical binding shadows a higher level lexical binding of the same variable.

7.10 The special forms **let** and **multiple-value-bind** may be used to create local bindings for their variables. Are these bindings visible within other functions which are nested within the **let** and **multiple-value-bind** constructs?

Chapter 8

Predicates and Boolean Operators

Like other programming languages, much of the decision-making in LISP is based upon the outcome of some sort of test. The test may relate to the value of an expression, the type of a data object, the magnitude of a number, whether a list is empty, or how one data object compares to another.

Many of the tests used to form the basis of such branching decisions are carried out by a family of LISP functions called *predicates*. The principal purpose of this chapter will be to review the most common predicates and show how they are used. The use of *Boolean operators* to combine the results of two or more predicate tests will also be explored.

In this chapter we will look at:

- the use of *recognizer predicates* to determine whether or not a LISP data object has some particular attribute
- the group of recognizer predicates which test for *object type*
- the use of *comparator predicates* in comparing one data object versus another as regards some particular attribute
- the various kinds of tests for equality which can be made with eq, eql, and equal
- the use of member and member-if to determine whether a given data object is a member of a particular set
- the manner in which *user-defined predicates* can be created
- the use of the Boolean logic operators AND, OR, and NOT for combining the results of two or more predicate tests

8.1 Predicates are used to test or to compare their arguments

In LISP terms – as opposed to conventional grammar – a *predicate* is a test of something which calls for a true-or-false response. Is X an atom (true or false)? Is X is a member of the list Y (true or false)?

If the assumption being tested is correct, a predicate function usually returns T, although some predicates such as **member** return other non-NIL values which for test purposes are equivalent to T. If false, a predicate returns NIL. Depending on the value returned, and using the conditional statements which will be discussed in Chapter 9, LISP can make appropriate decisions as to which course of action to take.

GCLISP has an assortment of about 60 predicates which test for a wide variety of properties. Predicates are characterized by a trailing 'p' as in **symbolp, consp, listp**, etc. to provide a clue as to their nature, although a few mavericks such as **atom** and **member** do not follow this practice. Where a word such as **upper-case** is hyphenated, by convention the trailing p of the corresponding predicate is also hyphenated, for example, **upper-case-p**.

Some of the more common predicates are reviewed below. Other predicates will be reviewed in the chapters dealing with the specific data objects to which they apply, for example, functions, characters, arrays, and strings.

8.2 Recognizer predicates test their single argument against a particular criterion

The most common type of predicate, which we can call a *recognizer predicate*, evaluates its single argument and tests to see whether the argument (after evaluation) meets some particular criterion.

For example, the predicate **symbolp** tests whether its argument is a symbol (as opposed to being some other type of data object). If it is a symbol the function returns T; if it is some other kind of data object the function returns NIL:

```
* (setf item 'peaches)
PEACHES
* (symbolp item)
T
```

Since **item** evaluates to a symbol, PEACHES, the function returns T. On the other hand:

```
* (setf item '(my friend))
(MY FRIEND)
* (symbolp item)
NIL
```

In this case **item** evaluates to something other than a symbol, that is, a list, so **symbolp** returns **NIL**.

We may at this point recall a peculiarity of **NIL**, which is unique in LISP in that it is both a symbol and a list!

```
* (symbolp nil)
T
* (listp nil)
T
```

This illustrates that all predicates are not necessarily mutually exclusive. For instance, an integer will pass the test for **integerp**, **numberp**, and **atom** since it is a member of all these data types.

Another recognizer predicate which deserves special mention is **null**, which tests whether its argument is **NIL** or the empty list:

```
* (setf item nil)
NIL
* (null item)
T
* (null ())
T
```

You will find yourself using this predicate frequently to test whether a data object has a **NIL** value. It can also be used as a terminating test for loops which end when a list has been **cdr**'d down to **NIL**, although the predicate **endp** (Section 8.8) is preferred for this particular purpose.

8.3 Many predicates are available to test for data type

One of the most common uses of a predicate is to test the data type of its argument. To save space we will list this group of predicates with commentary as to what they are testing for.

Predicate	*Tests to see whether*
(atom x)	x is a symbol, or a number, or NIL
(consp x)	x is of type cons (but not NIL)
(listp x)	x is a list (including NIL)
(numberp x)	x is a number
(integerp x)	x is an integer
(floatp x)	x is a floating point number
(characterp x)	x is a character
(rationalp x)	x is rational (integer only)
(stringp x)	x is a string
(simple-string-p x)	x is a simple string

Predicate	*Tests to see whether*
(vectorp x)	x is a vector
(simple-vector-p x)	x is a simple vector
(arrayp x)	x is an array
(packagep x)	x is a package
(functionp x)	x is a function definition
(compiled-function-p x)	x is a compiled function
† (stack-group-p x)	x is a stack group
(commonp x)	x is a Common LISP data type

† GCLISP-specific; not a Common LISP predicate

All of the above predicates are used with a single argument in exactly the same way as the **symbolp** example given previously, and all return T or **NIL**.

8.4 Other predicates test for numerical qualities

Various other recognizer predicates are designed to be applied to numbers to check their qualities.

Predicate	*Tests to see whether*
(zerop x)	x is zero
(plusp x)	x is a positive number
(minusp x)	x is a negative number
(evenp x)	x is an even number
(oddp x)	x is an odd number

See Section 3.10 for further discussion of the above.

8.5 Comparator predicates test one argument against another

Whereas recognizer predicates test their single argument for some particular property, *comparator predicates* compare one argument against another.

Predicate	*Tests to see whether*
(typep x y)	x is of type y
(subtypep x y)	x is a subtype of type y
(samepnamep x y)	the print names of x and y are the same
(> x y)	the number x is greater than the number y
(< x y)	the number x is less than the number y

Many other comparator predicates which apply to numbers, characters, and strings are discussed in the respective chapters dealing with these data objects.

8.6 How equal is 'equal'?

One of the more important types of predicate in LISP is the test for equality, since branching decisions are frequently made based on whether a variable has a certain value at that point in time. GCLISP includes three types of equality predicate: **equal**, **eql**, and **eq**, in increasing order of 'equality.'

The most general-purpose of these predicates, and the least demanding from the equality standpoint, is **equal**. One expression is **equal** to another if it is isomorphic to it, that is, structurally the same. For example, if we independently assign the same quoted list as a value to **x** and **y**:

```
* (setf x '(my friend) y '(my friend))
(MY FRIEND)
```

and then compare them for equality using **equal**:

```
* (equal x y)
T
```

The predicate returns **T** since the two objects are structurally the same, even though they share no **cons** cells.

At the other extreme, the most demanding predicate **eq** returns **T** only if the objects are **identical**, that is, represent the exact same structure in memory.

```
* (eq x y)
NIL
```

The test fails since although the values of **x** and **y** are structurally the same, they occupy different locations in memory. On the other hand, if we assign the value of **x** to **z**:

```
* (setf z x)
(MY FRIEND)
* (eq x z)
T
```

the test succeeds, since by the nature of **setf** the identical structure in memory has been assigned as the value of **z**. Put in other terms, the value pointer of **z** is now pointing to exactly the same structure as the value pointer of **x**.

Finally, the intermediate predicate **eql** is true if either two structures are identical, as in **eq**; or if they are numbers of the same type with the same value; or if they are character objects which represent the same character.

There is therefore a gradient of equality in the use of the three predicates. It follows that if any two expressions are **eq** they must also meet the test for **eql** and **equal**; and if they are **eql** they must be **equal** as well. Keep in mind that **equal** is computationally more expensive than the other two predicates since it must check each individual element of a list; **eq** is computationally least expensive since it merely has to verify that two address pointers are pointing to the same location. For testing purposes you should therefore use the predicate which is computationally most efficient while still serving the purpose.

For convenience in testing whether two arguments are *not* equal, GCLISP includes the un-Common LISP predicates **neq** and **neql**, which return **T** if the arguments are not **eq** or not **eql**, respectively:

```
(neq x y) = (not (eq x y))
(neql x y) = (not (eql x y))
```

where **not** (see Section 8.12) reverses the Boolean truth value of its single argument.

A corresponding negative form does not exist for **equal**; for the negative case you have to specify **(not (equal x y))**.

8.7 **member** and **member-if** test for membership in a set

One of the most commonly used comparator predicates is **member**, which tests to see whether its first argument (which may be an atom or a list) is **eql** to any top-level element of its second argument (which must be a list):

```
* (setf fruits '(apples pears grapes oranges))
(APPLES PEARS GRAPES ORANGES)
* (member 'pears fruits)
(PEARS GRAPES ORANGES)
* (member 'pineapples fruits)
NIL
```

If the test is successful **member** returns the balance of the list rather than **T**. For test purposes this constitutes a non-**NIL** value and is equivalent to **T**.

It should be noted that **member** includes the optional keyword **:test**, where the value of this keyword relates to the kind of equality test to be carried out. The full syntax of the function is:

```
(member <item> <list> :test <test-specification>)
```

where **<test-specification>** defaults to **#'eql**. If you are testing for the presence of an *atomic element* in the list the optional keyword can be omitted. However if you are testing for the presence of an *embedded list* you have to override the normal **:test** default and specify **#'equal**:

```
(member <item> <list> :test #'equal)
```

since quoted lists can never be **eql**. (See the comments on equality in Section 8.6; see also Section 6.13 for reasons for the use of the sharp-sign macro **#'**.)

member-if is a predicate which tests whether any element of the list meets a specified test. The syntax of this predicate is:

```
(member-if <predicate-test> <list>)
```

where <predicate-test> is successively applied to each element of <list> until one is found which passes the test. If such an element is found, the tail of the list is returned, similarly to **member**. For example:

```
* (member-if #'numberp '(able baker hotdog 5 you-all))
(5 YOU-ALL)
```

8.8 endp and tailp operate on lists

endp is a useful predicate designed to test for the end of a list. When **cdr**'ing down a list to carry out some operation or test on each element of the list, a test must be built in to indicate when the end of the list has been reached. This can be done with **null** (see Section 8.2) or with **endp**, which takes the syntax:

```
(endp <list>)
```

The CLRM indicates that **endp** is the recommended way to test for the end of a list: it returns **NIL** for a (nonempty) list, **T** for an empty list, and an error message if applied to any other kind of data object.

tailp tests whether its first argument is a sublist consisting of one of the **cons** structures making up its second argument, for example:

```
* (setf list '(one two three four))
(ONE TWO THREE FOUR)
* (setf sub-list (cddr list))
(THREE FOUR)
* (tailp sub-list list)
T
```

but:

```
* (tailp '(three four) '(one two three four))
NIL
```

since the data objects being compared do not share **cons** cells.

8.9 User-defined predicates can easily be created

We can readily create our own predicates to meet special needs. Let's say we have the list of fruits used in the previous example (bound to the symbol

fruits) and we want to establish a predicate to test whether a given fruit is a member of this list. We can define **fruitp** as follows:

```
* (defun fruitp (x)
    (member x fruits))
FRUITP
```

This predicate will return a non-**NIL** value if its argument is member of the list fruits, and **NIL** otherwise.

```
* (fruitp 'pears)
(PEARS GRAPES ORANGES)

* (fruitp 'pineapples)
NIL
```

It will be noted that **fruitp**, if successful, returns the value of the last expression evaluated, that is, the **member** predicate. As noted previously, this non-**NIL** value is for all practical (test) purposes equivalent to **T**.

8.10 Boolean logical AND requires that all arguments be non-NIL

Sometimes it may be necessary to have more than one test associated with a given branching decision. For instance, it may be required that two or more conditions be satisfied simultaneously in order for a test to succeed. Alternatively the test may succeed if any one of two or more alternative tests is satisfied. These situations may be handled through the use of the Boolean **AND** and **OR** special forms. These are not predicates, but rather control structures which may be used logically to combine two or more predicate tests to render a single true-or-false result.

The **AND** special form returns a non-**NIL** value if and only if every one of its arguments returns a non-**NIL** value. Any number of arguments can be included, as per the following syntax:

```
(and <arg1> <arg2> ... <argn>)
```

where each argument may be any LISP expression. The arguments are evaluated in left-to-right order. If an argument returns a non-**NIL** value, the program continues on to evaluate the following argument. Providing that none of the arguments returns **NIL**, the process continues until the last argument after the **AND** expression is exited, returning the value of the last argument. However if any single one of the arguments returns **NIL**, the expression is immediately exited without any of the remaining arguments being evaluated and a value of **NIL** is returned.

8.11 Boolean logical OR only requires that any single argument be non-NIL

The OR special form goes to the other extreme. In this case, if any single argument returns a non-NIL value, the control structure as a whole returns that same value. The syntax of an OR expression is:

```
(or <arg1> <arg2> ... <argn>)
```

The arguments are evaluated from left-to-right. If an argument evaluates to NIL, the next argument is tested. As soon as any one argument evaluates to non-NIL, the OR expression is immediately exited, returning that value, without any of the remaining arguments being evaluated. Otherwise the program proceeds until the last argument; only if this too is NIL does the OR expression return NIL.

Through use of OR, any single condition which may permit a test to succeed may be lumped together with other such conditions such that the passing of any one test will satisfy the requirements.

8.12 Boolean NOT reverses the value of its argument

The other Boolean operator which finds common use in LISP is the function NOT, which reverses the value of its single argument:

```
* (not t)
NIL

* (not nil)
T
```

NOT is often used to reverse the value of a test expression in a conditional clause so that an expression which would otherwise return NIL is transformed into a non-NIL value, or vice versa.

SUMMARY

Summarizing the key points of this chapter:

- *predicates* are used to test the nature of their arguments, or to test one argument against another
- *recognizer predicates* test their single argument against some criterion and return **T** or **NIL** according to whether or not the criterion is met
- *comparator predicates* compare their first argument against their second argument and return a non-**NIL** value or **NIL** depending on whether the comparative test is true or false
- **equal**, **eql**, and **eq** test for various levels of '*equality*'
- **member** and **member-if** test whether a given object or type of object is a member of a list
- it is easy to create *user-defined predicates* for special purposes
- The Boolean logical forms **AND** and **OR** may be used to combine two or more predicate tests
- Boolean **NOT** reverses the truth value of its single argument

EXERCISES

8.1 What values do the following predicates return?

(a) (symbolp "apples and pears")

(b) (symbolp nil)

(c) (listp nil)

(d) (eql '(my friend) '(my friend))

(e) (member 'cain '(able baker cain dog easy))

(f) (not (listp '(now is the time)))

(g) (endp ())

(h) (integerp 1.25)

(i) (and (integerp 10)(listp 'apples))

(j) (or (symbolp '(apples pears))(symbolp 'apples))

8.2 Given arg-1 and arg-2 as arguments, write the expressions which would be used to test whether arg-1 is:

(a) structurally the same as arg-2

(b) either identical to arg-2 or the same (constant) number

(c) identical to arg-2

8.3 The function **length** may be used to return the number of characters in a string, for example:

```
* (length "Now is the time")
15
```

Using **length** in conjunction with a numerical comparator predicate (see Section 8.5), define the predicate **short-string-p**, which returns **T** if its single argument is a string equal to or less than 10 characters in length. Use an **AND** relationship to assure that the necessary conditions are simultaneously satisfied.

8.4 Define the predicate **big-integer-p**, which returns **T** if its single argument is both an integer and larger than 255.

8.5 Define the predicate **two-or-more-p**, which takes two arguments and returns a non-**NIL** value if the first argument is contained at least twice as an element of the second argument, which must be a list. Provide for the contingency that the first argument may be a list.

8.6 Define the predicate **palindromep**, which takes a list as its single argument and returns **T** if the elements of the list are the same whether read from right to left or vice versa. Return **NIL** if an atom is entered as its argument.

8.7 Define the predicate **nilp**, which tests for whether a data object is **NIL** based on the fact that it passes the test of being both a symbol and a list.

8.8 Assume that our implementation of GCLISP does not contain a predicate for testing for a floating-point number. Using an **AND** relationship, create the predicate **test-float-p**, which makes such a test based on the data object being a number but not an integer.

8.9 Assume that our implementation of GCLISP does not contain a general predicate for testing for a number, but does contain the predicates **integerp** and **floatp** to test for these subtypes. Create the predicate **test-number-p**, which makes such a test based on the data object being either an integer or a floating-point number.

8.10 An iterative operation may be executed using the special form **loop**. Forms enclosed within a **loop** construct are repetitively evaluated until the construct is exited with a **return** statement which may be located at any point within the loop, that is:

```
(loop
  <forms-to-be-evaluated>
  (return <value>)
  <forms-to-be-evaluated>)
```

The <**value**> form which follows **return** is evaluated and determines the value returned by the **loop** construct. Using such a construct, define **count-numbers** which takes a single argument which must be a list and returns the number of numeric elements in the list. (Hint: Use **member-if** with a suitable test to isolate the numeric elements, and use **and** where necessary as a branching device to tie together forms in which the second form will only be evaluated if the first form returns a non-**NIL** value.)

Chapter 9
Branching Operations

At one or more points in any computer program, a branching point is reached where a decision has to be made as to what to do next, depending on circumstances. In LISP these circumstances typically relate to the current value or data type of a variable, the magnitude of a number, whether or not a list is empty, how some attribute of a data object compares with that of another object, or whether or not the value returned by an expression matches some test value.

These branching choices, which are made with *if/then/else* statements in procedural languages, are handled in LISP by *conditional* functions which are often used in conjunction with the predicate tests outlined in the previous chapter.

In this chapter we will look at:

- the manner in which *conditional statements* are structured
- the use of *default clauses*
- how *side effects expressions* are used to extend conditional statements
- the use of **if** and **ifn** to replace conditional statements in simple applications
- the use of **when**, **unless**, and **case** for other situations
- how Boolean operators can be used in conditional statements

9.1 Conditional statements are the LISP equivalent of if/then/else statements in procedural languages

In procedural languages, such as BASIC or PASCAL, branching decisions are made by if/then/else statements.

In LISP, the test which determines the **if** is frequently carried out by using one of the predicate functions described in Chapter 8 although, as we shall see, other expressions which evaluate to a non-**NIL** value will serve as well. The results of this test are incorporated into a **cond** (for CONDitional) statement, which can be represented in its most simple form as:

```
(cond (<if> <then>))
```

We can alternatively think of it in the form:

```
(cond (<test> <action-to-be-taken>))
```

wherein the first expression in the clause which follows the name of the special form **cond** represents some test to be made, and the second expression represents the action that should be taken in the event the test succeeds, that is, returns a non-**NIL** value.

The manner in which LISP handles the evaluation of an if/then clause of a conditional statement may be summarized as follows:

- If the value returned by the first expression in the clause is anything other than **NIL**, then the test is considered to have succeeded. The program then proceeds to the second expression, carries out whatever action may be specified there, and exits the **cond** construct, returning whatever value was returned by the second expression.
- If the value returned by the first expression is **NIL**, then the test is considered to have failed. In this case, the program totally ignores the second form and immediately exits the **cond** construct, returning **NIL** as a value.

For example:

```
* (setf apple 'fruit)
FRUIT

* (cond ((equal apple 'fruit)(format t "%An apple is a fruit")))
An apple is a fruit
```

The test passes and the action form is evaluated. (We will ignore the **NIL** value returned by a **format** statement at the top level.)

On the other hand:

```
* (cond ((equal apple 'grape)(format t "%An apple is a grape")))
NIL
```

The **equal** test fails and the **cond** function returns **NIL** without evaluating the action expression.

9.2 A conditional statement may have various test/action clauses

It is possible to have more than one conditional clause within the **cond** construct in which case if one test fails, rather than exiting the construct the program proceeds to test the following clause. A **cond** construct with multiple test/action clauses may be generally represented as follows:

```
(cond (<test1> <action1>)
      (<test2> <action2>)
            .
            .
      (<testn> <actionn>))
```

which corresponds to an extended if/then/else statement in a procedural language. Hence if the first test fails (returns **NIL**), control jumps to the second statement and tries out **<test2>**; if that fails it tries the next one, and so forth. If any one of the tests succeed its associated **<action>** expression is evaluated, that value is returned, and the **cond** construct is exited without processing any other clauses which may remain. In the event none of the tests pass, **cond** returns **NIL**.

What happens if you just include the **<test>** and leave out the **<action>** expression in a conditional statement? Assuming that the test succeeds, the value of the test itself will be returned as the value, rather than the value of the (nonexistent) action form. Hence a statement such as:

```
(cond (<test>))
```

is perfectly valid, and will return either the value of the test expression or **NIL**, depending on whether or not the test succeeds. (Note however that in the event a single test expression generates multiple values, only the first value will be returned; see Section 17.11.)

Such a construction is useful, for example, in a format such as:

```
(cond (<retrieve some value>)
      (<other tests and/or actions>))
```

wherein if the first test (which might be some sort of retrieval function) returns with a non-**NIL** value, this value is returned to the next higher level calling function; otherwise different methods of retrieval and/or default actions may be pursued by subsequent clauses.

9.3 A default clause is frequently included in case everything else fails

In the event that all tests fail, it is frequently desirable to take some default action rather than simply returning **NIL** as the value of the **cond** construct. Most **cond** statements therefore include a default clause at the very end:

```
(cond (<test1> <action1>)
      (<test2> <action2>)
           .
           .
      (<testn> <actionn>)
      ( t       <default action>))
```

All tests from **1** to **n** having failed, the program arrives at the final clause in which the test expression is simply the atom **T**. This of course evaluates to a non-**NIL** value, so the program continues on to the following expression to carry out whatever default action may be specified there.

Let's define the simple function **test-number** to illustrate the basic workings of the **cond** function:

```
* (defun test-number (number)
    (cond ((not (numberp number))
              (format t "That's not a number!"))
          ((> number 0)
              (format t "Number is positive"))
          ((< number 0)
              (format t "Number is negative"))
          ( t (format t "Number is zero"))))
TEST-NUMBER

* (test-number 10)
Number is positive

* (test-number 'hotdog)
That's not a number!
```

The first test uses the predicate **numberp** to test whether the input is a number. If it isn't, **(not (numberp number))** reverses the **NIL** value returned by **numberp**, thereby converting the overall form into a non-**NIL** value. The action expression prints a suitable admonishment and the **cond** construct is exited. Otherwise two subsequent tests check whether the number is positive or negative and print out testimonials to this effect. If none of the foregoing tests succeed, the number must be zero and the default statement is executed.

9.4 Side effects expressions may be included in extended conditional statements

Depending on the nature of the decision being made at a branching point, it may be desired to carry out various different actions – not just a single action – in the event that a test is successful. In procedural languages this is straightforward, since these actions can be listed one after another in that part of the program which follows the **then**. However LISP does it a bit differently.

Most LISP implementations contain what is known as an *extended conditional* special form, meaning that one or more so-called *side effects expressions* may be sandwiched in between the test and final action expressions. These might be thought of as additional expressions which are getting a 'free ride' in the event the test is successful. As has been mentioned earlier, the term side effects in its most basic sense refers to changes in list structure which persist after a function has been exited. For example, **setf** leaves side effects in the form of a new symbol data object whch has been created and/ or a change in a value pointer of an existing object. However, used in connection with conditional statements the term is used to emphasize the fact that the expressions are being included solely for the *effects* they produce rather then for the *values* they return. Used in this context, side effects expressions may include activities such as **format** statements which do not effect any lasting changes in list structure.

The general format of an extended conditional statement would be as follows, where **se** = side effects expression:

```
(cond (<test> <se1> <se2> ... <sen> <action>))
```

Assuming that the test succeeds, LISP proceeds to evaluate each of the side effects expressions one by one, after which it evaluates the final action expression. Although each side effects expression returns a value, this value is 'lost' within the body of the **cond** structure; only the value returned by the last action clause is visible to the next higher level calling function. Hence side effects expressions are included either for actions (such as printing) which they carry out, or for the changes in list structure which they produce – *not* for any values which they may return.

The overall format of an extended conditional function with multiple clauses is therefore as follows:

```
(cond (<test1> <... se clauses ...> <action1>)
      (<test2> <... se clauses ...> <action2>)
               .
               .
      (<testn> <... se clauses ...> <actionn>)
      (  t     <... se clauses ...> <default action>))
```

As noted, the default statement may include some side effects clauses of its own.

9.5 Conditionals can be nested within other conditionals

In line with LISP's flexibility in these matters, it is perfectly feasible to nest **cond** statements. Such nested statements could be inserted as side effect or final action expressions. Assuming that the initial test succeeded, upon reaching the embedded **cond** statement an additional branching activity would take place depending on the results of the new series of tests being presented. Ultimately of course the value returned by the embedded conditional expression would be returned to the higher level **cond** statement and evaluation of the latter would continue.

The syntax of a typical such construction might therefore be:

```
(cond (<test> (cond (<test><actions>)) <other-actions>))
```

9.6 if and ifn provide a simpler syntax for branching

cond provides a very flexible LISP control structure, allowing an unlimited number of test situations. However very often we may have only a simple **if/then/else** situation in which a single branching alternative is involved and no side effects clauses are required. This may be handled by the simpler special form **if**, which takes the following format:

```
(if <test>
   <then-action>
   <else-action>)
```

The syntax is considerably less complicated than that of the **cond** structure with its clauses and embedded expressions. **if** is immediately followed by a test expression which may be an atom or a list. If the test (after evaluation) returns a non-**NIL** value, the **then** action is evaluated and its value is returned as the value of the **if** expression. If the test returns a **NIL** value, the **else** action is evaluated instead. The **else** action may be left out, in which case **if** will simply return **NIL** in the event the test does not pass. As implied above, no side effects clauses can be explicitly included; however an equivalent effect can be achieved by grouping such forms within a single **progn** statement (see Section 13.10).

The above **if** function therefore corresponds to the following equivalent cond statement:

```
(cond (<test> <then-action>)
      ( t     <else-action>))
```

Since **if** is syntactically simpler and reflects its purpose more clearly than **cond**, it should where possible be used for this kind of simple **if/then/else** situation.

The alternative un-Common LISP special form **ifn** is provided by GCLISP to cover cases in which the test conditions are reversed, that is, the test passes if something is *not* true. The format is similar to **if**:

```
(ifn <test>
    <then-action>
    <else-action>)
```

The equivalent conditional statement would be:

```
(cond ((not <test>) <then-action>)
      ( t            <else-action>))
```

Aside from the reversed nature of the test, all of the comments made in connection with **if** equally apply to **ifn**.

9.7 **when** provides a simple if/then test

We saw above how **if** and **ifn** provide a simpler syntax for expressing branching operations where only one test is involved and no side effects expressions are required. Another related function is **when**, which takes the syntax:

```
(when <test> <action1> <action2> ... <actionn>)
```

In this case, if the test succeeds each of the following expressions is evaluated and the value of the last expression is returned as the value of the **when** function. If the test fails, none of the expressions are evaluated and **NIL** is returned.

when therefore provides the equivalent of a single **cond** statement with side effects forms:

```
(cond (<test> <action1> <action2> ... <actionn>))
```

9.8 **unless** provides an equivalent if-not/then test

unless is related to **when** in much the same way as **ifn** is related to **if**. It takes the syntax:

```
(unless <test> <action1> <action2> ... <actionn>)
```

In this case, if the test *fails* all of the actions are carried out; otherwise **NIL** is returned. **unless** therefore provides the equivalent of the single **cond** statement:

```
(cond ((not <test>) <action1> <action2> ... <actionn>))
```

9.9 **case** selects its branching choice based on a key

Whereas other types of branching functions test for a non-**NIL** value returned by the test form, **case** evaluates a key which can be any LISP expression and then tries to match this key against a list of possible choices. The syntax of **case** is:

```
(case key-form
  (key-spec1 <action1.1> ... <action1.n>)
  (key-spec2 <action2.1> ... <action2.n>)


  (otherwise <actionn.1> ... <actionn.n>))
```

key-form is any LISP expression which can be evaluated to provide a selector-key, which may be an object of any type. This key will subsequently be compared against the key-specs in the clauses which follow, which may take various forms. A key-spec may be a list of keys, in which case the test passes if **(member selector-key key-spec)** returns a non-**NIL** value. Alternatively, a key-spec may be a single (atomic) key, in which case the test passes if **(eql selector-key key-spec)** returns **T**. **key-spec** forms are not evaluated and must consist of symbols, keywords, numbers or lists of these atomic elements. As in **cond** statements, a default value can be provided by including a **T** key-spec; the alternative key-word **otherwise** can also be used.

If a test succeeds, all of the following expressions are evaluated and the value of the last is returned; otherwise **NIL** is returned.

As an example, suppose that we are printing out ordinal numbers which range from from 1 to 9, that is, 1st, 2nd, 3rd, etc. We want to design a function – say, **ordinal-suffix** – which will return an appropriate suffix depending on the digit. The suffix could then be incorporated into a **format** statement (see Section 12.5). Such a function might take the form:

```
(defun ordinal-suffix (digit)
  (case digit
    (1 "st")
    (2 "nd")
    (3 "rd")
    (otherwise "th")))
```

case evaluates the key-form **digit** to obtain the number, searches through the clauses which follow, and returns an appropriate suffix.

9.10 Boolean expressions can sometimes be used as a substitute for conditional statements

The manner in which Boolean expressions are evaluated provides a way in which they can be used in some cases to substitute for conditional statements. For example, in the **AND** expression:

```
(and <test1> <test2>)
```

if **<test1>** does not return a non-**NIL** value, **AND** immediately discontinues evaluation and exits from the function; otherwise **<test2>** is evaluated as well. **AND** with two arguments therefore gives results similar to the following conditional expression:

```
(cond (<test1> <action1>))
```

Similarly in the **OR** expression:

```
(or <test1> <test2>)
```

if **<test1>** returns a non-**NIL** value, **OR** immediately discontinues evaluation and exits from the function; otherwise **<test2>** is evaluated as well. Applying reverse logic to the case of **AND** above, **OR** gives results somewhat similar to the following conditional expression:

```
(cond ((not <test1>)(<action1>))
```

noting however that a different value will be returned in the event the first argument to **OR** evaluates to a non-**NIL** value.

SUMMARY

Summarizing the main points of this chapter:

- *conditional statements* are used in LISP to carry out if/then/else branching decisions
- *side effects expressions* may be included in a conditional clause
- a *default clause* provides for some default action to be carried out in the event all other tests fail
- the special forms **if** and **ifn** may be used in simple if/then/else situations where no side effects or default clauses are required.
- **when** and **unless** may be used in situations where various actions must be carried out whether a test passes or not, but no default actions or other test clauses are required
- **case** provides for branching based on the matching of a key against a list of possible choices
- Boolean functions may sometimes be used by themselves to provide the equivalent of an if/then branching operation

EXERCISES

9.1 Define the function numberp-1, which tests its single argument and prints "The argument is a number" if the test succeeds. Use a cond construct.

9.2 Define the function numberp-2, which is similar to Exercise 9.1 except that it also prints "The argument is NOT a number" if the test does *not* succeed. Use a cond construct with default clause.

9.3 Define the function air-con-1, which takes a single argument whose value is the temperature of the room. If the temperature is less than 75, print "The room is comfortable". Use a when construct.

9.4 Define the function air-con-2, which is similar to Exercise 9.3 except that if the temperature is 75 or more, print "Please turn on the air conditioner". Use an if construct.

9.5 Define the function booze-up-1, which takes a single argument whose value is your age. If your age is less than 21, print the message "You're too young to drink!". Use an unless construct.

9.6 Define the function booze-up-2, which is similar to Exercise 9.5 except that if your age is 21 or more, print "What'll you have?". Use an ifn construct.

9.7 Construct a simple daily calendar for each of the five weekdays which issues a printed reminder of something to be done on that day, for example: for Monday: "Attend Women's Lib meeting". Define the function daily-diary-1 which takes the day as its single argument and prints the reminder for that day. Generate an appropriate error message if the argument is not a weekday. For example:

```
* (daily-diary 'wednesday)
Picnic at Grand Canyon
```

Use a series of cond statements with a default clause to structure the above.

9.8 Repeat exercise 9.7 using case to structure the operation.

9.9 Assume that weather conditions may be defined as the value of the global variables sun, warm, rain, and cold, each of which may have a value of either yes or no. Using AND'd clauses, define the function weather-report-1 which prints "Weather is fine" if the current values of sun *and* warm are yes, "Weather is lousy" if wind *and* cold are yes, and "Weather is so-so" for any other combinations. (NB: Assume that sun and rain cannot be yes at the same time.)

9.10 Using Boolean OR and NOT operators, define a more complex function weather-report-2 which reports that the weather is fine if either it is sunny and warm OR if it is warm and not raining; lousy weather if it is either not sunny and cold OR it is raining; and so-so for any other combination.

Chapter 10

Input Functions

Information is read into our LISP system in two principal ways. While operating interatively as we are doing now, most of the input will come from the keyboard. While working with the editor and loading program files, much input will come from disk files. All of this input will be read into the system using the LISP function read or one of its variants.

In this chapter we will look at:

- the use of read as LISP's basic input mechanism
- how eof-error-p and eof-value can be used to exit under control when end-of-file is reached
- the use of read-char for reading a single character
- the use of read-line to read in a line of characters as a string
- how read-from-string can be used to read a single expression from a string
- how to create a special *stream* to permit data to be read from a disk file
- the use of *read-base* to establish the radix base in which integers are read into the system

10.1 read is the basic input mechanism for LISP

The basic purpose of the **read** function is to read in a single LISP character or expression, create a corresponding data object, and return a pointer to this object, as shown in Fig. 10.1.

If the data is a *symbol* the **read** function looks up the symbol on the Object List, creating it if necessary, and returns a pointer to the symbol. If the data is a *number* it is read in accordance with the current value of ***read-base*** (see Section 10.10), a numeric data object is created, and a pointer to the data object returned. (In the case of small **fixnums**, the binary representation of the number is directly contained in the pointer itself; hence in a manner of speaking the pointer *itself* is the data object!) If the data is a *list*, as in the example below, the corresponding linked-list structure is created and a pointer to this structure is returned. If the data is a *string* a vector containing the sequence of characters is created and a pointer to this vector is returned.

Chapter 29 provides further details as to the manner in which **read** operates at the machine language level.

read's syntax is:

```
(read &optional <input-stream> <eof-error-p>
                <eof-value> <recursive-p>)
```

read has a number of optional arguments which we will review presently. However this function will frequently be employed without arguments (that is, utilizing default values) and used simply to read a single valid S-expression into the system from the keyboard.

read is used within the system in two ways: as an integral part of the **read/eval/print** cycle, in a manner which is more or less transparent to the user, and explicitly within user-defined functions and top-level experiments

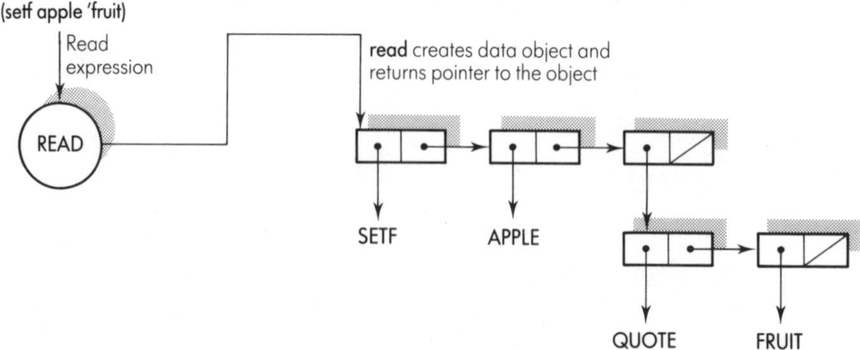

Fig. 10.1 **read** creates an internal data object.

at the keyboard. We have already reviewed the first category in Chapter 2. Let's now look at ways in which **read** can be used explicitly.

At the keyboard, we can simply call **read** and type in any valid S-expression:

```
* (read)<cursor is waiting here>
```

The first thing that happens when we call **read** is that nothing seems to happen! As noted in Chapter 2, **read** has in turn called the input routine of our computer's operating system and they are now both waiting for us to type something into the keyboard. Therefore when calling **read** explicitly we should normally precede this function call with some kind of printed statement to let the user know that the system is not hung up – it's just waiting for input.

If we now type in something:

```
* (read)(hot dog)
(HOT DOG)
```

we note that the list **(HOT DOG)** is returned as a value by **read**, with no complaints regarding the fact that **hot** is not a valid function. This is because **read**'s only purpose is to input a valid LISP expression and return a pointer to the corresponding data object in memory. No evaluation is carried out.

When used explicitly in a user-defined function **read** does essentially the same thing except that the pointer to the form is picked up by whatever function is in turn calling **read**. Typically this might be an assignment function as in the following example:

```
* (setf apple (read))(hot dog)
(HOT DOG)

* apple
(HOT DOG)
```

The pointer returned by **read** is picked up by **setf**, which puts the value returned into the value cell of **apple**. Thereafter **(HOT DOG)** is returned to the console – this time as the value returned by the **setf** function rather than by the **read** function.

10.2 read takes various optional arguments

read can take various arguments, all of which are optional. The first argument is the input stream from which it is reading. When using **read** in a program to solicit input from the console or when experimenting at the top level (as we are doing now), the default value of **input-stream** is ***standard-input*** (see Section 19.2). The default value of ***standard-input*** is, in turn, the keyboard. Hence the **input-stream** argument can be ignored until such time as you may want specifically to utilize **read** to get input from some other source such as a disk file or a peripheral device (see Section 10.9 and Chapter 19, 'Working with Streams').

10.3 end-of-file can be exited under control through use of eof-error-p and eof-value

The next two arguments relate to the possibility that you may reach **eof** (end of the file, that is, nothing left to read) while doing a **read** operation. This can occur if, for instance, you are reading S-expressions out of a file. After reading the last expression, the next iteration of the loop tries to **read** another expression but there are none left. This would normally signal an **end-of-file** error message and everything would grind to a halt. However you can use **eof-error-p** and **eof-value** to provide a terminating condition so as to exit the loop under control.

In this case **eof-error-p** must be specified as **NIL** and some expression – say, **'eof** – specified as the value to be returned as **eof-value.** When **end-of-file** is reached the next iteration of the loop returns the value of whatever expression is specified as **eof-value.** A simple test is built into the loop which causes a return when this condition is reached. For example, say we are reading expressions from a program file. As each expression is read in, it is printed on the console and evaluated:

```
(loop
 (setf <some-symbol> (read <input-stream> nil 'eof))
 (if (eq <some-symbol> 'eof)
    (return))
 (eval (print <some-symbol>)))
```

(In the unlikely event that **'eof** itself might be one of the symbols read from the file, a unique **cons** cell could be constructed for this purpose with a **(let ((eof (list 'eof)))** statement built in before the loop, and the symbol **eof** used as the **eof-value.**)

Another *end-of-file* circumstance *not* covered by the above arguments occurs when trying to read a file in which **eof** occurs in the middle of an S-expression, that is, before the necessary balancing closing parentheses have been parsed. If, for instance, the last entry in a file is the following incomplete expression:

```
(setf apple '(red fruit)
```

and you are reading from the file, **eof** will be reached before balancing the expression and an error will be generated. However this kind of *end-of-file* situation cannot be handled with the **eof** arguments mentioned above.

10.4 **recursive-p** finds use in recursive applications of **read**

recursive-p finds use in certain arcane applications where a call to **read** is embedded recursively in higher-level calls to **read**, for example, during the execution of macro characters. For more discussion on this subject see Section 20.9 and the CLRM pp. 374–5.

10.5 **read-preserving-whitespace** retains the delimiting space

When **read** is used for input of a LISP expression, the space following a token is interpreted as an otherwise meaningless delimiter and is discarded (along with other surplus spaces which may follow). In some specialized applications (see the CLRM pp. 366–7 for an example) it may be desirable to provide a means whereby the system can determine that the delimiter was a space, as opposed to some other terminating character. **read-preserving-whitespace** is provided for such situations. The syntax of this function includes the same optional arguments as for **read**.

If the **recursive-p** argument to **read-preserving-whitespace** is not **NIL**, this function behaves exactly like **read**.

10.6 **read-char** and **read-byte** read a single character or byte from the input stream

read-char reads a single character from the current input stream and returns a numerical value corresponding to its ASCII character code (see Chapter 20 for more details). Assuming that the normal default value of ***print-base*** (see Section 11.8) is in effect, this value will be expressed in decimal. The syntax of **read-char** includes the same optional arguments as for **read**. When experimenting as we are at the top level, **read-char** can be used to read in a single character from the keyboard:

```
* (read-char)A
65
```

Like **read**, **read-char** provides no prompts and waits until you provide some input. As soon as a single character has been typed **read-char** reads it and returns a number corresponding to the (ASCII decimal) value of the character code. Unlike **read**, **read-char** is unaffected by macro characters and simply returns their ASCII values in the same manner as for other characters.

A complementary function **unread-char** replaces the character just read by **read-char** at the front of the input stream again. Syntax of this function is:

```
(unread-char character &optional input-stream)
```

This function would not normally be used explicitly by the user, but would be used internally by the system to replace a terminating macro character back on the front of a stream so that it can be parsed as a separate token on the next **read** operation.

read-byte is similar to **read-char**, but it reads a single 8-bit byte from the current input stream and returns the value as a **fixnum** from 0 to 255. Syntax is:

```
(read-byte &optional <binary-input-stream> <eof-error-p>
                     <eof-value>)
```

The difference between **read-char** and **read-byte** is that the former returns a *character object*, as represented by its ASCII code, whereas the latter returns a true *number*. We will further explore the difference in Chapter 20.

10.7 **read-line** invites input of a string

read is used whenever you want to input an atom or a list. If you want to input a string you can do it in either of two ways: use **read** and enclose whatever you type in double quotes:

```
* (setf sentence1 (read))"I don't, do you?"
"I don't, do you?"
* sentence1
"I don't, do you?"
```

or use **read-line**, which reads in a line of text (terminated by a Newline) as if it were a single string:

```
* (setf sentence2 (read-line))I don't, do you? <cr>
"I don't, do you?"
* sentence2
"I don't, do you?"
```

read-line is particularly useful for input of natural language since it obviates the need to enclose the input in double quote marks, does away with parentheses, and permits input of characters such as the period, comma, and apostrophe which would otherwise clobber the input and/or provoke strange messages from the system.

This function has the same syntax and optional arguments as **read**. However it differs in that it returns *two* values: the string which has been input, and a flag which indicates how the line was terminated. (See Section 17.6 for further discussion of LISP functions which return multiple values.) Unlike the two values returned by **read-from-string** (see below), the second value is not displayed on the console; you just have to know it is there. This value is **NIL** if the line has been terminated normally and **T** if end-of-file occurred partway through the string, that is, before it was properly terminated with a **Newline**. When reading from a file, **eof** processing can be controlled with **eof-error-p** and **eof-value** in the same manner as discussed previously for **read**.

When typing in a sentence from the keyboard you will only be interested in the string returned by **read-line**; the fact that it returns a second value can be ignored. If you want to explore the fact that it *does* return two values, these can be captured using **multiple-value-setq** (see Section 17.9) which assigns each value to its respective parameter, for example:

```
(multiple-value-setq (input flag)(read-line))Hot dog!
"Hot dog!"
* input
"Hot dog!"
* flag
NIL
```

The first value returned by **read-line** has been bound to **input** and the second value **NIL** bound to **flag**.

The corresponding Common LISP output function **write-line** is not supported by GCLISP.

10.8 read-from-string reads a single token from a string

As noted above, **read-line** reads in English sentences (or other data) and returns the input in the form of a string. Since LISP's ability to manipulate strings is somewhat limited, it is often desirable to convert this string into a list for further processing. We can do this using **read-from-string** to read a token at a time from the string while accumulating these tokens into a list. **read-from-string** takes the following syntax:

```
(read-from-string <string> &optional <eof-error-p> <eof-value>
                           &key :start
                                :end
                                :preserve-whitespace)
```

The optional arguments **eof-error-p** and **eof-value** are used in the same way as discussed for **read**. Deferring discussion of the optional keywords for a moment, let's apply **read-from-string** to a simple string:

```
* (setf simple-string "How now brown cow!")
"How now brown cow!"
* (read-from-string simple-string)
HOW
4
```

read-from-string is a another unusual function which returns *two* values, both of which are displayed on the console. The first value is what we expected: the first token from the string. The second value is the index position of the first following character in the string which has not yet been read. Considering that the first character is index position 0 and that a single whitespace has been read after **HOW**, the next (unread) character will be at index position 4. This value can be used to reset the **read-from-string** pointer to the next token to be read.

Let's use **read-from-string** to read tokens from a string and accumulate these tokens into a list. For this purpose we can define **read-ex-string**:

```
* (defun read-ex-string (input-string)
    (let   ((word nil)
            (pointer 0)
            (sentence nil))
     (loop
      (multiple-value-setq (word pointer)
            (read-from-string input-string nil 'eof
              :start pointer
              :preserve-whitespace nil))
      (if    (equal word 'eof)
             (return (reverse sentence)))
      (setf sentence (cons word sentence)))))
READ-EX-STRING
```

After using **let** to create and initilize variables for temporary use, a loop is set up to read successive tokens from the string. As each token is read, it is **cons**'d to the list **sentence**. The two values returned by **read-from-string** are captured by **multiple-value-setq**, which binds the token to **word** and the index to **pointer**. The updated index is then used on the next pass to point to the start of the next word to be parsed. When **eof** is reached, the loop terminates, **sentence** is reversed to restore normal word order, and the resulting list is returned.

Trying out our new function:

```
* (read-ex-string "How now brown cow!")
(HOW NOW BROWN COW!)
```

Our input string has been converted to a list in which each word is now represented by an individual symbol.

If you experiment with the above function you will observe that the above process only works so long as macro characters such as commas, periods, and apostrophes are not included in the words. (For a more flexible way of handling English input, see Exercise 10.8.) It should also be noted that, in spite of the fact that **NIL** is the default value of the **:preserve-whitespace** keyword, when using GCLISP Version 1.0 this keyword/argument must be specifically included in the call to **read-from-string** if the index pointer is to be incremented properly on each successive pass. (NB: Version 1.1 has corrected this bug.)

read-ex-string can easily be amended to take additional arguments such as the initial pointer position and final pointer limit if desired to read only a certain number or total length of tokens from a string. If you are reading *all* the tokens from a string, a quicker way to do it is by using **string-append** (see Section 21.11) to graft a pair of parentheses onto each end of the string and then use **read-from-string** to read the whole list in one fell swoop. We can define **list-ex-string** to illustrate this:

```
* (defun list-ex-string (input-string)
    (let ((sentence nil))
      (setf input-string
        (string-append "(" input-string ")"))
      (setf sentence (read-from-string input-string))))
LIST-EX-STRING
* (list-ex-string "How now brown cow!")
(HOW NOW BROWN COW!)
```

10.9 A special stream provides for input from a disk file

In somewhat the same manner as LISP expressions are read from the keyboard, they may also be read from a text file. Such a file may be created with the GMACS editor, with a WordStar-type text editor, or interactively from the keyboard using appropriate LISP commands to open the file, print expressions to it, and close it.

In order to access a file it is necessary to create a special data object called a *stream*. (See Chapter 19 and Sections 11.10 and 11.11 for more information on streams.) The purpose of a stream in this case is to establish an interface between the LISP interpreter and the disk file. Once this interface has been established, the various **read** functions can be utilized to extract data from the file in exactly the same manner as if they were reading the information from keyboard input. Just as expressions explicitly read from the keyboard are not evaluated, neither is data read from a file evaluated unless specific provision is made for doing so (see Exercise 10.9).

Before proceeding further we should use GMACS or a word processor such as WordStar to create a file which we can use for test purposes. (If you use WordStar, remember to add a **.LSP** extension for consistency with GMACS, and to create the file in nondocument mode.) In this case we will call the file **b:testfile** (you may use an alternate drive and/or directories) and we will put the following expressions into it:

```
(setf apples 10)
(setf pears 15)
(defun add-em-up (one two)
    (+ one two))
(add-em-up apples pears)
```

Having created the file and input a series of valid expressions, we can return to the interpreter and open a stream to the file with the expression:

```
* (setf in-stream (open "b:testfile" :direction :input))
#<CLOSURE nnnn:nnnn>
```

where **in-stream** is a (mnemonic) name which we will give to the stream, and the file name assumes that we have used drive B. We have specified **:direction :input** in order to be explicit, but since this is the default we could have left it out. After evaluation of the above expression the necessary stream has been created and we can now read expressions from the file.

Depending on the kind of data in the file, different **read** functions may be used to access the data. In this case, since we have put expressions into the file, we must use **read** to access them on an expression-by-expression basis. If the file had contained lines of text terminated by Newlines we might use **read-line** for this purpose. In a file containing continuous text or binary bytes we might use **read-char** or **read-byte** to access the data on a byte-by-byte basis.

Trying our first read operation:

```
* (read in-stream nil 'eof)
(setf apples 10)
```

It will be noted that we have specified the name of the stream to override the normal default of ***standard-input***, and we have included **eof-error-p** and **eof-value** arguments.

The first expression has now been read from the file and the file pointer has been advanced to the beginning of the next expression. If we attempt another **read** operation we will get back the next expression. As discussed previously, when **end-of-file** is reached we will get back the value **'eof** and can use a test for this value to exit the read loop under control.

The above example illustrates the type of file which would normally be created with the GMACS editor, containing valid LISP expressions such as **defvar** statements, function definitions, etc. When you use a **load** operation to transfer the contents of such a file into the LISP environment, the system reads in the expressions one after another and at the same time evaluates them. The same process can be duplicated manually (see Exercise 10.9).

We will look at other aspects of accessing text files in Chapter 23.

10.10 *read-base* controls the radix base in which integers are read into the system

The global variable ***read-base*** controls the radix base in which integers are read into the system. The default for this variable is 10, but it can be set to any value between 2 and 36, inclusive, by a suitable **setf** or **defparameter** statement. For example:

```
* (setf *read-base* 16)
16
```

Any integers which we now read into the system will be taken to be in hexadecimal, for example:

```
* FF
255
```

Although the number is *read* in hexadecimal, a different global variable ***print-base*** (see Section 11.8) controls the manner in which the value returned is *printed*. Since the default value of ***print-base*** is 10, the value is returned in decimal. To return to normal decimal mode after the above experiment, execute **(setf *read-base* 0A)**.

SUMMARY

Summarizing the main points of this chapter:

- **read**, which is LISP's basic input mechanism, converts the printed representation of the input into an internal LISP data object
- **read** takes several optional arguments, the first of which is the input stream from which data is read. If this stream is unspecified, it defaults to ***standard-input***
- **End-of-file** can be exited under control through use of the optional arguments **eof-error-p** and **eof-value**
- **read-preserving-whitespace** preserves the delimiting space after a token
- **read-char** and **read-byte** are used to read in a single character from the input stream
- **read-line** reads in a line of text terminated by a Newline and returns it in the form of a string
- **read-from-string** reads a single token from a string and returns two values: the token and the index position of the next following character which has not yet been read
- a special input *stream* must be created to be able to read from a disk file
- ***read-base*** is a global parameter which determines the radix base in which integers are read into the system

EXERCISES

10.1 Output statements which include both text and data can be built up using **princ** (see Section 11.5) which supresses quotation marks around strings and does not start a new line. Using **princ** to generate output, define the function **get-symbol-value**, which prompts for input of a symbol. **get-symbol-value** checks as to whether a symbol has been entered and, if so, whether it has a value, and generates one of three kinds of statements:

> **Symbol <symbol-name> does not have a value.**
>
> **The value of <symbol-name> is <symbol-value>.**
>
> **<symbol-name> is not a symbol!**

10.2 Define the function **get-list-value** which is similar to Exercise 10.1 except that it prompts for input of a list. **get-list-value** checks as to whether a list has been entered and, if so, whether the first element of the list is the name of a function, and generates one of three kinds of statements:

> **<first-element> has no function definition!**
>
> **<input-expression> evaluates to <value-returned>**
>
> **<input-expression> is not a list!**

10.3 Define the function **yes-or-no** which prompts for input of either **y** or **n**. Provide for either lower- or uppercase input. Use **read-char** to read in the character and print a statement which says that the answer was **yes** or **no**, or that an invalid character was entered.

10.4 Define the function **count-character** which asks which character you want to count, prompts for input of a sentence, and counts the number of times the character appears in the sentence. Use **read-char** in a loop to read the sentence on a character-by-character basis until a Newline (ASCII 10) is typed, after which the program informs you how many times the character has appeared in the sentence. Use **string** (see Section 21.7) to convert the ASCII values returned by **read-char** to their string equivalents for printing on the console.

10.5 Define the function **sentence-length** which prompts for input of a sentence and uses **read-line** for this purpose. Use **length** (see Section 5.14) to ascertain the number of characters in the sentence and print "**The length of the sentence is <length>**".

10.6 Define the function **look-for-word**, which prompts successively for a word and then a sentence, uses **read-from-string** to ascertain whether the word is contained in the sentence, and prints an appropriate message to this effect.

10.7 Define the function **sentence-to-list-1**, which prompts for input of a sentence. Use **read-from-string** to read successive tokens from the string returned by **read-line**, accumulate these tokens into a list, and return the list.

10.8 Define the function **sentence-to-list-2**, which prompts for input of a sentence. In this case use **read-char** to read in the sentence character by character, using **string** (see Section 21.7) when required to convert the ASCII values returned by **read-char** to their string equivalents for printing on the console. Wherever an apostrophe, comma, or period (ASCII 39, 44, and 46) are encountered, insert a *single escape character* to nullify the macro effects of the character. Whenever a space (ASCII 32) is encountered, add the new token to the sentence. When all characters have been read, return the sentence in list form. For example:

```
* (sentence-to-list-2)
Please input a sentence: I can't, and neither can you.
(I CAN\'T\, AND NEITHER CAN YOU\.)
```

10.9 Using the GMACS editor (or a WordStar-type text editor), create the file **testfile.lsp** on any convenient drive and put the following expressions into it:

```
(setf x "apples")
(setf y "pears")
(princ
   (string-append
      "Who says you can't add " x " and " y "?"))
```

Define the function **read-from-file** which prompts for the name of the file, opens a stream to the file, and uses **read** successively to retrieve the expressions from the file. As each expression is read, evaluate it and print the value returned in the same manner as if the expressions were being typed in at the keyboard. Use **eof-error-p** and **eof-value** to control exit from the loop and print "**All expressions have been read**" when end-of-file is reached.

10.10 Define the function **hexadecimal** which changes the global variable ***read-base*** so that all integers are read in hexadecimal. Prompt for repetitive input of hexadecimal integers and return the decimal equivalents. Return ***read-base*** to its normal default value of 10 and exit the function when the word **exit** is entered in response to the prompt.

Chapter 11

Output Functions

The previous chapter looked at the different ways in which we can read information into a LISP system. This chapter will review the ways in which we can generate output from the system.

In Chapter 2 we reviewed the manner in which the print portion of the read/eval/print cycle provides a printout to the console of the final value returned at the top level. Other kinds of output from the system include printouts to the printer and transfer of data to disk files, most of which are carried out by some variant of print.

In this chapter we will look at:

- the basic purpose of *printing functions*
- the effect of *escape characters* on the printout
- the use of print as LISP's basic output mechanism
- how prin1 and princ provide for special printing needs
- how terpri is used to generate blank lines
- the manner in which print functions are controlled by *global print parameters*
- the use of pprint to provide for indented pretty-printing
- how to create a stream for directing output to the *printer*
- how to create a stream for directing output to a *file*

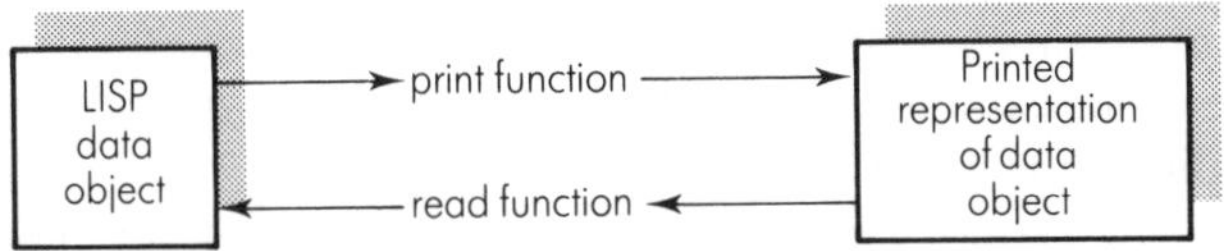

Fig. 11.1 **print** generates a printed representation of a data object.

11.1 Printing functions generate a visual representation of a LISP data object

The basic purpose of a printing function is to generate a *printed representation* of a LISP *data object*. This contrasts with the purpose of **read**, which works in the other direction to create a data object from a printed representation (see Fig. 11.1).

print resorts to varying strategies to generate a printed representation depending on the type of data object involved. If the data object is a *symbol*, the print name of the symbol is used for the printout. If the object is a *number*, the number is printed out in an appropriate representation depending on the current value of ***print-base*** (see Section 11.8) and on the type of number. If the object is a *string*, the string is printed with or without the enclosing quotation marks, depending on which **print** function is used. If the object is a *list*, right and left parentheses are printed to reflect the depth of nesting, and embedded symbols and numbers are handled as noted above. If the data object is a stream, package, closure, array, or other structure which does not directly lend itself to printed representation, the LISP implementation will provide some appropriate way to represent it in print, for example, **#<PACKAGE USER 29BF:36033>**.

Figure 11.1 flags out the interrelated nature of **print** and **read**. For instance, when you print something to a file, the printed representation within the file should be such that the data can be properly read back again when required. As we shall see, some print functions such as **princ** do not meet this criterion.

Before proceeding further, let's look at the way in which *escape characters* may be used to tailor printed output, since one of the differences which distinguish printing functions is the manner in which they handle such escape characters.

11.2 Escape characters can be used to tailor the output

There are instances, particularly in connection with the input of English language text, where it is desirable to suppress evaluation of what would otherwise be construed as *macro characters*, for example, the comma, period, and apostrophe. In other instances it may be desired to formulate unusual symbol names containing macro characters and/or spaces, or to preserve the upper- and lowercase characteristics of a symbol's print name. Such capability is provided by *escape* characters.

The *single escape character* \ can be used before any character to signal that the character should be accepted in its literal form, for example:

```
* (setf contraction 'don\'t)
DON\'T
```

As will be noted from the value returned, the system has incorporated the escape character directly into the print name of the symbol. \ nullifies the macro effects of the apostrophe which follows. The complete print name, including the escape character, is printed out during the course of the **read/eval/print** cycle since **print** faithfully gives back whatever it finds. As we will see shortly, we can edit out such escape characters with **princ**, a variant of **print**.

In constructions such as file pathnames, a \ can be incorporated into the pathname by preceding it with another \.

The *double escape character* | can be used, in a manner somewhat similar to quotation marks, to delimit any sequence of characters which are meant to be accepted literally, for example:

```
* (setf word-group '|I don't|)
|I don't|

* word-group
|I don't|
```

However, there is a significant difference between the string "**I don't**" and the symbol '|**I don't**|, although as we will subsequently see with **princ** their printout may be identical after editing. The version in quotation marks is a *string*, whereas the version enclosed in escape characters is a true *symbol*. This can be quickly demonstrated by trying to **setf** values to them:

```
* (setf |I don't| 'group-symbol)
GROUP-SYMBOL

* (setf "I don't" 'group-symbol)
ERROR:
SETQ: wrong type argument: "I don't"
A SYMBOL was expected
1>
```

11.3 print is the basic output mechanism for LISP

The function **print** is the primary means by which LISP generates output. Like **read** and **eval**, this third member of the **read/eval/print** triumvirate can be used explicitly to print data to any output stream (see Chapter 19 for more information on streams). The syntax of **print** is:

```
(print <object> &optional <output-stream>)
```

where **<object>** is any LISP object which can be evaluated and **<output-stream>** specifies the stream to which the printout is to be directed. If left unspecified **<output-stream>** defaults to ***standard-output***, which is usually the console.

print can be used to print information to a file or to other peripheral devices, but for the moment we will limit ourselves to its use for console output. Prior to printing the representation of its (evaluated) argument, **print** outputs a Newline (that is, a carriage return and linefeed); afterwards it follows the printout with a single space.

When operating at the top level, the **print** mechanism results in a somewhat peculiar double printout of the argument:

```
* (print 'apples)
APPLES
APPLES
```

The first printout is the result of evaluation of the **print** function as it does what you want it to do, that is, print out the value of its argument. The second printout represents the value returned by the function, which in this case produces an identical result. This would only happen at the top level when experimenting interactively at the console (or in the somewhat unlikely event that a **print** statement happened to be the last function called in a program).

We can use **progn** (see Section 13.10) conveniently to string together a number of **print** statements which can later be compared against other types of printing functions:

```
* (progn
    (terpri)
    (print '(I DON\'T THINK SO\.))
    (print '| double escape symbol |
    (print "and a string")
    (values))
(I DON\'T THINK SO\.)
| double escape symbol |
"and a string"
```

As noted, **print** automatically generates a Newline before printing out the value of its argument. Otherwise, **print** provides an accurate representation of the data object, including quotation marks and escape characters. (We have included a final call to **values** (see Section 17.8) to suppress the additional printout associated with the value returned of the final **print** statement.)

11.4 prin1 omits the Newline and space

Sometimes it is necessary to print various different items on the same line. prin1, which is exactly like print except that it does not output the Newline and space, may be used for this purpose. As a matter of interest, in assembler language print calls on prin1 to do the actual printing job:

```
PRINT    CALL NEWLINE    ;output Newline
         CALL PRIN1      ;do all the printing dogwork
         CALL SPACE      ;print out a space
         RET             ;return to calling routine
```

prin1's syntax is similar to that of print:

```
(prin1 <object> &optional <output-stream>)
```

Using progn again conveniently to string together several prin1 statements:

```
* (progn
    (terpri)
    (prin1 '(I DON\'T THINK SO\.))
    (prin1 '| double-escape symbol |
    (prin1 "and a string")
    (values))
  (I DON\'T THINK SO\.)| double-escape symbol |"and a string"
```

Like print, prin1 includes quotation marks and escape characters in its printout. Therefore when printing to a file various expressions which go on the same line prin1 should be used, since it will leave these characters intact for a later read operation. However when printing such output to the console princ, which edits out these characters, is usually more useful (see below).

11.5 princ edits out quotation marks and escape characters

princ is similar to prin1 in that it does not output a line feed and carriage return before the printout nor does it add a space after. What it does do is to edit out any single or double escape characters which are included in the expression, as well as the quotation marks which enclose a string. princ's syntax is similar to that of print:

```
(princ <object> &optional <output-stream>)
```

Repeating our previous printout, this time with princ:

```
* (progn
    (terpri)
    (princ '(I DON\'T THINK SO\.))
    (princ '| double-escape symbol |
    (princ "and a string")
    (values))
(I DON'T THINK SO) double-escape symbol and a string
```

It should be noted that in the course of its printing operation princ physically *removes* the escape characters and quotation marks from the data structure. As far as readable console output is concerned, the effect is exactly what you want. However it also illustrates that you should never use princ for printing such expressions to a file, since the relevant characters will be irretrievably lost. Later, when you try to read the expressions back from the file, the absence of these characters may cause parsing problems.

11.6 terpri generates a carriage return and line feed

The function terpri, an acronym for TERminate PRInting, generates a carriage return and line feed and is therefore used when you want to print out a blank line. terpri's syntax is:

```
(terpri &optional <output-stream>)
```

in which, like other printing functions, <output-stream> defaults to *standard-output*. Like any law-abiding LISP function, terpri returns a value (NIL), but of course the function is always used for its side effect rather than for the value returned.

```
* (progn (terpri)(terpri))
<cursor skips over two spaces>
NIL
```

We can also generate a Newline with (write-char #\Newline). In the next chapter we will see yet another way of printing a Newline through use of the *format directive* ~%.

11.7 pprint provides for indented pretty-printing

So far we have presented complex algorithms in a form known as '*pretty-printing*,' meaning that various elements are printed on separate lines and indented a number of spaces in proportion to their depth of nesting. This makes the whole expression easier to read and makes no difference to the read function of the LISP interpreter, which totally ignores line feeds, carriage returns, and extra spaces within an expression.

GCLISP includes the function pprint in the form of a special file in the directory \LISPLIB on the Utilities 2 diskette which can be autoloaded either from the bare interpreter or from the GMACS editor. When pprint is called up by a program or at the top level, the system automatically autoloads it from the library directory if it has not yet been defined.

Assume for example, that we have previously defined the function factorial:

```
* (symbol-function 'factorial)
(LAMBDA (N)(COND ((ZEROP N) 1)(T (* N (FACTORIAL (1-N))))))
```

The whole function stretched out as a single long list is not very easy to read. pprint rearranges the format:

```
* (pprint (symbol-function 'factorial))
; Autoload: PPRINT from "PPRINT" in "C:\\GCLISP\\LISPLIB\\".
(LAMBDA (N)
  (COND ((ZEROP N)
          1)
        (T (* N (FACTORIAL (1-N))))
        ))
```

pprint follows a complex pattern of rules for printing the output depending on whether the expression being printed is a normal function, a special function, an atom, or a list; on the present location of the cursor; on whether the current expression will fit within the right border of the screen, etc. The general goal is to indent expressions commensurate with their depth of nesting and to align expressions of equal depth along the same vertical column. Aside from making functions easier to read, pprint can come in handy when you are debugging a complex algorithm and want to check whether your parentheses are in proper order. (Although the *overall* parentheses may balance, it is easy to get closing parentheses mixed up in nested cond expressions and functions involving deeply embedded lists.)

The pretty-printing executed by pprint may not always suit your fancy. The above example might look a little neater as:

```
(LAMBDA (N)
  (COND ((ZEROP N) 1)
        (T (* N (FACTORIAL (1- N)))) ) )
```

When using the GMACS editor you are of course free to format your function definitions in whatever order appeals to your sense of logic. The obvious goal should be to make them easy to read, easy to understand, and easy to debug.

11.8 Printing operations are controlled by global parameters

GCLISP utilizes various global parameters to control the manner in which certain types of printing will be carried out. Although all parameters come bound to preset default values, these values may be changed before or during a program to suit specialized printing needs.

print-escape controls whether or not escape characters will be printed to the current output stream. Although the system default is T (meaning that escape characters will be printed), *print-escape* is reset automatically to the appropriate value by whatever print function is being used at the time. prin1 (and by extension print, which uses prin1 to do its work) will set it to T and princ will set it to NIL.

print-base controls the radix in which integers are printed to the current output stream. The system default is 10, but this can be changed with a setf operation to any value between 2 and 36. (See Chapter 22 for an explanation of this range.) For example:

```
* (setf *print-base* 16)
10
```

The value returned is momentarily misleading! In fact, setf is as usual returning the value of its second argument, 16, but this is now being expressed in hexadecimal, that is, 16(dec) = 10(hex)! It follows that any such radix reassignment will always return a value of 10, and that any evaluation of *print-base* will return 10. We can however check on the current value of *print-base* by executing:

```
* (1- *print-base*)
F
```

The foregoing change in *print-base* in effect turns our LISP interpreter into a radix base converter. We can continue to type in decimal integers and get them immediately converted into the alternative radix base. For example, now that we are in hexadecimal:

```
* 255
FF
```

Whereas *print-base* determines the radix in which integers are to be *printed*, *read-base* (see Section 10.10) determines the radix in which they are to be *read*. The system default for this variable is also 10. It will be noted that *print-base* and *read-base* may be different, that is, numbers may be read in a different radix base than that in which they are printed. In the above example where we evaluated the integer 255 the system was reading the number in base 10, and returning to eval a pointer to the fixnum corresponding to 255(dec); however upon being printed *print-base* caused the output to be expressed in hexadecimal.

print-radix controls the printing of radix specifiers. The system default is NIL, so that such specifiers are normally not printed. If we execute (setf *print-radix* t) all decimal integers will be printed with a trailing decimal point and all integers in other radix bases will be printed with appropriate prefixes, namely, #b for binary, #o for octal, #x for hexadecimal, and #nr for other bases where n is the radix base.

print-level controls the number of levels of a nested data structure which will be printed. The Common LISP default for *print-level* is NIL, meaning that *all* levels will be printed, but the parameter can be changed with a setf assignment:

```
* (setf level '(1 (2 (3 (4 (5 (6 (7 (8 (9 (10)))))))))))
(1 (2 (3 (4 (5 (6 (7 (8 (9 (10))))))))))
* (setf *print-level* 4)
4
* level
(1 (2 (3 (4 #))))
```

with all more deeply nested lists being represented by a single hash symbol #. Needless to say, the internal data structure of level still contains all of the elements; they are merely abbreviated during the printing process. (NB: Version 1.0 of GCLISP initialized the default of *print-level* to 4.)

print-length similarly controls the number of elements of a list which will be printed. The Common LISP default for *print-length* is NIL, meaning that *all* elements will be printed, but the parameter can be changed with a setf assignment:

```
* (setf length '(1 2 3 4 5 6 7 8 9 10 11 12 13 14 15))
(1 2 3 4 5 6 7 8 9 10 11 12 13 14 15)
* (setf *print-length* 10)
10
* length
(1 2 3 4 5 6 7 8 9 10 ...)
```

with all following elements being represented by three ellipsis dots (...). (NB: Version 1.0 of GCLISP initialized the default of *print-length* to 10.)

11.9 write-char and write-byte output a single character or byte to the output stream

write-char and write-byte are structured as follows:

```
(write-char <character> <output stream>)
(write-byte <integer> <output stream>)
```

where the first function outputs a character to the stream and returns <character> (see Exercise 11.10) and the second outputs an integer and returns <integer>. We will discuss these functions further in Chapter 20 which deals with characters.

We can demonstrate an example of **write-char** with the following function **type-it-slow**, which takes a single integer argument to define the rate at which the text is to be typed. This function reads text from a file and prints it on the screen at a speed determined by **rate**:

```
(defun type-it-slow (rate)
  (let ((text-stream nil)
        (char nil))
    (terpri)
    (princ "Type in the name of a file: ")
    (setf text-stream
      (open (read-line) :direction :input))
    (loop
      (setf  char (read-char text-stream nil 'eof))
      (when (equal char 'eof)
            (close text-stream)
            (return))
      (dotimes (wait rate))
           (write-char char))))
```

The **dotimes** function (see Section 13.5) causes a delay in the loop proportional to the rate. Try out this function with an initial rate of 10 and vary it from there. **type-it-slow** comes in handy in English language applications where you want a 'robot' to respond at a rate approximating the rate of human speech.

11.10 A special stream provides for output to the printer

During the course of your programming you will often wish to direct output to the printer to provide a hard-copy record of a session or to preserve data generated by a program.

MS-DOS recognizes the normal printer connected to the parallel output port as the device **prn** or alternatively **lpt1**. Either of these device codes will work with GCLISP output. (**lpt3** doesn't work and **lpt2** hangs up the system, necessitating a complete reboot and reload of GCLISP.) DOS is constructed in such a way that you can use a device name anywhere a file name can be used. You can therefore direct DOS to get information *from* a device, such as a modem, or direct information *to* a device, such as a printer.

These activities are coordinated between GCLISP and the MS-DOS operating system through the creation of *streams*, which serve as a kind of interface between GCLISP and external entities such as files and peripherals. We will get into more detail on streams in Chapter 19. For the moment, accept the fact that we have to create an *output stream* which will direct output to the printer. This stream, which we will mnemonically call **print-stream**, will be explicitly assigned as the <**stream**> argument for the **print** function.

```
(defun write-to-printer ()
  (let ((char nil))
   (terpri)
   (princ "Please type in text, ")
   (princ "followed by a carriage return:")
   (terpri)
   (setf print-stream (open "prn" :direction :output))
   (loop
    (setf   char (read-char))
    (when (equal char 10)
          (princ (string 10) print-stream)
          (close print-stream)
          (return))
    (write-char char)
    (write-char char print-stream))))
```

print-stream is created to interface with the printer device "**prn**". Since **:direction :input** is the normal default, it is necessary to add the keywords **:direction :output** to show that information is being printed *to* rather than *from* the printer.

A loop is set up to read in characters from the keyboard. As each character is read in, the ASCII value returned is converted to a character and printed out to the console and to the printer. This process continues until a Newline (ASCII 10) is parsed, after which the output stream is closed and the function exited.

If you start typing text into the keyboard and permit the text to wrap around the console screen without typing a carriage return, there will be a delay before the initial characters start to be printed. This is because the text is being accumulated into the printer's storage buffer. Nothing will emerge at the printer until the buffer is completely full. Once full, any further text pushed into one end of the buffer will cause the entire contents to be disgorged, after which the buffer starts accumulating a new batch (see Fig. 11.2).

After defining and calling up **write-to-printer**, keep count as you type characters into the keyboard. From your observations, how many

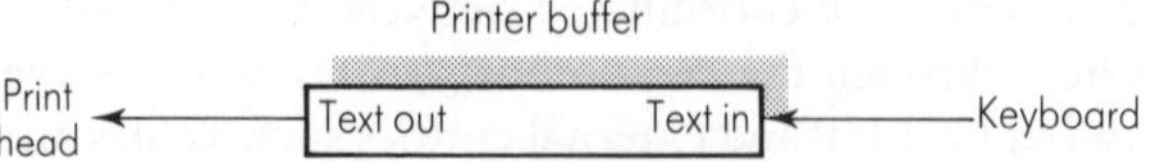

Fig. 11.2 Characters are accumulated into the printer buffer.

characters can be stuffed into the buffer before the first batch is disgorged from the other end? (Our printer stored 512.) When you have finished entering text, the final Newline causes the print stream to be closed. This Newline also causes all characters currently stored in the buffer to be flushed to the print head, leaving the buffer empty.

Further operations with the printer are explored in Chapter 23, 'Interfacing with File Systems.'

11.11 A special stream provides for output to a disk file

In the same manner as it was necessary to create a special stream to direct output to the printer, it is necessary to go through a similar procedure to create and/or send data to a file. We will discuss this in more detail in Chapter 19, "Working with Streams," but for now we can illustrate a simple example of writing to a file by modifying our **write-to-printer** function as follows:

```
(defun write-to-file ()
  (let ((char nil))
   (terpri)
   (princ "Please type in file name: ")
   (setf filename (read-line))
   (princ "Please type in text, ")
   (princ "followed by a carriage return:")
   (terpri)
   (setf file-stream
     (open filename :direction :output))
   (loop
     (setf   char (read-char))
     (when (equal char 10)
           (princ (string 10) file-stream)
           (close file-stream)
           (return))
     (write-char char)
     (write-char char file-stream))))
```

The filename may be preceded by a drive letter, for example, **b:test-file.lsp**. (We will routinely add the extension **.lsp** to be consistent with the GMACS editor.) If the file does not yet exist, the mere fact of opening the stream to it will create it. You can check that the file has been created and the text put into it by switching over to MS-DOS with the command **(sys:dos)** and accessing the file with the normal DOS commands **dir** and **type**. You can then return to GCLISP with the DOS command **exit**.

SUMMARY

Summarizing the main points of this chapter:

- printing functions generate a *printed representation* of a LISP data object
- *single* and *double escape characters* can be used to suppress evaluation of the following character or the enclosed group of characters
- the basic output mechanism of LISP is print, which precedes the printout of its single (evaluated) argument with a Newline and follows it with a single space
- prin1 is like print, but excludes the Newline and space
- princ is like prin1, but omits quotation marks and escape characters from its printout
- terpri is used to output a carriage return and line feed
- pprint provides an indented form of printout, referred to as *pretty-printing*, which is easier to read and debug
- the global variables *read-base* and *print-base* control the radix in which integers are read into the system and printed out by the system, while *print-radix* controls the printing of the radix specifiers
- the global variables *print-level* and *print-length* control the depth of nested lists and the number of list elements which will be printed
- a special output stream must be provided to direct output to the printer, which may use device codes prn or lpt1
- a special output stream must be provided to direct output to a disk file

EXERCISES

11.1 We wish to print the statement (THE TEMPERATURE IS 68 DEGREES FAHRENHEIT), where 68 is the value of the variable temp. Using progn to collect the expressions into a single group, show how this can be done with a single print statement. (Ignore the extra value returned at top level.)

11.2 Using progn and a series of prin1 expressions, generate a printout of the same statement as in Exercise 11.1, but without parentheses. (Hint: Use (write-char #\space) for generating a blank space between words.)

11.3 Using progn and a series of princ expressions, print the same statement as generated by Exercise 11.2.

11.4 Define the function blank-lines, which takes a single integer input and generates that many blank lines. Check the input and generate an error message if it is not an integer. Using an iterative construct with loop (see Section 13.2), generate the required number of terpri's followed by the statement "<integer> blank lines have been printed".

11.5 Define the function pretty-print, which takes the name of a function as its single argument and pretty-prints the function definition. Generate an error message if the argument is not the name of a function.

11.6 Define the function test-print-level, which prompts for input of a (revised) print level, prompts for input of a list, prints out the list using the revised print level, and returns *print-level* to its original value. Test the function with a deeply nested list.

11.7 Define the function test-print-length, which is similar to the function defined in Exercise 11.6 except that it applies to the global variable *print-length*. Test the function with a list containing many elements.

11.8 Define the function print-phone-numbers, which repetitively prompts for a name and phone number and prints this information on the printer. Discontinue input when a Newline is entered in response to the prompt.

11.9 Define the function file-phone-numbers, which does the same thing as Exercise 11.8 but instead prints the information to file b:telephon.lsp (or an alternate drive).

11.10 Define the function copy-file, which prompts for the name of the file to be copied from and the name of the file to be copied to, accesses the first file, and transfers the contents character-by-character to the second file. As characters are transferred, echo them to the console.

Chapter 12

Formatting Printed Output

In the previous chapter we looked at different types of print functions and the manner in which they direct output to the console or to external devices such as a printer or a disk file. The printouts generated by these print functions are used in many ways: to prompt the user for input, to display the results of a calculation as text or in tabular form, to signal an error of some kind, etc. Aside from the basic question of getting the data printed, another area of interest concerns the manner in which such output can be *formatted* so as to permit mixing text with data and in general enhancing the quality of communication between the system and the user.

In this chapter we will look at:

- how cons and append can be used to build up lists to print output messages
- the use of backquote to achieve easier formatting
- how princ may be used to provide a sequence of strings and tokens to make up an output message
- how format can be used to create a specially formatted output string
- how format may be used to carry out radix conversion
- other types of *formatting operations*
- how error and cerror are used to format and print error messages
- the use of flatc and flatsize in formatting a table
- the use of *user-query predicates* in eliciting a response

12.1 Output statements frequently combine text strings and data

For straightforward prompts or messages containing only a simple line of text, the simplest way to effect a printout is to use a **princ** statement with a string containing the text, for example:

```
(princ "Please type in your name: ")
```

However we will more often find it necessary to print out statements which combine text with data, for example:

```
The temperature is 68 degrees Fahrenheit
```

where the first and last word groups are strings and the number is the value of some variable.

In this chapter we will look at various ways in which text and data can be combined to produce the desired printout, and at ways in which this information can be formatted on the screen.

12.2 **cons** and **append** can be used to build up an output list

Since we are normally dealing with symbols and lists, a natural approach to formatting printed output is to build up the text using symbolic elements and quoted lists. Using the previous example, and assuming that the value of variable **temp** is **68**, we could build up the required list of symbols through a sequence of **cons** and **append** operations:

```
* (setf output (append '(the temperature is)
                       (cons temp '(degrees Fahrenheit))))
(THE TEMPERATURE IS 68 DEGREES FAHRENHEIT)
```

after which the list could be printed:

```
* (print output)
(THE TEMPERATURE IS 68 DEGREES FAHRENHEIT)
```

We note that the automatic conversion process has produced an uppercase message and that the printout includes the enclosing parentheses.

If we find the parentheses annoying we can devise a simple function which reads tokens from the list one by one and prints them out individually:

```
* (defun print-from-list (list)
    (terpri)
    (loop
      (if (endp list)
          (return))
      (princ (car list))
      (princ " ")
      (setf list (cdr list))))
PRINT-FROM-LIST
```

```
* (print-from-list output)
THE TEMPERATURE IS 68 DEGREES FAHRENHEIT
```

There are various other ways of manipulating such a list so as to convert it back to a string, revert back to lowercase letters, etc. (see also **dolist** (Section 13.4) for a more elegant way of printing tokens from a list), but for the moment let's look at some other methods of formatting printed output.

12.3 backquote provides a template for formatting printouts

The **backquote** character, which we will find particularly useful when we start writing macros (see Sections 16.6 and 16.7), provides another means of mixing text and values in a printout. The character itself is a kind of backward-slanting quote mark ` and it tells the system not to evaluate any of the elements of the form which follows it *except* elements preceded by a comma. For example:

```
* (setf pears '(those yellow fruits))
(THOSE YELLOW FRUITS)
* `(apples grapes ,pears)
(APPLES GRAPES (THOSE YELLOW FRUITS))
```

The expression has been left unevaluated, as with **quote**, except for the element **pears**, which was evaluated since it is preceded by a comma.

We can use the backquote mechanism to create **templates** for formatting printouts in which the quoted text is unevaluated and the symbols which provide the necesssary values are evaluated. Restructuring our previous example around **backquote**:

```
* (setf output `(the temperature is
   ,temp degrees Fahrenheit))
(THE TEMPERATURE IS 68 DEGREES FAHRENHEIT)
```

If the comma in a backquote expression is immediately followed by the at-sign modifier @, the form following the comma is evaluated to produce a list of objects which is then spliced into the overall template in somewhat the same manner as **append** splices a list of elements onto one end of another list. For example, given the previously assigned value of pears:

```
* `(apples grapes ,@pears)
(APPLES GRAPES THOSE YELLOW FRUITS)
```

Instead of using the ,@ construction, another option is to use a comma-and-period combination ,. which does the same thing as ,@ but permits destructive modification (rather than copying) of the list being evaluated. In the above example, rather than splicing a copy of the list

(THOSE YELLOW FRUITS) into the backquoted list ,. would splice in the original list itself.

The backquote mechanism therefore provides a convenient way of mixing values with quoted text without the need for a lot of extra cons or append operations as in the earlier example. However we are still stuck with somewhat unsightly uppercase messages enclosed in parentheses. Let's now look at some ways to incorporate values into text strings which can be printed out in a more natural way, in upper- or lowercase and without parentheses.

12.4 princ can be used to output a sequence of strings

A simple expedient to provide attractive text mixed with values is to use a series of princ statements:

```
* (progn ()
    (terpri)
    (princ "The temperature is ")
    (princ temp)
    (princ " degrees Fahrenheit")
    (values))
The temperature is 68 degrees Fahrenheit
```

Although a bit long-winded, this achieves the desired result.

In some cases it may be desirable to pre-construct the entire statement in the form of a single string in order to be able to assign it as the value of some variable. We can chain together such a mixture of strings and values but the values must first be converted to strings, using functions such as make-string-output-stream (see Section 19.10), whereupon the strings can be concatenated with string-append (see Section 21.11). An even simpler solution is to use the Common LISP format function.

12.5 format facilitates complex formatting

format is a powerful facility which provides a variety of options for formatting text, including provision for Newlines built into the formatted text string (thus avoiding the need for explicit terpri's), different modes of printing to simulate prin1 or princ, conversion of numbers to different radix bases, inclusion of embedded functions to calculate on-the-run values to be inserted in the text string, and other features. GCLISP includes about half of the 30 or so *format directives* supported by Common LISP.

A format statement takes the following syntax:

```
(format <destination> <control-string> <arguments>)
```

The <**destination**> specifies what you want to do with the string which is produced by the **format** operation. The three possible options include **t**, **nil**, or the name of a stream. If you specify **t**, the formatted string is printed to the stream corresponding to ***standard-output***, after which the **format** function returns **NIL**. Since ***standard-output*** is normally the console, you will probably most often be using this option when using **format** in a program.

If the destination is **NIL**, the output is returned as a value by **format**, that is, would not be printed on the console but would be returned as a value to the next higher level calling function, which might choose to do something else with it. If the destination is the name of some (output) stream, the output would be printed to that stream, for example, to a file or a peripheral such as a printer.

The *control string*, which may contain embedded *format directives*, and the (optional) arguments which follow are used to generate the output string. Let's look first at an example without format directives or arguments:

```
* (format t "How now brown cow!")How now brown cow!
NIL
```

In this basic example, **format** simply prints out the string wherever the cursor happens to be at the moment.

However the real power of **format** lies in the use of format directives which are designed to take one or more arguments which follow the control string and incorporate these arguments into the output string in different ways, according to the type of directive used. A *format directive* consists of a tilde character ~ followed by a character which indicates the kind of formatting to be applied to the argument. Let's assign a few values and look at an example:

```
* (setf when "now")
"now"

* (setf color "brown")
"brown"
```

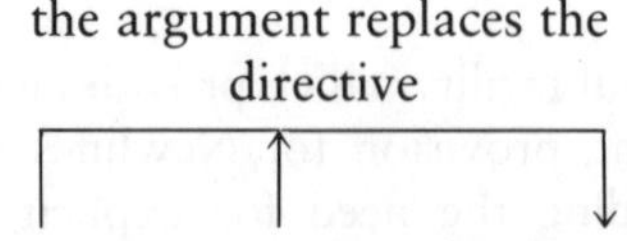


```
* (format t "How now ~a cow!" color)How now brown cow!
NIL
```

The format directive **~a** (or **~A**; directives are insensitive to case) tells the **format** function to take the argument which follows the control string, evaluate it, and incorporate the value into the string in the same manner as if it were printed by **princ**.

The format directive ~s operates similarly but incorporates the argument as if it were printed by **prin1**:

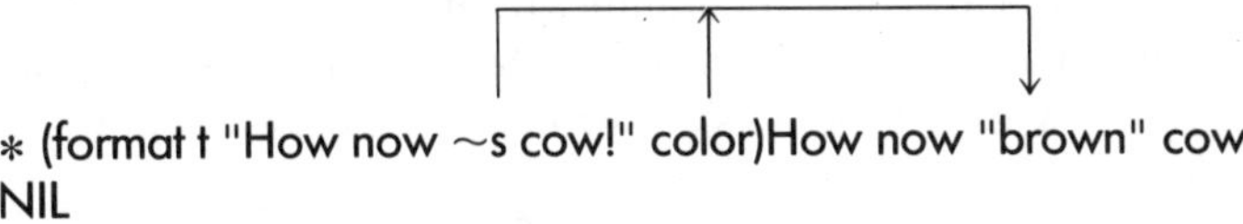

```
* (format t "How now ~s cow!" color)How now "brown" cow!
NIL
```

When using arguments which evaluate to strings, we would normally use ~a to edit out the quotation marks. In other instances we might wish to preserve quotation marks and/or escape characters, in which case we would use ~s.

Any number of format directives may appear in the control string, provided only that there are sufficient arguments to match the directives. If there are fewer arguments than directives an error message will be generated; however if there are surplus arguments the extra ones will be ignored. As **format** proceeds along the control string each subsequent format directive, as encounted, is applied to each subsequent argument:

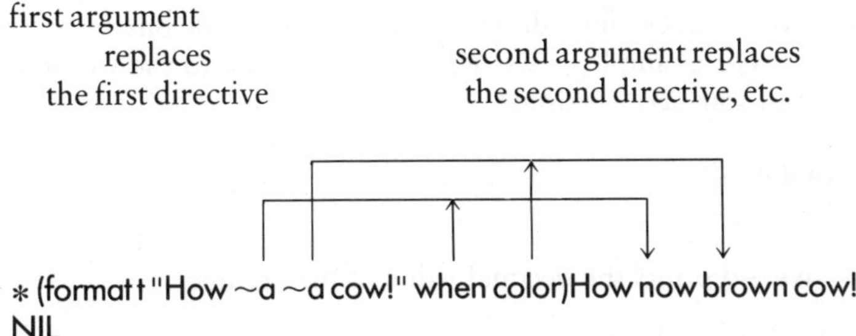


```
* (format t "How ~a ~a cow!" when color)How now brown cow!
NIL
```

12.6 The format directive ~% can be used in place of **terpri**

Rather than having to use **terpri**'s in the program to provide Newlines before and/or after the printout, these can be built directly into a format statement using the *Newline directive* ~%, which generates a carriage return and line feed. GCLISP does not support the Common LISP feature which allows an optional number to be inserted between the ~ and the % to specify how many blank lines are desired. However any number of consecutive ~%s may be incorporated into a format statement to achieve the same effect:

```
* (format t "~%~%~a~%~%" "Skip some lines!")
Skip some lines!
<cursor has now been advanced to here>
```

Note that it is not necessary to leave a space between a format directive and whatever precedes or follows it, except where a space is required to separate a text word from whatever is inserted in place of the directive. Also, as is probably self-evident, directives such as ~% do not consume arguments and hence are excluded from our earlier comment that the number of arguments must at least equal the number of directives.

The alternate *freshline directive* ~& is similar to ~%, with the difference that ~& only generates a Newline if the cursor is not already at the beginning of a line.

If we therefore include a single ~% at the start of the text, the printout will be located on the following line:

```
* (format t "~%How now ~a cow!" color)
How now brown cow!
NIL
```

12.7 Numerical directives provide for radix conversion

format also includes a number of **numerical directives** which provide for conversion of numbers into different radices: decimal, binary, octal, and hexadecimal. For example, if we assign the value **12** to the variable **x** and then carry out some conversions:

```
* (setf x 12)
12
```

The directive ~**d** prints the decimal value of the argument:

```
* (format t "~d" x)12
NIL
```

The directive ~**b** prints the binary value of the argument:

```
* (format t "~b" x)1100
NIL
```

The directive ~**o** prints the octal value of the argument:

```
* (format t "~o" x)14
NIL
```

The directive ~**x** prints the hexadecimal value of the argument:

```
* (format t "~x" x)C
NIL
```

Although lacking the flexibility of ***read-base*** and ***print-base***, these directives can be used in a limited way to convert between radix bases (see Exercise 12.5).

12.8 Other directives extend the scope of format operations

Other format directives supported by GCLISP are as follows.

The directive ~<Newline> permits you to continue typing on the next line in preference to the (somewhat disorderly) alternative of simply letting the text wrap around when you reach the end of the line. The <Newline> and any white space preceding the additional text will be ignored upon subsequent printout. The modifiers @ or : may be inserted between the tilde and the <Newline>, in which case @ will ignore only the additional whitespace (but not the Newline) and : will ignore only the Newline (but not the additional whitespace). If both modifiers are used together only the : will take effect.

The directive ~c prints the character corresponding to its argument, and the directive ~~ permits you to print the tilde itself as a character.

The directive ~? treats the next corresponding argument, which must be a string, as a control string; and the following argument, which must be a list, as the list of arguments to this control string. The net effect is that of another format operation nested within the original format (see pp. 399–400 of the CLRM for more information on this option).

The directive ~[str0~;str1~; ... ~;strn~] provides for the embedding of a number of subordinate control strings within the basic control string. The argth string, ranging from 0 upwards, is chosen depending on the value of the corresponding current argument, that is, if arg evaluates to 1 then str1 would be chosen as the basic control string. If arg evaluates to a higher number than there are strings available, none of them are processed; except that if the last entry is preceded by ~:; it is processed as a default string (see Exercise 12.6).

The directive ~:[false~;true~] is somewhat similar to the foregoing except that it contains only two subordinate control strings, choosing either the first or the second according to whether arg evalutes to NIL or non-NIL (see Exercises 12.7 and 12.10.)

The directive ~@[true~] tests its corresponding argument. If the argument evaluates to NIL it is consumed and the clause is not processed. If the argument evaluates to non-NIL it is not consumed and the clause true is processed.

12.9 error and cerror provide for formatting error messages

When the printed message is specifically related to an error of some sort, the functions error and cerror provide alternative ways to format such messages, while at the time time providing a clear indication of their purposes in the program code. In addition, they provide other features related to *debugging* (see Sections 24.2 and 24.3).

The syntax of error is:

```
(error <format-string>
       &rest <arguments>)
```

This function signals a fatal error, that is, one from which operations cannot be continued.

The syntax of cerror is:

```
(cerror <continue-format-string>
        <error-format-string>
        &rest <arguments>)
```

This function signals a continuable, that is, nonfatal error from which operations may proceed after calling (continue) or pressing Ctrl-P. Note that any arguments which follow &rest are shared by both format statements. This can create a problem in GCLISP, which does not support ~* directives for skipping over arguments. A solution is to replace either string with an embedded format statement containing its own argument(s), for example:

```
(cerror (format nil <continue-format-string> &rest args)
        <error-format-string> &rest <arguments>)
```

Although both error and cerror operate somewhat similarly to format, no destination need be specified since the printout will be sent automatically to the stream currently bound to *error-output*. (In GCLISP the printout is instead sent to *debug-io*, which normally defaults to *standard-output*.)

12.10 flatc and flatsize help to format tables

From time to time you may find it necessary to provide output in tabular form, for example:

Name	Address	Phone
John Doe	12 Whitney Drive	111-1111-1111
George Bush	The White House	222-2222-2222
Alfred E. Neumann	c/o Mad Magazine	333-3333-3333

Since GCLISP does not support the Common LISP format directive ~T for advancing to a given column, it is necessary to resort to more devious means of lining up the data. To assist in this, GCLISP provides two un-Common LISP functions flatc and flatsize, which return the number of characters in the printed representation of an object. flatc returns the number of characters without escape characters, as would be printed by princ, whereas flatsize includes escape characters, as would be printed by prin1.

```
* (flatc '|harry|)
5

* (flatsize '|harry|)
7
```

Tabulations such as the above (in which escape characters are not printed) can be lined up by using **flatc** to measure the length of the printed object, and printing additional blank spaces to bring the cursor up to the next column location (see Exercises 12.8 and 12.9).

length (see Section 5.14) can be used directly in place of **flatc** if the object to be printed is a string. Alternatively, if the object is a symbol, **length** can be applied to the print name of the symbol:

```
* (length "harry")
5

* (length (symbol-name 'harry))
5
```

12.11 User-query predicates are handy for eliciting a yes-or-no response from the user

GCLISP provides the query predicates **y-or-n-p** and **yes-or-no-p** to prompt for yes or no answers from the user. Both predicates return **T** if a 'yes' answer is provided and **NIL** if a 'no' answer is provided.

y-or-n-p is used for simple situations in which no great harm is done if the user types in the wrong letter. The user types in either **y** or a Space to indicate a 'yes' response and either **n** or a Rubout to indicate a 'no' response.

yes-or-no-p is used for more serious decision-making ('Are you *sure* you want to fire the missile???') in which the user is forced specifically to type **yes** or **no**, immediately followed by a Newline.

Both predicates can either be used alone (in which case some sort of question would normally precede them) or can be encapsulated along with a format statement in the following form:

```
(y-or-n-p <format-string> <arguments>)
```

in which case the formatted string will be printed out first, followed by the (Y or N) message generated by the predicate. (No format destination is required in this instance; destination is assigned the value of ***query-io*** which, unless otherwise provided for, is the console.) At this point the cursor will stop and wait for you to type something. We can define a simple function y-or-n for demonstration purposes:

```
* (defun y-or-n ()
    (terpri)
    (y-or-n-p "Please give a response"))
Y-OR-N
* (y-or-n)
Please give a response (Y or N)<cursor is now here>
```

Typing y or n in upper- or lowercase results in a printout of Yes or No, followed by a T or NIL on the next line representing the value returned by the y-or-n-p *predicate*. The whole expression can therefore be incorporated as a conditional test and used to control a branching decision. yes-or-no-p takes a similar format. If an incorrect response is provided, the system will continue to generate (Y or N) messages until the required character or word is input.

SUMMARY

Summarizing the main points of this chapter:

- it is frequently necessary to combine *text* strings and variable *values* in printed output
- princ can be used to concatenate strings and values, or lists can be built up with cons and append
- the backquote mechanism provides a template for formatting printouts
- format provides a flexible means of formatting output through the use of *control strings* and *format directives*
- *numerical directives* can be used to effect radix conversion
- error and cerror provide formatted error messages
- tabular arrangements can be facilitated by using flatc to measure the length of a string
- *user-query predicates* elicit yes-or-no responses from the user which may then be used to condition branching decisions

EXERCISES

12.1 Use appropriate list manipulation functions such as **cons** or **append** to build up the following message:

(TEMPERATURE IS 68 DEGREES AND HUMIDITY IS 80 PERCENT)

where the variables **temp** and **humid** have the values 68 and 80, respectively.

12.2 Use **backquote** to generate the same message as in Exercise 12.1.

12.3 Use a series of **princ** statements to generate the same message as in Exercise 12.1.

12.4 Use a **format** statement to generate the same message as in Exercise 12.1.

12.5 Define **convert-number**, a function which uses format directives to convert any (decimal) integer into its equivalent in binary, octal, or hexadecimal. Using **format** statements, generate a menu, prompt for input of a number, and print out the (converted) number in the following format:

```
Convert number to: (1) Binary
                   (2) Octal
                   (3) Hexidecimal
                   (4) Quit program
Your choice? <enter option number>
Number to be converted: <enter number>
<radix-base> equivalent is: <converted number>
```

Also using **format**, generate error messages if an invalid option is entered or if the number entered is not an integer.

12.6 Define the function **get-digit** which repetitively prompts for and reads a single digit from 0 to 3 from the keyboard. Use **format** to **prompt Please type in a digit from 0 to 3:** and use the ~[str0~; ... ~:;default~] directive to generate statements such as **That's a 0** identifying which digit has been typed in. If any other character is entered, generate a default message **Invalid character!** and exit the function. (NB: ASCII character codes for the digits 0, 1, 2, 3 are 48, 49, 50, 51.)

12.7 Define the function **test-predicate** which uses **format** to prompt for input of a predicate function. Depending on the value returned, use the ~:[false~;true~] directive to print **The predicate is false** (or '**true**'), for example:

```
* (test-predicate)
Please input a predicate function:
(equal 5 6)
The predicate is false!
```

12.8 Create a list which contains three embedded lists each of which contains a name, an address, and a phone number. Define **address-list** which retrieves this data and prints it out in the tabular format shown in Section 12.10. In order to align the printouts, define the auxiliary function **spaces** which takes two arguments: the string just printed and the total number of spaces between columns. **spaces** should print enough blank spaces to advance the cursor to the next column.

12.9 Create the function print-address-list which creates the same tabulation as Exercise 12.8, but directs the output to the printer as well as to the console. Create the necessary auxiliary function print-spaces to align columns as in Exercise 12.8.

12.10 Define the function yes-or-no which prints the question:

Have you stopped beating your dog?

and demands a yes or no answer. If the answer is yes, the function responds About time, you dirty rascal!; if no, the function responds Why not?. Use yes-or-no-p embedded in a format statement to achieve this result.

Chapter 13
Iterative Programming

We are often called upon in programming to carry out repetitive operations of some type. In procedural languages we would most often be dealing with numbers and be required to perform some operation *x* number of times, or until some specified condition has been satisfied. In LISP, which involves symbol manipulation, we might additionally be required to carry out such a repetitive operation on each of the elements of a list or on some other type of sequence. Programmed repetition of this type is referred to as *iteration*.

Such repetitive operations in LISP may be carried out in a so-called *structured* manner, using macros of the do family, or in an *unstructured* manner – much like the goto of BASIC – using a prog construct.

In this chapter we will look at:

- the manner in which *repetitive operations* may be carried out on the elements of a list or on sequences of integers
- the use of the simple loop construct to carry out indefinite iteration
- the use of do as a powerful mechanism for general iteration
- the use of dolist and dotimes for carrying out iteration on lists and number sequences
- the use of prog for carrying out unstructured iteration
- the use of other prog-*type constructs* for effecting the sequential evaluation of two or more forms

13.1 Iteration typically works on elements of a list or on sequences of integers

In general, the term *iteration* refers to any process which is carried out in a repetitive manner. For discussion purposes we can conveniently think of iteration in LISP as being divided into two broad categories: iteration as applied to the *elements of a list*, and iteration as applied to *sequences of integers*.

As regards lists, we will most often be thinking in terms of *lists of data*, that is, quoted lists of symbols which have some associative relationship such as a list of groceries (APPLES CORNFLAKES SOAP PEARS GRAPES RAT-TRAP BEER). We might want to traverse such a list on an item-by-item basis for various reasons: to count the number of items on the list, to reverse the order of the items, to see whether a given item is included in the list, to segregate those items which are fruits, etc.

As regards numbers, various mathematical operations involve the need to carry out some particular operation x number of times. The factorial of integer x involves successive multiplications of x by ever-lower numbers. An exponential calculation such as y to the xth power involves multiplying y by itself x times.

As is intuitively obvious, any iterative operation must have a *terminating condition* which calls a halt to the process. In the case of lists, such a condition is usually based on when the list has been cdr'd down to NIL; alternatively, using functions such as member, the operation may be discontinued when some element of the list passes a particular test. In the case of numbers, iteration is usually carried out on a countdown basis until some variable reaches a designated level.

Let's look now at the various iterative constructs which are provided by Common LISP.

13.2 loop is a simple construct for indefinite iteration

The function loop provides the most simple mechanism for effecting iteration. The basic syntax of loop is:

```
(loop
 form-1
 form-2
 ...
 form-n)
```

in which the various forms which follow loop are evaluated in much the same manner as a progn construct (see Section 13.10). After evaluation of the last form, program control returns to the beginning and a new round of evaluation commences.

In our initial discussions on the GCLISP interpeter, we illustrated (see Section 2.8) an example of a **loop** construct which included no provision for terminating the iteration:

```
* (loop)
```

A never-ending cycle was put into motion and the keyboard hung up. As you will recall, such a cycle can be broken with the keychord Ctrl-Break followed by Ctrl-C to return to the top level. (This reminder is included here in case you run into similar problems in the course of your hands-on experiments in this chapter.)

In order to exit from a **loop** construct we have to include a terminating test followed by a call to **return**. We will review the nature of **return** in more detail under the subject of **blocks** and **exits** (see Section 17.1), but for the moment it may simply be considered as a mechanism for exiting the **loop** function. If an argument is provided to **return** it will be evaluated and returned as the value of the **loop** construct; otherwise **NIL** will be returned.

Let's look at an example of **loop** as it might be used to handle a problem involving iteration over the elements of a list. We will take the grocery list cited earlier and define the function **count-groceries** which uses a **loop** construct to count the number of items on the list:

```
* (setf grocery-list
    '(apples cornflakes soap pears grapes rat-trap beer))
(APPLES CORNFLAKES SOAP PEARS GRAPES RAT-TRAP BEER)

* (defun count-groceries-1 (some-list)
    (let ((count 0))
     (loop
      (cond ((endp some-list)(return count))
            (t  (setf some-list (cdr some-list))
                (setf count (1+ count)))))))
COUNT-GROCERIES-1
```

Trying out our new function:

```
* (count-groceries-1 grocery-list)
7
```

After initializing the value of the temporary variable **count**, a loop is set up to '**cdr** down' the list of groceries. On each iteration the list is reduced by one item and the count of items is incremented by 1. When the list has been reduced to **NIL**, the value of **count** is returned.

Now let's look at an instance of **loop** as used to handle a problem involving iteration over a sequence of integers. We can use such an iteration to derive the **factorial** of a number x, written $x!$, which is equivalent to $x(x-1)(x-2)\ ...\ 1$:

```
* (defun factorial (x)
    (let ((fact 1))
      (loop
        (cond ((zerop x)(return fact))
              (t (setf fact (* fact x))
                 (setf x (1- x)))))))
FACTORIAL
* (factorial 5)
120
```

On the first pass the temporary variable **fact** is set to the value of **x**, and **x** is decremented by 1. On each successive pass **(setf fact (* fact x))** accumulates the growing factorial value until **x** has been decremented to zero at which time the value is returned. (The terminating condition also reflects the convention that the factorial of 0 is 1.)

In the above examples we had to include **let** constructs explicitly to provide for binding of variables used temporarily for programming purposes. In the next section we will look at the more sophisticated iteration function **do**, which automatically incorporates the temporary binding mechanisms of **let** into its syntax.

13.3 do provides a general iteration facility

As compared to **loop**, the function **do** provides a more powerful and general mechanism for iteration. The syntax of **do** is:

```
(do (<list of index-variable specifiers>)
  (<terminating test><value to be returned>)
  <forms to be evaluated>)
```

The first element of **do** is a list of *index-variable specifiers* which takes the general format:

```
((var1 init1 step1)(var2 init2 step2) ... (varn initn stepn))
```

This construct is somewhat analogous to **let** in that it permits a series of temporary variables to be defined and initializes their bindings. However it has an important added feature in that, on each successive iteration, the binding of the variable is modified in accordance with the *stepping-form* provision.

The stepping-form may be left out, in which case the variable is not automatically changed on each successive iteration. (However it could be changed by a **setf** assignment embedded in the third element: see the **count-groceries-3** example below.) Finally, the *initial value* may be left out as well, in which case the variable – as in a let construct – may be represented as a symbol and will be initialized to NIL.

The second element provides for a terminating test to be carried out. If the test passes, the form which follows is evaluated and this value is returned as the do macro is exited.

If the test does not pass, control continues to the third element which includes various forms to be evaluated. After completion of evaluation of these forms, control returns to the list of index-variable specifiers; the variables are modified in accordance with their respective step provisions; and the whole process is repeated.

Using do instead of loop we can repeat the exercise illustrated earlier:

```
* (defun count-groceries-2 (some-list)
    (do ((rest-list some-list (cdr rest-list))
         (count 0 (1+ count)))
        ((endp rest-list) count)))
COUNT-GROCERIES-2
```

In this instance – and as will frequently be the case with simple iterations using do – there is no need to incorporate the third element of additional forms to be evaluated since all the work is done within the index-specifier construct. However, to illustrate the process we could leave out the step provision and carry out the modification of the index variables explicitly:

```
* (defun count-groceries-3 (some-list)
    (do ((rest-list some-list)
         (count 0))
        ((endp rest-list) count)
        (setf rest-list (cdr rest-list))
        (setf count (1+ count))))
COUNT-GROCERIES-3
```

Normally of course we would want to take advantage of the automatic stepping provisions as in our earlier example.

To illustrate the use of do with sequences of integers we can modify our earlier example of factorial (see Section 13.2).

```
* (defun factorial-1 (x)
    (do ((fact 1 (* fact element))
         (element x (1- element)))
        ((zerop element) fact)))
FACTORIAL-1
* (factorial-1 5)
120
```

The associated macro do* is exactly the same as do except with regard to the sequence of evaluations and bindings to the index variables. In do these activities are carried out in much the same manner as psetq assignments, for example, all inits and/or stepping forms are evaluated in parallel, followed by bindings to their respective variables on a left-to-right basis. The evaluations and bindings carried out with **do***, on the other hand, are analagous to **setq** in which evaluations and bindings are carried out sequentially, such that a subsequent form can refer to the new bindings of the forms which precede it. In this sense, **do/do*** constructs behave similarly to the analogous **let/let*** constructs.

Note also that the body of every **do**-type macro is structured as an implicit **tagbody** (see Section 13.7) within which tags and **go** statements may be used to transfer program control in an unstructured manner.

13.4 dolist iterates over the elements of a list

As mentioned earlier, one of the common patterns of iteration involves stepping through some or all of the elements of a list. This operation can of course be accomplished with a **do** macro; and if the situation requires the use of temporary index variables **do** should preferentially be used, since it provides for automatic stepping of such variables and also avoids the need for a **let** construct. However where the operation involves only a straightforward iteration over the elements of a list, without the need for auxiliary index variables, **dolist** provides a somewhat simpler syntax:

```
(dolist (<variable> <list-form> <result-form>)
   <forms to be evaluated>)
```

dolist successively binds **<variable>** to each element of the list returned by evaluation of **<list-form>** and evaluates the forms which comprise the body of this macro. After the final element of the list has been processed **<variable>** is bound to **NIL**, and **<result-form>** is evaluated and its value returned. Since **dolist** is implicitly wrapped in a block named **NIL**, an explicit **return** statement may be used to terminate the iteration at any time and return a specified value. Note that **<result-form>** is optional; if omitted, **dolist** will return **NIL**. Also, if **return** is used to explicitly exit the construct, the value specified in the **return** statement will override any **<result-form>** which may be specified.

We see some of the shortcomings of **dolist** if we try to repeat our grocery list example using this macro:

```
* (defun count-groceries-4 (some-list)
    (let ((count 0))
      (dolist (element some-list count)
        (setf count (1+ count)))))
COUNT-GROCERIES-4
* (count-groceries-4 grocery-list)
7
```

We see that it is necessary to incorporate a **let** construct to provide for the auxiliary index variable **count**; furthermore we get no particular use out of the index variable **element**. Hence this macro is principally useful only when it is desired to do something specific with (other than merely counting) each individual element of a list and when additional index variables are not required. For example, **dolist** would be handy if we merely wanted to print out the items from the list:

```
* (defun print-groceries (some-list)
    (terpri)
    (dolist (element some-list)
      (princ element)
      (princ " ")))
PRINT-GROCERIES
* (print-groceries grocery-list)
APPLES CORNFLAKES SOAP PEARS GRAPES RAT-TRAP BEER
NIL
```

As an alternative, where it is desired to carry out some operation on each element of a list, a *mapping operation* may be more suitable (see Chapter 15).

13.5 **dotimes** iterates over a sequence of integers

As opposed to **dolist**, which provides for iteration over the elements of a list, **dotimes** provides for iteration over a sequence of integers. The syntax of **dotimes** is:

```
(dotimes (<variable> <count-form> <result-form>)
  <forms to be evaluated>)
```

where **<count-form>** must evaluate to an integer. **dotimes** successively binds **<variable>** to integers ranging from 0 to **<count-form>** − 1 and evaluates the forms which comprise the body of the function. After the last iteration **<variable>** is bound to the integer **<count-form>**, and **<result-form>** is evaluated and its value returned. As noted previously in connection with **dolist**, an explicit **return** statement may be used to exit the construct, in which case the value returned overrides that of the (optional) **<result-form>**.

dotimes has similar shortcomings to **dolist**, as we can see if we try to repeat our earlier example with **factorial**:

```
* (defun factorial-2 (x)
    (let ((fact 1))
      (dotimes (element x fact)
        (setf fact (* fact x))
        (setf x (1-x)))))
FACTORIAL-2
```

```
* (factorial-2 5)
120
```

Again we get no particular use out of the index variable <element> and it is still necessary to incorporate an explicit **let** construct to handle the scratch-pad variable **fact**.

In its simplest form, with neither <result-form> used to return a value nor a body of forms to evaluate, **dotimes** is useful for establishing timing delays in applications programs. For example,

```
* (dotimes (n 300))
NIL
```

runs through 300 iterations for a time delay of about 1 second on a PC operating at a clock rate of 4.77 MHz. (Earlier dynamically scoped versions of GCLISP would require a much larger number.) Other times can easily be set by experimenting with the value used for <count-form>. In earlier versions of GCLISP which limit maximum integer size to 32767, longer times can of course be arranged by nesting additional **dotimes** forms within the body of the construct, for example, for 1000000 iterations:

```
(dotimes (n 10000)
  (dotimes (n 100)))
```

As one application we can use **dotimes** to cause text to be scrolled onto the screen at varying rates, for example, to create robot responses which simulate normal speech generation. For example:

```
(defun speech-rate (count)
  (let ((sentence nil)
        (char nil))
   (format t "~%~%Please input a sentence:~%")
   (setf sentence
         (make-string-input-stream (read-line)))
   (terpri)
   (loop
    (setf char (read-char sentence nil 'eof))
    (if (equal char 'eof)
        (return nil))
    (write-char char)
    (dotimes (var count)))))
```

The above function uses **read-line** (see Section 10.7) to convert input into a string and **make-string-input-stream** (see Section 19.9) to convert the string to an input stream. Thereafter a loop is set up and **read-char** (see Section 10.6) is used to read a character at a time until the end of the string is reached. As each character is read it is printed onto the console, followed by a time delay. Experiments with different values of **count** provide varying rates of printout. On a PC operating at the above-mentioned clock rate, a value of 10 approximates the rate of normal human speech.

13.6 Other do constructs iterate over symbols in packages

Various other **do**-type constructs are available to iterate over the symbols contained in packages. These include the macros **do-symbols**, **do-all-symbols**, and **do-external-symbols**. These are covered in more detail in Section 25.9.

13.7 tagbody and go provide for unstructured iteration

Common LISP provides a facility similar to the **goto** mechanism of BASIC, whereby unstructured jumps can be made from one part of a program to another. This facility, which is built into macros such as **prog** and **prog*** (see below), as well as the **do** macros previously discussed, can be provided explicitly through the use of **tagbody** which takes the general syntax:

```
(tagbody
    <expressions to be evaluated>
  tag1
    <more expressions to be evaluated>
  tag2
    <more expressions to be evaluated>
  tag3
    etc.)
```

Any number of **tags**, which may be either symbols or integers, may be scattered throughout the body of the **tagbody** special form. Program flow is controlled by one or more **go** statements which take the syntax:

```
(go <tag-name>)
```

and which cause control to be transferred to the point immediately following the tag in question.

We can restructure our **count-groceries** example to illustrate the use of the **tagbody** construct:

```
(defun count-groceries-5 (some-list)
  (let ((rest-list some-list)(count 0))
    (tagbody
     again
       (cond ((endp rest-list)
              (go end))
             (t  (setf rest-list (cdr rest-list))
                 (setf count (1+ count))
                 (go again)))
```

```
        end
             (format t "~%~a~" count))))

* (count-groceries-5 grocery-list)
7
NIL
```

As long as any elements remain to be counted in **rest-list**, the default clause of the cond expression carries out the necessary updating of **rest-list** and **count**, and the second **go** statement causes control to jump back to the point following the tag **again**. Otherwise, when the terminating condition is reached the first **go** statement transfers control to the tag **end** and the value of **count** is printed to the console.

It should be noted that the **(go <tag>)** construct, together with the associated tags, may also be used within the various **do** macros, all of which incorporate an implicit **tagbody**.

Although **tagbody** and **go** may be useful in occasional special situations, their use results in an unstructured flow of control which should generally be avoided if possible.

In the above example we had to include an explicit **let** construct to provide for local binding of the scratch-pad variables **rest-list** and **count**. Now let's look at another macro which provides a built-in feature which precludes the need for a **let** statement.

13.8 LISP includes provision for a 'program' feature

The historic origins of **prog** are related to the fact that early versions of LISP did not permit multiple expressions to be evaluated within a single function body, nor were constructs such as **do** available to provide for structured iteration. Although still a valid Common LISP special form, **prog** is not used so frequently in modern LISP programming.

The syntax of **prog** is:

```
(prog ((var1 init1)(var2 init2) ... (varn initn))
      <implicit tagbody form>)
```

The macro name is followed by a list of so-called *program variables* together with their initial values, which are bound in the same manner as for a **let** construct. A simple **var** may be included in lieu of a **(var init)** pair, in which case the variable in question will be initialized to **NIL**.

Thereafter may follow a mixture of tags and statements, which are evaluated as described previously for tagbodies. Since the **prog** construct is implicitly wrapped in a block named **NIL** (see Section 17.1), a **return** statement may be used to terminate the evaluation process and return a specified value, similarly as in the **loop** construct. (This would be the usual way to exit a **prog** being used for iterative purposes.) Alternatively a **prog** macro may simply be permitted to 'run off the end,' in which case it returns the value of the last form evaluated.

Restructuring our grocery list example in **prog** form:

```
* (defun count-groceries-6 (some-list)
    (prog ((rest-list some-list)(count 0))
      again
        (cond ((endp rest-list)
                  (return count))
              (t  (setf rest-list (cdr rest-list))
                  (setf count (1+ count))
                  (go again)))))
COUNT-GROCERIES-6
* (count-groceries-6 grocery-list)
7
```

Flow of control is generally similar to that of **count-groceries-5** described previously, the only difference being that the need for an explicit **let** construct has been obviated by the fact that **prog** provides its own binding environment. Also, the use of **return** permits the final value of **count** to be returned directly as the value of the **prog** construct.

The associated function **prog*** differs from **prog** only in the manner in which program variables are initialized. As with **do** and **do***, the **(var init)** pairs of **prog** are evaluated in parallel whereas the **(var init)** pairs of **prog*** are evaluated sequentially.

13.9 progv binds variables to a list of values

The special form **progv** is somewhat similar to **prog** except for the manner in which its program variables are established and initialized. The syntax of **progv** is as follows:

(progv <**symbol-list**><**value-list**><forms to be evaluated>**)**

The program variables are named by symbols which are elements of the list which results from evaluation of <**symbol-list**>; and their respective values are elements of the list which results from evaluation of <**value-list**>. During the initial binding process, the *n*th symbol of <**symbol-list**> is bound to the *n*th value of <**value-list**>. Note that the lists of symbols and values are *computed* quantities rather than the explicit listings as used in **prog** and **let** constructs.

After the establishment of variable bindings, the forms which follow are evaluated in the usual manner and **progv** is exited, returning the value(s) of the last form.

13.10 Other prog-type special forms are used for sequencing

The special forms progn, prog1, and prog2 are used for sequencing the evaluation of two or more forms. They all take the general syntax:

```
(progn
  <first form to be evaluated>
  <second form to be evaluated>
  ....
  <nth form to be evaluated>)
```

and differ only in the value which is returned: prog1 returns the value of the first form, prog2 of the second form, and progn of the last form. In the event that evaluation of the form in question returns multiple values, it should be noted that prog1 and prog2 only return one of these values; and none of these simple constructs include provision for go, tags, or return.

In general, prog constructs are a carry-over from earlier days when LISP did not provide for evaluation of multiple forms within a single function call. However aside from their historical value they still come in handy for special purposes. For example, progn is useful when you have a binary choice, such as in an if construct, but want to incorporate multiple consequents in the event of a successful test, for example:

```
(if <some-test>
  (progn
    <various forms to evaluate IF <some-test> succeeds>)
  (progn
    <alternative forms to evaluate ELSE>))
```

For pedagogical purposes, progn also comes in handy when you want to demonstrate the effect of a sequence of function calls without the bother of illustrating intervening prompt symbols or values returned:

```
* (progn
    <first function call>
    ...
    <nth function call>)
  <visible effects of intermediate function calls>
  <LAST-VALUE-RETURNED>
```

Finally, it may be noted that the body of a defun statement is an implicit progn, in that all of its forms are evaluated in turn and the value of the last form is returned. Other LISP functions such as let, cond, when, unless, and the consequents of a do terminating test also contain implicit progn constructs.

prog1 and prog2 retain the values returned by their first and second forms, respectively, and hence can be used to preserve this information even if subsequent forms modify these values in some way. For example, assuming that we have created a global variable ***stack*** to represent a stack, **prog1** can be used to simulate a popping of the stack:

```
* (defun our-pop (stack)
    (prog1
      (car stack)
      (setq *stack* (cdr stack))))
OUR-POP
```

in which the value popped <**car stack**> is preserved and later returned without the need to save this element temporarily as the value of some variable.

SUMMARY

Summarizing the key points of this chapter:

- a process which is carried out in a repetitive manner is referred to as *iteration*
- the various constructs available in LISP to carry out iteration are principally applied either to the *elements of a list* or to *sequences of integers*
- the most simple construct for iteration is the special form **loop**, which recycles indefinitely until exited with a **return** statement
- the **do** macro is a powerful general mechanism for carrying out iteration, and includes three elements: a list of *index-variables*, with provision for initializing the variables and for updating them with stepping forms; a *terminating test* which triggers the return of a value; and a body of *forms* which are re-evaluated on each iteration
- the associated macros **dolist** and **dotimes** are specialized macros designed to perform iteration on the *elements of a list* and on *sequences of integers*, respectively
- the special form **prog** can be used to carry out iteration in an unstructured manner, using **go** and tags to transfer flow of control
- other **prog**-type constructs such as **progn**, **prog1**, and **prog2** are useful for effecting sequential evaluation of two or more forms and returning the value of a selected form

EXERCISES

13.1 Define **mini-eliza**, a program which simulates a Rogerian therapist dealing with a troubled patient. After inviting input with the opening **HOW CAN I BE OF ASSISTANCE?**, use **loop** to create a system in which, after each typed input from the 'patient,' the 'doctor' comes back in round-robin fashion with one of the three responses **HOW INTERESTING!**, **PLEASE GO ON.**, and **TELL ME MORE.** When the patient types in **bye**, the doctor says **THANK YOU, GOODBYE!** and the program terminates. Leave a space between input/response pairs and generate the doctor's replies in uppercase for contrast. For example:

```
* (mini-eliza)
HOW CAN I BE OF ASSISTANCE?

I think my mother is becoming an alcoholic.
HOW INTERESTING!

She goes through a whole bottle of gin every night!
PLEASE GO ON.

<etc., etc.>

Bye
THANK YOU, GOODBYE!
```

13.2 Define the function **our-reverse-1**, which takes a single argument which must evaluate to a list and returns a list in which the order of elements is reversed. Use a **loop** construct.

13.3 Define **our-exponent**, which takes an integer and an exponent as its two arguments and uses a **do** construct to calculate and return the integer raised to the power of the exponent.

13.4 Use a **do** construct to define the predicate **our-member**, which tests to see if its first argument, which may be an atom or a list, is a member of the list which constitutes its second argument. If the test succeeds, return the tail of the list, similarly to Common LISP's **member**.

13.5 Using a **do** construct, define **pattern-match**, a function which takes two arguments each of which must evaluate to a list, uses **equal** to check that each element of the first list is the same as the corresponding element of the second list, and returns **T** or **NIL** as appropriate.

13.6 Using the grocery list as defined in Section 13.2, define the function **print-fruits** which uses **dolist** to print out those items on the list which are fruits, for example:

```
* (print-fruits grocery-list)
APPLES PEARS GRAPES
```

Develop an auxiliary predicate **fruitp** to assist in identifying which items are fruits. **fruitp** may obtain this information from property lists associated with fruit symbols or may simply refer to a global checklist of fruits.

13.7 Joe Milquetoast has a teacher who always repeats instructions several times. Using **dotimes**, define **tell-them-again** which takes two arguments, the first of which must evaluate to a string and the second to an integer. When called,

tell-them-again repeats the (string) instruction the specified number of times, for example:

```
* (setf command "Get your books out!"
"Get your books out!"
* (tell-them-again command 3)
Get your books out!
Get your books out!
Get your books out!
```

13.8 Using a **prog** construct, define **our-intersection**, a function which takes two lists as its arguments and returns a list of elements common to both lists.

13.9 Using a **prog** construct, define **our-nth-element**, of which the first argument must evaluate to a list and the second element to an integer. **our-nth-element** returns the **nth** element of the list. Maintain consistency with the Common LISP convention that the first element of a list is the 0'th element.

13.10 Use a **prog** construct to create **our-reverse-2**, which does the same thing as **our-reverse-1** in Exercise 13.2.

Chapter 14
Writing Recursive Functions

In the previous chapter we looked at ways in which repetitive operations might be carried out by various kinds of iterative constructs. In this chapter we will look at another way to carry out equivalent operations using recursive techniques. *Recursion*, which is a way of breaking down a problem into smaller versions of itself, does not involve specific constructs such as **dotimes** or **dolist**; rather, it is a *style* of programming in which functions incorporate a nested call to themselves in their own function definitions.

In this chapter we will look at:

- various ways in which the term '*recursion*' may be used in LISP
- how recursion solves a problem by breaking it down into smaller versions of itself
- the essential elements of a *recursive function definition*
- how recursion, like iteration, may be applied to lists or to sequences of numbers
- the manner in which recursive definitions may have multiple terminating cases and/or recursive cases
- tail-recursive operations which simply return T or NIL

14.1 The definition of 'recursion' can be elusive

To the beginner to LISP, the concept of *recursion* is difficult to grasp perhaps because, even within the narrow domain of LISP, the word may be used in three subtly different ways.

In its most general sense recursion refers to the manner in which LISP functions call upon ever more deeply nested functions to get the work done. The term is being used in this broad sense when we are told that 'LISP has a *recursive* control structure.'

However the term is more often used in a more specific sense, that is, to describe a situation in which a LISP function *calls itself*. Looking at two simple examples of recursion:

```
* (+ 4 (+ 2 6))
12

* (+ 4 (* 2 (+ 3 1)))
12
```

In the first instance a + function calls directly upon another + function. In the second instance a + function calls upon a * function which in turn calls upon another + function. These two cases are equally recursive in the second sense that we use the word; the fact that an intervening function call is involved is irrelevant to the definition.

The third and most specific use of the word recursion, and the one which most interests us here, is the situation in which a function *calls itself within its own function definition*. This is a somewhat startling concept, but it provides a powerful and elegant mechanism for carrying out operations which would otherwise have to be done by iterative procedures. As we will see in the examples which follow, the nature of recursion as used in this sense involves breaking a problem down into ever smaller versions of itself.

14.2 Recursion breaks a problem into smaller versions of itself

In the previous chapter we developed various iterative techniques for counting the elements of a list. This involved cdr'ing down the list, counting as we went, until a *terminating condition* (the end of the list) was reached, at which point we discontinued the process and returned the accumulated value. Let's now explore a *recursive* way of achieving the same thing.

The essence of recursion is to break a problem down into smaller versions of itself, and to use the values returned by the smaller versions to contribute to the overall solution at higher levels. To illustrate, let's create a small list of symbols and use a recursive technique to count the elements in that list:

```
* (setf symbol-list '(A B C))
A B C

* (defun count-elements (some-list)
    (if (endp some-list)
        0
        (1+ (count-elements (cdr some-list)))))
COUNT-ELEMENTS

* (count-elements symbol-list)
3
```

The body of the function is a simple **if** construct which tests to see if the argument passed to the function is the empty list. If it is of course there are no elements; the **if** part of the test is satisfied and **0** is returned. In recursive definitions such as this, the test **(endp some-list)** is used as a terminating condition in much the same way as in iterative constructs, that is, to stop the procedure at some point.

However suppose the list is *not* empty. The **else** part of the **if** construct then executes the form **(1+ (count-elements (cdr some-list)))**, which in effect adds 1 to whatever value is returned by the recursive call to **count-elements**. At this point evaluation of the top-level function is put on hold and the system drops down one level to evaluate the nested call to **count-elements**.

This process continues until the terminating condition is satisfied at which time, rather than invoking another recursive call, the currently active version of **count-elements** simply returns 0. This value is passed upwards to the next higher level function in the normal manner, which adds 1 to it and passes the resulting value upwards to the next higher level function, and so on until the top level is reached and a final value is returned. We can illustrate the process diagrammatically, as shown in Fig. 14.1.

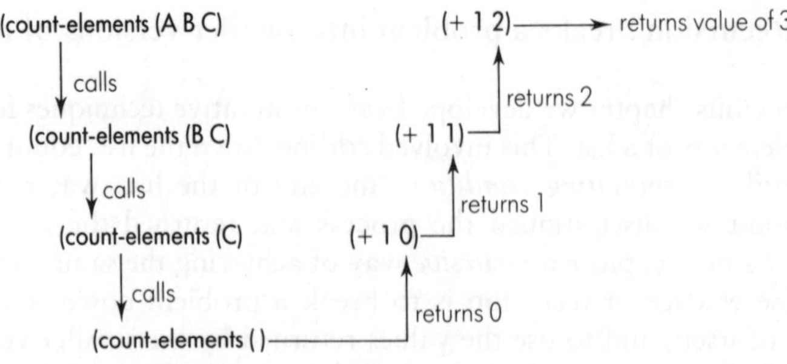

Fig. 14.1 **count-elements** calls itself recursively.

The **trace** facility (see Section 24.7), which is autoloaded from the utility diskette the first time it is called, provides a convenient way of following what is going on in a recursive operation such as the above. When given one or more symbol names as arguments, **trace** provides a printout of the arguments and values returned each time the function named by the symbol is called and exited:

```
* (trace count-elements)
; Autoload: TRACE from "TRACE" in "C:\\GCLISP\\LISPLIB\\".
T

* (count-elements symbol-list)

Entering: COUNT-ELEMENTS, Argument list: ((A B C))
  Entering: COUNT-ELEMENTS, Argument list: ((B C))
    Entering: COUNT-ELEMENTS, Argument list: ((C))
      Entering: COUNT-ELEMENTS, Argument list: (NIL)
      Exiting: COUNT-ELEMENTS, Value: 0
    Exiting: COUNT-ELEMENTS, Value: 1
  Exiting: COUNT-ELEMENTS, Value: 2
Exiting: COUNT-ELEMENTS, Value: 3
3
```

with the final value returned printed after the **trace** printout.

A function which contains a single call to itself is referred to as being *singly recursive*.

14.3 Definition of a recursive function involves identification of a terminating condition and a recursive relation

As may be intuitively apparent from the above example, there are two principal elements involved in the design of a recursive function: the presence of a so-called *recursive relation* and a potential *terminating condition*.

Taking the second element first, it is evident that a *terminating condition* must eventually be reached if the function is not to call itself indefinitely. The terminating condition in a recursive operation has a parallel in iterative constructs, in which iteration also continues until some terminating condition has been reached. Where *list recursion* is being used to operate on the elements of a list, the terminating condition typically occurs (as in iteration) when the list has been **cdr**'d down to **NIL**. Where *numeric recursion* is used to operate on a sequence of integers, the terminating condition typically occurs when some number has been decremented to zero or incremented to some predetermined quantity. As we will see subsequently, in some cases more than one terminating condition may be required.

The *recursive relation* refers to the manner in which a nested function call effectively breaks the problem down into a smaller version of itself. For example, (count-elements (cdr some-list)) is a simpler problem than (count-elements some-list) since the former has one less element to worry about. Aside from simplifying the problem, another key feature of the recursive relation is that the nested function call must represent a step nearer to the terminating condition which has been defined.

14.4 Recursive techniques may be applied to lists or to sequences of integers

In Chapter 13, we saw that iteration might be applied to lists or to sequences of integers. Recursion can be applied with a similar degree of flexibility. In the above example we saw an instance of recursion being applied to count the elements of a list. Now let's review a classic numerical example: the use of recursion to calculate the factorial of a number.

As we mentioned earlier, the factorial of a number n is $n \times (n - 1) \times (n - 2) \times ... \times 1$. For example, the factorial of 4, written 4!, has a value of $4 \times 3 \times 2 \times 1 = 24$. The key point to note about the above operation is that at each stage of the series a number is being multiplied by the factorial of the next lower number, for example, 4! is equivalent to 4 x 3!, 3! in turn is equivalent to 3 x 2!, etc. Based on this we can develop a recursive definition of factorial:

```
* (defun factorial (n)
    (if (zerop n)
        1
        (* n (factorial (1- n)))))
FACTORIAL
* (factorial 4)
24
```

Each call to factorial multiplies its current argument by the factorial of the next lower number until the terminating condition is reached. In the case of factorial, this takes place when the argument has been decremented to zero; rather than making another recursive call on factorial, the function simply returns 1. Thereafter each higher level function multiplies its value of n by the value received back from the lower level until the ultimate value of n! has been generated. As before, we can use trace to follow the course of the above call to factorial.

The above definition of factorial assumes that a positive integer will be entered as an argument. If we enter a negative integer we will wind up with a stack overflow, since ever-more-negative numbers will be passed as arguments to factorial and the terminating case will never be reached!

14.5 The Towers of Hanoi problem may be solved recursively

The Towers of Hanoi is a well-known AI problem which lends itself nicely to a recursive solution. A classical myth has it that somewhere in Vietnam, time is being marked off by a group of monks who are busy transferring 64 disks from one peg to another. The universe as we know it will end when they are done. Fortunately, their task will take considerable time, since they are constrained by the following rules:

- only one disk at a time may be moved
- no disk can ever be placed on top of a smaller disk

Initially the disks, all of which are of different diameters, are located on a single peg, with the smallest disk at the top and disks becoming ever larger towards the bottom of the stack, that is, each disk rests on the next larger disk.

Review of the disk logistics reveals that this problem has recursive potentials. Let us assume that we have three pegs to work with: A, B, and C; that all of the disks are initially located on peg A; and that we are required to transfer the disks to peg C, using peg B as a spare. Assuming that we have n disks to start with we see that in order to transfer the lowest, or largest, disk from peg A to peg C we have first to transfer all of the rest, that is $(n - 1)$ disks to the spare peg. For example, with 4 disks, we must first transfer the top 3 disks from peg A to peg B, before moving the bottom disk to peg C (see Fig. 14.2).

After this has been accomplished, the remaining $(n - 1)$ disks can be transferred from peg B to peg C. Of course this implies that a similar strategy be carried out, that is, that $(n - 2)$ disks be transferred back to peg A (now using this as a spare peg), so that the bottom disk on peg B can be transferred over to peg C.

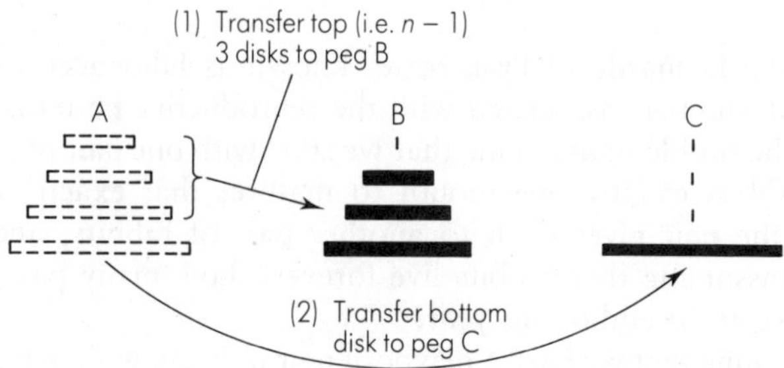

Fig. 14.2 The Towers of Hanoi problem may be solved recursively.

Using similar recursive techniques as discussed earlier, we can define an algorithm to make the required transfers:

```
(defun hanoi (n from spare to)
   (cond ((= n 1)(move-disk from to))
          (t  (hanoi (1- n) from to spare)
              (move-disk from to)
              (hanoi (1- n) spare from to))))
```

The above algorithm reflects the fact that as the lowest disks are progressively transferred to peg C, the stack of remaining disks is shifted back and forth between peg B and peg A. (Note that the order of arguments **from spare to** changes between function calls to **hanoi** to reflect the direction in which disks are being transferred at any given moment.)

Each time we have transferred all of the disks except for the largest one at the bottom we stop, transfer that bottom disk over to peg C, and repeat the process. The terminating condition is therefore the point at which only one disk is left on the peg from which disks are currently being transferred, that is, (= n 1). At this point we call on **move-disk** to print out a message to the effect that the disk is being transferred over to peg C:

```
(defun move-disk (from to)
   (format t "~%Move a disk from ~a to ~a" from to))
```

The **trace** facility comes in handy for seeing what is going on during the course of a call to **hanoi**. Exercise 14.10 may be worked out to provide a printout of all of the moves, including the status of the stack of disks on each peg after each move.

As in the case of **count-elements** and **factorial**, **hanoi** is a *singly recursive* function in that it requires only a single terminating condition and only makes a single call upon itself at any given stage of the problem. In more complex situations we may find that two or more terminating conditions are required and/or the function may call upon itself more than once.

14.6 Multiple terminating and/or recursive cases may be involved

In 1202, one Leonardo of Pisa, better known as Fibonacci, explored the sequence of numbers associated with the reproductive patterns of rabbits. He posed the problem: assuming that we start with one pair of rabbits; that it takes rabbits exactly one month to mature; that exactly one month thereafter the pair gives birth to another pair of rabbits; and so on *ad infinitum* (assuming that rabbits live forever), how many pairs of rabbits will we have at the end of one year?

Assuming that we have a newborn pair to begin with, we find that we wind up with a sequence like 1, 1, 2, 3, 5, 8, ..., in which each new number, representing the number of rabbits we have at the end of any month *n*, is equal to the sum of the two previous numbers. Recognizing that the first two numbers in the series are special cases, we can develop the following rules.

Value of n	*Rabbits at end of month n*
1	1
2	1
>2	$f(n-1) + f(n-2)$

(The alert reader will note a mild anomaly which can be resolved by assuming that new rabbits are born one minute after midnight on the first day of the month!)

Based on the recursive relation intrinsic in the above rules, we can define the function **fibonacci** to generate the *n*th number in the series:

```
* (defun fibonacci (n)
    (if (or (= n 1)(= n 2))
        1
        (+ (fibonacci (- n 1))
           (finonacci (- n 2)))))
FIBONACCI
```

and use it to calculate the rabbit population at the end of one year:

```
* (fibonacci 12)
377
```

Comparing the above function to the previous example we note several points of interest. Firstly, since the first two numbers in the Fibonacci series represent special cases, two possible terminating conditions must be defined. (For efficiency these have been combined into a single **or** statement.) Secondly, two recursive function calls have been incorporated to calculate the preceding Fibonacci numbers. The **fibonacci** function is therefore said to be *doubly recursive.*

If we trace the details of a function call to **fibonacci** we note an intrinsic inefficiency. For the calculation of $f(n)$, we have to calculate $f(n-1)$ and $f(n-2)$. But $f(n-2)$ corresponds to the $f(n-1)$ as calculated for the previous Fibonacci number; that is, we wind up calculating $f(n-2)$ twice! The moral of this is that recursive solutions, although elegant, may not not always be the best way to do things. (In the case of Fibonacci, a mathematical solution may be preferable: see Knuth, 1973, pp. 78–83 for all you ever wanted to know about Fibonacci numbers.)

14.7 Some recursive operations merely return T or NIL

Our previous examples of list and numeric recursion have been designed to return some specific value which has been accumulated either by **cdr**'ing down a list or by manipulating a number until some terminating condition is reached. However a recursive operation may simply return T or NIL, depending on whether it manages to get as far as the terminating case without running into some hazard along the way.

One of the more useful applications of LISP is in *pattern matching* wherein an argument, the *datum*, is compared in some way against a template, the *pattern*. In pattern matching we are generally looking to see whether the datum is like the pattern in some way, rather than exactly the same. (If we were looking for the latter we could simply use a predicate of the equal family.)

However for purposes of this recursive example we will assume that we are looking for an exact match:

```
(defun match (pat dat)
   (cond ((and (null pat)(null dat))
            t)
         ((equal (car pat)(car dat))
            (match (cdr pat)(cdr dat)))))
```

If we now establish a pattern, say, '(A B (C D) E F), and attempt to match this pattern against some datum, we will get back T or NIL depending on whether an exact match has been found for each and every element of both lists.

The terminating case occurs when both lists have been cdr'd down to NIL. Assuming that the operation reaches this point without mishap, an exact match has been demonstrated and the lowest function call of match returns T, which value is passed up the line to the top level. If on the other hand (car pat) is not equal to (car dat) at any point along the comparison, NIL is immediately returned, the recursive operation comes to a halt, and NIL is passed back up the line.

14.8 Tail recursion can result in more efficient calculations

In the above pattern-matching example it will be noted that the final value returned by the lowest level of recursion – T or NIL – was passed back up the line to the top level without change. This is in contrast with earlier examples such as count-elements which, at each level, had to 'remember' some value which would later be added to the value returned by the nested function call. In deeply nested recursive expressions, considerable stack space must be taken up in storing all of these intermediate values, and there is an associated overhead in returning to and exiting all of the intermediate function calls.

A procedure such as match is said to be *tail recursive* if the value returned by a lower level recursive call is simply passed back up the line without change, such that the function does not have to remember anything.

A tail-recursive procedure can be converted into an equivalent procedure which carries out the same calculation without using recursion. Some LISP systems take advantage of this and carry out such a conversion internally, resulting in a faster execution of tail-recursive functions.

SUMMARY

Summarizing the key points of this chapter:

- *recursion* is a programming technique in which functions include a call to themselves in their own definition
- recursion involves breaking a problem down into smaller versions of itself
- a recursive function definition must include a *terminating case*; and each successive nested function call must come closer to that terminating case
- *list recursion* may be applied to the elements of a list or *numeric recursion* to sequences of numbers
- recursive function definitions may involve multiple *terminating* and/or *recursive cases*
- a *tail-recursive* procedure may be converted into a more efficient procedure which provides the same result without using recursion

EXERCISES

14.1 Define our-reverse, which takes a list as its single argument and operates recursively to return a list in which all of the elements have been listed in reverse order.

14.2 Define our-filter, which, given two arguments of which the second must be a list, operates recursively to return a list from which all instances of the first argument have been removed.

14.3 Define our-intersection, which takes two arguments both of which must be lists and operates recursively to return a list containing those elements common to both lists. (Do not list elements more than once.)

14.4 Define our-union, which takes two arguments both of which must be lists and operates recursively to return a list containing all elements of both sets.

14.5 Define **our-member**, which given two arguments of which the second must be a list, operates recursively to test whether the first argument is an element of the second argument. If it is, **our-member** returns the tail of the list, as does Common LISP's **member**; otherwise it returns **NIL**.

14.6 In the Towers of Hanoi, a tower is comprised of *n* disks which must be transferred to another tower. Write a recursive function **tower-stack** which takes as a single argument the number of disks on the tower and returns a list of the disk numbers counting from top to bottom, for example:

```
* (tower-stack 5)
(1 2 3 4 5)
```

(NB: The solution to this exercise will be used in Exercise 14.10.)

14.7 Define **our-exponent**, which, given two arguments *m* and *n*, operates recursively to calculate *m* to the *n*th power.

14.8 Define **count-atoms**, which takes a single list argument and operates recursively to return a list of all of the atoms contained in the list, including those contained in nested list elements.

14.9 Define **our-substitute**, which takes three arguments of which the third is a list and replaces each occurrence of the second argument in the list with the first argument.

14.10 Referring to the Towers of Hanoi example in Exercise 14.6, augment the algorithms to provide a printout indicating the number of the disk being moved at each stage and the status of the towers after each move. For instance, the function call **(towers-of-hanoi 3 'a 'b 'c)**, where tower arguments are entered in the order **from-spare-to**, would generate a printout as follows:

```
Move disk 1 from A to C
Tower A = (2 3)
Tower B = NIL
Tower C = (1)
Move disk 2 from A to B
Tower A = (3)
Tower B = (2)
Tower C = (1)
```

and so on, where disks are numbered from top to bottom. Use the algorithm developed in Exercise 14.6 to initialize the stack representing the disks on the first tower.

Chapter 15
Mapping Functions

At times it is desirable to carry out the same operation on each of the various elements of one or more lists. This may be done iteratively by setting up a loop, individually accessing the constituent elements of the list(s), and operating on each element in turn. Alternatively a recursive approach may be possible. However it becomes much simpler if we have access to primitive LISP functions which do this kind of job automatically.

LISP has a family of functions called *mapping functions* which are designed to work on lists in just this manner. GCLISP supports all of the principal Common LISP mapping functions with the exception of map (CLRM p. 249).

In this chapter we will look at:

- the nature of *mapping functions*, which successively apply a function to the elements of one or more lists
- the manner in which mapcar operates on the elements of a list and accumulates the results into a single list
- the use of maplist, which operates on the successive cdr's of a list
- the use of mapcan to filter out those products of a mapping operation which do not meet a certain test
- the use of the mapping predicates some and every, which apply a test to every element of a list

15.1 Mapping functions successively apply a function to the elements of one or more lists

The CLRM (p. 128) puts it succinctly:

> 'Mapping is a type of iteration in which a function is successively applied to pieces of one or more sequences. The result of the iteration is a *sequence* containing the respective results of the function applications.'

Mapping functions take the following general syntax:

```
(map-name <function> <list> &rest <more-lists>)
```

The first argument <function>, which must be a functional object (see 6.13) represents some function which is to be successively applied to each of the elements of <list>. Additional arguments, which must also be lists, may be included. <function> must take as many arguments as there are lists to be operated upon.

The six basic mapping functions supported by GCLISP are discussed below.

15.2 mapcar operates on each element of a list

The most commonly used mapping function is mapcar, which applies its functional argument to each of the elements of the list or lists which make up its remaining arguments and returns a new list containing the results of these operations. We can preface our discussion of mapcar by first looking at a number of other ways to achieve a similar result.

Let's assume that we have a simple list of four numbers, which we will assign as the value of the symbol first-list:

```
* (setf first-list '(1 2 3 4))
(1 2 3 4)
```

and further assume that we wish to carry out some particular operation successively on each of the elements of this list and return a list containing the results of these operations.

As a simple example, we will increment each of the numbers by 1. We can easily define an iterative construct to do this, which we will call map-1:

```
* (defun map-1 (some-list)
    (let ((work-list nil))
     (loop
      (if (endp some-list)
          (return work-list))
```

```
        (setf work-list
          (append work-list
                  (list (1+ (car some-list)))))
        (setf some-list (cdr some-list)))))
MAP-1

* (map-1 first-list)
(2 3 4 5)
```

A somewhat simpler algorithm can be achieved through the use of a do construct. Calling our improved algorithm map-2:

```
* (defun map-2 (some-list)
    (do ((work-list some-list (cdr work-list))
         (new-list nil (append new-list
                                (list (1+ (car work-list))))))
         ((endp work-list) new-list)))
MAP-2

* (map-2 first-list)
(2 3 4 5)
```

The simplest version is however achieved through the use of mapcar, which is specifically designed to carry out just this kind of iterative operation:

```
* (mapcar #'1+ first-list)
(2 3 4 5)
```

noting that the dispatching macro #' (see Section 6.13) is used to identify a functional object.

As a matter of interest, we can define mapcar in terms of other Common LISP primitives to simulate the manner in which the machine language version carries out its task. Assuming for the moment only a single list argument, and calling the simulated function our-mapcar so as not to obliterate the function pointer of the real mapcar, which is a built-in LISP primitive:

```
* (defun our-mapcar (function-name some-list)
    (if (null some-list)
        nil
        (cons (funcall function-name (car some-list))
              (our-mapcar function-name (cdr some-list)))))
OUR-MAPCAR

* (our-mapcar #'1+ first-list)
(2 3 4 5)
```

15.3 mapcar can also operate on two or more lists

mapcar can take additional optional arguments all of which must be lists. The number of lists provided as arguments must match the number of arguments of the function being applied.

Let's define two more lists of numbers, which we can call second-list and third-list, and use mapcar to add the elements of all three lists together:

```
* (setf second-list '(2 3 4 5 6))
(2 3 4 5 6)
* (setf third-list '(3 4 5 6 7 8))
(3 4 5 6 7 8)
* (mapcar #'+ first-list second-list third-list)
(6 9 12 15)
```

Normally one would be using lists of the same length for such an exercise. However as will be evident from this example, the mapcar operation is terminated when the shortest list – which in this case is first-list – runs out of elements. Excess elements in the other lists are ignored.

In the above example we applied the + function, which by its nature can take any number of arguments. If on the other hand we had defined a function which takes a specific, and different, number of arguments and tried to apply it to the above lists:

```
* (defun add-em-up (number-1 number-2)
    (+ number-1 number-2))
ADD-EM-UP
* (mapcar #'add-em-up first-list second-list third-list)
ERROR:
Too many arguments for: NIL
while evaluating: NIL
```

Hence, unless we are applying a function like + which takes an indefinite number of arguments, the number of lists must match the number of arguments for the function being applied.

15.4 Lambda expressions can also be directly applied

As illustrated by our previous examples, we can use mapcar to apply either primitive functions or user-defined functions to its arguments. Indeed any functional argument can be used so long as it is acceptable to apply; it cannot be a macro definition or the name of a special form.

If we do not want to define a special function for a one-time application we can directly use a lambda expression instead. For example, to multiply the elements of first-list by 3, if we were following our previous method of operation we would define the function **triple**:

```
* (defun triple (x)
    (* 3 x))
TRIPLE
```

and apply it with **mapcar**:

```
* (mapcar #'triple first-list)
(3 6 9 12)
```

However we can alternatively use a lambda expression:

```
* (mapcar #'(lambda (x)(* 3 x)) first-list)
(3 6 9 12)
```

For one-shot usage, and where the function is not required to be generally available for use by other functions, the direct use of a lambda expression avoids tying up space on the Oblist for an otherwise unneeded symbol.

15.5 mapc is like mapcar but does not accumulate results

Like **mapcar**, **mapc** applies the function successively to each element of the list(s) which make up its argument(s). However it differs in that whereas **mapcar** is generally used for the sake of the value it returns (that is, the new list which is generated from the operations on its arguments), **mapc** is used for its side effects and merely returns the value of its first argument.

Let's devise an example in which we have a list of cities and a list of the states in which these cities are located. We would like to take each state name and place it on the property list of the corresponding city under the indicator **location**. Creating the necessary lists and function, which we can call **city-state**:

```
* (setf city-list '(dallas albany stanford))
(DALLAS ALBANY STANFORD)
* (setf state-list '(texas (new york) california))
(TEXAS (NEW YORK) CALIFORNIA)
* (defun city-state (city-name state-name)
    (setf (get city-name 'location) state-name))
```

If we now use **mapc** to apply the function **city-state** to the two lists:

```
* (mapc #'city-state city-list state-list)
(DALLAS ALBANY STANFORD)
```

we see that only the first list is returned. However we can readily check that the required operations have in fact been carried out:

```
* (get 'albany 'location)
(NEW YORK)
```

Hence, where we want to carry out an iterative mapping operation in which the side effects are of principal importance and the list returned by **mapcar** would not be put to any useful purpose we should use **mapc** in lieu of **mapcar**.

15.6 maplist operates on the successive cdr's of a list

maplist is something like **mapcar** except that, instead of applying the function to each element of the list, **maplist** first applies it to the entire list, then to the **cdr** of the list, then to the **cddr** of the list, and so on until the list has been decremented to **NIL**. **maplist** returns a list representing the **cons**'ing together of all of the successive values. For example:

```
* (maplist #'list first-list)
(((1 2 3 4))((2 3 4))((3 4))((4)))
```

As Wilensky (1986, p. 137) perceptively points out, it is hard to think of a noncontrived example of the use of **maplist** (although see Section 15.7 for an example of the use of its counterpart **mapl**.)

15.7 mapl is like maplist but does not accumulate results

mapl bears the same relationship to **maplist** as **mapc** does to **mapcar**, that is, it is used for its side effects, does not accumulate the results of successive applications of the function into a single list, and merely returns the value of its first argument. (See Section 30.15 for an example of the use of **mapl** in searching for a variable and updating its value on a lexically scoped rib list.)

15.8 mapcan provides for filtered accumulation of a mapcar operation

There may be times when we want to apply a **mapcar**-type operation to one or more lists, but segregate out only those elements which meet some particular criterion. For instance, suppose we have a list of groceries:

```
*(setf groceries '(apples soap pears beans fish grapes))
(APPLES SOAP PEARS BEANS FISH GRAPES)
```

and further assume that we wish to extract from the list only those elements which are fruits and accumulate them into a separate list, which in this case would be **(APPLES PEARS GRAPES)**.

Firstly, we can define a function to identify whether or not an element is a fruit, assuming that the value **fruit** is placed on its property list under the indicator **type**; and if it is a fruit, return its name as a list:

```
(defun find-fruit (x)
  (if (equal (get x 'type) 'fruit))
    (list x)))
```

If we use this function together with **mapcar** to scan our groceries list we get the following result:

```
* (mapcar #'find-fruit groceries)
((APPLES) NIL (PEARS) NIL NIL (GRAPES))
```

We can now extract the list we want by the following:

```
* (apply #'append (mapcar #'find-fruit groceries)
(APPLES PEARS GRAPES)
```

We can directly carry out such a *filtering operation* using **mapcan**, which effectively combines the results of **append** and **mapcar** to produce a list in which **NIL** values have been filtered out:

```
* (mapcan #'find-fruit groceries)
(APPLES PEARS GRAPES)
```

In actual fact, rather than using **append**, **mapcan** uses **nconc** (see Section 5.15) to achieve the same result. As discussed in Chapter 5, **nconc** is a destructive operation in which the **cdr** cell of each original list is altered to point to the next list (as opposed to **append**, which works with copies of lists). Assuming a single list argument, we can therefore define **our-mapcan** in terms of other Common LISP primitives as follows:

```
(defun our-mapcan (function-name some-list)
(apply 'nconc (our-mapcar function-name some-list))
```

where **our-mapcar** is as previously defined in Section 15.2.

15.9 mapcon filters a maplist operation

mapcon bears the same relation to **maplist** as **mapcan** does to **mapcar**, that is, applies **nconc** to generate a (destructively) concatenated filtered list of the elements returned by **maplist**.

The GCLRM contains an interesting application of **mapcon**, where elements of one list are transferred over to another list. As the transfer is made, **and** is inserted between adjacent elements:

```
* (mapcon #'(lambda (x)
              (if (null (rest x))
                  (list (first x))
                  (list (first x) 'and))) '(a b c d e))
(A AND B AND C AND D AND E)
```

15.10 Mapping predicates apply a test to every element of a list

The predicates **some** and **every** may be used to see whether at least one or more elements of a list meet some particular test, or whether every element meets the test. As a variant on the Common LISP standard, the GCLISP versions of these functions work only on lists but not vectors. **some**, which takes the syntax:

```
(some <predicate> <sequence> &rest <more-sequences>)
```

applies the predicate test to each element of the sequence (or sequences) and returns **T** (or some other non-**NIL** value) if an element is found which meets the test. If no such element is found **some** returns **NIL**.

```
* (some #'evenp '(1 2 3 4))
T
```

every takes a syntax similar to **some**, and similarly applies the predicate test to each element of the list. If any element is found which does not meet the test, **every** returns **NIL**; only if all elements meet the test does **every** return **T**.

```
* (every #'numberp '(1 2 3 4))
T
```

SUMMARY

Summarizing the key points of this chapter:

- *mapping functions* are designed to iterate over the elements of one or more lists in a successive manner, applying the same function to each element or set of elements
- **mapcar** applies its function to each individual element of its list argument(s) and returns a new list containing the results of each of the operations. The associated function **mapc**, which simply returns its first list argument, is used when only the side effects are of significance; otherwise it carries out the same operations as **mapcar**
- **maplist** carries out an iterative operation similarly to **mapcar**, except that the function is applied to the whole list(s) and to successive **cdr**'s of these lists. The associated function **mapl** carries out the same operations as **maplist**, but like **mapc** is used when only the side effects are significant.
- **mapcan** provides for filtering the list returned by **mapcar** so that all **NIL** elements are eliminated. **mapcon** is the equivalent filtering function for the results returned by **maplist**.
- the mapping predicates **some** and **every** may be used to test whether some or all of the elements of their list argument(s) meet some particular criteria

EXERCISES

15.1 What are the values returned by the following expressions:

(a) (mapcar #'list '(a b c) '(d e f))

(b) (mapcar #'* '(2 3 4) '(5 6 7))

(c) (mapc #'* '(2 3 4) '(5 6 7))

(d) (maplist #'list '(1 2 3 4))

(e) (mapl #'list '(1 2 3 4))

15.2 The function pairlis, which takes the syntax:

(pairlis <key-list> <datum-list> <a-list>)

augments the association list <a-list> by combining corresponding elements of <key-list> and <datum-list> and appending them to the front of <a-list>. Define a similar function our-pairlis, which does the same thing, using mapcar to join the key/datum pairs.

15.3 Define convert-temp, which converts a temperature from degrees Fahrenheit to degrees Centigrade (Centigrade = 5/9 × (Fahrenheit − 32). Use truncate to round off the Centigrade equivalent to the next lower integer. Finally, define f-to-c, a function which takes a list of temperatures, for example, (75 78 81 73 84) and uses mapcar and convert-temp to generate the corresponding list of Centigrade temperatures.

15.4 Define matchmaker, which takes a list of men's names and a list of women's names and uses mapcar to generate a list of potential marriage partners.

15.5 Define hooliganp, which checks whether a name is Spike or Skinhead. Then define bovver which takes a list of men's names and uses some to check a list of people at a soccer match to determine whether any hooligans are present. If the results are negative, bovver prints the message "Safe to attend the soccer match".

15.6 Define check-even, which takes a list of numbers and uses every to check whether they are all even numbers. Return an appropriate message indicating whether they are or not.

15.7 Define find-number, which checks its single argument and returns it as a list if it is a number. Then, assuming that the value of mixed-list is a list of symbols and numbers, write a mapcan function which will return a list of only the numbers.

15.8 In our discussion on mapcar we defined the function our-mapcar in terms of other Common LISP primitives, to operate on a single list argument. Modify the algorithm shown in Section 15.2 to work with two list arguments.

15.9 Using other Common LISP primitives define our-mapc, which takes two list arguments, and test it on the city-state example illustrated in Section 15.5. Check that all property lists have been appropriately modified.

15.10 Using other Common LISP primitives define our-maplist, based on taking a single list as its argument, and test it on first-list (see Section 15.6).

Chapter 16
Creating and Using Macros

Up to now we have been using defun to define the functions which are the principal mechanisms for executing procedures in LISP. In this chapter we will look at a related mechanism for defining procedures: the *macro*. A macro definition is much like a function definition in that it includes a name, a lambda list, and a body. However instead of evaluating its arguments, a macro expands into another form which is then evaluated in the normal manner. Macros can be therefore be used as a kind of template to create complex structures for evaluation. Through this mechanism macros permit the writing of code which is clear and straightforward at the user level but which, when invoked, expands into code of the required degree of complexity.

In this chapter we will look at:

- the manner in which a *macro* provides a template for creating a function-like procedure
- the use of defmacro for defining a macro definition
- how the backquote mechanism may be used to simplify the writing of a macro definition
- how macroexpand can be used to obtain the (expanded) definition of a macro
- the use of macro-function for retrieval of the expansion function which actually executes the macro
- how the *destructuring mechanism* provides a mapping between the input parameters and the body of a macro
- how possible name conflicts in macros may be avoided through the use of gensym

16.1 Macros provide a kind of template for the construction of generalized procedures

A macro may be thought of as a means of providing a kind of *template* of a LISP procedure to be carried out. The (unevaluated) arguments to the macro are fitted into this template and the resulting structure evaluated. Macro calls actually go through at least *two* levels of evaluation. On the first pass, recognizing that a macro call is involved, **eval** carries out a process of *macro expansion*, in which the macro's arguments are mapped into the template provided by the body of the macro. On the second pass, **eval** carries out an evaluation of the structure which results from the expansion, as shown in Fig. 16.1.

The use of macros offers several advantages over standard function calls:

- macro arguments are *not* evaluated; hence flexible syntactic constructs can be defined which take any sort of argument, including functional expressions
- in compiled systems, macros produce faster code than function calls since they avoid the overhead associated with function calls

In an interpreted system such as GCLISP, which does not yet support a compiler, the second advantage is not applicable.

However macros also have certain shortcomings:

- macro calls cannot be **trace**'d and hence are harder to debug than normal function calls
- macros cannot be used with **funcall**, **apply**, or any of the mapping functions
- in a compiled system, if you redefine a macro you have to recompile all the individual functions that call the macro

Again, in an interpreted system the last disadvantage is not applicable.

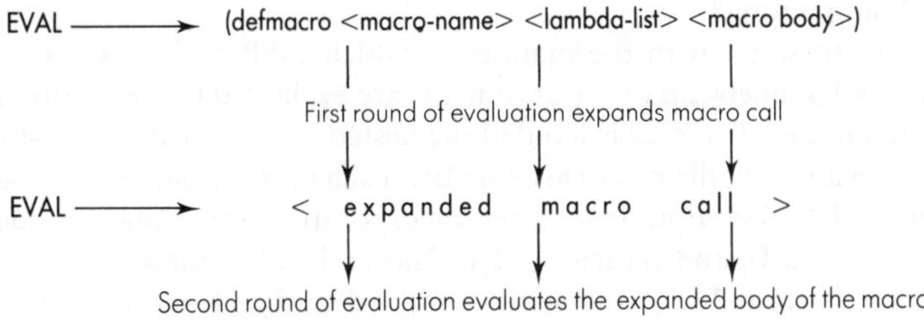

Fig. 16.1 **eval** carries out a process of macro expansion.

16.2 Macros do not evaluate their arguments

An essential aspect of a macro operation is that the arguments to the macro are not immediately evaluated. Let's look at how macros and standard functions differ in this regard.

Assume our implementation of LISP does not include a special form for **if**. If we tried to come up with a standard function definition of **our-if** to simulate the branching control provided by the **if** construct, its format would likely be as follows:

```
* (defun our-if (predicate then-clause &optional else-clause)
    (cond (predicate then-clause)
          (t else-clause)))
OUR-IF
```

Now that the function has been defined we can try it out. Let's incorporate it within another function used to determine whether an (unknown) number is greater than or less than zero and print out an appropriate statement to that effect. For example:

```
* (defun test-number (number)
    (our-if (> number 0)
          (format t "~%Number is greater than zero")
          (format t "~%Number is less than zero")))
TEST-NUMBER

* (setf unknown-number 5)
5

* (test-number unknown-number)
Number is greater than zero
Number is less than zero
NIL
```

test-number can't seem to make up its mind! First the number is greater than zero, then less than zero, and finally **NIL** is returned. We do not get such a rash of printouts when we use the **if** special form of Common LISP. Where are we going wrong?

The answer lies in the manner in which LISP evaluates a standard function call, namely, *all* of the arguments are evaluated before applying the function. Hence when **eval** is handed the nested function call to **our-if** in the course of evaluating the call to **test-number**, each of the arguments to **our-if** is evaluated. The 1st argument, after incorporating the value of **number**, equates to **(> 5 0)** and returns **T**. The 2nd and 3rd arguments, which are **format** (see Section 12.5) statements designed to direct output to the console, both return **NIL** *after* causing their respective strings to be printed on the console. All of these values are stored on the stack. Subsequently, when

our-if is applied to them, the body of the function is effectively reduced to:

```
(cond (t nil)
      (t nil))
```

and the first clause returns **NIL**, which is printed after the two **format** statements. Not quite what we wanted!

What we really wanted was for the body of the **our-if** function to reflect the following forms:

```
(cond ((> 5 0)(format t "~%Number is greater than zero")
      (t       (format t "~%Number is less than zero")))
```

in other words, for evaluation of all of the arguments to **our-if** to be deferred until *after* they had been inserted into the **cond** construct which makes up the body of **our-if**. Such deferred evaluation is an essential feature of the **defmacro** mechanism by which macros are defined.

16.3 defmacro is used to create a macro definition

defmacro, which is itself a macro, provides for the definition of macros. Its syntax is much like **defun**:

```
(defmacro <macro-name> <lambda-list> <body>)
```

Let's use **defmacro** to create an **our-if** macro along the lines discussed above:

```
* (defmacro our-if (predicate then-clause &optional else-clause)
    (list 'cond (list predicate then-clause)
                (list 't else-clause)))
; Autoload: DEFMACRO from "DEFMAC" in "C:\\GCLISP\LISPLIB\
\".
OUR-IF
```

The **defmacro** macro is not built in as a GCLISP primitive and must be autoloaded.

We have created our *macro template* by using **list** to group together the various elements of the template, including quoted elements such as **'cond** and **'t**, and variables such as **predicate**, **then-clause**, and **else-clause** to which the arguments will be bound.

If we now call **our-if** with the same arguments as before:

```
* (our-if (> 5 0)
          (format t "~%The number is greater than zero")
          (format t "~%The number is less than zero"))
The number is greater than zero
NIL
```

On the first round of evaluation the argument (> 5 0) is bound to the formal parameter **predicate** and the two **format** statements are respectively bound to **then-clause** and **else-clause**. The **list** functions are applied to their respective arguments, and the result of the expansion becomes:

```
(cond ((> 5 0)(format t "~%Number is greater than zero"))
      (t      (format t "~%Number is less than zero")))
```

On the second pass, the above structure will be evaluated in the normal manner and the expected value will be returned.

16.4 macroexpand expands the macro

Having created a macro it is a good idea to check on whether it is being expanded in accordance with your expectations. A useful function for this purpose is **macroexpand**, which takes the entire (quoted) macro call as its single argument and provides a printout of the macro after expansion. (**macroexpand** actually returns two values: the expanded form and **T**. If the macro name does not represent a valid macro definition, **macroexpand** simply returns the symbol name and **NIL**.)

For convenience we can bind the macro call to a symbol to avoid the need for typing it in repetitively:

```
* (setf if-example
    '(our-if
       (> 5 0)
       (format t "~%The number is greater than zero")
       (format t "~%The number is less than zero")))
(OUR-IF (> 5 0)(FORMAT T "~%The number is greater than
zero")(FORMAT T "~%The number is less than zero"))
```

We can then apply **macroexpand** to ascertain the manner in which the macro is being expanded:

```
* (macroexpand if-example)
(COND ((> 5 0)(FORMAT T "~%The number is greater than
zero"))((T (FORMAT T "~%The number is less than zero")))
T
```

thus verifying that **our-if** is being expanded in the desired manner. We can alternatively arrange for pretty-printing (see Section 11.7) of the value returned by **macroexpand** to format the output in a more readable manner:

```
* (pprint (macroexpand if-example))
; Autoload: PPRINT from "PPRINT" IN "C:\\GCLISP\\LISPLIB\\".
(COND ((> 5 0)
        (FORMAT T "~%The number is greater than zero"))
       (T
        (FORMAT T "~%The number is less than zero"))
       )
```

When debugging a long and complex macro you may wish to print out the expanded macro call on the printer so as to have it available for reference while you are doing other things on the console. Again pretty-printing the format, we can define **pprint-expanded-macro** for this purpose:

```
(defun pprint-expanded-macro (macro-call)
  (setf printer (open "prn" :direction :output))
  (pprint (macroexpand macro-call) printer)
  (princ (string 10) printer)
  (close printer))
```

In the above example, a single expansion was all that was required to convert the macro call to a form ready for final evaluation. However it is of course possible to nest macros within macros in which case multiple expansions will be required, one for each additional level of macro-within-macro nesting. In such cases **macroexpand** operates automatically to carry out additional expansions until a final form has been reached which permits of no further expansion. To do this, **macroexpand** repetitively calls **macroexpand-1**, a subordinate function which carries out a single expansion at a time.

16.5 Additional lambda-list keywords &body and &whole may be used with macros

Like the lambda-list used for normal function definitions, the macro-lambda-list may contain the keywords **&rest**, **&aux**, and **&optional**, all of which are used in the same way. However the macro-lambda-list also allows the use of the special keywords **&body** and **&whole.** (Note that in GCLISP these keywords can only be used in top-level lambda-lists; see the discussion of *structuring* in Section 16.9)

The keyword **&body**, which has exactly the same meaning as **&rest**, is used stylistically to indicate that whatever follows comprises the body of the macro call (as opposed, say, to a parameter list).

As regards **&whole**, the GCLRM advises: 'The keyword **&whole** binds the variable which follows it to the entire macro-call form. If **&whole**

is used, it must be the first element of a lambda-list.' See the CLRM pp. 145 and 149–51 for further discussion of the use of **&whole.**

16.6 Backquoting provides more readable macro definitions

The **backquote** mechanism (see Section 12.3) provides an easier way of writing macro definitions without the need for all of the **list** function calls used in the previous example. Like **quote**, the **backquote** character applies to the single expression which follows it. All of the elements of a backquoted expression are taken verbatim, without evaluation, except for any expression preceded by a comma, which *is* evaluated. The previous example can therefore alternatively be written:

```
* (defmacro our-if (predicate then-clause &optional else-clause)
    `(cond (,predicate ,then-clause)
           (t ,else-clause)))
OUR-IF
```

Expansion of this backquoted version of **our-if** results in exactly the same expression as was previously generated using **list**. The backquoted version is clearly much more readable.

16.7 At-sign and dot modifiers splice lists into backquoted expressions

If a comma followed by an at-sign ,@ is used in lieu of a simple comma in a backquoted expression, the elements of the list which results from evaluation of the variable are spliced into the backquoted expression in much the same manner as **append** splices elements of one list onto the front of another list:

```
* (setf some-list '(one two three))
(ONE TWO THREE)
* `(able baker ,@some-list cain dog)
(ABLE BAKER ONE TWO THREE CAIN DOG)
```

The original list is left unchanged. However if a comma followed by a dot ,. is used instead, the *original* list is spliced into the expression:

```
* `(able baker ,.some-list cain dog)
(ABLE BAKER ONE TWO THREE CAIN DOG)
```

Like a **rplaca** operation, this list surgery has had fatal effects on the original list:

```
* some-list
(ONE TWO THREE CAIN DOG)
```

and hence should only be used in one-shot situations where there will be no further use for the list being spliced in.

16.8 macro-function returns the macro expansion function

Although macroexpand provides an indication of the form to which the macro is expanded before final evaluation, there is somewhat more to the processing of a macro call than the expansion itself. For example, a check must be made as to whether sufficient arguments have been provided to match the parameters of the macro definition. defmacro therefore creates a special function which is designed to make these checks and to effect the actual implementation of the macro call. This function, which is referred to as a *macro expansion function*, may be displayed by use of macro-function which takes as its single argument the (quoted) name of the macro.

We can try out macro-function on our previous example of our-if with the following function call:

```
(macro-function 'our-if)
```

We can make more sense out of the (somewhat long-winded) value returned by macro-function by using pretty-print (see Section 11.7) to format it more agreeably:

```
* (pprint (macro-function 'our-if))
(LAMBDA (LISP::*MACROARG*)
  (AND (OR (< (LENGTH LISP::*MACROARG*) 3)
           (> (LENGTH LISP::*MACROARG*) 4))
       (ERROR "Wrong number of args to macro:
         ~S" LISP::*MACROARG*))
  (LET ((PREDICATE (CAR (CDR LISP::*MACROARG*))))
    (LET ((THEN-CLAUSE (CAR (CDR (CDR LISP::*MACROARG*)))))
      (LET ((ELSE-CLAUSE
              (CAR (CDR (CDR (CDR LISP::*MACROARG*))))))
        (LET ((LISP::*MACROARG1*
                (LIST 'COND (LIST PREDICATE THEN-CLAUSE)
                (LIST 'T ELSE-CLAUSE))))
          (IF (CONSP LISP::*MACROARG1*)
              (RPLACB LISP::*MACROARG* LISP::*MACROARG1*)
              LISP::*MACROARG1*))))))
```

As will be noted from perusal of the above, the entire body of the macro call is bound to the global variable *MACROARG1*. The macro expansion function then checks that the number of arguments provided to the macro call are correct, and in addition creates a nested series of let constructs within which the arguments are bound to the formal parameters of the macro definition.

As with **macroexpand**, we can easily define **pprint-macro-function** to provide a printout of this listing on the printer:

```
(defun pprint-macro-function (macro-name)
  (setf printer (open "prn" :direction :output))
  (pprint (macro-function macro-name) printer)
  (princ (string 10) printer)
  (close printer))
```

You can apply **pprint-macro-function** to the definition of **defmacro** itself to get a printout of the **defmacro** procedure. It will be noted that **defmacro** in turn calls upon the primitive special form **macro** to do much of the donkey-work. This primitive, which is also used by **autolaod**, is used internally by the system and should not normally be used at the top level for creating macro definitions.

16.9 Destructuring can simplify macro definitions

The macro handling facilities of LISP include provision for a feature called *destructuring*, which permits a direct mapping between the structural patterns of arguments supplied to a macro call and the structural patterns of the formal parameters of the macro definition. This facility simplifies the writing of a macro definition, as illustrated by the following example:

Let's create the macro definition **our-dotimes**, which carries out numerical iteration similarly to **dotimes** (see Section 13.5), which takes the syntax:

```
(dotimes (<variable><count><result>)
  <forms-to-be-evaluated>)
```

After initializing **<variable>** to 0, **dotimes** evaluates the forms which make up the body of the macro. This process is carried out in a repetitive manner, incrementing the value of **<variable>** by 1 on each pass. When this value equals that of **<count>** (which must evaluate to an integer), **<result>** is evaluated and its value is returned.A macro which would do the trick is:

```
(defmacro our-dotimes-1 (arglist &body body)
  `(do ((limit ,(cadr arglist))
        (,(car arglist) 0 (1+ ,(car arglist))))
      ((= ,(car arglist) limit) ,(caddr arglist))
      ,@body))
```

where **arglist** evaluates to a list of the three arguments (**<variable> <count><result>**) as noted above.

However this version is not as clear as it could be, due to the need to dig the three individual arguments out of **arglist** by applications of **car**, **cadr**, and **caddr**. We can simplify our task by taking advantage of **defmacro**'s *destructuring facility* which permits us to replace **arglist** with its nested equivalent (<variable><count><result-form>). The arguments within this list may then be directly mapped to the macro definition without the need for digging them out of **arglist**:

```
(defmacro our-dotimes-2 ((variable count result) &body body)
  `(do ((limit ,count))
       (,variable 0 (1+ ,variable)))
    ((= ,variable limit) ,result)
    ,@body))
```

In cases where the macro parameters and their arguments are structured as complex and deeply nested lists, the destructuring mechanism facilitates writing of the code and results in a more readable definition.

NB: In Common LISP the above lambda-list would normally include the keyword **&optional** before the last argument, reflecting that <result> may be omitted (in which case the macro returns **NIL**). Since GCLISP Version 1.1 does not allow keywords in nested lambda-lists, if we try to define **our-dotimes-2** with the lambda-list **((variable count &optional result) &body body)** we will get back the message:

```
ERROR:
&OPTIONAL can only be used in top-level lambda lists
```

However **&optional** is not actually required, since **macroexpand** will bind parameters which lack arguments to **NIL**, for example:

```
* (defmacro test-macro ((var count result) &body body)
    `(list ,var ,count ,result . ,body))
TEST-MACRO

* (macroexpand '(test-macro (1 2)(print "foo")))
(LIST 1 2 NIL (PRINT "foo"))
```

16.10 Variable name conflicts can occur in macros

Because a macro's arguments are not evaluated before it is expanded this can lead to situations in which variables contained in the (unevaluated) arguments conflict with index variables used in the macro definition. The CLRM (p. 147) provides a clear example of how such conflicts may be avoided:

```
(defmacro arithmetic-if (test neg-form zero-form pos-form)
  (let ((var (gensym)))
   `(let ((,var test))
     (cond ((> ,var 0) ,neg-form)
           ((= ,var 0) ,zero-form)
           (t ,pos-form)))))
```

Prior to entering the backquoted main body of the macro, the index variable **var** is bound to the symbol created by the use of **gensym** (see Section 25.13). Since this symbol is unique, any possible name conflicts are avoided.

SUMMARY

Summarizing the key points of this chapter:

- **macros** provide a method for defining function-like procedures of any degree of structural complexity by providing a template into which arguments can be slotted
- macro arguments are not evaluated, but rather are bound directly to the parameters of the macro call
- during the first round of evaluation, a macro is expanded to the format as defined by the macro definition, including arguments which may or may not be evaluated in the course of expansion; on the second round of evaluation, the expanded macro is evaluated in the usual manner
- **defmacro** is used to create a macro definition
- the function **macroexpand**, which takes the entire (quoted) macro call as an argument, provides an indication of the expanded form of the macro
- the **backquote** mechanism may be used to create more readable macro definitions
- the function **macro-function** provides a display of the *macro expansion function* which is created by **defmacro** to implement the macro call
- the *destructuring* feature permits the elements of *nested* lambda-lists to be directly mapped to corresponding elements within the macro parameters
- name conflicts can be avoided in macro definitions by incorporating a **let** construct in which index variables are bound to unique values through the use of **gensym**

EXERCISES

16.1 Define the macro **our-setq**, which does the same thing as **setq**. Use **set**.

16.2 Define the macros **our-first** and **our-rest**, which do the same thing as **car** and **cdr**.

16.3 Assuming that our implementation of LISP does not contain composite car/cdr functions, define the macro our-caadr, which returns the result of a combined (car (car (cdr (<list>)))) operation.

16.4 Define the macros our-when and our-unless, which carry out the same branching operations as when (see Section 9.7) and unless (see Section 9.8).

16.5 If a *stack* is represented by a list of elements, define the macro our-push, which takes another element as its first argument and the stack as its second argument, adds the new element to the front of the stack, and returns the value of the (augmented) stack. Also define the macro our-pop, which takes the stack as its single argument, removes the first element from the stack, and returns the element.

16.6 Design the macro our-dolist, which does the same thing as dolist (see Section 13.4). Assuming that the Common Lisp functions do and do* are available for use, which one should be used?

16.7 Design the macro our-mapcar, which takes as its two arguments the name of a function and a list. Like mapcar (see Section 15.2), our-mapcar returns a list of the values returned by successive applications of the function to each element of the second argument.

16.8 Design the macro our-let, which expands into a lambda expression and which does the same thing as let (see Section 6.8).

16.9 The function progv (see Section 13.9), which takes the syntax (progv <symbol-list> <value-list> <forms-to-be-evaluated>), is like prog except that the list of program variables are the result of evaluating <symbol-list> and the values initially bound to them are the result of evaluating <value-list>. If excess values are supplied these are ignored; if excess symbols are supplied these are made to have no value, using makunbound (see Section 4.12). Design the macro our-progv which does the same thing.

16.10 Assuming that our implementation of LISP does not have the general iterative construct do (see Section 13.3), design the macro our-do which does the same thing. Include provision for evaluation of optional side effects statements within the test clause.

Chapter 17

Blocks, Exits, and Multiple Values

There are times when we would like to be able to exit from a function immediately and return a value without bothering to evaluate the remaining expressions of the function. In deeply nested programs it may also be desirable to exit from a lower level function and return a value directly to some higher level function, without having to pass the value upward through a number of intervening functions. LISP provides several mechanisms for handling such situations, which we shall look at in this chapter.

As another matter related to the flow of control in LISP, we may also want to write functions which return multiple values, as well as to receive and process such values.

In this chapter we will look at:

- the manner in which a block construct may be created to permit a function to be exited immediately upon execution of a **return** statement
- the use of **catch** and **throw** for dynamically exiting a function and returning a value directly to some higher level function
- how **unwind-protect** may be invoked to assure that critical expressions are evaluated after a throw or a system error
- the use of **values** and **value-list** in returning multiple values from user-defined functions
- the use of various functions such as **multiple-value-setq** which are designed to receive and process multiple values

17.1 **block** establishes a structured exit facility

The special form **block** provides an environment in which forms are evaluated sequentially until a **return-from** statement is encountered. At that time the block construct is immediately exited, returning whatever value was specified by the **<result-form>** which follows the **return-from**. The syntax of **block** is:

```
(block <name><forms-to-be-evaluated>)
```

The block **<name>** is not evaluated and must be a symbol (although see note below regarding GCLISP). The forms are evaluated in order, as in a **progn** construct. The value(s) of the last form will be returned unless a **return-from** call occurs during the execution of the forms, in which case evaluation of forms is discontinued and **block** is immediately exited, returning the result(s) specified by the **return** statement. If **<result-form>** has not been specified, **NIL** will be returned.

(NB: Since **eq** is used as a test for the block identifier, a fixnum can also be used as a block name in GCLISP. However this would be considered bad style, and in any case inconsistent with Common LISP.)

The **return-from** statement takes the format:

```
(return-from <block-name> &optional <result-form>)
```

If the optional **<result-form>** is omitted, **NIL** will be returned. It should be noted that it is also possible to name a block **NIL** explicitly, in which case the simpler format **(return &optional <result-form>)** may be used to exit the block (see Section 17.2).

Let's look at some examples of **block**:

```
* (defun test-block-1 ()
    (block single-block
      (format t "~%Evaluating form one~%")
      (return-from single-block
        (format t "Returning to single-block"))
      (format t "~%Evaluating form two")))
TEST-BLOCK-1

* (test-block-1)
Evaluating form one
Returning to single-block
```

The **return-from** statement causes an immediate transfer of control back to **single-block** which exits, after printing out the **format** statement. The final form is not evaluated. (In this and other examples the final top level **NIL** returned by **format** statements will be ignored for clarity.)

We can nest blocks within blocks, and can return to any outer block so long as it is still active, that is, has not yet been exited:

```
* (defun test-block-2 ()
    (block outer-block
      (format t "~%Evaluating form one")
      (block inner-block
        (format t "~%Evaluating form two~%")
        (return-from outer-block
          (format t "Returning to outer-block")))
        (format t "~%Evaluating form three")))
TEST-BLOCK-2
* (test-block-2)
Evaluating form one
Evaluating form two
Returning to outer-block
```

Now let's look at a final example in which an intervening function call separates two block constructs:

```
* (defun test-block-3 ()
    (return-from outer-block
      (format t "~%Returning to outer-block")))
TEST-BLOCK-3
* (block outer-block
    (test-block-3))
ERROR:
RETURN-FROM: name OUTER-BLOCK not found.
```

Although this example will work in the dynamically scoped Version 1.01 of GCLISP, it will *not* work in the lexically scoped Version 1.1, since the expression **(block outer-block...** is outside of the lexical scope of the function **test-block-3** and cannot be 'seen' from within that function.

As another difference to be noted, user-defined functions in Common LISP are enclosed in an implicit block of the same name as the function, such that the function can be exited at any time by using a **return-from** statement. As the next experiment indicates, GCLISP does not support this feature:

```
* (defun test-block-4 ()
    (format t "~%Evaluating form one")
    (return-from test-block-4
      (format nil "~%Returning to test-block-4"))
    (format t "~%Evaluating form two"))
TEST-BLOCK-4
```

```
* (test-block-4)
Evaluating form one
ERROR:
RETURN-FROM: name TEST-BLOCK-4 not found
```

Therefore in GCLISP a block expression must be explicitly built in as the first statement in a function definition if you wish to use a **return** or **return-from** mechanism to exit the function.

The **block/return** construct provides a relatively efficient way to discontinue evaluation of forms and immediately return a value. Another way to achieve a similar effect through the **catch/throw** mechanism will be discussed below.

17.2 Some LISP constructs are surrounded by implicit blocks

A number of Common LISP constructs are surrounded by an implicit block named **NIL**. These include the iterative constructs **loop, do/do***, **dotimes**, **dolist**, and **prog/prog***. Any of these constructs can be exited immediately with the simplified return statement:

```
(return &optional <result-form>)
```

As noted above, this simpler form will also work on a block which has explicitly been named **NIL**. As a matter of interest, if we apply **macroexpand** (see Section 16.4) to a **return** expression we will find that **return** is actually a macro which expands to the format **(return-from nil &optional <result-form>)**. Hence the longer form could also be used to exit from any block – implicit or explicit – named **NIL**.

17.3 Blocks can be used to control mapping functions

In Chapter 15 we looked at various *mapping functions*, all of which are designed to traverse completely the lists or elements of a list which make up their arguments. At times it may be desirable to cut short a mapping operation when some specific goal has been reached, rather than letting it continue to the end. We can use a **block** construct for this purpose.

Let's resuscitate our old grocery list, together with some of the necessary infrastructure, using the following expressions:

```
(setf grocery-list
  '(soap beans pears apples fish grapes))
(defun find-fruit (x)
  (if (equal (get x 'type) 'fruit)
     (list x)))
```

```
(setf (get 'pears 'type) 'fruit
      (get 'apples 'type) 'fruit
      (get 'grapes 'type) 'fruit)
```

Rather than using mapcan (see Section 15.8) to filter out the list of items which are fruits, let's just use mapcar to apply find-fruit to look for fruits and, if it finds a single instance of a fruit, to immediately return T. Otherwise it will traverse the whole list and eventually return NIL. If we build in provision to print out each item as it is examined:

```
* (defun fruit-yes-or-no (some-list)
    (block found-fruit
      (mapcar #'(lambda (x)
                  (format t "~%~a" x)
                  (if (funcall #'find-fruit x)
                      (return-from found-fruit
                        (format t "~%Found a fruit!"))))
              some-list)
      nil))
```

we can verify the manner in which the mapcar operation is cut short by the return-from:

```
* (fruit-yes-or-no grocery-list)
SOAP
BEANS
PEARS
Found a fruit!
```

17.4 catch and throw permit dynamic exits

In our earlier experiment with test-block-3 we saw that we could not exit to a block which was outside of the lexical scope of the function.

However Common LISP also provides a way for returning control to a higher level calling function in a dynamic manner. The point to which control is to be returned is signaled by the special form catch, which takes the following syntax:

```
(catch <tag> <forms to be evaluated>)
```

The catch <tag> combination is used in much the same way as the block <name> combination, the principal difference being that the latter normally only works within the lexical scope of the function in which it appears, whereas catch can be separated from the ultimate point of return by any number of intervening function calls. (In the dynamically scoped Version 1.01 of GCLISP, the two constructs work similarly, except that the catch/throw combination also permits use of unwind-protect (see below).)

The forms following a catch statement (which may include nested function calls to any depth) are evaluated in a manner similar to the block construct, that is, they simply 'run off the end' unless a throw statement is encountered. The latter takes the syntax:

```
(throw <tag> <result-form>)
```

tag is evaluated to produce an object (which may be any LISP object) which names the catch. Flow of control jumps back to the earlier catch statement, and the value of <result-form> is returned.

catch and throw permit an immediate return from a deeply nested function without the need to pass a value all the way up the line. This avoids the overhead of requiring all of the intermediate functions to handle and pass along the value returned. We may wish to return immediately, either because we have finally found a desired solution at the lower level, or because at some point we have decided to abort the whole exercise.

In the latter context catch and throw come in particularly handy for processing errors which may occur at different levels of the program. Depending on how and where things went wrong, throw can call a halt to the whole process and return an appropriate error message to the catch location.

17.5 unwind-protect cleans up after a throw

There may be instances in which, before returning from a throw to a previous catch, some clean-up work is required. For example, perhaps a file (which would otherwise have been closed by some expression following the throw statement) is left open without updating the file pointer. This would of course cause problems the next time the file was accessed.

The unwind-protect feature provides a manner of carrying out such clean-up activities. Syntax of this construct is:

```
(unwind-protect <protected-form> <clean-up forms>)
```

The first argument is the single form to be protected. (Multiple forms can as usual be incorporated within this argument through use of a progn construct.) The remaining forms constitute the items to be 'cleaned up.' A typical unwind-protect construct, used in conjunction with catch and throw, would take the general form:

```
(catch <tag>
  (unwind-protect
    (progn
      (<some forms to be evaluated>)
      (if <some-test>
        <continue with what you were doing>
        <otherwise (throw <tag> <result-form>))
      (<some clean-up forms-to-be-evaluated>))))
```

If things work out such as to cause **throw** to return the flow of control to **catch**, the following activities will be carried out:

- the **<result-form>** following the throw will be evaluated and the value saved
- the **clean-up forms** will be evaluated up to the end of the **unwind-protect** form
- any bindings of program variables established subsequent to the **catch** will be undone
- the value or values returned by **<result-form>** will be returned by **catch**

We can illustrate a practical instance of **unwind-protect** in connection with opening and closing a file:

```
* (defun protect-file ()
    (catch 'close-file
      (let  ((file-stream nil)
             (sentence nil))
        (unwind-protect
          (progn
            (setf file-stream
              (open "c:testfile" :direction :output))
            (terpri)
            (loop
              (format t "Please input a sentence: ")
              (setf sentence (read-line))
              (print sentence file-stream)
              (if  (equal sentence "bye")
                   (throw 'close-file
                    "Th-th-THAT'S ALL FOLKS!"))))
              (format t "~%Clean-up form 1 being evaluated")
              (format t "~%Clean-up form 2 being evaluated")
              (close file-stream))))
PROTECT-FILE

* (protect-file)
Please input a sentence: How now brown cow!
Please input a sentence: The rain is in Spain!
Please input a sentence: bye

Clean-up form 1 being evaluated
Clean-up form 2 being evaluated
<file closed by third expression>
"Th-th-THAT'S ALL FOLKS!"
```

Everything within the **progn** expression, up to the end of the **throw** statement, constitutes the **<protected-form>**. The three expressions which follow simulate the **<clean-up forms>**.

The **loop** invites repetitive input of sentences, which are printed to file **c:test-file** until **bye** is typed, at which time **throw** returns control to **catch**. However the three cleanup forms are evaluated before doing so, which is the whole point of **unwind-protect**. Thereafter the (saved) **<result-form>** is returned.

unwind-protect is employed in this same manner in the course of defining the macro **with-open-file** which is used to access a file and thereafter close it automatically. In this case the **catch** and **throw** mechanism is not required. The use of **unwind-protect** in this macro may be illustrated by evaluating the following:

```
* (pprint (macroexpand
    '(with-open-file
        (out-stream "c:test.2.lsp" :direction :output)
        (print "Now is the time!" out-stream))))
(LET ((OUT-STREAM (OPEN"c:test-2.lsp" :DIRECTION :OUTPUT)))
  (UNWIND-PROTECT
    (PRINT
      "Now is the time!"
      OUT-STREAM)
      (CLOSE OUT-STREAM)))
```

17.6 LISP provides mechanisms for generating and processing multiple values

Ordinarily when we call a LISP function we get back a single LISP object as the 'value returned.' However there are instances where the nature of a function is such that it is desirable to return two or more values. We saw an instance of this with **read-from-string** (see Section 10.8) which, in the course of reading tokens from a string, returned *two* values: the token just read and the index position of the next unread character in the string. Another example is the arithmetic function **truncate**, which takes the syntax:

```
(truncate <number> &optional <divisor>)
```

truncate divides **<number>** by **<divisor>** and returns two values: an integer and a remainder:

```
* (truncate 10 3)
3
1
```

In earlier LISP systems such functions were required to return their (multiple) values in the form of a list or a vector, or else temporarily assign the values to two or more global variables. Modern implementations have provided facilities whereby multiple values can be returned directly by a function, and have provided auxiliary functions to receive and process such multiple values.

Aside from the relatively small number of LISP primitives such as **read-from-string** and **truncate** which are specifically designed to return multiple values, we can use **values** (see Section 17.7) to create user-designed functions which return more than one value. Using primitives of the **multiple-** family (see Sections 17.9 and 17.10) we can also create other functions geared up to receive and process more than one value.

17.7 values provides a means of returning multiple values

We can create user-defined functions which return more than one value through the use of **values**, which takes the syntax:

```
(values &rest <value-forms>)
```

The elements of <**value-forms**> are evaluated in sequential order (like **setq**), and the multiple values resulting from these evaluations are returned. For example:

```
* (values (+ 1 2)(- 10 3)(* 3 3))
3
7
9
```

When employed in a user-defined function to return multiple values, **values** would usually be the last form to be evaluated so as to provide the value(s) returned by the function (but see comments on **values-list** below).

If **values** is used in such a manner as to return multiple values to a (normal) function which is geared up to receive only a single value, the extra values will be ignored:

```
* (setf number (values (+ 1 2)(- 10 3)(* 3 3)))
3

* number
3
```

In this case only the first value has been utilized; the remainder have been 'lost.' In effect, **values** places its multiple values on a stack from which they may be retrieved by a function (see Sections 17.9 and 17.10) designed to handle multiple values. If a normally single-valued function like **setf** then accesses the stack to retrieve its expected single value, the remaining values are simply flushed from the stack before the next form is evaluated.

A related function **values-list** returns as multiple values all of the elements of the list which constitutes its second argument:

```
* (values-list '(3 hotdog (my dog has fleas)))
3
HOTDOG
(MY DOG HAS FLEAS)
```

values-list comes in handy when evaluation of some form returns multiple values but for some reason you don't want to return these values right away. You can execute a statement such as:

```
(setf <some-symbol> (multiple-value-list (eval <form>)))
```

which evaluates the form in question, uses **multiple-value-list** (see Section 17.10) to collect the values returned by the form into a list, and assigns this list as the value of **<some-symbol>**. Later, when you *do* want to return the values, you can execute:

```
(values-list <some-symbol>)
```

which will return the (multiple) values in the order in which they appear in the list. (See the **time-elapsed** macro in Section 24.15 for an example of such usage.)

17.8 A LISP function can return no value at all

If the concept of returning multiple values appears alien at first sight, another surprise is yet in store: it is possible for a function to return no value at all! In Common LISP a call to **(values)** without any arguments returns '*no value*.'

The idea of 'no value' is mildly confusing when considered from the standpoint of a function which normally expects to receive a value and, incomprehensibly, receives none. What does it do? As Woody Allen might put it, how does it *cope*?

Most normal functions simply assume that they have received **NIL** and proceed on this basis. However some functions of the **read** family *are* specially designed to handle a 'no value' situation. The return of 'no value' occurs principally in connection with the creation of user-defined macro characters designed to encapsulate commentary within a function definition. Using 'no value,' this can be done in such a manner that, when the definition is read in from the keyboard or a file, no trace of the commentary is left to confuse the evaluation process (see Section 20.10 for an example).

17.9 multiple-value-setq carries out multiple assignments

One of the more useful functions for handling multiple values is **multiple-value-setq**, which takes the syntax:

```
(multiple-value-setq <var-list> <values-form>)
```

<values-form> is evaluated, and then the variables named by the <var-list> are assigned the values returned by <values-form>, the *n*th value being assigned to the *n*th variable. If there are more variables than values, the excess variables are bound to NIL; if there are more values than variables, the excess values are discarded. Although the first value returned by <values-form> is returned, the main purpose of **multiple-value-setq** is to produce side-effects, that is, to establish the value assignments to the variables.

An example of a function utilizing **multiple-value-setq** is **read-ex-string** (see Section 10.9) which is useful for processing English language input. **read-ex-string** prompts for input of a sentence, reads successive tokens from the resulting input string, and accumulates the tokens into a list:

```
(defun read-ex-string ()
  (format t "~%Please input a sentence: ")
  (let ((input (read-line))
        (word nil)
        (pointer 0)
        (sentence nil))
   (loop
    (multiple-value-setq (word pointer)
       (read-from-string input nil 'eof
         :start pointer
         :preserve-whitespace nil))
       (if (equal word 'eof)
          (return (reverse sentence)))
          (setf sentence (cons word sentence)))))
```

read-ex-string works its way along the string of text, token by token. As each token is read, two values are returned: the token itself and a pointer to the next unread character in the string. These values are assigned to **word** and **pointer**, respectively, by **multiple-value-setq**. The **word** is added to the **sentence** being accumulated, and the **pointer** is used to control the point at which **read-ex-string** starts trying to parse the next token. When end-of-file on the stream created by **read-ex-string** is reached, the list of words is reversed (to restore original word order) and returned.

17.10 Other special forms are available to receive and process multiple values

In the foregoing section we looked at **multiple-value-setq**, which assigned multiple values to a series of variables. A related function is **multiple-value-bind**, which takes the syntax:

```
(multiple-value-bind <var-list> <values-form> <body>)
```

This function in effect combines the facilities provided by a **let** construct with the assignment features of **multiple-value-setq**. In this case the values are temporarily *bound*, rather than assigned; thereafter the remaining forms which make up the body of the function are evaluated as an implicit **progn** and the value(s) of the last form will be returned.

A related function **multiple-value-list** takes the syntax:

```
(multiple-value-list <values-form>)
```

and returns a list containing the values returned by its single argument. For example:

```
* (multiple-value-list (values 1 2 3))
(1 2 3)
```

This function is useful in situations where you cannot anticipate exactly how many values will be returned by <**values-form**>, so you collect them all into a single list for subsequent processing.

Finally, the function **multiple-value-prog1** which takes the syntax:

```
(multiple-value-prog1 <form-1> <other forms>)
```

is a multiple-value version of **prog1**, in that it evaluates the forms which follow in sequential order, and returns the value(s) of the first form. The only difference from **prog1** is that multiple values may be returned. As mentioned previously in connection with sequencing forms (see Section 13.10), **prog1** and **prog2** only return a single value even if the form which determines their value returns multiple values.

GCLISP does not support the Common LISP function **multiple-value-call**, which takes as its arguments the value produced from the first actual argument plus a list of all the values produced from the remaining arguments. The first argument, which should be a function, is **apply**'d to the resulting list. However we can design a user-defined function which achieves the same effect (see Exercise 17.10).

17.11 Handling of multiple values is not always consistent

There are occasional instances in LISP where the passing back of multiple values is handled in a somewhat inconsistent manner. For example, although **cond** returns multiple values when the **form** producing them is the last form in the clause:

```
* (cond ((equal 5 5)(values 1 2 3)))
1
2
3
```

it only returns a single value if the form producing multiple values is the (single) predicate in the clause:

```
* (cond ((values 1 2 3)))
1
```

Along somewhat analogous lines, the logical operators **AND** and **OR** pass back multiple values from the last subform but not from subforms other than the last.

Other than the above examples, those functions which are geared up to handle multiple values generally do so consistently. The fine points of the rules governing the passing of multiple values are covered in the CLRM pp. 137–9.

SUMMARY

Summarizing the main points of this chapter:

- the **block** construct provides a means of effecting an immediate exit from a function, without evaluating all of the forms which follow the **return** statement
- if a **block** is exited by a return statement, the value of the **<result-form>** is returned; otherwise evaluation of forms continues to the end of the construct and 'runs off the end,' as with a **prog** construct
- **catch** and **throw** provide a dynamic means of exiting a function and returning a value directly to some higher level function
- **unwind-protect** can be used to provide for evaluation of critical forms after a **throw** operation or after a system error
- **values** and **value-list** provide a mechanism for returning multiple values from a user-defined function
- **multiple-value-setq** and other related functions are geared up to handle and process multiple values

EXERCISES

17.1 Define **get-numbers-1**, which repetitively invites the input of a number from the console. Use a **block** construct to encase the body of the function. If anything other than a number is typed in, execute a **return** statement to exit the function with the message "**That's not a number!**".

17.2 Define **get-numbers-2**, which does the same thing as Exercise 17.1 but uses a **catch/throw** construct.

17.3 Define **get-numbers-3**, which does the same thing as Exercise 17.1 but which writes the numbers entered to file **c:number** and uses **unwind-protect** to close the file automatically when the function is exited.

17.4 Define the function **our-substitute**, which takes three arguments: a new element to be substituted, an old element to be replaced, and a list which may or may not contain instances of the old element. **our-substitute** returns two values: a (possibly amended) list, and **T** or **NIL** depending on whether any substitutions were made.

17.5 Define **parents-names-1**, which successively solicits the input of your father's and mother's names from the console and returns the two values.

17.6 Define **parents-names-2**, which does the same thing as Exercise 17.5 but uses **values-list** to return the names in the form of a list.

17.7 Write an expression in which **multiple-value-setq** uses the function defined in Exercise 17.5 as its second argument, and assigns the values of the father's and mother's names to the global variables ***father*** and ***mother*** respectively.

17.8 Write an expression in which **multiple-value-bind** carries out an operation similar to Exercise 17.7 but temporarily binds the values of the names to the variables **father** and **mother**, and uses these values in a format statement which responds "**I understand your father's name is <father> and your mother's name is <mother>**". Ignore differences in case in the printout.

17.9 Using **multiple-value-list**, write an expression which carries out an operation similar to Exercise 17.8 but returns the two names in the form of a list.

17.10 The Common LISP function **multiple-value-call** takes the syntax:

```
(multiple-value-call <function-name> <forms>)
```

After evaluating **<function-name>**, which must evaluate to a function, **multiple-value-call** evaluates the forms which follow, gathers all of the values returned by these forms into a single list, **apply**'s the function to the list, and returns whatever is returned by the function. For example:

```
* (multiple-value-call #'+
  (truncate 10 3)(truncate 20 7))
12
```

Define the function (or macro) **our-multiple-value-call**, which achieves the same effect.

Chapter 18
Property and Association Lists

A powerful feature of LISP is the ability to associate one or more properties with a symbol name. To the extent a symbol is thought of as representing a real-world object, a property list can be used to store the real-world attributes of such an object. If, for instance, we have a friend named Harry, some of the descriptive attributes of Harry such as the fact that his age is 30, his weight is 150 pounds, and his hobbies are golf and tennis can be captured on his property list.

Whereas the property list is generally used to store a variety of information related to a particular symbol, the association list provides a more general way of storing information in the form of key/datum pairs. In this sense an association list may be compared to a simple lookup table.

In this chapter we will look at:

- the nature of *property lists* and how they are related to a symbol
- how information is added to and retrieved from a property list
- how the whole property list can be retrieved
- the manner in which *association lists* are similar to property lists and how they differ
- how association lists are created and accessed
- how entries in an association list may be replaced or deleted

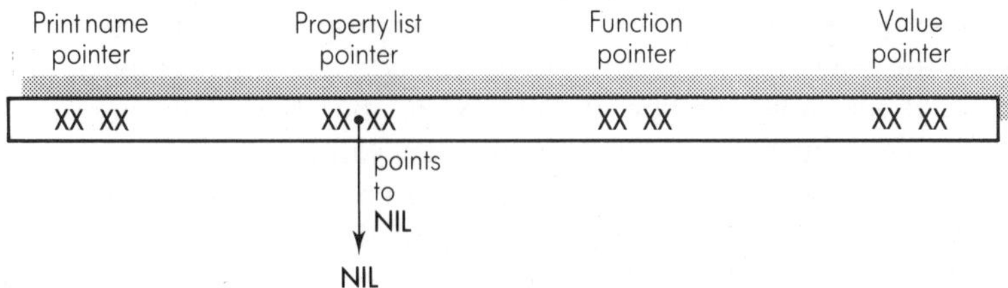

Fig. 18.1 Property lists are initialized to point to **NIL**.

18.1 The property list pointer is a special symbol cell

As discussed in Chapter 4, the property list is one of the four principal attributes of a symbol. When a symbol is initially created, its property list pointer is initialized to point to **NIL**, as shown in Fig. 18.1.

Subsequently, when a property list is created for this symbol, the associated list structure is stored in the general area reserved for lists and a pointer to the list is placed in the symbol's property list cell.

It should be noted that a number of GCLISP primitives have non-NIL property lists which are used to store various kinds of system information related to their use. If you are interested in pursuing this, evaluate the following:

```
(do-symbols (symbol 'lisp)
  (print symbol)
  (terpri)
  (princ " ")
  (prin1 (symbol-plist symbol)))
```

which prints a list of LISP primitives followed by their property lists (if any). The function **symbol-plist** (see Section 18.3) returns the entire property list of a symbol.

18.2 setf is used to assign an indicator and its value

Older implementations of LISP, and many current microcomputer implementations, utilize the function **put** or **putprop** to add a property indicator and its value to a property list. In line with Common LISP's use of the generalized **setf** function, GCLISP uses **setf** for this purpose. The typical format for adding the property indicator **age** and its value **30** to Harry's property list would therefore be as follows:

```
* (setf (get 'harry 'age) 30)
30
```

which uses **get** (see Section 18.4) to access the property list structure and **setf** to insert the relevant value. If the indicator **age** does not yet exist, **get** will create it. If the indicator **age** already exists, the above **setf** operation will cause the old value to be replaced by the new value.

It will be noted that properties come in pairs, where the name of the property is referred to as the *indicator* and the value of the property is referred to as the *value*. A property indicator must be a symbol. It is physically possible to assign a list as an indicator:

```
* (setf (get 'harry '(red fruit)) 'apple)
APPLE
```

and the resulting indicator/value pair will be stored on the property list:

```
* (symbol-plist 'harry)
((RED FRUIT) APPLE AGE 30)
```

However the retrieval mechanism will not work:

```
* (get 'harry '(red fruit))
NIL
```

since **get** looks for indicators which are **eq**, and two quoted lists can never be **eq** (see Section 8.6).

Since GCLISP represents a fixnum within the pointer itself, it is possible to use a fixnum as a value:

```
* (setf (get 'harry 12) '(the twelfth property))
(THE TWELFTH PROPERTY)
```

since the pointers of two identical fixnums will be the same, and **eq** basically compares pointers. This may or may not work in other implementations of Common LISP.

The property *value* can be any LISP data object.

18.3 The whole property list can be retrieved with symbol-plist

As we add new indicator/value pairs to Harry's property list they will be appended to the front of the list. (This pertains to GCLISP and may be handled differently in other implementations of Common LISP.) Having added the properties **weight 150** and **hobbies (tennis golf)** in that order (and ignoring our earlier experiment with apples), we can retrieve the entire list for inspection with **symbol-plist**:

```
* (symbol-plist 'harry)
(HOBBIES (GOLF TENNIS) WEIGHT 150 AGE 30)
```

From which we see that Harry's property list has been structured as shown in Fig. 18.2.

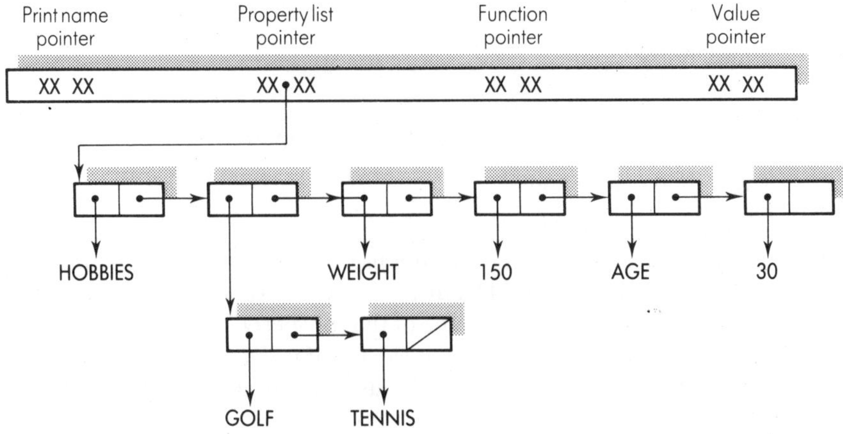

Fig. 18.2 Harry's property list.

It is possible to use **setf** in conjunction with **symbol-plist** to create a whole property list in one fell swoop:

```
* (setf (symbol-plist 'moo) '(how now brown cow))
MOO

* (symbol-plist 'moo)
(HOW NOW BROWN COW)
```

Further experimentation will reveal that the retrieval mechanism for property lists only recognizes the odd-numbered elements as potential indicators. A **get** operation on **HOW** and **BROWN** will return the corresponding 'values' **NOW** and **COW**; but **NIL** will be returned if an attempt is made to get the values of **NOW** and **COW**.

Use of **setf** to create a property list in the above manner is potentially dangerous, since the new property list will completely replace any previous property list the symbol may have had. This could result in a loss of critical data.

18.4 A property may be retrieved with get

A property value is retrieved with **get**, which takes the syntax:

```
(get <symbol> <indicator> &optional <default>)
```

where **<symbol>** is the name of the symbol to which the property list is attached, **<indicator>** is the property indicator, and the optional argument **<default>** is the value to be returned in the event the indicator does not exist. The default value of **<default>** itself is **NIL**.

We can therefore retrieve Harry's age as follows:

```
* (get 'harry 'age)
30
```

If we try to retrieve the value of a nonexistent property:

```
* (get 'harry 'wife-name)
NIL
```

A source of past confusion in the use of property lists was that if a particular property was set to **NIL** during the course of a program, and if an attempt was made to retrieve the value of that property, there was no way of knowing if the property simply did not exist or if it *did* exist but had a value of **NIL**. The <**default**> argument can be used to circumvent this problem. For example:

```
* (setf (get 'harry 'hobbies) nil)
NIL
* (symbol-plist 'harry)
(HOBBIES NIL WEIGHT 150 AGE 30)
* (get 'harry 'hobbies 'no-such-indicator)
NIL
```

but:

```
(get 'harry 'wife-name 'no-such-indicator)
NO-SUCH-INDICATOR
```

thus discerning between a property with a value of **NIL** and a nonexistent property. (The value of <**default**> should of course be some data object which would never be the same as any possible property value.)

18.5 getf provides a more general way of retrieving a value

getf is a function which provides for a more general way of retrieving a value from a list of indicator/value pairs which is not necessarily the property list of a given symbol. The syntax is:

```
(getf <place> <indicator> &optional <default>)
```

where <**place**> must evaluate to a list. For example, let's create a sort of imitation property list which is the value of the symbol **rita**:

```
(setf rita '(age 40 profession lecturer))
(AGE 40 PROFESSION LECTURER)
```

We can retrieve a value from this list using **getf**:

```
* (getf rita 'age)
40
```

We can also add new indicator/value pairs to this list with a **setf** operation similar to that which we used to augment a property list:

```
* (setf (getf rita 'home) 'Singapore)
(HOME SINGAPORE AGE 40 PROFESSION LECTURER)
```

noting the difference that we do not quote the symbol name (since we want it to be evaluated), and that the entire list is returned.

18.6 **get-properties** searches for an indicator

The function **get-properties**, which takes the syntax:

```
(get-properties <place> <indicator-list>)
```

searches a list of indicator/value pairs contained on the list which is the value of <place>, looking for an indicator which is a member of <indicator-list>. If no indicator meeting the test is found, **get-properties** returns *three* values, all of which are **NIL**. If an indicator meeting the test is found, the three values returned by **get-properties** are the indicator, the value associated with that indicator, and the tail of the list commencing with the indicator/value pair just found. For example:

```
* (setf place-list '(one sun two shoe three tree four door))
(ONE SUN TWO SHOE THREE TREE FOUR DOOR)
* (get-properties place-list '(five six seven)
NIL
NIL
NIL
```

but:

```
* (get-properties place-list '(two four six eight))
TWO
SHOE
(TWO SHOE THREE TREE FOUR DOOR)
```

In the case of a successful retrieval, the third (non-**NIL**) value returned by **get-properties** can be used (after removal of the first two elements) as data for further comparison against the list of indicators.

18.7 **remprop** removes an indicator/value pair

remprop, which takes the syntax:

```
(remprop <symbol> <indicator>)
```

removes an indicator/value pair from a property list by destructively splicing the list to exclude it. For example:

```
* (remprop 'harry 'weight)
T
```

If the removal operation is successful, **T** is returned. If we now check Harry's property list:

```
* (symbol-plist 'harry)
(HOBBIES (GOLF TENNIS) AGE 30)
```

we see that the **weight 150** indicator/value pair has been deleted.

18.8 remf is the generalized variable version of remprop

In much the same way as we used **getf** to add an indicator/value pair to a generalized property list, we can use **remf** destructively to remove an indicator/value pair from such a list:

```
* (remf rita 'age)
T
```

As with **remprop**, **remf** returns **T** if a removal operation has been successful; otherwise it returns **NIL**. Checking our generalized property list:

```
* rita
(HOME SINGAPORE PROFESSION LECTURER)
```

we see that the **age 40** pair has been removed.

18.9 Property value assignments made to a locally bound symbol persist after the function is exited

It is of interest to note that property value assignments made to a symbol while that symbol is locally bound within a function persist after the function is exited. For example:

```
* (setf (get 'harry 'status) 'not-said-hello-to)
NOT-SAID-HELLO-TO
* (defun say-hello (name)
    (setf (get name 'status) 'said-hello-to)
    (format nil "HELLO, ~a!" name))
SAY-HELLO
* (say-hello 'harry)
"HELLO, HARRY!"
* (get 'harry 'status)
SAID-HELLO-TO
```

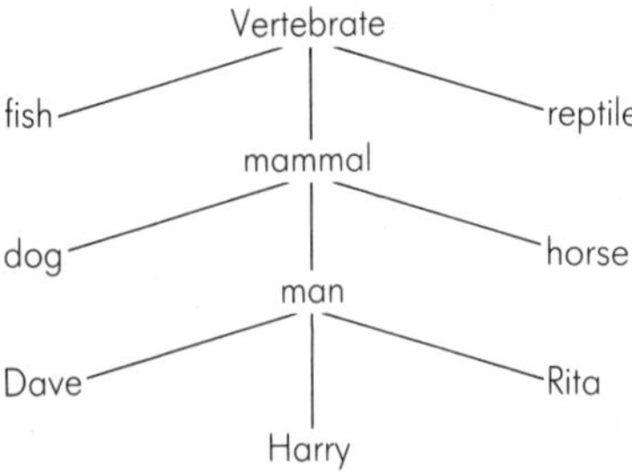

Fig. 18.3 Hierarchical retrieval structure can be created.

Although the property assignment was made to the symbol **harry** while this symbol was bound within **say-hello**, the effect of the property assignment persisted after the function was exited. (The same thing would be true of a function definition assigned to **harry** while bound as a local variable.) Hence it is only the **value** of the symbol which is transient during the time it is locally bound and which reverts to its former value after the function is exited.

18.10 The is-a property facilitates a hierarchical retrieval structure

An interesting extension of the property list concept is to link property lists with higher level property lists in a hierarchical fashion. If we consider the hierarchy in Fig. 18.3 we see that we can set up a kind of data base in which certain symbols can inherit information from higher level symbols. For example, if we should wish to ask whether Harry has a skeleton and the information is not readily available on Harry's property list, we should be able to look at the property list of a higher level symbol. To the extent that the information sought is extremely general, say, relating to the basic characteristics of a vertebrate, it may be necessary to work our way all the way up to the vertebrate property list before we find the answer.

Such a hierarchical structure may be linked with the **is-a** property. For instance, **Harry**'s property list would include the indicator **is-a** with the value **man**; similarly, the **is-a** property on **man**'s property list would have the value **mammal**, etc. We can define appropriate functions which, if the information being sought is not contained in a given property list, will see if an **is-a** property exists and, if so, will search the next higher level property list for the answer (see Exercise 18.7). We will see this concept extended later when we get into AI applications involving the use of **frames**.

18.11 Association lists are somewhat similar to property lists

Another mechanism for storing data related to a particular key is through use of an *association list*, which consists of a series of *key/datum pairs* in a manner somewhat similar to a property list. However there are some important differences.

- Whereas a property list generally serves to collect a variety of properties associated with some particular symbol, an association list gathers together key/datum pairs in which the keys generally have something in common and each datum is in some way related to its key.
- Whereas property lists store their information in the form of a continuous list of indicator/value elements, association lists store their information as a series of dotted pairs (see Section 5.7).
- Similarly to a property list, a new key/datum pair is added to the front of an association list. However whereas an indicator only appears once on a property list, the same key can appear more than once on an association list. When searching an association list, the most recent key, that is, the one nearest the front of the list, is used as a basis for retrieving a value.
- Whereas the indicator in a property list must be a symbol, the key in an association list may be either a symbol or a list.

The most common way of creating an association list is by using a simple **setf** statement, in which the list consists of a series of dotted pairs:

```
* (setf city-list '((dallas . texas)(albany new york)
    ((las vegas) . nevada)))
((DALLAS . TEXAS)(ALBANY NEW YORK)((LAS VEGAS) . NEVADA))
```

in which each city can later be accessed with a retrieval function to ascertain the state in which it is located. Note that it is unnecessary to include the dot where the second element of the pair is itself a list.

18.12 pairlis can be used to create an association list

Another way of creating an association list is with **pairlis**, which takes the syntax:

```
* (pairlis <key-list> <datum-list> &optional <a-list>)
```

This function returns an association list which is formed by adding the pairs created by combining one element from <**key-list**> with the corresponding element from <**datum-list**>. For example:

```
* (setf food-list '(spaghetti snails (paella valenciana)))
(SPAGHETTI SNAILS (PAELLA VALENCIANA))
* (setf city-list '(rome paris madrid))
(ROME PARIS MADRID)
```

```
* (setf where-to-eat (pairlis food-list city-list))
((SPAGHETTI . ROME)(SNAILS . PARIS)
  ((PAELLA VALENCIANA) . MADRID))
```

The optional argument <a-list> may be used where it is desired to append the list produced by **pairlis** to the front of an existing **a-list**.

18.13 A new key/datum pair can be added with acons

Once an association list has been created we can augment it with **acons**, which takes the syntax:

```
(acons <key> <datum> <a-list>)
```

and adds a new key/datum pair to the front of the list. For example:

```
* (setf where-to-eat
  (acons '(hot dogs) '(coney island) where-to-eat)
(((HOT DOGS) CONEY ISLAND)(SPAGHETTI . ROME)
  (SNAILS . PARIS)((PAELLA VALENCIANA) . MADRID))
```

again noting that dotted pair notation is not required when the second element of the pair is itself a list.

18.14 assoc is used to search an association list

Having created an association list by one of the above methods, **assoc** can be used to retrieve the datum associated with a particular key. This function takes the syntax:

```
(assoc <item> <a-list> &key :test)
```

where <**item**> is the key and <**a-list**> is the name of the association list.

The optional keyword **:test**, which defaults to #'**eql**, must be a functional predicate of some kind. If a simple match is being sought against a symbol name (or, conceivably, a number), the default may be used. However if the key is a list, **:test** #'**equal** must explicitly be specified to cover this contingency (see Section 8.6). Alternatively, other user-defined predicate tests may be specified to test the acceptability of the key.

assoc returns the key/datum pair:

```
* (assoc 'snails where-to-eat)
(SNAILS . PARIS)
```

Hence some additional list manipulation with **cdr** (*not* **cadr**, since we are dealing with dotted pairs) is required to extract the datum, that is:

```
* (cdr (assoc 'snails where-to-eat))
PARIS
```

Note that if the key element is a list, the above syntax would not work. We would have to include explicitly the **:test** keyword:

```
* (assoc '(hot dogs) where-to-eat :test #'equal)
((HOT DOGS) CONEY ISLAND)
```

Athough the above example has used a mixture of symbols and lists to illustrate the flexibility of association lists, in practice it is desirable to maintain structural consistency between the data objects being used as keys and as values, so that standardized access functions can be used to retrieve information in a consistent manner.

18.15 rassoc searches for the datum rather than the key

Whereas **assoc** searches the association list looking for a *key*, **rassoc** works in the reverse manner to find a *datum* and returns the key/datum pair. The syntax is similar to **assoc**

```
(rassoc <item> <a-list> &key :test)
```

For example:

```
* (rassoc 'paris where-to-eat)
(SNAILS . PARIS)
```

Similarly as noted for **assoc**, it would be necessary to specify **:test #'equal** explicitly if the datum, for example **(CONEY ISLAND)** is a list.

18.16 copy-alist copies an association list

copy-alist may be used to copy an association list. It takes the syntax:

```
(copy-alist <a-list>)
```

and returns an exact copy of the association list.

18.17 Association list pairs can be deleted

Since an association list is of type *sequence*, it is possible to remove an association list pair using the functions **remove** or **delete** (Section 26.9), for example:

```
* (delete (assoc 'snails where-to-eat) where-to-eat)
(((HOT DOGS) CONEY ISLAND)(SPAGHETTI . ROME)
   ((PAELLA VALENCIANA) . MADRID))
```

SUMMARY

Summarizing the key points of this chapter:

- a special cell associated with each symbol is used to point to the *property list* of the symbol
- a property list consists of a set of *indicator/value pairs* in which the indicator is used as a key
- **setf** is used to assign an indicator and its value to a property list
- a property may be retrieved with **get**. The whole property list can be retrieved with **symbol-plist**. **getf** is the generalized variable equivalent of **get**.
- **get-properties** searches for an indicator which matches one of those on a list
- a property indicator/value pair may be removed with **remprop**. **remf** is the generalized variable equivalent of **remprop**
- the **is-a** property facilitates a hierarchical retrieval structure based on inheritance
- *association lists* are somewhat similar to property lists, and can be created by a **setf** assignment or by using **pairlis**
- a key may be duplicated in an association list, in which case a search will return the value associated with the key nearest the front of the list
- **assoc** is used to search an association list for a key; **rassoc** is used to search for a datum
- a new key/datum pair can be added to an a-list with **acons**
- **copy-alist** copies an association list

EXERCISES

18.1 Some microcomputer versions of LISP use the function **put** to add a key/datum pair to a property list. Write your own version of **put**, which takes the syntax:

```
(put <symbol-name> <indicator-name> <value>)
```

and returns the value.

18.2 Many implementations of LISP store key/datum information in the form of dotted pairs instead of a single extended list. Define the function put-prop, which adds to or updates such a property list. Use put-prop to redefine the property list for Harry as per Section 18.3, such that symbol-plist would return the following value:

((HOBBIES GOLF TENNIS)(WEIGHT . 150)(AGE . 30))

In other respects, put-prop is similar to put.

NB: You may wish to use assoc to find the key/value pair. Since setf cannot be used to invert a value returned by assoc, one permissible solution is to delete the old key/value pair before cons'ing the replacement pair to the front of the property list.

18.3 Define the function get-prop, which accesses the kind of property list described in Exercise 18.2 and returns only the datum rather than the entire key/datum pair. If the key does not exist or if the associated value is NIL, get-prop returns NIL.

18.4 Define the function rem-prop which destructively removes the key/datum pair from the property list described in Exercise 18.2. If the pair is successfully found and removed then rem-prop returns the pair; otherwise it returns NIL.

18.5 Define the function get-indicators which takes as its single argument the name of a symbol and returns a list of all of the indicator keys on that symbol's property list.

18.6 Create place-list as per Section 18.6 and define the function search-place-list which takes the syntax:

(search-place-list <place-list> <indicator-list>)

For any given <indicator-list>, search-place-list uses get-properties to compare the two lists and returns a list containing all of the key/datum pairs in which there was a successful match. For example, using the indicator list '(ONE THREE), search-place-list should return the list ((ONE SUN)(THREE TREE)).

18.7 Define the function get-inherit (see Section 18.10), which operates on a property list like get except that if the property indicator does not exist or its value is NIL, get-inherit operates recursively to explore higher level property lists connected by is-a links. get-inherit returns the first value found in a higher level list, or NIL if no values are found.

18.8 Create the association list book-list in which each key is an author's (last) name and the datum is a string containing the title of a book. Define the function add-book which repetitively prompts for the name of an author and then for a title (which is input in the form of a string), and adds the key/datum pair to the list. Exit the loop if 'exit' is input in response to either prompt.

18.9 Define the function get-book which prompts for the (last) name of an author, searches the list created by Exercise 18.8, and returns the title of the most recent book written by that author. If there is no such author on the list, print a message to this effect.

18.10 Define the function **get-author** which prompts for the title of a book (which is input in the form of a string), searches the list created by Exercise 18.8, and returns the author's name. If there is no such book on the list, print a message to this effect.

Chapter 19

Working with Streams

In the course of an interactive session with our LISP interpreter, information is passing in and out of the system in the form of expressions typed in at the keyboard, values printed out on the console, data sent to files, and perhaps characters directed to the printer. In order to provide for the proper routing of all this data from one location to another, Common LISP (and GCLISP) utilize a kind of data object called a *stream*.

Unlike other LISP data objects, streams cannot readily be visualized as a kind of structure. Rather, they represent a mechanism for interfacing between the various components of your operating system. If you are only typing in expressions on the keyboard and getting back responses on the console there is little need to worry about streams, since you are operating with the default streams *standard-input* (= the keyboard) and *standard-output* (= the console). However when you start accessing files or directing output to the printer you must create specific streams to provide an interface with these devices.

In this chapter we will look at:

- the nature of *streams*, and how they are used to permit communication between input and output devices
- the seven standard streams supported by Common LISP, how they are used, and what they default to
- the manner in which streams are created (opened) and how they are closed
- the use of with-open-file which closes a file automatically after a read or write operation
- the use of make-string-input-stream to create a stream to access a string of characters
- how make-string-output-stream and get-output-stream-string may be used to accumulate and retrieve a string
- the manner in which streams may be used as functions

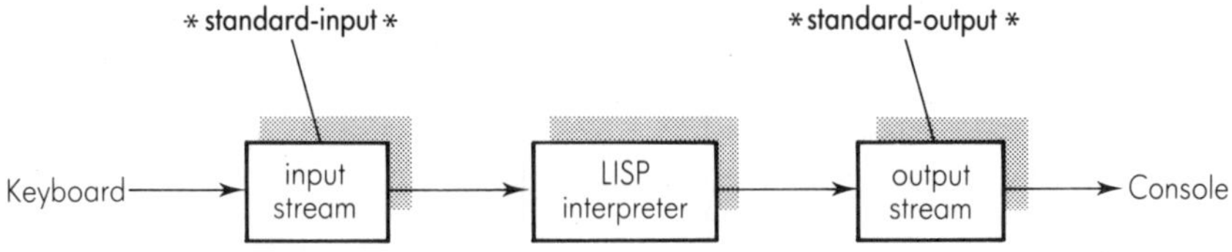

Fig. 19.1 Streams create an interface with peripheral devices.

19.1 Streams provide an interface with peripherals and files

Information inevitably flows *from* someplace *to* someplace. In this context a stream may be thought of as a kind of conduit which connects the two places and facilitates the flow of data between them. Another way of thinking of a stream is as a kind of *data-handling* manager which:

- establishes an interface between the input device and the LISP interpreter, and provides for the receipt of information from the input device in accordance with the kind of read function which is being used to input the data
- establishes an interface between the LISP interpreter and the output device, and provides for the delivery of information in accordance with the kind of print or write function which is being used to output the data

When you use the interpreter in interactive mode you are actually using two streams: one to provide for input of data and the other to print the values returned on the console. Since these streams are the system defaults you don't have to specify them explicitly (see Fig. 19.1).

Input from the keyboard is handled by the stream *standard-input* which in effect provides an interface between the keyboard and the LISP interpreter. The value returned by the read/eval/print process is handled by the stream *standard-output* which provides the interface between the interpreter and the console.

19.2 GCLISP supports seven standard streams

Seven standard streams are provided by GCLISP to handle a variety of input/output situations. These may be diagramatically illustrated as shown in Fig. 19.2. The most basic stream is *terminal-io* which provides for input from the keyboard and output to the console. The 'io' (in/out) refers to the fact that this is a type of stream which can handle information flowing two ways. This stream should never be changed by the user, since it represents

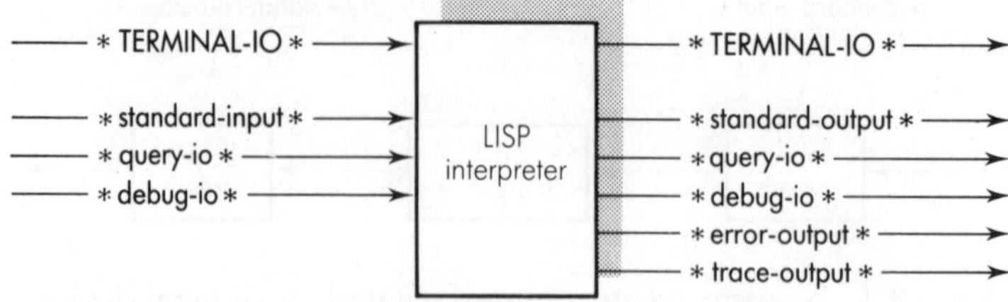

Fig. 19.2 GCLISP supports seven standard streams.

the most basic mode of communication between the interpreter and the outside world.

The streams *standard-input* and *standard-output* control the manner in which data is currently being input and output, respectively. When you are typing in data at the keyboard and getting values returned on the console, both of these streams are in turn initialized to default to the value of *terminal-io*. When you wish to get data from some other source you have to create a special stream for this purpose and specify it as an argument to a read operation (which otherwise is using *standard-input* as a default). Similarly, when directing data to some other output device you have to create a special stream and specify it as an argument to a print operation, which otherwise is using *standard-output* as a default.

The *query-io* stream is used to handle y-or-n-p and yes-or-no-p queries (see Section 12.11) which may arise in the course of a program. Unless otherwise specified, *query-io* defaults to *terminal-io*, which is where you would normally want to have it, that is, with queries being printed on the console and the user's response entered at the keyboard.

The *debug-io* stream is used to handle interactive debugging, and similarly defaults to *terminal-io* which is where you would normally want to carry out debugging activities. (NB: The GCLISP error system functions error and cerror use this stream instead of *error-output*.)

The *error-output* stream has been included in GCLISP for compatibility with Common LISP; however the GCLISP error functions instead utilize the *debug-io* stream. The *error-output* stream defaults to *standard-io*.

The *trace-output* stream is used to handle the output of the trace function. This stream defaults to *standard-io* which is where you would normally want trace printouts to appear, that is, the console.

When you boot up GCLISP you can check the values of all of the above streams by evaluating the stream-name variables, for example:

```
* *standard-input*
#<DYNAMIC CLOSURE 30B5:E34>
```

If you do this with all of the stream variables you will find that all of the streams except *terminal-io* will be bound to the same closure. This closure is in turn a synonym stream (see below) for *terminal-io*, which means that until such time as any of these streams are specifically changed to something else the input for all of them will come from the keyboard and the output from all of them will be printed on the console.

19.3 Output streams are needed to print data to a file

Whenever your LISP program is required to access anything other than the keyboard or the console for input or output, a special stream must be created to serve as an interface between the program and the external device or file. Such streams may be created with open, which takes the syntax:

```
(open pathname &key :direction <direction>
                    :element-type <element-type>)
```

The pathname, which must be entered in the form of a string, for example, "b:testfile.lsp", specifies the location of the external device or file. This will be explored in more detail in Chapter 23. For the moment, assume that a pathname to a file may be simply represented as a string possibly containing a disk drive code, as in the above example referring to the file named testfile.lsp on drive B. If you are directing output to the printer it may be referred to as prn or lpt1; either designation is recognized by GCLISP and MS-DOS.

The keyword argument :direction refers to whether the stream being opened will be used for output *to* a device, in which case the argument :output would be specified, or whether the stream will be used for input *from* a device, in which case :input would be specified (or left blank, since :input is the default). Version 1.1 of GCLISP also supports :io streams, which permit both input and output operations to be carried on to a file.

If you specify (or take by default) :direction :input, or if you specify :direction :io, the sytem will assume that you want to read information from a file and will check to see if file <path-name> exists. If it does, an input or in/out stream will be created to provide the necessary interface. If it does not, an error message will be generated.

If you specify :direction :output the system will similarly check to see if file <pathname> exists and will create an output stream to the file. If the file does not exist a new file will automatically be created. If the file already exists, the file pointer will be reset to 0 so that anything you write will *overwrite* the previous contents of the file. (The Common LISP :append option to the :if-exists keyword, which permits data to be added to the end of an existing file, is not supported by GCLISP. Later, in Chapter 23, we will devise ways of adding data to the end of a existing file.)

The keyword argument :element-type specifies the type of data to be supplied to or from the stream. GCLISP supports only the two options string-char, which is the default, and unsigned-byte.

When creating a stream with **open** you will usually assign the stream as the value of some symbol with **setf**, for example:

```
(setf <some-symbol-name>)
  (open <some-pathname> :direction <direction>)
```

with the added keyword **:element-type** required only when handling unsigned bytes. The symbol-name will then be used as the **<stream>** argument for the various **read** and **print** functions.

Let's look at an output example in which we will create the file **test-01.lsp** on drive B and put some data into it. (For consistency with the GMACS editor we will use the **.lsp** extension for all of our test files.) Arbitrarily calling the stream **out-stream**:

```
* (setf out-stream (open "b:test-01.lsp" :direction :output))
#<DYNAMIC CLOSURE nnnn:nnnn>
```

The act of opening a stream creates a data object called a **dynamic closure** (see Chapter 30 for more on closures), which is returned as a value by **open.** We can now output data to the file with any appropriate **print** function. Let's output two lines of text to the file:

```
* (print "How now brown cow!" out-stream)
"How now brown cow!"
* (print "Now is the time" out-stream)
"Now is the time!"
```

The next thing we want to do at this stage is to check whether the file has been created and, if so, whether the text has been put into the file. Assuming that we have created the file on drive B, we can check the first item by temporarily returning to DOS with a **(sys:dos)** command, logging on to drive B, and scanning the directory. We find the file listed as follows:

TEST-01 LSP 0 <today's date and time>

Although the file has been created, we are mildly disconcerted to note that there appears to be no data in it. If we try a **type** command to display the contents of the file nothing is displayed. If we go back to GCLISP and try to read from the file we immediately get an **EOF** error. Has some bug gotten into our **print** operation?

In fact, the two lines of text are in the file. The only problem is that the file has not yet been **closed**. The file pointer, which was set to 0 when the file was created, has therefore not been updated to reflect the new text which has just been added. The moral is: when you write data to a file, before you can **read** that data you have first to **close** the file to update the file pointer.

19.4 close-all-files and close are used to terminate streams

The function **close-all-files** may be used to close, in one fell swoop, all streams which are connected to files. This function returns a list of the pathnames of all of the streams which were closed. If no streams are currently open it simply returns **NIL**.

Let's use it to close the file which we have just been working on:

```
* (close-all-files)
(#.(PATHNAME "B:TEST-01.LSP"))
```

If we now repeat the previous exercise with DOS and the directory scan, we see that the file is listed as follows:

TEST-01 LSP 24 <today's date and time>

The act of closing the file has updated the file pointer, and we can now access the contents via an input stream. As illustrated by the above example, it is good practice to close a file as soon as you have finished printing to it.

Whereas **close-all-files** only closes streams connected to files, the related function **close** can be used to close *any* stream. Its syntax is simply:

```
(close <stream-name>)
```

Unlike **close-all-files**, close merely returns **NIL** when it closes a stream.

19.5 Input streams are needed to read data from a file

If we want to **read** from the file we must now create a different stream, this time to get input *from* the file. Arbitrarily calling our input stream **in-stream**:

```
* (setf in-stream (open "b:test-01.lsp" :direction :input)
#<DYNAMIC CLOSURE nnnn:nnnn)
```

Since we put two strings of text into the file with a print operation, which left the double quote marks intact, it would be appropriate to read them out again using **read**:

```
* (read in-stream)
"How now brown cow!
* (read in-stream)
"Now is the time!"
```

If we try another **read** operation:

```
* (read in-stream)
ERROR:
EOF on stream: #<DYNAMIC CLOSURE nnnn:nnnn)
1>
```

Since we reached end-of-file and made no specific provisions for this contingency, an error message was generated. Normally we would set up a loop to read text lines in a manner similar to that illustrated by read-ex-string (see Section 10.8), including a NIL value for eof-error-p and some suitable value (say, 'eof) for eof-value. If we had done this, the previous read operation would have had the syntax and would have generated the result as follows:

```
* (read input-stream nil 'eof)
EOF
```

We can use this value returned in a terminating test to exit the loop under control in the same manner as we did for read-ex-string.

19.6 with-open-file opens a file, evaluates forms, and automatically closes the file

As we saw above, open merely creates a stream to permit access to a file, after which we have to close it explicitly. A much easier way to access files is by using with-open-file, which provides more extensive features including automatic closing of the file after the desired operations have been carried out. The syntax of this macro is:

```
(with-open-file
  (<stream-name> <pathname> &optional
    :direction <direction>
    :element-type <element-type>)
  <form1> <form2> ... <formn>)
```

Following the macro name is a separate embedded list containing the arguments as shown. The <stream-name>, which must be a symbol, is bound to the stream which is opened by with-open-file. This name may therefore be used as the stream argument in subsequent read or print statements which may be included among the forms. The <pathname> is the same as described above for open. The (optional) keywords are the same as those used with open and are evaluated in the same manner. Following the argument list may be any number of forms which are evaluated, with the value of the last form being returned by the function.

The purpose of with-open-file is to permit you to open a file, do something with it (put data in or take data out), and close the file, all within the aegis of a single function call. We can duplicate the operations we carried out previously on b:test-01.lsp but this time using with-open-file and creating a new file **b:test-02.lsp**:

```
* (with-open-file
    (out-stream "b:test-02.lsp" :direction :output)
    (print "Now is the time!" out-stream)
    (print "For all good men!" out-stream))
; Autoload: WITH-OPEN-FILE from "MACRO" in
    "C:\\GCLISP\\LISPLIB\\."
"For all good men!"
```

If this is the first time **with-open-file** has been called during the current session, there will be a brief pause while the system loads the definition from the utility file, after which the above function call will be evaluated. **with-open-file** creates (in this case) and opens a stream to **b:test-02.lsp**, prints the data into the file, and closes the file. The value returned by the last **print** statement is returned.

Since we don't have any other files open at the moment, we can use **close-all-files** as a quick check that **with-open-file** has indeed actually closed the file:

```
* (close-all-files)
NIL
```

We can now use **open** and **read**, as illustrated in Section 10.9, to examine the contents of the file. Alternatively we can return to DOS and type out the contents. As a third alternative, we can use **with-open-file** again, this time in input mode:

```
* (with-open-file
    (in-stream "b:test-02.lsp" :direction :input)
    (let (phrase)
      (loop
        (setf phrase (read in-stream nil 'eof))
        (if (equal phrase 'eof)
            (return))
        (terpri)
        (princ phrase))))
Now is the time!
For all good men!
NIL
```

In this case **with-open-file** opened the file, created an input stream to it, read the two strings from the file, and automatically closed the file when end-of-file was reached. In view of these convenient features you would normally use **with-open-file** rather than **open** and **close** when accessing disk files.

19.7 with-open-stream automatically closes a stream after use

The related macro with-open-stream takes the syntax:

```
(with-open-stream (<var><stream>) <forms>)
```

The form <stream> is evaluated and must return a stream object. The variable <var> is bound to this stream as its value. After evaluating the following forms, as in an implicit progn, the stream is automatically closed, no matter whether the exit is normal or abnormal.

19.8 make-synonym-stream permits an alternative name to be specified for the same stream

The function make-synonym-stream sets up a relationship between two symbols such that they are both bound to the same stream; moreover, if the first symbol becomes bound to a different stream, the second symbol will automatically follow suit. The syntax is as follows:

```
(make-synonym-stream <symbol>)
```

which creates and returns a so-called *synonym stream*. Its use is best illustrated by example:

```
* (setf first-stream
    (open "b:test-03.lsp" :direction :output)
#<DYNAMIC CLOSURE nnnn:nnnn>
```

We have now established a new stream bound to the symbol first-stream. This output stream is linked to the file test-03.lsp which has just been created on drive B. If we now create a new symbol second-stream and assign it the value of first-stream

```
* (setf second-stream first-stream)
#<DYNAMIC CLOSURE nnnn:nnnn>
```

the second symbol becomes bound to the same stream as the first symbol, and we can use *either* stream name to direct output to file B:test-03.lsp. If at this point we change the binding of first-stream to some other stream, second-stream will remain bound to the original output stream linked to B:test-03.lsp.

However we may want to arrange matters such that, if some different stream is bound to first-stream, the change in binding will also carry over to second-stream. We can do this as follows:

```
* (make-synonym-stream second-stream)
#<DYNAMIC CLOSURE nnnn:nnnn>
```

which effectively establishes a linkage between **second-stream** and **first-stream** such that any changes in the binding of the latter are automatically applied to the former as well.

As mentioned earlier, all of the six standard streams ***standard-input***, ***standard-output***, ***query-io***, ***debug-io***, ***error-output***, and ***trace-output*** are initially bound to synonym streams which pass all operations on to the stream that is the value of ***terminal-io***.

19.9 make-string-input-stream turns a string into a stream

In Chapter 10 we looked at **read-from-string**, a function which permitted us to read a single atom or list from a string. However there will be times, particularly when working with English language, when we will want to use **read-char** to access a string on a character-by-character basis. In order to provide for such sequential access an input stream must be created. **make-string-input-stream**, which may be used for this purpose, takes the following format:

```
(make-string-input-stream <string> &optional <start> <end>)
```

Deferring discussion of the optional arguments for a moment, let's apply the function to a string:

```
* (make-string-input-stream "abc")
#<DYNAMIC CLOSURE nnnn:nnnn>
```

The function has returned an input stream which contains the sequence of characters contained in the string "**abc**". However in order to utilize the stream as a source of characters we have to give it a name which can be provided as the optional <**stream**> argument to **read-char**. Calling our input stream **in-stream**:

```
* (setf in-stream (make-string-input-stream "abc"))
#<DYNAMIC CLOSURE nnnn:nnnn>
```

We can now use **read-char** to read characters from the stream:

```
* (read-char in-stream)
97

* (read-char in-stream)
98
```

It will be noted that **read-char** is reading its way character by character through the string, returning the decimal ASCII character codes. We can envision a pointer moving along the string which is updated each time a **read-char** operation is carried out, as illustrated in Fig. 19.3.

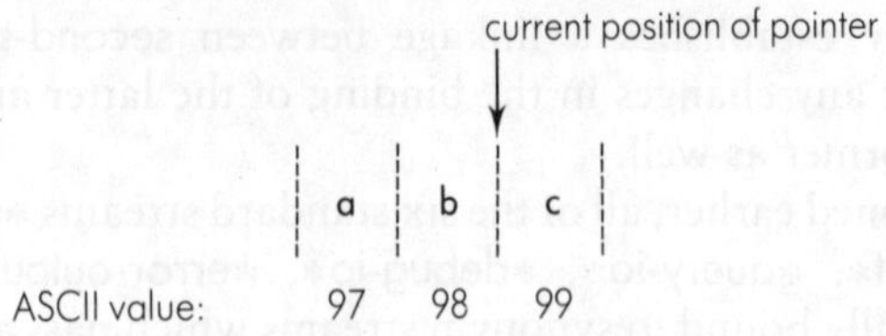

Fig. 19.3 The string pointer is updated by each **read-char** operation.

Since ASCII values are not too illuminating, let's convert the next character we read back to graphic form with **string**:

```
* (string (read-char in-stream))
"c"
```

Our pointer has now been advanced to the end of the string. What happens if we try to read another character?

```
* (read-char in-stream)
ERROR:
EOF on stream: #<DYNAMIC CLOSURE nnnn:nnnn>
1>
```

Again, we have reached end-of-file without making specific provisions for this contingency. The same comments apply as in our earlier example with **read**.

Before looking at the manner in which the optional arguments may be used, it may be useful to define a function to check the contents of a stream. (We will use this function shortly to see if the <start> and <end> arguments are working properly.) Calling the function **char-ex-string**:

```
* (defun char-ex-string (string-input-stream)
    (let (character)
     (terpri)
     (loop
      (setf character
        (read-char string-input-stream nil 'eof))
      (if (equal character 'eof)
         (return nil))
      (princ (string character)))))
```

As each character is read it is converted to its graphic form and printed on the console. When end-of-file is reached **read-char** returns 'eof, the **if** test succeeds, and the loop is exited under control.

If we create a new input stream and try out **char-ex-string**:

```
* (setf in-stream (make-string-input-stream "hello"))
#<DYNAMIC CLOSURE nnnn:nnnn>
```

```
* (char-ex-string in-stream)
hello
NIL
```

What happens if we repeat the call to **char-ex-string**?

```
* (char-ex-string in-stream)
NIL
```

Since the stream has been completely read by the first application of **char-ex-string** the file pointer is at end-of-file; hence there is nothing left to read and the function returns **NIL**.

The optional arguments <**start**> and <**end**> can be used to specify the limits of the substring to be read from a given string. Keeping in mind that the first character is index position 0, we can extract a substring by applying the <**start**> and <**end**> arguments:

```
* (setf in-stream
   (make-string-input-stream "abcdefghijk" 3 7))
   #<DYNAMIC CLOSURE nnnn:nnnn>
```

We can now use our previously defined function **char-ex-string** to check the results:

```
* (char-ex-string in-stream)
defgh
```

We see that the substring from **d** (index position 3) to **h** (index position 7) has been properly transferred to **in-stream**.

For further examples of accessing strings created by **make-string-input-stream**, see Exercises 19.5 and 19.8.

19.10 make-string-output-stream permits characters to be accumulated into a string

There may be instances where you want to generate groups of characters in individual batches and periodically recover each batch as a separate string. Also there may be times when you want to convert the **value** of a symbol into a string. (The name of the symbol itself can be directly supplied as a string with **symbol-name**.) Alternatively you may want to take a list and convert it to a string for further string-oriented manipulations. All of this can be accomplished by using **make-string-output-stream**, which creates an output stream into which *any* input – be it an atom, a list, or a string – is evaluated and the value converted into a string. The resulting string can then be recovered using **get-output-stream-string** (see below), after which the output string index pointer will be reset to 0 in preparation to receive the next batch of characters. **make-string-output-stream**, which takes no arguments, creates the stream and returns it:

```
* (setf out-stream (make-string-output-stream))
#<CLOSURE nnnn:nnnn>
* (princ "abcdef" out-stream)
"abcdef"
```

Note that this is one of the rare instances when we use **princ** for printing to other than the console or printer. If we used **prin1**, upon subsequent recovery of the string with **get-output-string-stream** we would find ourselves with an extra set of embedded quotation marks.

Let's now recover the string with **get-output-stream-string**:

19.11 get-output-stream-string collects the accumulated characters from the output string

As each batch of characters is accumulated into the output string it may be recovered by **get-output-stream-string**, which takes as a single argument the name of the stream. Applying this function to the above stream:

```
* (get-output-stream-string out-stream)
"abcdef"
```

The available characters having been read, the output-stream index pointer is reset to 0. If we try to read from it again:

```
* (get-output-stream-string out-stream)
""
```

Since there are no characters to read we get an empty string "" and will continue to get this value until such time as a print or write operation puts something back into **out-stream**.

At times we may wish to convert a symbol's value into a string. In Chapter 12 we discussed ways in which to generate an output string such as **"The temperature is 68 degrees Fahrenheit"**, representing a mixture of two strings and a value. Assuming that **temp** still has the value **68**, we can incorporate it into the string as follows:

```
* (princ temp out-stream)
68
* (setf output (string-append
    "The temperature is "
    (get-output-from-string out-stream)
    " degrees Fahrenheit"))
 "The temperature is 68 degrees Fahrenheit"
```

The combined string has thus been assigned as the value of **output** and can be printed with a single (**princ output**) statement. Using **make-string-output-**

stream we can also define a substitute for Common LISP's **princ-to-string**, which is not supported by GCLISP (see Exercise 19.6).

Finally, we can convert a list to a string using **make-string-output-stream**:

```
* (princ '(This is a quoted list) out-stream))
"(THIS IS A QUOTED LIST)"
* (get-output-from-string out-stream)
"(THIS IS A QUOTED LIST)"
```

19.12 Streams can be used as functions

As we discussed before, streams are an unusual kind of data object in that they provide an interface between the LISP interpreter and external devices. A further unique property of GCLISP streams is that they may be used as a kind of *function* in a manner reminiscent of **object-oriented programming**. As an example, if we have created an output stream called ***out-stream*** and want to write a character to it we can use the following syntax:

```
(funcall *out-stream* :write-char <character>)
```

The manner in which **funcall** is operating on ***out-stream*** denotes the latter's use as a function. The first argument after the **<stream>** function must be a *keyword* (preceded by colons), which indicates the *operation* that the stream function is to perform on the rest of the arguments. In this case the keyword is **:write-char** (see below) and its single argument is the character to be written. GCLISP also provides a function **send** which is exactly the same as **funcall** except that it better indicates the flavor of message-passing to the user. In subsequent examples we will use **send**.

Input streams explicitly support the following three basic operations:

- **:read-char** which, like the function **read-char**, inputs a single character from the stream. If no character is available it will be waited for. If end-of-file has been reached, **NIL** will be returned.
- **:unread-char** which, like the function **unread-char**, returns the most recent character read to the front of the stream.
- **:which-operations** which returns a list of keywords each of which names an operation supported by the stream

Output streams explicitly support the **:which-operations** operation as well as **:write-char** which, like the function **write-char**, outputs a single character to the stream.

By 'explicitly support' we mean that GCLISP has built into its input and output streams only these specific operations. However other operations can be incorporated by the user (see **stream-default-handler** below).

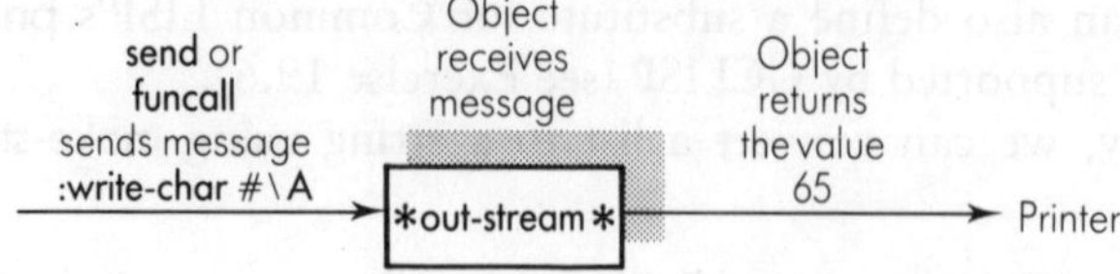

Fig. 19.4 GCLISP streams can be used as functions.

Let's open file **b:test-04** in the usual manner and write a character to it, this time using the stream as a function:

```
* (setf *out-stream* (open "b:test-04" :direction :output))
#<CLOSURE nnnn:nnnn>

* (send *out-stream* :write-char #\A)
65
```

Using **close-all-files** to close the file and update the end-of-file pointer:

```
* (close-all-files)
(#.(PATHNAME "B:TEST-04"))
```

If we now go back to DOS and type the file contents, we see that the character 'A' has been put into the file. Reversing the procedure to read from the file:

```
* (setf *in-stream* (open ":b:test-04" :direction :input)
#<DYNAMIC CLOSURE nnnn:nnnn>

* (send *in-stream* :read-char)
65
```

and we retrieve the character code of 'A.' If we try another read operation:

```
* (send *in-stream* :read-char)
NIL
```

the stream object simply returns **NIL** as a value, rather than generating an **eof** error message as we experienced earlier when using **read-char** as a function operating on a stream.

The object-oriented nature of a GCLISP stream used in this manner can be illustrated diagrammatically, as shown in Fig. 19.4, where **:write-char** acts as the message name, **#\A** as the message argument, and the value returned by the function call acts as the object returned by the receiver object.

19.13 Users can create their own streams

GCLISP permits users to define their own streams in exactly the same manner as functions are defined. User-defined input and output streams must handle, as a minimum, at least the operations listed above, that is: :read-char and :unread-char for input streams, :write-char for output streams, and :which-operations for both types of stream.

The GCLRM provides the following example of a user-defined input stream:

```
(defun newline-input-stream (operation &optional arguments)
  (case operation
    (:read-char #\Newline)
    (:unread-char)
    (:which-operations
      '(:read-char :unread-char :which-operations))
    (otherwise
      (error "Unknown input stream operation: ~s"
             operation))))
```

If we define the above and try it out:

```
* (newline-input-stream :read-char)
10
```

the :read-char clause reads in the ASCII code corresponding to a Newline. Other arguments will return values as per the case statement.

The GCLRM also provides the following example of a user-defined output stream:

```
(defparameter *list* '())

(defun list-output-stream (operation &optional arguments)
  (case operation
    (:write-char
      (setf *list* (append *list* (list arg))))
    (:which-operations
      '(:write-char :which-operations))
    (otherwise
      (error "Unknown output stream operation: ~s"
             operation))))
```

This output stream collects the actual characters which are output into a single list, which is the value of the global variable *list*. If we try it out with the character #\A:

```
* (list-output-stream :write-char #\A)
(65)
```

If we input more characters they will be added to *list* and the value of *list * returned. Other arguments will return values as per the case statement.

19.14 **stream-default-handler** extends the number of operations which a stream can handle

As noted above, the standard GCLISP streams are only structured to handle the four basic operations shown. A special function **stream-default-handler** is provided to handle any other operations which you might wish to create on a stream. In such a case, the **otherwise** option of the **case** could be used to pass on the operation and its arguments to **stream-default-handler**, in which case the last **case** clause in the above example would be amended to:

```
(otherwise
  (stream-default-handler <stream-name> <operation>
    &optional <arguments>))))
```

Assuming that the operation was nonstandard, the **:write-char** and **:which-operations** tests of **case** would not succeed, and the **otherwise** clause would call **stream-default-handler** to do the necessary work. (The error message would be transferred over to the last **case** clause of **stream-default-handler**.)

See pp. 187–8 of the GCLRM for the various additional operations which can be handled using **stream-default-handler**.

SUMMARY

Summarizing the main points of this chapter:

- *streams* are special data structures which provide an interface between the LISP interpreter and external devices such as the keyboard, console, printer or disk files
- GCLISP supports seven standard streams: *terminal-io*, *standard-input*, *standard-output*, *query-io*, *debug-io*, *error-output*, and *trace-output*
- the functions open and close may be used to create and close individual streams
- close-all-files may be used to close all open streams which are currently connected to files
- with-open-file is a convenient function which creates a stream, permits various operations to be carried out, and automatically closes the stream upon completion
- alternative symbol names can be used to refer to the same stream with make-synonym-stream
- a string can be connected to a stream with make-string-input-stream
- any LISP object can be converted to a string representation through use of make-string-output-stream, from which the string can be retrieved with get-output-stream-string
- a stream may be considered as a type of function and users can define functions which can be used as streams
- the number of operations which a stream can handle can be extended using stream-default-handler

EXERCISES

19.1 Using open and close, create an output stream to access the file test-01 on any convenient drive and print the following expressions to the file:

```
'(setq apples 10 pears 15 grapes 20)
'(defun add-em-up (one two three)
   (+ one two three))
'(add-em-up apples pears grapes)
```

Use progn to tie all of the necessary functions together into a single statement. After executing the progn, switch over temporarily to DOS and type the file contents to verify that the expressions have been filed properly.

19.2 Repeat Exercise 19.1 with a new file **test-02**, this time using **with-open-file.** Check with DOS and type the file contents to verify that the expressions have been filed properly.

19.3 Using **open** and **close**, create an input stream to read the expressions back from the file created in Exercise 19.1. As each expression is read, evaluate it and print the value returned on the console.

19.4 Repeat Exercise 19.3 using **with-open-file** to read from file **test-02.**

19.5 Define the function **string-to-list**, which displays an appropriate prompt and uses **read-line** to input a line of text. After creating a stream of the resulting string with **make-string-input-stream**, use **read** to retrieve the individual tokens, accumulate the tokens into a list, and return the list.

19.6 Define the Common LISP function **princ-to-string** which evaluates its single argument and returns the value in the form of a string. Use **make-string-output-stream** and **get-output-stream-string** to accumulate and retrieve the string.

19.7 Define the function **make-string-list** which converts a string to a list of tokens. Display an appropriate prompt and use **read-char** to read the input on a character-by-character basis. Accumulate the characters into a string created by **make-string-output-stream.** If an apostrophe, comma or period is encountered (ASCII character codes 39, 44 or 46), precede it with a single escape character. Parsing spaces (ASCII 32) as delimiters, use **get-output-stream-string** to retrieve each completed token, convert it into a symbol, and add it to a list. When the end of the text has been reached as indicated by a Newline (ASCII 10), return the list.

19.8 Define the function **make-list-string** which converts a list to a string of tokens. Display an appropriate prompt and use **read** to input a list. (Generate an error message if the input is not a list.) Convert the list into a string with **make-string-output-stream** and transfer it to an input stream with **make-string-input-stream** and **get-output-stream-string.** Using **read-char,** transfer the characters from this string back to the same output stream, deleting any parentheses (ASCII 40 and 41) which are encountered. At end-of-file, use **get-output-stream-string** again to retrieve and return the string of tokens.

19.9 After creating **file-stream-1** to output data to file **test-03** on any drive, create **file-stream-2**, a synonym stream for **file-stream-1**.

19.10 Create the user-defined function **string-output-stream** which reads a character from the keyboard and adds it to the string which is the value of ***string***, in the same manner as **list-output-stream** (see Section 19.13) adds the character to the list which is the value of ***list***.

Chapter 20

What's in a Character?

In 8-bit CP/M systems, as Gertrude Stein might have said, a character is a character is a character. The limited (64K) amount of on-board memory does not permit the luxury of full-fledged character data objects.

MS-DOS, on the other hand, provides a great deal more room to work with, and a full character readtable can be implemented. Using such a readtable we can assign a number of properties to a character. In GCLISP we will find that a character can be assigned a special print name, can be assigned a macro definition, and can be modified by use of the Control and Alt keys to take on some special significance over and above its printout characteristics.

In this chapter we will look at:

- the nature of a *character data object*
- *ASCII characters* and the extended character set
- the types of *syntax* which a character may have
- the nature of *terminating macro characters*
- use of the standard *dispatching macro* character #
- how to define your own macro character functions
- how to copy the syntactic properties of one character to another
- the use of *names* for special characters
- the use of :control and :meta bits
- the *predicates* which are available to test characters
- conversion of characters to upper and lowercase

20.1 Character data objects are contained in a readtable

As outlined in Chapter 2, which described the nature of the **read/eval/print** cycle, input to the LISP system is read on a character-by-character basis by **read-char**, which looks up the character on a readtable and then decides what action to take. Conceptually, a character data object on the readtable can be represented by Fig. 20.1.

- The *character code*, a number ranging from 0 to 1023, is used as the basis for lookup on the readtable, and the remaining nodes on the diagram represent various kinds of properties which can be associated with any given character.
- The *macro definition* of the character is the function which is automatically executed when **read-char** reads a macro character during an input operation.
- The *character syntax* specifies the kind of character it is and the manner in which it will be used by the system.
- The *print name* of the character is a string which may be assigned as the name of the character.
- The *font attribute* refers to the style in which the characters are to be printed, for example, italic. (We can ignore this particular attribute here since GCLISP, like most LISPs designed for use on microcomputers, provides for only a single font.)
- The *bits attribute* permits extra flags to be associated with a character, for example, as an indication that other keys such as the Control key or Alt key have been pressed in combination with a keyboard character to give it some special programming significance. GCLISP supports two such bits, **:control** and **:meta**, the use of which will be discussed below.

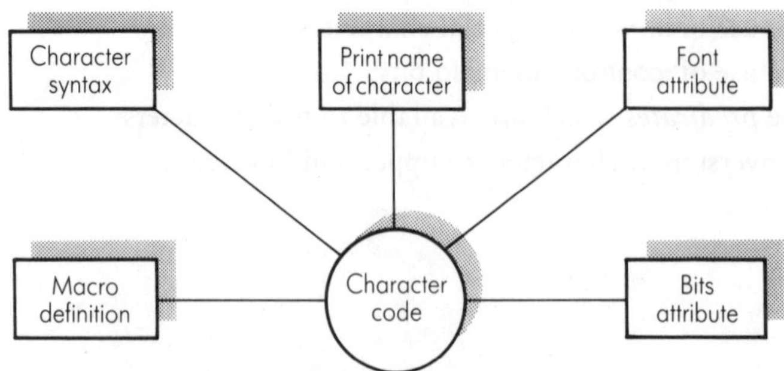

Fig. 20.1 A character data object has various attributes.

20.2 Printed characters are represented as binary numbers

Given the binary nature of data storage within a computer, a printed character must be represented by a pattern of bits. This pattern inevitably corresponds to some binary number. When the time comes to retrieve and print the character, the computer must have some way of knowing that the binary number retrieved from storage in fact represents a character; and must also have recourse to a lookup table whereby the number can be converted back into a suitable pattern of pixels to generate the corresponding character on a screen or printer.

In Common LISP this number, which uniquely identifies a given character, is referred to as the *character code*. As we will see, characters in GCLISP are synonymous with their codes, which are returned to output streams as decimal integers (assuming that ***print-base*** is set to its normal default value of 10).

The number of characters which can be accomodated within a given character set is directly related to the number of bits-per-character which one is prepared to allocate for this purpose. A common scheme for representing characters is the ASCII character set, which utilizes the first seven bits of a byte; the other bit is usually reserved as a parity bit whereby a check can be made at the other end of a transmission line as to whether the remaining seven bits – that is, the ASCII character – have been received properly (see Fig. 20.2).

Having seven bits at its disposal, the ASCII character set comprises $2^7 = 128$ possible characters. These include all of the 96 commonly used characters referred to by GCLISP as the *Standard Character Set*, which includes the following 94 non-blank printing characters:

GCLISP Standard Character Set

! " # $ % & ' ( ) * + , – . / 0 1 2 3 4 5 6 7 8 9 : ; < = > ?
@ A B C D E F G H I J K L M N O P Q R S T U V W X Y Z [\ ] ^ –
` a b c d e f g h i j k l m n o p q r s t u v w x y z { | } ~

plus the space character **#\Space** and the linefeed/carriage return character **#\Newline**. The balance of the normal ASCII set includes 32 control

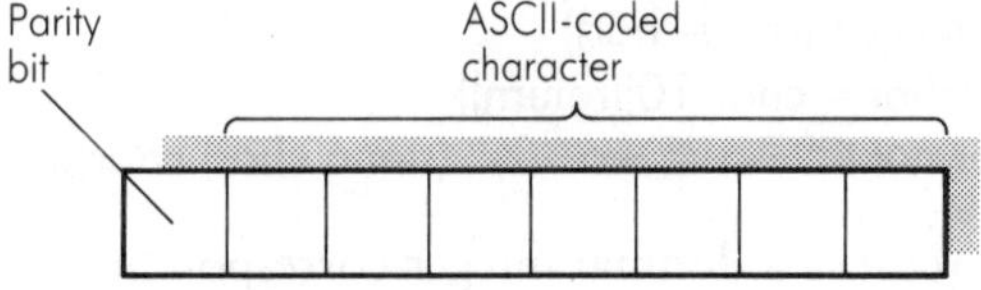

Fig. 20.2 ASCII characters are represented by seven bits.

characters, generated by combining the Control key with the 26 letters of the alphabet plus the six characters @, [, \,], ^, and _.

Assuming that we dedicate a whole byte to character representation and are willing to forego use of the parity bit, our character set can be further expanded to 256 characters, corresponding to character codes from 0 to 255 inclusive. Such an *extended character set* has been implemented in MS-DOS and is utilized by GCLISP. (See Fig. 20.3 for a summary of the extended character set.)

20.3 get-char-ascii returns the character code

We can retrieve the numerical code corresponding to a character with **char-code**:

```
* (char-code "A")
65
```

Alternatively:

```
* (char-code #\A)
65
```

We can also retrieve this code by the use of **read-char** (see Section 10.6), which reads in a single character from the keyboard (or other source) and returns the code. Like **read**, **read-char** provides no prompt signals and merely waits for you to type something in:

```
* (read-char)A
65
```

Based on the use of **read-char** we can define a simple function **get-char-ascii** to provide the ASCII code of any character typed into the keyboard:

```
(defun get-char-ascii ()
  (let (char)
    (format t "~%Type in characters; ~
       press Enter when finished:~%~%")
    (loop
      (setf char (read-char))
      (if (char= char 10)(return))
      (format t " ~a = ~a~%" (string char) char))))
```

Since **read-char** returns a decimal integer corresponding to the ASCII code of the character, this must be converted to its string equivalent using **string** (see Section 21.7). Using **get-char-ascii** we can experiment with all of the characters which can be generated by our keyboard, for example:

```
* (get-char-ascii)
Type in characters; press Enter when finished:
a = 97
S = 83
7 = 55
<Enter>
NIL
```

You may wish to define **get-char-ascii** and use it to explore the character codes generated by your particular keyboard (see Exercise 20.1).

20.4 get-ascii-char reverses the above process

We can also define an alternative function **get-ascii-char**, which works in reverse and provides the character corresponding to any integer typed in at the keyboard:

```
(defun get-ascii-char ()
  (let (ascii-value)
    (format t "~%Type in ASCII values; ~
      enter '10' when finished:~%~%")
    (loop
      (setf ascii-value (read))
      (if (= ascii-value 10)(return))
      (format t "~a = ~a~%"
        ascii-value (string ascii-value)))))
```

In this case, since more than one character may be required, we use **read** followed by <enter> to input the number. We then use the ASCII code for #**Newline**, 10, as a signal to exit the loop.

```
* (get-ascii-char)
Type in ASCII values; enter '10' when finished:
42
42 = 8
67
67 = b
10 <signal for exit>
NIL
```

20.5 display-ascii-char displays the entire character set

If we experiment with the keyboard (see Exercise 20.1) we will find that we can only generate the standard character set plus a few odd characters associated with the Function keys, Backspace key, etc. How do we get to look at the rest of the 256 possible characters?

We can of course use **get-ascii-char**, manually type in the numbers from 0 to 255, and see what we get. An easier way is to define another function which does this for us and lines up a display in tabular format.

```
(defun display-ascii-char (from to)
  (let (ascii-value col-num)
   (terpri)
   (setf ascii-value from)
   (loop
    (if (eql ascii-value to)
       (return))
    (setf col-num 1)
    (terpri)
    (princ " ")
    (loop
     (if (or (eql col-num 8)
             (eql ASCII-value to))
        (return))
     (princ ascii-value)
     (cond ((< ascii-value 10)(princ " = "))
           ((> ascii-value 99)(princ " = "))
           (t (princ " = ")))
     (if (or (eql ascii-value 9)
             (eql ascii-value 10))
        (princ " ")
        (princ (string ASCII-value)))
     (princ " ")
     (setf col-num (+ 1 col-num))
           ascii-value (+ 1 ascii-value)))))
```

We can use the above function to display the full range of characters from 0 to 255, corresponding to Fig. 20.3

20.6 The character's syntax determines how it is used

Assuming that **read-char** is being used for input from the keyboard (as opposed to, say, reading from a file), each key or key-chord combination generates an integer value which can vary from 0 to 1023, representing the 256 characters of the extended character set augmented by up to two leading bits associated with the Control and Alt keys. This value is looked up on the readtable and the syntax associated with the character is examined.

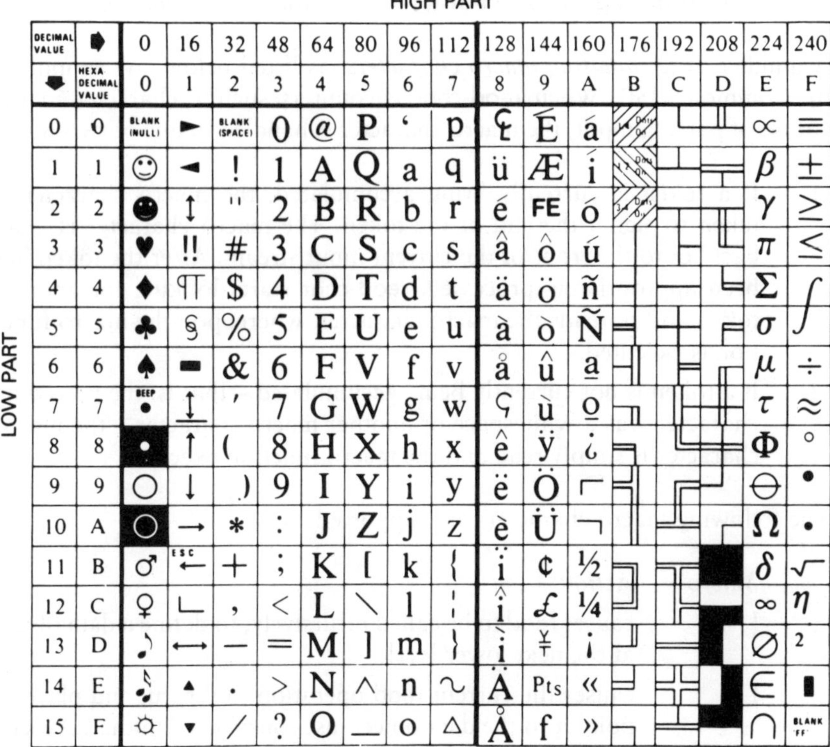

Fig. 20.3 The extended character set comprises 256 characters.

A character may fall into one of the following syntactic categories:

- *constituent*, in which case the character is collected into a numeric or symbolic token
- *escape*, in which case the following character or characters are taken literally (see also Section 11:2)
- *whitespace*, in which case the current token is terminated; additional whitespaces thereafter are ignored
- *terminating macro*, in which case the current token is terminated and whatever macro action may be associated with the character is executed
- *standard # macro*, which provides a means of abbreviating other types of syntax

20.7 Terminating macro characters terminate a token

A number of *terminating macro characters*, as listed below, are supported by Common LISP. When **read-char** encounters such a character in the course of parsing input, the macro character is handled in one of two ways:

(1) If a token is currently bring accumulated, the macro character is taken to signal the end of the token. The macro character is 'read back' onto the front of the current input stream. After the token has been appropriately processed, **read-char** starts looking for another token and re-reads the macro character, whereupon the macro function is executed.

(2) If a token is not currently being accumulated – that is, the preceding character was a whitespace or another macro character – the macro character is simply read and the macro function executed.

The following macro characters are supported:

Macro	*Action*
(	causes **read** to be called recursively, to define a data object at the next lower level
)	causes the current **read** operation to return, and places a pointer to the data object just constructed in the CAR cell at the next higher level
' (quote)	causes the S-expression following the macro to be quoted
`	causes the S-expression following the macro to be back-quoted
, (comma)	causes the S-expression following the macro to be evaluated, and replaced with its value
"	causes whatever sequence of characters between adjacent " macros to become a string
;	causes whatever sequence of characters between the macro and the next Newline to be taken as a comment and ignored by the program

See Chapter 29 on the **read/eval/print** cycle for further discussion of the handling of macro characters during input.

20.8 # is the standard dispatching macro character

The nonterminating macro character # provides a special syntactical form for different purposes. The principal ways in which this character can be used are listed below:

Syntax	*Represents*
#' <function>	abbreviation for (function<function>)
#: <symbol>	abbreviation for uninterned <symbol>
#\ <character>	a character object
#a <array>	array <array>
#s <structure>	a structure defined by defstruct

Other forms such as #b, #c, #o, #r, and #x are used to indicate the use of various radix bases for expressing numbers. The uses of # will be discussed in more detail in the sections dealing with the structures which they represent.

#\<character> reads in the character data object which represents <character>. For example:

```
* #\A
65
```

Normally there would be no need to use #\ in this context, since the character can be read in directly. However the syntax is useful when providing for output of nonprinting characters within a program, for example:

```
* #\Newline
10
```

(See Section 20.12 below for other character names supported by GCLISP which can be represented in this manner.)

20.9 Macro functions can be defined for any character

We can supplement the standard macro characters which are built into our implementation by assigning our own macro definitions to specified characters. Such definitions can be assigned through the use of set-macro-character, which takes the following syntax:

```
(set-macro-character <char> <function>)
```

where <char> is a character data object and <function> may be either a user-defined function or a directly applied lambda definition. Once such a definition has been assigned, when the LISP reader encounters <char> in the stream being read it executes the specified <function>. (See Chapter 29 on the read/eval/print cycle for a more detailed description.)

Needless to say, once we define a character as a macro character we can no longer use it as a normal constituent character. The Common LISP standard reserves the following characters for the user: !, ?, [,], {, and }, so we would tend to use these for user-defined macro purposes.

The function to be executed must have exactly two arguments, the first being the current input stream and the second the character. These dummy arguments are usually called **stream** and **char** for obvious mnemonic reasons.

Let's assume that we wish to use the question mark character as a quote macro, that is, having the same properties as '. We can define a specific function for this purpose; let's call it **quote-it**:

```
* (defun quote-it (stream char)
     (list (quote quote)(read stream t nil t)))
QUOTE-IT

* (set-macro-character #\? #'quote-it)
T
```

Trying out our newly defined macro:

```
* ?(ab?cd)
(AB (QUOTE CD))
```

The use of the form **(read stream t nil t)** requires some elaboration. As you will recall from Chapter 10, **read** (see Section 10.2) takes four optional arguments, the first three of which are the **stream** being read from followed by two arguments to determine the means of handling end-of-file conditions. In this case we are including the normal default values of **t** and **nil** for **eof-error-p** and **eof-value** solely in order to pave the way for specifying the last argument, **recursive-p**.

recursive-p is specified as **t** to reflect the fact that the **read** operation currently going on is recursively embedded in a higher level **read** function. This in effect permits the lower level function calls to 'remember' certain conditions established during higher level calls to **read**, for example, whether **read-preserving-whitespace** is in effect. If we do not include **recursive-p** and specify the above form simply as **(read stream)**, some applications of our macro may work and some may not. If as an exercise we redefine **quote-it** in this manner, reassign it to the question mark character with **set-macro-character**, and carry out a few experiments, we will find that we get erratic results on trials such as **?(ab?cd)**. Hence all of the optional arguments should be included in calls to **read** within a character macro definition, with **recursive-p** always specified as **t**. (For more discussion on this subject see pp. 374–5 of the CLRM.)

In the above example we explicitly defined the function **quote-it** and assigned this function to the character. However it is easier directly to assign the equivalent lambda definition:

```
* (set-macro-character #\?
    #'(lambda (stream char)
        (list (quote quote)(read stream t nil t))))
T
```

which achieves the same results.

20.10 Some macro functions should not return a value

In a case such as that discussed above, the top-level **read** operation is temporarily held up while the quote macro recursively calls **read** to input the next S-expression. Ultimately the macro returns the value **(QUOTE <S-expression>)** which is spliced into the data object being accumulated at the top level.

However there are times when we don't want *any* value to be returned! For instance, the macro ; indicates that all text following this macro up until the next Newline is to be interpreted as commentary text and otherwise ignored by the program. This means that we can include comments in the course of defining a function, for example:

```
* (defun test-comment ()
    (setf x 'y)      ;this is a test comment
    (setf y 'z))
TEST-COMMENT
```

with which we can document various aspects of the program. If we **load** the above definition from the file and then retrieve the function definition:

```
* (symbol-function 'test-comment)
(LAMBDA TEST-COMMENT NIL
   (SETF X (QUOTE Y))
   (SETF Y (QUOTE Z)))
```

we find that the comment is not reflected in any way. This means that the ; macro causes itself as well as the following text to be skipped over and left out of the function definition. This in turn implies that the macro returns *no value* to the top-level **read** function.

Let's see what happens if we try to define a macro for reading comments. Using the left curly bracket for our character:

```
* (set-macro-character #\{
    #'(lambda (stream char)
        (loop
         (if     (char= #\newline (read-char stream t nil t))
                 (return)))))
```

If we now use this macro in the course of writing a function definition:

```
* (defun test-macro ()
    (setf apples '(red fruits))    {this is a comment
    (setf pears '(yellow fruits)))
TEST-MACRO
```

and subsequently retrieve the function definition:

```
* (symbol-function 'test-macro
(LAMBDA TEST-MACRO NIL                      ↓
   (SETF APPLES (QUOTE (RED FRUITS))  [NIL]
   SETF PEARS (QUOTE (YELLOW FRUITS))))
```

we see that we have picked up a surplus **NIL** following the first **setf** expression, representing the value returned by the { macro. Although in some cases an extraneous **NIL** might not adversely effect the function, in other instances it could be disastrous.

We can avoid returning a value through use of the function **values** (see Section 17.8), called without arguments. As the last function called in the definition, **(values)** determines the value returned by the function which is, in this case, no value at all! Needless to say, **read** is designed to handle this contingency, and totally ignores such an 'invisible' data object. We can therefore modify the last line of our lambda expression from **(return)))))** to:

```
(return (values))))))
```

which will have the desired effect. If we redefine the { macro function along these lines and repeat the experiment with **test-macro**, we will now find that the **NIL** has disappeared from the function definition, reflecting that **set-macro-character** is now returning no value. (See also Exercise 20.4.)

(NB: Version 1.01 of GCLISP does not support **(values)** with no arguments, but provides an equivalent way of handling the situation. The macro function may be set up to return one or two values. If two values are returned and if the second value is non-**NIL**, the macro character and any characters read by its function are excluded from the data object currently being constructed by **read**. Hence the above ending would be amended to **read: (return (values t t))))))**.)

20.11 The syntactic properties of a character can be copied to another character

The function **set-syntax-from-char** can be used to copy the syntactic properties of one character over to another character. The function:

```
(set-syntax-from-char <to-char> <from-char>)
```

copies the readtable syntax information from <from-char> to <to-char>, and returns T. This function copies the syntactic type of the character, that is, whether it is constituent, terminating macro, etc.), and also copies any macro definitions which may be associated with it.

Paralleling the previous example, we can convert the left bracket [to display the same macro properties as the single quote mark:

```
* (set-syntax-from-char #\[ #\')
T
```

If we now try out our new macro character:

```
*(setf fruits '(apples [pears grapes))
(APPLES (QUOTE PEARS) GRAPES)
```

we see that [has inherited the macro characteristics of '.

20.12 Names have been assigned to some characters

Common LISP assigns names to certain specific characters. Whether a particular character has a name or not may be ascertained through use of (char-name <char>), which returns the print-name of the character in the form of a string:

```
* (char-name 10)
"Newline"

* (char-name 32)
"Space"
```

where 10 and 32 are the respective ASCII character codes.

All Common LISP implementations support the names Newline and Space. We can check as to which additional characters have names in our implementation by defining get-char-name:

```
(defun get-char-name ()
  (let ((char 0))
    (loop
      (if (char= char 256)
        (return))
      (if (char-name char)
        (format t "~%~a = ~a"
          char (char-name char)))
      (setf char (1+ char)))))
```

If we execute this function with GCLISP, all the printable characters from 0 to 255 will be scrolled on the screen and we will find that the following semi-standard names are supported:

ASCII	*Name*	*ASCII*	*Name*
8	Backspace	13	Return
9	Tab	27	Esc
12	Page	127	Rubout

None of the remaining characters have names. The naming of characters is implementation-specific and there is no way that you can assign your own special name to a character.

(Name-char <name>) attempts to return the character named by <name>. If **name** matches the name of some character (using **string-equal**) that character is returned; otherwise **NIL** is returned. For example:

```
* (string-equal "Newline" (char-name 10))
T

* (name-char "Newline")
10

* (name-char "Hotdog")
NIL
```

20.13 A single character font is supported by GCLISP

Common LISP supports the concept of *font bits* whereby it is possible to specify the manner in which printout is to be printed, for example, in italics or some other special font. Microcomputer LISPs do not support this relative luxury; hence only the normal character set supported by MS-DOS can be printed.

The GCLISP value for **char-font-limit** is therefore 1, meaning that there is only one (default) font for printing GCL output. (In view of this limit, GCL does not support the Common LISP function **char-font**.)

20.14 GCLISP provides for :control and :meta bits

Common LISP refers to the use of up to four additional bits which may be associated with a character, including **:control**, **:meta**, **:super**, and **:hyper**, which carry respective 'weights' of 1, 2, 4, and 8. GCLISP supports only the first two of these bits.

Conceptually, we can expand the single-byte concept of a character which we considered earlier into a two-byte format (see Fig. 20.4), in which only the right-most 10 bits are utilized by GCLISP. The first byte is used for the character code; the first bit of the second byte for a flag corresponding

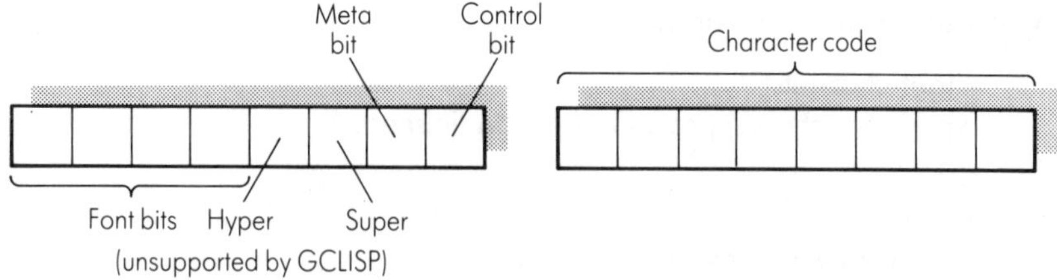

Fig. 20.4 GCLISP provides for **:control** and **:meta** bits.

to the Control key; and the second bit for a flag corresponding to the Alt key. (It will be noted that this reflection of the use of the Control key differs from the ASCII character set.)

GCLISP therefore represents characters internally as numbers in the (decimal) range of 0 to 1023, in which 0 to 255 represent characters with no Control or Alt key pressed, 256–511 as characters with the Control key pressed, 512–767 as characters with the Alt key pressed, and 768–1023 as characters with both keys pressed. (NB: The latter is more theoretical than practical, since pressing both keys returns a value as if only the Alt key had been pressed.)

20.15 char-bit tests for the presence of a bit

The function (char-bit <char><name>) can be used to test for the presence of a particular bit, where <char> is any character object and <name> is the name of the bit, that is, :control or :meta. This function can therefore be used to test for whether the Control or Alt key has been pressed in conjunction with a character. We can define a simple test function get-char-bits by modifying get-char-ascii slightly:

```
(defun get-char-bits ()
  (let (char)
  (format t "~%Type in keychords; ~
                   press Enter when finished~%~%")
  (loop
   (setf char (read-char))
   (if (eq char 10)
      (return))
   (format t "~a = ~a~%" (string char) char)
   (cond ((char-bit char :control)
          (princ "Control key has been pressed"))
         ((char-bit char :meta)
          (princ "Alt key has been pressed"))
         (t (princ "No special keys have been pressed")))
   (terpri))))
```

Trying out our new function:

```
* (get-char-bits)
Type in keychords; press Enter when finished:
<a>
a = 97
No special keys have been pressed
<Shift-a>
A = 65
No special keys have been pressed
<Ctrl-a>
A = 321
Control key has been pressed
<Alt-a>
A = 577
Alt key has been pressed
```

Further experiments will reveal that Alt-Ctrl-a provides the same results as Alt-a; and that both the Control and Alt keys include an (implicit) shift key effect, that is, convert the printed representation of the character to upper case.

20.16 Other functions relate to the bits component

Several other functions are provided which relate to bits. (char-bits <char>) returns the bits attribute of <char>:

```
* (char-bits 321)
1
```

The value returned is the binary value of the two bits which may be set and may thus vary from 0 to 3.

(set-char-bit <char><bit-name><new-value>) returns the character with the specified bit set to the new value. The bit name must be either :control or :meta.

```
* (set-char-bit 65 :control 1)
321
```

In this case the value returned corresponds to the letter A with the Control key pressed.

(code-char <code> &optional <bits><font>) returns a character object which has the specified code, bits, and font attributes. The bits and font attributes default to 0.

```
* (code-char 65 1 1)
321)
```

20.17 Various character-testing predicates are available

A variety of predicates are provided to test the various qualities of a character, as follows:

- (standard-char-p <char>) returns a boolean value indicating whether or not the character in question is part of the 'standard character' set. GCLISP standard characters have zero bits and font attributes; hence any character with non-zero attributes will not pass the 'standard-char' test (see Exercise 20.8).
- (alpha-char-p <char>) is true if char is an alphabetic character.
- (upper-case-p <char>) is true if char is an uppercase character.
- (both-case-p <char>) is true if char has both an upper- and lowercase representation, that is, is one of the 26 letters of the alphabet.
- (digit-char-p <char> &optional <radix>) is true if char is a digit of the specified radix (if not, the radix defaults to 10). If true, this predicate returns the weight of the digit in the specified radix (see Exercise 20.9). For example:

  ```
  * (digit-char-p C 16)
  12
  ```

  meaning that the character C has a (decimal) weighting of 12 in a hexadecimal system.
- (char= <char> &rest <more-chars>) is true if all of its arguments are the same character. Comparing uppercase A's:

  ```
  * (char= 65 65 65)
  T
  ```

- (char-equal <char> &rest <more-chars>) is true if the arguments are all the same character, ignoring differences in case. Comparing upper- and lowercase A's:

  ```
  * (char-equal 65 65 97 97)
  T
  ```

- (char-lessp <char> &rest <more-chars>) is true if the arguments are characters which are monotonically increasing from left to right, ignoring differences in case:

  ```
  * (char-lessp 65 66 67)
  T
  ```

It should be noted that GCLISP differs slightly from Common LISP as regards its handling of characters. Common LISP characters are supposed to be of a separate object type but in GCLISP they are indistinguishable from fixnums up to 1023:

```
* (characterp 1023)
T
* (characterp 1024)
NIL
```

20.18 Characters can be converted to upper- or lowercase

When handling English language text, the alphabetic characters A to Z can appear in either upper or lower case. Conversion functions are available to convert from one case to another.

(char-upcase <char>) attempts to convert char to its uppercase equivalent. For example, converting a lowercase 'a' = ASCII 97:

```
* (char-upcase 97)
65
```

where 65 is the ASCII value for uppercase 'A.' If char does not have an uppercase equivalent, <char> is simply returned. For example, attempting to convert the question mark (ASCII 63):

```
* (char-upcase 63)
63
```

(char-downcase <char>) does the reverse, that is, attempts to convert an uppercase character to its lowercase equivalent, and simply returns <char> if the attempt is unsuccessful.

SUMMARY

Summarizing the key points of this chapter:

- during a **read** operation, each character parsed is looked up on a *readtable* to determine how it is to be handled
- character data objects are identified by their *character codes*, which range from 0 to 1023. The lower 8 bits of the code identify the printed representation of the character in the *extended character set*
- the *syntax* of a character determines how it is used by the system. Characters may be classed as *constituent*, *escape*, *whitespace*, *terminating macro*, and the standard *dispatching macro #*
- macro functions can be defined for any character by means of **set-macro-character**. Alternatively the syntax and macro definition can be copied from one character to another using **set-syntax-from-char**
- special handling is required using **values** in cases where it is desired that a macro not return a value to **read**
- names may be assigned to nonprinting characters. All Common LISP implementations support the names **Newline** and **Space**
- GCLISP supports **:control** and **:meta bits** to indicate when the Control or Alt keys have been used in conjunction with a character
- a variety of predicates are provided to test the qualities of a character
- functions are available to convert uppercase characters to lowercase and vice versa

EXERCISES

20.1 Draw a rough diagram of your computer keyboard and use **get-char-ascii** to retrieve the codes corresponding to all possible key and/or keychord combinations. How many of the possible 256 characters can you generate? Which keys are significant when used in conjunction with another key? Of these particular keys, if two or more are pressed simultaneously, which one takes precedence?

20.2 Define the function print-char, which is somewhat like display-ascii-char (see Section 20.5), except that it prints each character on the console on a separate line in the format:

65 = A
66 = B
etc.

and at the same time copies the output to the printer. (Hint: To get the printer to print each character as it is generated rather than storing it in the buffer, output a linefeed after each character.) What do you notice as integers from 0 to 255 are displayed? What special arrangements must be built into the function to prevent the printout from being turned off?

20.3 In some LISP applications you may wish to include provision for the use of function keys. Define the function function-keys which prompts for any function key to be pressed and prints an appropriate message as to which key was pressed. Exit the function if any other key is pressed. If you have not done Exercise 20.1, the following are the character codes:

F1 – 224	F2 – 225	F3 – 226	F4 – 227	F5 – 232
F6 – 233	F7 – 234	F8 – 236	F9 – 237	F10 – 238

20.4 Modify the left curly bracket macro function (see Section 20.10) so that the comment text is terminated by a right curly bracket rather than a Newline, thus permitting a comment to be embedded anywhere within a program. The program should ignore both curly brackets and the text which lies between them.

20.5 Define the function copy-syntax, which prompts for a character from which the syntax is to be copied, prompts for the character to which the syntax is to be copied and carries out the copying operation.

20.6 setf the variable *text* to the following string: "This is a string of text in which all characters which fall between a left curly bracket { and a right curly bracket } are to be printed in italics." Then define the function print-italics which reads from the above string and prints the text to the printer, printing all text which lies between curly brackets (but not the brackets themselves) in italics. (NB: If the high bit is set, the printer will print in italic characters.)

20.7 Define the function get-char-names, which is similar to get-char-name (see Section 20.12) but prints a list of only those particular characters which have names. Display the characters in the format:

ASCII	*Name*
8	backspace
10	newline
127	rubout
	etc.

20.8 Define the function get-standard-char which examines the ASCII character list and prints all characters which pass the standard-char-p test. Print the characters in groups of 10 on each succeeding line of the display.

20.9 Define the function **get-digit-char** which takes a single argument equal to the radix base and prints "**The following characters represent digits of radix base <radix>**", followed by a list of the digits. Where letters are involved in radices over 10, display the uppercase characters only.

20.10 Define the function **get-both-case-char** which prints a listing of lowercase characters followed by their uppercase equivalent in the format:

a → A
b → B
etc.

Chapter 21
Working with Strings

In the course of writing LISP programs we will find ourselves using strings a great deal, principally for textual output such as data printout, table headings, and error messages. In English language processing we will be using strings to handle input as well as to generate computer responses.

In this chapter we will look at:

- the nature of a *string* as a one-dimensional vector
- various common ways in which strings can be created
- how other LISP data objects may be converted into strings using stream functions
- how a string may be converted into a stream with make-string-input-stream
- how strings may be compared for equality
- the use of string-append in concatenating strings
- how to search a string for a specified substring

21.1 A string is a one-dimensional vector of characters

In most microcomputer implementations, when a string is created it is placed in a certain area of memory reserved for strings. During the evaluation process, if an address pointer is found to point into this area, the data object pointed to may be assumed to be a string and is processed accordingly. The form of a string is a simple one-dimensional vector of characters, terminated by a null character. This area also includes the print names of atoms. We will follow this conceptual convention in the discussion which follows. (However it should be noted that implementations which support *packages* will handle print names in a somewhat different manner.)

During a read operation, each token parsed potentially represents a new symbol and is accumulated, character by character, into the string area starting at a point just beyond the end of the last string. This location is of course kept track of by a pointer. When parsing of the token is complete, the Object List is surveyed to see if the atom already exists. If it does, the string just accumulated is ignored (since the print name of the atom already exists elsewhere), the string pointer is left unchanged, and the next string will overwrite this area. If the atom is a new one, a data object for the new atom is created with the print name pointer pointing to the string just created, a null is added to terminate this string, and the string pointer is updated to point to the next following byte.

When printing out a value corresponding to a string, the print (and prin1) operation prints a double quote character " before and after the printout, in a manner somewhat analogous to its printing '(' and ')' before and after a list. princ simply prints the string without the quote marks.

The simplest way to create a string is by enclosing one or more characters in double quote marks:

```
* (setf apples "red fruits")
"red fruits"
```

Assuming that apples is a new symbol just being created, the new atom data object and the end of our string storage area will now look like Fig. 21.1 (converting bytes to their ASCII equivalent). Note that although read has converted the symbol name to uppercase, the quoted string retains its lowercase identity.

The print name of a symbol in the form of a string can be retrieved using symbol-name:

```
* (symbol-name 'apples)
"APPLES"
```

As regards evaluation, a string always evaluates to itself:

```
* "red fruits"
"red fruits"
```

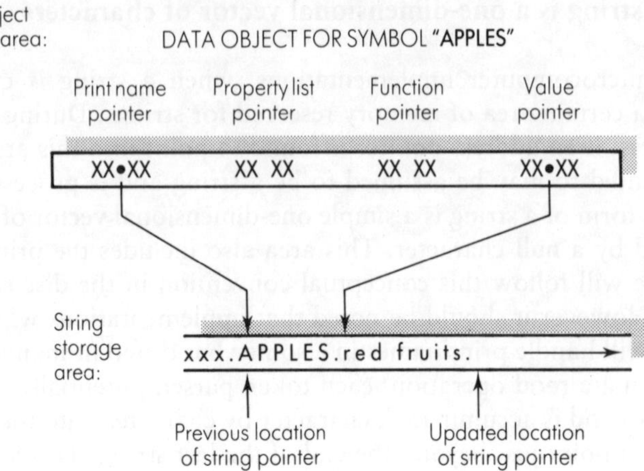

Fig. 21.1 Strings are stored in a special area.

21.2 Strings may also be created using a **format** statement

Another common way of creating strings is by using a **format** statement (see Section 12.5). As discussed previously, **format** makes it possible to mix predetermined strings together with as-yet-unkown values to produce an overall string. This may be compared with the manner in which **backquote** mixes quoted data objects with values to produce an overall quoted list.

Using our previously generated value of **apples**:

```
* (setf fruit-statement
    (format nil "Apples are an example of ~a" apples))
"Apples are an example of red fruits"
```

Use of the format destination **NIL** causes the data object created by the **format** statement to be returned as a value (rather than being printed as by **princ**). The top-level printout flags out the fact that a *string* has been created.

As a matter of comparison, we could do something similar with **backquote** (see Section 12.3), but we would have to set the value of **apples** to a list and we would wind up with a quoted list in uppercase:

```
* (setf apples '(red fruits))
(RED FRUITS)
* (setf fruit-statement
    '(apples are an example of ,@apples))
(APPLES ARE AN EXAMPLE OF RED FRUITS)
```

(NB: The foregoing discussion has been of a conceptual nature. GCLISP handles strings as separate individual data objects. The difference, which is of course transparent to the user, may be explored by using some of the low-level utility functions described in Section 26.1.)

21.3 read-line reads in a line as a string

Another common way to create a string, particularly in the course of processing English language input, is with read-line (see Section 10.7), which takes a complete line of input, terminated by a Newline, and converts it into a string:

```
* (setf sentence (read-line))Now is the time for all men!<CR>
"Now is the time for all men!"

* sentence
"Now is the time for all men!"
```

21.4 make-string creates a simple string

The function make-string, which takes the syntax:

```
(make-string <size> &key :initial-element)
```

creates a simple string of length <size>, each of whose characters has been initialized to the :initial-element argument.

```
* (setf string-01 (make-string 10 :initial-element #\A)
"AAAAAAAAAA"
```

If the (optional) :initial-element argument is not provided, the string is initialized in an implementation-dependent way.

21.5 LISP data objects may be converted to strings using make-string-output-stream and get-output-string-stream

It is sometimes desirable to convert another kind of data object such as a list or a number to a string, in order to permit it to be handled by string-manipulation functions or to be spliced into a format statement. This may be accomplished by printing (using princ) the data object to a special output stream created by make-string-output-stream, and then reading the resulting string back from the stream using get-output-stream-string. (See Sections 19.10 and 19.11 for more details.)

NB: The Common LISP function princ-to-string can be used to convert other LISP data objects to strings; however this function is not supported by GCLISP (see Exercise 19.6).

A related function **with-output-to-string** similarly permits the collection of data into a string. This macro takes the syntax:

```
(with-output-to-string (<var> &optional <string-name>)
                       <forms-to-evaluate>)
```

A stream bound to <var> is created and thereafter any output to that stream is collected into the string bound to <string-name>. If no string name is specified, the string of collected output is returned as the value of **with-output-to-string**; otherwise this macro returns the value of the last form evaluated.

21.6 A string may be used as an input source through use of make-string-input-stream

Having created a string there are various ways to manipulate it. As we will see below, the string can be concatenated, that is, appended, to other strings using **string-append**. Various other operations are designed to dissect strings into substrings, or to convert strings back into list form.

read-from-string (see Section 10.8) reads a single expression – which may be a symbol, a number, or a list – from a string. The index limits between which the expression is to be read may be specified by additional optional arguments.

An entire string can be converted back to a list by using **string-append** (see Section 21.11) to graft parentheses onto each end of the string, followed by **read-from-string** to read the resulting list in one fell swoop (see **list-ex-string** in Section 10.8).

Finally, **read-char** may be used to access a string on a character-by-character basis. For this purpose it is necessary to convert the string into a stream using **make-string-input-stream**. See Section 19.9 for details.

21.7 string converts its argument to a string representation

The function **string** tests its single argument for type and returns various values depending on what it finds.

Perhaps the most common application for **string** is to convert the numeric representation of a character data object to its string equivalent for printout on the console or printer:

```
* (string 65)
"A"
```

If the object is a symbol, **string** returns its print name:

```
* (string 'apples)
"APPLES"
```

If the object is a string, **string** merely returns that string:

```
* (string "roses are red")
"roses are red"
```

As might be expected, trying to apply **string** to other data objects generates an error.

21.8 char accesses the index'th character of a string

The function (char <string><index>) returns the index'th character of a string in the form of the decimal integer corresponding to the ASCII representation:

```
* (setf test-string "roses are red")
"roses are red"

* (char test-string 2)
115
```

The ASCII value of 115 corresponds to the 3rd character in the string, a lowercase 's' (remembering that the first character of a string has an index value of 0). If the printed representation of the character is desired, a further conversion must be carried out using **string** (see Section 21.7).

The related function **schar**, which takes the same syntax as **char**, may be used to to extract the index'th character from a *simple string*, which is a one-dimensional vector without a fill-pointer (see Section 22.9). The CLRM indicates that in some implementations **schar** may be faster than **char** in retrieving a character.

Note that **setf** can be used with either **char** or **schar** to replace the index'th character of a string, after which the (integer) character will be returned:

```
* (setf string "abc")
"abc"
* (setf (char string 2) #\z)
122
* string
"abz"
```

21.9 string= and string-equal compare two strings for equality

Strings or substrings of strings may be compared for equality with **string=**, which takes the syntax:

```
(string= <string1> <string2> &key :start1 :end1 :start2 :end2)
```

string= makes a case-sensitive comparison. Hence:

```
* (string= "roses are red" "roses are red")
T
```

but:

```
* (string= "ROSES ARE RED" "roses are red")
NIL
```

The optional keyword arguments **:start1** and **:end1** specify the range of positions in **string1** to be included in the comparison, where **:start1** is the inclusive lower bound and **:end1** is the exclusive upper bound. The remaining keyword arguments are similarly defined for **string2**.

string-equal is similar to **string=** except that characters are compared ignoring differences in case. Using **string-equal**, the second test above would have returned **T**.

21.10 string< and string-lessp test whether one string is lexicographically less than another string

string< is a case-sensitive predicate which compares its two arguments and returns **T** if **string1** is lexicographically less than **string2**, that is, if **string1** comes before **string2** in an alphabetically sorted list. Syntax is as follows:

```
(string< <string1><string2> &key :start1 :end1 :start2 :end2)
```

For example:

```
* (string< "aaaa "aaab")
3
```

If the test succeeds, **string<** returns as a value the index position of the first character which differs.

The optional keyword arguments **:start1** and **:end1** specify the range of positions in **string1** to be included in the comparison, where **:start1** is the inclusive lower bound and **:end1** is the exclusive upper bound. The remaining keyword arguments are defined analagously for **string2**.

string-lessp carries out a similar comparison, but ignores differences in case.

21.11 string-append concatenates two or more strings

string-append, which is a GCLISP function similar to Common LISP's **concatenate**, permits strings to be appended to one another. Syntax is as follows:

```
(string-append <string1> <string2> ... <stringn>)
```

string-append takes any number of strings as its arguments and concatenates copies of them into a single string. If we **setf aaa** to '**roses,**' **bbb** to '**are,**' and **ccc** to '**red,**' we can combine them all into a single string:

```
* (string-append aaa bbb ccc)
"rosesarered"
```

We note from this that if we wish to retain a space between words the space must either be incorporated into each individual string, that is, 'roses ', or appended as separate data objects, that is:

```
* (string-append aaa " " bbb " " ccc)
"roses are red"
```

21.12 Characters can be trimmed from the ends of a string

There are times when it may be desirable to prune unwanted characters from one end or another of a string. Characters may be pruned from either or both ends of a string with **string-trim**, **string-right-trim** or **string-left-trim**, all of which take a similar syntax:

```
(string-trim       <character-bag> <string>)
(string-right-trim <character-bag> <string>)
(string-left-trim  <character-bag> <string>)
```

The first argument, conventionally referred to as the *character-bag*, is a listing of one or more characters to be pruned from the end of the string. The second argument is the string to be trimmed. As may be inferred from the names, **string-trim** will trim characters from both ends of the string, whereas the other functions trim from the back and the front of the string, respectively.

Let's assume that we have a list which we wish to convert to a string. Leaving out considerations of case for the moment, we can convert the list to a string and then use string trim functions to prune the parentheses from each end. For example, we might convert the list **(HOW NOW BROWN COW)** to a string as follows:

```
* (setf list '(how now brown cow))
(HOW NOW BROWN COW)

* (setf string (format nil "~a" list))
"(HOW NOW BROWN COW)"

* (Setf char-bag "()")
"()"

* (setf trimmed-string
    (string-trim char-bag string))
"HOW NOW BROWN COW"
```

Any of these functions will continue to prune its end of the string until a character is reached which is not contained in <character-bag>. It should be noted that not only are char-bag characters trimmed, but also any trailing or leading blank spaces which may be present between the innermost character to be trimmed and the next non-space character.

Although you would normally specify <character-bag> as a string, it can alternatively be specified in the form of a list, in which case the characters must be listed as character data objects. In the above example, either '(#\(#\)) or '(42 43) could have been assigned to char-bag.

21.13 Strings may be searched for a substring

GCLISP provides several string search functions corresponding to Common LISP's search function as applied specifically to a string sequence.

string-search, which takes the following syntax, may be used to search for a substring of a string:

```
(string-search <sub-string> <string> &optional <from> <to>)
```

If the substring is found, string-search returns the index to the first character of the substring. For example, if we setf word to 'are' and string to 'roses are red':

```
* (string-search word string)
6
```

keeping in mind that the first character is index position 0.

The optional keywords <from> and <to> represent integer arguments which may be included in the function call to delimit the area of search. <from>, which defaults to 0, refers to the first character in the search area, and <to>, which defaults to the length of the string, refers to the character immediately following the search area. (It will be remembered that the *length* of the string is actually one more than the index of the last character in the string, given that the first character is index 0.)

string-search carries out its search in a case-sensitive manner. The corresponding function string-search* is similar except that case is ignored.

As a matter of programming interest, the empty string "" is a substring of each and every string:

```
* (string-search "" string)
0
```

21.14 **stringp** tests for a string data object

The predicate **stringp** may be used to determine whether or not the value of its single argument is a string:

```
* (stringp "roses are red")
T
```

but

```
* (stringp '(hot dog))
NIL
```

21.15 Various sequence operations can be carried out on strings

Strings, in common with lists, contain an ordered sequence of elements. Therefore various Common LISP sequence operations can be used on strings as well as lists. The GCLISP sequence functions which work on strings are as follows.

length returns the number of characters in the string:

```
* (length "roses are red")
13
```

Like **flatc** and **flatsize** (see Section 12.10), **length** can be used to calculate the number of spaces required to align columns when structuring tables (see also Exercise 12.8).

subseq returns a substring of its first argument, commencing with the index position corresponding to its second argument. The syntax is as follows:

```
(subseq <sequence> <start> &optional <end>)
```

The optional third argument specifies an exclusive bound for the index position of the end of the substring:

```
* (subseq "roses are red" 2 9)
"ses are"
```

Although the CLRM states that **setf** may be used in conjunction with **subseq** to replace the specified substring destructively with an alternative string of characters, this feature is not currently supported by GCLISP.

SUMMARY

Summarizing the main points of this chapter:

- a *string* is a one-dimensional vector of characters, which is maintained in a special area set aside for atom print names and strings
- strings may be created by enclosing a group of characters within double quote marks, by using **read-line** to input data, or by using a **format** operation
- the function **make-string** may be used to create a simple string and to initialize its elements
- other LISP data objects may be converted to strings by using **make-string-output-stream** and **get-output-string-stream**
- the function **string** finds frequent use in converting a character code to its printed representation
- **string=** and **string-equal** may be used to compare strings for equality; **string<** and **string-lessp** test whether one string is lexicographically less than another string
- **string-append** may be used to concatenate two or more strings
- characters may be trimmed from either end of a string using **string-left-trim** and **string-right-trim**
- **string-search** may be used to look for a substring within a string
- sequence operations such as **length** and **subseq** can be carried out on strings

EXERCISES

21.1 Execute an operation which uses **setf** to assign the following string values to the symbol **test-string**:

(a) the print name of the symbol **apple**

(b) the phrase "**I like apples!**"

(c) the statement "**The temperature is 68 degrees**", where **68** is the value of the symbol **temp**

21.2 Execute an operation which reads in an English language sentence and uses **setf** to assign the resulting string as the value of the symbol **sentence**.

21.3 Define the function print-char, which prompts for input of integer values and repetitively uses string to convert the integers to their printed character equivalent. Exit the function when something other than an integer is input.

21.4 Define the function count-char, which prompts for input of a string followed by a prompt for a single character. Use char to test each successive character in the string until the end, compare it to <character>, and indicate how many times the character has appeared in the string.

21.5 Define the function equal-strings, which prompts for input of two strings, compares them using string=, and issues a message as to whether or not the two strings are equal.

21.6 Define the function unequal-strings, which prompts for input of two strings, compares them using string<, and issues a message as to whether or not the first string is lexicographically less than the second string.

21.7 Define the function test-string, which prompts for input of an S-expression, evaluates it, tests the resulting value with stringp, and generates a message as to whether or not the object is a string.

21.8 Define the function punctuation-trim, which invites input of an English language sentence, trims one or more punctuation marks from the end, and returns the (trimmed) sentence.

21.9 Define the function string-search, which prompts for input of a line of text followed by a prompt for a substring, searches the line of text for all occurrences of the substring, and reports how many times the substring is found.

21.10 Define the function print-name, which prompts for a name and an address and prints this information as per the following format:

```
Name?         : George Bush
Address?      : The White House

George Bush     The White House
```

where the address commences in column 30. Use a do construct to generate the required amount of blank spaces between the name and the address, using length to ascertain the length of the name.

Chapter 22

Numbers, Arrays, and Structures

Basic LISP functions which carry out arithmetic operations on numbers were reviewed in Chapter 3. In this chapter we will look further at the types of numbers supported by GCLISP and at the other kinds of operations which may be carried out on these numbers.

We will also look at a new data type: the *array*. Arrays are useful for storing large quantities of data in a manner which minimizes storage requirements and at the same time permits speedier access to the individual elements of the array.

Finally, we will consider a complex macro named **defstruct** whereby a user can define his or her own type of data structure, create new instances of the structure, and access and modify any data element of the structure.

In this chapter we will look at:

- the four types of *integer* and *floating-point numbers* supported by GCLISP
- the kinds of *recognizer* and *comparator predicates* which may be applied to numbers
- the use of various functions for carrying out *arithmetic*, *exponential*, *logarithmic*, and *bit-wise* operations on numbers
- the use of **make-array** for creating an array and **aref** for accessing the elements of an array
- how a *fill pointer* may be used for stack-like operations with an array
- the use of an *array leader* to hold additional information about an array
- the use of **defstruct** to create a user-defined data type
- the manner in which automatic *constructor* and *access* functions are created by **defstruct**
- the *optional keywords* which may be used with **defstruct**

22.1 GCLISP supports four types of numbers

GCLISP supports four types of numbers: *fixnums*, *bignums*, *single-floats*, and *double-floats*.

(1) A *fixnum* is represented by a two-byte binary number of which the high bit is used for the sign and the other 15 bits used to represent an integer in the range -2^{15} to $2^{15} - 1$. There is no pointer as such to a fixnum; in a manner of speaking the fixnum *is* the pointer. This leads to very speedy execution of arithmetic operations on small integers.

(2) A *bignum* may range from -2^{32} to $2^{32} - 1$, and occupies 32 bits. An error is signaled if an integer operation results in a number outside of this range.

(3) A *single-float* number is represented in Intel 8087 short real format, occupies 32 bits, can represent 6 to 7 significant digits, and has a range from $8.43*10^{-37}$ to $3.37*10^{38}$ (in both positive and negative numbers).

(4) A *double-float* number is represented in Intel 8087 long real format, occupies 64 bits, can represent 15 significant digits, and has a range from $4.19*10^{-307}$ to $1.67*10^{308}$ (in both positive and negative numbers).

An error is signaled if a floating-point computation casues the exponent to overflow or underflow.

22.2 A variety of recognizer and comparator predicates may be applied to numbers

The recognizer predicate **numberp** tests whether a data object is a number. Other predicates **integerp** and **floatp** test for the type of number. The predicates **plusp**, **minusp**, and **zerop** test whether a given number is positive, negative or zero. The predicates **evenp** and **oddp** may be used to indicate whether an integer is odd or even. (These predicates were covered in Sections 8.3 and 8.4.)

All of these predicates take a single argument and are couched in the same format, for example:

```
* (plusp 45)
T
```

Finally, a variety of comparator predicates are available to compare a number against one or more other numbers:

=	equal
/=	not equal
<	less than
>	more than
<=	equal or less than
>=	equal or more than

Where two or more arguments are provided, each successive argument must meet the same test as compared to the next following argument if the overall test is to succeed, for example:

```
*(<= 5 5 6 8 9 9 12 14)
T
```

The comparator predicates **equal**, **eql**, and **eq** (see Section 8.6) may also be applied to two numbers as a test for equality. However **eq** will only return T when applied to fixnums, since two bignums or floating-point numbers, like lists, may occupy different locations in memory and hence not be 'identical' to the standards required by **eq**. (In implementations other than GCLISP, **eq** may or may not be dependably used on fixnums.)

22.3 The basic arithmetic operations include +, −, *, and /

The basic arithmetic operations are carried out in LISP by the following functions:

addition :	(+ &rest <numbers>)	Section 3.4
subtraction :	(− <number> &rest <more-numbers>)	Section 3.7
multiplication:	(* &rest <numbers>)	Section 3.7
division :	(/ <number> &rest <more-numbers>)	Section 3.7

These were covered in Chapter 3, as indicated.

22.4 incf and decf increment and decrement generalized variables

The concept of a generalized variable was introduced in Section 4.11. Two functions are available which may be used to increment or decrement the value currently associated with the variable. If this value is not a number an error will be generated.

(incf <place> &optional <delta>) adds the value of **<delta>** to the number stored at **<place>** and returns the sum. Both values must be numbers. If not given, **<delta>** defaults to 1.

(decf <place> &optional <delta>) operates like incf, but decrements the number instead.

22.5 Common LISP provides for various exponential and logarithmic functions

Of the various exponential and logarithmic functions supported by Common LISP, GCLISP supports the following:

- (abs <number>) returns the absolute value of <number>.
- (signum <number>) returns −1, 0, or 1 depending on whether <number> is negative, zero, or positive.
- (exp <number>) returns the natural logarithm e raised to power <number>.
- (expt <base-number> <power-number>) returns <base-number> raised to the power <power-number>.
- (log <number> &optional <base>) returns the logarithm of <number> in the base <base> (which defaults to 10).
- (sqrt <number>) returns the principle square root of <number>.
- (isqrt <number>) returns the integer square root of <number>, that is, the largest integer that is less than or equal to the exact positive square root of the number.
- (sin <radians>) returns the sine of <radians>.
- (cos <radians>) returns the cosine of <radians>.
- (tan <radians>) returns the tangent of <radians>.
- (atan <y> &optional <x>) returns an arc tangent in radians. Given one argument, atan returns its arc tangent. Given two arguments, the arc tangent of <y>/<x> is returned.

The GCLRM (p. 234) provides documentation on the use of the function sys:8087-fpp, which is provided to control the use of or emulation of an auxiliary 8087 chip for making floating-point calculations.

22.6 Type conversions and component extractions may be made

When integers and floating-point numbers are compared or combined by a numerical function, the rule of *floating-point contagion* is followed. This means that dissimilar types of numbers are converted so that they all become the same type prior to applying the numerical operator. When combined with floating-point numbers, integers are converted to a floating-point number of the same format; in similar vein, single-float numbers are converted to double-float when appropriate.

Although the above conversions are carried out automatically, Common LISP also provides several functions to do them explicitly. The function **float**, which takes the syntax:

```
(float <number> &optional <template>)
```

converts **<number>** to a floating-point number, that is, an object of type **float**. If **<template>** is not given, the number is converted to a single-float number; otherwise it is converted to a number of the same type as **<template>**.

The function **coerce**, which takes the syntax:

```
(coerce <object> <result-type>)
```

returns an object of type **<result-type>** which is equivalent to **<object>**, and can be used to make conversions between types of numbers as well as other data objects.

Other functions extract components from a number and return some significant result. **truncate**, which takes the syntax:

```
(truncate <number> &optional <divisor>)
```

converts **<number>** to an integer by truncating towards zero. If a divisor is included, **truncate** returns the integer resulting from the division plus an integer or floating-point number equal to the remainder. **<divisor>** defaults to 1. For example:

```
* (truncate 10 3)
3
1
```

Other functions in this general category are:

- **(floor <number>)** returns the greatest integer that is less than or equal to **<number>**, that is, truncates toward negative infinity.
- **(ceiling <number>)** returns the least integer that is *not* less than **<number>**, that is, truncates toward positive infinity.
- **(round <number>)** returns the integer that is closest to **<number>**. If two integers are equally close, the even integer is returned.
- **(mod <integer> <divisor>)** returns the smallest integer remainder of **<integer>/<divisor>** that is the same sign as **<divisor>**. Both arguments must be integers.
- **(rem <integer> <divisor>)** returns the smallest integer remainder of **<integer>/<divisor>** that is of the same sign as **<integer>**. Both arguments must be integers.

22.7 Bit-wise logical operations may be carried out on numbers

Decimal integers, when converted into binary notation, produce a vector of 0 and 1 bits. Such vectors may be used, for instance, to represent a set of objects, with the presence or absence of elements in the set being mapped against to 0-or 1-bits in the vector.

Common LISP provides various functions to carry out logical operations on such vectors. The interested reader is referred to the CLRM p. 220–5 for more discussion on this subject. GCLISP supports the following Common LISP functions:

- **(logior &rest <integers>)** returns an integer which is the result of a bit-wise logical **inclusive or** of all of its arguments. If no arguments are given, zero (the identity for this operation) is returned.
- **(logxor &rest <integers>)** returns an integer which is the result of a bit-wise logical **exclusive or** of all of its arguments. If no arguments are given, zero is returned.
- **(logand &rest <integers>)** returns an integer which is the result of a bit-wise logical **and** of all its arguments. If no arguments are given, −1 is returned.
- **(logeqv &rest <integers>)** returns an integer which is the result of a bit-wise logical **equivalence** (that is, the **exclusive nor**) of all of its arguments. If no arguments are given, −1 is returned.
- **(lognot <integer>)** returns an integer which is the bit-wise logical **not** of integer.
- **(logtest <integer1> <integer2>)** is a predicate which is true iff there is a bit in **<integer1>** and a bit in the same position in **<integer2>** which are both one-bits.
- **(logbitp <index> <integer>)** is a predicate which is true iff the **<index>**'th bit of **<integer>** is a one-bit
- **(ash <integer> <count>)** arithmetically shifts **<integer>** by **<count>** bit positions. If **<count>** is a non-negative integer, **<integer>** is shifted **<count>** positions to the left (filling with zeros on the right and discarding bits on the left). If **<count>** is a negative integer, **<integer>** is shifted **<count>** positions to the right (copying the sign bit on the left and discarding bits on the right.) NB: Since integers are of fixed size, an arithmetic shift can cause the sign to change.
- **(lsh <integer> <count>)** shifts **<integer>** by **<count>** bit positions. If **<count>** is a non-negative integer, **<integer>** is shifted **<count>** positions to the left (filling with zeros on the right and discarding bits on the left). If **<count>** is a negative integer, **<integer>** is shifted **<count>** positions to the right (filling with zeros on the left and

discarding bits on the right). (NB: This is not a standard Common LISP function.)

22.8 Arrays are useful for storing large sets of data

Up to now we have been using the *list* as the primary data object for the storage of data. Miscellaneous collections of objects such as pocket contents or groceries have been grouped together in the form of a list; properties and their values have similarly been contained in lists; and associations and their values have been stored in a somewhat more structured way as nested elements of lists.

Although lists are useful in this regard, providing considerable flexibility as regards information storage, retrieval, and general manipulation, they have some shortcomings as a data storage mechanism. Retrieval of a particular item from a long list involves time-consuming search operations using car/cdr combinations or other mechanisms such as nth or match. Lists are also relatively wasteful of storage, since each item requires the allocation of an extra address cell for the sole purpose of pointing to the next item.

Common LISP provides an alternative mechanism – the *array* – to provide for holding large sets of data. An array is a more efficient means of storing information, since the data is placed in contiguous bytes of memory which require no pointers to the next piece of data, and functions are available which can quickly retrieve a piece of data from any specified array location.

An array may be a *general array*, meaning that each element may be any LISP object; or it may be a *specialized array*, meaning that each element must be of a particular specified type.

The components of an array are arranged according to a rectilinear coordinate system specified in terms of its number of dimensions. Common LISP implementations generally support a minimum of seven dimensions. An array with one dimension (which is the maximum supported by GCLISP) is referred to as a *vector*. Vectors whose elements are restricted to type string-char are called *strings*.

22.9 make-array creates and returns a one-dimensional array

Creation of an array is effected by use of the function make-array, which takes the syntax:

```
(make-array <dimension> &key :element-type
                             :initial-element
                             :initial-contents
                             :fill-pointer
                             :leader-length
                             :named-structure-symbol)
```

GCLISP arrays differ from the Common LISP standard in that only a single dimension is permitted. The Common LISP keywords **:adjustable**, **:displaced-to**, and **:displaced-index-offset** are not supported; but two additional (nonstandard) keywords are provided: **:leader-length** and **:named-structure-symbol**, the uses of which are described below.

The <**dimension**> specifies the length of the vector and must be a non-negative integer.

The argument to **:element-type** specifies what type of element may be stored in the vector. If it is **T** (the default), the array is a general array and any LISP object may be stored in it. Other possible types include **string-char** and **(unsigned-byte 8)**.

If the keyword **:initial-element** is provided, each element of the vector is initialized to the value of its argument, which must be an object of the type specified by **:element-type**.

The keyword **:initial-contents** is used to initialize the contents of the vector. Its argument must be a list whose length is equal to <**dimension**>; and the elements of the list must be of the type specified by **element-type**. The *n*th element of the vector is initialized to the *n*th element of the list. The keywords **:initial-element** and **:initial-contents** may not both be specified. If neither is specified, the initial values of the vector elements are undefined.

A vector may optionally be provided with a *fill pointer*, which is used to keep track of where you are along the vector when adding elements to or deleting them from the vector. The value of **:fill-pointer** may be **T**, **NIL** (the default), or a non-negative integer less than or equal to **dimension**. If **NIL**, the vector will not have a fill pointer; otherwise it will be provided with a fill pointer which is initialized to either the end of the vector (by specifying **T**) or to some particular offset location (by specifying an integer).

The argument to **:leader-length**, if this keyword is used, must be a non-negative integer. If specified, the vector will have an *array leader* of that length. (This amounts to prefixing the array with additional elements which can be used to contain special information related to the use of the array.) Note that the elements in an array leader are of type **T**, no matter what the element-type of the array.

The keyword **:named-structure-symbol**, whose argument must be a symbol, provides a means of assigning a *type* designation to the array which is being created. The object returned by **make-array** will be of type **structure** with the name <**symbol**>.

(Caveat: Early versions of GCLISP do not enforce a number of the documented constraints. Even if **:element-type** is specified, data objects of other types are accepted into the array without complaint, whether by way of values initialized through use of **:initial-element** or **:initial-contents**, or by subsequent use of **setf/aref**. Also, the former two keywords are not mutually exclusive; if both are used, the values associated with **:initial-contents** will override.)

index	*contents*	
9	0	
8	0	
7	0	
6	0	
5	0	← fill
4	E	pointer
3	D	
2	C	
1	B	
0	A	

Fig. 22.1 An array of 10 elements with fill pointer.

Let us create an array of 10 elements, of which the first five will be initialized with letters from A to E. A fill pointer will be specified at index position 5. (Note that indices start from position 0.) In order to access the array later we have to give the object a name, say, **our-array**:

```
* (setf our-array
    (make-array 10 :initial-contents '(A B C D E)
                   :fill-pointer 5))
#<VECTOR T 10 891C:FB26>
```

We have now created an array which corresponds to Fig. 22.1. The elements which have not been specifically initialized have been set to 0. The fill pointer has been set to point to the 6th element, that is, index position 5. Elements located at or above the location of the fill pointer are said to be *inactive*; those below the pointer are said to be *active*.

Now that we have created the array, the next step is to find the means of accessing the information in the array and/or changing the contents of the array elements.

22.10 aref accesses an array location

The contents of an array may be retrieved by use of **aref**, which takes the syntax:

```
(aref <array> <index>)
```

and which returns the <index>'th element of <array>. The <index> must be a non-negative integer less than the dimension of the <array>. (Since indices start at 0 the highest possible index will be one less than the dimension.) Hence **aref** can access *any* element in <array>, regardless of whether of not the element is active, relative to the location of a fill pointer if one exists.

```
* (aref our-array 3)
D
```

Since it is convenient to be able to scan the entire contents of the array during our experiments, we can define **check-array** to iterate over the elements of the array and display them on the screen:

```
* (defun check-array (array)
    (dotimes (index (array-length array))
      (format t "~%Element at index ~a = ~a"
                  index
      (aref array index))))
CHECK-ARRAY
```

Using our new function on the array which we have just created:

```
* (check-array our-array)
Element at index 0 = A
Element at index 1 = B
Element at index 2 = C
Element at index 3 = D
Element at index 4 = E
Element at index 5 = 0
Element at index 6 = 0
Element at index 7 = 0
Element at index 8 = 0
Element at index 9 = 0
NIL
```

Uninitialized elements of arrays in Common LISP are generally undefined. (NB: GCLISP initializes all such elements to 0, irrespective of the types of elements which may be specified for the array.)

The related function **svref**, which takes the same general syntax as **aref**, is used to return an element of a simple vector.

22.11 setf can be used to alter the contents of an array

Using **aref** to define the generalized variable location, the **setf** macro can be used to modify an element of an array:

```
* (setf (aref our-array 7) 'hotdog)
HOTDOG
* (setf (aref our-array 8) '(How now brown cow!))
(HOW NOW BROWN COW!)
```

The fact that these values have been inserted into the respective array elements may be quickly verified using **check-array**.

22.12 The fill pointer permits a vector to be used as a stack

The current position of the fill pointer can be ascertained using **fill-pointer**, which takes the syntax **(fill-pointer <vector>)**. (An error is signaled if the argument to **fill-pointer** is not a vector with a fill pointer.)

```
* (fill-pointer our-array)
5
```

In some applications the fill pointer can be used in much the same way as a stack pointer, that is, to permit use of the array as a stack. The array-access functions **vector-push** and **vector-pop** support such usage.

The first function, which takes the syntax **(vector-push <element> <vector>)**, attempts to extend the active length of **<vector>** by storing **<element>** into the location currently pointed to by the fill pointer, and increments the fill pointer to point to the next higher element. Referring to our earlier example of **our-array**:

```
* (vector-push 24 our-array)
5
```

pushes the integer 24 into location 5, which is currently being pointed to by the fill pointer, and advances the pointer upwards to location 6. In the event the fill pointer is already at the top of the vector, **<vector>** is left unchanged and **NIL** is returned; otherwise the index where **<element>** was stored is returned.

The associated function **(vector-pop <vector>)** decreases the active length of **<vector>** by one and returns the value of the element extracted from the location now pointed to by the fill pointer. If the fill pointer is already at zero, vector-pop returns unpredictable values (rather than signalling an error as indicated in the GCLRM); hence, a fill pointer check should be made before carrying out a vector-pop.

Finally, **array-has-fill-pointer-p** is a predicate which is true iff its single argument **<vector>** has a fill pointer.

22.13 An array leader can hold special information about an array

Through use of the un-Common LISP keyword **:leader-length** it is possible to preface a GCLISP array with a specified number of so-called 'leader elements.' Such elements are general in nature and can be used to contain any sort of information which might be useful in processing the elements of the array, in storing a total or average of (numerical) elements of the array, etc.

Functions which relate to leader elements are the following:

- (array-has-leader-p <vector>) is a predicate which is true iff <vector> has an array leader.
- (array-leader-length <vector>) returns the length of <vector>'s array leader, if it has one, and NIL otherwise.
- (store-array-leader <element> <vector> <index>) stores <element> in the <index>'th position of <vector>'s array leader. <object> is returned. (Alternatively a setf assignment can be made using array-leader (see below) as an access form.)
- (array-leader <vector> <index>) returns the index'th element of <vector>'s array leader.

If a fill pointer is specified for a vector, it will be noted that array-has-leader-p will return T when tested against the vector, and array-leader-length will return 1. This is because GCLISP prefixes such vectors with a single leader element and uses that element to store the current index of the fill pointer.

As we previously defined check-array, we can similarly define check-array-leader for printing out the contents of the leader elements:

```
(defun check-array-leader (array)
  (ifn (array-has-leader-p array)
       (format t "~%Array ~a has no leader" array)
       (dotimes (index (array-leader-length array))
         (format t "~%Leader element at index ~a = ~a"
                   index
                   (array-leader array index)))))
```

22.14 Elements may be copied from one array to another

The contents of one array may be copied over to another array using copy-array-contents, which takes the syntax (copy-array-contents <from-array> <to-array>).

A new array can be created, named, and copied into all in one fell swoop with an expression such as:

```
(copy-array-contents <existing-array>
  (setf <new-array-name>
    (make-array <dimension>)))
```

which does all the appropriate work and returns T.

If <from-array> has more elements than <to-array>, the excess <from-array> elements are ignored. If <to-array> has more elements than

<from-array> its excess elements are filled with NIL (if it is a general array) or zero (if it is a string-char or (unsigned-byte 8) array. Fill pointers which may exist in either array are ignored.

22.15 Various functions provide information about an array

Various functions are available which provide different kinds of information about an array.

The function array-in-bounds-p takes the syntax:

```
(array-in-bounds-p <vector> &rest <index>)
```

and is a predicate which is true iff <index> is greater than 0 and less than the length of <vector>.

array-active-length, which takes the array name as its single argument, returns the fill pointer of <array> if it has one; otherwise it returns the total number of elements in <array>.

array-length, which takes the array name as its single argument, returns the total number of elements in <array>, regardless of the fill pointer. (Note that since GCLISP supports only vectors, array-length in effect performs a subset of the functionality of the Common LISP function array-total-size.)

22.16 vector creates a simple general vector

The function vector, which takes the syntax:

```
(vector &rest <objects>)
```

creates and returns a simple general vector whose initial contents are <objects>. For example:

```
* (setf our-vector (vector 2 4 6 8 10))
#<VECTOR T 5 891C:276C>
```

creates a five-element vector containing the objects listed. Hence this operation produces essentially the same result as:

```
(make-array n :initial-contents (list obj1 obj2 ... objn))
```

Now that we have seen the use of arrays as a mechanism for storing data, let us look at another way in which information can be stored in the form of a user-defined data structure.

22.17 **defstruct** permits the user to create new data types

In Chapter 18 we looked at the *property list* as a means of storing information about a particular object. In the example we used, the hobbies, weight, and age of a person named Harry were put on Harry's property list, from which they could later be retrieved via a **get** operation. Alternatively the whole property list could be retrieved using **symbol-plist**:

```
* (symbol-plist 'harry)
(HOBBIES (GOLF TENNIS) WEIGHT 150 AGE 30)
```

If we have a lot of people in our data base it would be desirable to have some way of creating a special data object for *person* so as to be able to assign and retrieve data directly rather than having to use expressions such as **(setf (get 'harry 'age) 30)**.

The macro **defstruct** provides such a facility. **defstruct** permits you to create a new data type, much like a record in PASCAL or other languages which support records. Components of this structure may be named in much the same manner as record fields are named; the necessary constructor, access, and assignment functions are automatically created when we create the new data type.

The **defstruct** macro takes the general form:

```
* (defstruct (<name> :conc-name
                     :constructor
                     :predicate
                     :print-function
                     :type
                     :named
                     :initial-offset)
    <slot-description-1>
    <slot-description-2>


    <slot-description-n>)
```

where each **<slot-description>** roughly corresponds to the name of an indicator on a property list. (GCLISP does not support the slot options described in the CLRM p. 310.)

The macro name is followed by a list consisting of the name of the structure to be created and various optional keywords. If no keywords are specified, the name may be entered either as a list or as a symbol. If keywords are specified, each keyword and its argument must be entered as a sublist, for example, **(:type list)**. Since all of the keywords are optional we will ignore them for the time being and consider only the basic case of **defstruct**. We will use this macro to create a data type called **person**, and then look at the auxiliary functions which can be used to create an instance of this data type named **Harry**.

First, using **defstruct** to create the new data type:

```
* (defstruct person
             hobbies weight age)
; Autoload: DEFSTRUCT from "DEFSTRUC" in "C:\\GCLISP\\etc".
PERSON
```

Since we are using no keywords, the structure name **person** can be entered as a symbol rather than enclosing it in a list. If this is the first time **defstruct** is being called it will be autoloaded.

After defining the new data structure, **defstruct** returns the name of the structure. It should be noted that **defstruct** does not actually *create* a structure; rather, it defines a *template* for it. The template will later be used by the constructor function (see Section 22.19) which creates *instances* of the structure. Aside from creating the template, **defstruct** also creates a number of auxiliary functions with which the structure may be accessed and otherwise manipulated.

There is no specific function provided for printing out a summary of the elements and keywords which were used in creating a structure. However if you remember the structure name you can use **apropos-list** (see Section 25.10) to provide information on the slot names, as well as on the functions automatically defined by **defstruct**:

```
* (apropos-list "person")
(PERSON-HOBBIES PERSON MAKE-PERSON PERSON-WEIGHT
PERSON-AGE PERSON-P)
```

apropos-list, which takes a string as its single argument, makes a search through all of the system packages and returns a list of all variables and symbols which contain the argument as a substring.

As an additional exercise you may wish to define a retrieval function which takes a structure name as its single argument, uses **apropos-list** to generate a list as above, weeds out irrelevant elements such as **PERSON-P**, uses **apply** on the remaining elements to extract values from the slots of a structure, and prints out the slot names and their values on the console.

22.18 Default initialization values may be specified

At the time of defining the structure, default initialization values may be specified for some or all of the slots. For example, if our data base concerns boy scouts we might initialize the value of **sex** as **male**. When a slot is provided with a value, the **slot-name/value** pair must be entered as a list:

```
* (defstruct boy-scout
        age weight badges (sex 'male))
BOY-SCOUT
```

22.19 defstruct automatically creates a constructor function

As part of the complex **defstruct** procedure, when a new data structure is created a *constructor function* is also created with the name **make-<name>**, where **<name>** is the name of the structure. Hence, when we created the **person** structure in the above example, a constructor function named **make-person** was also (automatically) created. We can readily check as to whether it has indeed been created by evaluating:

```
(pprint (symbol-function 'make-person))
```

(NB: In Version 1.0 the above should be preceded by the expression **(setf *print-level* nil)** to assure a full printout of the function definition.)

We can use **make-person** to create an *instance* of the structure **person**. As with arrays, streams, etc. we have to have some handle with which to access the resulting structure, so we will use **setf** to give it a name at the same time as we create it. We can create a structure in which none of the slots are initialized (other than with default values which may have been incorporated into the basic call to **defstruct**):

```
* (setf harry (make-person))
#s(PERSON :HOBBIES 0 :WEIGHT 0 :AGE 0)
```

Since this leaves us with the job of updating all of Harry's slots, we would more often explicitly initialize some or all of these values when we create the structure:

```
* (setf harry (make-person :hobbies '(golf tennis)
                           :weight 150
                           :age 35))
#s(PERSON :HOBBIES (GOLF TENNIS) :WEIGHT 150 :AGE 35)
```

We have now created a data object of type **person** and have assigned this object as the value of the symbol **harry**. Since objects created by **defstruct** are not directly printable as such, the special syntax **#s(PERSON <slots values>)** is used to represent the structure.

It will be noted that the slot names are expressed as keywords, prefixed with a colon. This reflects that when a new data object is created, **defstruct** interns each of the slot names in GCLISP's **keyword** package (see Section 25.3).

22.20 Various type tests can be applied to structures

The act of creating a structure with **defstruct** causes the structure's name to become a valid type specifier which may be tested with the functions **type-of** and **typep**.

type-of takes a single argument and returns its type:

```
* (type-of harry)
PERSON
```

typep is a predicate which confirms whether its first argument is of the type specified by its second argument:

```
* (typep harry 'person)
T
```

22.21 A predicate and a copier function are also defined

defstruct also automatically creates two additional functions: a predicate which may be used to check if a given object is a structure defined by **defstruct**, and a function which may be used to copy an existing structure.

The predicate takes the syntax **(<structure-name>-p <object>)**, and returns **T** or **NIL** as appropriate:

```
* (person-p harry)
T
```

The copier function takes the syntax **(copy-<structure-name> <object>)**, and can be used to create a copy of a structure.

22.22 Access functions are created for each defstruct slot

In the same manner as the constructor function was automatically created by **defstruct**, a number of *access functions* are also created. An access function, which takes the form **(<structure-name>-<slot-name>)** is created for each slot in the structure. The function takes a single argument: the structure being accessed. We can therefore retrieve Harry's age with the access function for that particular slot:

```
* (person-age harry)
35
```

22.23 defstruct slots can be updated with setf

The macro setf can be used to update a defstruct slot. For example, if we want to change Harry's age to 40:

```
* (setf (person-age harry) 40)
40
* (person-age harry)
40
```

Note that the macros incf and decf can also be used to increment or decrement the value in a slot, providing that the value is an integer.

22.24 defstruct supports a number of optional keywords

As noted in Section 22.17, a number of optional keywords may be included in a call to defstruct. These keywords are used as follows:

- :conc-name, which defaults to the structure name plus a hyphen, permits you to specify some other prefix to the access functions which are automatically created by defstruct. If NIL is used as the argument then *no* prefix is used, and the access function name becomes the same as the slot name.
- :constructor permits you to specify some other name for the constructor function. (Note that the *by-position constructor functions* described in the CLRM p. 315 are not supported by GCLISP.)
- :predicate permits an alternative name to be specified for the type predicate.
- :print-function (which may only be used if the :type option is not specified) permits you to arrange for printout of the structure to some other stream such as the printer (see the CLRM p. 314 for more detailed discussion). If left unspecified, a default printing function is provided which will print out all the slots of a structure using the #S syntax as noted in the preceding examples.
- :type explicitly specifies the printed representation to be used for the structure, that is, as a general vector, a specialized vector, or a list (see Section 22.25 below).
- :named may be used in conjunction with the :type keyword so that the name of the structure is recoverable from the structure itself, if a choice has been made to represent the structure as a vector or a list (see Section 22.26 below).
- :initial-offset allows you to specify that slots be allocated beginning at an element other than the first (see the CLRM pp. 315 and 319–20 for more detailed discussion).

22.25 Structure representation may be explicitly specified

There may be occasions when we wish to use a structure created by **defstruct** for storage of information, and yet find it desirable to maintain the data in the form of a vector or a list. As noted above, the **:type** option may be used to force the structure into such a representation. Revising our earlier **person** example:

```
* (defstruct (person (:type list))
             hobbies weight age)
PERSON
* (setf harry (make-person :hobbies '(golf tennis)
                           :weight 150
                           :age 35))
((GOLF TENNIS) 150 35)
```

Firstly, we note that the structure **person** is no longer being printed with the **#<PERSON>** syntax, but rather as a list, reflecting that we have forced it into this representation through use of the **:type** keyword. If we experiment a bit we will find that the access functions created by **defstruct** still work properly and that we can update slot values with **setf** in the same manner as before. However:

```
* (typep harry 'person)
NIL
* (type-of harry)
CONS
```

that is, the structure **person** is no longer recognized by **typep** as a valid type of data object. The CLRM refers to such a structure as a 'conceptual' data type because it is not made a part of the Common LISP type system. Furthermore, although the structure has been created by a **defstruct**-type operation, there is no way to recover that it is a **person** structure from the structure itself, as we could do previously with **type-of**.

We can partially get around the structure identification problem by explicitly naming the structure and defining our own predicate to recognize it.

22.26 The :named keyword permits a structure to be named

For structures which have been forced into a list or vector representation through use of the **:type** keyword, the **:named** option can be used to name the structure explicitly. This is done by inserting the name as the first element of the list or vector:

```
* (defstruct (person (:type list) :named)
            hobbies weight age)
PERSON
* (setf harry (make-person :hobbies '(golf tennis)
                           :weight 150
                           :age 35))
(PERSON (GOLF TENNIS) 150 35)
```

Although PERSON is still not a valid type specifier, the fact that the name is now contained as the first element in the list lends itself to identification with a user-defined type predicate, say:

```
(defun person-p (x)
  (and (consp x)
       (eq (car x) 'person)))
```

See the CLRM pp. 317–19 for in-depth discussion of the finer points of named and unnamed structures. (NB: The :named keyword may cause errors in early versions of GCLISP.)

Several un-Common LISP functions are provided by GCLISP to aid in identification of a named structure

The function named-structure-p, which takes <object> as its single argument, returns NIL if <object> is not a named structure (whether by virtue of being a normal product of defstruct or an explicitly named structure). If <object> is a named structure, its name is returned.

The function named-structure-symbol, which takes <object> as its single argument, returns <object>'s name (a symbol) if the object is a named structure.

SUMMARY

Summarizing the main points of this chapter:

- GCLISP supports *four types of numbers* including *fixnums*, *bignums*, and two types of floating-point numbers
- various *recognizer predicates* can be used to test the type of a number; whether it is positive, negative, or zero; and whether it is odd or even
- various *comparator predicates* can be used to test the magnitude of a number versus that of another number or numbers
- a wide range of functions is available in Common LISP to carry out various *arithmetic*, *exponential*, *logarithmic*, and *bit-wise* operations on numbers
- *arrays* are useful for storing large sets of data, since they minimize storage requirements and at the same time permit speedy access to any element of the array
- the function **make-array** can be used to create an array, and the function **aref** to access an element of an array
- array elements may be modified through the use of **setf** together with an array access function
- the *fill pointer* of an array keeps track of the highest active element, and can control use of an array as a stack
- additional information related to an array can be stored in the *array leader* elements
- the macro **defstruct** permits the user to create a new data type, and at the same time automatically creates functions for constructing an instance of the data structure and for accessing and modifying elements of the structure
- the representation of a structure created with **defstruct** can be explicitly specified through use of the **:type** keyword

EXERCISES

22.1 Given the symbol **N**, write expressions to test whether **N** is:

(a) a number

(b) an integer

(c) a floating-point number

22.2 Given the integer X, write expressions to test whether X is:

(a) a positive number
(b) a negative number
(c) zero
(d) an odd number
(e) an even number

22.3 Given the numbers X and Y, write expressions which will return T if:

(a) X is equal to Y
(b) X is not equal to Y
(c) X is less than Y
(d) X is greater than Y

22.4 Assume that it is Harry's birthday today and write an expression which increments his age by 1. Assume that Harry's age is the value associated with the indicator age on his property list.

22.5 Write two alternative expressions which create a vector of dimension 15, containing all of the digits from 0 to F in hexadecimal, and assign this vector as the value of hex-array.

22.6 Define the function get-hex-array which takes the array created in Exercise 22.5, uses a subsidiary function hex-to-dec to convert the elements of the array from hexadecimal to decimal, and lists the converted values on the console in the typical format:

Element 15 = F (hex) = 15 (dec)

Store the function name of hex-to-dec in an array leader element of our-array and use array-leader to retrieve it when required by get-hex-array.

22.7 Define the function convert-array, which takes the array created in Exercise 22.5, iterates over each of its elements, and replaces the hexadecimal element with its decimal equivalent. Store the conversion function hex-to-dec in an array leader element as in Exercise 22.6.

22.8 Using defstruct, define the structure show-dog with the slots pedigree-name, breed, sex, and age. Create an instance of this data type with the slot values "Steeleblade Beaulieu Woofniks", boxer, male, and 5, respectively, and assign the structure as the value of the symbol BEAUDOG.

22.9 Define a show-dog structure as in Exercise 22.8, but assume that all dogs in the kennel are male boxers and provide appropriate default values for these slots.

22.10 Redefine the structure created in Exercise 22.9 such that it is represented as a list; include provision for naming the structure; and define the predicate show-dog-p which tests whether an object is of the conceptual type show-dog.

Chapter 23

Interfacing with File Systems

In the course of working with our LISP interpreter we will inevitably find ourselves using one or more files. At the very least we will have a file to contain the principal expressions which constitute an applications program: function definitions, macro definitions, and assignment statements which initialize the global variables used by the program. Such files, which are given the extension .lsp to identify them as LISP program files, are normally created during program development on the GMACS editor, but may also be created with a standard text editor such as WordStar. These files are stored on a floppy disk or in a directory on the hard disk from which they may be load'ed when required. Aside from LISP program files, we may also wish to access and manipulate ASCII text files used for the storage of text and/or data base information.

Common LISP provides a standardized system of *pathnames* which are used to specify the manner in which the operating system can gain access to such files.

In this chapter we will look at:

- the concept of a *pathname*, which provides a standardized specification of the way in which a file may be accessed
- the use of make-pathname and merge-pathnames to create pathnames, including optional default provisions
- the use of *defaults-pathname-defaults* for providing a set of default pathname components
- the various Common LISP functions which are available for identifying pathname objects or retrieving the components of a pathname
- the use of open and with-open-file for creating a file and/or opening a stream for transmittal of data to or from a file
- the use of close and close-all-files for closing the stream associated with a file

23.1 A pathname provides a standardized way of accessing a file

In order to provide for consistency in accessing files, the location of any Common LISP file may be expressed in the form of a standardized *pathname* which is made up of six components. The *host*, a term used in networking, is the name of the file system on which the file resides. The *device* is the name of the (logical or physical) device containing the file. The *directory* is the name given to a group of related files. The *name* is the name of the specific file in question. The *type* is an extension which is usually used to indicate the nature of the file, for example **.COM**, **.BAS**, **.LSP**, etc. Finally, the *version* is a number which is incremented each time the file is modified. (GCLISP, designed to run on MS-DOS machines, supports neither the *host* nor the *version* components.)

Therefore if we have a file named **testfile.lsp** in our WordStar **(ws)** directory on hard disk drive C, it may be accessed by the namestring **"C:\ \ws\ \testfile.lsp"**. As shown in Fig. 23.1, this is converted by the LISP system into the pathname used to access the file, with double backslash separators between device/directory and directory/filename. The first backslash, which is parsed as LISP's single escape character, causes the second separator to be taken literally.

(NB: GCLISP also allows input of pathnames using a single slash in lieu of double backslash, for example:

```
(load "c:/ws/testfile.lsp")
```

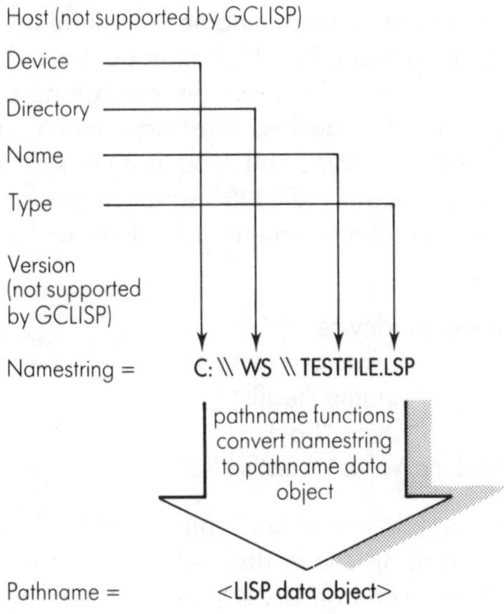

Fig. 23.1 A pathname is made up of six components.

but for the balance of this chapter we will use the double backslash convention for consistency with the values returned by most pathname functions.)

When encountered in the context of a command such as **open** (see Section 19.3) or **with-open-file** (see Section 19.6), the system automatically converts our namestring into a pathname through a process referred to as *parsing*. Alternatively we can explicitly create such pathnames through use of some of the functions outlined in this chapter.

Another operation which we will encounter involves the input of partial namestrings which lack certain components. The system has the capability of filling in the missing components from a set of default values, through a process referred to as *merging*.

23.2 make-pathname synthesizes a pathname from components

One of the ways in which we can explicitly create a pathname is through use of **make-pathname**, which takes the syntax:

```
(make-pathname &key :device
                    :directory
                    :name
                    :type
                    :defaults)
```

and which returns a pathname whose components are specified by the keyword arguments.

The general intent of **make-pathname** is to build up a pathname from a group of individual components which may be derived from somewhere within the program or may be obtained by prompting the user for input. The arguments provided for **:device, :directory, :name**, and **:type** must be either strings, **NIL**, **:wild** (for **:name** and **:type** only) or symbols, in which case their print names are used. Since GCLISP supports neither host nor version components, the corresponding Common LISP keywords are not supported. For example:

```
* (make-pathname :device "c:"
                 :directory "\\ws"
                 :name "testfile"
                 :type "lsp")
#.(PATHNAME "c:\\ws\\testfile.lsp")
```

Since a pathname is not a data object which can be visualized and which lends itself to printing, the #. dispatch character is used to precede an equivalent *printed representation* (CLRM pp. 355–6). (Note that it is necessary to prefix the directory name with double slash characters, which are otherwise inserted automatically between the directory and file name.)

A **:defaults** keyword argument may be provided, in which case those components of the (new) pathname which were left unspecified are filled by the corresponding components in the **:defaults** keyword argument. This argument may be a string, a pathname, or a variable such as ***default-pathname-defaults***, which evaluates to a string or to a pathname. Otherwise no default provisions are built into **make-pathname**, in which respect it differs from **merge-pathname** (see below).

Note that the mere fact of creating a pathname does not in itself create or open the corresponding file; it just specifies how to access the file once it exists. To create a file it is necessary to use the pathname in conjunction with a stream-opening function such as **open** or **with-open-file.**

23.3 **merge-pathnames** uses defaults to create a new pathname

When we create a new file it is likely that we will want the file to be put into the same drive and directory as other files on which we are currently working. We may also wish to tag the file with a similar extension, such as **.lsp.**

Rather than explicitly supplying all of the components to the new file name we may wish to take advantage of the automatic defaulting built into **merge-pathnames**, which takes the syntax:

```
(merge-pathnames <pathname> &optional <defaults>)
```

This function creates and returns a new pathname object that is a copy of **<pathname>** except that unspecified (that is, **NIL**) components are replaced with components from **<defaults>**. In this sense it is different from **make-pathname** in which a **:default** keyword argument must be explicitly included if any defaulting is to be carried out.

During the evaluation process all of the specified (that is, non-**NIL**) components of **<pathname>** are mapped onto corresponding components in the new pathname object. Then any components which remain unspecified are filled in with the defaults. For example:

```
* (setf *default-pathname-defaults* "c:\\ws\\filename.lsp")
"c:\\ws\\filename.lsp"
* (merge-pathnames "newfile")
#.(PATHNAME "C:\\WS\\NEWFILE.LSP")
```

Hence when we want to create (or open an existing) file called **"newfile"** with extension **.lsp** in directory **ws** on drive **C:**, assuming that the default pathname is as noted, we can open a stream as follows:

```
(setf file-stream
  (open (merge-pathnames "newfile") :direction :output))
```

and the default system will do the rest.

23.4 *default-pathname-defaults* provides a set of standard default values

The global variable ***default-pathname-defaults*** is used to provide any default values which may be required during a call to **merge-pathnames.** The value of this variable may be any object acceptable to the function **pathname**, that is, a string such as "C:\\ws\\filename.lsp", a pathname, or a symbol whose print name will be used.

For use with the GMACS editor, GCLISP initially binds ***default-pathname-defaults*** to #.(PATHNAME "C:\\GCLISP\\FOO.LSP"), assuming that the interpreter is instaled on the hard disk.

23.5 Some pathname functions return a pathname object

A variety of miscellaneous functions are available which return a pathname object or test whether an object is a pathname.

(pathname <pathname>) parses <pathname> and returns an equivalent pathname object. <pathname> may be a string, a symbol (whose print name is used), or a pathname object (which is simply returned). No defaulting is carried out. Pathname components which are left unspecified in <pathname> are set to **NIL** in the pathname object.

For convenience, we can assign a pathname object as the value of a variable to avoid the need for repetitive typing of the namestring:

```
* (setf file-path (pathname "c:\\ws\\testfile.lsp"))
#.(PATHNAME "C:\\WS\\TESTFILE.LSP")
* (setf file-stream (open file-path :direction :output))
#<DYNAMIC CLOSURE 78F1:4FC5>
```

(parse-namestring <pathname>) parses <pathname> and returns an equivalent pathname object. (Since GCLISP does not support the Common LISP optional and keyword arguments for this function, **parse-namestring** is for all intents and purposes identical to **pathname**.)

(parse-directory-namestring <namestring>) parses <namestring> as if it were a directory and returns an equivalent pathname object. The **name** and **type** components are always set to **NIL**. (This is not a Common LISP standard function.)

(pathnamep <object>) is a predicate which is true iff <object> is a pathname object.

23.6 Other functions return a pathname component

Certain other pathname functions are available which return a specific component of a pathname.

(pathname-device <pathname>) returns the device component of <pathname>. If <pathname> includes a device, its name is returned as a string; otherwise NIL is returned.

```
* (pathname-device file-path)
"C:"
```

Other functions return the remaining components.

(pathname-directory <pathname>) returns the directory component of <pathname>. If <pathname> does not have a specified directory component, NIL is returned. Otherwise if the directory component of <pathname> consists of a single subdirectory then a string which represents it is returned; otherwise if the directory component is composed of more than one subdirectory (that is, it is a hierarchy) then an ordered list of the subdirectories (each represented by a string) is returned.

```
* (pathname-directory "c:\\ws\\testfile.lsp")
("\\" "WS")
```

(pathname-name <pathname>) returns the name component of <pathname>. This function and the one which follows may return either NIL, :wild, or a string depending on whether the name component was unspecified, wild, or a specific name, respectively.

(pathname-type <pathname>) returns the type component of <pathname>.

23.7 Other functions return component strings

Other functions are available which convert all or part of a pathname back into its namestring equivalent.

(namestring <pathname>) returns the namestring which represents <pathname>:

```
* (namestring file-path)
"C:\\WS\\TESTFILE.LSP"
```

(file-namestring <pathname>) operates in a similar manner but returns a string which includes only the name and type components of <pathname>.

(directory-namestring <pathname>) operates similarly but returns a string which includes only the directory component.

23.8 **open** and **with-open-file** can be used to open a file

The function open (see Section 19.3), which takes the syntax:

```
(open <pathname> &key :direction <direction>
                      :element-type <element-type>)
```

returns a new stream that is connected to the external file named by <pathname>. The keyword arguments specify what kind of stream to connect to the file and how to handle opening the file. A list of keyword arguments and their allowed values is:

```
:direction
   :input (default) or :output
:element-type
   string-char (default) or unsigned-byte
```

If <pathname> is opened in the **:output** direction and such a file already exists, it is overwritten. (GCLISP does not support the Common LISP **append** option to the **:if-exists** keyword. See Exercise 23.8 for a way to add data to an existing file.)

A more convenient way to open a file is with the macro **(with-open-file** (see Section 19.6), which takes the syntax:

```
(with-open-file
   (<stream-name> <pathname> &optional
      :direction <direction>
      :element-type <element-type>)
   <form1> <form2> ... <formn>)
```

This macro establishes a connection between the named <**stream**> and the file named by <**pathname**>, within which the <**forms**> are evaluated as an implicit **progn**. The file named by <**pathname**> is opened as if by **open**, in compliance with the specified options. The variable named by the symbol <**stream**> is bound to the resulting stream. The <**forms**> are then evaluated as an implicit **progn** and the value of the last form is returned.

The purpose of **with-open-file** is to permit you to open a file, do something with it (put data in or take data out), and close the file, all within the aegis of a single function call. See Section 19.6 for a detailed discussion of **with-open-file**; see also Section 17.5 for a discussion of the use of **unwind-protect** in connection with the automatic closing of files.

23.9 File streams support an extended set of operations

A so-called *file stream* is created when an external file is opened by a call on **open** (see Section 19.3) or **with-open-file** (see Section 19.6). In Section 19.12 we discussed the manner in which a stream might be used as a kind of function in an object-oriented manner through the use of **funcall** or **send**.

In addition to the standard operations **:read-char**, **:unread-char**, **:which-operations**, etc. which are supported by *all* input and output streams, file streams additionally support the following extended operations peculiar to the use of files:

```
:set-pointer <n>
:read-pointer
:fill-array <array> :dump-array <array>
:pathname
```

The first two operations may be used, respectively, to set the file pointer of a file to some particular location and to retrieve that location. For example:

```
* (defun file-test-01 ()
    (with-open-file (outfile "c:\\ws\\file-01.lsp"
                        :direction :output)
      (format t "~%File pointer is at ~a"
                        (send outfile :read-pointer))
      (princ "ABCDEFGHIJKLMNOPQRSTUVWXYZ" outfile)
      (format t "~%File pointer is now at ~a"
                        (send outfile :read-pointer))
      (format t "~%Setting file pointer to 9")
      (send outfile :set-pointer 9)
      (format t "~%File pointer is now at ~a"
                        (send outfile :read-pointer))))
FILE-TEST-01
* (file-test-01)
File pointer is at 0
File pointer is now at 26
Setting file pointer to 9
File pointer is now at 9
NIL
```

As will be noted, upon opening a file the file pointer is set to 0, that is, pointing to the first byte in the file. After a **read** operation the file pointer will be advanced to the next byte following the last character read. Otherwise we can use **:set-pointer** to set the file pointer to any desired location, thereby permitting random access of the file.

:fill-array and **:dump-array** can be used to transfer blocks of text from one file to another, using an intermediate array (which we must create as part of the transfer process) as a buffer. Let's say we want to transfer 10 bytes from the file which we just created to a new file, **infile**, starting from the 10th byte. We can do this as follows:

```
* (defun file-test-02 ()
    (with-open-file (outfile "c:\\ws\\file-01.lsp")
      (with-open-file (infile "c:\\ws\\file-02.lsp"
                          :direction :output)
        (send outfile :set-pointer 9)
```

```
            (let ((letter-array
                    (make-array 10 :element-type 'string-char)))
              (send outfile :fill-array letter-array)
              (send infile :dump-array letter-array)))))
FILE-TEST-02

* (file-test-02)
"JKLMNOPQRS"
```

noting that we do not have to specify the default value of **:direction :input** for **outfile**, and that file pointers, like sequences, commence with 0 as the first element. In the above example we created the array **letter-array** of length 10, used a **:fill-array** operation to transfer 10 characters from the **outfile** stream to this array, followed by a **:dump-array** operation to move the contents of the array to the **infile** stream.

We can now check the contents of the new **file-02** to which we have transferred the partial contents of **file-01**:

```
* (defun file-test-03 ()
    (with-open-file (infile "c:\\ws\\file-02.lsp")
      (let (letter)
        (format t "~%Reading from file ~a"
                      (send infile :pathname))
        (terpri)
        (loop
          (setf letter (send infile :read-char))
          (if (null letter)
              (return))
          (format t "~a" (string letter))))))
FILE-TEST-03

* (file-test-03)
Reading from file #.(PATHNAME "C:\\WS\\FILE-02.LSP")
JKLMNOPQRS
NIL
```

The above example also illustrates the manner in which the **:pathname** operation can be used to retrieve the pathname of the file connected to the stream.

Note that the **:read-char** operation returns **NIL** at end-of-file; hence we used a **null** test on **letter** to trigger the return from the loop. This compares to the use of **read-char** as a distinct *function* (rather than a stream operation), in which we evaluated something like **(read-char <some-stream> nil 'eof)** and compared the value returned against **'eof** to test for end-of-file.)

23.10 Files can be closed individually or in batches

The functions for closing files are discussed in detail in Section 19.4, but will be reviewed briefly here in view of their relevance to interfacing with file systems.

The function close-all-files, which takes no arguments, closes all streams which are currently connected to files. We can use it to close the test file which we created previously:

```
* (close-all-files)
(#.(PATHNAME "C:\\WS\\TESTFILE.LSP")
```

As will be noted, this function returns the pathname(s) of whatever files have been closed. If no such streams are currently open close-all-files simply returns NIL. Since we will normally be using with-open-file to manage the closing of a file automatically there should be little need to use close-all-files. Also as noted in Section 24.11, close-all-files should not be called while dribble is being used to accumulate a history of a LISP session, since it will also close the dribble file.

Whereas close-all-files only closes streams connected to files, the related function close can be used to close any stream. Its syntax is:

```
(close <stream-name>)
```

Unlike close-all-files, close simply returns NIL when it closes a stream.

23.11 Other file operations include renaming and deleting

A number of utility functions permit the existence of a file to be checked, and allow for renaming and deleting of files while still in the LISP environment.

The function probe-file, which takes the pathname of the file as its single argument, checks whether or not an external file corresponding to <pathname> exists. If one does, the true pathname of the file is returned; otherwise NIL is returned.

```
* (probe-file "c:\\ws\\testfile.lsp")
#.(PATHNAME "C:\\WS\\TESTFILE.LSP")
```

A file name may be changed with rename-file, which takes the syntax:

```
(rename-file <pathname> <new-name>)
```

and which changes <pathname> to <new-name>. If the file is successfully renamed, three values are returned: the <new-name> pathname with no missing components, the old <pathname>, and the new truename of <pathname>. Otherwise if the file cannot be successfully renamed, an error is signaled. (Note that as per the CLRM, the *truename* may be different from the **pathname** because of 'file links, version numbers, or other artifacts of the file system.' Within GCLISP, the two should normally be identical.)

We can use this function to change the name of the file we previously created to, say, **newfile.lsp**:

```
* (rename-file "c:\\ws\\testfile.lsp" "c:\\ws\\newfile.lsp")
#.(PATHNAME "C:\\WS\\NEWFILE.LSP")
#.(PATHNAME "C:\\WS\\TESTFILE.LSP")
#.(PATHNAME "C:\\WS\\NEWFILE.LSP")
```

The function **file-info** (which is not a Common LISP standard function) takes the pathname of the file as its single argument and returns MS-DOS encoded information about the file, namely:

```
(file-info <pathname>) => attribute
                          filesize-hi
                          filesize-lo
                          creation-date
                          creation-time
```

Although GCLISP does not support the Common LISP function **file-length**, we can implement it using **file-info**:

```
(defun file-length (filepath)
  (multiple-value-bind (ignore hi lo)
                       (file-info filepath)
    (+ (* 65536 hi) lo)))
```

Finally, we can delete a file from the system with **delete-file**, which takes the pathname of the file as its single argument. If the file in question is found, it is deleted and its pathname returned; otherwise **NIL** is returned.

```
* (delete-file "c:\\ws\\newfile.lsp")
"c:\\ws\\newfile.lsp"
```

23.12 Various options are available during loading of files

The principle type of file with which we will normally be working is a **.lsp** program file containing top-level forms such as **defun**, **defmacro**, and **defvar/parameter/constant**, which define the functions and variables of the program. Such a file is loaded into the LISP environment with the function **load**, which takes the syntax:

```
(load <pathname> &key :verbose
                      :print)
```

GCLISP does not support Common LISP's **:if-does-not-exist** keyword.

The value of the keyword **:verbose** determines whether some sort of message will be printed to the screen when a file is loaded. If left out,

:verbose defaults to the current value of the global variable ***load-verbose***, which GCLISP initializes to **T**. The pathname of the file is printed as the value returned by **load**:

```
* (load "c:\\ws\\files-23.lsp")
; Reading file C:\WS\FILES-23.LSP
   <file is loaded>
#.(PATHNAME "C:\\WS\\FILES-23.LSP")
```

If the **:print** argument (which defaults to **NIL**) is set to **T**, the value of each expression is printed to ***standard-output*** as the file is loaded. This feature comes in particularly useful when you have been simultaneously editing a number of function definitions and, upon **load**'ing the file, get some kind of end-of-file error message. If you set the **:print** argument to **T**, the values returned from (successful) evaluation of the definitions will be printed one by one until the erroneous definition is reached, that is, the last thing printed on the screen before the error will be the value of the last successful form, so the error will be in the next form.

(fasload <pathname>), which is not a standard Common LISP function, loads the compiled-code file named **<pathname>**. If **<pathname>** has a missing type component, it defaults to **fas**. If the current value of ***load-verbose*** is non-**NIL**, **fasload** prints the name of the file being loaded in the form of a comment (like **load**).

23.13 **autoload** provides for automatic loading of supplementary functions and macros

In larger computer systems the complete implementation of Common LISP is available in on-board or virtual memory. However in small systems, such as MS-DOS, directly addressable memory is limited. In the interest of maximizing the amount of memory available for running programs, a number of lengthy functions are not built in as compiled code, but rather are stored in various files in the **LISPLIB** directory from whence they may be retrieved as needed.

The function cells of the symbols which name these functions are specially tagged so that when the function or macro is called for the first time, a special **autoload** routine is called to load the definitions from the file. As these definitions are loaded and evaluated, pointers to the lambda expressions or macros are placed in the function pointer cells of the associated symbols. Thereafter the definitions are accessed and executed in the same manner as for any user-defined function or macro.

Over a period of time in the course of your programming work you will inevitably create a number of useful 'utility' functions which you would like to have on tap as and when you need them, without having to include them explicitly as part of the source code of every applications program.

Once incorporated into some general file – say, UTILITY.LSP– such a function can be made accessible by including a top-level **autoload** statement somewhere in the program, with the following syntax:

```
(autoload <name> <file-name> &optional <library-path>
                                      <library-diskette>)
```

There are basically three ways in which you can execute the above **autoload** statement. Assuming that you have created the definition of **factorial** and put it in file **utility.lsp**:

(1) If file **utility.lsp** is stored in some directory, say, "C:\\WS\\" on your hard disk, you can provide for autoloading it by the statement:

```
* (autoload factorial "utility.lsp" "c:\\ws\\")
("utility.lsp" "c:\\ws\\" NIL)
```

noting that the directory name must be both preceded *and* followed by double slashes. The **autoload** function returns the so-called **file-access-list**. Subsequently, the first call to **factorial** in a program will generate an autoload message:

```
* (factorial 5)
; Autoload: FACTORIAL from "utility.lsp" in "C:\\WS\\"
120
```

(2) As the second hard disk option, you may wish to add your utility file to directory C:\\GCLISP\\LISPLIB\\, which is the default directory for autoloaded files. Although this directory contains GCLISP .FAS (compiled) files, you can also store your **utility.lsp** file in this directory. In that case your autoload statement can be reduced to:

```
* (autoload factorial "utility.lsp")
("utility.lsp" SYS::*LISP-LIBRARY-PATHNAME* NIL)
```

where the parameter **SYS::*LISP-LIBRARY-PATHNAME*** is bound to the default directory pathname \\GCLISP\\LISPLIB\\.

(3) Finally, if you are working without a hard disk, you can specify a file on a drive, for example:

```
* (autoload factorial "utility.lsp" "A:\\lisplib\\" "A:")
```

in which the drive is explicitly specified as the second optional argument. In the above case, if the directory and file cannot be found in the drive you will be prompted to insert it.

GCLISP Version 1.1 contains several auxiliary global parameters which may be used in conjunction with autoloading facilities

If the value of **sys::*al-log-stream*** is a stream object, information will be logged to this stream when a file is autoloaded. For example, assuming that we had previously defined **factorial** (see Section 13.2) and now wanted to pretty-print the definition; that we had not previously caused **pprint** to be autoloaded; and that we want the information to be logged into file **auto.lsp** in directory **ws** on drive **C**:

```
* (with-open-file (sys::*al-log-stream* "c:\\ws\\auto.lsp"
                   :direction :output)
    (pprint (symbol-function 'factorial)))
; Autoload: PPRINT from "PPRINT" in "c:\\GCLISP\\LISPLIB\\".
<factorial definition is pretty-printed>
```

If we now modify **file-test-03** (see Section 23.9) to read the above new file **auto.lsp** (instead of **file-02.lsp**):

```
* (file-test-03)
Reading from file #.(PATHNAME "C:\\WS\\AUTO.LSP")
Autoload LISP:PPRINT from "PPRINT" in "C:\\GCLISP\\LISPLIB\\"
```

we see that the autoloading of **pprint** has been logged into the file. This facility would be useful to determine those specific GCLISP functions which have been autoloaded by a given applications program. For example, it might be desirable to incorporate these definitions specifically into the program source code to preclude run-time delays associated with autoloading.

The parameter **sys::*autoload-verbose***, which defaults to **T**, controls the printing of information about files being autoloaded to the ***trace-output*** stream (normally the console), as in the above example.

The parameter **sys::*print-al-errors***, which defaults to **NIL**, similarly controls the printing of error messages triggered by problems in trying to log the autoload information.

Note that *double* colons are required when referencing the above parameters, since they are not external to package **SYS**.

23.14 Directories may be changed or otherwise accessed

A point to note in connection with the use of directories is that at any point in time MS-DOS and GCLISP may each be operating with a different default directory.

All things being equal, the MS-DOS default directory is whichever one you were in when you called up GCLISP, or when you returned from MS-DOS to the interpreter with the **exit** command. This is also the directory you will find yourself in when you temporarily leave the interpreter with the **(sys:dos)** command.

The GCLISP default directory, on the other hand, is whichever one is currently specified by the pathname bound to ***default-pathname-defaults***.

As mentioned earlier, this is initialized to the pathname "C:\\GCLISP\\FOO.LSP".

The function **cd** (Change Directory), which takes the syntax **(cd &optional <pathname>)**, changes the MS-DOS default drive and directory to those specified in **<pathname>**. At the same time, **cd** updates the value of ***default-pathname-defaults*** to reflect the new MS-DOS default drive and directory. The new value of ***default-pathname-defaults*** is returned. The argument to **cd** must be either a pathname object or a namestring; if the latter, it is converted to a pathname using **parse-directory-namestring.** If **cd** is called without an argument, it updates the value of ***default-pathname-defaults*** to correspond to the current MS-DOS default drive and directory.

Another useful function is **directory,** which takes a single **<pathname>** argument. **directory** returns a list of all of the pathnames which match **<pathname>**, whose components may be wild. **(directory "*.* ")** can be used to retrieve the names of all files in the current default drive/directory without leaving the interpreter. For example, if you have just booted up GCLISP from drive A:

```
* (directory "*.*")
(#.(PATHNAME A:\\CONFIG.LSP)
#.(PATHNAME A:\\CONFIGGC.LSP)
#.(PATHNAME A:\\INIT.LSP)
#.(PATHNAME A:\\USERINIT.LSP)
#.(PATHNAME A:\\GCLISP.COM))
```

A more readable listing can be obtained by extracting the actual file names from the **PATHNAME** statements (see Exercise 23.4).

SUMMARY

Summarizing the main points of this chapter:

- a *pathname* provides a standardized means of defining the access path to a file by specifying the device, directory, name, and type of the file
- pathnames can be created by *parsing* a namestring or by *merging* a partial pathname together with the default values bound to the global variable ***default-pathname-defaults***
- various functions are available to retrieve components of a pathname, or to test whether a LISP data object is a pathname
- a stream to a file may be opened using the functions **open** or **with-open-file**; the latter is preferable since it provides for automatic closing of the file
- *file streams* support an extended set of operations, including **:set-pointer**, **:read-pointer**, **:fill-array**, **:dump-array**, and **:pathname**
- a stream to a file may be closed using the function **close**, which closes a specific stream, or **close-all-files**, which closes all file streams which are currently open
- the function **load**, which loads LISP program files into the environment of the interpreter, includes various keyword options which provide for the printing of messages and echoing of values to the console
- GCLISP includes provision for **autoload**'ing of supplementary macro and function definitions from the Utilities 2 diskette

EXERCISES

23.1 Define **get-pathname**, which prompts the user for all necessary components, uses **make-pathname** to build up the pathname, and returns the pathname. Make provision for automatic insertion of "\\" before the directory name.

23.2 Write the two expressions required to establish directory **lispprog** as the default directory on drive **B:** and **.lsp** as the default file type; and to create a pathname, using **merge-pathnames**, to file **lispfile** in that same directory.

23.3 Define **check-file**, which prompts for the pathname of a file and advises whether or not the file exists.

23.4 Define **get-files**, which prompts for the name of a device and directory, and prints a list of the names of all the files in that directory.

23.5 Assuming that the file **our-file.lsp** exists in directory **ws** on drive C:, write expressions which return:

(a) the pathname to the file

(b) the drive on which the directory is located

(c) the directory name

(d) the file name

(e) the file type

23.6 Using **with-open-file**, create a file called **my-file.lsp** in directory **ws** on drive C (or an alternate directory and/or drive to suit your system) and put into it the expression **(SETF *PRINT-BASE* NIL *PRINT-LEVEL* NIL)**. Then temporarily return to DOS and check that the file has been created and the data entered.

23.7 Write an expression which accesses the file created in Exercise 23.6 and prints the expressions contained therein to the printer.

23.8 GCLISP does not support Common LISP's **:if-exists** keyword and its **append** option to permit data to be added to an existing file. Devise a series of expressions whereby the function definition for **factorial** (see Section 13.2) can be added to the data already existing in the file created in Exercise 23.6. (Hint: Create a new file, transfer the data from the existing file, and add the new data.)

23.9 Write an expression which **load**'s the file created in Exercises 23.6 and 23.8 and prints the contents of the file to the console as they are being evaluated.

23.10 Assuming that the **load** function of your system has suddenly packed up, define an alternative function **our-load** which does the same thing. Ignore the need to provide for **:verbose**, **:print**, and **:if-does-not-exist** keywords.

Chapter 24

Debugging, Tracing, and Timing

As with any software, a LISP application program is prone to error during the development stage and will inevitably require some degree of debugging. Due to the highly interactive nature of LISP, debugging is generally easier than in other languages. The **break** mechanism is particularly useful, since, in a manner of speaking, you can stop and *query* the interpreter as to what is going wrong! Other facilities such as **trace** permit you to monitor the arguments being passed to functions and the values which are being returned; and **step** permits you actually to accompany an evaluation step by step.

For testing and improving real-time applications in which quick response time is important, other functions are available to measure the exact time it takes to execute a function call, as well as to run benchmarks to test your implementation of LISP against other versions.

In this chapter we will look at:

- the kinds of *error messages* which are generated by a LISP program, and how these error traps can be built into your function definitions
- how you can call a temporary halt to the evaluation process with the *break* mechanism, and use a subordinate **read/eval/print** cycle to inspect the current state of the environment
- the use of **trace** and **untrace** to check on the arguments which are being supplied to a function call, as well as the values being returned by the function
- how the **step** option may be used to review, on a step by step basis, the evaluations which take place during a call to a function
- the use of **dribble** to capture the history of an interactive LISP session
- how to halt program execution for a specified number of seconds
- how to measure the *elapsed time* required to execute a function call

24.1 Common LISP includes provision for error handling

As anyone who has ever worked on interactive software will testify, a substantial amount of coding is dedicated to testing keyboard input to assure that proper kinds and/or ranges of values are being supplied in response to prompts, and to generating appropriate messages if such is not the case. LISP provides several facilities for the latter purpose.

There are two kinds of errors which can be committed during the course of running a program: *fatal errors* and *nonfatal errors*. As the names imply, a fatal error is one in which the error is such that evaluation must be brought to a halt – for example, when a symbol is provided as an argument when a number is expected. A nonfatal error is one in which something is not quite as expected but, assuming that you know about it and provide a waiver, the program can continue operation.

24.2 Fatal errors are signaled with error

Fatal errors may be signaled with **error**, which takes the syntax:

```
(error <format-string> &rest <args>)
```

The **<format-string>** (see Section 12.5) may be used to generate the error message. To the extent format directives are included, the **<args>** which follow are applied to the directives.

We can build **error** into our program so as to generate an appropriate message if something goes wrong. Taking a simple example, let us define a function which simply adds two numbers. We can build in a test which assures that numerical arguments are being supplied and complains if this is not the case:

```
(defun add-em-up (x y)
  (if (not (numberp x))
     (error "Not a number: ~a" x))
  (if (not (numberp y))
     (error "Not a number: ~a" y))
  (+ x y))
```

Assuming the evaluation process can work its way through the minefield of error traps, the arguments must be legitimate numbers and the final function call to + can be carried out with confidence.

In the above case we are of course preempting Common LISP's own built-in system of error messages. If we defined **add-em-up** as simply:

```
(defun add-em-up (x y)
   (+ x y))
```

and tried it out with anything but numbers, we would get the same kind of error message from the LISP interpreter, which is set up to test for such things. Hence we would normally reserve the explicit use of **error** in programs for things which the interpreter could not be counted on to intercept automatically.

When a fatal error is encountered in our program, an error message is generated and we are put into *break* mode at the first *listener level* with a number to indicate the level:

```
* (+ 'apples 'pears)
ERROR:
+: wrong type argument: APPLES
A NUMBER was expected.
1>
```

We can return to the top level by executing the function **(sys:clean-up-error)**, which can either be explicitly typed in or, more conveniently, can be invoked simply by pressing the Ctrl-G keychord. If we are at a lower break level, Ctrl-G will return us to the next higher level; alternatively if we are at a deeply nested break, we can use Ctrl-C to jump us directly back to the top level.

It should be noted that the use of **(sys:clean-up-error)** automatically ensures that any **unwind-protect** clean-up forms are evaluated before returning, for example, to close files which might otherwise have been left open, etc. (See Section 17.5 for a discussion of **unwind-protect** and Section 12.9 for discussion of the formatting aspects of **error**.)

24.3 Nonfatal errors are signaled with cerror

Nonfatal errors are signaled with **cerror**, which permits you to continue program execution and which provides for an additional message indicating what will happen if you choose this option. The syntax of **cerror** is:

```
(cerror <continue-string> <format-string> &rest <args>)
```

Like **error**, **cerror** puts us in break mode after generating its messages. The difference between the two is that, after a **cerror** message has been generated, we can cause program evaluation to continue by executing the keyboard command **(continue)** or by pressing Ctrl-P. Alternatively we can stop evaluation and return to the top level with Ctrl-G or Ctrl-C, as with **error**. To illustrate the format of messages generated by **cerror**:

```
* (setf number 'hotdog)
HOTDOG

* (unless (numberp number)
        (cerror   "Number defaults to 0"
                  "Not a number: ~a" number)
        (setf number 0))
```

```
ERROR:
Not a number: HOTDOG
If continue with (CONTINUE): Number defaults to 0
1>
```

In the above example, use of the **(continue)** option would cause the program to evaluate the next following form, which would reset **number** to 0.

Arguments can be incorporated into both the <**continue-string**> and the <**format-string**>, but special arrangements must be made (see Section 12.9) to segregate which arguments apply to which string.

Although ***error-output*** is defined for compatibility with Common LISP, GCLISP does not use this stream for the generation of error messages. Instead it uses the ***debug-io*** stream, which initially defaults to ***terminal-io***. Like other streams, ***debug-io*** can be changed under program control to output error messages via other streams. (See Section 19.2 for more discussion on **streams**.)

24.4 ignore-errors provides for special handling of errors

The un-Common LISP special form **ignore-errors**, which takes the syntax:

```
(ignore-errors <forms>)
```

causes <**forms**> to be evaluated in much the same manner as **progn**. In the event an error is encountered, **ignore-errors** immediately returns **NIL** as its first value and a string describing the error as its second value, for example:

```
* (ignore-errors (+ 'apples 'pears))
NIL
"+: wrong type argument: APPLES
A NUMBER was expected."
```

Hence **ignore-errors** can be built into a program as a sort of predicate so that in the event of an error the above values can be returned to a higher level calling function without halting execution of the program (see Exercise 24.5).

If no error occurs while **ignore-errors** is being evaluated, it returns two values: the first result returned by the last form and **NIL**:

```
* (ignore-errors (setf apples 5 pears 10))
10
NIL
```

Note that multiple values (except the first) will be lost when using **ignore-errors**.

24.5 The break key permits a program to be interrupted

A program may be interrupted in the middle of the **read/eval/print** cycle in either of two ways: by pressing the Ctrl-Break keychord or by explicitly building a **(break)** function call into a program.

The first method must be used in cases where the program seems to be taking an inordinately long time to do something and you feel that perhaps it has been caught in an endless loop. As discussed previously (see Section 2.8) we can artificially create such a situation by simply executing a function call to **(loop)**. The Ctrl-Break keychord puts us in break mode, exactly as discussed above in connection with error situations, except that Ctrl-C rather than Ctrl-G must be used to get us back to the top level.

Several global parameters are used in connection with breaks. The value of **sys:*break-event*** must be a function, which is invoked whenever the user types the break key-sequence. The initial value of **sys:*break-event*** is, not surprisingly, the function **break**. In other words, when you use the break key you get exactly the same effect as if a function call to **(break)** had been explicitly incorporated into the program at that point. Note that any function to which **sys:*break-event*** is bound should not simply return, since it can corrupt storage in GCLISP. It should do a **throw**, or a **break**, or something similar. Note also that 0 arguments are passed to the function.

The variable **sys:*break-level*** represents the number of nested break points or errors that are waiting to be handled; this is the number which is displayed along with the prompt (see below).

The global value of **sys:*break-prompt*** is a function which is called each time through a break-level **read/eval/print** loop. The purpose of this function is simply to print a break prompt to the ***debug-io*** stream. Like the subroutine which generates the normal prompt symbol of *, this break prompt function is called just before **read**, and prints the value of **sys: *break-level*** followed by the string "> ".

While in break mode, another **read/eval/print** cycle has effectively been nested within the previous cycle which was operating up until the break. Using this nested cycle, you can type in the names of variables to see what their current value is and in general carry out any evaluation which provides information about the status of the program. You can also generate side-effects – such as **setf**'ing new values to variables – which will be carried over when you return to normal program operation at the higher level.

24.6 An explicit break statement may also be used to halt a program

For debugging purposes, the function **(break)** may be explicitly built into a program to cause it to halt at that point to permit inspection of variable values, etc. **break** takes the syntax:

```
(break &optional <format-string> &rest args)
```

If you have only built a single break into the program, naturally there is no need to bother with the format statement since you know where you are when the program halts. In more complex situations, two or more breaks may be built into the program with unpredictable branching possibilities so that it is necessary to identify at which particular break you are. For this purpose a format statement may be built into the function call in a manner similar to that described for **error** and **cerror** above.

After making the required tests at the break level, execution of the program may be continued by executing **(continue)** or Ctrl-P from the keyboard. In this case Ctrl-G doesn't work and Ctrl-C returns us to the top level rather than causing program operation to resume.

As an example of the use of **break**, let's modify our addition function to incorporate a break:

```
* (defun add-em-up (x y)
    (break)
    (+ x y))
ADD-EM-UP
* (add-em-up 5 10)
BREAK, (CONTINUE) or Ctrl-P to continue
1>
```

Immediately upon calling the function, the first form to be evaluated is the **break** statement. The program halts and issues a break prompt, and we now have a new **read/eval/print** cycle at our disposal to explore the current status of variables, for example:

```
1> x
5
1> y
10
```

We see that the formal parameters have been bound to the arguments as expected. Since there is not much else we can investigate in this case, we continue operation:

```
1> <Ctrl-P>
15
```

The interpreter resumes evaluation where it had left off and returns the final value.

Note that the foregoing example works in Version 1.0 of GCLISP and in normal implementations of Common LISP; however there is a bug in Version 1.1 such that only global values of a variable are visible during a break. Hence during the debugging stage a special declaration must be temporarily built into the function, for example:

```
(defun add-em-up (x y)
  (declare (special x y))
  (break)
  (+ x y))
```

in order that the local bindings of the variables may be accessed during the break. Since this can conceivably effect the behavior of the function, another alternative is to build in temporary **format** statements to indicate the current (lexical) value of the variables:

```
(defun add-em-up (x y)
  (format t "~%Value of x is ~a" x)
  (format t "~%Value of y is ~a" y)
  (+ x y))
```

24.7 trace provides a running display of how a function is performing

trace is a useful function which provides a display of the arguments which are being passed to each (traced) function, and the values which are being returned by these functions. **trace**, which takes the syntax:

```
(trace <function-names>)
```

causes the evaluation of each function named by **<function-names>** to be traced. In effect **trace** temporarily *replaces* each function definition with a modified definition. The modified definition provides additional facilities which, as each function is called, print out the arguments to the function, and as each function is exited print out the value returned. Furthermore the printouts are indented to a degree commensurate with the depth of nesting.

When called with no arguments, **trace** returns a list of the functions which are currently being traced.

We can review an earlier example from our chapter on recursion, in which the function **count-elements** was called recursively to count the number of elements in a list:

```
* (defun count-elements (some-list)
    (if    (null some-list)
           0
           (1+ (count-elements (cdr some-list)))))
COUNT-ELEMENTS
* (trace count-elements)
; Autoload: TRACE from "TRACE" in "C:\\GCLISP\\LISPLIB\\".
T
```

```
* (count-elements '(A B C))
ENTERING: COUNT-ELEMENTS, ARGUMENT LIST: ((A B C))
  ENTERING: COUNT-ELEMENTS, ARGUMENT LIST: ((B C))
    ENTERING: COUNT-ELEMENTS, ARGUMENT LIST: ((C))
      ENTERING: COUNT-ELEMENTS, ARGUMENT LIST: (NIL)
      EXITING: COUNT-ELEMENTS, VALUE: 0
    EXITING: COUNT-ELEMENTS, VALUE: 1
  EXITING: COUNT-ELEMENTS, VALUE: 2
EXITING: COUNT-ELEMENTS, VALUE: 3
3
```

with the final value returned printed after the **trace** printout.

Output from **trace** is routed to the stream ***trace-output***, which defaults to ***terminal-io*** (see Section 19.2). The value of ***trace-output*** could of course be modified under program control to direct output to some other stream such as a file or the printer.

The associated function **untrace**, which takes a syntax similar to that of **trace**, undoes the effect of the **trace** function and returns the named functions to normal (untraced) operating mode. If one of the symbolic arguments to **untrace** has a function definition which is currently being traced, **untrace** replaces the (trace-modified) function definition with the original function definition; otherwise it ignores the symbol. **untrace** returns a list of the functions which were actually untraced.

Several caveats should be mentioned in connection with **trace**, namely, (1) don't try to **trace trace**, or you will wind up in an endless loop as it tries to trace itself! and (2) the use of **trace** on common primitives such as **cons**, **car**, etc. may appreciably slow down your program if it involves a lot of **cons**'ing or other list manipulations, and (3) a function which is in the middle of a **trace**'d execution should not be **untrace**'d – for example during a break – or the interpreter will get corrupted.

24.8 sys:backtrace displays contents of the control stack

As nested functions are called during the course of evaluation, the interpreter needs temporarily to store and keep track of the names of higher level function calls as well as the evaluated and/or unevaluated arguments associated with these functions. All of this information is maintained on a so-called *control stack*. At each level on the stack, a *stack frame* is created which keeps track of the pending state of evaluation of a given form. The most recent stack frame corresponds to the most deeply nested form currently being evaluated.

The **sys:backtrace** facility (not defined in Common LISP) may be used to display the contents of this control stack. When **sys:backtrace** is called, each form which has been given to the evaluator but which has not yet been completely evaluated is displayed on a separate line in reverse chronological order, that is, the form most recently given to the evaluator is displayed first. Working back up the line, one can usually spot where some value has gone wrong or some invalid operation has been attempted.

As a rough and highly contrived example:

```
(defun test-backtrace ()
  (prog (x y)
    (setf y 10)
    (setf x (+ 5 (car y)))
    (format t "~%Value of x is ~a" x)))
TEST-BACKTRACE

* (test-backtrace)
ERROR:
CAR or CDR of non-LIST object: 10
1>
```

If at this point in the break we call (sys:backtrace):

```
1> (sys:backtrace)
(SYS:BACKTRACE)
(CAR Y)
(+ 5 (CAR Y))
(TEST-BACKTRACE)
NIL
1>
```

the control stack is displayed in reverse order, with the most recent form under evaluation, that is, the one which caused the error (CAR Y), on top. Higher level forms for which evaluation is still in suspension are displayed lower down the list (subject to exceptions as noted below) with the original function call at the very bottom.

In GCLISP the usefulness of sys:backtrace is somewhat limited since macros such as setf and special forms such as setq and prog are not displayed. Since these types of constructs frequently constitute a large percentage of a function definition, the resulting backtrace display may leave out a lot of the forms which are pending evaluation.

24.9 step permits step-by-step review of the evaluation process

The step macro provides a very flexible means whereby you can review the evaluation process step by step. This macro takes the syntax:

```
(step <form-to-be-evaluated>)
```

When called in this manner, the <form-to-be-evaluated> is displayed immediately below the function call. Thereafter various option keys from the numeric keyboard may be used to carry out the stepping operation. (Make sure that the Number Lock key is not currently active, since this disables the functional use of these option keys.) Pressing of any key other than one of the step function keys causes the list of stepping options to be displayed. Using the example from the GCLISP User's Guide:

```
* (step (+ 1 (+ 2 3)))
; Autoload : STEP from "STEPPER" in "C:\\GCLISP\\LISPLIB\\".
(+ 1 (+ 2 3)) <press any key at this point>
STEP commands are:
   arrow-dn →  Step to next level down
   arrow-rt →  Value of this form
   arrow-up →  Step to next level up
   arrow-lt →  PrettyPrint current form
   Ctrl-Break → Enter Break level
   END →       Complete without more Stepping
```

The arrow-down option causes a step-wise evaluation of the form to take place, starting with the smallest subforms within the form and working towards the right. As each subform is evaluated its value is printed and the next subform to the right is displayed. The arrow-right option evaluates the (whole) current form being displayed and prints the next form onto the screen. The arrow-up option evaluates the current form which is displayed and the form which encloses it. The arrow-left option causes the current form (which may be long and complex) to be pretty-printed on the screen for improved readability. The End key (the #1 key) causes the remaining evaluation to be carried out to completion and returns you to the top level.

At any time during a stepping operation you can use Control-Break to cause a break to occur, in which case the phrase STEPPER BREAK is printed below the current form and the break prompt is displayed. At this point you are in standard break mode and can carry out break-type experiments. To return to stepping mode you have to use (continue) or Ctrl-P; Ctrl-G doesn't work and Ctrl-C takes you directly back to the top level.

24.10 Pretty-printing can flag out parentheses errors

As mentioned above, pprint (see Section 11.7) can be useful in outputting the printed representation of its single argument in a manner which provides for easy readability. Aside from use within a stepping operation, pprint can be called up at any time to check the construction of a user-defined function (or a macro; see Section 16.4). Its principal advantage in this regard is to check on the manner in which those troublesome parentheses have been distributed. For example, the parentheses may balance overall but you may have an extra parenthesis after one expression and be lacking a parenthesis after another. Pretty-printing will show this up in a graphical manner. For instance, in the following function:

```
(defun test-cond (number)
  (cond ((> number 0)(format t "~%Number is positive"))
        ((< number 0)(format t "~%Number is negative"))
        (t           (format t "~%Number is zero))))
```

If we pretty-print the above (properly formed) definition, we get a nicely balanced printout:

```
* (pprint (symbol-function) 'test-cond)
(LAMBDA (NUMBER)
   (COND ((> NUMBER 0)
          (FORMAT T "~%Number is positive"))
         ((< NUMBER 0)
          (FORMAT T "~%Number is negative"))
         (T
          (FORMAT T "~%Number is zero"))
         ))
NIL
```

If, on the other hand, we have left out a parenthesis after the second **cond** clause and compensated for it by an extra parenthesis at the end of the function, the bottom six lines of the printout would have appeared as follows:

```
         ((< NUMBER 0)
          (FORMAT T "~%Number is negative")
          (T (FORMAT T "~%Number is zero")))
         ))
NIL
```

giving us an immediate visual indication of where parentheses have been misplaced.

24.11 **dribble** captures the history of an interactive session

For various purposes, including debugging, it is often desirable to record the history of an interactive session. Some microcomputer implementations provide for setting printer control variables so that all transactions are echoed to the printer. Common LISP provides the function **dribble**, which takes the syntax:

```
(dribble &optional <pathname>)
```

which causes all input and output from the stream ***terminal-io*** to be recorded to a file named **<pathname>**. When called with no arguments, dribble terminates the recording of input and output and closes file <pathname>. For example, the following sequence will record the interactive history to file "history" on drive B:

```
* (dribble "b:history")
; Autoload: DRIBBLE from "DRIBBLE" in <pathname>
T
* "How now brown cow!"
"How now brown cow!"
* (car 10)
ERROR:
CAR or CDR of non-LIST object: 10
1> <Control-C>
Top-Level
* (dribble)
```

If we now temporarily exit GCLISP with (sys:dos) and check drive B we will find a new file history has been created which contains a record of the above input and output.

When using dribble, remember to close other files explicitly. Don't use the catch-all close-all-files, since this will close the dribble file as well.

24.12 Your PC keeps track of the session date and time

Time measurements are occasionally required for general use, for measuring how long it takes to execute some function critical to a real-time application, or for comparing the efficiency of your LISP implementation versus a system running on another machine.

Your PC has an internal clock which, once initialized, keeps automatic track of the date and time. This data may be updated at any time using the DOS commands date and time:

```
A:\>date
Current date is Tue 1-01-1980 <the MS-DOS default date>
Enter new date (mm-dd-yy):
A:\>time
Current time is 0:01:18.59 <random time>
Enter new time:
```

Since the date and time are automatically stored in the directory at the time a file is created or modified, it is a good idea to keep this information up to date if for no other purpose than to help identify the latest version of a file. The commands date and time may be built into your startup AUTOBAT.BAT file in order to provide automatic prompts for this information each time the PC is booted up.

24.13 **get-decoded-time** returns the current time

For retrieving the date and time for general use, the Common LISP primitive **get-decoded-time** taps into the PC clock and returns the current time in the form of multiple values: second, minute, hour, date, month, year. For example:

```
* (get-decoded-time)
4
38
17
1
1989
```

where the month is expressed as a digit, that is, 1 = January.

We can readily define the macro **get-elapsed-time**, which calculates the total time required to execute a given form. This macro uses **multiple-value-setq** (see Section 17.9) to assign the time values returned by **get-decoded-time** to appropriate variables. For our purposes we will assume that only the seconds and minutes will be required:

```
(defmacro get-elapsed-time (form)
  `(let ((min-1 0)(min-2 0)(min 0)
       (sec-1 0)(sec-2 0)(sec 0))
    (multiple-value-setq
       (sec-1 min-1) (get-decoded-time))
    (eval ,form)
    (multiple-value-setq
       (sec-2 min-2) (get-decoded-time))
    (setf sec (– sec-2 sec-1))
    (if (minusp sec)
       (setf sec (+ sec 60) min-2 (1– min-2)))
    (setf min (– min-2 min-1))
    (if (minusp min)
       (setf min (+ min 60)))
    (format t "~%Elapsed time is ~a:~a"
       min sec)))
```

However since **get-decoded-time** only measures time to the nearest second, the above macro is only suitable for rough time measurements. For real-time applications, the macro **time** (see Section 24.15) provides for more accurate measurement.

A related function **get-internal-real-time** returns a single integer that represents the number of hundredths of a second since midnight:

```
* (get-internal-real-time)
; Autoload: GET-INTERNAL-REAL-TIME from "UTIL" in <pathname>
3377505
```

24.14 Time delays can be built into a program

Under certain circumstances it may be desirable to halt program execution under control for a certain time. The function **sleep**, which takes a single integer argument, causes execution to cease for the number of seconds specified, for example:

```
* (progn
    (format t "~%Start of 5-second time delay")
    (sleep 5)
    (format t "~%End of 5-second time delay"))
Start of 5-second time delay
<screen hangs up for 5 seconds>
End of 5-second time delay
```

See also Exercise 24.9.

24.15 time measures elapsed time to 100ths of a second

The Common LISP macro **time**, which takes the syntax:

```
(time <form>)
```

evaluates **<form>** and measures the time required for the evaluation. The values returned by **<form>** are returned by the overall **time** construct. In addition, **time** prints a report on the elapsed time to the stream which is the current value of ***trace-output***.

In GCLISP this activity is performed by the macro **time**, which with its subordinate function **eval-time** is stored in the directory **LISTLIB** on the Utilities 2 diskette. These macros/functions take the same general form as the modified versions **get-time** and **time-elapsed** shown below:

```
(defmacro get-time x
  `(time-elapsed ',(car x)))

(defun time-elapsed (form)
  (let (start finish hun-1 hun-2
        sec-1 sec-2 min-1 min-2 vals)
    (multiple-value-setq (nil nil nil min-1 start)
        (sys:%sysint #x21 #x2c00 0 0 0))
    (setq vals (multiple-value-list (eval form)))
    (multiple-value-setq (nil nil nil min-2 finish)
        (sys:%sysint #x21 #x2c00 0 0 0))
    (setq hun-1 (logand start #x0ff)
```

```
          hun-2 (logand finish #x0ff)
          sec-1 (lsh start -8)
          sec-2 (lsh finish -8)
          min-1 (logand #x0ff min-1)
          min-2 (logand #x0ff min-2))
    (setq hun (- hun-2 hun-1))
    (if (minusp hun)
      (setq hun (+ hun 100)
            sec-2 (1- sec-2)))
    (setq sec (- sec-2 sec-1))
    (if (minusp sec)
      (setq sec (+ sec 60)
            min-2 (1- min-2)))
    (setq min (- min-2 min-1))
    (if (minusp min)
      (incf min 60))
    (format t "~%Elapsed time is ~a:~a.~a" min sec hun)
    (values-list vals)))
```

As will be noted, time-elapsed taps directly into the registers of the CPU chip using sys:%sysint (see Section 26.1) to obtain the current time. (GCLISP's versions of the foregoing have been slightly modified to permit more general use in the exercises which follow.)

24.16 Gabriel benchmarks provide standardized tests for LISP systems

It is of interest to be able to compare the relative efficiency of a LISP implementation running on one type of computer with the efficiency of another version running on another type of machine. For this purpose, so-called *benchmarks* have been devised which provide a standardized basis for comparison.

The primary source of such benchmarks is Richard P. Gabriel's book *Performance and Evaluation of LISP Systems*, which documents about 20 different benchmarks devised to measure various kinds of LISP capabilities, for example, general function calls, cons'ing, numerical operations, destructive list operations, traversal of tree structures, iteration, search, pattern-matching, etc. Many of these 'Gabriel benchmarks' have become industry standards.

An example is tak, the first benchmark in the book, of which Gabriel writes:

> 'The TAK benchmark is a variant of the Takeuchi function that Ikuo Takeuchi of Japan used as a simple benchmark. Because Tak is

function-call-heavy, it is representative of many LISP programs. On the other hand, because it does little else but function calls (fixnum arithmetic is performed as well), it is not representative of the majority of LISP programs. It is only a good test of function call and recursion, in particular.'

tak is defined as follows:

```
(defun tak (x y z)
  (if (not (< y x))
    z
    (tak (tak (1- x) y z)
         (tak (1- y) z x)
         (tak (1- z) x y))))
```

Used as a standard benchmark, tak is called with the following arguments:

```
(tak 18 12 6)
```

With these arguments tak makes 63609 function calls and performs 47706 subtractions by 1. The result returned by the function is 7.

Using our get-time macro to run tak on our PC:

```
* (get-time (tak 18 12 6))
  <go out and make some coffee>
  Elapsed time is 0:5:27.35
```

Gabriel makes a number of relevant observations in connection with benchmarking, namely, that:

- Benchmarking is most effective when carried out in conjunction with an analysis of the underlying LISP implementation and computer architecture.
- Performance is not the only – or even the most important – measure of a LISP implementation. Trade-offs are often made that balance performance against flexibility, ease of debugging, and address space.

In connection with the analysis aspect, a substantial part of the book is dedicated to a discussion of the architectures of a number of principal machines on which the benchmarks were run. A wealth of interesting detail is provided as to the manner in which architecture influences the observed performance when running the different benchmarks.

SUMMARY

Summarizing the key points of this chapter:

- error traps for fatal and nonfatal errors can be built into your programs using **error** and **cerror**, both of which can include formatted error messages
- the special form **ignore-errors** can be used to identify an error condition and otherwise permit a program to continue execution
- a program may be interrupted through use of Control-Break or by explicit inclusion of the **(break)** function so as to permit debugging evaluations to be carried out at a lower listener level
- the **trace** function is useful in reviewing the arguments which are passed to a function and the values returned by that function
- the **sys:backtrace** mechanism permits review of the *control stack* to assist in debugging
- a step-by-step review of the evaluation process may be carried out using the **step** feature
- LISP's *pretty-printing* mechanism can be usefully employed to check on the proper placement of parentheses
- a complete history of the input and output occurring at the top level of an interactive LISP session may be captured to file using **dribble**
- various macros and functions such as **get-decoded-time** and **time** are available for ascertaining the current time or for measuring how long it takes to execute a function call
- program execution can be halted for a specified number of seconds using the **sleep** function
- *Gabriel benchmarks* represent industry-recognized standard tests for evaluating LISP systems

EXERCISES

24.1 Define **get-name**, which prompts for your name and returns it as a value. If anything other than a symbol is entered, print the fatal error message "**Not a symbol: <input>**".

24.2 Define plus-or-minus, which prompts for input of an integer and prints a message as to whether the number is positive, negative, or zero. If anything other than an integer is entered, print the fatal error message "Number is not an integer: <number>".

24.3 Define get-file-name, which prompts for the name of a file and returns this name as a value. If the file name is longer than eight characters, print the nonfatal error message "File name <file-name> longer than 8 characters" with the (continue) option message "Truncating to 8 characters".

24.4 Define what-time, which generates three prompts for the current time in the format:

```
Please input the time:
  Hours :
  Minutes:
  Seconds:
```

and returns the three values. If anything other than a positive integer is entered in response to any prompt, and/or if hours are more than 23, or minutes or seconds more than 59, print an appropriate nonfatal error message with the (continue) option message "<Time> defaults to 00".

24.5 Define the function add-integers, which takes two integer arguments and adds them together. If the sum is within GCLISP's allowable integer limit the function prints "The sum is <sum>"; otherwise it prints "Sum is greater than the allowable limit". Use ignore-errors to avoid halting progress of the evaluation.

24.6 Define timing-cycle, a simple function which takes two integer arguments x and y and initiates a dotimes cycle of the format (dotimes (a x)(dotimes b y)). Then define break-interrupt, a function which permits the above cycle to be interrupted through use of the Control-Break keychord, at which time the iteration is discontinued and timing-cyle returns the message:

```
Timing cyle was interrupted with the following values:
  a = <value of a>
  b = <value of b>
```

24.7 Define trace-factorial, which takes a single integer argument and calculates its factorial (see Section 14.4). Build in provision so that the function is automatically trace'd when called, and the trace is turned off prior to exiting the function.

24.8 Define the function tell-time, which uses get-decoded-time to get the date and time and prints the information in the following typical hh:mm:ss format:

```
It is 16:35:04 on January 29, 1989
```

24.9 Assuming that we do not have the function sleep available to us, define time-delay which takes a single integer argument and creates a time delay of this many seconds. Is it better to do this by comparing successive readings of get-decoded-time or by devising a nested timing loop into which <seconds> can be bound directly as an argument?

24.10 Utilizing the **get-time** macro developed in Section 24.15, define **multiple-time-elapsed**, the intent of which is to simulate timing measurements on a program which uses three nested function calls. **multiple-time-elapsed** makes three successive calls to a nested **dotimes** construct of the format:

```
(dotimes (n 2000)
  (dotimes (n <arg>)))
```

and takes three integer arguments which are bound to the three successive **dotimes** <arg>'s. The time elapsed to execute each timing loop is measured, the total time calculated, and printouts generated as per the following example:

```
* (multiple-time-elapsed 3 5 7)
Time elapsed in loop 1 = 00:4.78
Time elapsed in loop 2 = 00:5.38
Time elapsed in loop 3 = 00:5.99

Total time elapsed = 00:16.15
```

Assume that time elapsed will be limited to seconds and minutes only, and include appropriate provision for carryover of multiples of 100ths seconds to seconds and multiples of 60 seconds to minutes.

Chapter 25
Packages

Up to this point we have based our discussions on a simple LISP system featuring a single Object List on which all symbols are maintained. This approach is practical in a small microcomputer-based system with a single user, where the applications programs are of modest size, the number of symbols is limited, and any potential name conflicts can be quickly resolved.

In larger systems, where programs become more complex and various users may access the system, the problem of *name collisions* can arise. This happens when two different programmers try to use the same symbol name for different data objects. Efforts to avoid this problem have given rise to the development of *packages*, which are basically lookup tables which map a symbol print name to a symbol data object. Each user may have his or her own package which becomes the *current package* when that user is using the system. In the event other users have used the same name for some of their symbols, these names are hidden within other packages and are invisible to the current user.

In this chapter we will look at:

- the nature of a *package*, and how a package serves to map a print name of a symbol to the symbol data object
- the standard packages which are supplied with a Common LISP interpreter
- how the user may define a package
- the manner in which symbols may be present as *internal* or *external* symbols in a package
- how one package can gain access to and use the symbols in another package
- the various facilities which are available to retrieve information about a package and the symbols in the package
- the manner in which program subsystems may be loaded in the form of *modules*

25.1 A package is a lookup table for symbols

A *package* is a special kind of data structure which serves as a lookup table and which provides a *mapping* between the *print name* of a symbol and the corresponding *data object* on the Object List.

In our earlier discussions of the Object List we assumed that the symbols were referenced directly by their print names, which in turn were strings pointed to by the address in their print name pointer cells. This is the system employed by most microcomputer implementations and by older LISP systems. We will maintain the concept of the Object List as a place where symbol data objects are stored; however let us modify the manner in which these symbols are linked to their print names. For this purpose we will introduce a separate lookup table, or *package*, in which the print name of each symbol is stored together with a pointer to the symbol data object on the Object List. In place of the *print name pointer cell* as one of the four attributes of the symbol, we will have a *package pointer cell* which points to the package lookup table.

Harking back to one of our earlier examples where we created a new symbol called **hotdog** (see Section 4.4), the internal structure might look more as shown in Fig. 25.1, where the package pointer cell of the symbol data object points to the particular package in which the symbol is located, and the package lookup table includes two addresses for each symbol data object: one which points to the print name of the symbol and one which points to the data object on the Object List.

The lookup mechanisms used by **read** are generally similar to those which we outlined in our review of the **read/eval/print** cycle, except that instead of directly accessing the symbol data object by means of its print name as pointed to by the data object itself, **read** first looks in the current package, finds the print name, and follows the associated pointer to the symbol data object. An additional step is therefore required; however this is

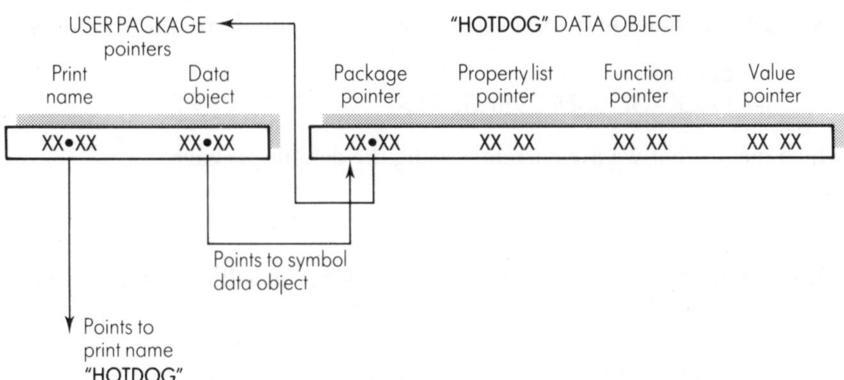

Fig. 25.1 A package maps a print name to a data object.

necessary if provision is to be made for using packages to segregate groups of symbol names within the same system.

When we create a new symbol it is automatically placed in the current package and is said to be *interned* in that package. Conversely, the package is said to be the *home package* of the symbol and may also be said to *own* the symbol.

25.2 Various packages are built into Common LISP

When we initialize a Common LISP interpreter, four standard packages are made available for our use. These include:

- LISP, which contains all of the Common LISP functional primitives and global parameters
- KEYWORD, which contains all of the keywords used by built-in or user-defined functions
- USER, which is the default package into which all of our user-defined symbols will be placed
- SYSTEM, which may be used for implementation-dependent system interface functions

GCLISP provides the additional package GCLISP which contains all of the un-Common LISP extensions provided. When using the GMACS editor, the package GMACS will also be loaded.

As noted above, USER is the default user package. Unless we create another package and specify it to be the current package, all new symbols defined by us will be placed in package USER, whether during our top-level experiments or at the time we load a program, that is, a .LSP file, into the system. The package in current use is bound to the global variable *package*:

```
* *package*
#<PACKAGE USER 29BF:3603>
```

which means that we are currently using the default package.

25.3 symbol-package identifies the package in which a symbol is interned

When we define a new symbol it is added to our current package and is said to be *interned* in that package. We can identify the package in which a particular symbol is interned through use of symbol-package, which takes as its single argument the (quoted) name of the symbol. For example:

```
* (setf hotdog 'sausage)
SAUSAGE
* (symbol-package 'hotdog)
#<PACKAGE USER 29BF:3603>
* (symbol-package 'sausage)
#<PACKAGE USER 29BF:3603>
```

In the course of the above **setf** operation, both of the new symbols were added to the current default package **USER**.

LISP primitives and control variables (including ***package*** itself) are contained in the **LISP** package:

```
* (symbol-package 'setf)
#<PACKAGE LISP 29BF:35B5>
* (symbol-package *package*)
#<PACKAGE LISP 29BF:35B5>
```

It is possible to intern symbols in any package by making that package the current package (see Section 25.5) and then creating the new symbols; however it is bad practice to utilize any of the system packages for this purpose except for **KEYWORD**.

Irrespective of what package we are in at the moment, any symbol which commences with a colon is considered to be a keyword (which evaluates to itself); and this keyword is added to the **KEYWORD** package where it remains for the balance of the current session.

```
* :monkey
:MONKEY
* (symbol-package :monkey)
#<PACKAGE KEYWORD 29BF:358E>
```

A symbol can be tested to see whether it is a keyword using the predicate **keywordp**:

```
* (setf test-word :monkey)
:MONKEY
* (keywordp test-word)
T
```

25.4 make-package creates and returns a new package

The basic purpose of the package concept is to permit the symbols used by different users on a system to be located in different lookup tables in order to avoid name conflicts. A new package may be created for this purpose with **make-package**, which takes the following syntax:

```
(make-package <package-name> &key :nicknames :use)
```

<package-name> may be a string or a symbol; in the latter case the print name of the symbol is utilized.

The optional keyword **:nicknames** provides for a listing of alternative names which will be recognized as the same package, ie, permitting an abbreviated version to be typed in. For instance we could create a package **EDITOR** but provide it with a nickname such as **ED** to save time when typing it in.

The optional keyword **:use** may be followed by a listing of other (existing) packages whose external symbols are to be inherited by the new package (see **use-package** in Section 25.6). Other than any packages which may be specified by **:use**, all symbols contained in the packages **LISP** and **GCLISP** are automatically inherited by any user-defined package.

The purpose of **make-package** is to create a new package into which symbols may be interned by the current user and thus kept separate from symbols in other packages currently resident in the system. For example:

```
* (setf *package* (make-package 'john))
; Autoload: MAKE-PACKAGE from "MAKEPACK" in <pathname>
; Autoload: LISP::CONVERT-TO-PACKAGE (from "SHADOW")
#<PACKAGE JOHN 8C2C:A5C5>
JOHN:
```

By virtue of executing the above function we have created the new package **JOHN** and are currently in that package, as evidenced by the new prompt **JOHN:**. Any symbols we create from now on will be interned in **JOHN** for the rest of the session or until we modify ***package*** again.

If we are sharing a large system where we want to use our own package in this manner, it is evident that an assignment statement such as the above (or an alternative **in-package** statement; see Section 25.5) must precede other top-level declarations and function definitions in an applications program so that when we load that program into the system, all symbols will automatically be interned in the correct package.

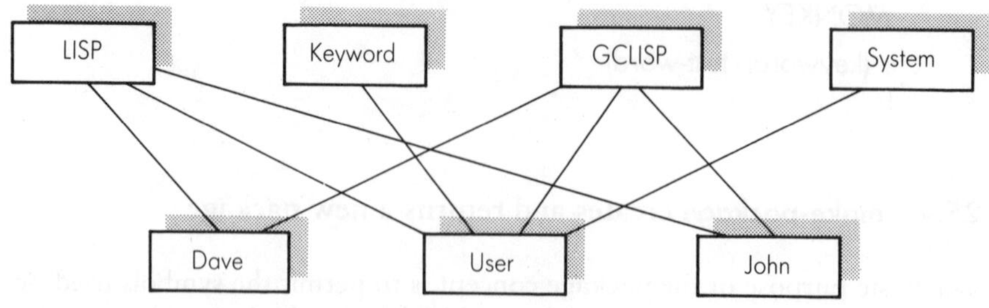

Fig. 25.2 New packages can be created by the user.

Assuming that we have created the two new packages DAVE and JOHN, in addition to the USER package which is automatically created by the system, the current status of our packages can be illustrated as in Fig. 25.2. All of the primitives and global variables present in the packages LISP and GCLISP (but not KEYWORD or SYSTEM) are automatically accessible in the user-defined packages DAVE and JOHN, as well as in the the default package USER.

Having created a package, we can change its name with rename-package, which takes the syntax:

```
(rename-package <package> <new-name>
  &optional <new-nicknames>)
```

The old name and all of the old nicknames of <package> are eliminated and replaced by <new-name> and <new-nicknames>.

25.5 in-package directs symbols into the specified package

The associated function in-package takes a syntax similar to that of make-package:

```
(in-package <package-name> &key :nicknames :use)
```

If the package named already exists, in-package adds any new names in the :nicknames list and/or any new packages in the :use list. If the package does not already exist, in-package creates it similarly to make-package. In either case, in-package assigns the package that it returns to the variable *package*.

Like make-package, this function is generally intended to be placed at the beginning of a subsystem which is to be loaded into the main system. Assuming that other parts of our applications package have already been loaded, with symbols placed into our special package JOHN, we could use an in-package statement to precede the additional material loaded to indicate any additional nicknames or, more likely, to indicate additional packages to be used in connection with the additional program material.

We can use in-package to move from one package to another:

```
JOHN: (in-package 'user)
#<PACKAGE USER 29BF:3603>
*
```

25.6 Symbols from one package can be made available for use by other packages

Let us assume that various symbols are interned in the package JOHN which we would like to use for another program currently resident in the system, whose symbols are interned in package **DAVE**. LISP provides various means of doing this.

To permit symbols from one package to be made available for use by other packages it is necessary first to *externalize* the symbols. This simply means changing their status from *internal* symbols to *external* symbols, thereby advising as to their availability for use elsewhere. The function **export** is used for this purpose, and takes the syntax:

```
(export <symbols> &optional <package-name>)
```

where **<symbols>** may be a single (quoted) symbol or a (quoted) list of symbols, and **<package-name>** defaults to the current package. A conventional use of **export** is as a statement at the start of a file to indicate which of the symbols in the current package are intended to be used by other packages.

Once symbols have been externalized they may be referenced by another program operating in another package by referring to them by their symbol name and their package name, separated by a colon. For example, while operating in the package **DAVE** we could utilize the externalized symbol **test-numb** in package **JOHN** by referring to it as **john:test-numb**. Alternatively we may **import** such a symbol into package **DAVE** with a function of the same name which takes the syntax:

```
(import <symbols> &optional <package-name>)
```

where **<symbols>** are a (quoted) list of **package-name:symbol** designations like **john:test-numb** and **<package-name>** defaults to the current package into which the symbols are being imported. Once imported, the symbols are said to be permanently *present* in package **DAVE**, meaning that it is no longer necessary to reference them with the prefix **john:**. Furthermore the imported symbols will become available to any other package which wishes to use symbols from the package **DAVE**.

Alternatively the function **use-package**, which takes the following syntax, provides for a package to inherit *all* of the external symbols of another package or packages:

```
(use-package <package-names> &optional <package-name>)
```

where the first argument is a (quoted) list of the package names from which the symbols are to be inherited and the optional argument defaults to the current package.

There is a difference between **use-package** and **import** in that the symbols *inherited* through the use of **use-package** are said to be *accessible* in the current package, rather than being *present*. This in turn means that such symbols are not inherited by other packages which use the current package. In any case, the ownership of the symbols remains in their original home package.

25.7 Symbols may be explicitly interned into a package

A symbol may be searched for and/or interned within a given package by **intern**, which takes the syntax:

```
(intern <symbol-name-string> &optional <package>)
```

This function (which is principally used by the LISP reader for looking up symbols during the **read/eval/print** process) returns two values: a symbol whose print name is **<symbol-name-string>** and a value indicating whether or not the symbol was created by this invocation of **intern**. If we experiment with **intern**:

```
* (intern "PAVAROTTI")
PAVAROTTI
NIL
```

NIL is returned as the second value, indicating that the symbol was created by this invocation of **intern**. Once the symbol is present:

```
* (intern "PAVAROTTI")
PAVAROTTI
:INTERNAL
```

The second value returned for an already existing symbol may be one of three values:

:INTERNAL	The symbol was already present in **<package>** as an interned symbol
:EXTERNAL	The symbol was present as an external symbol
:INHERITED	The symbol was inherited and hence accessible in **<package>**

intern is case-sensitive and will if necessary encapsulate the input in double escape characters to preserve lowercase characters:

```
* (intern "maria callas")
|maria callas|
NIL
```

A related function **find-symbol** takes a similar syntax:

```
(find-symbol <symbol-name-string> &optional <package>)
```

This function merely tests whether a symbol whose print name is **<symbol-name-string>** is accessible in **<package>**. If the symbol is accessible, the same values are returned as for **intern**; otherwise **NIL** is returned.

```
* (find-symbol "kiri te kanawa")
NIL
```

```
* (find-symbol "PAVAROTTI")
PAVAROTTI
:INTERNAL
```

25.8 Various functions reverse the availability process

Symbols which have been declared external through use of **export** may be changed back to internal status through use of the function **unexport**, which takes the syntax:

```
(unexport <symbol-names> &optional <package>)
```

Similarly, symbols which have been inherited through the use of **use-package** may be returned to their former status with **unuse-package**, which takes the syntax:

```
(unuse-package <package-names> &optional <package>)
```

This function removes the external symbols associated with <**package-names**> from being accessible within <**package**>, which defaults to the current package.

Having imported a symbol, there is no way to reverse this process other than by *uninterning* the symbol (see Section 25.12).

25.9 **do-symbols** iterates over the symbols available in a package

do-symbols is a macro which provides iteration over the symbols that are accessible in a package. The syntax is:

```
(do-symbols (<var> <package> <result-form>)
   <tags | statements>)
```

The <**result-form**> can be omitted, in which case the macro returns **NIL**. The iteration can be terminated prematurely with a return. For example, if we want to print out the first three symbols in package LISP:

```
* (let ((count 0))
    (do-symbols (symbol 'lisp)
      (if (= count 3)
        (return))
      (print symbol)
      (setf count (1+ count))))
SIMPLE-VECTOR-P
LISP::CONSTANT-P
LISP::STEP-INDENT
NIL
```

do-external-symbols is similar to **do-symbols** but only the external symbols of the specified package are scanned.

do-all-symbols is similar to **do-symbols** but every symbol contained in every package is scanned. (This may result in multiple processing of symbols which are present through having been imported into more than one package.)

Although these iterative constructs were not supported in Version 1.0 of GCLISP, equivalent macros can be created using **apropos-list** (see Section 25.10).

25.10 apropos may be used to simulate some of the do-symbols functions

You may forget the exact name of a system variable or function, but remember some element of its name, say, "**find-<something>**". You can institute a search for all symbols whose names contain the substring "**find**" using **apropos**, which takes the syntax:

```
(apropos <string> &optional <package>)
```

This function searches through **<package>**, which must be a package data object, and displays all of the symbol print names which contain the substring **<string>**, for example:

```
* (apropos "find" 'lisp)
LISP::FIND-VIOLATIONS
FIND-PACKAGE -function
LISP::MY-FIND-SYMBOL -function
FIND-ALL-SYMBOLS -function
FIND-SYMBOL -function
```

A related function **apropos-list** is similar but returns a list of the symbol names which meet the substring criterion:

```
* (apropos-list "find" 'lisp)
(LISP::FIND-VIOLATIONS FIND-PACKAGE LISP::MY-FIND-SYMBOL
   FIND-ALL-SYMBOLS FIND-SYMBOL)
```

Since the empty string "" is a substring of any string, either of the **apropos** functions can be used with the empty string to return *all* of the symbols in a given package.

apropos and **apropos-list** may be incorporated into user-defined functions to simulate the effects of **do-symbols** and other iterative constructs: see Exercises 25.6 to 25.10.

A related function **find-all-symbols**, which takes the syntax:

```
(find-all-symbols <string-or-symbol>)
```

performs a case-sensitive search in every package in the system to find every symbol whose print name matches the specified string, and returns a list of all the symbols found.

25.11 Symbols may be shadowed by other symbols

When importing a symbol from one package to another, it is possible that the symbol may already be accessible in the importing package. If the symbol is *present* in the package, whether by virtue of having been directly interned in the package or having been imported from another package, **import** has no effect. However if the symbol is *accessible* through inheritance from another package due to previous use of use-package, an error message is generated by **import**.

The above error can be precluded by use of **shadowing-import**, which takes the syntax:

```
(shadowing-import <symbols> &optional <package>)
```

In this case, if a symbol already accessible in <package> has the same print name but is distinct from a symbol being imported, the latter takes its place and the former is uninterned.

The related function **shadow** takes the syntax:

```
(shadow <symbols> &optional <package>)
```

and provides for somewhat different handling depending on whether the (duplicated) symbol was accessible in the package by virtue of being present or being inherited. The interested reader is referred to the CLRM pp. 178–81 for a discussion of the finer points of shadowing and name conflicts.

Having used **shadow** and/or **shadowing-import** to establish shadowing relationships within a package, the function **package-shadowing-symbols** can be used to return the list of shadowing symbols in <package>. This function takes the syntax:

```
(package-shadowing-symbols <package>)
```

in which <package> can be a package data object or the name of a package.

25.12 Uninterned symbols have no home package

An uninterned symbol is a symbolic data object which has no home package. The pointer in the package cell of an uninterned symbol points to **NIL**.

Not being in any package, such a symbol cannot be accessed directly by the user. It can be *indirectly* accessed provided that it is pointed to by some other data object. An uninterned symbol is identified during printout by the prefix #:.

We can unintern an existing (interned) symbol using **unintern**, which takes the syntax:

```
(unintern <symbol> &optional <package>)
```

If **<symbol>** is present in **<package>** it is removed from the package as well as from the shadowing-symbols list of the package if it appears there. If the package in question is the symbol's home package, the symbol becomes *homeless*.

An uninterned symbol can also be explicitly created with the function **make-symbol**, which takes a single printname string as an argument:

```
* (make-symbol "HOTDOG")
#:HOTDOG
```

Like **intern** and **find-symbol**, **make-symbol** is sensitive to case and will encapsulate the name in double escape characters if necessary to preserve lowercase letters.

Although we have created the symbol, there is no direct way to access it since it is not in any package:

```
* (symbol-package '#:HOTDOG)
NIL
```

A related function **copy-symbol**, which takes the syntax:

```
(copy-symbol <symbol> &optional <copy-props-p>)
```

creates and returns an uninterned symbol with the same print name as **<symbol>**. If the optional argument is **NIL** (the default), the new symbol will be unbound, have no function definition, and have an empty property list. If **<copy-props-p>** is **T**, the value and function definition of the new symbol will be the same as those of **<symbol>**, and the property list will be a copy of that of **<symbol>**.

25.13 gensym creates uninterned symbols

For some programming purposes it is desirable to be able to generate symbols automatically which can in turn be used to keep track of repetitive items such as the individual sentences in a dialogue, objects in a domain, etc. The function **gensym** (for GENerate SYMbol), which takes the following syntax, may be used for this purpose:

(gensym &optional <reset>)

Used without the optional argument, **gensym** generates a series of uninterned symbols in the format #:Gn, where each successive integer n is one more than the preceding integer:

```
* (gensym)
#:G1
* (gensym)
#:G2
```

If <reset> is a positive integer, the next symbol generated by **gensym** will be reset to this number and will continue from there. If <reset> is a string, the string will replace the default prefix G and will continue to be used until changed:

```
* (gensym "sen-")
#:sen-3
* (gensym 15)
#:sen-15)
```

25.14 Various functions provide information about a package

A variety of functions are available to retrieve different kinds of information about packages:

(find-package <package-name>) returns a package object if the package in question exists:

```
* (find-package 'user)
#<PACKAGE USER 29BF:3603>
```

The name or nickname of the package may be supplied as a string or (quoted) symbol; in the latter case the print name of the symbol will be used.

(package-name <package>) and (package-nicknames <package>) return the name of the package in the form of a string, or a list of the nicknames of the package, respectively. The single argument must be the package data object (not the package name).

(package-use-list <package>) and (package-used-by-list <package>) return a list of the packages used by <package> and a list of the packages which use <package>, respectively. The single argument may be either the package data object or the name of the package.

(list-all-packages) returns a list of all the existing packages in the system.

25.15 Program subsystems may be loaded in the form of modules

In extremely large applications programs it may be desirable to organize the coding into separate smaller subsystems. The coding for such subsystems may be contained in several files, and may involve more than one package. Common LISP refers to such a subsystem as a *module*, and provides several primitive functions and global parameters for loading and otherwise keeping track of such modules. If only a single package is involved the name of the module would normally be the same as the name of the package.

The variable ***modules*** is a global parameter used for keeping track of the modules which have been loaded into a LISP system up to any given point in time. This list is used by the various module functions discussed below. The initial value of ***modules*** after loading and initialization of the LISP interpreter is **NIL**.

The function **provide**, which takes the syntax:

```
(provide <module-name>)
```

simply adds the name of a module being loaded to the ***modules*** list. A top-level **provide** statement should be included at the start of each module; otherwise an error message will be generated when **require** is called to load the module. Module names are maintained as strings (if a symbol is entered, its print name will be used), and ***modules*** will therefore accumulate a list of string elements.

GCLISP additionally provides the un-Common LISP function **unprovide**, which takes a similar syntax and which removes the name of the module from the list. (However it would not remove the associated module coding from memory.)

Loading of a module into the system is carried out by use of the function **require**, which takes the syntax:

```
(require <module-name> &optional <pathname>)
```

This function checks the ***modules*** list to see whether **<module-name>** is already present, in which case it takes no action. Otherwise it proceeds to load the appropriate set of files pointed to by **<pathname>**, which may be a single pathname or a list of pathnames. If **<pathname>** is **NIL**, or is not provided, the system will load the file with the same name as **<module-name>** in the default directory.

The CLRM pp. 189–92 provides an example of the manner in which a module can be created, together with guidance as to the order in which the various function calls related to packages should be grouped.

SUMMARY

Summarizing the key points of this chapter:

- a *package* serves as a lookup table to map symbol names to their corresponding data objects
- users can define their own packages so as to avoid *symbol name conflicts* with other users on the system
- Common LISP provides the three built-in packages **LISP**, **KEYWORD**, and **SYSTEM** to contain primitive functions, parameters, and keywords, as well as **USER** as a default package for the user
- GCLISP provides the additional package **GCLISP** to contain extensions to Common LISP
- symbols are *interned* in a package in the course of the normal **read/eval/print** cycle, or may be *imported* from other packages
- iterative constructs such as **do-symbols** may be used to carry out some operation on all of the symbols in a package
- **apropos** and **apropos-list** may be used to search for all symbols whose names contain a specified substring
- **gensym** may be used to create unique uninterned symbols

EXERCISES

25.1 Name the four basic packages built into Common LISP and describe the purpose of each.

25.2 Write expressions which will return the following values:

(a) the name of the current user package
(b) the name of the package containing the symbol '**hotdog**
(c) the package data object containing LISP keywords

25.3 Write an expression to create a new package named **SCREEN-EDITOR**, which can be abbreviated '**ED**' and which uses external symbols from the packages **DAVE** and **JOHN**.

25.4 Write expressions which will:

(a) externalize the symbols **GIN** and **BEER** in package **DAVE**
(b) import the above symbols into the current user package
(c) make *all* external symbols from packages **JOHN** and **DAVE** accessible from within the current user package

25.5 Define **check-package-symbols**, which takes as an argument a (quoted) list of symbols and prints the packages in which they are located, for example:

```
* (check-package-symbols '(setf :test check-package))
SETF is contained in #<PACKAGE LISP 9016:19224>
TEST is contained in #<PACKAGE KEYWORD 9016:19185>
CHECK-PACKAGE is contained in #<PACKAGE USER 9016:19263>
```

25.6 Define **get-package-symbols**, which takes a package name as its single argument and prints to the console all of the symbols currently accessible in that package. If the package named does not exist, generate an appropriate error message.

25.7 Define **print-package-symbols**, which is similar to Exercise 25.6 except that it prints all of the symbols onto the console in two columns, for example:

```
0001 <symbol-name>        0002 <symbol-name>
0003 <symbol-name>        0004 <symbol-name>
etc.
```

Start the second column of numbers at column 40.

25.8 Define **count-package-symbols**, which checks packages **LISP**, **KEYWORD**, **SYSTEM**, and **USER** and prints the number of symbols currently accessible in each package in the format:

```
Package      Symbols
LISP         <number>
KEYWORD      <number>
etc.
```

Build in provision for the necessary spacing to right-justify the package names as well as the numbers.

25.9 Define **package-symbol-lengths**, which takes a package name as its single argument, surveys all of the symbols in the package, and prints a breakdown of the lengths of the symbol names, for example:

```
Package:     <package-name>
Length       Symbols
1             8
2             4
3            14
etc.
```

Include the total number of symbols at the end.

25.10 Assume that your LISP implementation does not support the Common LISP macro **do-symbols** (see Section 24.8), and define the macro **our-do-symbols** which does the same thing. (Ignore the need to provide for the use of return to terminate the iteration prematurely.)

Chapter 26

Other Features of GCLISP

A number of other functions are provided by GCLISP to carry out a range of miscellaneous activities. The purpose of this chapter is to summarize these features and in general to discuss whatever remaining items have not already been covered. Much of the material here is of an implementation-specific nature and will not necessarily correspond to functions found in other Common LISP implementations.

In this chapter we will look at:

- GCLISP functions used to interface with the system at the machine level
- functions which are used to run external *executable programs* from within GCLISP
- functions used to *merge and sort* a list
- *typing* of data objects
- functions related to *documentation*
- functions which provide *general information* about the system and the environment
- functions which carry out operations on *unsigned fixnums*
- functions which operate on *sequences* or lists
- *hash table* functions
- functions which are used to assist with *memory management*
- functions used in connection with *garbage collection*
- other miscellaneous functions and global variables

26.1 Low-level functions carry out activities at the machine language level

GCLISP provides a number of functions which permit you to interface with the interpreter at the machine language level. These functions are as follows:

sys:%pointer	returns the machine language location of a data object
sys:%unpointer	returns the data object which is found at a certain location
sys:%unpointer-offset	returns the data object offset by *n* bytes from a certain location
sys:%structure-size	returns the size in bytes of a data object
sys:%contents	returns the contents of the byte, word, and next word at a certain location
sys:%contents-store	stores data at a certain location
sys:%move-mem	moves a block of memory from one location to another
sys:%io-port	transfers data to or from an i/o port
sys:%sysint	performs a software interrupt on the 8088 chip

These functions are described in more detail below.

sys:%pointer, which takes the syntax:

(sys:%pointer <object>)

returns the logical address of <object>. For example, we can use sys:%pointer to find out where GCLISP places a symbol data object as well as the value assigned to that object:

```
* (setf quotation '(how now brown cow!))
(HOW NOW BROWN COW!)
* (sys:%pointer 'quotation)
16367
-29652
* (sys:%pointer quotation)
21978
30961
```

indicating that the symbol quotation has been placed on GCLISP's Object List at base/offset location −29652:16367; and the list representing its value has been placed at base/offset location 30961:21978. (sys:%pointer returns the offset address first, followed by the base address.) Negative numbers reflect cases where address components larger than 32767 are being translated as if they were negative numbers in twos-complement form.

(NB: The addresses returned by your experiments will likely differ from the above.)

The related function **sys:%unpointer**, which takes the syntax:

(sys:%unpointer <base-address> <offset-address>)

returns the object at the address specified by **<base-address>** augmented by **<offset-address>**. Using the address data returned by our previous use of **sys:%pointer**, we can retrieve the symbol data object and its value from their respective locations:

```
* (sys:%unpointer -29652 16367)
QUOTATION
* (sys:%unpointer 30961 21978)
(HOW NOW BROWN COW!)
```

Caveat: There must be a valid LISP object at the address specified, otherwise an error message is generated, for example:

```
* (sys:%unpointer 1111 1111)
ERROR:
Unprintable object, type code 248 at 457:457
```

The fact that GCLISP returns some messages with addresses in decimal and others in hexadecimal can at times be confusing. A quick way to convert from decimal to hexadecimal is through the use of a **format** statement (see Section 12.7) using an ~x directive:

```
* (format t "~x" 1111) 457
```

This works, since ***read-base*** is normally set to decimal. To convert from hexadecimal to decimal we have to change ***read-base*** (see Section 1.11) to hexadecimal and use the format statement with a ~d directive:

```
* (setf *read-base* 16)
16
* (format t "~d" 457) 1111
```

Upon completion of these gymnastics don't forget to change ***read-base*** back to decimal with a **(setf *read-base* a)** statement (remembering that '**a**' is 10 in base 16!).

The related function **sys:%unpointer-offset**, which takes the syntax:

(sys:%unpointer-offset <object1> <count>)

offsets into **<object1>** by **<count>** bytes, and returns the LISP object stored at that position. For example, if we offset five bytes into a list structure we get the **cdr** of the list:

```
* (sys:%unpointer-offset quotation 5)
(NOW BROWN COW)
```

(The extra byte is due to the fact that the first byte of a cons is used as a type indicator.)

sys:%structure-size, which takes the syntax:

```
(sys:%structure-size <object>)
```

returns the physical size, in bytes, of <object>. If <object> is of type fixnum, 0 is returned since fixnums are represented directly as a special type of pointer. We can check the size of the symbol which we created in the %pointer example:

```
* (sys:%structure-size 'quotation)
30
```

reflecting that a (Version 1.1) GCLISP symbol data object is 21 bytes in length plus one byte for each character of the name, giving a total of 30 (see Exercise 26.10). Version 1.0 was 4 bytes shorter.

The use of %structure-size on lists provides a uniform result:

```
* (sys:%structure-size quotation)
9
```

reflecting only the type byte plus the first cons cell of the list. As an interesting exercise you may wish to develop a function which traces the pointers in the car and cdr cells of a list down to the final leaves (symbols) of the tree to ascertain the true size of the list structure.

sys:%contents, which takes the syntax:

```
(sys:%contents <base-address> <offset-address>)
```

accesses the memory location described by the two addresses and returns three values: the byte stored at that address, the (two-byte) word stored at that address, and the (two-byte) word stored at the next higher contiguous address.

Taking the address of our symbol data object from the %pointer example:

```
* (sys:%contents -29652 16367)
14
-9714
-3755
```

The related function sys:%contents-store, which takes the syntax:

```
(sys:%contents-store <base-address> <offset-address>
   <value> <data-size>)
```

provides a means of storing data in a given address location. If <data-size> is NIL, then <value> is stored in the single byte addressed. If <data-size> is T, then <value> is assumed to be a two-byte value and is stored in the (two-byte) word addressed. Otherwise <data-size> must be an integer, and both

<value> and <data-size> are stored in the addressed double-word, with <value> being stored in the lower-addressed word.

Experiments with **sys:%contents-store** should be carried out with extreme caution, since the contents of memory locations which may affect your program may be altered. In addition, GCLISP storage could become corrupted, forcing a reboot of GCLISP and/or of the operating system.

The function **sys:%move-mem**, which takes the syntax:

```
(sys:%move-mem <source-segment> <source-offset>
   <dest-segment> <dest-offset> <count>)
```

moves a block of memory of length <count>, starting at the source segment and offset, to the destination segment and offset. If <count> is 0, a 64K block will be transferred.

sys:%ioport, which takes the syntax:

```
(sys:%ioport <io-address> <value> <word-p>)
```

either transfers <value> to the output port at <io-address> (and returns <value>), or returns the current value of the input port at <io-address>.

If <value> is **NIL**, **sys:%ioport** returns the current value of the input port at <io-address>. Otherwise <value> must be an integer, which is transferred to the output port at <io-address> and returned by **%ioport**.

If <word-p> is **T**, a word is actually being transferred to/from <io-address+1:io-address>. Otherwise if <word-p> is **NIL**, a byte is being transferred to/from <io-address>.

The function **sys:%sysint**, which takes the syntax:

```
(sys:%sysint <interrupt-type> ax bx cx dx &optional ds es)
```

generates a software interrupt whose type code is <interrupt-type>. Basically, it executes the Intel 8086/8088 **INT** instruction with <interrupt-type> as its operand.

Before generating the interrupt, **sys:%sysint** loads the AX, BX, CX, DX, and optionally the DS and ES registers with ax, bx, cx, dx, ds, and es, respectively. Following the return from the interrupt, **sys:%sysint** returns the contents of the FLAGS, AX, BX, CX, and DX registers. (See Section 24.14 for an example of **sys:%sysint** as used to generate an interrupt for purposes of extracting time from the system clock).

26.2 Other MS-DOS programs can be run while in GCLISP

The function **sys:exec**, which takes the syntax:

```
(sys:exec <program-pathname> <command-string>)
```

may be used to run an external executable program from within GCLISP. The <command-string> will be passed to the program as a command line. If the program cannot be invoked due to insufficient memory, **exec** will return the MS-DOS error code; otherwise the program will be loaded and executed after which **exec** will return **NIL**. Error codes returned by **sys:exec** are:

2: COMMAND.COM not found
3: Executable file not found
4: (Probably) too many files open
8: Insufficient memory

In order for the **exec** function to work properly, sufficient memory must be reserved for the operating system (see the function **allocate**) and the specified program must be accessible. (The function cannot be run from GMACS since the latter allocates all available memory to the interpreter.)

Another function which interfaces with MS-DOS is **select-page**, which takes the syntax:

```
(select-page <active-page>)
```

and which selects a new active display page. This function is only valid in BIOS alpha mode. **<active-page>** must be an integer in the range 0 to 7 (inclusive) for 40×25 modes and must be an integer in the range 0 to 3 (inclusive) for 80×25 modes.

The value of the variable **sys:*display-page***, which is set by the function **select-page**, is an integer which represents the active display page.

26.3 merge and sort functions order the elements of a list

Since the **sort** function is undefined in early verions of GCLISP, you may find the following functions useful. They are based upon the **list merge sort** algorithm described in Volume 3 of Knuth (1973), *The Art of Computer Programming*, with the sorting time of a list proportional to *n* log *n*, where *n* is the length of the list.

```
(defun sort (list test)
  (cond ((null list) nil)
        ((null (cdr list)) list)
        (t (setq list (cons (sort (split list) test)
                            (sort list test)))
         (merge (cdr list)(car list) test))))
```

For example:

```
* (setf letter-list '(q w e r t y u i o p a s d f g h j k
  l z x c v b n m))
(Q W E R T Y U I O P A S D F G H J K L Z X C V B N M)
* (sort letter-list #'string-lessp)
(A B C D E F G H I J K L M N O P Q R S T U V W X Y Z)
```

sort sorts the elements of **list** by recursively splitting the list into ever smaller lists and then successively merging these lists back together, applying **test** to determine the ordering of the elements. **Test** must be an appropriate two-argument comparator predicate.

The auxiliary functions **merge, split,** and **split-aux** are defined as follows:

```
(defun merge (lst1 lst2 test)
  (cond ((atom lst1) lst2)
        ((atom lst2) lst1)
        (t (if (funcall test (string (car lst2))
                             (string (car lst1)))
               (rplacd lst2
                 (merge lst1 (cdr lst2) test))
               (rplacd lst1
                 (merge (cdr lst1) lst2 test))))))
```

merge takes two lists of ordered elements and merges them together in accordance with the ordering of **test**.

```
(defun split (lst)
  (if (atom lst)
      lst
      (split-aux lst (cdr lst))))

(defun split-aux (head tail)
  (cond ((atom tail)
         (prog1 (cdr head)(rplacd head nil)))
        (t (pop tail)
           (cond ((atom tail)
                  (prog1 (cdr head)(rplacd head nil)))
                 (t (split-aux (cdr head)(cdr tail)))))))
```

split divides a list into two equal parts. The front half of the list remains bound to the symbol which names the list; **split** returns the back half of the list. If there is an odd element it is included in the front half.

Another method for sorting a list is the **bubble sort** (see Exercise 26.6).

26.4 A data object may be identified by a type specifier

Many of the branching operations in LISP are predicated on whether the value represented by a symbol is of a given *type*. It is often necessary also to check the type of data object used as an argument when applying a particular type of function to it. For instance, prior to carrying out an arithmetic operation on some data object it is necessary to verify that it is of type **number**; otherwise an error message will be generated.

The 36 pre-defined data types in GCLISP are as follows:

array	integer	sequence
atom	keyword	short-float
bignum	lexical-closure	single-float
character	list	stack-group
common	long-float	standard-char
compiled-function	nil	string
cons	null	string-char
double-float	number	structure
dynamic-closure	package	symbol
fixnum	pathname	t
float	random-state	unsigned-byte
function	scanned-special-form	vector

Some of these data types are *subtypes* of another data type. For instance, single-float, short-float, and long-float are subtypes of float, which is in turn a subtype of number. At any particular moment the above data types may be supplemented by other types created by defstruct (see Section 22.17). The CLRM pp. 11–35 provides comprehensive coverage of the data types supported by Common LISP.

A type specifier can also be a list, such as (unsigned-byte 8), in which the first element of the list is a symbol and the rest of the list provides additional type information. Such a type specifier should always be quoted, since the symbol unsigned-byte has no functional implications.

The type of a data object can be ascertained through use of type-of, for example:

```
* (type-of (symbol-function 'car))
COMPILED-FUNCTION
* (type-of '(how now brown cow))
CONS
```

The related function typep is a predicate which tests whether a data object is of the specified type:

```
* (typep '(how now brown cow) 'cons)
T
```

(The above would also return T if tested against 'list.)

26.5 Documentation functions return documentation information

The syntax of a function or macro definition includes provision for a so-called *documentation string* to be included as the first element immediately after the lambda-list. As the name implies, a documentation string is useful for documenting the purpose of the function, so that someone else will be able to read and understand your program more easily. For example:

```
* (defun add-em-up (x y z)
    "This is a function for adding up three variables"
    (+ x y z))
```

Although the documentation string is shown during the printout of a .LSP file it is ignored by the interpreter when evaluating the function. The string can be retrieved by use of the documentation function, which takes the syntax:

```
(documentation <symbol> <doc-type>)
```

in which <symbol> must evaluate to a symbol and <doc-type> must be either 'variable, 'function, or 'type. The variable type refers to documentation strings entered in connection with defvar, defparameter, or defconstant global assignments (see Section 7.2). The function type refers to strings included in function or macro definitions.

For example, having defined add-em-up as above, we can retrieve the documentation string:

```
* (documentation 'add-em-up 'function)
"This is a function for adding up three variables"
```

(NB: Although GCLISP permits a documentation string to be included in a function or macro definition, this string is subsequently discarded and documention cannot be used to retrieve it. As an exercise you may wish to write your own version of load (see Exercise 23.10 for a start) which reads in a .lsp file, extracts any documentation strings from function or macro definitions, and puts these strings on the property list of the symbols concerned. You will at the same time have to write a retrieval function, since of course documentation will not work in this case.)

Another function related to documentation is sys:doc, which takes the syntax:

```
(sys:doc <symbol> &optional <doc-type>)
```

This un-Common LISP function prints GCLISP doumentation describing the use of <symbol> when used as type <doc-type>. For example:

```
* (sys:doc 'car 'function)
CAR is a FUNCTION
(car LIST) -> FIRST-ELEMENT
<plus other information about car>
```

Other information about a function or macro definition can be obtained with the un-Common LISP function sys:lambda-list, which takes the syntax:

```
(sys:lambda-list <name> &optional <dont-search-p>)
```

and which returns information about the parameter list of the function named by <name>. For example:

```
* (sys:lambda-list 'add-em-up)
(X Y Z)
```

The value of the optional parameter <dont-search-p> controls the action taken in the event the function definition in question is compiled.

26.6 Other functions provide general information about the system and the environment

The function **describe**, which takes the syntax:

```
(describe <object>)
```

prints useful information about <object>, which may be any type of data object, to the ***standard-output*** stream. For example:

```
* (describe 'add-em-up)
ADD-EM-UP is a symbol.
  Its global value is unbound.
  Its function definition is: (LISP::SCANNED LAMBDA
    ((X Y Z)(+ X Y Z))).
  Its property list is empty.
```

The function **identity**, which takes the syntax:

```
(identity <object>)
```

simply returns the value of <object>. The value returned by this function is used primarily as a functional argument.

The value of the global variable **sys:*obarray*** is a general array (with a two-element leader) which is used internally to manage the GCLISP name space. The second leader element contains an association list which maps macro characters to their respective functions. (See Exercise 26.8.)

The function **lisp-implementation-type** may be used to idenfify a particular implementation of Common LISP. When used with GCLISP this function simply returns the string "GOLDEN COMMON LISP".

The function **lisp-implementation-version** identifies the current version of the particular implementation of Common LISP. (When used with Version 1.1 this function returns "1.1, Small Memory".)

The global variable ***features*** is bound to a list of symbols which name special 'features' provided by a particular Common LISP implementation. In Version 1.1 of GCLISP this variable is bound to the list **(SYS:IBMPC GCLISP)**.

The function **sys:get-environment-string** takes a namestring (which must be in uppercase) as its single argument, searches the environment for a variable with that name, and returns the string value of that variable; otherwise it returns **NIL**.

The parameter **sys:*psp-selector*** is bound to a value corresponding to the segment address of GCLISP's Program Segment Prefix. The PSP contains internal information such as the command line, the address of the environment, and the initial Disk Transfer Address.

The parameter **sys:*command-line*** is bound to a string array containing the command line.

26.7 Stack group functions are based on ZetaLISP

A *stack group* is a kind of functional object which contains data related to the state of its own evaluation and to its binding environment. It has many of the characteristics of a *task* or a *process*. (Although supported by Version 1.0 of GCLISP, stack groups are not explicitly supported by Version 1.1.)

The term 'stack group' derives from the existence of the two stacks which comprise the group: the *control stack*, or regular PDL (push-down-list), and the *dynamic environment stack*, or special PDL. The control stack is used to keep track of the state of the computation, that is, which function is currently running, which function called it, and so forth, in a manner reminiscent of the display generated by use of the **backtrace** command. The environment stack, as its name implies, keeps track of pending bindings in somewhat the same manner as a shallow-binding list keeps track of the bindings in a dynamically scoped interpreter (see Section 30.11).

GCLISP (Version 1.0) functions related to stack groups are as follows.

```
(make-stack-group <name> &key :regular-pdl-size
                              :special-pdl-size)
```

creates and returns a stack group named **<name>**. Internal state information of the created stack group is undefined, and must be initialized by use of **stack-group-preset** (see below).

```
(stack-group-preset <stack-group> <function> &rest <arguments>)
```

initializes <**stack-group**> so that when it is resumed, both stacks are cleared and <**function**> is applied to <**arguments**>.

```
(stack-group-unwind)
```

resets the currently active stack group. Both stacks are cleared, all bindings are undone, and any existing **unwind-protect** clean-up forms are evaluated. The function call **(top-level)** is made the initial function call of the stack group, and the stack group is resumed.

(stack-group-resume <stack-group> <object>)

resumes **<stack-group>**, transmitting **<object>** in the process.

(stack-group-return <object>)

resumes the current stack groups **resumer**, transmitting **<object>** to it.

Two global variables are used in connection with stack groups. The value of ***initial-stack-group*** is the stack group which is created when GCLISP is initialized. The value of ***current-stack-group*** is the stack group which is currently active.

The scope of this book does not permit an exhaustive treatment of stack groups. The GCLRM (Version 1.0) pp. 82–9 provides more details on their use. Also, in view of the fact that GCLISP stack groups were inspired by ZetaLISP, the reader is referred to the LISP Machine Manual pp. 256–66 for an in-depth discussion.

26.8 Operations can be carried out on unsigned fixnums

The following un-Common LISP functions are provided for carrying out comparisons and arithmetic operations on unsigned *fixnums*, which are stored as full 16-bit integers:

<&	tests whether the first argument is less than the second argument
>&	tests whether the first argument is greater than the second argument
+&	returns the sum
−&	returns the difference
***&**	returns the product
/&	returns the quotient

In Version 1.0 these functions permit manipulation of integers in excess of the normal (signed) limit of 32767. (The printed representation of results between 32767 and 65535 will be expressed as negative numbers.)

New functions to operate on unsigned fixnums introduced in GCLISP Version 1.1 include:

+%	returns the sum of two unsigned fixnums
−%	returns the difference of two unsigned fixnums
<=%	compares two unsigned fixnums

Other new functions include **(ash% <fixnum> <count>)**, which shifts the fixnum argument **<count>** positions and returns the low order 16 bits as a fixnum, and **%bn-to-uw** and **%uw-to-bn** which perform numerical conversions.

The function ****, when applied to two unsigned fixnums, returns the remainder of the first argument divided by its second argument.

26.9 Some functions are designed to work with sequences

A *sequence* is an ordered set of elements. The two types of data objects, *lists* and *vectors*, each of which can be used to represent an ordered set of elements, are therefore considered subtypes of type **sequence.** (Although this term is used in a generic sense to refer to those types of structures which lend themselves to operations on ordered sets of elements, it is not a recognized data type in Common LISP, that is, it is not reflected in a corresponding predicate **sequencep.**)

Of the functions which operate on sequences, as outlined in the CLRM p. 245, GCLISP supports **length** (see Section 5.14), **subseq** (see Section 21.14), **reverse** and **nreverse** (see Section 5.8), **sort** (see Section 26.3), and **some** and **every** (see Section 15.10). (Of these, only **length** and **subseq** work on both lists and vectors.) The following functions are also supported:

remove, which takes the syntax:

```
(remove <item> <sequence>)
```

returns a copy of **<sequence>** with all elements **eql** to **<item>** removed. This function is the nondestructive counterpart of **delete** (see below).

```
* (remove 'apples '(grapes apples nuts beans apples pears))
(GRAPES NUTS BEANS PEARS)
```

Like **member** (see Section 8.7), the additional keyword **:test** is supported in the event the first argument is required to meet some other test of equality, for example, **:test #'equal** if embedded lists are involved.

The related function **remove-if** takes the syntax:

```
(remove-if <test> <sequence>)
```

and removes from **<sequence>** all items which satisfy **<test>**:

```
* (remove-if #'numberp '(apples 3 5 grapes 5 pears 8 9))
(APPLES GRAPES PEARS)
```

delete takes the same syntax as **remove**; it supports use of the keyword **:test**, and carries out the same operation. However **delete** works on a destructive basis, modifying and returning the original list rather than a copy.

delete-if is similarly the destructive counterpart of **remove-if.**

Although documented in the chapter on sequences for compatibility with Common LISP, the GCLISP versions of **remove** and **delete** work only on the single subtype **list.**

26.10 Other functions are used to operate on lists

In addition to the functions discussed in Chapter 5, a number of other functions are available to operate on lists.

copy-list takes a list as its single argument and returns a copy of that list.

copy-tree takes any LISP object as its single argument, recursively copies every **cons** in the object, and returns the copied structure.

push, which takes the syntax:

```
(push <object> <place>)
```

replaces the list stored in the generalized variable <place> with a list created by **cons**'ing <object> onto the original list. Using this macro, a list of elements can be used as a push-down stack.

pushnew is like **push** but only carries out the push provided that the object is not already included somewhere in the list (see **adjoin** below).

pop is the opposite of **push** and takes the syntax:

```
(pop <place>)
```

The first element of the list is returned, and the list is replaced by the **cdr** of the list.

butlast, which takes the syntax:

```
(butlast <list> &optional <n>)
```

creates and returns a (copy of) <list> containing all but the last <n> elements of the list.

nbutlast is the destructive counterpart of **butlast**, that is, it operates on the original list.

ldiff, which takes the syntax:

```
(ldiff <list> <sublist>)
```

creates and returns a list containing those elements of <list> which appear before <sublist>.

The un-Common LISP function **snoc**, which takes the syntax:

```
(snoc <cons> <object>)
```

replaces the **cdr** of <cons> with the **ncons** of <object>.

subst, which takes the syntax:

```
(subst <new> <old> <tree>)
```

returns a tree with <new> substituted for every occurrence of <old> within <tree>. The original tree is not modified.

sublis, which takes the syntax:

```
(sublist <a-list> <tree>)
```

uses an association list to perform multiple substitutions on the elements of <tree>, and returns the resulting tree. The original tree is not modified.

adjoin takes the same syntax as **cons**:

```
(adjoin <item> <list>)
```

and operates similarly, but with the difference that, if <item> is already an element of <list>, it is not **cons**'d. If <list> is thought of as representing a set of objects, **adjoin** operates to add a new element to the set only if it is not already there.

26.11 GCLISP supports the hash function sxhash

Although GCLISP does not generally support hash table functions, the primitive hash function **sxhash** is provided, which takes the syntax:

```
(sxhash <object>)
```

Given an object of any type, this function will return a non-negative integer, called the *hash code* of the object.

```
* (sxhash 'apples)
2801
* (sxhash '(my dog has fleas))
7809
```

sxhash hashes on the tree structure of <object>, implying that:

```
(equal x y) implies (= (sxhash x) (sxhash y))
```

See Exercise 26.5 for creation and use of a small hash table.

26.12 Memory management functions allocate memory for use by the interpreter

Memory management is normally carried out automatically. However GCLISP includes provision for allocating additional storage space for atoms and cons cells through use of the function **sys:allocate**, which takes the following syntax:

```
sys:allocate <number-of-paragraphs> <parts-cons-space>
    <parts-atom-space> <reserve-p>)
```

The first argument, which must be an integer, specifies the number of 16-byte 'paragraphs' to allocate or reserve. The second and third arguments, which must also both be integers, specify that the space to be allocated should be divided between cons space and atom space according to the ratio <parts-cons-space>/<parts-atom-space>. Either argument may be zero, in which case *all* the memory in question is allocated to the other type of data object.

If <**reserve-p**> is **T**, *all* available memory except for <**number-of-paragraphs**> paragraphs is allocated to GCLISP. If <**reserved-p**> is NIL, only <**number-of-paragraphs**> paragraphs are allocated to GCLISP.

If <**reserved-p**> is an integer, <**number-of-paragraphs**> paragraphs are allocated to GCLISP, beginning at address <**reserved-p**>. This allows the user to specify a memory address that is outside the normal range of MS-DOS memory management, for example, >640K.

Once memory has been allocated to GCLISP, it cannot be returned to the operating system. Note that the cons/atom ratio of allocated memory can only be changed by allocating additional memory with a different ratio.

Information on internal storage management is provided by the function **room**, which takes the syntax:

(room &optional <detail-p> <gc-p>)

If <**detail-p**> is **NIL** (the default), only summary information is printed; otherwise detailed information is printed. If <**gc-p**> is non-**NIL** (the default), the garbage collector is invoked (via the **sys:gc** function) before any information is gathered; otherwise no garbage collection is carried out.

Further information on the manner in which memory is allocated in GCLISP may be obtained by evaluating the global variable **sys:*gc-data***. This evaluates to an unsigned 8-bit byte vector with a two-element leader that contains information about the allocation of memory. Leader element 0 acts as a gc-in-progress flag, and contains a non-**NIL** object if a garbage collection is in progress. It should always contain **NIL** when accessed by the user. Leader element 1 contains an integer that represents the number of garbage collections which have taken place since GCLISP was invoked.

The main vector cosists of 9-byte groups, each of which represents a *region descriptor* with the following format:

Byte 0	Contains a code indicating the type of data obtained in the region, that is: 0 – dynamic cons space 1 – dynamic atom space 2 – static cons space 3 – static atom space If the value of this byte is 255, then the previous region descriptor was the last valid descriptor.
Bytes 1/2	Segment offset address of region
Bytes 3/4	Segment base address of region
Bytes 5/6	Length of region
Bytes 7/8	Number of free bytes remaining after last garbage collection. If the region descriptor is a dynamic cons, these bytes contain the number of free cons cells remaining.

26.13 Garbage collection functions recover cons cells which are no longer in use

When space becomes exhausted in a particular segment which is being written to, the garbage collector is automatically called to recover cons cells and/or other data objects which are no longer in use. During the time the garbage collector is in operation the notice **GC** is displayed in reverse image at the lower lefthand corner of the screen, and the system temporarily hangs. The function **sys:gc** can also be used at any time explicitly to force a garbage collection.

The value of the global variable **sys:*gc-light-p*** may be used to control the display of the **GC** notice. Normally this variable is bound to the fixnum 112, which is used as a bit vector 01110000 to specify *reverse video* to the display controller. Other alternatives include setting **sys:*gc-light-p*** to **T**, in which case the letters are displayed in the normal manner; or to **NIL**, in which case the letters are simply not displayed.

GCLISP also includes provision for carrying out a special user-defined procedure after a garbage collection, for example to display or record the amount of memory recovered, advise as to the amount of memory still available, etc. The value of the global variable **sys:*gc-event*** may be either **NIL** or a function. After a garbage collection is carried out, if the value of this variable is a function the function will be called with no arguments (see ***break-event***, Section 24.5, for an analogous operation in connection with breaks). If **NIL**, no action will be taken.

SUMMARY

To summarize the main points of this chapter:

- the function **sys:%pointer** returns the MS-DOS address at which a data object is located; **sys:%unpointer** returns the object located at a given address; and **sys:%unpointer-offset** returns the object located at offset <**count**> bytes from the given address
- the function **sys:%contents** returns the byte, double word, and next contiguous double word stored at a given address; **sys:%contents-store** stores a value at a given address
- other low-level functions include **sys:%structure-size**, which returns the size in bytes of a data object; **sys:%move-mem**, which moves a block of memory; **sys:%io-port**, which transfers values to and from an io port; and **sys:%sysint**, which generates a software interrupt and extracts data from the 8088 registers
- **sort** and the auxiliary functions **merge** and **split** may be used to sort a list
- all LISP data objects have a particular type designation, which may be ascertained through use of **type-of**; the predicate function **typep** tests whether an object is of the specified type
- the function **sxhash** can be used to create hash tables
- the function **sys:allocate** permits the user explicitly to allocate storage space for use by atoms and cons cells
- information on GCLISP internal storage management can be retrieved through use of **room** and/or by evaluation of the global variable **sys:*gc-data***
- garbage collection is carried out automatically, or may be invoked explicitly through use of the function **gc**

EXERCISES

26.1 An object of unknown type has been assigned as the value of the symbol **hotdog**. Write an expression which first tests to see whether the value of this data object is a list. If it is, the expression returns **T**; otherwise it ascertains what the type is and returns that type as a value.

26.2 We have a very long grocery list and decide that we only have time to purchase the first 10 items on the list. Write an expression which uses **butlast** to rewrite **grocery-list**, eliminating all items after the 10th.

26.3 A shuffled deck of cards is represented by the 52-element list card-deck, with cards being represented by symbols in which the first character represents the suit, for example, D03. Write an expression which uses pop to deal five cards off the top of this deck and push to collect these cards into the list poker-hand.

26.4 Define the predicate diamondp which tests whether a given card in the deck of Exercise 26.3 is a diamond. Then write an expression which removes all diamonds from the deck and returns the remainder of the deck.

26.5 A large data base of names and phone numbers may be accessed more quickly if a hashing mechanism is used to split the data into 'buckets.' Create phone-array, a general array of 10 elements each of which is initialized to an empty association list. Then define file-phones, which repetitively prompts for a first name followed by a phone number, for example, DAVE 2566596. Use the hash code of the name to add the name/phone as a dotted pair to the association list in one of the 10 'buckets' of the array. If the name is already on the association list replace the old phone number with the new one. Then define the related function retrieve-phones which prompts for a name, accesses the association list in the appropriate bucket, and returns the phone number.

26.6 The list merge sort discussed in Section 26.3 is only one method of sorting a list. Another method is the bubble sort, which works upward through a list, comparing each symbol against the symbol which follows it and interchanging the relative position of the symbols if the first symbol is lexicographically greater than the second symbol. The list is scanned repeatedly until no further interchanges are required, at which point the sort is complete. Define bubble-sort, which takes a list as an argument and sorts it in this manner.

26.7 If you are interested in exploring the internal structure of GCLISP it is helpful to have a function such as display-bytes, which operates like the Display option of a CP/M or MS-DOS debug program. display-bytes takes the syntax:

```
(display-bytes <base-address> <offset-address> &optional sign)
```

and prints out a listing of the decimal content of each byte starting from <segment-base-address> and <segment-offset-address>, with a separate listing of the ASCII formats at the right side of the screen, for example:

```
* (display-bytes 10738 11853)

Base:   10738                                String
Offset  chr  chr chr chr chr chr chr  chr  chr equivalent
11853     0   67  65  82   8   4   1    0    0 . C A R . . . . .
11863     0    0   0  44   0  67  65   82   32 . . . . . C A R . o
11873   114   32  67  68  82  32 111  102   32 r . C D R . o f . n
11883   111  110  45  76  73  83  84   32  111 o n - L I S T . o b
etc.
```

Define display-bytes. Provide for a listing of 10 characters on each line (the last chr column is left out in the above example for lack of space), and skip a space after every 10 lines.

display-bytes works upward or downward in accordance with the (optional) sign of 1 or −1, respectively, with 1 as the default, until stopped with a **break**. Generate an error message if a sign argument other than 1 or −1 is entered. Also, if working downward, reverse the order of the character printout at the right side of the screen so that text is printed in its normal order.

26.8 The value of the global variable ***obarray*** is a general array which is used internally to manage GCLISP name space. Define **get-obarray**, which accesses this array and prints out the data in the following format:

```
*obarray* leader elements:
  0: NIL
  1: NIL
*obarray* elements:
  0: ((2 IGNORE *** 0 SLOT-ACCESSOR)(6 0 *GMACS-RA* etc)
  1: ((2 0 DEFST-TYPE BITS)(4 *GC-DATA* 0))
  2: ((2 INTERNAL-TIME-UNITS-PER-SECOND 0)(3 0 NUM))
etc.
```

Provide for proper indenting of index numbers, skip a space after each group of five elements, and provide for a 3-space margin at the beginning and end of each new page.

26.9 Define the function **file-symbol-list**, which takes a package name as its single argument and prints a list of all of the symbols in the package to file **symbols.lsp** on a suitable disk file. Then define **get-symbol-list** which accesses the above file and prints a listing of all the symbols on the console.

26.10 A GCLISP symbol data object may be located by using a call to **(%pointer '<symbol-name>)**. Using the symbol list functions developed in Exercise 26.9, define **symbol-data-objects**, which takes a package as its argument, extracts all of the symbols in the package, and prints information onthe symbols to the console in the format shown below.

```
* (symbol-data-objects 'lisp)
Package: USER          Value     Plist      Funct
Symbol-name            Pointer   Pointer    Pointer
SIMPLE-VECTOR-P        10687     9286        6646
  10687: 3858              0        0           0
GENSYM                 10687     9286        2812
  10687: 17292             0        0      -18527
INSPECT                10687     9286       16879
  25668: 21313             0        0       19008
etc.
```

Include provision for an optional extra argument which, if of a non-**NIL** value, causes the listing to be printed to the printer in addition to the console. (NB: The value pointer cell is offset +1 from the start of the symbol data object, the property list pointer cell offset +5, and the function pointer cell +11. In all cases the first two bytes contain the offset address and the next two bytes the base address.)

Chapter 27
Using the GMACS Editor

At some early point during your study of this tutorial you will want to start using the GMACS editor to enter and debug solutions to the exercises. For even a short program of a half dozen lines, it can get very tiresome typing in the lines over and over as you search for the right way to express an algorithm. With the GMACS editor you can instantly make a change and test it without even leaving the editor.

Design of the GMACS editor was based on EMACS, a LISP display editor created by Richard M. Stallman at the MIT Artificial Intelligence Laboratory in the mid-1970s. The acronym is derived from Editing MACros, based on the original use of macro expressions to support the editing operation. Although EMACS was an impressive editor for its time, it has since been overshadowed by the many efficient word processors which have come onto the market. Most of the GMACS key bindings are based on standard EMACS bindings; hence if you are familiar with EMACS you can skim much of this chapter.

The knowledge of only a few basic commands is sufficient to start using the editor. In the first part of this chapter we will cover the 'quick and dirty' essentials to get you started. These will more than suffice for your work with the exercises at the end of each chapter. Later, as you start doing serious program development work, you can explore the more sophisticated features of the editor at your leisure.

In this chapter we will look at:

- the essential features of the *GMACS editor*
- how to *move* and *copy* blocks of text
- *backward* and *forward search* for a specified string
- the use of *split edit windows* to merge texts
- the use of *multiple edit buffers*
- *numeric arguments* and other features of GMACS
- GMACS *help facilities*

27.1 The basic operations of GMACS may be summarized diagramatically

Before getting into the details of how to use the editor, it may be helpful to provide an overview in the form of a diagram (see Fig. 27.1) which illustrates the basic relationships between the editor, the interpreter, the MS-DOS operating system and the file to be edited.

The following concentrated summary of editor operations assumes that we are operating with GCLISP installed on our hard disk:

(1) Once we have booted up MS-DOS and are in a given directory, we can check whether a file exists in this directory using the **dir** command and can review its contents on the screen with the **type** command.

(2) Once in the GCLISP directory we can call up the bare interpreter with the **gclisp** command, or can load the interpreter together with the editor with the **gmacs** command. When in the interpreter we can temporarily return to MS-DOS with a call to **(sys:dos)**. While back in MS-DOS we can execute various DOS commands without affecting the integrity of the interpreter, after which we can return to the interpreter with an exit command. Finally, we can permanently exit from the interpreter with a call to **(exit)**.

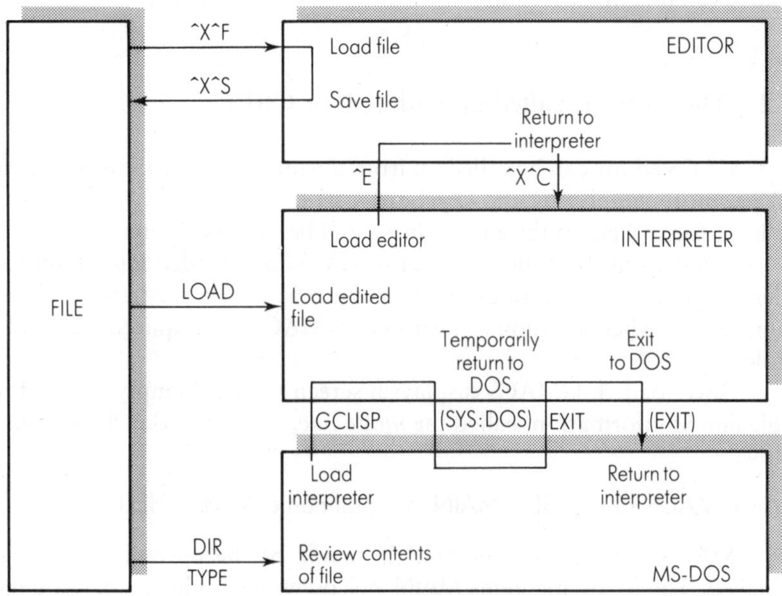

Fig. 27.1 Relationships between the editor, interpreter and MS-DOS.

(3) While in the interpreter we can load a **.LSP** file (or any other file containing an ASCII-coded LISP program) with the command **(load "<filename>")**. Although we can make modifications to the program while in the interpreter, we cannot save these modifications to file; for this we need the editor.

(4) Assuming that we have loaded the editor, we can get into editor mode from the interpreter with a call to **(ed)** or by simply pressing the keychord Ctrl-E. Once in the editor we can call up a particular file for editing using Ctrl-X Ctrl-F, followed by typing in the file pathname in response to the prompt. If the file does not already exist, a new file of that name will be created. We can add or delete material from the file, or modify existing material through the use of the numeric keyboard keys supplemented by the Space key and Rubout key. We can save the edited version of the file using Ctrl-X Ctrl-S. We can temporarily return to the interpreter with Ctrl-X Ctrl-C to load and test the program. From the interpreter we can return to edit mode with **(ed)** or Ctrl-E without having to reload the editor. We can permanently exit from the interpreter to MS-DOS with **(exit)**.

The foregoing provides a general overview. We will now look at the details of using the interpreter, concentrating on the most basic edit mechanisms. These basics will get you by until such time as you have the time and/or inclination to explore some of the more powerful time-saving commands available in GMACS.

27.2 The editor is called up with (ed) or Ctrl-E

The GMACS editor can be called up from the interpreter with the command **(ed)** or, more simply, by the keychord Ctrl-E. (Certain other options are available for calling up the editor; these will be discussed later.)

Initially only a minimal subset of GMACS is loaded into memory in order to leave a maximum amount of space available for testing the program. As and when additional features of GMACS are required they will be autoloaded.

Once loaded, GMACS displays a screen which is empty except for a single line of information, called the *mode* line, at the bottom. This looks as follows:

```
GMACS V2.1 (USER) MAIN: null pathname Alt-H = HELP
```

The GMACS version number and the name of the current package are displayed. The following items **MAIN: null pathname** indicate that you have an empty edit buffer with the default name of '**MAIN**' which is ready for use, and as yet this buffer is not associated with any particular file.

There are two things you can do with this edit buffer:

- create and edit a new file
- retrieve and edit the contents of an existing file

The so-called *buffer* is simply an area in memory that GMACS sets aside for editing a single file. As the file is created and/or added to, the buffer expands to accomodate the growing text. The operation is in principle exactly like the creation of a document in a word processor. In a typical word processor, once in the top-level menu you indicate that you wish to edit a file and provide the filename. If the file already exists the contents will be displayed; if it does not yet exist, a new file of that name will be created. GMACS works the same way.

GMACS provides for more than one buffer to be present in memory, each associated with a different file, and provides means whereby you can switch back and forth from one buffer to another. For the moment we will just consider the single buffer in which you will be starting to edit, which is referred to as the *current buffer*. We will initially look at the first option: to create and edit a new file; in Section 27.7 we will look at the second option of retrieving and editing an existing file.

27.3 Arrow and paging keys move the cursor around the screen

At this point we are ready to create a new LISP program file (which has not yet been named) in the buffer. Although GMACS has a plethora of bells and whistles to carry out any conceivable editing task, we find that initially we can get by quite well with only the basic numeric keypad keys to move the cursor around, supplemented by a few keychords to get us in and out of the editor.

Basically, editing consists of moving the cursor to some location on the screen and then carrying out some operation there: deleting text, adding text, or shifting text backward or forward. We may also wish to copy or move blocks of text to other locations (see Section 27.5).

Movement of the cursor on the screen may be effected by use of keys on the numeric keypad or by keychord commands. Since use of the keypad is more straightforward we will use these keys to get started. The keys in question are as shown in Fig. 27.2; the comments at left describe what each key does.

Initially the cursor is in the Home position on the screen. If we try to move the cursor about with the numeric keyboard keys the system will beep in protest. This is because the cursor can only be moved when there is an existing text field in which to move, and as yet we have created no text. Let's

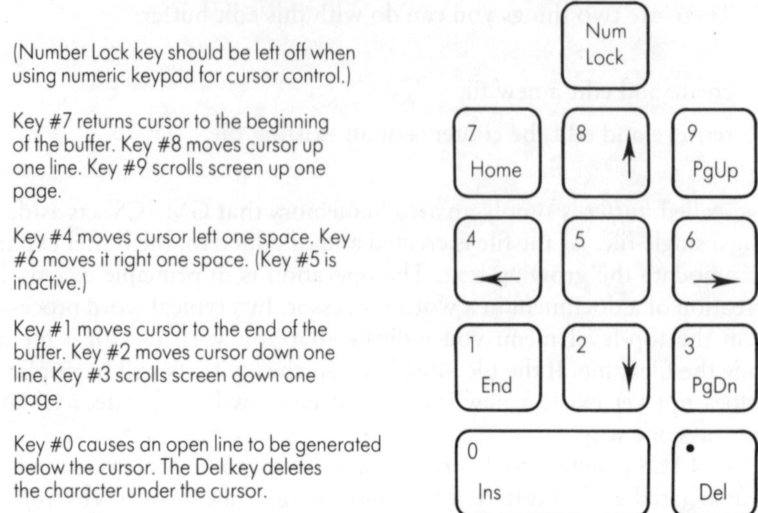

(Number Lock key should be left off when using numeric keypad for cursor control.)
Key #7 returns cursor to the beginning of the buffer. Key #8 moves cursor up one line. Key #9 scrolls screen up one page.
Key #4 moves cursor left one space. Key #6 moves it right one space. (Key #5 is inactive.)
Key #1 moves cursor to the end of the buffer. Key #2 moves cursor down one line. Key #3 scrolls screen down one page.
Key #0 causes an open line to be generated below the cursor. The Del key deletes the character under the cursor.
Num Lock
7 Home
8
9 PgUp
4
5
6
1 End
2
3 PgDn
0 Ins
• Del

Fig. 27.2 The numeric keypad provides for various cursor movements.

do so by typing in the following:

```
;FACTORIAL calculates the factorial of a number
(defun factorial (n)
  (if (zerop n)
      1
      (* n (factorial (1- n)))))<cursor is now here>
```

We can enter text in either upper- or lowercase. (Strings aside, the interpreter will convert all S-expressions to uppercase anyway when the file is loaded.) A semicolon anywhere on the line indicates that the material which follows is a comment to be ignored by the interpreter.

We can easily type in the above example by using only a few keys in addition to the text characters themselves. The *Enter*, or *Carriage Return*, key advances the cursor to the start of a new line; and the *Space Bar* advances the cursor to the right. We can use the *Backspace* key to back up over (and delete) a mistake. If we get to the end and find that we have made a mistake somewhere we can move the cursor back to the desired location with the *Left Arrow* key and make modifications by deleting characters with the *Delete* key and/or typing in new characters.

Since one of the classic problems in writing LISP programs has been related to those Lots of Irritating Silly Parentheses, GMACS includes some features to help us in this area. We note that when we get to the end of the above expression, the first parenthesis before the defun is blinking, indicating that it is 'balanced' by the parenthesis just to the left of the cursor. If we move the cursor one position to the left with the Left Arrow key, we see that a different balancing parenthesis is now flashing. And if we add a surplus parenthesis after the **factorial** definition we will get a beep complaint and an **Overbalanced close parenthesis** message. These features provide a check on the number and placement of parentheses during the writing of a program.

When we reach the bottom of the window in which we are currently working, the next **Newline** operation suddenly causes the text to scroll upward by about half a screen to provide room for inserting additional lines. This may be occasionally frustrating since the first line of a function may suddenly disappear above the top of the screen, making it impossible to see whether the first parenthesis is flashing in balance with the final parenthesis.

The best way to deal with this is to move the cursor to about the middle of the function definition and use Ctrl-L. This will move the display so that the current line is at the middle of the screen, thus centering the function definition to the extent possible. You can fine-tune the screen position thereafter by moving the cursor up or down by one line and using Ctrl-L again.

(Another solution which springs to mind is to split the screen (see Section 27.10) on a single buffer and scroll the respective half-screens, so that the front end of the definition will be in the top buffer and the bottom end in the bottom buffer. Unfortunately, the flashing parenthesis feature does not bridge split screens.)

Having created the above function definition we would now like to save it to some (new) file, say, **C:\\WS\\TESTFILE.LSP**. To do this we use keychord Ctrl-X Ctrl-S, whereupon the following is displayed below the mode line:

Write file: <<= >
Default: C:\GCLISP\FOO.LSP

prompting us for the name of the file. If we type in the above pathname **C:\\WS\\TESTFILE** (to which GMACS will automatically add the **.LSP** extension), GMACS will look for a file of that name in the relevant directory. If the file exists, GMACS will overwrite it with the new material; if the file does not exist, GMACS will create it and write the new material to it. After completing this task, the message **File written** is displayed at the bottom of the screen.

(NB: Rather than use the double backslash notation, we can use a single slash, that is, **"C:/WS/TESTFILE.LSP"**.)

After saving material to file, GMACS leaves you in the same buffer so that you can continue with your editing. Like word processors, this feature permits you to save text periodically so as to minimize the loss of work should the system crash for some reason.

Your choice as to the file pathname will of course be dictated by your disk drive configuration. If you have a hard disk you will probably have GCLISP installed in its own directory and can keep your **.LSP** files in this or some other directory. If you have a word processor on the hard disk, this is a good place in which to keep .LSP files on which you are working, for several reasons. You can use the word processor, with which you may be more comfortable than GMACS, to modify them and/or to transfer 'boilerplate' blocks of text from one program to another. You can also copy your LISP programs to reports which describe the programs, etc. For purposes of this discussion we will assume that you are storing your file in (WordStar) directory WS on drive C.

We now wish to test our new function. Although some testing can be carried out without leaving editor mode (see Section 27.12), we will for the moment use the interpreter for this purpose. This will give us practice in saving the edited material to the file and moving back and forth between the editor and the interpreter.

27.4 Moving back and forth between the editor and the interpreter

We can now jump over to the interpreter with the Ctrl-X Ctrl-C command. Once in the interpreter we can try out our new function:

```
* (factorial 5)
ERROR:
Undefined function: FACTORIAL
While evaluating (FACTORIAL 5)
1>
```

As this illustrates, the fact that we have defined a function in the editor doesn't necessarily mean that the interpreter knows about it! In this sense the editor and interpreter are two separate operating environments. Therefore, before testing the program we have to **load** the program file into the interpreter:

```
* (load "c:\\ws\\testfile" :print t)
; Reading file C:\WS\TESTFILE.LSP
FACTORIAL
#.(PATHNAME "C:\\WS\\TESTFILE.LSP")
```

GMACS automatically adds the .LSP extension before making the search, so we don't have to include it in the specification. We have added the **:print t** option to **load**, which causes the value returned by each expression loaded from the file to be echoed to the console (see Section 23.12).

The fact that no error has been signaled means that our parentheses are in balance and that all expressions in the file have been evaluated without syntax errors. We can now test our factorial function:

```
* (factorial 5)
120
```

We can now, if we wish, return to the editor with Ctrl-E and work on the program some more, remembering that after each round of modifications we have to save them with Ctrl-X Ctrl-S, return to the interpreter, and re-load the file before testing.

27.5 Blocks of text may be copied or moved to another location

The foregoing minimal operations are sufficient to create and edit a small LISP program. However one additional feature with which you should be familiar is the GMACS system for deleting, copying, and moving blocks of text. This can save you a lot of time when copying blocks of 'boilerplate' from one function definition to another.

If massive restructuring of your program is involved, and if you have a word processor with which you are familiar, at times it may be quicker to move the program into the word processor and edit the major changes there, rather than doing it with the GMACS editor. Remember to do this in 'N' nondocument mode; otherwise you will get page-advance and/or other characters carried over which will cause syntax errors when you start evaluating expressions which have been loaded from the file (although these will be visible on the GMACS edit screen and can be removed).

As compared to the straightforward method used by word processors to move or copy blocks of text, GMACS has a somewhat complicated system in which a block of text, referred to as a *region*, is first *killed* to a push-down stack. Subsequently it may be *yanked* from the stack and copied into a new location.

The so-called region is marked out by first moving the cursor to one end of the region and pressing the keychord Ctrl-@ which sets a mark at that location. Although the mark is not echoed on the console, the message Mark set appears below the mode line. The cursor is then moved (either backward or forward) to mark out the other end of the region. At this point either of the following keychords may be used to move the region of text to the so-called *kill history* push-down stack:

- Ctrl-W deletes the region of text and moves it to the kill history stack. This is equivalent to a Move operation with a word processor.
- Alt-W copies the region of text to the kill history stack, but otherwise leaves it as it is. This is equivalent to a Copy operation with a word processor.

Having put the block of text into the kill history stack, the cursor is then moved to the location where the text is to be copied or moved, and the keychord Ctrl-Y is pressed. This command 'yanks' the block of text from the kill history stack and copies it into the new location.

It should be noted that after having been 'yanked,' the block of text still remains on the kill history stack. As and when other blocks of text are 'killed,' they will be pushed onto the kill history stack on top of the previous block of text until a maximum of five blocks have been accumulated; thereafter the lowermost blocks will be popped off the bottom of the stack and discarded. Blocks lower down on the stack can be retrieved by a series of yank (Ctrl-Y) and yank-pop (Alt-Y) operations in which each lower nested block replaces the current one on a round-robin basis until you work your way down to the one you want.

27.6 Other cursor motion commands are available

A number of keychords are available which duplicate the cursor motions effected by keys of the numeric keypad. If you do a lot of editing and are an accomplished typist you may be able to use these keys more efficiently than the keypad:

Keychord	*= Keypad key*	*Keychord*	*= Keypad key*
Ctrl-F	Right Arrow	Ctrl-V	PgDn
Ctrl-B	Left Arrow	Alt-V	PgUp
Ctrl-P	Up Arrow	Esc <	Home
Ctrl-N	Down Arrow	Esc >	End
Ctrl-D	Delete	Ctrl-H	Rubout

Other combinations also permit you to jump backwards and forwards by one word, or to the beginning or end of the sentence:

Keychord	*Moves cursor to*	*Keychord*	*Moves cursor to*
Alt-F	Forward one word	Ctrl-A	Beginning of line
Alt-B	Backward one word	Ctrl-E	End of line

Finally, various commands are available to delete the word in front of or behind the cursor, as well as the rest of the line following or preceding the cursor:

Keychord	*Deletes*	*Keychord*	*Deletes*
Alt-D	Word after cursor	Ctrl-K	Line after cursor
Ctrl-Rubout	Word before cursor		

It should be noted that the foregoing deletions are kill commands which move the deleted item to the kill history stack. Hence, if you inadvertently delete something you shouldn't have, you can recover it with a yank or yank-pop command (see Section 27.5).

Other deletion commands (which do *not* move the item deleted to the kill history stack) include Esc \, which deletes all space before and after the current cursor location, and Ctrl-Z ^, which deletes any space at the front of the line on which the cursor is located and then appends this line to the line above.

Since GMACS is specifically designed to edit LISP program files, it includes a multitude of specialized expressions to move the cursor forward or backward to the beginning or end of the expression in which the cursor is currently located; to the beginning or end of a list or function definition; downward into the next more deeply nested list, etc. These commands are summarized in Section 27.16; and more details are provided in the GCLRM.

27.7 Ctrl-X Ctrl-R reads in a file

Rather than use the **MAIN** buffer to create a new program file, we will often be using it to call up and edit an existing program. In this case, once we have the buffer at our disposition we can press the keychord combination Ctrl-X Ctrl-R to indicate to GMACS that we want to load and edit a file, whereupon the following is displayed below the mode line:

```
GMACS V2.1 (USER) MAIN: null pathname          Alt-H = HELP
   Read file: <<= >
Default: C:\GCLISP\FOO.LSP
```

with the cursor positioned after the **Read File** prompt to type in the name of the file.

There are actually *two* ways in which we can proceed at this point.

(1) We can type in the pathname of an existing file on which we want to do some more editing work, in which case the file will be loaded and displayed in the buffer. At such time as we are finished editing, we can use Ctrl-X Ctrl-S to save the file. The edited version will overwrite the previous version.

(2) We can type in the pathname of a (new) file which does not exist, in which case we will be presented with an empty buffer in which we can create a new program. This is similar to the first option which we looked at earlier, the difference being that the buffer is now associated with a specific file which will automatically be created when we save the new material.

For purposes of this exercise let's assume that we wish to carry out additional editing on an existing file **C:\\WS\\TESTFILE**. At this point you may wish to exit to MS-DOS and reload GMACS to simulate this situation, using the factorial file which you just created in Section 27.3).

In response to the prompt, we will therefore enter:

C:\\WS\\TESTFILE

GMACS will access the existing file, and the factorial definition will be displayed on the screen, available for further editing.

Note that use of Ctrl-X Ctrl-F (see following section) is generally preferable to Ctrl-X Ctrl-R, since it preserves whatever may be in the current buffer rather than writing over it.

27.8 More than one buffer can exist at a time

In the course of program development you may be operating with just a single .LSP file being edited in a single buffer. However there are times when it may be desirable to create one or more additional buffers to hold files from which you are copying text (see Section 27.10 below).

You can create a new buffer with the *find-file* command Ctrl-X Ctrl-F, which prompts for the name of the file and creates a new buffer for it. This buffer then becomes the *current buffer* and the buffer your were working on previously becomes the *previous buffer*. You can return to the previous buffer with the command Ctrl-Z L. In general, having created two or more buffers, you can switch from one buffer to another with the *select-buffer* command Ctrl-X B, which prompts for the buffer name and then makes that buffer the current buffer. Note that for buffers other than MAIN the buffer name is simply the name of the file without the .LSP extension; and that given a (bare) filename GMACS assumes the same drive and directory as defaults.

Various other commands are available to deal with multiple buffers. A listing of currently existing buffers may be obtained using the *list-buffers* command Ctrl-X Ctrl-B, which lists the name of each edit buffer and the name of the file associated with it. A buffer can be deleted with the *kill-buffer* command Ctrl-X K.

If you have made any changes to a buffer since it was last saved to file, the *buffer status* asterisk * is displayed after the pathname on the mode line. If you try to exit from the interpreter without saving the most recent modifications a warning message will be generated. However you can instruct the system to ignore any such modifications with the *unmodify-buffer* command Esc ~, which clears the buffer status asterisk from the mode line.

27.9 Ctrl-S and Ctrl-R provide for forward and backward search

There will inevitably be occasions when you wish to search for a specific string of characters in the file. Perhaps, when loading a (supposedly debugged) program, you get the message: **ERROR: Unbound variable: formd.** You have used the variable **forms** in a number of places throughout the program, and have apparently mistyped a **d** instead of an **s** in one of them.

Assuming that your program is still in the current buffer you can return to the editor, position the cursor to the beginning of the buffer with the Home key, and press the keychord Ctrl-S to effect a forward search for the string. If you type in **formd** in response to the prompt for a search string and press the Esc key, the system will institute a search through the file for the first instance of **formd**. When found, the cursor will stop just after the end of the string and you can make the necessary corrections. If you want to check whether any other instances of **formd** exist in the file you can press Ctrl-S again. This time **formd** is displayed as the *default string*, and you can just press Esc to cause the search to continue without having to type in the string again.

Whereas Ctrl-S initiates a search in a *forward* direction, Ctrl-R searches *backward* from the current cursor position. Caveat: In earlier versions of GCLISP, if you inadvertently hit Ctrl-R and then change your mind, be sure to use Ctrl-G to abort the command in the event a default string has not been established by an earlier search. If you simply press Esc again, with no search string specified, the system will completely hang up, necessitating a reboot and causing you to lose any edited material which has not been saved.

GMACS also includes provision for a *search and replace* operation. Pressing the keychord Alt-% will prompt for two inputs: a search string and another string to replace it with. The system will then search forward for instances of the search string, stopping at each instance to query **(y-or-n?)** whether you want to effect the replacement on this particular instance. The search will automatically continue until end-of-file is reached. (NB: An alternative option ! permits *all* instances to be replaced without further recourse to you.)

27.10 Editing can be carried out in two separate windows

A very convenient feature of GMACS is the ability to split the screen into two half-screen windows, in each of which a separate file – or different regions of the same file – can be displayed and edited. The single screen is transformed into two half-screen windows with the keychord combination Ctrl-X 2.

Each of the windows is associated with a particular buffer. When you split the screen, the upper half displays the contents of the current buffer, with the cursor positioned in the approximate center of the window. If only one buffer is currently active, the lower window displays the same buffer as the top window; otherwise it displays the previous buffer. Hence, if you want to copy some text from **FILE-2** into the file which you are currently editing, use Ctrl-X Ctrl-F to create a new buffer for FILE-2 and then split the windows: FILE-2 will be in the upper window and the file being edited will be in the bottom window. Since both of these edit windows share the same kill history stack, text can be transferred from one file to another by killing a region in one window and then moving to the other window and yanking it into the other file.

The command Ctrl-X O moves you back and forth between windows. While operating in either window, all the normal screen edit commands apply to that window only.

When you are finished editing with two windows, you can return to single-window mode with Ctrl-X 1. Since the file from which you were copying text is now in the current buffer, you will have to use the command Ctrl-Z L to re-display the *previous buffer* which now holds the file you were editing.

27.11 Numeric arguments and other miscellaneous features

At times you may wish to execute a GMACS command a certain number of times. GMACS provides a *numeric argument* feature whereby this can be accomplished. If a command is preceded by the key sequence:

```
Ctrl-U <number> ...
```

then the command which follows that sequence will be executed <number> of times. If <number> is left out it defaults to 4.

Several commands are available for operating on directories. The *display-directory* command Ctrl-X Ctrl-D prompts for the pathname of a directory and displays a listing of the files in that directory. The *change-directory* command Ctrl-X C changes the default directory to the one you name in response to the prompt.

Other commands provide for specifying the type case of a single word or of a whole region (see Section 27.16).

Information about LISP code can be displayed using Alt-H Alt-L, which displays the lambda list of the current function in which the cursor is located; Alt-H Alt-D, which displays the full Help documentation of the current function; and Esc @, which displays the macro-expansion of the S-expression immediately to the right of the cursor.

As mentioned previously, there are other ways of calling up the editor. A call to (ed "<filename>") bypasses the empty MAIN buffer operation and puts you directly into a current buffer with the desired file. A call to (ed t) provides you with a new empty MAIN buffer and preserves the MAIN buffer from a previous invocation, if any.

Finally, several commands are available (see Section 27.16) which provide for indenting of a line of LISP code to reflect the nesting level of the current form.

27.12 Evaluation of expressions can be carried out in the editor

Up to now we have been testing our programs by moving back to the interpreter with Ctrl-X Ctrl-C, loading the modified file with a (load "<file-name>") command, and testing the function(s). GMACS also makes provision for carrying out such evaluations on the spot without leaving the editor.

The *eval-definition* command Ctrl-X Ctrl-E evaluates the current expression in which the cursor is located (the expresssion which would be found by the command beginning-of-definition). This comes in handy for checking whether your parentheses are in balance on a long function definition. Evaluation of a function definition will of course only return the function name. If you want to try out the function you have to type a function call into the editor, for example, (factorial 5) and evaluate *that*. (Obviously such test expressions, which would not be part of a normal program file, should be purged from the editor after use.)

27.13 Function keys are associated with common commands

For operating convenience, GMACS has associated the ten function keys with commonly used commands.

Key	*Command*	*Key*	*Command*
F1	exit-editor	F6	prefix key – Meta
F2	ed-help	F7	find-file
F3	select-buffer	F8	read-file
F4	select-previous-buffer	F9	save-file
F5	prefix key – Control	F10	abort command/beep

27.14 GMACS provides help facilities

While in the GMACS environment, a variety of on-line Help facilities are available. Typing Alt-H causes a short menu of help options to be displayed, any of which can be invoked by typing in the indicated letter:

- A 'Apropos': displays the keychords for all GMACS commands which contain the substring entered in response to the prompt.
- D 'Documentation: displays the documentation on all of the GMACS commands containing the substring.
- K 'Keychord binding': displays the GMACS command bound to a particular keychord.

T 'Teach GMACS': invokes the GMACS on-line tutorial. This consists of three text files which you can scroll and read, and which provide a guided tutorial on the use of GMACS.

? Redisplays the above menu.

27.15 GMACS functions can be unloaded after use

When finished with GMACS we can recover some of the space used by the editor with unload-gmacs, which takes the syntax:

(unload-gmacs &optional <and-kernel>)

This function maps fmakunbound to functions used by GMACS such that the space used by these definitions will be retrieved during the next garbage collection. If <and-kernel> is non-NIL, then functions that are required to enter the editor will also be unloaded; otherwise these functions will be left and only the functions that implement additional features will be unloaded.

If we use room (see Section 26.12) to check memory availability before and after the use of unload-gmacs, we find that only a modest amount of memory appears to be recovered. In order to maximize the amount of memory available for use with a program it is therefore advisable to return to the operating system, reload GCLISP from scratch, and load the program file directly into the (bare) interpreter.

An associated function unload-lisplib, which takes no arguments, similarly maps fmakunbound to functions previously autoloaded from the LISPLIB and LISPLIB\PACKAGES directories. These functions will subsequently be autoloaded again whenever required.

27.16 Summary of GMACS commands for quick reference

All of the GMACS commands are summarized below, by category of operation, for quick reference.

Cursor Motion Commands

Ctrl-F or Right Arrow	FORWARD-CHAR
Ctrl-B or Left Arrow	BACKWARD-CHAR
Alt-F or Ctrl-Right Arrow	FORWARD-WORD
Alt-B or Ctrl-Left Arrow	BACKWARD-WORD
Ctrl-A	BEGINNING-OF-LINE
Ctrl-E	END-OF-LINE
Ctrl-N or Down Arrow	NEXT-LINE
Ctrl-P or Up Arrow	PREVIOUS-LINE
Home or Esc <	BEGINNING-OF-BUFFER
End or Esc >	END-OF-BUFFER

Edit window commands

Ctrl-V or PgDn	NEXT-SCREEN
Alt-V or PgUp	PREVIOUS-SCREEN
Ctrl-X 1	ONE-WINDOW
Ctrl-X 2	TWO-WINDOWS
Ctrl-X O	OTHER-WINDOW
Ctrl-Z V	SCROLL-OTHER-WINDOW
Ctrl-L	RECENTER-SCREEN

Text deletion commands

Rubout or Ctrl-H	RUBOUT
Ctrl-D or Del	DELETE-CHAR
Ctrl-H or Rubout	RUBOUT
Ctrl-Z ^	DELETE-INDENTATION
Esc \ or Esc Space	DELETE-HORIZONTAL-SPACE
Alt-D	KILL-WORD
Ctrl-Rubout or Esc Rubout	BACKWARD-KILL-WORD
Ctrl-K	KILL-LINE
Alt-X command-name	BACKWARD-KILL-LINE
Ctrl-W	KILL-REGION
Ctrl-Z K	KILL-SEXP
Ctrl-Z Rubout	BACKWARD-KILL-SEXP
Ctrl-Z ;	KILL-COMMENT

Buffer and file commands

Ctrl-X Ctrl-F or F7	FIND-FILE
Ctrl-X Ctrl-R or F8 or Ctrl-X Ctrl-V	READ-FILE
Ctrl-X Ctrl-S or F9	SAVE-FILE
Ctrl-X B or F3	SELECT BUFFER
Ctrl-X K	KILL-BUFFER
Ctrl-Z L or F4	SELECT-PREVIOUS-BUFFER
Ctrl-X Ctrl-B	LIST-BUFFERS
Esc ~	UNMODIFY-BUFFER
Ctrl-X Ctrl-W	WRITE-FILE
Ctrl-X C	CHANGE-DIRECTORY
Ctrl-X Ctrl-D	DISPLAY-DIRECTORY
Ctrl-M	EXIT-MINIBUFFER
Ctrl-Z : or Ctrl-X P	SET-BUFFER-PACKAGE

Search and replace commands

Ctrl-S	FORWARD-SEARCH
Ctrl-R	REVERSE-SEARCH
Alt-%	QUERY-REPLACE

Case-setting commands

Alt-C	UPPERCASE-INITIAL
Alt-L	LOWERCASE-WORD
Alt-U	UPPERCASE-WORD
Ctrl-X Ctrl-U	UPPERCASE-REGION
Ctrl-X Ctrl-L	LOWERCASE-REGION

Commands for editing LISP

Ctrl-Z F or Ctrl-PgDn	FORWARD-SEXP
Ctrl-Z B or Ctrl-PgUp	BACKWARD-SEXP
Ctrl-Z N	FORWARD-LIST
Ctrl-Z P	BACKWARD-LIST
Ctrl-Z D	DOWN-LIST
Ctrl-Z U or Ctrl-Z (	BACKWARD-UP-LIST
Ctrl-Z)	FORWARD-UP-LIST
Ctrl-Z A, or Ctrl-Home	BEGINNING-OF-DEFINITION
Ctrl-Z E or Ctrl-End	END-OF-DEFINITION
Alt-! or Esc !	EVAL-SEXP
Ctrl-X Ctrl-E	EVAL-DEFINITION
Ctrl-Z I or Ctrl-Z Q	INDENT-SEXP
Ctrl-I	INDENT-TO-LEVEL
Esc ;	INDENT-FOR-COMMENT
Ctrl-J or Ctrl-Enter	INDENT-NEWLINE
Alt-H Alt-L	DISPLAY-LAMBDA-LIST
Alt-H Alt-D	DISPLAY-DOCUMENTATION
Esc @ or Ctrl-Z M	DISPLAY-MACROEXPANSION

Region and kill history commands

Ctrl-X Ctrl-X	EXCHANGE-POINT-AND-MARK
Ctrl-@ or Ctrl-Space or Ctrl-2 or F5 Space	SET-POP-MARK
Alt-W	SAVE-REGION
Ctrl-Y	YANK
Alt-Y	YANK-POP
Ctrl-Z W	APPEND-NEXT-KILL

Miscellaneous

Ctrl-X Ctrl-C or F1 or Ctrl-X Ctrl-Z	EXIT-EDITOR
Ctrl-G or Ctrl-X Ctrl-G or Ctrl-Z G	ED-BEEP
Alt-H ? or F2 or Alt-H Alt-H or Alt-H H or F2 H	ED-HELP
Alt-H A or F2 A	ED-APROPOS

Miscellaneous (cont.)

Alt-H K or Esc ? or F2 K	ED-KEYCHORD
Alt-H D or F2 D	ED-DOC
Alt-X	EXTENDED-COMMAND
Enter	NEWLINE
Ctrl-O or Ins	OPEN-LINE
Ctrl-U	NUMERIC-ARG
Ctrl-Q	QUOTED-INSERT
Ctrl-T	EXCHANGE-CHARACTERS
Ctrl-X Ctrl-^	CONTROL-PREFIX

SUMMARY

Summarizing the main points of this chapter:

- GMACS is a full-screen *display editor*, based on the original EMACS editor designed at MIT by Richard M. Stallman
- the editor maintains one or more *edit buffers*, each of which may be associated with a .LSP program file
- a full range of keychords and keychord combinations is available for moving the cursor around the screen, and for adding or deleting text
- facilities are provided to effect *backward* and *forward search* for a specified string, as well as to replace one or more instances of a string with a replacement string
- *split edit windows* may be used to merge texts
- *numeric arguments* permit repetitive execution of a GMACS command
- the most common GMACS commands are linked to *function keys*
- GMACS provides various kinds of *help facilities*

Chapter 28
Inside a LISP Interpreter

To further enhance your understanding of LISP and the manner in which it operates, it is of interest to gain some familiarity with the internal structure and operation of a LISP interpreter. The discussion in this chapter will center on a relatively simple interpreter designed for an 8-bit CP/M-80 system. However the general principles are applicable to larger systems. GCLISP, which is designed for a 16-bit MS-DOS system, provides many more features and is considerably more complex.

In this chapter we will look at:

- the manner in which a simple LISP interpreter allocates and uses memory
- the nature of the *initialization* process
- the manner in which the *Object List* is created
- the *layout* of a typical microcomputer LISP interpreter
- the nature of *garbage collection*, and some mechanisms for carrying out this operation
- how the *LISP environment* may be saved to a .SYS file
- the concept of cdr-*coding* as a means of minimizing space requirements for list structures
- the nature of *compilation* and how it speeds up performance of a LISP system

28.1 A simple LISP interpreter uses memory in five basic ways

The basic components of a LISP interpreter and the manner in which it utilizes memory can be discussed in terms illustrated in Fig. 28.1. The diagram reflects the following five principal areas of memory usage:

(1) main body of the interpreter
(2) dynamic flags
(3) Object List
(4) heap storage
(5) control stack

The *main body of the interpreter* is the object code for the interpreter itself. After the interpreter has been loaded into onboard memory by loading a .COM file, various initialization steps are taken including display of a logon message; allocation of available memory space for storage of numbers, strings, lists, and the control stack; creation and initialization of the Object List; and invocation of the top level **read/eval/print** loop.

The *dynamic flags* area is an area of memory reserved for address pointers which change in the course of using the system. When recreating a LISP environment all of these addresses have to be reset to reflect the state of the previous environment (see Section 28.6).

The *Object List* serves as a lookup table for LISP symbols. This list is initialized to contain all of the primitives built into the LISP system. Symbols subsequently defined by the user are added onto the end of this list.

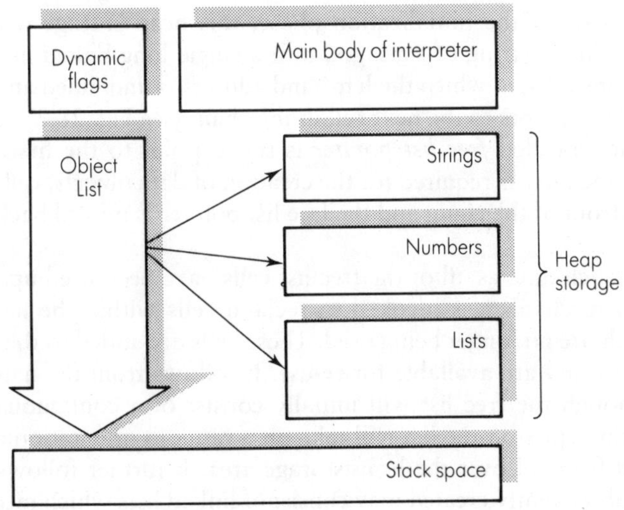

Fig. 28.1 Allocation of memory within a LISP interpreter.

Heap storage refers to the bulk of on-board memory which is left after loading the interpreter, creating the Object List, and providing for the needs of the operating system itself. The manner in which this memory is allocated and utilized is discussed in more detail in Section 28.2.

Finally, the *control stack* is used to keep track of the status of function calls and their arguments during the evaluation process.

28.2 Memory is allocated during the initialization process

Since the size of user-defined procedures and data is not determined until run-time, there is no way of predicting in advance the amount of storage which they may take up. This situation therefore dictates the use of *heap storage*, in which a large block of memory is set aside as a source of cons cells for use by the interpreter as and when needed. Such heap storage may be allocated in a single block for general use by all kinds of LISP data objects, or may be split into sections each dedicated to a certain type of data object.

In the most general application of this concept, the entire block of memory is used for all of the different kinds of data objects involved in a LISP program. Aside from symbols (which are maintained on the Object List) these would typically include lists (whether used for functional procedures or data), numbers, strings, arrays, and structures. During the initialization process, the total amount of available storage is determined by ascertaining the amount of on-board memory available and subtracting the required amounts of storage to be allocated to the control stack and to the Object List. Whatever is left may be used as heap storage.

As part of the initialization phase, this heap storage is connected, somewhat like a string of sausages, into a single long linked list of double address cons cells, in which the left-hand address is undefined and the right-hand address points to the next cell in the chain (see Fig. 28.2).

The so-called *free list pointer* is set to point to the first cell in the chain. As memory is required for the creation of data objects, cells are taken from the front of the chain and the free list pointer is moved back along the chain.

At such time as all of the free list cells have been used up, a garbage collection mechanism is invoked to reclaim cells within the heap storage area which are no longer being used. These cells are added to the tail end of the free list and are available for re-use. It follows from the nature of this that, although the free list will initially consist of a contiguous listing of cells, as time goes on the list will take on a random orientation as cells are reclaimed from all over the heap storage area. It further follows that data objects subsequently created may consist of linked lists which meander over the whole range of free storage. However none of this effects the efficiency of the system since the manipulation of linked lists in no way depends on a

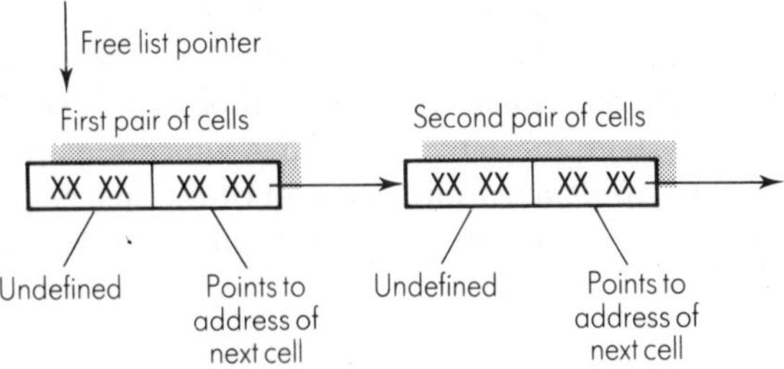

Fig. 28.2 The free list serves as a source of **cons** cells.

subsequent cell in the chain being physically contiguous to the previous cell. (Some LISP systems have explored the benefits to be gained by using contiguous cells for linked lists, thereby precluding the need for pointers between cells. See the commentary on **cdr**-coding in Section 28.7.)

The generalized use of heap storage for any and all data objects has both advantages and disadvantages, as compared to selective allocation of memory to specific types of data objects. The advantages are that:

- the entire heap storage is available for use by any and all data objects, precluding the need for decision-making as to how much storage to allocate to what types of data object for a given AI application, and precluding the need for reallocation of blocks to alternative uses if the initial guess was incorrect;
- once a data object has been created there is never any need to change its location in memory or to adjust any of the pointers which reference it.

The disadvantages are that:

- a specific system such as bit markers must be devised so that the system can tell, when it accesses a data object, exactly what type of object is being accessed. This is a consequence of the fact that LISP is a weakly typed language in the sense that a symbol's type is only determined at runtime; subsequently the same symbol can be used to represent any kind of data object. In a CP/M-80 system, space is found for such bit markers by locating cons cells on even 4-byte boundries such that the lower two bits of the address are always '00' and can temporarily be 'borrowed' for bit markers. In larger systems, higher-order bits which are not required as part of the address may be used for this purpose;
- development of a LISP interpreter based on generalized heap storage is much harder to debug than one in which specific data objects are assigned to specific heap storage areas, and particularly to contiguously located free list cells.

As an alternative to generalized heap storage, the total amount of available memory may be allocated to specific kinds of data objects. For example, separate blocks of memory may be allocated to strings, numbers, and lists. In such a system, the active structures which remain after garbage collection are usually *compacted* into one end of the space. This manner of memory allocation has its advantages and disadvantages. The advantages are that:

- data types may be quickly determined by testing the address of the data object;
- as data objects are created, contiguous cells are used to build up the object, building downward or upward from the initially defined boundaries of the storage space. Hence the entire data object is located in one compact location in memory, rather than being spread out all over the heap storage area. This simplifies the algorithms to create the data objects, particularly in handling of number vectors, and vastly simplifies debugging.

The disadvantages are that:

- there is some loss in flexibility as compared to having the entire heap storage available for any and all data objects. If one area runs out of space, space can be reallocated from another area but only at the expense of relocating existing data structures in that area and resetting all of the pointers which reference these data structures;
- garbage collection is more troublesome, since existing data objects must be compacted back to their space borders and all pointers which reference these objects must be reset.

A mixed method of memory allocation is used by some interpreters, which initially allocate a limited amount of heap storage to certain data types, holding the remainder in reserve. As the allocated space becomes used up, additional chunks of heap storage are allocated. If and when all memory has been used up it has presumably been allocated in a manner proportional to the needs of the particular program being run.

28.3 The Object List is also created during initialization

The Object List is created during the initialization process which takes place after the interpreter has been loaded. We can define seven areas of code of particular interest in connection with this operation, which may be represented diagramatically, as shown in Fig. 28.3.

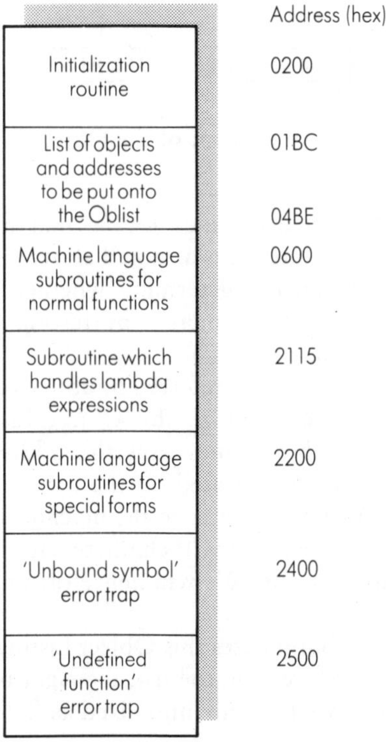

	Address (hex)
Initialization routine	0200
List of objects and addresses to be put onto the Oblist	01BC 04BE
Machine language subroutines for normal functions	0600
Subroutine which handles lambda expressions	2115
Machine language subroutines for special forms	2200
'Unbound symbol' error trap	2400
'Undefined function' error trap	2500

Fig. 28.3 Areas of code which relate to the Object List.

Addresses are arbitrary, are in hexadecimal notation, are appropriate to a 64Kbyte CP/M-80 system, and are included for use in the accompanying discussion.

When the interpreter is loaded, the first routine to be called displays a logon message to the console which identifies the implementation and version, and usually includes a copyright message. Immediately thereafter the initialization routine is called. Although this routine carries out certain other duties, the following discussion will be limited to the manner in which it initializes the Object List.

In the smaller microcomputer implementations which do not support macros, three types of objects are included in the Object List:

(1) normal functions, all of whose arguments are evaluated

(2) special forms, which handle the evaluation of their arguments in a nonroutine manner

(3) special symbols such as NIL and T, and global variables which are principally used to control the manner in which read and print operations are carried out

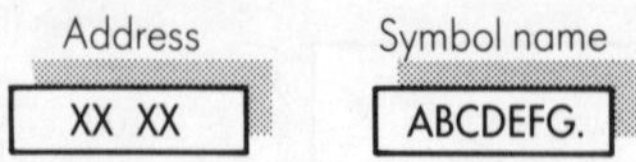

Fig. 28.4 An element of the Object Listing.

The machine language routines for normal functions and special forms are contained in separate areas as noted above.(During the evaluation process the system can quickly determine whether it is dealing with a normal function or special form merely by testing into which area the function pointer is pointing.)

The second area of memory referred to above contains a list of all of the symbols to be used to initialize the Object List. This comprises a contiguous listing of symbol names and the addresses at which their machine language routines are located, in the format shown in Fig. 28.4, where the address represents a pointer to the machine language routine and the symbol name is a sequence of ASCII characters terminated by a null byte (.) to mark the end of the string. We will henceforth refer to this list as the *Object Listing*.

The initialization routine uses this Object Listing to set up the Object List. Starting with the first item on the list, the eight bytes which represent each symbol data object are typically initialized as follows:

Bytes	*Address pointer*	*Points to*
2	Print name	Address of print name string on Object Listing
2	Property list	NIL
2	Function	Subroutine address as per Object Listing
2	Value	'unbound symbol' error trap

The *print name* pointer is the starting address of the print name on the Object Listing, as noted above.

The *property list* pointer is initialized to point to NIL, since none of the primitive symbols has a property list associated with it (although one could be added later by the user).

The *function* pointer address is taken from the first element of the Object Listing as noted above. Since most of the primitives will be functions or special forms, this address will point to a machine language subroutine in one of the two areas as noted in the previous diagram. Where lambda or nlambda is involved, the address will point to a special routine for handling lambda expressions. For the remaining special symbols such as NIL or T and/ or for global variables, this address will be set to point to an *undefined function* error trap. Hence if one attempts to use a variable as the first

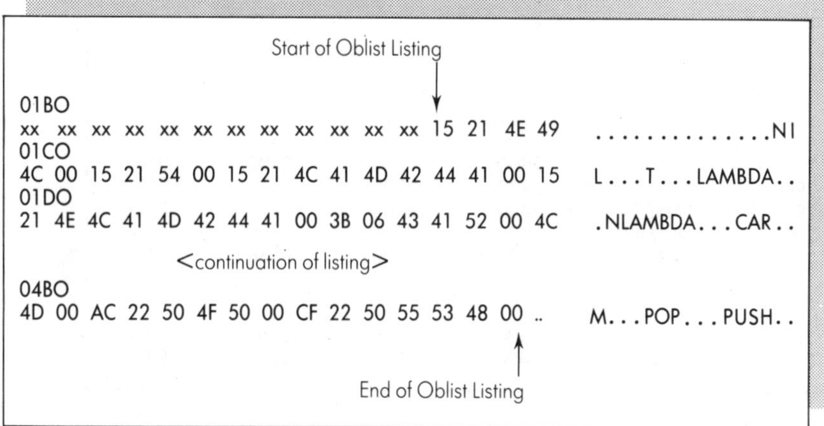

Fig. 28.5 The Object Listing for a microcomputer interpreter.

element of a list to be evaluated, for example, **(nil <some-symbol>)**, an 'undefined function' error will be generated.

The *value*, with exceptions as noted below, is set to an *unbound symbol* error trap. Hence if one attempts to use a primitive in a situation requiring that it be evaluated as a symbol, for example, **(setf symbol-name car)**, since **car** does not have a value an 'unbound symbol' error message will be generated.

As an example of the manner in which an Object List is initialized, we will briefly look at the Object Listing for a popular CP/M-80 based LISP interpreter. The listing commences at memory location 01BC. Using the *debug* utility to print out the relevant machine code, the printout shown in Fig. 28.5 is generated. As will be noted, the listing is comprised of contiguous pairs of addresses and print names (addresses first). The print names, followed by a null byte (.), are reflected in the printout of ASCII characters at right; nonprintable characters such as addresses are also printed as a dot.

The initialization routine uses the above Object Listing to set up the Object List in the manner previously described. Starting with the first item on the list, the eight bytes which represent each data object are generally initialized in the manner as noted previously.

After loading all primitives, the Oblist structure is as shown in Fig. 28.6. After loading of the last primitive, the address in the Oblist pointer cell is 2C08, which is the location at which the first user-defined symbol will be added to the list. Thereafter, as each new symbol is defined, it will be added to the Object List and the Oblist pointer advanced 8 bytes to the next following location.

Further comments on the Object List follow (refer back to addresses as shown in Fig. 28.3).

Starting memory location	Primitive	Value	Property list	Function	Print name
		Object List			
2900	NIL	2900	2900	2500	01BE
2908	T	2908	2900	2500	01C4
2910	LAMBDA	2400	2900	2115	01C8
2918	NLAMBDA	2400	2900	2115	01D1
2920	CAR	2400	2900	063B	01DB
		<continuation of Object List>			
2BF8	POP	2400	2900	22AC	04B4
2C00	PUSH	2400	2900	22CF	04BA

Fig. 28.6 Object List addresses.

- NIL and T are special symbols in that they evaluate to themselves, that is, their value pointers point to their own addresses as data objects.
- The other symbols listed do not have pre-defined values; hence their value pointer points to the 'unbound symbol' error trap at 2400. (An error trap is simply a machine language routine which generates a specific kind of error message and halts the program.)
- The property list pointers of all primitives point to 2900, that is, the address of NIL.
- The function pointers of NIL and T, which have no function definition, point to the 'undefined function' error trap at 2500; function pointers of LAMBDA and NLAMBDA to the special handling routine at 2115; the function pointer of CAR to the normal function routine at 063B; and the function pointers of POP and PUSH to special form routines at 22AC and 22CF, respectively.

If we follow the function pointer for CAR, for example, and disassemble (and document) the machine code at location 063B, we will wind up with something like the following:

```
063B  7E    CAR  MOV A,M   ;low byte to accumulator
063C  23         INX H     ;increment H/L pointer
063D  66         MOV H,M   ;high byte to H register
063E  6F         MOV L,A   ;low byte to L register
063F  C9         RET       ;return
```

which subroutine extracts the CAR address from the first cell of the list data object pointed to and places this address in the H/L register, from which it will be retrieved by the next higher level calling function.

- The print name pointers of all primitives point to the start of their respective name strings in the Object Listing area.

28.4 Layout of a typical small CP/M interpreter

Fig. 28.7 indicates the manner in which the above-mentioned interpreter allocates available memory in a 64K CP/M-80 system. The salient features are as follows.

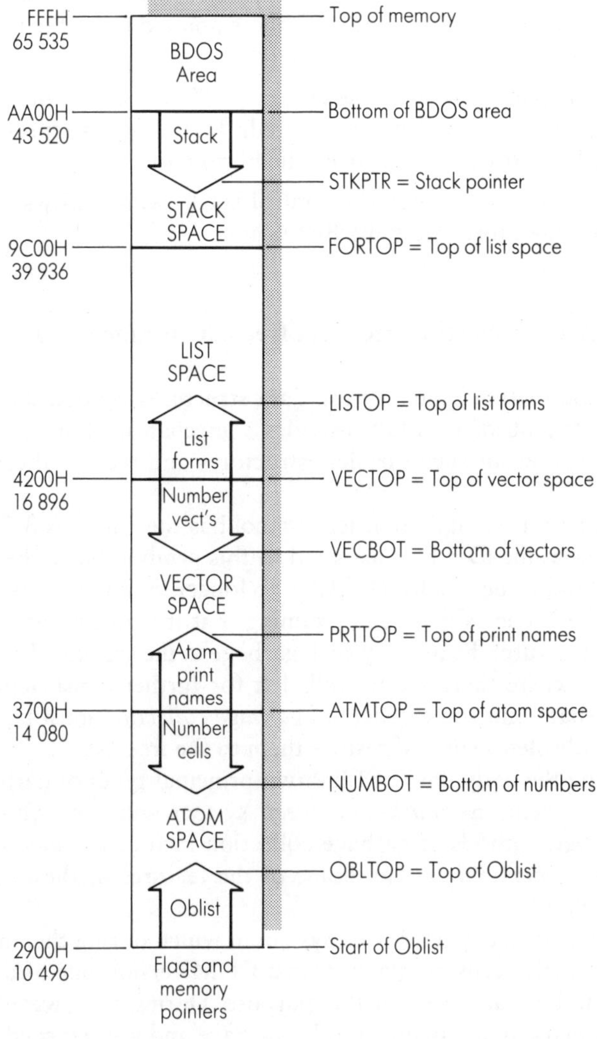

Fig. 28.7 Allocation of memory in a 64K interpreter.

- *Atom space* takes up an area from 2900H to 3700H, or 3584 bytes. This space is used for atomic data objects, which include symbols and numbers. The symbols are placed on the Object List which starts at 2900H and, after initialization, extends up to 2C08, consuming a total of 776 bytes. (This comprises 97 compiled primitives at 8 bytes each.) Any symbols which are created subsequently by the user in interpretive mode are added onto the end of this list.
- *Vector space* takes up an area from 3700H to 4200H, or 2816 bytes. The lower part of this area is used for print names of new symbols which are added to the Oblist, and for strings. The upper part of the vector space is used for number vectors, which contain the actual binary representation of the numbers pointed to by the number data objects in atom space.
- *Pointer space* represents the largest (70%) allocation of memory and is used for lists. As lists are created, the linked list representation of these lists grows upward from the bottom of the space.
- *Stack space* is used for the control stack, which grows downwards from AA00, just below the BDOS area.

28.5 Garbage collection recovers free list storage space

Over a period of time, some of the data structures created during a LISP session become obsolete. LISP provides a mechanism known as *garbage collection* to seek out such obsolete structures and recover their cons cells for re-use.

Assume for example that **test-symbol** has the value **(A B C)**, and at a later time the value **(D E F)** is assigned to this symbol. Since the new value replaces the old value, the list **(A B C)** is no longer 'pointed to' by **test-symbol** and therefore becomes *garbage* (assuming that it is not pointed to by any other data structure). Eventually such garbage in the system will accumulate to the point where there are no cells left for further construction of data objects. At that point some system of *garbage collection* must be invoked to reclaim the obsolete cells and restore them to the free list.

During the early days of LISP two principal types of garbage collection were utilized: the *mark-and-sweep* system and the *reference count* system. Newer methods of garbage collection include the *incremental* system and the *ephemeral* system. Some of the features of these systems are described below.

Mark-and-sweep refers to a system in which during the 'mark' phase all currently active cells are flagged. In a CP/M version one of the two low bits in the address are used for this purpose. During the 'sweep' phase, all cells not so marked are assumed to be garbage and are returned to the free list. (At the same time, those cell bits which were marked are reset to zero for the next garbage collection.) Cells are assumed to be active if they are pointed to, directly or indirectly, by some symbol on the Object List.

The mark-and-sweep system has the advantage that it is relatively simple to implement and requires no additional memory space. Its principal disadvantage is that garbage collection tends to be carried out in large batches, thus holding up operation of the system for some finite period. This can result in intolerable delays in real-time AI systems.

A *reference count* system keeps track of the number of pointers which reference a given data structure. When an additional reference is created the count is incremented by one; when a reference is removed the count is decremented. When the reference count for a given structure drops to 0 the structure is automatically garbage collected and returned to the free list.

The reference count system has the advantage that garbage collection is carried out on an incremental as-needed basis and tends to be transparent to the user, thus making it better for real-time systems. The disadvantage is that a substantial amount of memory is required to maintain the reference count table, which must contain a pointer to each data structure and a number corresponding to the current reference count for that structure.

The *incremental* system of garbage collection is a method of weaving so-called *scavenger* steps in with the execution of the user's program, so that the cost of garbage collection is amortized over the entire execution period. Scavenger steps may also be performed whenever the processor is momentarily idle. The system is described by Touretzky and Gabriel (1987):

> 'The scheme works by dividing the address space into two halves called NewSpace and OldSpace. New cons cells are allocated sequentially at one end of NewSpace, while cells in OldSpace are gradually copied to the other end of NewSpace. There are no freelists.
>
> Each cons operation is accompanied by a few scavenging steps. The scavenger copies a cell from OldSpace into NewSpace and leaves a forwarding pointer in OldSpace. As the program executes, all accessible objects in OldSpace will eventually be copied to NewSpace. Thus, when scavenging is complete, all objects in OldSpace have either been replaced with forwarding pointers or are garbage. Scavenging must complete before NewSpace fills up, so the system usually does several scavenger steps for each cons operation.
>
> When NewSpace fills up, a "flip" occurs. This means NewSpace and OldSpace switch roles, and the system once again begins copying all accessible structures from one half of the address space to the other. The details of the algorithm may be found in Baker's 1978 paper.'

The incremental system is very effective in minimizing disturbances in real-time performance due to garbage collection. The principal disadvantage is that it requires twice the space that is being garbage collected.

Touretzky and Gabriel (1987) go on to point out that the *ephemeral* system is an improvement upon the incremental system and provides a way of ensuring that the space allocated to short-lived objects (ones that more quickly become garbage) is copied and flipped most often. Storage is divided into static space (for objects that almost never change, and thus don't need to be garbage collected, like compiled code), dynamic space (for objects that change slowly, and should eventually be garbage collected), and one or more ephemeral levels. Random cons'ing is done at the lowest ephemeral level. The lowest level is copied very frequently; higher levels are copied less often, and may flip only when the first level does. Objects in one level that prove to be long-lived (by surviving a flip) migrate to the next higher ephemeral level, or from the highest ephemeral level to dynamic space. Since most of the garbage collector's activity is concentrated in the lowest ephemeral levels, where most of the garbage is to be found, this is a more efficient strategy than ordinary incremental garbage collection.

28.6 A LISP environment may be saved as a .SYS file in some implementations

As we have noted, LISP programs are stored in an ASCII text file which contains the sequence of LISP expressions which make up the program. Such files usually include a file extension such as .LIB or .LSP to identify their nature.

Some implementations also permit the current operating environment to be saved in a different kind of file, usually referred to as a .SYS (= SYStem) file. This file contains a machine language image of the dynamic elements of the interpreter environment, so that when it is loaded into the system it effectively recreates the LISP environment which existed when it was saved. The operations involved in saving and reloading such a file are carried out as described below.

When a .SYS file is save'd, a garbage collection is first carried out to winnow out list structure which is no longer active, after which the remaining active list data objects are compacted into the bottom of the list storage area. The purpose of compaction is to minimize the amount of material to be saved and stored. A pointer to the top of the compacted list storage determines the upper limit of memory to be saved to the .SYS file. Thereafter a machine language image of system memory, starting at the bottom of the dynamic flags area and extending to the top of the compacted list storage, is saved to the file.

When such a .SYS file is later load'ed, the first step carried out by the interpreter is to re-initialize the system, including allocation of memory, construction of the Object List, etc. This step of course wipes out whatever environment currently exists. The .SYS file is then loaded in such a manner as to overlay the areas of which it represents a mirror image, that is, from

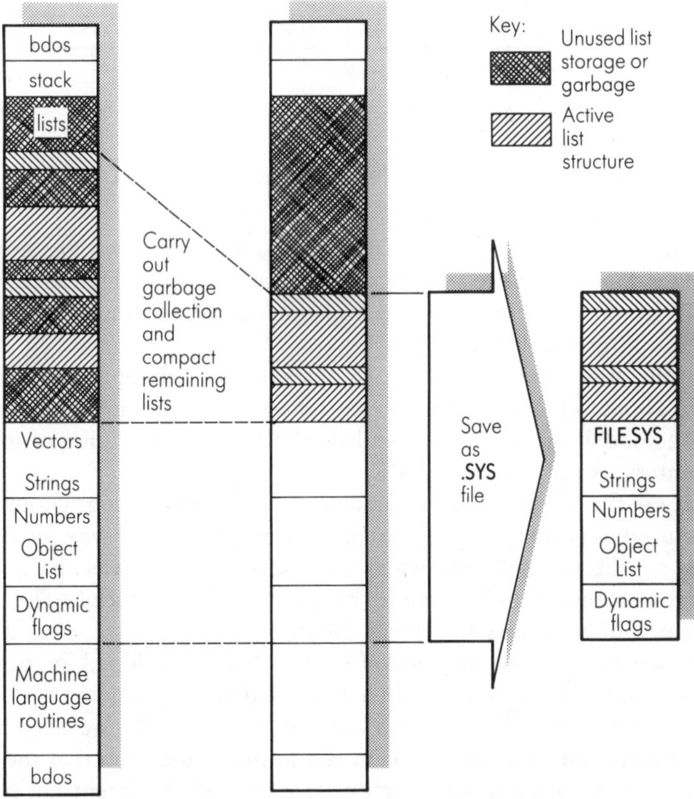

Fig. 28.8 Creation of a .SYS file.

the bottom of the dynamic flags area to the top of compacted list storage. The net effect is to recreate the environment which existed at the time the file was saved.

Fig. 28.8 illustrates the concepts involved.

28.7 cdr-coding reduces list storage space requirements

Since LISP programs and data are typically stored in the form of linked lists it is of interest to explore ways in which the space consumed by such lists may be minimized. One popular method of optimizing storage of lists is referred to as cdr-*coding*.

In normal list structure, the car cell of each node points to some data object and the cdr cell points to the next node in the chain. Hence up to 50% of the total space required for a list may be taken up by such pointers.

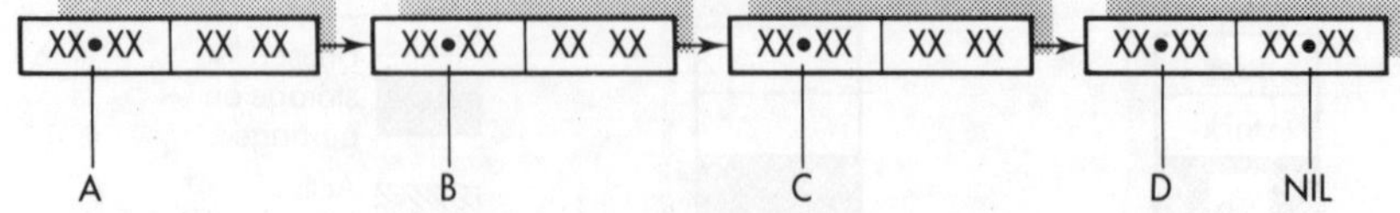

Fig. 28.9 Standard list structure for (A B C D).

For example, in the list (A B C D), and assuming that we are using an 8-bit CP/M-80 system, we have a structure as shown in Fig. 28.9, where XX XX XX XX represents two 16-bit hexadecimal addresses contained in four 8-bit contiguous bytes.

In the above example, of the 16 bytes required to represent the list, 6 bytes or about 38% of the total are taken up by pointers to the next following node. If the list were extended infinitely, the allocation of space to such pointers would approach 50%.

If, on the other hand, we had a system wherein contiguous bytes could be used to point to successive data objects, with some way (other than pointing to NIL) of knowing when the end of the list was reached, the amount of storage required could be considerably reduced. The above example would be compacted to Fig. 28.10.

A scheme known as cdr-*coding* has been developed in order to achieve the above space savings. In a cdr-coded system only the car cells of each node are stored. Within each car cell, two tag bits are allocated to providing information about the next cell in the chain, such that these bits effectively replace the normal function of a cdr cell. Different tag codings may be used by different machines. The codings for the LISP Machine are:

Bits	*Meaning*	*Intepretation*
00	CDR-NIL	This is the last cell in the list, the cdr of which points to NIL
01	CDR-NORMAL	The next node in the chain is *not* the next contiguous word; however the address of the next node is stored in the next word.
10	CDR-NEXT	The cdr of this node is a cell located at the next contiguous word.
11	CDR-ERROR	It is an error to try to take the cdr of this word since it is not a list object.

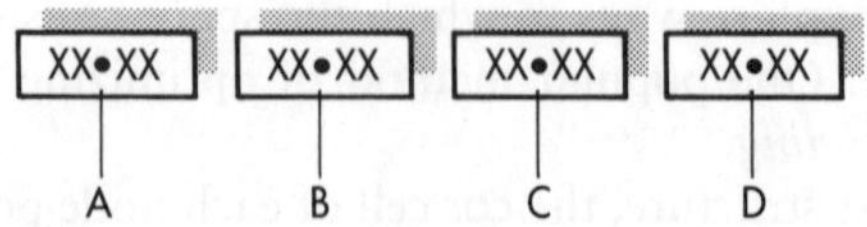

Fig. 28.10 Compacted list structure for (A B C D).

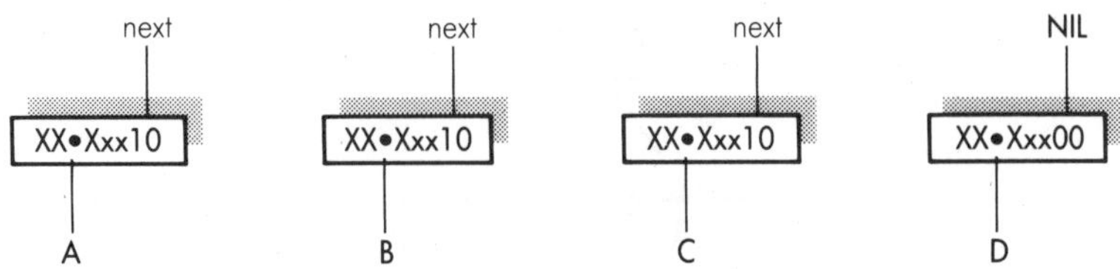

Fig. 28.11 cdr-codes for compacted list structure.

In a cdr-coded representation of the above list, assuming that the last two bits were being used for the code, we might have something like Fig. 28.11, in which we have replaced the lowest hexadecimal representation X of each address with its corresponding four bits xxxx, with real values for the lowermost two bits. As noted from the above table, the cdr-codes of the first three cells indicate that the cdr of the list is contained in the next contiguous word; and the cdr-code of the last cell indicates that the cdr is NIL.

It is assumed, for purposes of the above example, that the lowest two bits of a 2-byte CP/M address could be utilized for this purpose, based on the fact that all data objects referenced by such pointers commence at an even-multiple-of-four address for which these bits are zero, that is, they can be masked out by the system after extracting the cdr-coding information. (In practice cdr-coding is impractical in a CP/M system, since these bits must be used for other purposes including garbage collection markers and/or type tags. However it might be practicable for use in MS-DOS systems in which, due to limits in on-board memory as compared to addressing capabilities, more high-level bits could become available.)

Touretzky and Gabriel observe that cdr-coding carries with it certain disadvantages. Coding becomes more complex and therefore larger and more difficult to debug. Performance can be degraded if there is destructive modification to the cdr of a cell, since more complex manipulations are required as compared to the simple replacement of a cdr pointer with a rplacd operation.

Another observation of interest is that in more modern LISP systems, vectors and structures find increasing use (as compared to conventional lists) since they are computationally more efficient than lists for many applications. The availability of generic sequence functions makes vectors more convenient to use than in previous implementations. Since the amount of memory allocated to lists is smaller in Common LISP than in earlier systems, the potential gains from cdr-coding are correspondingly smaller.

28.8 A compiler can greatly improve execution speed of a program

The purpose of a LISP compiler is to transform user-defined function definitions written in LISP into machine language code which the interpreter

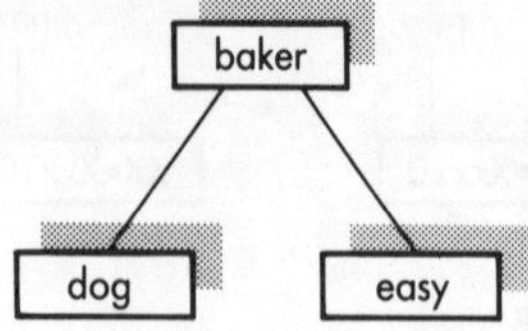

Fig. 28.12 A program of compiled functions.

can use in the same fashion as LISP primitives. Compilation greatly speeds up the execution of an applications program since it cuts out the need for the intermediate interpretive step.

Compilation in LISP differs from compilation of procedural languages in two principal respects:

(1) compilation of LISP functions can be carried out on a selective basis wherein some functions are compiled and others are left to be interpreted

(2) even after compilation, the compiled functions are still called up and used in an interpretive environment

As a simple example, let's assume that we have the LISP functions **baker**, **dog**, and **easy**, which interact as illustrated in Fig. 28.12. Within the environment of the interpreter we can call up an *incremental compiler* to compile all of these definitions on an individual basis. When we next call **baker**, we will find that the overall program runs much faster, since all three elements have now been converted to machine language routines.

Still in interpretive mode, we can define other functions which use the above compiled modules, as shown in Fig. 28.13, in which **able** and **foxtrot** are normal user-defined functions which are stored as lambda definitions and are interpreted in the usual manner, and **baker**, **dog**, and **easy** are compiled functions which are applied in much the same manner as built-in LISP primitives. Hence, unlike procedural languages, we can end up with a system in which some of the functions are compiled and some interpreted.

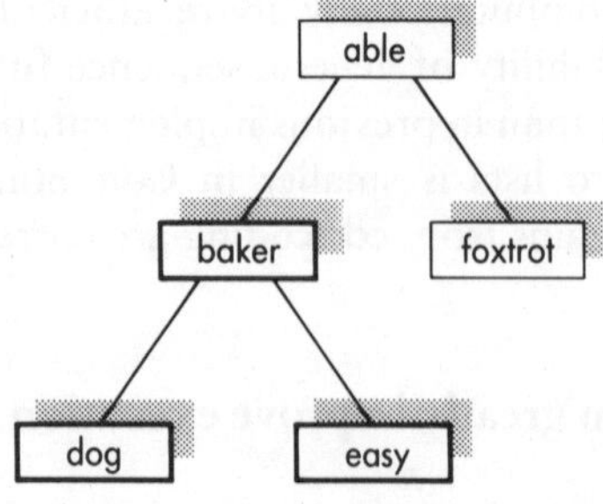

Fig. 28.13 A mixture of interpreted and compiled functions.

Alternatively we can define all of the above functions in the usual interactive manner, save them to file, and then call up a *file compiler* to compile all of the functions in the file in one fell swoop as it loads the file into the system.

Aside from generating machine language compiled functions, the compiler translates certain LISP primitives directly into so-called 'inline' code. Operations which lend themselves to such conversion include car, cdr, and their derivatives if, cond, and certain other functions depending on the implementation. Inline code executes much more rapidly than code which sets up arguments and carries out function calls in the normal manner. When using a compiler you should therefore be familiar with those LISP functions which are converted to inline code, and endeavor to use them in preference to others, all things being equal.

SUMMARY

Summarizing the main points of this chapter:

- a simple *LISP interpreter* uses memory for five basic purposes: the body of the interpreter; dynamic flags; the Object List; heap storage for LISP data objects; and the control stack
- the purpose of the *initialization process* is to create the Object List and to allocate available memory for different purposes
- *heap storage* can be allocated for general use by all LISP data objects, in which case some sort of tag mechanism is required to identify the type being pointed to; alternatively heap storage can be allocated to specific types of data objects
- various techniques are used for *garbage collection*, in which no-longer-accessible list structure is purged from the system and cons cells recovered for re-use
- a LISP environment may be saved as a .SYS file in some implementations
- cdr-*coding* is a technique for reducing list storage space requirements
- *compilation* can greatly speed up the execution of a LISP program

Chapter 29
The read/eval/print Cycle

As we have seen throughout the course of this book, the so-called **read/eval/print** cycle is the heart of the LISP interpreter. The purpose of this chapter is to fine-tune your understanding of the manner in which LISP operates by examining the way these interrelated functions work in more detail.

In this chapter we will look at:

- the manner in which a nested **read/eval/print** loop can be invoked through the use of **listener**
- the nature of the separate routine which displays the **prompt** symbol, and how this symbol can be tailored
- the manner in which LISP input is received into a *buffer* prior to processing
- the manner in which **read** parses a single form, creates an internal representation of that form, and returns a pointer to the data object which has been created
- the use of *macro characters*, which are parsed at read time
- the steps by which **eval** carries out evaluation of atoms, quoted forms, special forms, and macros
- the manner in which **eval** calls upon **apply** to process normal functions and their arguments
- the manner in which **print** operates to create a printed representation of a LISP data object
- the functions which are available to *recall* recently processed forms and their values

29.1 A call to **sys:listener** invokes a **read/eval/print** loop

The function **sys:listener**, which takes the syntax:

```
(sys:listener &optional <herald-string>)
```

invokes a **read/eval/print** loop. When GCLISP is booted up, this function is automatically called, at which time **<herald-string>** is initialized to a value of **"Top-Level"**. This string is assigned as the value of the global variable **sys:*listener-name***:

```
* sys:*listener-name*
"Top-Level"
```

A nested **read/eval/print** loop can be invoked through an explicit call to **sys:listener**, using an appropriate herald string to indicate which loop you are currently in.

When calling **sys:listener**, the new **<herald-string>** is automatically bound to **sys:*listener-name***. However the modified herald string does not take effect until an intervening break or error occurs and Ctrl-G is used to return you to the top level of the loop. (See also **sys:*prompt*** below.)

While in a nested listener loop, Ctrl-G will return you to the top level within that loop. However Ctrl-C will jump over any and all nested loops and return you directly to the top-level loop.

29.2 A separate routine is used to display the prompt

Since **read** has been designed to be used explicitly as well as to be used as a part of the **read/eval/print** cycle, display of the prompt symbol is handled by a separate subroutine.

The un-Common LISP global variable **sys:*prompt*** is bound to a function which prints '*' to the ***standard-output*** stream:

```
* sys:*prompt*
#<COMPILED FUNCTION 0AFB:20EC>
```

If the current package is something other than **USER**, the function prints the name of the current package followed by ':' as a prompt.

In the unlikely event you wish to generate a prompt different from the one provided by GCLISP, you can do so by creating an alternative prompt function, say:

```
* (defun prompt-symbol ()
    (format t "~%Sock it to me: "))
```

and assigning this function as the value of **sys:*prompt***:

```
* (setf sys:*prompt* (symbol-function 'prompt-symbol))
PROMPT-SYMBOL

Sock it to me:
```

The new prompt will not take effect until you have invoked a lower level **read/eval/print** loop with **listener**, or until an intervening break or error has occurred and Ctrl-G is used to return you to the top level of the loop. Thereafter it will remain in effect until otherwise modified.

29.3 read accepts input of a single form

After calling subroutine **prompt** to output the prompt symbol to the console, subroutine **read** is called next to invite input of a form for evaluation. In GCLISP you will see this prompt symbol as a single asterisk, with the cursor blinking alongside:

```
* <cursor>
```

At this point **read** has in turn called the MS-DOS input routine and both of them are sitting there waiting for you to type something in.

The nature of the **read** operation is such that it accepts input of a single LISP form for evaluation. This form will generally consist of either a symbol, a number, a string or a list. As soon as input of the form has been completed, GCLISP immediately proceeds to evaluate it without waiting for a carriage return, as in some other implementations. Basically this is carried out as follows.

- If the first character input is a left parenthesis, **read** keeps track of subsequent left and right parentheses as they are typed in (excepting those encased in escape characters) and commences evaluation as soon as a balancing right parenthesis is parsed.
- If the first character input is a double quote mark, the form is assumed to be a string and evaluation commences as soon as a balancing double quote mark is parsed.
- Otherwise evaluation of a symbol or number commences as soon as the token being accumulated is terminated by a whitespace or terminating macro character.

Some implementations delay evaluation until a carriage return is typed in. In such circumstances it is possible to input more than one form at a time in which case, depending on the implementation, an error message may be generated, only the first form may be accepted for evaluation, or all the forms will be evaluated in succession. This is emphatically not the case with GCLISP which immediately commences evaluation as soon as a single valid form has been entered.

29.4 read parses input on a character-by-character basis

Accumulation of characters into the MS-DOS input buffer is terminated by one of the above criteria having been met, at which time the read subroutine commences to parse the input. The object of such parsing is to build up an internal representation of the LISP data object corresponding to the printed input. Parsing is carried out on a character-by-character basis in accordance with Fig. 29.1, which has been adapted from the comprehensive summary provided in the CLRM pp. 335–8.

Let's assume for the moment that a single symbol – say, *print-base* – has been input for evaluation. As soon as the whitespace following the symbol is parsed, input is discontinued and the string of characters is parsed by read. Since each of the characters is a normal constituent character, the token *print-base* is gradually accumulated. This process continues until the trailing whitespace (which is included along with the input string) is encountered. Since the whitespace is considered as a *terminating macro character*, a complete token with the print name *print-base* is assumed to have been parsed.

At this point read consults the name lookup table of the current package to see if *print-base* already exists as an established symbol name. In this case it does, so no further action is required. In the event it did not, read would add it to the lookup table and would create a symbol data object on the Object List to represent it in the manner outlined in Chapter 3. If we have simply typed in a (new) symbol name, the fact that this has no value will of course cause problems later when we get to eval; however this is not read's concern.

Having either verified the presence of an existing symbol or created a new symbol, read returns a value in the form of a pointer to the symbol data object, which is typically put into some convenient CPU register from which it will be retrieved by the next function called (in this case eval).

Other variants in the handling of a symbolic token include the presence of single or double escape characters, the effects of which are incorporated into the flow diagram.

If the input form is an atom, read tests whether it is a symbol or a number and, if the latter, whether it is an integer or a floating-point number. Integers are identified by the fact that all of the characters which make up the token are digits within the radix base which is the current value of *read-base*, for example, if *read-base* = 16, the digits from 0 to 9 and the letters A to F would be acceptable as digits. The pointer which is returned for a *fixnum* contains a tag identifying it as such, and the binary value of the fixnum is contained in two bytes of the pointer itself. If a

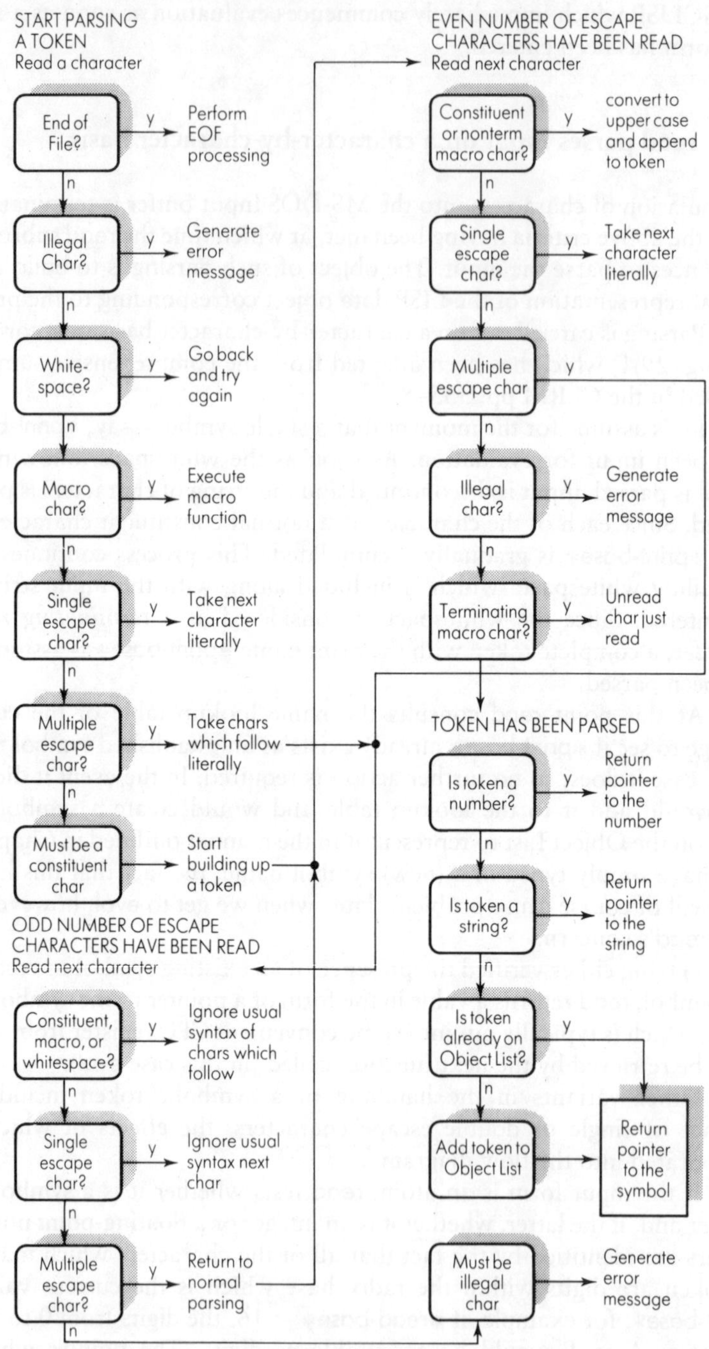
START PARSING
A TOKEN
Read a character
End of File?
y
Perform EOF processing
n
Illegal Char?
y
Generate error message
n
White-space?
y
Go back and try again
n
Macro char?
y
Execute macro function
n
Single escape char?
y
Take next character literally
n
Multiple escape char?
y
Take chars which follow literally
n
Must be a constituent char
Start building up a token
ODD NUMBER OF ESCAPE
CHARACTERS HAVE BEEN READ
Read next character
Constituent, macro, or whitespace?
y
Ignore usual syntax of chars which follow
n
Single escape char?
y
Ignore usual syntax next char
n
Multiple escape char?
y
Return to normal parsing
n
EVEN NUMBER OF ESCAPE
CHARACTERS HAVE BEEN READ
Read next character
Constituent or nonterm macro char?
y
convert to upper case and append to token
n
Single escape char?
y
Take next character literally
n
Multiple escape char
n
Illegal char?
y
Generate error message
n
Terminating macro char?
y
Unread char just read
TOKEN HAS BEEN PARSED
Is token a number?
y
Return pointer to the number
n
Is token a string?
y
Return pointer to the string
n
Is token already on Object List?
y
n
Add token to Object List
Return pointer to the symbol
Must be illegal char
Generate error message

Fig. 29.1 Parsing is carried out on a character-by-character basis.

bignum or floating-point number is parsed, an internal binary representation of the number is created in a special space reserved for such numbers and a pointer to the address is returned.

If the input form is a string, the sequence of characters is placed into a one-dimensional vector in a special space reserved for strings, and a pointer to the vector is returned.

29.5 read operates as a recursive-descent parser to create list structure

A more complex procedure, referred to as *recursive-descent parsing*, takes place when a list is input, for read must create a data object in memory corresponding to the list. It does this by calling itself recursively to create a binary tree, corresponding to the list structure, in which the lowest level calls to read return pointers to the symbol data objects corresponding to the 'leaves' of the tree.

Let's say we input the list (setq apple '(red fruit)), which will be transformed into the structure shown in Fig. 29.2. We can trace the recursive descent process as follows.

(1) The initial left parenthesis is parsed as a macro character. This particular macro sets up a routine whereby, if the next character is a closing parenthesis, the empty list or NIL is returned by the current read operation. Otherwise read is called recursively.

(2) The recursive call to read is applied to the balance of the input string which follows the first left parenthesis. In due course the token setf is parsed and a pointer to this data object is returned to the top-level read, which creates the first cons cell of the structure. The car of this

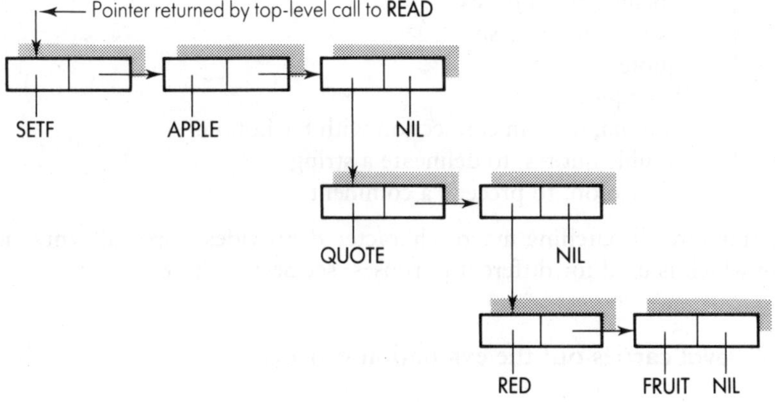

Fig. 29.2 read constructs an internal data object.

cell contains the address pointer just returned by the earlier recursive call to **read**; the contents of the cdr cell are as yet undefined.

(3) Another recursive call to **read** is invoked. If at this point a right-hand parenthesis were to be parsed and returned, the top-level **read** would insert a pointer to **NIL** in the **cdr** of the cons cell and would return a pointer to the list **(setf)**. However instead the token **apple** is parsed and returned. At this point the top-level **read** appropriates another cons cell from the free list, places the address of **apple** in the **car** of this cell, and places a pointer to the new cons cell in the **cdr** of the previous cons cell.

(4) On the next recursive call to **read**, the macro character ' is parsed. This macro sets up a subroutine in which a nested list is created containing a pointer to the symbol **quote** in the **car** of the first cons cell, and a pointer to the single form following the macro character ' in the **car** of the following cell. A pointer to this whole structure is returned as a value to the top level **read** operation, which places the address in the next following cons cell in exactly the same manner as it did with **setf** and **apple**.

(5) On each pass, prior to invoking a recursive call to **read**, the top level **read** looks ahead to see if the next character is a closing parenthesis. At this point it is, so a pointer to **NIL** is placed in the **cdr** of the last cell, and the top level **read** returns a pointer to the whole data structure which has just been created.

29.6 Macro characters are executed at read time

A variety of macro characters (see Section 20.7) are included in Common LISP. Those characters supported by GCLISP include:

(opening parenthesis
) closing parenthesis
' quote
` backquote
, comma, used in connection with backquote
" double quotes, to delineate a string
; semicolon, to precede a comment

The standard dispatching macro character # provides a special syntactical form which is used for different purposes; see Section 20.8.

29.7 **eval** carries out the evaluation process

Once **read** has returned a pointer to the data structure which it has created to correspond to the printed input, **eval** is called to evaluate this structure.

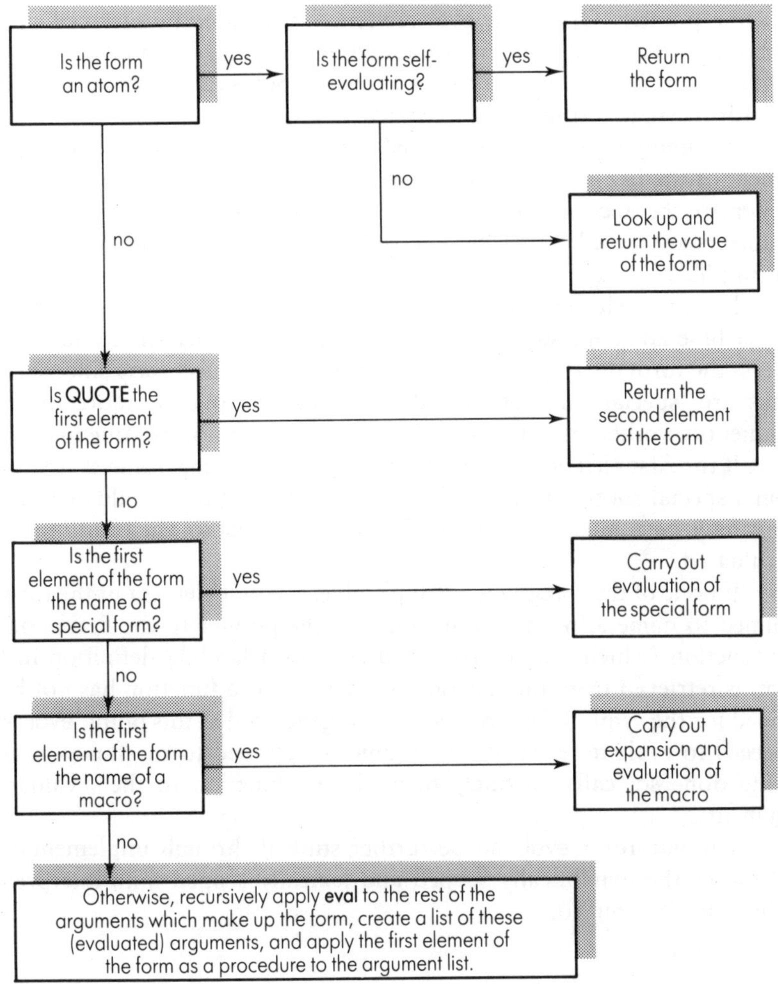

Fig. 29.3 Steps in evaluation of a form.

The steps in evaluation of a form are summarized in Fig. 29.3.

As mentioned previously, **eval** retrieves from an appropriate register of the CPU an address pointer to the data object just created by **read. eval** then ascertains the type of data object being pointed to, and tailors the evaluation process accordingly. The type may be ascertained in one of two basic ways: by testing tag bits built into the address pointer which identify the type of object being pointed to, or by consulting a lookup table to see what kind of object is being stored in the address area being pointed to.

If the data object is a symbol, **eval** makes a further test to see whether it is a self-evaluating symbol such as **NIL**, **T**, a number, a keyword, or a character. If the symbol falls into one of these categories **eval** simply returns the same pointer. Otherwise **eval** references the value pointer cell of the symbol and returns a pointer to the address contained in that cell. In the event no value has yet been assigned to the symbol, **eval** causes an appropriate error message routine to be executed.

Assuming that the form is a list, **eval** checks to see whether the first element of the list is the symbol **quote**, in which case **eval** simply returns a pointer to the second element of the list. In the event any additional arguments are included they are ignored; a call to **quote** without arguments returns **NIL**.

If the first element of the form is the name of a special form, **eval** uses the machine language subroutine pointed to by the function cell address to process the form on a 'special-handling' basis. This is necessary since special forms are 'special' in that they do not evaluate one or more of their arguments or otherwise process their arguments in a non-routine manner.

If the first element of the form is the name of a macro, **eval** first calls upon a special routine to expand the macro. After the (unevaluated) arguments have been incorporated into the expanded macro, the resulting form is evaluated.

If none of the foregoing are applicable, the first element of the form is assumed to name a 'normal' function, and the pointer to the definition of this function (which may be compiled code or a lambda definition in list form) is retrieved from the function pointer cell. If a function has not been defined for the symbol, an error message is generated at this point. **eval** then proceeds to evaluate each of the arguments supplied to the function and, having done so, calls on **apply** to apply the function to the (evaluated) arguments.

The nature of **eval** can be further studied through implementation and use of the dynamically scoped and lexically scoped mini-interpreters outlined in Chapter 30.

29.8 **apply** is called upon to process normal functions

The function **apply** (see Section 6.15) is usually used in LISP to execute a function call in situations where neither the name of the function nor the arguments to which it is to be applied are known at run time. These elements are brought together in the course of executing the program and

(apply <function-name> <list-of-arguments>)

is then used to generate the effect of a function call. As well as being used explicitly in such situations, **apply** is also called by **eval** and used to process 'normal' functions. The value or values returned by **apply** in turn become the values returned by **eval**.

29.9 **evalhook** and **applyhook** call up special functions during the evaluation process

At times you may wish explicitly to modify the evaluation process so that, instead of executing **eval** in the normal manner, the system does something else instead. Such modifications might include provision to trace the evaluation of some or all forms, or to step through the evaluation process, providing a break at each step in order to permit debugging operations.

The modification process consists of defining some alternate function, called the **eval hook function**, which takes a form as its single argument. This function definition is then assigned as the value of the global variable ***evalhook*** (whose normal default value is **NIL**). When **eval** is called upon to evaluate a form, if the value of ***evalhook*** is non-**NIL** the form is passed over to the **eval hook function** for handling. The value returned by this function is handled as if it were the value returned by the normal **eval** process. (Note that the GCLISP implementation does not support Common LISP's optional **environment** argument.)

A related process permits the definition of an alternate **apply hook function** which takes two arguments: a function name and a list of arguments. This function may be assigned as the value of the global variable ***applyhook***. When **apply** is called upon to apply a function to an argument list, if the value of ***applyhook*** is non-**NIL** these arguments are instead passed over to the **apply hook function** for handling.

The related functions **evalhook** and **applyhook**, which take the syntax:

```
(evalhook <form> <eval-hook-func> <apply-hook-func>)

(applyhook <func> <args> <eval-hook-func> <apply-hook-func>)
```

are provided to facilitate the use of the hook features. These functions provide for automatic binding of ***evalhook*** and ***applyhook*** to the corresponding functional arguments. Furthermore, as the CLRM points out:

> 'The check for a hook function is bypassed for the evaluation of the form itself (for **evalhook**) or for the application of the function to the args itself (for **applyhook**), but not for the subsidiary evaluations and applications, such as evaluations of subforms. It is this one-shot bypass that makes **evalhook** and **applyhook** so useful.'

A simple tracing routine, using **evalhook**, is illustrated in the CLRM pp. 323–4. A similar program is reproduced below, with modifications to accommodate certain features not supported by GCLISP:

```
(defvar *hooklevel* 0)

(defun hook (hook-form-to-eval)
  (declare (special hook-form-to-eval))
  (let ((*evalhook* 'eval-hook-function))
    (eval hook-form-to-eval)))

(defun eval-hook-function (form &optional ignore)
  (let ((*hooklevel* (+ *hooklevel* 1)))
    (format t "~%~a"(indent *hooklevel*))
    (format t "Form: ~s" form)
    (let ((values (multiple-value-list
          (evalhook form
              #'eval-hook-function
              nil))))
        (format t "~%~a" (indent *hooklevel*))
        (format t "Value:~a" (print-values values))
        (values-list values))))

(defun indent (level)
  (do ((n 0 (1+ n))
       (spaces "" (string-append " " spaces)))
      ((eql n level) spaces)))

(defun princ-to-string (arg)
  (let ((string-stream (make-string-output-stream)))
    (princ arg string-stream)
    (get-output-stream-string string-stream)))

(defun print-values (value-list)
  (do ((work-list value-list (cdr work-list))
       (work-string ""
          (string-append
            work-string " " (princ-to-string (car work-list)))))
      ((null work-list) work-string)))
```

The indent function is required since GCLISP does not support the ~T format directive for cursor positioning; princ-to-string and print-values similarly get around the fact that GCLISP does not support the ~{str~} iteration construct.

If we create a simple function definition:

```
(defun fact (number)
  (declare (special number))
  (if (< number 2)
    1
    (* number (fact (1- number)))))
```

and apply **hook** in the same manner as illustrated in the CLRM:

```
* (hook '(fact 3))
  Form: (EVAL HOOK-FORM-TO-EVAL)
    Form: HOOK-FORM-TO-EVAL
    Value: (FACT 3)
    Form: (FACT 3)
      Form: 3
      Value: 3
      Form: (IF (< NUMBER 2) 1 (* NUMBER (FACT
      (1- NUMBER))))
        .
        .
        <lots more printing>
        .
        .
      Value: 6
    Value: 6
  Value: 6
6
```

It should be noted that in GCLISP variables in the functions that are 'hooked' must be declared special if the function is to work properly.

The special form **eval-when** is also supported by Version 1.1 of GCLISP; see the CLRM pp. 69–70 for use of this somewhat esoteric function. It is intended to allow specific pieces of code to be executed only at compile time, only at load time, or when interpreted but not compiled, and is presumably incorporated into GCLISP in anticipation of future plans to provide a compiler.

29.10 print also operates in a recursive-descent manner

print operates as a recursive descent printer in a manner exactly the opposite of **read**. Whereas **read** constructs an internal list structure from a printed representation, **print** creates a printed representation from an internal list structure.

print precedes any printed representation with a Newline, follows it with a single space, and operates as follows:

- if the pointer returned by **eval** points to a symbol, **print** accesses the symbol and prints out the namestring of the symbol
- if the pointer points to a numeric data object, **print** converts the binary representation to the corresponding printed format in accordance with the radix currently bound to ***print-base*** (see Section 11.8).

- if the pointer points to a string, print prints a double quote mark followed by the characters in the string. When the end of the string is reached, as signaled by a null byte, print prints a closing double quote mark

If the pointer points to a list structure, the print operation is somewhat more complex:

- if the car of the cons cell being scanned points to another list, a left-hand parenthesis '(' will be printed before print is called recursively to scan the next element of the structure
- if the car points to an atom, print prints out the atom as noted above and scans the cdr of the cons cell
- if the cdr of the cell points to NIL (or to an atom in the case of a dotted list), print prints out a right-hand parenthesis ')' and returns to the next higher level
- otherwise print follows the cdr pointer to the next cons cell and continues the process

Some types of data objects such as packages, arrays, structures, streams, etc. do not lend themselves to being printed out as described above. In these cases print uses a convention in which the hash character # is used together with angle brackets to represent the object, for example:

```
* (symbol-package 'self)
#<PACKAGE LISP 9015:19224>
```

29.11 Recent function calls and their results can be recalled

Common LISP provides a mechanism whereby a form recently handled by the read/eval/print cycle – or one or more of the values returned by that form – can be recalled to the screen. This is accomplished by binding certain values to the symbols –, +, * or /, which in this case are being utilized as global variables. The bindings are effected as follows:

–	The minus sign is bound to the form currently being evaluated at the top level.
+, ++, +++	The three combinations of + signs are bound to the most recent, second most recent, and third most recent form evaluated at the top level.

*, **, ***	The three combinations of * signs are bound to the first value returned by the most recent, second most recent, etc., form evaluated.
/, //, ///	The three combinations of / signs are bound to a list containing all of the values returned by the most recent, etc., etc., form evaluated.

As an example:

```
* (defun our-truncate (x y)
    (format t "~%Current form being evaluated is ~a~" -)
    (truncate x y))
OUR-TRUNCATE

* (our-truncate 10 3)
Current form being evaluated is (OUR-TRUNCATE 10 3)
3
1
```

The − sign is a temporary binding which is only in effect while the form is being evaluated; as soon as the function exists the value of − is passed over to +. (Hence − used explicitly at the top level will simply return −, since *that* is the form being evaluated at the moment.) After having called the above function, information associated with this 'most recent' function call could be recalled by evaluating any one of the variables as noted below:

```
* +
(OUR-TRUNCATE 10 3)

* *
3

* /
(3 1)
```

A little experimentation will reveal that these manipulations can only be done *once*, since the use of +, * or / is itself a form to be evaluated, and this will be reflected in the value returned by the next successive use of +, * or /. Hence, if we wanted all three of the above values associated with the function call, we would have to enter + followed by ** followed by /// to incorporate the effects of evaluating the intermediate variables.

SUMMARY

Summarizing the main points of this chapter:

- a new read/eval/print loop can be invoked through the use of listener, including provision for a *herald string* which is printed upon return to the top level of the loop
- the prompt symbol is generated by a separate subroutine, and can be tailored by the user
- the read function parses a single form, creates an internal representation of that form, and returns a pointer to the data object which has been created
- *macro characters*, which are parsed at read time, activate special routines to supplement the reading process
- the eval function directly evaluates symbols, numbers, strings, special forms, and macros
- eval calls upon apply to process normal functions and their arguments
- the print function operates in a recursive-descent fashion to create the printed representation of a LISP data object
- where a data object does not lend itself to normal printout, a #< ... > convention is utilized to represent it
- recent forms which have been evaluated, as well as the values returned by these forms, are bound to variables such as +++, ***, and ///, and can be recalled by evaluating these variables

Chapter 30

Lexical and Dynamic Scoping Mechanisms

One of the principal features which distinguishes one version of LISP from another is the method by which they handle evaluation of variables. In a *dynamically scoped* LISP, the value of a variable will reflect the most recent value which has been assigned to a variable of that name, whether it be bound within the function currently being evaluated, within some higher level function, or as a global variable at the top level. In a *lexically scoped* LISP, the value of a variable will reflect either its current binding as a local variable, the most recent value assigned to it as a special variable, or its binding within a closure.

The differences between the two types of scoping are difficult to grasp when described in a purely textual manner. A better way is to develop physical analogs and observe the manner in which they operate. We will therefore develop in this chapter several mini-interpreters, which follow different scoping rules, in order to observe at first hand how these systems handle their environments. In the course of these experiments we will have occasion to observe how careless use of a dynamically scoped interpreter can lead to the so-called *'funarg' problem.* Later we will explore the nature of *closures* and how they carry with them their own environments.

In this chapter we will look at:

- the concept of an *environment* in LISP
- how *scoping* of variables relates to the manner in which *environments* are handled
- development of mini-interpreters to simulate the effects of *dynamic scoping* with deep binding and shallow binding
- the manner in which dynamic scoping gives rise to the *'funarg problem'*
- the concept of a *lexical closure* in which a function can carry its own environment around with it
- development of a mini-interpreter to simulate the effects of *lexical scoping*

30.1 Interpreters for other languages can be developed 'on top of' a LISP interpreter

The remarkable flexibility of LISP makes it an ideal language for developing other languages which can be written 'on top of' the LISP interpreter. For example, one could write a LISP-BASIC interpreter in such a manner that, upon loading the LISP applications file, it would appear to the user that he was using a BASIC interpreter.

By extension, it is possible to simulate a LISP interpreter 'on top of' another LISP interpreter. Since such an interpreter-on-an-interpreter invokes two levels of interpretation, the speed of the program is slowed down considerably. However such an exercise is useful in demonstrating some of the scoping aspects of LISP.

In the following exercise we will develop a mini LISP interpreter based on *dynamic scoping* and *deep binding*. In subsequent exercises we will modify this interpreter to illustrate the differences between *deep* and *shallow binding* techniques. Finally we will modify the mini-interpreter to provide for handling of variables in a *lexically scoped* manner.

The LISP coding is an adaptation of the coding presented by David S. Touretzky and Richard P. Gabriel during their jointly conducted tutorial on *Advanced Common LISP Programming* which was presented at AAAI-87 in Seattle, Washington, in July 1987.

30.2 A collection of bindings is called an environment

As we have seen during the **read/eval/print** process (see Section 29.7), at some point during evaluation the system must have recourse to a lookup table from which the current value of a symbol may be retrieved. Such a table, which consists of a listing of variables and their current bindings, may be thought of as an *environment*. It follows intuitively that any given form must be evaluated with respect to some particular environment. It is the manner in which this environment is created, maintained, and made available during the course of evaluation which gives rise to the differences between *dynamic* and *lexical* scoping.

The concept of an environment may be broadened to include two kinds of environments: the *global environment* and the *activation environment*.

The *global environment* is the collection of symbols and their values and/or function definitions which are created during the initialization process and which are available at the top level when we start to use the interpreter. By their nature, the entities in this environment are *global* and can be accessed at any time and from any level of nesting within the program. As additional user-defined functions and special variables are created thereafter, these are added to the global environment.

The *activation environment*, on the other hand, is a dynamically changing environment which reflects the comings and goings of the bindings of local variables as functions are entered and exited. It is this environment which is principally of interest to us here, and which will be referred to as the 'environment' in the mini-interpreter which we will develop shortly.

To paraphrase the gist of the foregoing: during execution of a function call, the evaluation process effectively has recourse to two kinds of 'environments.' The current value of a bound variable will be located in the *activation environment*, whereas the value of a global variable or the definition of a function will be located in the *global environment*. (For purposes of this discussion we will ignore property lists, which would also be found in the global environment.)

How does the evaluation process know in which environment to look for the value of a given variable? The answer is, it doesn't, so it takes a trial-and-error approach. Against the possibility that the variable may be local it looks first in the activation environment. If the variable name cannot be found there it assumes that the variable is global and looks in the global environment. (If it can't be found there either an 'unbound variable' error message is generated.)

For purposes of our mini-interpreter we can simulate an activation environment by using an association list on which bound variables and their values are represented as **(variable . value)** dotted pairs. Given a variable name, we can then use **assoc** to search through this list to retrieve the value currently bound to the symbol of this name. Physically, the split between the activation environment and the global environment will be handled in the following manner. We will explicitly represent the activation environment as an association list and will build appropriate specialized constructs into our mini-interpreter for accessing and maintaining this environment. If and when we wish to access or maintain the global enviroment we will do so with the normal LISP assignment and access primitives.

As a quick preview, let us suppose that we execute the top-level assignment statement **(setf x 12 y 13)**. The global environment will be augmented by these assignments:

Activation environment ⟵	Global environment ⟶
NIL	<Oblist> (x . 12) (y . 13)

(As noted previously, for these top-level experiments we will use **setf** rather than **defvar** (see Section 7.2) for assigning such values, since the latter macro can only be used once for a given variable.)

The activation environment, being at top level, is still **NIL**. If we now call a function which has been previously defined as:

```
(defun square-it (x)(* x x))
```

and which also happens to have a formal parameter named **x**, during the period that the function is active we can imagine the activation environment being expanded by the temporary binding which takes place between the argument to **square-it** and its formal parameter **x**. For example, if we call **(square-it 8)**, during the time that this function is being processed our environments would appear as follows:

Activation environment	Global environment
←————————	————————→
(X . 8)	<Oblist> (x . 12) (y . 13)

wherein the local binding of **8** to **x** is reflected as the variable/value dotted pair **(X . 8)** which has been (temporarily) appended to the activation environment. In the event additional function calls were to be nested within **square-it**, the bindings associated with these functions would be appended to the activation environment as the functions were called, and would grow outward to the left. Such temporary bindings would '**shadow**' any previously established values – whether local or global – for the symbols in question, since the left-to-right nature of table lookup by **assoc** would mean that **eval** would stop searching as soon as it had encountered the first variable of that name.

The use of a table such as the foregoing, in which variable/value pairs pile up at the front end of the environment list and a left-to-right lookup strategy is required to locate a value, is referred to as *deep binding*. Using this concept, we will now develop a mini-interpreter to simulate a dynamically scoped LISP with deep binding.

30.3 **d-read-eval-print** sets up a mini **read/eval/print** cycle

We can simulate the **read/eval/print** cycle with **d-read-eval-print**:

```
(defun d-read-eval-print ()
  (let (form environment)
    (terpri)
    (loop
      (format t "~%d? ")
      (setf form (read))
      (if (equal form '(exit))
          (return))
      (format t "~%~s~%" (d-eval form environment)))))
```

This comprises a simple loop which prompts for input of a form and thereafter prints the value returned by the mini-interpreter evaluation function **d-eval**. A special prompt "**d?**" is generated to differentiate this cycle from the normal interpreter as well as from the shallow binding and lexically scoped mini-interpreters which we will develop later. The loop may be exited by executing **(exit)**, similarly to the normal GCLISP interpreter.

Being at the top level, the (activation) environment is initialized to **NIL**.

30.4 d-eval simulates the LISP evaluation process

The work of evaluating forms is split between the evaluation function **d-eval**, which directly evaluates atoms and special forms, and the function **d-apply**, which evaluates the remaining forms which are assumed to be normal functions (see Section 29.8). These functions may be called by name or may be passed to **apply** in the form of a lambda expression.

In contrast with the basic LISP interpreter, which of course handles the environmental question in a manner transparent to the user, we must explicitly include the environment for use by our mini-interpreter. (In any case, explicit handling of the environment is essential if we are to highlight the differences between dynamic and lexical scoping.)

Based on the foregoing table we can define **d-eval** as follows:

```
(defun d-eval (form environment)
  (cond ((atom form)
         (cond ((self-eval-p form) form)
               ((equal form 'environment) environment)
               (t (d-get-value form environment))))
        ((member (first form) '(quote function))
         (second form))
        ((eq (first form) 'setq)
         (d-setq (rest form) environment))
        ((eq (first form) 'if)
         (d-if (rest form) environment))
        (t (d-apply
            (first form)
            (mapcar #'(lambda (arg)
                        (d-eval arg environment))
                    (rest form))
            environment))))
```

(Only a few common special forms have been included for our experimentation purposes. A complete simulation of **eval** would of course have to include all of them.)

If **form** is an **atom**, **d-eval** uses the predicate **self-eval-p** to check whether it is self-evaluating:

```
(defun self-eval-p (form)
  (or (eq form 't)
      (eq form 'nil)
      (numberp form)
      (keywordp form)
      (characterp form)
      (stringp form)))
```

and returns **form** if it is. Special provision for the **atom environment** is included to permit the user periodically to check on its status. Otherwise **d-get-value** is called to retrieve the value of the variable from the a-list.

30.5 d-get-value looks up the value of a symbol

The function **d-get-value** looks up and returns the value of a symbol:

```
(defun d-get-value (symbol environment)
  (let ((result (assoc symbol environment)))
    (if result
        (cdr result)
        (symbol-value symbol))))
```

This function first uses **assoc** to search the activation environment to see if the symbol is bound as a local variable. If the variable value pair is found in this environment the currently bound value is returned. Otherwise it is assumed that the symbol is a global variable and **symbol-value** is used to retrieve its value directly from the global environment (Object List).

30.6 d-setq assigns a value to a symbol

Value assignments to a variable are effected by **d-setq**:

```
(defun d-setq (args environment)
  (let* ((variable (car args))
         (value (d-eval (cadr args) environment))
         (result (assoc variable environment)))
    (if result
        (rplacd result value)
        (setf (symbol-value variable) value))
    value))
```

which uses **let*** to initialize **variable** to the variable to which the value is to be assigned. A recursive call is made to **d-eval** to evaluate the form which is to be assigned as a value, and the resulting value is bound to **value**. Finally, **assoc** is used to search the enviroment for **variable**, and the value returned is bound to **result**.

If **result** is a non-**NIL** value, then **variable** is a locally bound variable and its current value is (destructively) replaced with **value**. If **result** is **NIL**, this means that the variable is not in the (activation) environment, that is, it is a global variable, and **setf** is used in conjunction with **symbol-value** to update its value. Athough we will likely not use it in the context of our mini-interpreter, **value** is returned for consistency with **setq**.

30.7 d-if simulates LISP's if special form

The mini-interpreter function **d-if** simulates the effects of the special form **if**. Its operation is generally self-explanatory:

```
(defun d-if (args environment)
  (cond ((d-eval (first args) environment)
         (d-eval (second args) environment))
        (t  (d-eval (third args) environment))))
```

30.8 d-apply applies functions to their arguments

Assuming that the form to be evaluated is a normal function (as opposed to a special form), the final default clause of the **cond** construct which makes up the body of **d-eval** turns over the evaluation process to **d-apply**:

```
(d-apply (first form)
         (mapcar #'(lambda (arg) (d-eval arg environment))
                   (rest form))
         environment))))
```

The value returned by **(first form)** may be the name of a user-defined function, the name of a LISP-compiled primitive, or a lambda expression. **mapcar** is used together with a lambda expression which recursively calls **d-eval** to generate a list of arguments which have all been evaluated with respect to the current environment.

We can define **d-apply** as follows:

```
(defun d-apply (procedure args environment)
  (cond ((symbolp procedure)
         (d-apply
           (symbol-function procedure)
           args environment))
```

```
((compiled-function-p procedure)
  (apply procedure args))
(t (let ((form-list (cddr procedure))
        (environment (d-create-bindings
                      (second procedure)
                      args
                      environment)))
     (loop
      (ifn form-list (return))
      (d-eval (first form-list) environment)
      (setf form-list (rest form-list)))))))
```

If the function name is a symbol, **symbol-function** is used to retrieve its function definition and **d-apply** is called recursively to apply the resulting functional data object to the (evaluated) arguments.

If the functional data object being applied is a compiled function, the LISP primitive **apply** is called to apply the function to its arguments.

If the first argument passed to **d-apply** is neither a symbol nor a compiled-function data object, the only possibility left is that it is a lambda expression or a closure.

The default clause provides for evaluation of such expressions. After initializing variables within a **let** construct, this expression sets up a loop in which **d-eval** is applied to each one of the forms. Evaluation is carried out in an environment which has been augmented by local variable bindings created by **d-create-bindings** (see below).

30.9 d-create-bindings binds arguments to function parameters

At the time a function is entered, the arguments to the function must be bound to the formal parameters of the lambda list and the resulting variable value pairs added to the environment. This is carried out by **d-create-bindings**:

```
(defun d-create-bindings (var-list val-list environment)
  (nconc (pairlis var-list val-list) environment))
```

pairlis is utilized to create an association list of variable-value bindings from **var-list** and **val-list**, and this list is appended to the front of the existing environment. The destructive function **nconc** is used for this purpose since there is no need to preserve the original association list; the next time the function is called a new environment will be created from scratch.

Once the foregoing code has been loaded we can make a function call to **(d-read-eval-print)** to activate the mini-interpreter:

```
* (d-read-eval-print)
d?
```

and can thereafter carry out tests to confirm that it is working properly.

30.10 Dynamically scoped variables give rise to the so-called 'funarg' problem

Dynamic scoping of a LISP interpreter can potentially lead to a situation in which the values of variables bound within one function can be changed by lower level nested functions which inadvertently refer to and modify these same variables. Such a bug is called the *functional argument* or *'funarg' problem.*

To demonstrate the nature of this problem, let's set up the following function definitions and test them with our dynamically scoped mini-interpreter. We have included format statements so as to display the changing value of the environment as the functions are entered and exited:

```
* (setf (symbol-function 'test-function-1)
    '(lambda (x y)
      (format t "~%Environment is ~a" environment)
      (format t "~%Entering test-function-2")
      (test-function-2 5)
      (format t "~%~%Environment is ~a" environment)))
* (setf (symbol-function 'test-function-2)
    '(lambda (x)
      (format t "~%~%Environment is ~a" environment)
      (format t "~%Setting x to 10 and y to 15")
      (setq x 10)
      (setq y 15)
      (format t "~%Environment is ~a" environment)
      (format t "~%Returning to test-function-1")))
```

test-function-1 binds its arguments to the local variables X and Y, and then calls test-function-2 with the arbitrary argument 5. The local variable X of test-function-2 happens to be the same as one of the variables of test-function-1. test-function-2 also happens to reference variable Y, which is the other local variable of test-function-1, as a free variable. The object of this exercise is to see what effect test-function-2's use of and/or referencing of the same symbols used as formal parameters by test-function-1 has on these variables, once control has returned to test-function-1.

Calling up our mini-interpreter, and calling test-function-1 with the arbitrary arguments 4 and 6:

```
* (d-read-eval-print)
d? (test-function-1 4 6)
Environment is ((X . 4)(Y . 6))
Entering test-function-2
```

```
Environment is ((X . 5)(X . 4)(Y . 6))
Setting x to 10 and y to 15
Environment is ((X . 10)(X . 4)(Y . 15))
Returning to test-function-1
Environment is ((X . 4)(Y . 15))
NIL
```

We note the following:

- **test-function-2**'s use of **x** as a local variable has no effect on the value of this variable within the environment of **test-function-1**, since its binding shadows that of **test-function-1**. This shadowed value is therefore unchanged, and is restored when **test-function-2** exits.
- However the modification to the value of the variable **y**, which **test-function-2** references as a free variable, persists after this function exits, causing a change to the value of the bound variable of the same name in **test-function-1**.

The significance of this is that the use of a dynamically scoped interpreter can result in bugs due to unforeseen changes in the values of bound variables. This can happen if the user is not careful to avoid duplication of formal parameter names by the names of free variables referenced at lower levels in deeply nested programs. Since this type of bug is associated with the manner in which values are assigned and/or modified during the course of nested function calls, it is traditionally referred to as the *functional argument* or *'funarg' problem*.

We will look shortly at the manner in which lexical scoping provides a solution to the 'funarg' problem. However, before we do so, let's look at a variation of dynamic scoping in which a shallow binding, rather than deep binding, technique is used to keep track of the values bound to local variables.

30.11 Shallow binding uses the global environment for variable lookup

Another technique for keeping track of bindings is referred to as *shallow binding*. Rather than maintain an environment in the form of an association list, the current value bound to a variable at any point in time is simply put into its value slot on the Object List, as if it were an assignment to a global variable. This means that a value can be directly retrieved from the symbol data object on the Oblist without the need to traverse an association list. Of course it remains necessary to retain the previous value of a bound variable so that it can be restored after a function is exited. This is done by maintaining a *binding stack* onto which the current value of a variable can be pushed when the variable becomes bound. After the function exits the old value can be popped back off the stack.

For instance, in the previous example if variables **x** and **y** had had global values of **12** and **13** prior to calling **test-function-1**, after this function had been entered the global environment and the binding stack would have looked as follows:

Global environment	Binding stack
(X . 4) (Y . 6) <rest of Oblist>	(X. 12) (Y . 13)

Upon exiting the function, the values of **X** and **Y** would have been popped off the binding stack and used to restore their values on the Object List. We will implement such a shallow binding system in the mini-interpreter version which follows.

30.12 A shallow binding system maintains a binding stack in lieu of an environment association list

In line with the foregoing comments on the use of a binding stack in lieu of an environment association list, the following revised functions define a mini-interpreter based on shallow binding:

```
(defvar *bind-stack* nil)

(defun s-read-eval-print ()
  (let (form *bind-stack*)
   (terpri)
   (loop
    (format t "~%s? ")
    (setf form (read))
    (if (equal form '(exit))
       (return))
    (format t "~%~s~%" (s-eval form)))))

(defun s-eval (form)
  (cond ((atom form)
         (cond ((self-eval-p form) form)
               ((equal form '*bind-stack*) *bind-stack*)
               (t (symbol-value form))))
        ((member (first form) '(quote function))
         (second form))
        ((eq (first form) 'setq)
         (s-setq (rest form)))
        ((eq (first form) 'if)
         (s-if (rest form)))
        (t  (s-apply
            (first form)
            (mapcar #'s-eval (rest form))))))
```

```
(defun s-setq (args)
  (setf (symbol-value (first args))
        (s-eval (second args))))

(defun s-if (args)
  (cond ((s-eval (first args))
         (s-eval (second args)))
        (t (s-eval (third args)))))

(defun s-apply (procedure args)
  (cond ((symbolp procedure)
         (s-apply (symbol-function procedure) args))
        ((compiled-function-p procedure)
         (apply procedure args))
        (t (prog2
             (mapc #'shallow-bind
                (second procedure) args)
             (let ((form-list (cddr procedure)))
                (loop
                  (ifn form-list (return))
                  (s-eval (first form-list))
                  (setf form-list
                    (rest form-list))))
                (mapc #'shallow-unbind
                  (reverse (second procedure)))))))

(defun shallow-bind (var value)
  (push (if  (boundp var)
             (symbol-value var)
             '$unbound$)
        *bind-stack*)
  (setf (symbol-value var) value))

(defun shallow-unbind (var)
  (let ((old-binding (pop *bind-stack*)))
    (if (eq old-binding '$unbound$)
       (makunbound var)
       (setf (symbol-value var) old-binding))))
```

NB: The definition of self-eval-p, as in Section 30.4, will also be used by this version of the interpreter.

We can modify the test functions as previously defined with the following statements:

```
(setf (symbol-function 'test-function-3)
  '(lambda (x y)
    (format t "~%~%X = ~a and Y = ~a" x y)
    (format t "~%Binding stack = ~a" *bind-stack*)
    (format t "~%Entering test-function-4")
```

```
    (test-function-4 5)
    (format t "~%~% X = ~a and Y = ~a" x y)
    (format t "~%Binding stack = ~a" *bind-stack*)))

(setf (symbol-function 'test-function-4)
  '(lambda (x)
    (format t "~%~%X = ~a and Y = ~a" x y)
    (format t "~%Binding stack = ~a" *bind-stack*)
    (format t "~%Setting x to 10 and y to 15")
    (setq x 10)
    (setq y 15)
    (format t "~%X = ~a and Y = ~a" x y)
    (format t "~%Binding stack = ~a" *bind-stack*)
    (format t "~%Returning to test-function-3")))
```

Repeating our earlier experiment, but this time with the shallow-binding interpreter:

```
* (setf x 12 y 13)
13
* (s-read-eval-print)

s? (test-function-3 4 6)
X = 4 and Y = 6
Binding stack = (13 12)
Entering test-function-4

X = 5 and Y = 6
Binding stack = (4 13 12)
Setting x to 10 and y to 15
X = 10 and Y = 15
Binding stack = (4 13 12)
Returning to test-function-3

X = 4 and Y = 15
Binding stack = (13 12)
NIL
```

Principal changes from the deep binding mini-interpreter are as follows.

- The current bindings of all variables are maintained in the global environment, that is, the Object List, and can be directly looked up there when required.
- Therefore it is no longer necessary to maintain an activation environment per se and pass it along as an argument to **s-eval**, **s-apply**, and other functions.

- A binding stack is maintained to store previous values of variables. As new values are bound to local variables, the old values are pushed onto this stack; as a function exits, previous values are restored by popping them from the stack.

One thing which has *not* changed is that we are still stuck with the funarg problem, as noted by the fact that upon return to **test-function-3**, the bound variable Y has been reset to 15.

Now that we have reviewed the two basic mechanisms for carrying out dynamic scoping, let's look at a mini-interpreter system for implementing lexical scoping.

30.13 Lexical scoping isolates the activation environment of one function from that of another

We saw in the previous example that an undesirable feature of dynamic scoping is that a nested function can inadvertently alter the value of a variable which is bound in a higher level function. This problem could be averted if each of the functions had a separate environment of its own, with no access to any variable within the environment of other functions. For example, after calling **test-function-4** we might have a situation as follows:

Test-function-3 Environment: (X . 4)(Y . 6)	Global environment: <Oblist> (X . 12) (Y . 13)
Test-function-4 Environment: (x . 5)	

in which each function could normally only access the variables bound within it, and could not tinker with the values of variables bound within other higher level calling functions. The operation of our lexically scoped mini-interpreter will clarify the manner in which these separate environments are maintained.

As usual, there will be exceptions to these rules. A lexically scoped interpreter *does* provide a mechanism whereby variables can be accessed in a manner similar to that observed in a dynamically scoped system: see Section 7.7 regarding the creation of special variables.

30.14 A closure encloses a function together with a set of bindings

Before getting into our lexically scoped mini-interpreter, let's look at a phenomenon peculiar to lexically scoped LISPs: the *closure*.

We have introduced the concept of maintaining a separate activation environment for each function being called. As illustrated above, such an environment would include only the bound variables of the function. However there may be instances in which we might wish to extend this environment to include not only the locally bound variables, but some free variables as well. We can imagine a function which uses some particular value in its operations, updates that value, and wishes to have the (updated) value available the next time it is called. We could of course handle this situation by means of a global variable, say ***value***, to which the function refers as and when needed. However such a global variable is always susceptible to being clobbered elsewhere in the program. It would be nice if we could arrange matters such that the function had this 'free' variable all to itself.

Common LISP provides such a mechanism, called a *closure*, which is a data object containing a function together with an 'enclosing' environment. Put in another way, one could say that the function carries its global environment around with it, much as a hermit crab carries its shell. When the function is subsequently called, the bindings of its formal parameters are used to augment this 'in-house' global environment.

A closure is created by applying the function **function** to a lambda expression, which operation returns a closure data object. This two-element object contains the lambda expression itself plus an environment consisting of all of the free variables referenced by the lambda expression together with their current values. The concept is best illustrated by example.

If we first assign a global value to variable **x** with a top level **setf** statement, we can then create a closure using an arbitrary lambda expression which refers to this (free) variable as well as to a bound variable of its own:

```
* (setf x 3)
3
* (function (lambda (y)
    (+ x y)))
#<LISP::SCANNED LAMBDA ((Y)(+ X Y))>
```

The above closure is in effect a two-element data object which may be conceptualized as illustrated in Fig. 30.1.

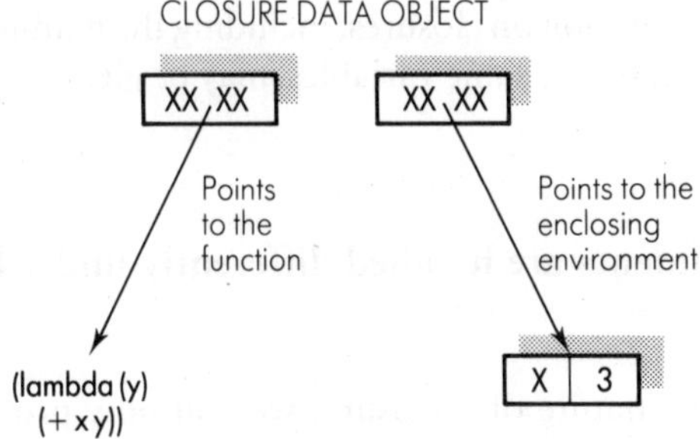

Fig. 30.1 A closure includes an enclosing environment.

As noted above, the first element points to the lambda expression and the second element points to an environmental lookup table which contains the free variable X, along with its value as of the time the closure was created. Should we now go back and modify the global value of X with another top level setf statement, the lookup table would remain unchanged. In this manner, the closure carries around with it a fixed value of X until such time as it may be changed by a subsequent application of the function call.

The CLRM (p. 87) incorporates the above example into the function definition of adder, with the difference that rather than taking the value of x from the global environment, the value is being established through the call to adder:

```
* (defun adder (x)
    (function (lambda (y) (+ x y))))
ADDER
```

For example, the result of (adder 7) is a function which will add 7 to its argument:

```
* (setf add7 (adder 7))
#<LEXICAL CLOSURE 78F1:4B60>
* (funcall add7 6)
13
```

As the CLRM points out, this works because function creates a closure of the inner lambda expression which is able to refer to the value 7 of the variable X even after control has returned from the function adder.

If the foregoing seems confusing, think of adder as being merely a kind of caretaker function through which the value of its argument can be channeled into the closure expression which makes up its body. Calling adder with some argument incorporates this argument into the lookup table of the closure created by the function expression, and returns the resulting closure as a value. When we then use setf as shown, we are effectively defining a function definition for add7 in the form of a closure which is carrying around a certain value for the variable X. Since the function is in the form of a closure we can't invoke it like a normal function; we have to use funcall or apply to activate it.

Further information on closures, including the manner in which two or more closures can share the same variables, may be gleaned by referring to the CLRM pp. 87–9.

30.15 Environments are handled differently under lexical scoping rules

Having defined the nature of a closure, we will now proceed to develop a *lexically scoped* mini-interpreter. This interpeter will be characterized by the following features.

- As each function is called,its bound variables and their values will be gathered into a so-called *rib list*, which provides a unique lexical environment for that function. (See **cons-rib** below for a description of how a rib list differs from the dotted-pair activation environment which we developed previously for our deep-binding interpreter.)
- Any special variables which are dynamically scoped will be handled by simply referring to the general Object List.
- The interpreter will be able to create and process lexical closures.

We can start by defining a function to simulate the **read-eval-print** loop, this time with a **l?** (lexically scoped) prompt:

```
(defun l-read-eval-print ()
  (let (form environment)
   (terpri)
   (loop
    (format t "~%l? ")
    (setf form (read))
    (if (equal form '(exit))
       (return))
    (format t "~%~s~%" (l-eval form environment)))))
```

The basic evaluation function is defined as follows:

```
(defun l-eval (form environment)
  (cond ((atom form)
          (cond ((self-eval-p form) form)
                ((equal form 'environment) environment)
                ((l-get-value form environment))))
        ((eq (first form) 'quote)
          (second form))
        ((eq (first form) 'function)
          (l-function (second form) environment))
        ((eq (first form) 'setq)
          (l-setq (rest form) environment))
        ((eq (first form) 'if)
          (l-if (rest form) environment))
        ((eq (first form) 'l-apply)
          (l-apply (l-function (second form) environment)
                   (mapcar #'(lambda (arg)
                               (l-eval arg environment))
                           (cddr form))))
        (t  (l-apply (l-function (first form) environment)
                   (mapcar #'(lambda (arg)
                               (l-eval arg environment))
                           (rest form))))))
```

We can make some general comments on the l-eval algorithm. Handling of atomic forms is carried out in a manner generally similar to that used for our dynamically scoped interpreters. The same self-eval-p predicate is used for identifying those atoms which evaluate to themselves.

A modified version of l-get-value is used to retrieve the value of a symbol from the rib list:

```
(defun l-get-value (var riblist)
  (block l-get-value
    (dolist (rib riblist)
      (mapc #'(lambda (x xval)
                (if (eq x var)
                    (return-from l-get-value xval)))
            (car rib)
            (cdr rib)))
    (symbol-value var)))
```

If the first element of the form to be evaluated is quote, the form itself is returned.

If the first element of the form is function, l-function is called to process it:

```
(defun l-function (procedure environment)
  (cond ((symbolp procedure)
         (if    (and   (boundp procedure)
                       (l-closurep (symbol-value procedure)))
                (symbol-value procedure)
                (symbol-function procedure)))
        (t (l-make-closure procedure environment))))
```

The purpose of l-function is to return an appropriate functional data object for use by l-apply. If a procedure is represented by a symbol it may be a closure, in which case the closure itself is returned; otherwise it is either a primitive, in which case a #<COMPILED FUNCTION> data object is returned, or a user-defined function, in which case the lambda definition associated with the function is returned. If the procedure is not represented by a symbol it must be in the form of a lambda definition, in which case l-make-closure is called to create a closure of this definition.

If the first element of the form is setq, l-setq is called to process it:

```
(defun l-setq (args environment)
  (block l-setq
    (let ((var (car args))
          (newval (l-eval (cadr args) environment)))
     (dolist (rib environment)
       (mapl #'(lambda (vars vals)
         (when (eq (car vars) var)
               (rplaca vals newval)
               (return-from l-setq newval)))
```

```
          (car rib)
          (cdr rib)))
       (setf (symbol-value var) newval))))
```

l-setq recursively calls **l-eval** to evaluate the argument representing the value to be assigned in the context of the current environment. That done, **dolist** is utilized to iterate through the rib list which represents the environment. (In our simple examples there will be only one 'rib' on the list.) **mapl** is used to traverse the successive **cdr**'s of the rib, searching for the variable to which the value is to be assigned. If it finds the variable, its value is updated with a **rplacd** operation; otherwise it is assumed that the variable is special and **setf** is used to update its value on the Object List. (A **block** is explicitly incorporated into **l-setq** to support the return, since this is not done automatically by GCLISP.)

If the first element of the form is **if**, the function **l-if** is called to process the branching operation. This function is identical to the dynamically scoped version:

```
(defun l-if (args environment)
  (cond ((l-eval (first args) environment)
         (l-eval (second args) environment))
        (t (l-eval (third args) environment))))
```

If none of the foregoing are applicable, it is assumed that the form represents a 'normal' function call and the default clause:

```
(l-apply (l-function (first form) environment)
         (mapcar #'(lambda (arg)
                     (l-eval arg environment))
                 (rest form)))
```

calls **l-apply** to take over the job of evaluating the form:

```
(defun l-apply (procedure args)
  (cond ((l-closurep procedure)
         (let*  ((lambdaexp (second procedure))
                 (environment (third procedure))
                 (arglist (second lambdaexp))
                 (body (third lambdaexp)))
           (l-eval body
             (cons-rib arglist args environment))))
        ((compiled-function-p procedure)
         (apply procedure args))
        (t  (let ((form-list (cddr procedure))
                  (environment (cons-rib
                                 (second procedure)
                                 args
                                 nil)))
```

```
(loop
  (cond ((not (second form-list))
         (return
           (l-eval (first form-list)
                   environment)))
        (t (l-eval (first form-list)
                   environment)
           (setf form-list
                 (rest form-list))))))))
```

The procedure to be applied is the value returned by **(l-function (first form) environment)**. Since symbols and special forms have already been processed by **l-eval**, such an expression must by default consist of either a *closure*, a *compiled function*, or the *lambda expression* associated with a user-defined function.

If the procedure is a closure it is evaluated as a lambda expression would be, but in the context of the environment which it is carrying around. This environment may include values for one or more of the free variables which are being referenced within the body of the lambda expression. To the extent the values of any of these free variables are altered during the course of evaluation, the modified values will be carried along within the closure until the next time it is applied.

If the procedure is a compiled function, **l-apply** simply applies the functional data object to its (evaluated) arguments.

If **procedure** is neither a closure nor a compiled function, the only possibility left is that it is a user-defined function. The default clause of **l-apply** binds the arguments to the formal parameters of the lambda expression, and sets up a loop to evaluate each of the forms which make up the body of the expression. The value of the last form is returned.

As mentioned previously, the default clause of **l-eval** applies **l-function** to a procedure before turning it over to **l-apply** to process. If the procedure is a lambda expression entered by the user, **l-function** calls **l-make-closure** to convert the expression into a closure:

```
(defun l-make-closure (procedure environment)
  (list '$closure$ procedure environment))
```

For purposes of our mini-interpreter, a closure is simulated by creating a list containing the symbol **$CLOSURE$**, followed by the lambda definition, followed by the environment in force at the time that the closure is created, for example:

```
($closure$ (lambda (x y)(+ x y)) environment)
```

The closure thus created is passed to **l-apply**, along with the list of (evaluated) arguments returned by the **mapc** operation.

The predicate **l-closurep** tests whether its argument is a closure:

```
(defun l-closurep (x)
  (and (consp x)
       (eq (car x) '$closure$)))
```

The function **cons-rib** adds variable/value pairs to the riblist:

```
(defun cons-rib (vars vals riblist)
  (cons (cons vars vals) riblist))
```

For example, assuming that a lambda expression with the parameter list (X Y Z) is applied to the argument list (2 3 4), **cons-rib** will append the rib ((X Y Z) 2 3 4) to the environment. (In our simple examples, since the environment is normally NIL, it would become (((X Y Z) 2 3 4)) after exiting cons-rib.)

We can test our lexically scoped mini-interpreter with the same functions **test-function-1** and **test-function-2** which were defined for the previous interpreters:

```
* (l-read-eval-print)

l? (test-function-1 4 6)
Environment is: (((X Y) 4 6))
Entering test-function-2

Environment is: (((X) 5))
Setting x to 10 and y to 15
Environment is: (((X) 10))
Returning to test-function-1

Environment is: (((X Y) 4 6))
NIL
```

The principal point to be noted is that the **setq** assignment to the free variable Y in **test-function-2** had no effect on the value of this (bound) variable within the lexical scope of **test-function-1**. It would of course alter the value of any special variable of this name which might exist. Furthermore, if the variable did not yet exist, such a **setq** statement would create and initialize it. (Needless to say, this would represent very poor programming practice!)

We can also simulate the closure as per the example in Section 30.14:

```
* (setf (symbol-function 'adder)
    '(lambda (x)
       (function (lambda (y)(+ x y)))))
(LAMBDA (X)(FUNCTION (LAMBDA (Y)(+ X Y))))

* (l-read-eval-print)
```

```
I? (setq add3 (adder 3))
($CLOSURE$ (LAMBDA (Y)(+ X Y)) (((X) 3)))
I? (l-apply add3 5)
8
```

30.16 Dynamic closures can be created explicitly in GCLISP

The earlier dynamically scoped Version 1.0 of GCLISP did not support the use of function together with a lambda expression to create a lexical closure. However means were provided to explicitly create a *dynamic closure* data object through use of the function closure, which takes the syntax:

```
(closure <variable-list> <function>)
```

This function creates and returns a closure data object which includes two elements: the function definition and an enclosed global environment representing the current bindings of each of the variables in <variable-list>.

Such a closure can be used as in a lexically scoped LISP, that is, it can be apply'ed or funcall'ed. When invoked in this manner, the values which have been carried around with the closure are bound to the corresponding free variables and the function is applied. Upon exiting the function, the enclosed bindings are updated to reflect any new values which may have been assigned during evaluation of the lambda body. These new values are carried along until the next application of the closure.

We can use GCLISP Version 1.0's explicit closure mechanism to duplicate the previous lexically scoped example:

```
* (defun adder (x)
    (closure '(x) #'(lambda (y)(+ x y))))
ADDER
* (setf add3 (adder 3))
#<DYNAMIC CLOSURE 322A:C6F3>
```

We can apply car and cdr to the closure data object:

```
* (car add3)
#<LEXICAL CLOSURE 322A:C6FC>
* (cdr add3)
(X 3)
```

and use funcall with the closure to obtain the same result as in the previous examples:

```
* (funcall add3 5)
8
```

For compatibility reasons, Version 1.1 continues to support **closure** in a slightly revised form. However the lexical closure mechanism should preferably by used for compatibility with Common LISP.

SUMMARY

Summarizing the main points of this chapter:

- an *environment* is the collection of variable/value bindings with respect to which the evaluation of a form is carried out
- *scoping* in LISP refers to the manner in which environments are handled, with particular reference to the manner in which values may be assigned to free variables
- in *dynamic scoping*, any variable may be referenced at any point in the program
- dynamic scoping gives rise to the *'funarg' problem*, in which a nested function can modify the values of variables bound within higher level functions
- dynamically scoped interpreters can utilize *deep binding* or *shallow binding* as mechanisms for keeping track of local variable bindings
- *lexical scoping* avoids the funarg problem by maintaining separate environments for each function as it is called
- a *closure* is a data object in which a function definition can be enclosed together with an environment of variable bindings

APPENDIX A

GCLISP Functions and Global Variables

	Section	CLRM	GCLRM V1.0	GCLRM V1.1
%BN-TO-UW	26.8	–	–	239
%CONTENTS	26.1	–	221	236
%CONTENTS-STORE	26.1	–	221	236
%FBOUNDP	6.16	–	–	60
%IOPORT	26.1	–	222	238
%MOVE-MEM	26.1	–	–	236
%POINTER	26.1	–	222	237
%STRUCTURE-SIZE	26.1	–	222	237
%SYSINT	26.1	–	223	237
%UNPOINTER	26.1	–	223	237
%UNPOINTER-OFFSET	26.1	–	–	237
%UW-TO-BN	26.8	–	–	239
* (multiplication)	3.7	199	116	122
*, **, *** (variables)	29.11	325	174	178
*&	26.8	–	118	125
AL-LOG-STREAM	23.13	–	–	213
APPLYHOOK	29.9	322	171	176
AUTOLOAD-VERBOSE	23.13	–	–	214
BREAK-EVENT	24.5	–	213	225
BREAK-LEVEL	24.5	–	206	218
BREAK-PROMPT	24.5	–	206	218
COMMAND-LINE	26.6	–	–	233
CURRENT-STACK-GROUP	26.7	–	88	–
DEBUG-IO	19.2	328	178	182
DEFAULT-PATHNAME-DEFAULTS	23.4	416	197	207
DISPLAY-PAGE	26.2	–	220	234
ERROR-OUTPUT	19.2	328	177	182
EVALHOOK	29.9	322	170	175
FEATURES	26.6	448	214	227
GC-DATA	26.12	–	217	230

	Section	CLRM	GCLRM V1.0	GCLRM V1.1
GC-EVENT	26.13	–	218	231
GC-LIGHT-P	26.13	–	216	229
INITIAL-STACK-GROUP	26.7	–	88	–
LISTENER-NAME	29.1	–	173	177
LOAD-VERBOSE	23.12	426	202	212
MODULES	25.15	188	–	115
OBARRAY	26.6	–	215	228
PACKAGE	25.2	183	101	107
PRINT-ALL-ERRORS	23.13	–	–	214
PRINT-BASE	11.8	371	186	195
PRINT-ESCAPE	11.8	370	185	195
PRINT-LENGTH	11.8	372	186	196
PRINT-LEVEL	11.8	372	186	196
PRINT-RADIX	11.8	371	186	195
PROMPT	29.2	–	175	179
PSP-SELECTOR	26.6	–	–	233
QUERY-IO	19.2	328	178	182
READ-BASE	10.10	344	184	191
STANDARD-INPUT	19.2	327	177	181
STANDARD-OUTPUT	19.2	327	177	181
TERMINAL-IO	19.2	328	178	182
TRACE-OUTPUT	19.2	328	178	182
+ (addition)	3.4	199	115	122
+, ++, +++ (variables)	29.11	325	173	177
+%	26.8	–	–	238
+&	26.8	–	118	124
− (subtraction)	3.7	199	115	122
− (variable)	29.11	325	174	178
−%	26.8	–	–	238
−&	26.8	–	118	125
/ (division)	3.7	200	116	123
/, //, /// (variables)	29.11	325	175	179
/&	26.8	–	119	125
/=	3.11	196	112	119
1+	3.8	200	117	123
1−	3.8	200	117	123
8087-FPP	22.5	–	221	234
<	3.11	196	113	119
<&	26.8	–	115	121
<=	3.11	196	113	120
<=%	26.8	–	–	238
=	3.11	196	112	119
>	3.11	196	113	120
>&	26.8	–	115	121
>=	3.11	196	114	120

	Section	CLRM	GCLRM V1.0	GCLRM V1.1
CHAR	21.8	300	162	165
CHAR-BIT	20.15	243	132	137
CHAR-BITS	20.16	240	130	135
CHAR-CODE	20.3	239	129	135
CHAR-DOWNCASE	20.18	241	131	136
CHAR=	20.17	237	129	135
CHAR-EQUAL	20.17	239	129	135
CHAR-LESSP	20.17	239	129	135
CHAR-NAME	20.12	242	131	136
CHAR-UPCASE	20.18	241	130	136
CHARACTER (type)	26.4	43	22	33
CHARACTERP	8.3	75	38	49
CLEAN-UP-ERROR	24.2	–	207	219
CLOSE	19.4	332	180	184
CLOSE-ALL-FILES	19.4	–	180	184
CLOSURE	30.16	–	81	89
CODE-CHAR	20.16	240	130	136
COERCE	22.6	51	24	35
COMMON (type)	26.4	43	22	33
COMMONP	8.3	76	41	51
COMPILED-FUNCTION (type)	26.4	43	22	33
COMPILED-FUNCTION-P	8.3	76	40	51
COND	9.1	116	64	72
CONS	5.3	262	141	146
CONS (type)	26.4	43	22	33
CONSP	8.3	74	37	48
CONTINUE	24.6	–	207	219
COPY-ALIST	18.16	268	145	149
COPY-ARRAY-CONTENTS	22.14	–	161	164
COPY-LIST	26.10	268	145	149
COPY-SYMBOL	25.12	169	98	102
COPY-TREE	26.10	269	145	149
COS	22.5	207	121	122
DECF	22.4	201	118	124
DECLARE	7.9	153	92	96
DEFCONSTANT	7.2	68	32	43
DEFMACRO	16.3	145	90	92
DEFPARAMETER	7.2	68	32	43
DEFSTRUCT	22.17	307	167	171
DEFUN	6.2	67	31	42
DEFVAR	7.2	68	32	42
DELETE	26.9	254	135	141
DELETE-FILE	23.11	424	201	211

DELETE-IF	26.9	254	136	141
DESCRIBE	26.6	441	211	224
DIGIT-CHAR-P	20.17	236	128	134
DIRECTORY	23.14	427	203	214
DIRECTORY-NAMESTRING	23.7	417	199	209
DO	13.3	122	67	75
DO*	13.3	122	68	77
DO-ALL-SYMBOLS	25.9	188	109	114
DO-EXTERNAL-SYMBOLS	25.9	187	109	114
DO-SYMBOLS	25.9	187	108	114
DOC	26.5	–	208	221
DOCUMENTATION	26.5	440	208	221
DOLIST	13.4	126	69	77
DOS	2.9	–	219	232
DOTIMES	13.5	126	69	78
DOUBLE-FLOAT (type)	26.4	43	22	33
DRIBBLE	24.11	443	212	224
DYNAMIC-CLOSURE (type)	26.4	–	–	33
ED	27.2	442	212	224
ENDP	8.8	264	142	146
EQ	8.6	77	41	52
EQL	8.6	78	42	53
EQUAL	8.6	80	43	53
ERROR	24.2	429	205	217
EVAL	29.7	321	170	175
EVALHOOK	29.9	323	171	176
EVAL-WHEN	29.9	69	–	44
EVENP	3.10	196	112	118
EVERY	15.10	250	135	140
EXEC	26.2	–	220	232
EXIT	2.9	–	219	231
EXP	22.5	211	119	125
EXPORT	25.6	186	105	111
EXPT	22.5	211	119	125
FASLOAD	23.12	–	203	212
FBOUNDP	6.16	91	50	60
FILE-INFO	23.11	–	202	212
FILE-NAMESTRING	23.7	417	199	209
FILL-POINTER	22.12	296	159	162
FIND-ALL-SYMBOLS	25.10	187	–	113
FIND-PACKAGE	25.14	183	102	108
FIND-SYMBOL	25.7	185	105	110
FIRST	5.13	266	142	147
FIXNUM (type)	26.4	43	22	33
FLATC	12.10	–	191	200

	Section	CLRM	GCLRM V1.0	GCLRM V1.1
FLATSIZE	12.10	–	191	200
FLOAT	22.6	214	122	128
FLOAT (type)	26.4	43	22	33
FLOATP	8.3	75	38	49
FLOOR	22.6	215	122	128
FMAKUNBOUND	6.16	92	53	63
FORMAT	12.5	385	191	201
FUNCALL	6.14	108	57	67
FUNCTION	6.13	87	48	58
FUNCTION (type)	26.4	43	22	33
FUNCTIONP	8.3	76	40	50
GC	26.13	–	216	229
GENSYM	25.13	169	98	102
GET	18.4	164	94	99
GET-DECODED-TIME	24.13	445	213	226
GET-ENVIRONMENT-STRING	26.6	–	–	233
GET-INTERNAL-REAL-TIME	24.13	446	–	226
GET-OUTPUT-STREAM-STRING	19.11	330	179	183
GET-PROPERTIES	18.6	167	96	101
GETF	18.5	166	96	100
GO	13.7	133	76	84
IDENTITY	26.6	448	215	227
IF	9.6	115	62	70
IFN	9.6	–	62	71
IGNORE-ERRORS	24.4	–	207	219
IMPORT	25.6	186	106	111
IN-PACKAGE	25.5	183	102	107
INCF	22.4	201	117	124
INTEGER (type)	26.4	43	22	33
INTEGERP	8.3	74	38	48
INTERN	25.7	184	104	109
ISQRT	22.5	205	–	126
KEYWORD (type)	26.4	43	22	33
KEYWORDP	25.3	170	99	103
LABELS	7.11	113	61	70
LAMBDA	6.7	59	30	41
LAMBDA-LIST	26.5	–	209	222
LAST	5.14	267	144	148
LDIFF	26.10	–	148	151
LENGTH	5.15	248	133	139
LET	6.8	110	59	69
LET*	6.8	111	60	69
LEXICAL-CLOSURE (type)	26.4	–	–	33

LISP-IMPLEMENTATION-TYPE	26.6	447	214	226
LISP-IMPLEMENTATION-VERSION	26.6	447	214	227
LIST	5.8	267	144	148
LIST (type)	26.4	43	22	33
LIST*	5.8	267	144	148
LIST-ALL-PACKAGES	25.14	184	104	109
LIST-LENGTH	5.15	265	142	147
LISTENER	29.1	–	172	177
LISTP	8.3	74	37	48
LOAD	23.12	426	202	212
LOG	22.5	204	119	126
LOGAND	22.7	221	124	130
LOGBITP	22.7	224	125	131
LOGEQV	22.7	221	124	130
LOGIOR	22.7	221	123	130
LOGNOT	22.7	223	124	130
LOGTEST	22.7	223	125	130
LOGXOR	22.7	221	124	130
LONG-FLOAT (type)	26.4	43	22	33
LOOP	13.2	121	67	75
LSH	22.7	–	126	131
MACRO	–	–	91	92
MACRO-FUNCTION	16.8	144	89	91
MACROEXPAND	16.4	151	91	93
MACROEXPAND-1	16.4	151	91	93
MAKE-ARRAY	22.9	286	156	159
MAKE-LIST	5.18	268	144	148
MAKE-PACKAGE	25.4	183	101	107
MAKE-PATHNAME	23.2	416	197	207
MAKE-STACK-GROUP	26.7	–	84	168
MAKE-STRING	21.4	302	–	168
MAKE-STRING-INPUT-STREAM	19.9	330	179	183
MAKE-STRING-OUTPUT-STREAM	19.10	330	179	183
MAKE-SYMBOL	25.12	168	97	102
MAKE-SYNONYM-STREAM	19.8	329	179	183
MAKE-WINDOW-STREAM	–	–	–	263
MAKUNBOUND	4.12	–	52	62
MAPC	15.5	128	71	80
MAPCAN	15.8	128	73	81
MAPCAR	15.2	128	70	78
MAPCON	15.9	128	74	81
MAPL	15.7	128	72	80
MAPLIST	15.6	128	71	79
MAX	3.9	198	114	120
MEMBER	8.7	275	150	154

	Section	CLRM	GCLRM V1.0	GCLRM V1.1
MEMBER-IF	8.7	275	151	154
MERGE-PATHNAMES	23.3	415	196	206
MIN	3.9	198	114	121
MINUSP	3.10	196	111	118
MOD	22.6	217	123	129
MULTIPLE-VALUE-BIND	17.10	136	78	86
MULTIPLE-VALUE-LIST	17.10	135	77	85
MULTIPLE-VALUE-PROG1	17.10	136	77	85
MULTIPLE-VALUE-SETQ	17.9	136	78	86
NAME-CHAR	20.12	243	131	137
NAMED-STRUCTURE-P	22.26	–	–	173
NAMED-STRUCTURE-SYMBOL	22.26	–	169	173
NAMESTRING	23.7	417	199	209
NBUTLAST	26.10	–	147	151
NCONC	5.16	269	145	150
NCONS	5.3	–	141	146
NEQ	8.6	–	42	52
NEQL	8.6	–	42	53
NIL (type)	26.4	43	22	33
NIL	2.13	72	34	45
NOT	8.12	82	44	54
NREVERSE	5.9	248	134	140
NTH	5.14	265	142	147
NTHCDR	5.14	267	143	148
NULL	8.2	73	36	47
NULL (type)	26.4	43	22	33
NUMBER (type)	26.4	43	22	33
NUMBERP	8.3	74	37	48
ODDP	3.10	196	112	118
OPEN	19.3	418	200	210
OR	8.11	83	45	55
PACKAGE (type)	26.4	43	22	33
PACKAGE-NAME	25.14	184	102	108
PACKAGE-NICKNAMES	25.14	184	103	108
PACKAGE-SHADOWING-SYMBOLS	25.11	184	103	109
PACKAGE-USE-LIST	25.14	184	103	109
PACKAGE-USED-BY-LIST	25.14	184	103	109
PACKAGEP	8.3	76	39	50
PAIRLIS	18.12	280	152	155
PARSE-DIRECTORY-NAMESTRING	23.5	–	196	206
PARSE-NAMESTRING	23.5	414	195	206
PATHNAME	23.5	413	195	205

PATHNAME (type)	26.4	43	22	33
PATHNAME-DEVICE	23.6	417	198	208
PATHNAME-DIRECTORY	23.6	417	198	208
PATHNAME-NAME	23.6	417	198	208
PATHNAME-TYPE	23.6	417	199	209
PATHNAMEP	23.5	416	197	208
PLUSP	3.10	196	111	118
POP	26.10	271	147	150
PPRINT	11.7	383	190	199
PRIN1	11.4	383	189	199
PRINC	11.5	383	190	199
PRINT	11.3	383	189	199
PROBE-FILE	23.11	424	202	212
PROCLAIM	7.5	156	–	96
PROG	13.8	131	74	83
PROG*	13.8	131	75	83
PROG1	13.10	109	58	68
PROG2	13.10	109	59	68
PROGN	13.10	109	58	67
PROGV	13.9	112	61	70
PROVIDE	25.15	188	–	115
PSETQ	4.7	92	52	62
PUSH	26.10	269	146	150
PUSHNEW	26.10	270	146	150
QUOTE	2.16	86	48	58
RASSOC	18.15	281	153	156
RANDOM-STATE (type)	26.4	43	22	33
RATIONALP	8.3	74	–	49
READ	10.2	375	187	197
READ-BYTE	10.6	382	189	198
READ-CHAR	10.6	379	188	197
READ-FROM-STRING	10.8	380	188	198
READ-LINE	10.7	378	187	197
READ-PRESERVING-WHITESPACE	10.5	376	187	197
REM	22.6	217	–	129
REMF	18.8	167	96	101
REMOVE	26.9	253	135	141
REMOVE-IF	26.9	253	135	141
REMPROP	18.7	166	95	100
RENAME-FILE	23.11	423	201	211
RENAME-PACKAGE	25.4	184	–	108
REQUIRE	25.15	188	–	115
REST	5.13	266	143	148
RETURN	17.2	120	66	75
RETURN-FROM	17.1	120	66	74
REVERSE	5.9	248	134	139

	Section	CLRM	GCLRM V1.0	GCLRM V1.1
ROOM	26.12	442	211	229
ROUND	22.6	215	123	129
RPLACA	5.17	272	148	152
RPLACB	5.17	–	149	152
RPLACD	5.17	272	148	152
SAMEPNAMEP	8.5	–	97	101
SCANNED-SPECIAL-FORM (type)	26.4	–	–	33
SCHAR	21.8	300	–	165
SECOND	5.14	266	143	147
SELECT-PAGE	26.2	–	220	234
SEND	19.12	–	181	185
SEQUENCE (type)	26.4	43	22	33
SET	4.8	92	52	62
SET-CHAR-BIT	20.16	244	132	137
SET-MACRO-CHARACTER	20.9	362	185	195
SET-SYNTAX-FROM-CHAR	20.11	361	184	194
SETF	4.11	94	54	64
SETQ	4.5	91	51	61
SHADOW	25.11	186	107	112
SHADOWING-IMPORT	25.11	186	107	112
SHORT-FLOAT (type)	26.4	43	22	33
SIGNUM	22.5	206	120	127
SIMPLE-VECTOR-P	8.3	75	–	50
SIMPLE-STRING-P	8.3	75	–	50
SIN	22.5	207	121	127
SINGLE-FLOAT (type)	26.4	43	22	33
SLEEP	24.14	447	–	226
SNOC	26.10	–	149	152
SOME	15.10	250	134	140
SORT	26.3	258	136	–
SPECIAL	7.9	157	–	96
SPECIAL-FORM-P	6.16	91	50	61
SPECIAL-P	7.4	–	–	97
SQRT	22.5	–	136	126
STACK-GROUP (type)	26.4	43	22	33
STACK-GROUP-P	8.3	–	41	51
STACK-GROUP-PRESET	26.7	–	84	–
STACK-GROUP-RESUME	26.7	–	86	–
STACK-GROUP-RETURN	26.7	–	86	–
STACK-GROUP-UNWIND	26.7	–	85	–
STANDARD-CHAR (type)	26.4	43	22	33
STANDARD-CHAR-P	20.17	234	127	133
STEP	24.9	441	210	223

	Section	CLRM	GCLRM V1.0	GCLRM V1.1
UNLESS	9.8	115	63	72
UNLOAD-GMACS	27.15	–	–	228
UNLOAD-LISPLIB	27.15	–	–	228
UNPROVIDE	25.15	–	–	115
UNREAD-CHAR	10.6	379	188	198
UNSIGNED-BYTE (type)	26.4	–	22	33
UNTRACE	24.7	440	210	222
UNUSE-PACKAGE	25.8	187	108	113
UNWIND-PROTECT	17.5	140	80	87
UPPER-CASE-P	20.17	235	128	134
USE-PACKAGE	25.6	187	107	113
VALUES	17.7	134	76	84
VALUES-LIST	17.7	135	77	85
VECTOR	22.16	290	157	160
VECTOR (type)	26.4	43	22	33
VECTOR-POP	22.12	296	160	163
VECTOR-PUSH	22.12	296	159	162
VECTORP	8.3	75	39	49
WHEN	9.7	115	63	72
WITH-OPEN-FILE	19.6	422	200	210
WITH-OPEN-STREAM	19.7	330	–	184
WITH-OUTPUT-TO-STRING	21.5	331	–	184
WRITE-BYTE	11.9	385	191	200
WRITE-CHAR	11.9	384	190	200
Y-OR-N-P	12.11	407	193	203
YES-OR-NO-P	12.11	408	194	203
ZEROP	3.10	195	111	118
\	11.2	338	7	7
\ \	26.8	–	–	125
|	11.2	338	7	7
` (backquote)	12.3	349	–	192

APPENDIX B

User-defined Functions

	Section	Exercise
ADD-BOOK		18.8
ADD-EM-UP	15.3	
ADD-EM-UP	24.2	
ADD-EM-UP	26.5	
ADD-INTEGERS		24.5
ADD3	30.14	
ADDER	30.14	
ADDRESS-LIST		12.8
AIR-CON-1		9.3
AIR-CON-2		9.4
ARITHMETIC-IF	16.10	
BIG-INTEGER-P		8.4
BLANK-LINES		11.4
BOOZE-UP-1		9.5
BOOZE-UP-2		9.6
BUBBLE-SORT		26.6
CHAR-EX-STRING	19.9	
CHECK-ARRAY	22.10	
CHECK-ARRAY-LEADER	22.13	
CHECK-EVEN		15.6
CHECK-FILE		23.3
CHECK-PACKAGE-SYMBOLS		25.5
CHECK-WINDOWS	1.8	
CIRCLE-AREA		6.1
CITY-STATE	15.5	
CONS-RIB	30.15	
CONVERT-ARRAY		22.7
CONVERT-NUMBER		12.5
CONVERT-TEMP		15.3
COPY-FILE		11.10
COPY-SYNTAX		20.5
COUNT-ATOMS		14.8
COUNT-CHAR		21.4
COUNT-CHARACTER		10.4

	Section	Exercise
COUNT-ELEMENTS	14.2	
COUNT-ELEMENTS	24.7	
COUNT-GROCERIES-1	13.2	
COUNT-GROCERIES-2	13.3	
COUNT-GROCERIES-3	13.3	
COUNT-GROCERIES-4	13.4	
COUNT-GROCERIES-5	13.7	
COUNT-GROCERIES-6	13.8	
COUNT-NUMBERS		8.10
COUNT-PACKAGE-SYMBOLS		25.8
D-APPLY	30.8	
D-CREATE-BINDINGS	30.9	
D-EVAL	30.4	
D-GET-VALUE	30.5	
D-IF	30.7	
D-READ-EVAL-PRINT	30.3	
D-SETQ	30.6	
DAILY-DIARY-1		9.7
DIAMONDP		26.4
DISPLAY-ASCII-CHAR	20.5	
DISPLAY-BYTES		26.7
ENTER-HOUSE	1.8	
ENVIRONMENT	1.7	
EQUAL-STRINGS		21.5
EVAL-HOOK-FUNCTION	29.10	
FACTORIAL	13.2	
FACTORIAL	14.4	
FACTORIAL-1	13.3	
FACTORIAL-2	13.5	
FIBONACCI	14.6	
FILE-PHONE-NUMBERS		11.9
FILE-PHONES		26.5

	Section	Exercise
FILE-TEST-1	24.9	
FILE-TEST-2	24.9	
FILE-TEST-3	24.9	
FIND-FRUIT	15.8	
FIND-NUMBER		15.7
FRUITP	8.9	
FRUITP	13.6	
FUNCTION-KEYS		20.3
GET-ASCII-CHAR	20.4	
GET-AUTHOR		18.10
GET-BOOK		18.9
GET-BOTH-CASE-CHAR		20.10
GET-CHAR-ASCII	20.3	
GET-CHAR-BITS	20.15	
GET-CHAR-NAME	20.12	
GET-CHAR-NAMES		20.7
GET-DIGIT		12.6
GET-DIGIT-CHAR		20.9
GET-ELAPSED-TIME	24.13	
GET-FILE-NAME		24.3
GET-FILES		23.4
GET-GC-DATA		26.8
GET-HEX-ARRAY		22.6
GET-INDICATORS		18.5
GET-INHERIT		18.7
GET-LIST-VALUE		10.2
GET-OBARRAY		26.9
GET-NAME		24.1
GET-NUMBERS-1		17.1
GET-NUMBERS-2		17.2
GET-NUMBERS-3		17.3
GET-PACKAGE-SYMBOLS		25.6
GET-PATHNAME		23.1
GET-PROP		18.3
GET-STANDARD-CHAR		20.8
GET-SYMBOL-VALUE		10.1
GET-TIME	24.12	
HANOI	14.5	
HEXADECIMAL		10.10
HOOK	29.10	
HOOLIGANP		15.5
IF-EXAMPLE	16.4	
INDENT	29.10	
L-APPLY	30.15	
L-CLOSUREP	30.15	
L-EVAL	30.15	
L-FUNCTION	30.15	

	Section	Exercise
L-GET-VALUE	30.15	
L-IF	30.15	
L-MAKE-CLOSURE	30.15	
L-READ-EVAL-PRINT	30.15	
L-SETQ	30.15	
LIST-EX-STRING	10.8	
LIST-OUTPUT-STREAM	19.13	
LOOK-FOR-WORD		10.6
MAKE-LIST-STRING		19.8
MAKE-STRING-LIST		19.7
MAP-1	15.2	
MAP-2	15.2	
MATCH	14.7	
MATCH-MAKER		15.4
MERGE	26.3	
MINI-ELIZA		13.1
MOVE-DISK	14.5	
MULTIPLE-TIME-ELAPSED		24.10
NEWLINE-INPUT-STREAM	19.13	
NILP		8.7
NUMBERP-1		9.1
NUMBERP-2		9.2
OUR-CAADR		16.3
OUR-DO		16.10
OUR-DOLIST		16.6
OUR-DO-SYMBOLS		25.10
OUR-DOTIMES-1	16.9	
OUR-DOTIMES-2	16.9	
OUR-EXPONENT		13.3
OUR-EXPONENT		14.7
OUR-FILTER		14.2
OUR-FIRST		16.2
OUR-IF	16.2	
OUR-INTERSECTION		13.8
OUR-LET		16.8
OUR-LOAD		23.10
OUR-MAPC		15.9
OUR-MAPCAN	15.8	
OUR-MAPCAR	15.2	
OUR-MAPCAR		16.7
OUR-MAPLIST		15.10
OUR-MEMBER		13.4
OUR-MEMBER		14.5
OUR-MULTIPLE-VALUE-CALL		17.10
OUR-NTH-ELEMENT		13.9
OUR-POP		16.5

APPENDIX C

The Diskette and Ordering Information

All of the LISP coding used in the book is contained on a 5-¼″ MS-DOS diskette which may be ordered as indicated below. Two (mnemonically named) files are included for each chapter:

START-01	SCOPE-07	ITERA-13	STREA-19	PACKA-25
INTER-02	PREDI-08	RECUR-14	CHARS-20	OTHER-26
ACQUI-03	CONDI-09	MAPIT-15	STRIN-21	GMACS-27
SYMBO-04	READS-10	MACRO-16	ARRAY-22	INSID-28
LISTS-05	PRINT-11	BLOCK-17	FILES-23	EVALU-29
FUNCT-06	FORMA-12	PROPS-18	DEBUG-24	MECHA-30

with extensions .FUN covering functions defined during the text of the chapter and .LSP covering answers to the exercises.

In addition, a number of AI applications programs with complete supporting documentation and commentary are included on the diskette:

ELIZA-31 includes a complete basic program for carrying on a dialogue with your computer along the lines of Weizenbaum's famous *Eliza* program, including built-in debugging facilities and provision for testing of elapsed CPU time for each element of dialog parsing and generation.

ELIZA-32 includes additional algorithms to 'fine-tune' the basic *Eliza* program to incorporate randomized responses, comparison of keywords against global lists to provide for more controlled responses, provision of the 'Earlier you mentioned...' memory feature, and facilities to save and print out the results of an *Eliza* dialogue.

FRAME-33 includes a set of algorithms to create and use a system of frames for storage of information, including class hierarchies, various modes of search for default information, and provision for :if-added, :if-deleted, and :if-needed demons.

TRANS-34 includes a basic set of algorithms for parsing natural language and mapping the results of the parse into nested list format reflecting the phrase structure and facilitating further processing.

EXPER-35 includes algorithms for establishing production rules, an inference engine for backward-and-forward chaining and constuction of an expert system shell

For the diskette, including airmail postage worldwide, send US$20 to:

David J. Steele
Farrer Road P.O. Box 9
Singapore 9128

Answers to Exercises

Chapter 2 The LISP Interpreter

2.1 The four elements of the basic interpreter cycle are:

prompt	which displays the asterisk prompt symbol
read	which reads in a single valid LISP expression
eval	which evaluates the expression read
print	which prints the results of the evaluation

2.2 quote is used to suppress evaluation of an expression.

2.3 Numbers and strings evaluate to themselves, as do the special symbols NIL and T.

2.4 LISP functions are used either for their values returned or for the side effects which they produce.

2.5 The next higher listener level is returned to using Ctrl-G.

2.6 Intermediate listener levels may be skipped over using Ctrl-C.

2.7 An endless loop may be exited using Ctrl-Break followed by Ctrl-C to return to the top level.

2.8 GCLISP may be exited temporarily by a call to (sys:dos).

2.9 Type exit to return from MS-DOS to GCLISP.

2.10 A call to (exit) will permanently exit from GCLISP.

Chapter 3 Getting Acquainted with Functions

3.1 (a) 33
(b) Undefined function: PLUS
(c) 5.0
(d) 100.0
(e) 3
(f) 6

(g) Wrong number of arguments for: EVENP
(h) T
(i) T

3.2 (/ (* base height) 2)

3.3 (/ (* pi diameter diameter) 4)

3.4 (+ (* x x)(* 2 x) 6)
(+ (* x (+ x 2)) 6)

3.5 (setf pear (+ 1 apple))
(setf pear (1+ apple))

3.6 (zerop grape)

3.7 (oddp (min 7 3 2 6 6 9))

3.8 (evenp (max 7 3 2 6 6 9))

3.9 (plusp (+ 4 −3 5 −7 −2 1))

3.10 (minusp (− 4 −3 5 −7 −2 1))

Chapter 4 Symbols as Data Objects

4.1 The Object List serves as a lookup table of all of the symbols which are recognized by the LISP interpreter.As initialized, the Object List contains LISP primitives and system parameters. As additional symbols are defined by the user, these are added to the Object List.

4.2 The four attributes of a symbol are its print name, its property list, its function definition, and its value.

4.3

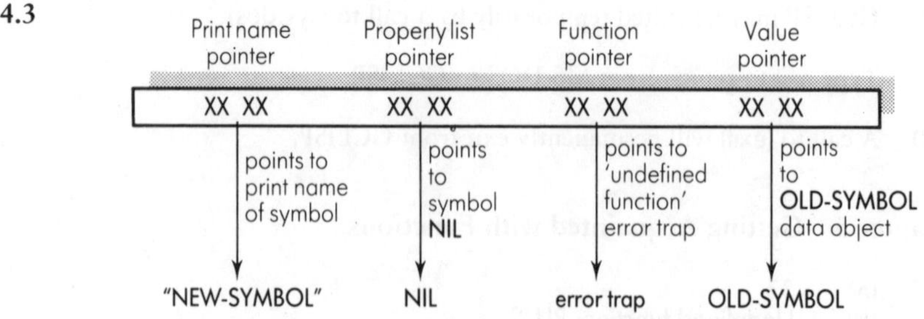

4.4 (b) returns 6, and the value of y = 6.

4.5 (b) returns NIL, and the value of y = 5.

4.6 (setq symbol-one "this is a string" symbol-two 'symbol-three
symbol-three '(one two three four) symbol-four 'symbol-two)

After executing the set assignments, the value of all the symbols will be (ONE TWO THREE FOUR)

4.7
(a) T
(b) T
(c) T
(d) NIL

4.8
(a) NEXT-SYMBOL
(b) 12
(c) Would display an error message:
ERROR:
SYMBOL VALUE: wrong type argument: 12
A SYMBOL was expected.

4.9
(a) "TEST-SYMBOL"
(b) "NEXT-SYMBOL"
(c) Would display an error message:
ERROR:
SYMBOL VALUE: wrong type argument: 12
A SYMBOL was expected.

4.10
(a) (setf test-symbol next-symbol)
(b) (setf test-symbol 'next-symbol)
(c) (setf (symbol-value test-symbol) next-symbol)
(d) (setf (symbol-value test-symbol) 'next-symbol)

test-symbol must evaluate to a symbol in (c) and (d).

Chapter 5 List Creation and Manipulation

5.1 (setf sentence (cons 'this (cons 'is (cons 'a (cons 'list nil)))))

5.2 (append '(the temperature is) (list temp) '(degrees))

5.3 Since list retains the character of the individual elements, it would be necessary to list the individual values, that is: (list 'the 'temperature 'is temp 'degrees).

5.4 (reverse palindrome)

5.5 (car (cdr (cdr '(now is the time))))
(caddr '(now is the time))
(third '(now is the time))
(nth 2 '(now is the time))

5.6
(a) HOW
(b) (THIS IS A LIST)
(c) (BROWN COW)
(d) ERROR: CAR or CDR of non-LIST object: A
(e) NIL

5.7 (a) HAS
(b) ERROR: CAR or CDR of non-LIST object: NOW
(c) NOW

5.8 (nth 4 '(now is the time for all good men))

5.9 (length '(one (two) three (four) five))

5.10

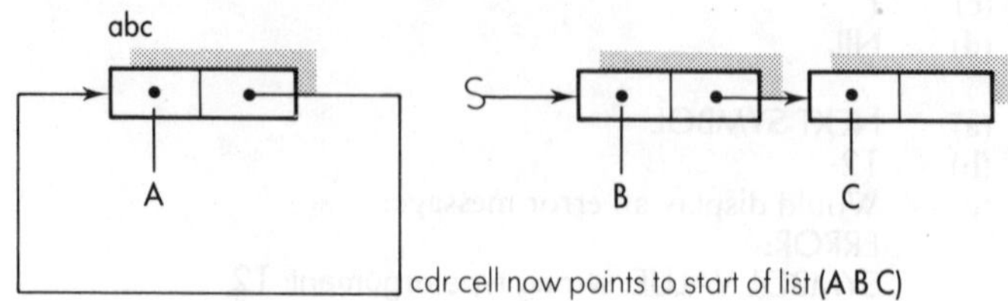

Chapter 6 Defining Your Own Functions

6.1 (defun circle-area (diameter)(/ (* 3.14 diameter diameter) 4))

6.2 (defun trapezoid-area (bottom top height)
(* (/ (+ bottom top) 2) height))

6.3 ((lambda (diameter)(/ (* 3.14 diameter diameter) 4)) 10)

6.4 ((lambda (bottom top height)(* (/ (+ bottom top) 2) height))
20 16 8)

6.5 (defun square-area (base)(* base base))
(symbol-function 'square-area)

6.6 (defun square-area (base)(expt base 2))
(setf (symbol-function 'square-area)
'(lambda (base)(expt base 2)))

6.7 (funcall '(lambda (bottom top height)
(* (/ (+ bottom top) 2) height)) 20 16 8)

6.8 (eval (quote (circle-area 10)))

6.9 (apply '(lambda (bottom top height)
(* (/ (+ bottom top) 2) height)) '(20 16 8))

6.10 (a) (fboundp 'test-symb)
(b) (special-form-p 'test-symb)
(c) (macro-function 'test-symb)

Chapter 7 Scoping of Variables

7.1 A special variable is normally defined at the top level and its binding is visible to the entire LISP program. A lexical variable is bound within a function, and its binding is normally only visible within the lexical scope of that function.

7.2 **defvar** is used to create and/or initialize a variable whose value is expected to be changed during the course of the program.

defparameter is used to create and initialize a variable whose value will be used as a parameter to control operation of the program.

defconstant is used to create and initialize a variable whose value is expected to remain constant during the course of the program.

7.3 Special variables can be created and initialized at the top level by using a **setf** statement or by using **proclaim** with a special declaration. Neither of these constructs allows documentation information to be incorporated, nor can variables created with **setf** be tested with the **special-p** predicate.

7.4 **(special-p '*cow*)**
Such a statement would return **T** if applied to special variables created with a **proclaim** statement, but **NIL** if applied to variables created with a **setf** statement.

7.5 Variable **x** would still be 10, since **defvar** does not update a pre-existing value.

7.6 The value of variable **y** would be updated to 20 by **defparameter.**

7.7 An error message would be generated, since once defined with **defconstant** the value of the variable is not expected to change.

7.8 The lexical binding of the local variable in **A** would not normally be visible in function **B**, but could be made so by incorporating the statement **(declare (special <variable-name>))** at the beginning of function **A**.

7.9 The term 'shadows' means that the variable takes on the new binding in lieu of the old binding; the value of the old binding is saved and later restored when the function is exited. We can carry out the following experiment to demonstrate the manner in which a local binding shadows a higher level local binding of the same variable:

```
(defun scope-16 (x)
  (format t "~%Now in scope-16")
  (format t "~%Value of x is ~a" x)
  (scope-17 10)
  (format t "~%~%Now back in scope-16")
  (format t "~%Value of x is ~a" x))

(defun scope-17 (x)
  (format t "~%Now in scope-17")
  (format t "~%Value of x is ~a" x))
```

Calling **scope-16** with some value other than 10, the printout will indicate the manner in which the value of **x** in **scope-17** will shadow the value of **x** in the higher level function.

7.10 Bindings of variables locally bound within a **let** or **labels** construct will be visible to all functions nested within these constructs if the variables are special, whether through a global proclamation or by virtue of having been declared special at some higher point in the program (or within the **let/labels** constructs themselves).

Chapter 8 Predicates and Boolean Operators

8.1 (a) NIL
(b) T
(c) T
(d) NIL
(e) (CAIN DOG EASY)
(f) NIL
(g) T
(h) NIL
(i) NIL
(j) T

8.2 (a) (equal arg-1 arg-2)
(b) (eql arg-1 arg-2)
(c) (eq arg-1 arg-2)

8.3
```
(defun short-string-p (arg)
  (and (stringp arg)(< (length arg) 11)))
```

8.4
```
(defun big-integer-p (arg)
  (and (integerp arg)(> arg 255)))
```

8.5
```
(defun two-or-more-p (one two)
  (member one
     (cdr (member one two :test #'equal)) :test #'equal))
```

8.6
```
(defun palindromep (arg)
  (and (listp arg)
       (equal arg (reverse arg))))
```

8.7
```
(defun nilp (arg)
  (and (symbolp arg)
       (listp arg)))
```

8.8
```
(defun test-float-p (arg)
  (and (numberp arg)
       (not (integerp arg))))
```

8.9
```
(defun test-number-p (arg)
  (or (integerp arg)
      (floatp arg)))
```

8.10
```
(defun count-numbers (arg)
  (let ((count 0))
    (loop
      (and (endp arg)(return count))
      (and (setf arg (member-if #'numberp arg))
           (setf count (1+ count)))
      (setf arg (cdr arg)))))
```

Chapter 9 Branching Operations

9.1
```
(defun numberp-1 (arg)
  (cond ((numberp arg)
         (print "The argument is a number"))))
```

9.2
```
(defun numberp-2 (arg)
  (cond ((numberp arg)
         (print "The argument is a number."))
        (t (print "The argument is NOT a number"))))
```

9.3
```
(defun air-con-1 (temp)
  (when (< temp 75)
        (print "The room is comfortable")))
```

9.4
```
(defun air-con-2 (temp)
  (if (< temp 75)
     (print "The room is comfortable.")
     (print "Please turn on the air conditioner")))
```

9.5
```
(defun booze-up-1 (age)
  (unless (> age 20)
          (print "You're too young to drink!")))
```

9.6
```
(defun booze-up-2 (age)
  (ifn (> age 20)
       (print "You're too young to drink!")
       (print "What'll you have?")))
```

9.7
```
(defun daily-diary-1 (day)
  (cond ((equal day 'monday)
            (print "Attend Women's Lib meeting"))
        ((equal day 'tuesday)
            (print "Write letter to George Bush"))
        ((equal day 'wednesday)
            (print "Picnic at Grand Canyon"))
        ((equal day 'thursday)
            (print "Recover from picnic"))
        ((equal day 'friday)
            (print "Hang loose till Monday"))
        (t (print "That's not a weekday!"))))
```

9.8
```
(defun daily-diary-2 (day)
  (case day
    (monday    (print "Attend Women's Lib meeting"))
    (tuesday   (print "Write letter to George Bush"))
    (wednesday (print "Picnic at Grand Canyon"))
    (thursday  (print "Recover from picnic"))
    (friday    (print "Hang loose till Monday"))
    ( t        (print "That's not a weekday!"))))
```

9.9
```
(defun weather-report-1 ()
  (cond ((and (equal sun 'yes)(equal warm 'yes))
          (print "Weather is fine"))
        ((and (equal rain 'yes)(equal cold 'yes))
          (print "Weather is lousy"))
        (t (print "Weather is so-so"))))
```

9.10
```
(defun weather-report-2 ()
  (cond ((or (and (equal sun 'yes)(equal warm 'yes))
             (and (equal warm 'yes)(not (equal rain 'yes))))
          (print "Weather is fine"))
        ((or (and (not (equal sun 'yes))(equal cold 'yes))
             (equal rain 'yes))
          (print "Weather is lousy"))
        (t (print "Weather is so-so"))))
```

Chapter 10 Input Functions

10.1
```
(defun get-symbol-value ()
  (let (symbol)
    (terpri)
    (princ "Please input a symbol: ")
    (setf symbol (read))
    (cond ((symbolp symbol)
            (cond ((not (boundp symbol))
                    (princ "Symbol ")
                    (princ symbol)
                    (princ " does not have a value.")
                    (terpri))
                  (t (princ "The value of ")
                    (princ symbol)
                    (princ " is: ")
                    (princ (symbol-value symbol))
                    (terpri))))
          (t (print symbol)
            (princ "is not a symbol!")
            (terpri)))))
```

10.2
```
(defun get-list-value ()
  (let (list)
    (terpri)
    (princ "Please input a list: ")
    (setf list (read))
    (cond ((listp list)
            (cond ((not (fboundp (car list)))
                    (print (car list))
                    (princ "has no function definition!")
                    (terpri))
                  (t (print list)
                    (princ "evaluates to: ")
                    (princ (eval list))
                    (terpri))))
```

```
        (t (print list)
          (princ "is not a list!")
          (terpri)))))
```

10.3
```
(defun yes-or-no ()
  (let (char)
    (terpri)
    (princ "Please indicate yes or no (y/n): ")
    (princ (string (setf char (read-char))))
    (terpri)
    (case char
      (#\Y (princ "The response is yes")(terpri))
      (#\y (princ "The response is yes")(terpri))
      (#\N (princ "The response is no")(terpri))
      (#\n (princ "The response is no")(terpri))
      (otherwise (princ "Invalid response")(terpri)))))
```

10.4
```
(defun count-character ()
  (let (char character (count 0))
   (terpri)
   (princ "Which character do you want to count? ")
   (princ (string (setf char (read-char))))
   (terpri)
   (princ "Please input a sentence: ")
   (loop
    (setf character (read-char))
    (cond ((equal character 10)
                (terpri)
                (princ "Character count is ")
                (princ count)
                (return))
            (t  (princ (string character))
                (if  (equal character char)
                     (setf count (1+ count))))))))
```

10.5
```
(defun sentence-length ()
  (let (line-length)
    (terpri)
    (princ "Please input a sentence: ")
    (setf line-length (length (read-line)))
    (princ "The length of the sentence is ")
    (princ line-length)
    (terpri)))
```

10.6
```
(defun look-for-word ()
  (let (word sentence token (pointer 0))
   (terpri)
   (princ "Please input a word: ")
   (setf word (read))
   (princ "Please input a sentence: ")
   (setf sentence (read-line))
```

```
    (loop
      (multiple-value-setq (token pointer)
          (read-from-string sentence nil 'end
            :preserve-whitespace nil
            :start pointer))
      (cond ((equal token 'end)
             (princ "Word is not contained in sentence")
             (return nil))
            ((equal token word)
             (princ "Word is contained in sentence")
             (return t))))))
```

10.7

```
(defun sentence-to-list-1 ()
  (let (input word (pointer 0) sentence)
    (terpri)
    (princ "Input a sentence: ")
    (setf input (read-line))
    (loop
      (multiple-value-setq (word pointer)
        (read-from-string input nil 'eof
              :start pointer
              :preserve-whitespace nil))
      (if (equal word 'eof)
        (return (reverse sentence)))
      (setf sentence (cons word sentence)))))
```

10.8

```
(defun sentence-to-list-2 ()
  (let ((punctuation-list '(39 44 46))(word "") sentence char)
    (terpri)
    (princ "Please input a sentence: ")
    (loop
     (setf char (read-char))
     (cond ((equal char 10)
            (ifn  (equal word "")
                  (setf sentence
                    (cons (read-from-string word)
                          sentence)))
                  (return (reverse sentence)))
           (t  (princ (string char))
               (cond ((member char punctuation-list)
                      (setf word
                        (string-append word "\\" char)))
                     ((equal char 32)
                      (setf sentence
                        (cons (read-from-string word)
                              sentence))
                      (setf word ""))
                     (t   (setf word
                        (string-append word char)))))))))
```

10.9

```
(defun read-from-file ()
  (let (in-stream value-read)
    (terpri)
    (princ "Please input name of file: ")
```

```
(setf in-stream (open (read-line) :direction :input))
(loop
 (setf value-read (read in-stream nil 'eof))
 (cond ((equal value-read 'eof)
          (terpri)
          (princ "All expressions have been read")
          (close in-stream)
          (return))
       (t  (print (eval value-read))))))
```

Note that if testfile is created with GMACS it must be called up as **testfile.lsp** to reflect the extension which is automatically added by GMACS

10.10
```
(defun hex-to-decimal ()
  (setf *read-base* 16)
  (let (number)
    (terpri)
    (princ "Please input hexadecimal integers: ")
    (loop
      (terpri)
      (setf number (read))
      (if (equal number 'exit)
        (return))
      (princ "= ")
      (princ number)))
  (setf *read-base* a))
```

Note that *read-base* must be reset to a(hex) = 10(dec)

Chapter 11 Output Functions

11.1
```
(progn
  (setf temp 68)
  (print (append '(the temperature is)
    (cons temp '(degrees Fahernheit)))))
```

11.2
```
(progn
  (setf temp 68)
  (terpri)
  (prin1 'the)(write-char #\space)
  (prin1 'temperature)(write-char #\space)
  (prin1 'is)(write-char #\space)
  (prin1 temp)(write-char #\space)
  (prin1 'degrees)(write-char #\space)
  (prin1 'fahrenheit))
```

11.3
```
(progn
  (setf temp 68)
  (terpri)
  (princ "THE TEMPERATURE IS ")
  (princ temp)
  (princ " DEGREES FAHRENHEIT"))
```

11.4
```
(defun blank-lines (lines)
  (let ((count 0))
   (cond ((integerp lines)
          (loop
            (when (= count lines)
                  (terpri)
                  (princ count)
                  (princ
                    " blank lines have been printed")
                  (return))
                  (terpri)
                  (setf count (1+ count))))
         (t (terpri)
            (princ "That's not an integer!")
            (terpri)))))
```

11.5
```
(defun pretty-print (function-name)
  (cond ((functionp function-name)
         (pprint (symbol-function function-name)))
        (t (terpri)
           (princ function-name)
           (princ " is not a function!")
           (terpri))))
```

11.6
```
(defun test-print-level ()
  (let (temp-print-level temp-list)
    (setf temp-print-level *print-level*)
    (terpri)
    (princ "New print level: ")
    (setf *print-level* (read))
    (princ "Input nested list: ")
    (setf temp-list (read))
    (print temp-list)
    (setf *print-level* temp-print-level)))
```

11.7
```
(defun test-print-length ()
  (let (temp-print-length temp-list)
    (setf temp-print-length *print-length*)
    (terpri)
    (princ "New print length: ")
    (setf *print-length* (read))
    (princ "Input list: ")
    (setf temp-list (read))
    (print temp-list)
    (setf *print-length* temp-print-length)))
```

11.8
```
(defun print-phone-numbers ()
  (terpri)
  (setf print-stream (open "prn" :direction :output))
  (setf data "")
  (princ "Input names and phone numbers: ")
  (terpri)
```

```
(loop
  (terpri print-stream)
  (setf data (read-line))
  (when (equal data "")
        (princ (string 10) print-stream)
        (close print-stream)
        (return))
  (princ data print-stream)))
```

11.9
```
(defun file-phone-numbers ()
  (terpri)
  (setf file-stream (open "b:telephon.lsp" :direction :output))
  (setf data "")
  (princ "Input names and phone numbers: ")
  (terpri)
  (loop
    (terpri file-stream)
    (setf data (read-line))
    (when (equal data "")(princ (string 10) file-stream)
          (close file-stream)(return))
    (princ data file-stream)))
```

11.10
```
(defun copy-file ()
  (let   (from-file to-file
          from-file-stream to-file-stream
          char letter)
    (terpri)
    (princ "File to be copied from? ")
    (setf from-file (read-line))
    (princ "File to be copied to? ")
    (setf to-file (read-line))
    (setf from-file-stream (open from-file :direction :input))
    (setf to-file-stream (open to-file :direction :output))
    (loop
      (setf char (read-char from-file-stream nil 'eof))
      (when (equal char 'eof)
            (close from-file-stream)
            (close to-file-stream)
            (return))
      (setf letter (string char))
      (princ letter)
      (princ letter to-file-stream))))
```

Chapter 12 Formatting Printed Output

12.1
```
(setq temp 68 humid 80)
(append '(temperature is)
  (cons temp
    (append '(degrees and humidity is)
      (cons humid '(percent)))))
```

12.2
```
(setq temp 68 humid 80)
`(temperature is ,temp degrees and humidity is ,humid percent)
```

12.3
```
(setq temp 68 humid 80)
(progn
  (princ "Temperature is ")
  (princ temp)
  (princ " degrees and humidity is ")
  (princ humid)
  (princ " percent"))
```

12.4
```
(setq temp 68 humid 80)
(format t "~%Temperature is ~a degrees and ~
  humidity is ~a percent" temp humid)
```

12.5
```
(defun convert-number ()
  (let (choice number)
  (terpri)
  (loop
   (format t "Convert number to: (1) Binary
                (2) Octal
                (3) Hexadecimal
                (4) Quit program ~%Your choice? ")
   (setf choice (read))
   (cond ((not (member choice '(1 2 3 4)))
             (format t "~a is not a viable option~%~%"
               choice))
         ((equal choice 4)(return))
         (t  (format t "Number to be converted: ")
             (setf number (read))
             (cond ((not (integerp number))
                      (format t "~a is not an ~
                        integer~%~%" number))
                   ((case choice
                      (1 (format t "Binary equivalent ~
                           is ~b~%~%" number))
                      (2 (format t "Octal equivalent ~
                           is ~o~%~%" number))
                      (3 (format t "Hexadecimal ~
                           equivalent is ~x~%~%" number)
                           )))))))))
```

12.6
```
(defun get-digit ()
  (format t "~%Please type in a digit from 0 to 3~%~%")
  (loop
    (setf char (read-char))
    (case char
      (48 (princ 0)(setf char 0))
      (49 (princ 1)(setf char 1))
      (50 (princ 2)(setf char 2))
      (51 (princ 3)(setf char 3))
      (otherwise (princ (string char))(setf char 4)))
    (format t "~[~%That's a 0~%~
        ~;~%That's a 1~%~
        ~;~%That's a 2~%~
        ~;~%That's a 3~%~
        ~:;~%Invalid character!~]" char)
    (ifn (member char '(0 1 2 3))(return))))
```

12.7
```
(defun test-predicate ()
  (let (value))
    (format t "~%Please input a predicate function:~%")
    (setf value (eval (read)))
    (format t "~:[~%The predicate is false~
      ~;~%The predicate is true~]" value))
```

12.8
```
(setf list
  '((|John Doe| (|12 Whitney Lane| 111-1111-1111))
    (|George Bush| (|The White House| 222-2222-2222))
    (|Alfred E. Neumann| (|c/o Mad Magazine| 333-3333-3333))))

(defun address-list ()
  (let (alist string)
   (terpri)
   (princ " Name ")
   (princ " Address ")
   (princ " Phone ")
   (terpri)
   (princ "--------------------")
   (princ "-----------------------")
   (princ "-------------")
   (setf alist list)
   (loop
    (ifn alist (return nil))
    (terpri)
    (setf string (princ (caar alist)))
    (spaces string 22)
    (setf string (princ (car (cadar alist))))
    (spaces string 25)
    (princ (cadr (cadar alist)))
    (setf alist (cdr alist)))))

(defun spaces (word tab)
  (let ((column (flatc word)))
   (loop
    (if (= column tab)
       (return column))
    (princ " ")
    (setf column (1+ column)))))
```

12.9
```
(defun print-address-list ()
  (let (print-stream alist string)
   (setf print-stream (open "prn" :direction :output))
   (terpri print-stream)
   (terpri)
   (princ " Name " print-stream)
   (princ " Name ")
   (princ " Address " print-stream)
   (princ " Address ")
   (princ " Phone " print-stream)
   (princ " Phone ")
   (terpri print-stream)
   (terpri)
   (princ "--------------------" print-stream)
```

```
      (princ "--------------------")
      (princ "----------------------" print-stream)
      (princ "----------------------")
      (princ "-------------" print-stream)
      (princ "-------------")
      (setf alist list)
        (loop
          (unless alist (princ (string 10) print-stream)
            (close print-stream)
            (return nil))
          (terpri print-stream)
        (terpri)
        (setf string (caar alist))
        (princ string)
        (princ string print-stream)
        (print-spaces string 22)
        (setf string (car (cadar alist)))
        (princ string)
        (princ string print-stream)
        (print-spaces string 25)
        (setf string (cadr (cadar alist)))
        (princ string)
        (princ string print-stream)
        (setf alist (cdr alist)))))

(defun print-spaces (word tab)
   (let ((column (flatc word)))
     (loop
       (if (= column tab)
          (return column))
       (princ " ")
       (princ " " print-stream)
       (setf column (1+ column)))))
```

12.10

```
(defun yes-or-no ()
      (terpri)
      (princ "Have you stopped beating your dog?")
      (format t "~:[~%Why not?~;~%About time, ~
         you dirty rascal!~]" (yes-or-no-p)))
```

Chapter 13 Iterative Programming

13.1

```
(defun mini-eliza ()
   (format t "~%HOW CAN I BE OF ASSISTANCE?~%~%")
   (let ((responses '("HOW INTERESTING!"
                      "PLEASE GO ON."
                      "TELL ME MORE.")))
     (loop
       (if (equal (read-line) "bye")
          (return (format t "THANK YOU, GOODBYE!")))
       (format t "~a~%~%" (car responses))
       (setf responses
         (append (cdr responses)
           (list (car responses)))))))
```

13.2
```
(defun our-reverse-1 (some-list)
  (let ((new-list nil))
    (loop
      (if (null some-list)
        (return new-list))
      (setf new-list (cons (car some-list) new-list))
      (setf some-list (cdr some-list)))))
```

13.3
```
(defun our-exponent (inte power)
  (let ((number 1))
    (loop
      (if (eql power 0)
        (return number))
      (setf number (* inte number))
      (setf power (1- power)))))
```

13.4
```
(defun our-member (arg1 arg2)
  (do ((remainder arg2 (cdr remainder)))
    ((null remainder) nil)
    (if (equal arg1 (car remainder))
      (return remainder))))
```

13.5
```
(defun pattern-match (list1 list2)
  (do ((rest1 list1 (cdr rest1))
       (rest2 list2 (cdr rest2)))
    ((not (equal (car rest1)(car rest2))) nil)
    (if (and (null rest1)(null rest2))
      (return t))))
```

13.6
```
(defun print-fruits (gro-list)
  (terpri)
  (dolist (fruit gro-list)
    (if (fruitp fruit)
      (format t "~a " fruit))))
(defun fruitp (gro-item)
  (member gro-item '(apples bananas pears grapes plums)))
(setf grocery-list
  '(apples cornflakes soap pears grapes rat-trap beer))
```

13.7
```
(defun tell-them-again (what how-many-times)
  (dotimes (count how-many-times)
    (terpri)
    (princ what)))
```

13.8
```
(defun our-intersection (list1 list2)
  (prog ((rest1 list1) inter-list element)
    again
    (if (null rest1)
      (return inter-list))
    (setf element (car rest1))
    (if (and (member element list2)
             (not (member element inter-list)))
      (setf inter-list (cons element inter-list)))
    (setf rest1 (cdr rest1))
    (go again)))
```

13.9
```
(defun our-nth-element (some-list inte)
  (prog ((rest-list some-list)(count inte))
    again
      (if (null rest-list)
          (return nil))
      (setf element (car rest-list))
      (if (zerop count)
          (return element))
      (setf rest-list (cdr rest-list))
      (setf count (1- count))
      (go again)))
```

13.10
```
(defun our-reverse-2 (some-list)
  (prog (new-list)
    again
      (if (null some-list)
          (return new-list))
      (setf new-list (cons (car some-list) new-list))
      (setf some-list (cdr some-list))
      (go again)))
```

Chapter 14 Writing Recursive Functions

14.1
```
(defun our-reverse (some-list)
  (if (null some-list)
      nil
      (append (our-reverse (cdr some-list))
        (list (car some-list)))))
```

14.2
```
(defun our-filter (item some-list)
  (cond ((null some-list) nil)
        ((equal (car some-list) item)
          (our-filter item (cdr some-list)))
        (t (cons (car some-list)
                 (our-filter item (cdr some-list))))))
```

14.3
```
(defun our-intersection (list1 list2)
  (cond ((null list1) nil)
        ((and (member (car list1) list2)
              (not (member (car list1)
                      (our-intersection (cdr list1) list2))))
              (cons (car list1)
                    (our-intersection (cdr list1) list2)))
        (t    (our-intersection (cdr list1) list2))))
```

14.4
```
(defun our-union (list1 list2)
  (cond ((null list1) list2)
        ((member (car list1) list2)
          (our-union (cdr list1) list2))
        (t  (cons (car list1)(our-union (cdr list1) list2)))))
```

14.5
```
(defun our-member (item some-list)
  (cond ((null some-list) nil)
        ((equal item (car some-list)) some-list)
        (t (our-member item (cdr some-list)))))
```

14.6
```
(defun tower-stack (n)
  (cond ((eql n 1)(list 1))
        (t (cons n (tower-stack (1- n))))))
```

14.7
```
(defun our-exponent (inte expt)
  (if (zerop expt)
     1
     (* inte (our-exponent inte (1- expt)))))
```

14.8
```
(defun count-atoms (object)
  (cond ((null object) 0)
        ((atom object) 1)
        (t (+ (count-atoms (car object))
              (count-atoms (cdr object))))))
```

14.9
```
(defun our-substitute (new old structure)
  (cond ((equal old structure) new)
        ((atom structure) structure)
        (t (cons (our-substitute new old (car structure))
                 (our-substitute new old (cdr structure))))))
```

14.10
```
(defun towers-of-hanoi (n from spare to)
   (let ((from-stack (tower-stack n))
         (spare-stack nil)
         (to-stack nil)
         (left from)
         (middle spare)
         (right to)
         (disk nil))
      (hanoi n from spare to)))

(defun tower-stack (n)
  (cond ((eql n 1)(list 1))
        (t (cons n (tower-stack (1- n))))))

(defun hanoi (n from spare to)
  (cond ((= n 1)(move-disk from to))
        (t (hanoi (1- n) from to spare)
           (move-disk from to)
           (hanoi (1- n) spare from to))))

(defun move-disk (from to)
  (adjust-tower-stacks from to)
  (setf printer (open "prn" :direction :output))
  (format printer "~%Move disk ~a from ~a to ~a" disk from to)
  (format printer "~%From stack = ~a" from-stack)
  (format printer "~%Spare stack = ~a" spare-stack)
  (format printer "~%To stack = ~a" to-stack)
  (princ (string 10) printer)
  (close printer))
```

```
(defun adjust-tower-stacks (from to)
  (cond ((eql from left)
            (setf disk (pop from-stack)))
         ((eql from middle)
            (setf disk (pop spare-stack)))
         (t  (setf disk (pop to-stack))))
  (cond ((eql to left)      (push disk from-stack))
         ((eql to middle) (push disk spare-stack))
         (t                (push disk to-stack))))
```

Chapter 15 Mapping Functions

15.1 (a) ((A D)(B E)(C F))
(b) (10 18 28)
(c) (2 3 4)
(d) (((1 2 3 4))((2 3 4))((3 4))((4)))
(e) (1 2 3 4)

15.2
```
(defun our-pairlis (key-list datum-list a-list)
  (append (mapcar #'list key-list datum-list) a-list))
```

15.3
```
(defun f-to-c (temp-list)
  (mapcar #'convert-temp temp-list))
(defun convert-temp (f)
  (truncate (* 5 (/ (- f 32) 9))))
```

15.4
```
(defun matchmaker (man-list woman-list)
  (mapcar #'list man-list woman-list))
```

15.5
```
(defun bovver (soccer-list)
  (ifn (some #'hooliganp soccer-list)
     (format t "~%Safe to attend the soccer match")))
(defun hooliganp (name)
  (or (equal name 'spike)
     (equal name 'skinhead)))
```

15.6
```
(defun check-even (number-list)
  (if (every #'evenp number-list)
    (format t "~%All the numbers are even")
    (format t "~%Not all the numbers are even")))
```

15.7
```
(defun find-number (x)
  (if (numberp x)
     (list x)))

(mapcan #'find-number mixed-list)
```

15.8
```
(defun our-mapcar (function-name list-1 list-2)
  (ifn (and list-1 list-2)
     nil
     (cons (funcall function-name (car list-1)(car list-2))
          (our-mapcar function-name
             (cdr list-1)(cdr list-2)))))
```

15.9
```
(defun our-mapc (function-name list-1 list-2)
   (do ((work-1 list-1 (cdr work-1))
         (work-2 list-2 (cdr work-2)))
      ((or (null work-1)(null work-2)) list-1)
      (funcall function-name (car work-1)(car work-2))))
```

15.10
```
(defun our-maplist (function-name list-1)
   (ifn list-1
      nil
      (cons (funcall function-name list-1)
            (our-maplist function-name (cdr list-1)))))
```

Chapter 16 Creating and Using Macros

16.1
```
(defmacro our-setq (name value)
   `(set ',name ,value))
```

16.2
```
(defmacro our-first (list)
   `(car ,list))

(defmacro our-rest (list)
   `(cdr ,list))
```

16.3
```
(defmacro our-caadr (list)
   `(car (car (cdr ,list))))
```

16.4
```
(defmacro our-when (test &rest others)
   `(cond (,test ,@others)))

(defmacro our-unless (test &rest others)
   `(cond ((not ,test) ,@others)))
```

We could alternatively use **&body** instead of **&rest** in both of the above examples.

16.5
```
(defmacro our-push (item stack)
   `(setf ,stack (cons ,item ,stack)))

(defmacro our-pop (stack)
   `(prog1 (car ,stack)
      (setf ,stack (cdr ,stack))))
```

Note that **prog1** (see Section 13.9) avoids the need for creating a temporary variable to store **(car stack)**.

16.6
```
(defmacro our-dolist (varlist &body body)
   `(do* ((lst ,(cadr varlist)(cdr lst))
          (,(car varlist)(car lst)(car lst)))
      ((null lst) ,(caddr varlist))
         ,@body))
```

do*, rather than **do**, is required in order to update the binding of **lst** to **(cdr lst)** *prior* to updating the binding of the list variable to **(car lst)**.

16.7
```
(defmacro our-mapcar (function list)
   `(do ((in-list ,list (cdr in-list))
         (out-list nil
             (append out-list (list (,function (car in-list))))))
        ((null in-list) out-list)))
```

16.8
```
(defmacro our-let (arg-list &body body)
   `((lambda ,(mapcar #'car arg-list) ,@body)
     ,@(mapcar #'cadr arg-list)))
```

The lambda expression creates a **prog**-like format in which the **let** variables, extracted by **(mapcar #'car arg-list)** comprise the lambda-list, followed by the body. The final **mapcar** expression splices onto the tail end of the lambda expression a list of the initial values to be bound to the program variables. The net result is as if a **let** construct was inserted in front of the body of forms. The best way to visualize the workings of the foregoing is to create an **our-let** statement, **setf** some symbol (say **example**) to the quoted statement (so you don't have to keep typing it in each time you experiment with it) and then execute **(pprint (macroexpand example))** which will provide a pretty-printed format of the expanded **our-let** macro.

16.9
```
(defmacro our-progv (symbols values &body body)
  `(do*    ((symbol-list ,symbols (cdr symbol-list))
            (value-list ,values (cdr value-list))
            (symbol (car symbol-list)(car symbol-list))
            (value (car value-list)(car value-list)))
      ((and    (null symbol-list)
               (null value-list)) ,@body)
      (cond    ((and value-list
                     (null symbol-list)))
               ((and symbol-list
                     (null value-list))
                  (makunbound symbol))
               (t  (set symbol value)))))
```

do* is used to provide for sequential evaluation since the bindings of **symbol** and **value** depend on the previous bindings of **symbol-list** and **value-list**.

16.10
```
(defmacro our-do (letlist testlist &body body)
   `((lambda ,(mapcar #'(lambda (var)
         (if (atom var)
             var
             (car var))) letlist)
      (loop
         (if ,(car testlist)
             (return
                (let ((restlist (cdr ',testlist))
                      (carlist nil))
                   (loop
                      (setf carlist (eval (car restlist)))
                      (setf restlist (cdr restlist))
                      (ifn  restlist
                            (return carlist))))))
```

```
,@body
(psetq
  ,@(mapcan #'(lambda (var)
        (if (atom var)
            nil)
        (if (caddr var)
            (list (car var)(caddr var))))
              letlist))))
  ,@(mapcar #'(lambda (var)
        (if (atom var)
            nil
            (cadr var))) letlist)))
```

As opposed to the previous example of **let**, singleton index variables are allowed. The first **mapcar** operation therefore uses a lambda construct to test for this case in order to return the appropriate (symbolic) value; the final **mapcar** operation carries out a similar exercise in order to provide a value of **nil** to be bound to a singleton index variable. After establishing initial bindings, a loop is set up to permit repetitive evaluation of the forms which make up the body of the macro; after each round of evaluation, stepping operations are carried out on the index variables. This is in turn achieved through a **mapcan** operation which traverses the variable list, identifies those index variables which include a stepping argument, and incorporates the variable/stepping-form pairs into an overall **psetq** function call to reflect that **do** evaluations are carried out in parallel.

Chapter 17 Blocks, Exits, and Multiple Values

17.1
```
(defun get-numbers-1 ()
  (block no-number
    (terpri)
    (loop
     (format t "Please input a number: ")
     (ifn (numberp (read))
          (return-from no-number
            (format t "That's not a number!"))))))
```

17.2
```
(defun get-numbers-2 ()
  (catch 'no-number
    (terpri)
    (loop
     (format t "Please input a number: ")
     (ifn (numberp (read))
          (throw 'no-number
            (format t "That's not a number!"))))))
```

17.3
```
(defun get-numbers-3 ()
  (catch 'no-number
    (terpri)
    (let ((file-stream nil)
          (number 0))
      (unwind-protect
          (progn
            (setf file-stream
              (open "c:number" :direction :output))
```

```
            (loop
                (format t "Please input a number: ")
                (setf number (read))
                (ifn (numberp number)
                    (throw 'no-number
                        (format t "That's not a number!"))
                    (print number file-stream))))
        (close file-stream)))))
```

17.4
```
(defun our-substitute (new old old-list)
  (do* ((work-list old-list (cdr work-list))
        (new-list nil (cons item new-list))
        (element (car work-list)(car work-list))
        (flag nil))
    ((null work-list)(values (reverse new-list) flag))
    (cond ((equal element old)
           (setf item new)
           (setf flag t))
          (t  (setf item element)))))
```

17.5
```
(defun parents-names-1 ()
  (let ((father nil)
        (mother nil))
    (format t "~%Please input father's name: ")
    (setf father (read))
    (format t "Please input mother's name: ")
    (setf mother (read))
    (values father mother)))
```

17.6
```
(defun parents-names-2 ()
  (let ((parents nil))
    (format t "~%Please input father's name: ")
    (setf parents (cons (read) parents))
    (format t "Please input mother's name: ")
    (setf parents (cons (read) parents))
    (values-list (reverse parents))))
```

17.7
```
(multiple-value-setq (*father* *mother*)
  (parents-names-1))
```

17.8
```
(multiple-value-bind (father mother)
  (parents-names-1)
  (format t "~%I understand your father's ~
    name is ~s and your mother's name is ~s"
    father mother))
```

17.9
```
(multiple-value-list (parents-names-1))
```

17.10
```
(defmacro our-multiple-value-call (function &rest rest)
  `(apply ,function
     (do* ((work-list '(,@rest) (cdr work-list))
           (value-list nil))
       ((null work-list)
        value-list)
```

```
        (setf value-list
          (append value-list
            (multiple-value-list
              (eval (car work-list)))))))
```

Chapter 18 Property and Association Lists

18.1
```
(defun put (symbol indicator value)
  (setf (get symbol indicator) value))
```

18.2
```
(defun put-prop (symbol indicator value)
  (let ((counter 0)
        (prop-list (symbol-plist symbol))
        (prop-length (length prop-list))
        (key (caar prop-list)))
  (loop
    (when (equal counter prop-length)
      (setf (symbol-plist symbol)
        (cons (cons indicator value)
          (symbol-plist symbol)))
      (return value))
    (when (equal key indicator)
      (setf (nth counter (symbol-plist symbol))
        (cons indicator value))
      (return value))
    (setf prop-list (cdr prop-list))
    (setf key (caar prop-list))
    (setf counter (1+ counter)))))
```

;Use of assoc to locate the key/value pair provides a shorter algorithm:

```
(defun put-prop (symbol indicator value)
  (let*   ((plist (symbol-plist symbol))
           (prop-pair (assoc indicator plist)))
    (when prop-pair
          (setf plist (delete prop-pair plist)))
    (setf (symbol-plist symbol)
      (cons (cons indicator value) plist))
    value))
```

18.3
```
(defun get-prop (symbol indicator)
  (if (setf prop-pair (assoc indicator (symbol-plist symbol)))
    (cdr prop-pair)))
```

18.4
```
(defun rem-prop (symbol indicator)
  (let (prop-pair)
    (when (setf prop-pair
            (assoc indicator (symbol-plist symbol)))
          (setf (symbol-plist symbol)
            (delete prop-pair (symbol-plist symbol)))
          prop-pair)))
```

18.5
```
(defun get-indicators (symbol)
  (let  ((prop-list (symbol-plist symbol))
         (indicator-list nil))
   (loop
    (ifn prop-list
        (return (reverse indicator-list)))
    (setf indicator-list
      (cons (car prop-list) indicator-list))
    (setf prop-list (cddr prop-list)))))
```

18.6
```
(setf place-list '(one sun two shoe three tree four door))

(defun search-place-list (list1 list2)
   (let (pairs-list)
      (loop
         (ifn list1
              (return (reverse pairs-list)))
         (multiple-value-setq (one two three)
            (get-properties list1 list2))
         (format t "~%one = ~a" one)
         (format t "~%two = ~a" two)
         (format t "~%three = ~a" three)
         (if three
            (setf pairs-list (cons (list one two) pairs-list)))
         (format t "~%Pairs list = ~a" pairs-list)
         (setf list1 (cddr three))
         (format t "~%List1 = ~a" list1 ))))
```

18.7
```
(defun get-inherit (symbol indicator)
   (let (value sym)
      (if (setf value (get symbol indicator))
         value
         (if (setf sym (get symbol 'is-a))
            (get-inherit sym indicator)))))
```

18.8
```
(defun add-book ()
   (let (book-list author title)
      (loop
         (format t "~%Author's name: ")
         (setf author (read))
         (if (equal author 'exit)
            (return))
         (format t "Book title : ")
         (setf title (read-line))
         (if (equal title "exit")
            (return))
         (setf book-list
            (acons author title book-list)))))
```

18.9
```
(defun get-book ()
  (let (author book-name)
   (format t "~%Author's name: ")
   (setf author (read))
```

```
        (if (setf book-name
              (cdr (assoc author book-list)))
            book-name
            (format t "There is no such author on the list"))))
```

18.10
```
(defun get-author ()
   (let (book-name author)
      (format t "~%Name of book: ")
      (setf book-name (read-line))
      (if (setf author
               (car (rassoc book-name book-list :test #'equal)))
          author
          (format t "There is no such book on the list"))))
```

Note that the optional **test** keyword must be specified as #'**equal** since the strings pointed to by the value cell of book-name and the cdr cell of the indicator/value pair are not the same data object

Chapter 19 Working with Streams

19.1
```
(progn
   (let (out-stream)
      (setf out-stream
         (open "b:test.1.lsp" :direction :output))
      (print '(setq apples 10 pears 15 grapes 20) out-stream)
      (print '(defun add-em-up (one two three)
         (+ one two three)) out-stream)
      (print '(add-em-up apples pears grapes) out-stream)
      (close out-stream)))
```

19.2
```
(with-open-file
   (out-stream "b:test.2.lsp" :direction :output)
   (print '(setq apples 10 pears 15 grapes 20) out-stream)
   (print '(defun add-em-up (one two three)
      (+ one two three)) out-stream)
   (print '(add-em-up apples pears grapes) out-stream))
```

19.3
```
(progn
  (let (in-stream input)
   (setf in-stream
     (open "b:test.1.lsp" :direction :input))
   (loop
    (setf input (read in-stream nil 'eof))
    (when (equal input 'eof)
          (close in-stream)
          (return))
    (print (eval input)))))
```

19.4
```
(with-open-file
   (in-stream "b:test.2.lsp" :direction :input)
   (let (input)
      (loop
         (setf input (read in-stream nil 'eof))
```

```
        (if (equal input 'eof)
           (return))
        (print (eval input)))))
```

19.5
```
(defun string-to-list ()
   (let (in-stream sentence token)
      (terpri)
      (princ "Please input a line of text: ")
      (setf in-stream (make-string-input-stream (read-line)))
      (setf sentence nil)
      (loop
         (setf token (read in-stream nil 'eof))
         (if (equal token 'eof)
            (return (reverse sentence)))
         (setf sentence (cons token sentence)))))
```

19.6
```
(defun princ-to-string (arg)
   (let (string-stream)
      (setf string-stream (make-string-output-stream))
      (princ arg string-stream)
      (get-output-stream-string string-stream)))
```

19.7
```
(defun make-string-list ()
   (let (out-stream p-list last-char char token sentence)
     (terpri)
     (princ "Please input a line of text: ")
     (setf out-stream (make-string-output-stream))
     (setf p-list '(39 44 46))
     (setf last-char 32)
     (loop
      (setf char (read-char))
      (when (equal char 10)
            (setf token
              (read-from-string
                (get-output-stream-string out-stream)))
            (if token (setf sentence (cons token sentence)))
            (return (reverse sentence)))
      (when (and (equal char 32)(not (equal last-char 32)))
            (setf token
              (read-from-string
                (get-output-stream-string out-stream)))
            (setf sentence (cons token sentence))
            (setf token nil))
      (cond ((member char p-list)
                (princ (string-append "\ \" (string char))
                   out-stream)
                (princ (string-append "\ \" (string char))))
            (t  (princ (string char) out-stream)
                (princ (string char))))
      (setf last-char char))))
```

19.8
```
(defun make-list-string ()
  (let (list out-stream char)
   (terpri)
   (princ "Please input a list: ")
   (setf list (read))
   (cond ((not (listp list))
          "That's not a list! Try again.")
         (t (setf out-stream (make-string-output-stream))
            (princ list out-stream)
            (setf in-stream
              (make-string-input-stream
                (get-output-stream-string out-stream)))
            (loop
             (setf char (read-char in-stream nil 'eof))
             (if (equal char 'eof)
                 (return (get-output-stream-string
                          out-stream)))
             (ifn (or (equal char 40)(equal char 41))
                  (princ (string char) out-stream)))))))
```

19.9
```
(progn
  (setf file-stream-1 (open "b:test.3" :direction :output))
  (setf file-stream-2 file-stream-1)
  (make-synonym-stream file-stream-2))
```

19.10
```
(defvar *string* "")
(defun string-output-stream (operation &optional arg)
  (case operation
    (:write-char
      (setf *string* (string-append *string* (string arg))))
    (:which-operations
      '(:write-char :which-operations))
    (otherwise
      (error "Unknown output stream operation: ~s"))))
```

Chapter 20 What's in a Character?

20.1 It is suggested that you draw a large diagram with space on each key to include the codes generated by the keychords as illustrated below.

You can generate only the standard character set plus a few odd characters corresponding to the function keys, backspace key, etc.

The Control, Alt, and Shift keys are significant when used in conjunction with another key. Both Control and Alt include an (implicit) Shift key effect; and the Alt key overrides the Control key (hence you cannot set *both* the :Control and :Meta bits with any keychord).

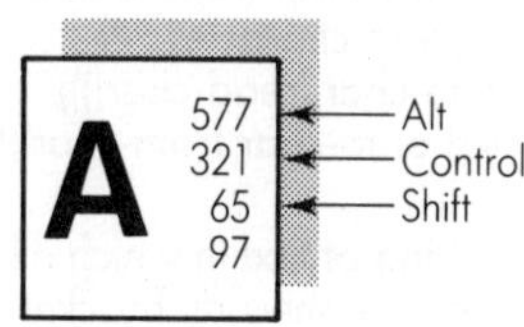

20.2
```
(defun print-char ()
  (let ((char 0) printer)
    (terpri)
    (loop
      (setf printer (open "prn" :direction :output))
      (when (char= char 256)
            (princ (string 10) printer)
            (close printer)
            (return))
      (format t "~a = ~a~%" char (string char))
      (if (or (char= char 19)(char= char 147))
         (princ (format nil "~a = Ctrl-S" char) printer)
         (princ (format nil "~a = ~a"
           char (string char)) printer))
      (princ (string 10) printer)
      (close printer)
      (setf char (1+ char)))))
```

Note that special handling is required to nullify the effects of ^S (ASCII 19 and its equivalent with the high bit set), which otherwise turns off the printer. Other odd effects are noted with ASCII 10, 11, and 23 which skip a space, 12 which causes a form feed, and 15 and 18 which condense and re-expand font size.

Also, when the high bit is set MS-DOS prints the standard character set in italics (see Exercise 19.6).

20.3
```
(setf f-list '((224 F1)(225 F2)(226 F3)(227 F4)(232 F5)
  (233 F6)(234 F7)(236 F8)(237 F9)(238 F10)))

(defun function-keys ()
  (let (key)
    (format t "~%Press a function key:~%")
    (loop
      (if (setf key (cadr (assoc (read-char) f-list)))
        (format t "You have pressed key ~a~%" key)
        (return)))))
```

20.4
```
(set-macro-character #\{
  #'(lambda (stream char)
     (loop
      (if (char= 125 (read-char stream t nil t))
          (return (values t t))))))
```

where ASCII 125 is a right curly bracket

20.5
```
(defun copy-syntax ()
  (let ((from-char 0)(to-char 0))
    (format t "~%Copy from character: ")
    (princ (string (setf from-char (read-char))))
    (format t "~%Copy to character : ")
    (princ (string (setf to-char (read-char))))
    (set-syntax-from-char to-char from-char)))
```

20.6
```
(setf *text* "This is a string of text in which all characters which fall between a
  left curly bracket { and a right curly bracket } are to be printed in italics.")
```

```
(defun print-italics ()
  (let (text-stream italics-flag print-stream char)
    (setf text-stream (make-string-input-stream *text*))
    (setf italics-flag nil)
    (setf print-stream (open "prn" :direction :output))
    (loop
      (setf char (read-char text-stream nil 'eof))
      (if (char= char 125)
        (setf italics-flag nil))
      (when (char= char 'eof)
            (princ (string 10) print-stream)
            (close print-stream)
            (return))
      (ifn italics-flag
          (princ (string char) print-stream)
          (princ (string (+ char 128)) print-stream))
      (if (char= char 123)
        (setf italics-flag t)))))
```

20.7

```
(defun get-char-names ()
  (let ((char 0))
   (format t "~%ASCII Name")
   (format t "~%---------------~%")
   (loop
    (if (char= char 128)
      (return))
    (when (char-name char)
          (cond ((> char 99)(princ " "))
                ((< char 10)(princ "   "))
                (t          (princ "  ")))
          (format t "~a ~a~%" char (char-name char)))
    (setf char (1+ char)))))
```

20.8

```
(defun get-standard-char ()
  (let ((char 0)(count 0))
    (loop
      (if (char= char 128)
        (return))
      (if (standard-char-p char)
        (princ (string char)))
      (setf char (1+ char))
      (setf count (1+ count))
      (when (equal count 10)
            (princ (string 10))
            (setf count 0)))))
```

20.9

```
(defun get-digit-char (radix)
  (let ((char 0))
   (format t "~%The following characters represent")
   (format t "~%digits of radix base ~a:~%~%" radix)
   (loop
    (if (char= char 128)
      (return))
```

```
      (if (and (digit-char-p char radix)
               (or (upper-case-p char)
                   (not (both-case-p char))))
        (princ (string char)))
      (setf char (1+ char)))))
```

20.10
```
(defun get-both-case-char ()
  (let ((char 0))
    (loop
      (if (char= char 128)
        (return))
      (if (and (both-case-p char)
               (not (upper-case-p char)))
        (format t "~%~a --> ~a"
          (string char)(string (char-upcase char))))
      (setf char (1+ char)))))
```

Chapter 21 Working with Strings

21.1 (a) `(setf test-string (symbol-name 'apple))`

(b) `(setf test-string "I like apples!")`

(c)
```
(setf temp 68)
(setf test-string (format nil
"The temperature is ~a degrees" temp))
```

21.2 `(setf sentence (read-line))`

21.3
```
(defun print-char ()
  (let (number)
    (format t "~%Please input an integer: ~%")
    (loop
      (setf number (read))
      (ifn (integerp number)(return))
      (format t "~a = ~a~%" number (string number)))))
```

21.4
```
(defun count-char ()
  (let (input-string string-length input-char
        (index 0)(count 0))
   (format t "~%Please input a string: ~%")
   (setf input-string (read-line))
   (setf string-length (length input-string))
   (format t "Please input a character: ~%")
   (setf input-char (read-char))
   (princ (string input-char))
   (loop
    (when (equal index string-length)
          (format t "~%The character ~a appears ~
            ~a times in the string"
            (string input-char) count)
          (return))
    (if (equal (char input-string index) input-char)
       (setf count (1+ count)))
    (setf index (1+ index)))))
```

21.5
```
(defun equal-strings ()
   (let (first-string second-string)
      (format t "~%Please input the first string: ~%")
      (setf first-string (read-line))
      (format t "Please input the second string: ~%")
      (setf second-string (read-line))
      (if (string= first-string second-string)
         (format t "The two strings are equal")
         (format t "The two strings are different"))))
```

21.6
```
(defun unequal-strings ()
   (let (first-string second-string)
      (format t "~%Please input the first string: ~%")
      (setf first-string (read-line))
      (format t "Please input the second string: ~%")
      (setf second-string (read-line))
      (if (string< first-string second-string)
         (format t "The first string is less")
         (format t "The first string is not less"))))
```

21.7
```
(defun test-string ()
   (format t "~%Please input an S-expression: ~%")
   (if (stringp (eval (read)))
      (format t "~%The object is a string")
      (format t "~%The object is not a string")))
```

21.8
```
(defun punctuation-trim ()
   (let (sentence char-bag)
      (format t "~%Please input a sentence: ~%")
      (setf sentence (read-line))
      (setf char-bag ".!?")
      (format t "Trimmed sentence is:")
      (format t "~%~a"
         (string-right-trim char-bag sentence))))
```

21.9
```
(defun search-string ()
   (let (sentence end-index sub-string
          (index 0)(count 0) value)
    (format t "~%Please input a line of text: ~%")
    (setf sentence (read-line))
    (setf end-index (length sentence))
    (format t "Please input a sub-string: ~%")
    (setf sub-string (read-line))
    (loop
          (when (equal index end-index)
                  (format t "The sub-string occurs ~a ~
                    times within the string" count)
                  (return))
          (cond  ((setf value
                         (string-search sub-string sentence index))
                      (setf index (+ value (length sub-string)))
                      (setf count (1+ count)))
                  (t (setf index end-index))))))
```

21.10
```
(defun print-name ()
  (let (name address)
    (format t "~%Name? : ")
    (setf name (read-line))
    (format t "Address? : ")
    (setf address (read-line))
    (do ((blank-spaces "" (string-append " " blank-spaces))
         (count 0 (1+ count)))
      ((= 30 (+ count (length name)))
      (format t "~%~%~a~a~a"
         name blank-spaces address)))))
```

Chapter 22 Numbers, Arrays, and Structures

22.1
(a) (numberp n)
(b) (integerp n)
(c) (floatp n)

22.2
(a) (plusp x)
(b) (minusp x)
(c) (zerop x)
(d) (oddp x)
(e) (evenp x)

22.3
(a) (= x y)
(b) (/= x y)
(c) (< x y)
(d) (> x y)

22.4 (incf (get 'harry 'age))

22.5
```
(setf hex-array
  (make-array 16 :initial-contents
    '(0 1 2 3 4 5 6 7 8 9 A B C D E F)))
(setf hex-array (vector 0 1 2 3 4 5 6 7 8 9 A B C D E F))
```

22.6
```
(defun hex-to-dec (digit)
  (if (integerp digit)
    digit
    (case digit
      (A 10)
      (B 11)
      (C 12)
      (D 13)
      (E 14)
      (F 15))))
(setf hex-array
  (make-array 16
    :initial-contents '(0 1 2 3 4 5 6 7 8 9 A B C D E F)
    :leader-length 1))
(store-array-leader 'hex-to-dec hex-array 0)
```

```
(defun get-hex-array (array)
  (let ((fun-def (array-leader array 0)))
    (dotimes (index (array-active-length array))
      (format t "~%Element ~a = ~a (hex) = ~a (dec)"
        index
        (aref array index)
        (funcall fun-def (aref array index))))))
```

22.7
```
(defun convert-array (array)
  (let ((fun-def (array-leader array 0)))
    (dotimes (index (array-active-length array))
      (setf (aref array index)
        (funcall fun-def (aref array index))))))
```

22.8
```
(defstruct show-dog
  pedigree-name breed sex age)

(setf beaudog
  (make-show-dog :pedigree-name "Steeleblade Beaulieu Woofniks"
                 :breed 'boxer
                 :sex 'male
                 :age 5))
```

22.9
```
(defstruct show-dog
  pedigree-name (breed 'boxer) (sex 'male) age)
```

22.10
```
(defstruct (show-dog (:type list) :named)
  pedigree-name breed sex age)

(defun show-dog-p (object)
  (and (consp x)
       (eq (car x) 'show-dog)))
```

Chapter 23 Interfacing with File Systems

23.1
```
(defun get-pathname ()
  (let (dev dir nam typ)
   (format t "~%Device name : ")
   (setf dev (read-line))
   (if (equal dev "")
       (setf dev nil))
   (format t "Directory name: ")
   (setf dir (string-append "\ \" (read-line)))
   (if (equal dir "\ \")
       (setf dir nil))
   (format t "File name : ")
   (setf nam (read-line))
   (if (equal nam "")
       (setf nam nil))
   (format t "Extension : ")
   (setf typ (read-line))
   (if (equal typ "")
       (setf typ nil))
```

```
(make-pathname :device dev
               :directory dir
               :name nam
               :type typ)))
```

23.2
```
(setf *default-pathname-defaults* "b:\\lispprog\\filename.lsp")
(merge-pathnames "lispfile")
```

23.3
```
(defun check-file ()
  (let (path)
    (format t "~%Pathname: ")
    (setf path (read-line))
    (if (probe-file path)
      (format t "File ~a exists" path)
      (format t "File ~a does not exist" path))))
```

Note that only one slash is required for input, since **read-line** automatically adds the other (single escape character) slash.

23.4
```
(defun get-files (pathname)
  (dolist (file-name (directory pathname))
    (format t "~%~a" (file-namestring file-name))))
```

23.5
(a) `(pathname           "c:\\ws\\our-file.lsp")`
(b) `(pathname-device    "c:\\ws\\our-file.lsp")`
(c) `(pathname-directory "c:\\ws\\our-file.lsp")`
(d) `(pathname-name      "c:\\ws\\our-file.lsp")`
(e) `(pathname-type      "c:\\ws\\our-file.lsp")`

23.6
```
(with-open-file (file-stream "c:\\ws\\my-file.lsp"
      :direction :output)
  (print '(setf *print-base* nil *print-level* nil)
    file-stream))
```

23.7
```
(with-open-file
  (file-stream "c:\\ws\\my-file.lsp" :direction :input)
  (with-open-file
    (print-stream "prn" :direction :output)
    (let (expression)
     (loop
      (setf expression (read file-stream nil 'eof))
      (cond ((equal expression 'eof)
             (print (string 10) print-stream)
             (return))
            (t (print expression print-stream)))))))
```

Note that a **with-open-file** can be nested within another **with-open-file** to permit transactions involving more than one file.

23.8
```
(with-open-file
  (new-stream "c:\\ws\\new-file.lsp" :direction :output)
  (with-open-file
    (file-stream "c:\\ws\\my-file.lsp" :direction :input)
    (let (expression)
     (loop
```

```
        (setf expression (read file-stream nil 'eof))
        (if (equal expression 'eof)
          (return)
          (print expression new-stream)))
      (print '(defun factorial (n)
               (if (zerop n)
                 1
                 (* n (factorial (1- n)))))
             new-stream))))
  (delete-file "c:\\ws\\my-file.lsp")
  (rename-file "c:\\ws\\new-file.lsp" "c:\\ws\\my-file.lsp")
```

23.9 `(load "c:\\ws\\my-file.lsp" :print t)`

23.10

```
(defun our-load (path)
  (cond ((not (probe-file path))
         (error "File ~a does not exist" path))
        (t (format t "~%Reading file ~a" (namestring path))
           (with-open-file (file-stream path :direction :input)
             (let (expression)
               (loop
                 (setf expression
                   (read file-stream nil 'eof))
                 (if (equal expression 'eof)
                   (return (pathname path)))
                 (eval expression)))))))
```

Chapter 24 Debugging, Tracing, and Timing

24.1

```
(defun get-name ()
  (let (name)
    (format t "~%Please type your name: ")
    (setf name (read))
    (ifn (symbolp name)
      (error "Name is not a symbol: ~s" name))
      name))
```

24.2

```
(defun plus-or-minus ()
  (let (number)
   (format t "~%Please input an integer: ")
   (setf number (read))
   (ifn (integerp number)
      (error "Number is not an integer: ~a" number))
   (cond ((> number 0)(format t "Number is positive"))
         ((< number 0)(format t "Number is negative"))
         (t           (format t "Number is zero")))))
```

24.3

```
(defun get-file-name ()
  (let ((file-name nil))
   (format t "~%Please input file name: ")
   (setf file-name (read-line))
   (when (> (length file-name) 8)
         (cerror "Truncating to 8 characters"
                 "File name is in excess of 8 characters")
         (subseq file-name 0 8))))
```

24.4
```
(defun what-time ()
  (let (hours minutes seconds)
    (format t "~%Please input the time: ~% hours : ")
    (setf hours (read))
    (if (or (not (integerp hours))
            (minusp hours)
            (> hours 23))
      (cerror "Hours defaults to 00"
              "Invalid entry for hours: ~a" hours))
    (format t " minutes: ")
    (setf minutes (read))
    (if (or (not (integerp minutes))
            (minusp minutes)
            (> minutes 59))
      (cerror "Minutes defaults to 00"
              "Invalid entry for minutes: ~a" minutes))
    (format t " seconds: ")
    (setf seconds (read))
    (if (or (not (integerp seconds))
            (minusp seconds)
            (> seconds 59))
      (cerror "Seconds defaults to 00"
              "Invalid entry for seconds: ~a" seconds))
    (values hours minutes seconds)))
```

24.5
```
(defun add-integers (num1 num2)
  (ifn (ignore-errors (+ num1 num2))
       (format t "~%Sum exceeds the allowable limit")
       (format t "~%The sum is ~a" (+ num1 num2))))
```

24.6
```
(defun timing-cycle (x y)
  (let ((sys:*break-event* #'break-interrupt))
    (catch 'resume
      (dotimes (a x)
        (declare (special a))
        (format t "~%a = ~a" a)
        (dotimes (b y)
          (declare (special b))
          (format t "~%b = ~a" b))))))

(defun break-interrupt ()
  (throw 'resume
    (format t "~%Timing cycle was interrupted ~
                        at the following values:
    a = ~a
    b = ~a" a (if (boundp 'b) b "UNBOUND"))))
```

24.7
```
(defun trace-factorial (n)
  (trace factorial)
  (eval (factorial n))
  (untrace factorial))

(defun factorial (x)
  (if (zerop x)
    1
    (* x (factorial (1- x)))))
```

24.8
```
(defun tell-time ()
  (multiple-value-bind
    (second minute hour date month year)
     (get-decoded-time)
  (case month
    (1  (setf month "January"))    (2  (setf month "February"))
    (3  (setf month "March"))      (4  (setf month "April"))
    (5  (setf month "May"))        (6  (setf month "June"))
    (7  (setf month "July"))       (8  (setf month "August"))
    (9  (setf month "September")) (10 (setf month "October"))
    (10 (setf month "November")) (12 (setf month "December")))
  (format t "~%It is ~a:~a:~a on ~a ~a, ~a"
    hour minute second month date year)))
```

24.9
```
(defun time-delay (seconds)
  (block nil
    (let ((sec-1 0)(sec-2 0))
      (setf sec-1 (get-decoded-time))
      (loop
        (setf sec-2 (get-decoded-time))
        (if (minusp (- sec-2 sec-1))
          (setf sec-2 (+ 60 sec-2)))
        (if (>= (- sec-2 sec-1) seconds)
          (return))))))
```

Using nested dotime loops with variable parameters is not a dependable way to establish time delays due to the variable amount of function-calling overhead involved.

24.10
```
(defun multiple-time-elapsed (one two three)
  (let ((count 1)(min-tot 0)(sec-tot 0)(hun-tot 0))
    (get-time (dotimes (n 5000)
      (dotimes (n one))))
    (setf hun-tot (+ hun hun-tot)
          sec-tot (+ sec sec-tot)
          min-tot (+ min min-tot)
          count 2)
    (get-time (dotimes (n 5000)
      (dotimes (n two))))
    (setf hun-tot (+ hun hun-tot)
          sec-tot (+ sec sec-tot)
          min-tot (+ min min-tot)
          count 3)
    (get-time (dotimes (n 5000)
      (dotimes (n three))))
    (setf hun-tot (+ hun hun-tot)
          sec-tot (+ sec sec-tot)
          min-tot (+ min min-tot))
    (loop
      (if (minusp (- hun-tot 100))
        (return)
        (setf hun-tot (- hun-tot 100)
          sec-tot (1+ sec-tot))))
```

```
(loop
   (if (minusp (– sec-tot 60))
      (return)
      (setf sec-tot (– sec-tot 60)
         min-tot (1+ min-tot))))
(format t "~%~%Total time elapsed = ~a:~a.~a"
   min-tot sec-tot hun-tot)))
```

Modify the **format** statement of the **time-elapsed** macro to read: **(format t "~%Time elapsed in loop ~a = ~a:~a.~a" count min sec hun)**

Chapter 25 Packages

25.1 The four basic packages built into Common Lisp are:

LISP	which contains LISP primitives and global variables
KEYWORD	which contains LISP and user-defined keywords
SYSTEM	which contains implementation-specific primitives
USER	which contains user-defined symbols

25.2 (a) ***package***
(b) **(symbol-package 'hotdog)**
(c) **(find-package 'keyword)**

25.3
```
(make-package "screen-editor" :nicknames ("ed")
                              :use ("dave" "john"))
```

25.4 (a) **(export '(dave::gin dave::beer) 'dave)**
(b) **(import '(dave::gin dave::beer))**
(c) **(use-package '(john dave))**

25.5
```
(defun check-package-symbols (fun-list)
   (do ((function-list fun-list (cdr function-list)))
      ((endp function-list))
      (format t "~%~a is contained in ~a"
         (car function-list)
         (symbol-package (car function-list)))))
```

25.6
```
(defun get-package-symbols (package-name)
   (let ((package (find-package package-name)))
      (if package
         (apropos "" package)
         (error "~a is not a package" package-name))))
```

25.7
```
(defun print-package-symbols (package-name)
   (let ((package (find-package package-name))
         (count 0)
         (toggle 0))
      (terpri)
      (cond ((not package)
                (error "~a is not a package" package-name))
            (t (dolist (symb (apropos-list "" package))
                  (incf count)
```

```
          (if (= toggle 0)
             (format t "~%~a~a ~a~a"
               (zeros count) count symb
               (spaces symb)))
          (if (= toggle 1)
             (format t "~a~a ~a" (zeros count)
               count symb))
          (if (= toggle 0)
             (setf toggle 1)
             (setf toggle 0)))))))

(defun zeros (numb)
  (cond ((< numb 10) "000")
        ((< numb 100) "00")
        ((< numb 1000) "0")
        (t              "")))

(defun spaces (item)
  (let ((blanks (- 35 (flatc item)))
        (skip-spaces ""))
    (dotimes (n blanks skip-spaces)
      (setf skip-spaces (string-append " " skip-spaces)))))
```

25.8

```
(defun count-package-symbols ()
  (let ((packages '(lisp keyword system user)))
    (format t "~%~%Package   Symbols")
    (format t "~%-------   -------")
    (dolist (item packages)
      (format t "~%~a~a" (item-spaces item) item)
      (let ((count
              (length (apropos-list "" (find-package item))
        (format t "~a~a" (count-spaces count) count)))))))

(defun item-spaces (symbol)
  (case symbol
    (lisp "   ")
    (keyword "")
    (system " ")
    (user "   ")))

(defun count-spaces (number)
  (cond ((< number 10) "          ")
        ((< number 100) "         ")
        ((< number 1000) "        ")
        (t              "       ")))
```

25.9

```
(defun package-symbol-lengths (package-name)
  (format t "~%~% Package: ~a" package-name)
  (format t "~% Length Symbols")
  (format t "~% ------------")
  (let ((pack-array (make-array 35 :element-type 'integer
                                   :initial-element 0))
        (count 0)
        (total-count 0))
```

```
(dolist (symbol
        (apropos-list "" (find-package package-name)))
  (setf count (flatc symbol))
  (incf (aref pack-array count)))
(dotimes (n 35 (format t "~%~% Total count: ~a"
           total-count))
  (setf count (aref pack-array n))
  (unless (or (zerop n)(zerop count))
           (format t "~%~a~a~a~a"
             (count-spaces n) n
             (count-spaces count) count)
           (setf total-count (+ count total-count))))))
```

NB: count-spaces from Exercise 25.3 is re-utilized for this Exercise

25.10
```
(defmacro our-do-symbols ((var package result-form) &body body)
  `(do* ((package-list
          (apropos-list "" (find-package ',package))
           (cdr package-list))
         (,var (car package-list)(car package-list)))
    ((endp package-list) ,result-form)
    ,@body))
```

Chapter 26 Other Features of GCLISP

26.1
```
(setf hotdog 'some-object)
(if (typep hotdog 'list)
  t
  (type-of hotdog))
```

26.2
```
(setf grocery-list
  '(a b c d e f g h i j k l m n o p q r s t u v w x y z))
(setf grocery-list
  (butlast grocery-list (- (length grocery-list) 10)))
```

26.3
```
(setf card-deck
  '(C0K S03 H10 S09 S0Q H03 C0A S10 H0K D04 C08 D02 D0A
    C05 C03 D08 C06 D06 H0J C10 C09 D07 C07 H07 D0Q H04
    D03 C04 H06 C02 S07 D0K H0A S08 S02 S0K D05 H09 H0Q
    D0J H08 S05 C0Q H05 S0J S06 S04 S0A H02 D09 D10 C0J))
(let (poker-hand)
 (dotimes (n 5 poker-hand)
   (push (pop card-deck) poker-hand)))
```

26.4
```
(defun diamondp (card)
  (equal #\D
    (read-char (make-string-input-stream (symbol-name card)))))
(remove-if #'diamondp card-deck)
```

26.5
```
(defvar *phone-array*
  (make-array 10 :element-type 'list
                 :initial-element nil))
```

```
(defun file-phones ()
  (let (name number bucket bucket-list)
   (loop
    (format t "~%Name : ")
    (setf name (read))
    (if (equal name 'exit)
       (return))
    (format t "Number : ")
    (setf number (read))
    (setf bucket (truncate (sxhash name) 3277))
    (setf bucket-list (aref *phone-array* bucket))
    (cond ((assoc name bucket-list)
              (delete (assoc name bucket-list))
              (acons name number bucket-list))
           (t  (setf bucket-list
                (acons name number bucket-list))))
    (setf    (aref *phone-array* bucket) bucket-list))))
(defun retrieve-phones ()
   (let (name bucket name-number)
     (loop
       (format t "~%Name : ")
       (setf name (read))
       (if (equal name 'exit)
         (return))
       (setf bucket (truncate (sxhash name) 3277))
       (setf name-number
         (assoc name (aref *phone-array* bucket)))
       (if name-number
         (format t "~a's number is ~a~%"
           name (cdr name-number))
         (format t "~a is not on the list.~%" name)))))
(defun display-phones ()
   (terpri)
   (dotimes (n 10)
     (format t "~%~a: ~a" n (aref *phone-array* n))))
```

26.6

```
(defun bubble-sort (list)
   (format t "~%~%Sorting")
   (let (previous newlist flag)
    (setf previous (car list))
    (loop
     (princ ".")
     (setf flag nil)
     (dolist (item (cdr list))
       (cond ((string= (symbol-name previous)
                        (symbol-name item))
               (push previous newlist)
               (setf previous item))
             ((string< (symbol-name previous)
                        (symbol-name item))
               (push previous newlist)
               (setf previous item))
             (t (push item newlist)
               (setf flag t))))
```

```
          (cond (flag
                    (setf list (reverse (push previous newlist)))
                    (setf previous (car list))
                    (setf newlist nil))
                  (t (return
                      (reverse (push previous newlist))))))))
```

26.7

```
(defun display-bytes (base offset &optional sign)
  (declare (special offset sign char))
  (ifn (or (eql sign 1)(eql sign -1)(eql sign nil))
     (error "Sign must be 1, -1, or left to default (= 1)"))
  (format t "~%~%Base:    ~a" base)
  (format t "~%Offset   chr chr chr chr chr chr chr chr chr ~
                        chr    string equivalent  ")
  (format t "~%------   --- --- --- --- --- --- --- --- --- ~
                        ---   -------------------")
  (setf char-array (make-array 10 :element-type 'integer))
  (let ((count 0))
   (loop
    (cond ((eql count 10)
             (terpri)(setf count 1))
          (t   (setf count (1+ count))))
    (format t "~%~a~a  " (o-space) offset)
    (if (not sign)
       (setf sign 1))
    (neg-update offset)
    (dotimes (n 10)
      (update offset)
      (setf char (sys:%contents base offset))
      (if (or (eql char 9)(eql char 10))
          (setf char 0))
      (setf (aref char-array n) char))
    (dotimes (n 10)
      (setf char (aref char-array n))
      (format t "~a~a" (char-space) char))
    (princ "    ")
    (cond ((eql sign 1)
             (dotimes (n 10)
               (format t "~a "
                 (string (aref char-array n)))))
          (t  (do((n 9 (1- n)))
               ((eql n -1))
               (format t "~a "
                 (string (aref char-array n))))))
    (update offset))))

(defun update (input)
  (if (eql sign 1)
     (setf offset (1+ input))
     (setf offset (1- input))))

(defun neg-update (input)
  (if (eql sign -1)
     (setf offset (1+ input))
     (setf offset (1- input))))
```

```
(defun char-space ()
  (cond
    ((> char 99) " ")
    ((> char 9) "  ")
    (t "   ")))

(defun o-space ()
  (cond ((> offset 9999) "  ")
        ((< offset -9999) "")
        ((> offset 999) "   ")
        ((< offset -999) "  ")
        ((> offset 99) "    ")
        ((< offset -99) "   ")
        ((> offset 9) "     ")
        ((< offset -9) "    ")
        ((>= offset 0) "      ")
        (t "     ")))
```

26.8

```
(defun get-obarray ()
  (with-open-file
    (printer "prn" :direction :output)
    (format printer "~% ")
    (format printer "LISTING OF *OBARRAY* ELEMENTS")
    (format printer "~%~%*obarray* leader elements:")
    (format printer "~% 1: ~a" (array-leader sys:*obarray* 0))
    (format printer "~% 2: ~a" (array-leader sys:*obarray* 1))
    (format printer "~%~%*obarray* elements:")
    (do ((n 1 (1+ n))(c 8) element)
      ((eql n 511)(format printer "~%~%~%"))
      (setf element (aref sys:*obarray* (1- n)))
      (format printer "~%~a~a: ~a"
        (ob-space (1- n)) (1- n) element)
      (when (zerop (second
                (multiple-value-list (truncate n 5))))
        (format printer "~%")
        (setf c (1+ c)))
      (if (> (length (princ-to-string element)) 75)
        (setf c (1+ c)))
      (setf c (1+ c))
      (cond ((eql c 63)
              (format printer "~%~%~%~%~%~%")
              (setf c 3))
            ((eql c 64)
              (format printer "~%~%~%~%~%")
              (setf c 3))
            ((eql c 65)
             (format printer "~%~%~%~%")
              (setf c 3))))))

(defun ob-space (n)
  (cond ((> n 99) "")
        ((> n 9) " ")
        (t "  ")))
```

```
(defun princ-to-string (arg)
  (let ((string-stream (make-string-output-stream)))
    (princ arg string-stream)
    (get-output-stream-string string-stream)))
```

26.9
```
(defun file-symbol-list (package)
  (with-open-file (symbol-stream "c:\\ws\\symbols.lsp"
      :direction :output)
    (let ((count 0))
      (do-symbols (symbol (find-package package) count)
        (print symbol symbol-stream)
        (setf count (1+ count))))))

(defun get-symbol-list ()
  (with-open-file (symbol-stream "c:\\ws\\symbols.lsp"
      :direction :input)
    (loop
      (setf symbol (read symbol-stream nil 'eof))
      (if (equal symbol 'eof)
        (return))
      (print symbol))))
```

26.10
```
(defun symbol-data-objects (package &optional print)
  (declare (special package))
  (file-symbol-list package)
  (with-open-file
    (printer "prn" :direction :output)
      (with-open-file (symbol-stream "c:\\ws\\symbols.lsp"
        :direction :input)
      (let (bas off dum va1 va2 pl1 pl2 fn1 fn2 do1 do2)
      (declare (special lisp-symbols bas off dum va1 va2 pl1
        pl2 fn1 fn2 do1 do2))
      (format t "~%Package: ~a~aValue   Plist   Funct   ~
        Doc" package (pack-space package))
      (if print
        (format printer "~%Package: ~a~aValue   Plist   ~
            Funct    Doc" package (pack-space package)))
      (format t "~%     Symbol-name       Pointer Pointer ~
        Pointer  Pointer")
      (if print
        (format printer "~%     Symbol-name       Pointer ~
            Pointer  Pointer  Pointer"))
      (format t "~%---------------------  -------  -------  ~
        -------  -------")
      (if  print
         (format printer "~%---------------------  -------  ~
          -------  -------  -------"))
      (loop
        (setf item (read symbol-stream nil 'eof))
        (if (equal item 'eof)
          (return))
        (multiple-value-setq (off bas)(sys:%pointer item))
        (multiple-value-setq
          (dum va2 va1)(sys:%contents bas (1+ off)))
```

```
        (multiple-value-setq
          (dum pl2 pl1)(sys:%contents bas (+ 5 off)))
        (multiple-value-setq
          (dum fn2 fn1)(sys:%contents bas (+ 11 off)))
        (multiple-value-setq
          (dum do2 do1)(sys:%contents bas (+ 17 off)))
        (format t "~%~a~a   ~a~a   ~a~a   ~a~a   ~a~a"
          item (item-space item)
               (ptr-space va1) va1 (ptr-space pl1) pl1
               (ptr-space fn1) fn1 (ptr-space do1) do1)
        (format t "~%~a~a:~a~a ~
                         ~a~a   ~a~a   ~a~a   ~a~a~%"
          (ptr-space bas) bas (ptr-space off) off
          (ptr-space va2) va2 (ptr-space pl2) pl2
          (ptr-space fn2) fn2 (ptr-space do2) do2)
        (when print
              (format printer
                "~%~a~a   ~a~a   ~a~a   ~a~a   ~a~a"
                item (item-space item)
                     (ptr-space va1) va1 (ptr-space pl1) pl1
                     (ptr-space fn1) fn1 (ptr-space do1) do1)
              (format printer "~%~a~a:~a~a            ~
                                   ~a~a   ~a~a   ~a~a   ~a~a~%"
               (ptr-space bas) bas  (ptr-space off) off
               (ptr-space va2) va2 (ptr-space pl2) pl2
               (ptr-space fn2)  fn2  (ptr-space do2) do2)))))))
(defun pack-space (package)
  (spaces (- 16 (flatc (package-name package)))))
(defun item-space (item)
  (spaces (- 22 (flatc item))))
(defun spaces (num)
  (do ((count 0 (1+ count))(space "" (string-append " " space)))
      ((eql count num) space)))
(defun ptr-space (ptr)
  (cond ((> ptr 9999) "  ")
        ((< ptr -9999) "")
        ((> ptr 999) "   ")
        ((< ptr -999) "  ")
        ((> ptr 99) "    ")
        ((< ptr -99) "   ")
        ((> ptr 9) "     ")
        ((< ptr -9) "    ")
        ((>= ptr 0) "      ")
        (t "     ")))
```

Bibliography

Abelson H. and Sussman G. J. (1985). *Structure and Interpretation of Computer Programs*. Cambridge MA: The MIT Press

Allen J. (1978). *Anatomy of LISP*. New York: McGraw-Hill

Anderson J. R. *et al.* (1987). *Essential LISP*. Reading MA: Addison-Wesley

Baker H. G. Jr (1978). List processing in real time on a serial computer. *Comm. ACM*, **21**(4), April

Berk A. A. (1985). *LISP, The Language of Artificial Intelligence*. London: Collins

Berkeley E. C. and Bobrow D. G., eds. (1966). *The Programming Language LISP: Its Operation and Applications*. 2nd Edn. Cambridge MA: The MIT Press

Bromley H. (1986). *LISP Lore: A Guide to Programming the LISP Machine*. Boston MA: Kluwer Academic

Brooks R. A. (1985). *Programming in Common LISP*. New York: John Wiley

Burge W. H. (1975). *Recursive Programming Techniques*. Reading MA: Addison-Wesley

Byte. August 1979, **4**(8) (issue dedicated to LISP)

Byte. February 1988, **13**(2) (an in-depth update of the current state of LISP as of 1988)

Charniak E. *et al.* (1987). *Artificial Intelligence Programming* 2nd Edn. Hillsdale NJ: Lawrence Erlbaum Associates

Chirlian P. M. (1986). *LISP*. Ohio: Weber Systems

Coxhead P. (1987). *Starting LISP for AI*. Oxford: Blackwell Scientific

Danicic I. (1983). *Lisp Programming*. Rockville MD: Computer Science Press

Dybvig R. K. (1987). *The Scheme Programming Language*. Englewood Cliffs NJ: Prentice-Hall

Eisenberg M. (1988). *Programming in Scheme*. Redwood City CA: The Scientific Press

Fladung B. J. (1987). *The XLISP Primer*. Englewood Cliffs NJ: Prentice-Hall

Foderaro J. (1979). *The Franz LISP Manual*. Berkeley CA: University of California

Franz, Inc. (1988). *Common LISP: The Reference*. Reading MA: Addison-Wesley

Friedman D. P. (1974). *The Little LISPer*. London: Science Research Associates

Friedman D. P. and Felleisen M. (1987). *The Little LISPer*. Cambridge MA: The MIT Press

Gabriel R. P. (1985). *Performance and Evaluation of LISP Systems*. Cambridge MA: The MIT Press

Glaser H. *et al.* (1984). *Principles of Functional Programming*. London: Prentice-Hall International

Gloess L. (1982). *Understanding LISP*. Sherman Oaks CA: Alfred Publishing Co.

Gnosis Inc. (1984). *Learning LISP*. Englewood Cliffs NJ: Prentice-Hall

Hasemer T. (1984). *A Beginner's Guide to LISP*. Menlo Park CA: Addison-Wesley (Also published under the title: *Looking at LISP*)

Henderson P. (1980). *Functional Programming: Application and Implementation*. London: Prentice-Hall International

Hekmatpour S. (1988). *Introduction to LISP and Symbol Manipulation*. Englewood Cliffs NJ: Prentice-Hall

Hekmatpour S. (1989). *LISP: A Portable Implementation*. Englewood Cliffs NJ: Prentice-Hall

Hilts P. J. (1982). *Scientific Temperaments: Three Lives in Contemporary Science*. New York: Simon & Schuster (biographical portrait of John McCarthy)

Holtz F. (1985). *LISP, The Language of Artificial Intelligence*. Blue Ridge Summit PA: TAB Books

Hughes S. (1986). *LISP Computer Language Handbook*. London: Pitman Publishing

Kaisler S. H. (1986). *INTERLISP: The Language and Its Usage*. NY: John Wiley

Keene S. E. (1989). *Object Oriented Programming in Common LISP*. Reading MA: Addison-Wesley

Kessler R. R. (1988). *LISP, Objects, and Symbolic Programming*. Glenview IL: Scott Foresman

Knuth D. E. (1973). *The Art of Computer Programming* Vol I, *Fundamental Algorithms* 2nd edn. Reading MA: Addison-Wesley

MacLennan B. J. (1983). *Principles of Programming Languages: Design, Evaluation, and Implementation*. New York: Holt, Rinehart and Winston

Mason I. A. (1986). *The Semantics of Destructive LISP*. CSLI Lecture Notes No. 5, Center for the Study of Language and Information, Stanford University CA

Milner W. L. (1988). *Common LISP: A Tutorial*. Englewood Cliffs NJ: Prentice-Hall

Maurer W. D. (1973). *A Programmer's Introduction to LISP*. New York: Elsevier

McCarthy J. (1960). Recursive functions of symbolic expressions and their computation by machine. *Comm. ACM*, April, 184–95.

McCarthy J. *et al.* (1962). *LISP 1.5 Programmer's Manual*. Cambridge MA: The MIT Press

McCarthy J. (1977). History of LISP. In *Proc. ACM Con. on the History of Programming Languages*, Los Angeles CA

Meehan J. R., ed. (1979). *The New UCI LISP Manual*. Hillsdale NJ: Lawrence Erlbaum Associates

Milner W. L. (1988). *Common LISP: A Tutorial*. Englewood Cliffs NJ: Prentice-Hall

Moon D. (1974). *MACLISP Reference Manual*. Cambridge MA: Laboratory of Computer Science, MIT

Moon D. *et al.* (1978). *LISP Machine Manual*. Cambridge MA: AI Laboratory, MIT

Narayanan A. and Sharkey N. E. (1985). *An Introduction to LISP*. UK: Ellis Horwood

Norman A. and Cattell G. (1983). *LISP on the BBC Microcomputer*. Cambridge, England: Acornsoft

Oakley S. (1984). *LISP for Micros*. Guildford, England: Butterworth

O'Shea T. and Eisenstadt M. eds. (1984). *Artificial Intelligence: Tools, Techniques, and Applications*. New York: Harper & Row

Peyton Jones S. L. (1987). *The Implementation of Functional Programming Languages*. Englewood Cliffs NJ: Prentice-Hall

Pitman K. M. (1983). *The Revised MACLISP Manual*. Cambridge MA: Laboratory of Computer Science, MIT

Pratt T. W. (1984). *Programming Languages: Design and Implementation*. 2nd edn. Englewood Cliffs NJ: Prentice-Hall

Queinnec C. (1984). *LISP*. London: MacMillan
Sammet J. E. (1969). *Programming Languages: History and Fundamentals*. Englewood Cliffs NJ: Prentice-Hall
Shapiro S. C. (1979). *Techniques of Artificial Intelligence*. New York: Van Nostrand
Shapiro S. C. (1986). *LISP: An Interactive Approach*. Rockville MD: Cognitive Science Press
Siklossy L. (1976). *Let's Talk LISP*. Englewood Cliffs NJ: Prentice-Hall
Slade S. (1987). *The T Programming Language: A Dialect of LISP*. Englewood Cliffs NJ: Prentice-Hall
Smith J. D. (1988). *Introduction to Scheme*. Englewood Cliffs NJ: Prentice-Hall
Steele G. L. Jr (1982). An overview of Common LISP. *Conf. Rec. of 1982 ACM Symp. on LISP and Functional Programming*
Steele G. L. Jr (1984). *Common LISP: The Language*. Digital Press
Tanimoto S. L. (1987). *The Elements of Artificial Intelligence: An Introduction Using LISP*. MD: Computer Science Press
Tatar D. (1987). *A Programmer's Guide to Common LISP*. Palo Alto CA: Digital Press
Teitelman W. *et al.* (1974). *INTERLISP Reference Manual*. Palo Alto CA: Xerox Corporation, Palo Alto Research Center
Texas Instruments (1988). *PC Scheme User's Guide and Language Reference Manual* Student Edn. Redwood City CA: The Scientific Press
Touretzky D. S. (1984). *LISP, A Gentle Introduction to Symbolic Computation*. New York: Harper & Row
Touretzky D. S. and Gabriel R. P. (1987). Advanced Common LISP Programming. Tutorial given at the *Sixth Nat. Con. on Artificial Intelligence*, Seattle WA
Tracton K. (1980). *Programmer's Guide to LISP*. Blue Ridge Summit PA: TAB Books
Weissman C. (1967). *LISP 1.5 Primer*. Belmont CA: Dickinson
Wertz H. (1988). *An Introduction to Programming in LISP*. Chichester, England: John Wiley
Wilensky R. (1984). *LISPcraft*. New York: Norton
Wilensky R. (1986). *Common LISPcraft*. New York: Norton
Winston P. H. and Horn B. K. P. (1989). *LISP* 3rd edn. Reading MA: Addison-Wesley
Yuasa T. and Hagiya M. (1986). *Introduction to Common LISP* (translated from Japanese). Boston MA: Academic Press
Yuasa T. (1988). *Common LISP Drill* (translated from Japanese). Boston MA: Academic Press

In addition to the above references, most of which are books and manuals, a large number of influential papers on LISP have been issued in the form of reports by the AI laboratories of universities such as MIT, Yale, Carnegie-Mellon, Stanford, etc. A catalog of the principal papers generated by MIT is available from:

MIT Artificial Intelligence Laboratory
545 Technology Square
Cambridge, MA 02139

Other seminal papers on LISP have been presented at the biannual *ACM Conference on LISP and Functional Programming* (1980, 1982, 1984, 1986 and 1988). Copies of the proceedings may be ordered from:

Association for Computing Machinery
11 West 42nd Street
New York, NY 10036

The Special Interest Group on Artificial Intelligence (SIGART) of the ACM periodically publishes a quarterly SIGART Newsletter with articles of interest.

Other papers on LISP have been presented at the (annual) AAAI and (biannual) IJCAI Conferences sponsored by the American Association for Artificial Intelligence. Membership information can be obtained from:

American Association for Artificial Intelligence.
445 Burgess Drive
Menlo Park, CA 94025

Copies of the proceedings for all of the above-mentioned conferences dating back to 1969 are available from:

Morgan Kaufmann, Inc.
95 First Street
Los Altos, CA 94022

Other articles related to Artificial Intelligence appear in the quarterly AI Magazine of the AAAI.

Publication of an international journal *LISP and Symbolic Computation*, edited by Richard P.Gabriel and Guy L. Steele Jr commenced in June 1988. Subscriptions may be obtained through:

Kluwer Academic Publishers
101 Philip Drive
Norwell, MA 02061

Many interesting articles on LISP programming appear in the following monthly magazines:

AI Expert
Miller Freeman Publications
500 Howard Street
San Francisco, CA 94105

PC AI
3310 West Bell Road, Suite 119
Phoenix, AZ 85023

Index